New Perspectives on

MICROSOFT® ACCESS 2000

Comprehensive Enhanced

JOSEPH J. ADAMSKI
Grand Valley State University

CHARLES HOMMEL
University of Puget Sound

KATHLEEN T. FINNEGAN

APPROVED COURSEWARE

EXPERT

COURSE TECHNOLOGY
THOMSON LEARNING

Australia • Canada • Mexico • Singapore • Spain • United Kingdom • United States

New Perspectives on Microsoft® Access 2000—Comprehensive Enhanced
is published by Course Technology.

Managing Editor
Greg Donald

Senior Editor
Donna Gridley

Series Technology Editor
Rachel Crapser

Senior Product Manager
Kathleen Finnegan

Acquisitions Editor
Christine Guivernau

Developmental Editor
Jessica Evans

Associate Product Manager
Melissa Dezotell

Editorial Assistant
Jessica Engstrom

Production Editors
Daphne Barbas, Melissa Panagos, Jennifer Goguen

Text Designer
Meral Dabcovich

Cover Art Designer
Douglas Goodman

PREFACE

The New Perspectives Series

About New Perspectives

Course Technology's **New Perspectives Series** is an integrated system of instruction that combines text and technology products to teach computer concepts, the Internet, and microcomputer applications. Users consistently praise this series for innovative pedagogy, use of interactive technology, creativity, accuracy, and supportive and engaging style.

How is the New Perspectives Series different from other series?

The **New Perspectives Series** distinguishes itself by **innovative technology**, from the renowned Course Labs to the state-of-the-art multimedia that is integrated with our Concepts texts. Other distinguishing features include sound **instructional design**, **proven pedagogy**, and **consistent quality**. Each tutorial has students learn features in the context of solving a realistic case problem rather than simply learning a laundry list of features. With the **New Perspectives Series**, instructors report that students have a complete, integrative learning experience that stays with them. They credit this high retention and competency to the fact that this series incorporates critical thinking and problem-solving with computer skills mastery. In addition, we work hard to ensure accuracy by using a multi-step quality assurance process during all stages of development. Instructors focus on teaching and students spend more time learning.

Choose the coverage that's right for you

New Perspectives applications books are available in the following categories:

Brief
2-4 tutorials

Brief: approximately 150 pages long, two to four "Level I" tutorials, teaches basic application skills.

Introductory
6 or 7 tutorials, or Brief + 2 or 3 more tutorials

Introductory: approximately 300 pages long, four to seven tutorials, goes beyond the basic skills. These books often build out of the Brief book, adding two or three additional "Level II" tutorials.

Comprehensive
Introductory + 4 or 5 more tutorials. Includes Brief Windows tutorials and Additional Cases

Comprehensive: approximately 600 pages long, eight to twelve tutorials, all tutorials included in the Introductory text plus higher-level "Level III" topics. Also includes two Windows tutorials and three or four fully developed Additional Cases. The book you are holding is a Comprehensive book.

Advanced
Quick Review of basics + in-depth, high-level coverage

Advanced: approximately 600 pages long, covers topics similar to those in the Comprehensive books, but offers the highest-level coverage in the series. Advanced books assume students already know the basics, and therefore go into more depth at a more accelerated rate than the Comprehensive titles. Advanced books are ideal for a second, more technical course.

Office

Office suite components
+ integration + Internet

Custom Editions

Choose from any of the
above to build your own Custom
Editions or CourseKits

Office: approximately 800 pages long, covers all components of the Office suite as well as integrating the individual software packages with one another and the Internet.

Custom Books The New Perspectives Series offers you two ways to customize a New Perspectives text to fit your course exactly: *CourseKits*™ are two or more texts shrinkwrapped together, and offer significant price discounts. *Custom Editions*® offer you flexibility in designing your concepts, Internet, and applications courses. You can build your own book by ordering a combination of topics bound together to cover only the subjects you want. There is no minimum order, and books are spiral bound. Contact your Course Technology sales representative for more information.

What course is this book appropriate for?

New Perspectives on Microsoft® *Access 2000—Comprehensive Enhanced* can be used in any course in which you want students to learn the basics of Windows 98 and all the most important topics of Microsoft Access 2000, including creating and maintaining database tables; defining table relationships; creating running, and saving queries; sorting and filtering records; creating and customizing forms and reports; publishing Access objects to the World Wide Web; replicating a database; creating and running macros; creating a switchboard; and writing Visual Basic code. It is particularly recommended for a full-semester course on Microsoft Access 2000 or a course preparing students to take the Microsoft Office User Specialist Expert Access exam.

What is the Microsoft Office User Specialist Program?

APPROVED COURSEWARE

The Microsoft Office User Specialist Program provides an industry-recognized standard for measuring an individual's mastery of an Office application. Passing one or more MOUS Program certification exams helps your students demonstrate their proficiency to prospective employers and gives them a competitive edge in the job marketplace. Course Technology offers a growing number of Microsoft-approved products that cover all of the required objectives for the MOUS Program exams. For a complete listing of Course Technology titles that you can use to help your students get certified, visit our Web sit at **www.course.com**.

  New Perspectives on Microsoft Access 2000 – Comprehensive Enhanced has been approved by Microsoft as courseware for the Microsoft Office User Specialist (MOUS) Program. After completing the tutorials and exercises in this book, students will be prepared to take the Expert MOUS exam for Microsoft Access 2000. For more information about certification, please visit the MOUS program site at **www.mous.net**.

Proven Pedagogy

CASE

Tutorial Case Each tutorial begins with a problem presented in a case that is meaningful to students. The case turns the task of learning how to use an application into a problem-solving process.

45-minute Sessions. Each tutorial is divided into sessions that can be completed in about 45 minutes to an hour. Sessions allow instructors to more accurately allocate time in their syllabus, and students to better manage their own study time.

1.

2.

3.

Step-by-Step Methodology We make sure students can differentiate between what they are to *do* and what they are to *read*. Through numbered steps – clearly identified by a gray shaded background – students are constantly guided in solving the case problem. In addition, the numerous screen shots with callouts direct students' attention to what they should look at on the screen.

TROUBLE? Paragraphs These paragraphs anticipate the mistakes or problems that students may have and help them continue with the tutorial.

Tutorial Tips Page This page, following the Table of Contents, offers students suggestions on how to effectively plan their study and lab time, what to do when they make a mistake, how to use the Reference Windows, MOUS grids, Quick Checks, and other features of the New Perspectives Series.

"Read This Before You Begin" Page Located opposite the first tutorial's opening page for each section of the text, the Read This Before You Begin Page helps introduce technology into the classroom. Technical considerations and assumptions about software are listed to save time and eliminate unnecessary aggravation. Notes about the Data Disks help instructors and students get their files in the right places, so students get started on the right foot.

Quick Check Questions Each session concludes with meaningful, conceptual Quick Check questions that test students' understanding of what they learned in the session. Answers to the Quick Check questions are provided at the end of each tutorial.

Reference Windows Reference Windows are succinct summaries of the most important tasks covered in a tutorial and they preview actions students will perform in the steps to follow.

File Finder Chart This chart, located at the back of the book, visually explains how students should set up their Data Disks, what files should go in what folders, and what they'll be saving the files as in the course of their work.

Mous Certification Chart In the back of this book, you'll find that a chart that lists all the skills for the Microsoft Office User Specialist Expert Exam on Access 2000. With page numbers referencing where these skills are covered in this text and where students get hands on practice in completing the skills, the chart can be used as an excellent study guide in preparing for the Access Expert MOUS exam.

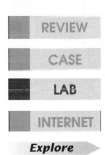

Task Reference Located as a table at the end of the book, the Task Reference contains a summary of how to perform common tasks using the most efficient method, as well as references to pages where the task is discussed in more detail.

End-of-Tutorial Review Assignments, Case Problems, Internet Assignments, and Lab Assignments Review Assignments provide students with additional hands-on practice of the skills they learned in the tutorial using the same case presented in the tutorial. These assignments are followed by four to five Case Problems that have approximately the same scope as the tutorial case but use a different scenario. In addition, some of the Review Assignments or Case Problems may include Exploration Exercises that challenge students, encourage them to explore the capabilities of the program they are using, and/or further extend their knowledge. Each tutorial also includes instructions on getting to the text's Student Online Companion page, which contains the Internet Assignments and other related links for the text. Internet Assignments are additional exercises that integrate the skills the students learned in the tutorial with the World Wide Web. Finally, if a Course Lab accompanies a tutorial, Lab Assignments are included after the Case Problems.

The Instructor's Resource Kit for this title contains:

- Electronic Instructor's Manual
- Data Files for Access tutorials
- Make Data Disk Program for Level I Windows 98 tutorials
- Solution Files
- Course Test Manager Testbank
- Course Test Manager Engine
- Figure files

These supplements come on CD-ROM. If you don't have access to a CD-ROM drive, contact your Course Technology customer service representative for more information.

The New Perspectives Supplements Package

Electronic Instructor's Manual. Our Instructor's Manuals include tutorial overviews and outlines, technical notes, lecture notes, solutions, and Extra Case Problems. Many instructors use the Extra Case Problems for performance-based exams or extra credit projects. The Instructor's Manual is available as an electronic file, which you can get from the Instructor Resource Kit (IRK) CD-ROM or download it from **www.course.com**.

Data Files Data Files contain all of the data that students will use to complete the tutorials, Review Assignments, and Case Problems. A Help file includes instructions for using the files. See the "Read This Before You Begin" page or the "File Finder" chart for more information on Data Files.

Solution Files Solution Files contain every file students are asked to create or modify in the tutorials, Review Assignments, Case Problems, and Extra Case Problems. A Help file on the Instructor's Resource Kit includes information for using the Solution Files.

Course Labs: Concepts Come to Life These highly interactive computer-based learning activities bring concepts to life with illustrations, animations, digital images, and simulations. The Labs guide students step-by-step, present them with Quick Check questions, let them explore on their own, test their comprehension, and provide printed feedback. Lab icons at the beginning of the tutorial and in the tutorial margins indicate when a topic has a corresponding Lab. Lab Assignments are included at the end of each relevant tutorial. The Labs available with this book and the tutorials in which they appear are:

Using a Mouse

Using a Keyboard

Databases

The Internet: World Wide Web

SQL Queries

| Tutorial 1 | Tutorial 1 | Tutorial 1 | Tutorial 7 | Tutorial 8 |
| Windows 98 | Windows 98 | Access 2000 | Access 2000 | Access 2000 |

Figure Files Many figures in the text are provided on the IRK CD-ROM to help illustrate key topics or concepts. Instructors can create traditional overhead transparencies by printing the figure files. Or they can create electronic slide shows by using the figures in a presentation program such as PowerPoint.

Course Test Manager: Testing and Practice at the Computer or on Paper Course Test Manager is cutting-edge, Windows-based testing software that helps instructors design and administer practice tests and actual examinations. Course Test Manager can automatically grade the tests students take at the computer and can generate statistical information on individual as well as group performance.

Online Companions: Dedicated to Keeping You and Your Students Up-To-Date Visit our faculty sites and student sites on the World Wide Web at **www.course.com**. Here instructors can browse this text's password-protected Faculty Online Companion to obtain an online Instructor's Manual, Solution Files, Data Files, and more. Students can also access this text's Student Online Companion, which contains Data Files and Internet Assignments and other useful links. Internet Assignments are additional exercises that integrate the database skills the students learned in the tutorial with the World Wide Web.

More Innovative Technology

Explore! CBT/WBT The back of this textbook contains an exciting new CBT learning product—Explore! Explore! places the student as an intern in a working company, AdZ, Incorporated. Students will gain computer skills through helping the other AdZ employees solve their business problems. The CD included in this textbook contains a CBT that teaches the basic operating system and file management skills of Microsoft Windows 2000 Professional. (Students do not need Microsoft Windows 2000 Professional to run Explore!, but the content may not match what students see on their computers if they are running Windows 95, 98, or NT.)

For more information, or to use the WBT version of Explore!, go to www.npexplore.com. Or, see the Technology Tools Appendix included in this textbook for step-by-step instructions on how to use Explore!

MyCourse.com MyCourse.com is an online syllabus builder and course enhancement tool. Hosted by Course Technology, MyCourse.com adds value to your course by providing additional content that reinforces what students are learning.

Most importantly, MyCourse.com is flexible. You can choose how you want to organize the material—by date, by class session, or by using the default organization, which organizes content by chapter. MyCourse.com allows you to add your own materials, including hyperlinks, school logos, assignments, announcements, and other course content. If you are using more than one textbook, you can even build a course that includes all of your Course Technology texts in one easy-to-use site!

Computer Buyer's Guide A helpful and comprehensive Computer Buyer's Guide is now available on our Office 2000 Enhanced Student Online Companion (www.course.com/newperspectives/office2000). Simply go to the Student Online Companion and click the link for the Buyer's Guide.

Course CBT Enhance your students' Office 2000 classroom learning experience with self-paced computer-based training on CD-ROM. Course CBT engages students with interactive multimedia and hands-on simulations that reinforce and complement the concepts and skills covered in the textbook. All the content is aligned with the MOUS (Microsoft Office User Specialist) program, making it a great preparation tool for the certification exams. Course CBT also includes extensive pre- and post-assessments that test students' mastery of skills. These pre- and post-assessments automatically generate a "custom learning path" through the course that highlights only the topics students need help with.

Course Assessment How well do your students *really* know Microsoft Office? Course Assessment is a performance-based testing program that measures students' proficiency in Microsoft Office 2000. Previously known as SAM, Course Assessment is available for Office 2000 in either a live or simulated environment. You can use Course Assessment to place students into or out of courses, monitor their performance throughout a course, and help prepare them for the MOUS certification exams.

WebCT WebCT is a tool used to create Web-based educational environments and also uses WWW browsers as the interface for the course-building environment. The site is hosted on your school campus, allowing complete control over the information. WebCT has its own internal communication system, offering internal e-mail, a Bulletin Board, and a Chat room.

Course Technology offers pre-existing supplemental information to help in your WebCT class creation, such as a suggested Syllabus, Lecture Notes, Figures in the Book/Course Presenter, Student Downloads, and Test Banks in which you can schedule an exam, create reports, and more.

Acknowledgments

I would like to thank the following reviewers for their helpful feedback: Calleen Coorough, Skagit Valley College; Bonnie Bailey, Moorhead State; Rick Wilkerson, Dyersburg State Community College; Rebekah Tidwell, Carson-Newman College; and Carol Beck, College of St. Mary. My thanks to all the Course Technology staff, especially Rachel Crapser for her guidance and encouragement; Melissa Dezotell and Karen Shortill for their support; Daphne Barbas for her excellent management of the production process; and John Bosco, Quality Assurance Project leader, and Nicole Ashton, John Freitas, Alex White, and Jeff Schwartz, QA testers, for ensuring the accuracy of the text. Special thanks to Jessica Evans for her outstanding editorial and technical contributions in developing this text, and to Joe Adamski for lending his insights and expertise. This book is dedicated in loving memory to Joe and Jeff, who left us too soon; with all my love and gratitude to my parents, Ed and Mary, and my mother-in-law, Elaine; and with hope and love to my two beautiful sons, Connor and Devon.

Kathleen T. Finnegan

I want to thank all those who helped in completing this book, including Nancy Acree of University of Puget Sound, and Joyce Strain of Green River Community College, who reviewed the first draft; Course Technology's great team, including Rachel Crapser, Donna Gridley, Karen Shortill, Melissa Dezotell, John Bosco, Daphne Barbas, and Jessica Evans; and all the others involved in creating this book. Also, my thanks to Kathy Finnegan, whose keen eye greatly improved the book. Finally, special thanks to Joan, who tolerated many late nights and lost weekends while I worked, and Anna, who helped with paste-ups and backups when she would have preferred a good game of checkers.

Charles Hommel

I would like to thank the dedicated and enthusiastic Course Technology staff, especially Rachel Crapser for her leadership; Jessica Evans for her excellence and positive attitude and influence and for going the extra mile; and Kathy Finnegan for her many contributions under very difficult circumstances. I wish the very best to Kathy, Connor and Devon.

Joseph J. Adamski

TABLE OF CONTENTS

Tutorial 2   AC 2.01

Maintaining a Database
Creating, Modifying, and Updating an Order Table

Tutorial 3   AC 3.01

Querying a Database
Retrieving Information About Restaurant Customers and Their Orders

Tutorial 4 — AC 4.01

Creating Forms and Reports

Creating an Order Data Form, a Customer Orders Form,
and a Customers and Orders Report

Tutorial 5   AC 5.03

Creating More Advanced Queries and Custom Forms

Making the Dining Database Easier to Use

Tutorial 6   AC 6.01

Customizing Reports and Integrating Access with Other Programs

Creating a Custom Invoices Report and a Report with an Embedded Chart and a Linked Document

Tutorial 10   AC 10.01

Using and Writing Visual Basic for Applications Code

Completing the FineFood Database User Interface

Reference Window List

Tutorial Tips

These tutorials will help you learn about Microsoft Windows 98 and Microsoft Access 2000. The tutorials are designed to be worked through at a computer. Each tutorial is divided into sessions. Watch for the session headings, such as Session 1.1 and Session 1.2. Each session is designed to be completed in about 45 minutes, but take as much time as you need. It's also a good idea to take a break between sessions.

Before you begin, read the following questions and answers. They will help you plan your time and use the tutorials effectively.

Where do I start?

Each tutorial begins with a case, which sets the scene for the tutorial and gives you background information to help you understand what you will be doing. Read the case before you go to the lab. In the lab, begin with the first session of a tutorial.

How do I know what to do on the computer?

Each session contains steps that you will perform on the computer to learn how to use Microsoft Access 2000. Read the text that introduces each series of steps. The steps you need to do at a computer are numbered and are set against a shaded background. Read each step carefully and completely before you try it. Some steps ask you to print. Check with your instructor to see if he or she wants you to provide printed documents.

How do I know if I did the step correctly?

As you work, compare your computer screen with the corresponding figure in the tutorial. Don't worry if your screen display is somewhat different from the figure. The important parts of the screen display are labeled in each figure. Check to make sure these parts are on your screen.

What if I make a mistake?

Don't worry about making mistakes—they are part of the learning process. Paragraphs labeled "TROUBLE?" identify common problems and explain how to get back on track. Follow the steps in a TROUBLE? paragraph only if you are having the problem described. If you run into other problems:

- Carefully consider the current state of your system, the position of the pointer, and any messages on the screen.
- Complete the sentence, "Now I want to…" Be specific, because identifying your goal will help you rethink the steps you need to take to reach that goal.
- If you are working on a particular piece of software, consult the Help system.
- If the suggestions above don't solve your problem, consult your technical support person for assistance.

How do I use the Reference Windows?

Reference Windows summarize the procedures you will learn in the tutorial steps. Do not complete the actions in the Reference Windows when you are working through the tutorial. Instead, refer to the Reference Windows while you are working on the assignments at the end of the tutorial.

How can I test my understanding of the material I learned in the tutorial?

At the end of each session, you can answer the Quick Check questions. The answers for the Quick Checks are at the end of that tutorial.

After you have completed the entire tutorial, you should complete the Review Assignments and Case Problems. They are carefully structured so that you will review what you have learned and then apply your knowledge to new situations.

What if I can't remember how to do something?

You should refer to the Task Reference at the end of the book; it summarizes how to accomplish tasks using the most efficient method.

How can I prepare for MOUS Certification?

The Microsoft Office User Specialist (MOUS) logo on the cover of this book indicates that Microsoft has approved it as a study guide for the Microsoft Access 2000 Expert MOUS exam. At the back of this text, you'll see a chart that outlines the specific Microsoft certification skills for Access 2000 that are covered in the tutorials. You'll need to learn these skills if you're interested in taking a MOUS exam. If you decide to take a MOUS exam, or if you just want to study a specific skill, this chart will give you an easy reference to the page number on which the skill is covered. To learn more about the MOUS certification program, refer to the preface in the front of the book or go to **www.mous.net**.

Now that you've read the Tutorial Tips, you are ready to begin.

New Perspectives on

MICROSOFT®
WINDOWS® 98

Read This Before You Begin

To the Student

Make Student Disk Program

To complete the Level I tutorials, Tutorial Assignments, and Projects, you need 2 Student Disks. Your instructor will either provide you with Student Disks or ask you to make your own.

If you are making your own Student Disks you will need 2 blank, formatted high-density disks and access to the Make Student Disk program. If you wish to install the Make Student Disk program to your home computer, you can obtain it from your instructor or from the Web. To download the Make Student Disk program from the Web, go to www.course.com, click Data Disks, and follow the instructions on the screen.

To install the Make Student Disk program, select and click the file you just downloaded from www.course.com, 5446-0.exe. Follow the on-screen instructions to complete the installation. If you have any trouble installing or obtaining the Make Student Disk program, ask your instructor or technical support person for assistance.

Once you have obtained and installed the Make Student Disk program, you can use it to create your student disks according to the steps in the tutorials.

Course Labs

The Level I tutorials in this book feature 3 interactive Course Labs to help you understand selected computer concepts. There are Lab Assignments at the end of Tutorials 1 and 2 that relate to these Labs. To start a Lab, click the **Start** button on the Windows 98 Taskbar, point to **Programs**, point to **Course Labs**, point to **New Perspectives Course Labs**, and click the name of the Lab you want to use.

Using Your Own Computer

If you are going to work through this book using your own computer, you need:

Computer System Microsoft Windows 98 must be installed on a local hard drive or on a network drive.

Student Disks You will not be able to complete the tutorials or exercises in this book using your own computer until you have your Student Disks. See "Make Student Disk Program" above for details on obtaining your student disks.

Course Labs See your instructor or technical support person to obtain the Course Lab software for use on your own computer.

Visit Our World Wide Web Site

Additional materials designed especially for you are available on the World Wide Web. Go to http://www.course.com.

To the Instructor

The Make Student Disk Program and Course Labs for this title are available on the Instructor's Resource Kit for this title. Follow the instructions in the Help file on the CD-ROM to install the programs to your network or standalone computer. For information on using the Make Student Disk Program or the Course Labs, see the "To the Student" section above. Students will be switching the default installation settings to Web style in Tutorial 2. You are granted a license to copy the Student Files and Course Labs to any computer or computer network used by students who have purchased this book.

In this tutorial you will:

- Start and shut down Windows 98

- Identify the objects on the Windows 98 desktop

- Practice mouse functions

- Run software programs and switch between them

- Identify and use the controls in a window

- Use Windows 98 controls such as menus, toolbars, list boxes, scroll bars, option buttons, tabs, and check boxes

- Explore the Windows 98 Help system

EXPLORING THE BASICS

Investigating the Windows 98 Operating System

LABS

Using a Keyboard

Using a Mouse

Your First Day on the Computer

You walk into the computer lab and sit down at a desk. There's a computer in front of you, and you find yourself staring dubiously at the screen. Where to start? As if in answer to your question, your friend Steve Laslow appears.

"You start with the operating system," says Steve. Noticing your puzzled look, Steve explains that the **operating system** is software that helps the computer carry out operating tasks such as displaying information on the computer screen and saving data on your disks. Your computer uses the **Microsoft Windows 98** operating system—Windows 98, for short.

Steve tells you that Windows 98 has a "gooey" or **graphical user interface (GUI)**, which uses pictures of familiar objects, such as file folders and documents, to represent a desktop on your screen. Microsoft Windows 98 gets its name from the rectangular work areas, called "windows," that appear on your screen.

Steve explains that much of the software available for Windows 98 has a standard graphical user interface. This means that once you have learned how to use one Windows software package, such as word-processing software, you are well on your way to understanding how to use other Windows software. Windows 98 lets you use more than one software package at a time, so you can easily switch between your word-processing software and your appointment book software, for example. Finally, Windows 98 makes it very easy to access the **Internet**, the worldwide collection of computers connected to one another to enable communication. All in all, Windows 98 makes your computer an effective and easy-to-use productivity tool.

Steve recommends that you get started right away by using some tutorials that will teach you the skills essential for using Microsoft Windows 98. He hands you a book and assures you that everything on your computer system is set up and ready to go.

SESSION 1.1	In this session, in addition to learning basic Windows terminology, you will learn how to use a pointing device, how to start and stop a program, and how to use more than one program at a time.

Starting Windows 98

Using a Keyboard

Windows 98 automatically starts when you turn on the computer. Depending on the way your computer is set up, you might be asked to enter your username and password.

To start Windows 98:

1. Turn on your computer.

TROUBLE? If prompted to do so, type your assigned username and press the Tab key. Then type your password and press the Enter key to continue.

TROUBLE? If this is the first time you have started your computer with Windows 98, messages might appear on your screen informing you that Windows is setting up components of your computer. If the Welcome to Windows 98 box appears, press and hold down the Alt key on your keyboard and then, while you hold down the Alt key, press the F4 key. The box closes.

After a moment, Windows 98 starts.

The Windows 98 Desktop

In Windows terminology, the area displayed on your screen represents a **desktop**—a workspace for projects and the tools needed to manipulate those projects. When you first start a computer, it uses **default** settings, those preset by the operating system. The default desktop, for example, has a plain teal background. However, Microsoft designed Windows 98 so that you can easily change the appearance of the desktop. You can, for example, add color, patterns, images, and text to the desktop background.

Many institutions design customized desktops for their computers. Figure 1-1 shows the default Windows 98 desktop and two other examples of desktops, one designed for a business, North Pole Novelties, and one designed for a school, the University of Colorado. Although your desktop might not look exactly like any of the examples in Figure 1-1, you should be able to locate objects on your screen similar to those in Figure 1-1. Look at your screen display and locate the objects labeled in Figure 1-1. The objects on your screen might appear larger or smaller than those in Figure 1-1, depending on your monitor's settings.

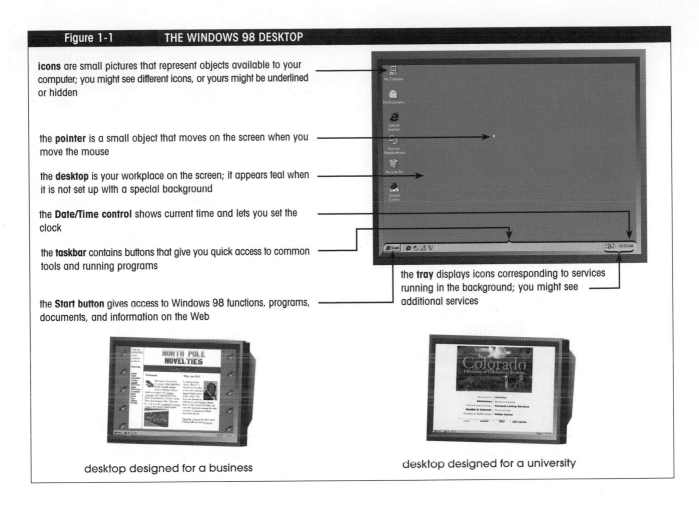

| Figure 1-1 | THE WINDOWS 98 DESKTOP |

icons are small pictures that represent objects available to your computer; you might see different icons, or yours might be underlined or hidden

the **pointer** is a small object that moves on the screen when you move the mouse

the **desktop** is your workplace on the screen; it appears teal when it is not set up with a special background

the **Date/Time control** shows current time and lets you set the clock

the **taskbar** contains buttons that give you quick access to common tools and running programs

the **Start button** gives access to Windows 98 functions, programs, documents, and information on the Web

the **tray** displays icons corresponding to services running in the background; you might see additional services

desktop designed for a business

desktop designed for a university

If the screen goes blank or starts to display a moving design, press any key to restore the Windows 98 desktop.

Using a Pointing Device

Using a Mouse

A **pointing device** helps you interact with objects on the screen. Pointing devices come in many shapes and sizes; some are designed to ensure that your hand won't suffer fatigue while using them. Some are directly attached to your computer via a cable, whereas others function like a TV remote control and allow you to access your computer without being right next to it. Figure 1-2 shows examples of common pointing devices.

The most common pointing device is called a **mouse**, so this book uses that term. If you are using a different pointing device, such as a trackball, substitute that device whenever you see the term "mouse." In Windows 98 you need to know how to use the mouse to manipulate the objects on the screen. In this session you will learn about pointing and clicking. In Session 1.2 you will learn how to use the mouse to drag objects.

You can also interact with objects by using the keyboard; however, the mouse is more convenient for most tasks, so the tutorials in this book assume you are using one.

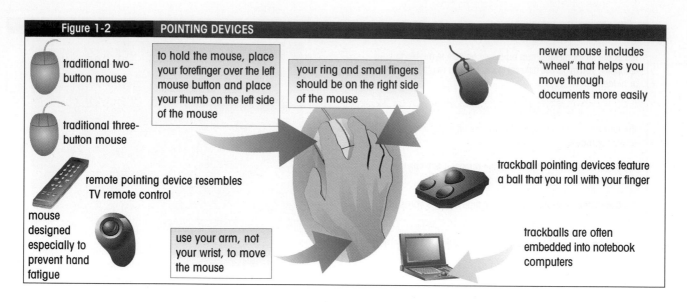

Figure 1-2   POINTING DEVICES

traditional two-button mouse

traditional three-button mouse

to hold the mouse, place your forefinger over the left mouse button and place your thumb on the left side of the mouse

your ring and small fingers should be on the right side of the mouse

newer mouse includes "wheel" that helps you move through documents more easily

remote pointing device resembles TV remote control

mouse designed especially to prevent hand fatigue

use your arm, not your wrist, to move the mouse

trackball pointing devices feature a ball that you roll with your finger

trackballs are often embedded into notebook computers

Pointing

You use a pointing device to move the pointer, in order to manipulate objects on the desktop. The pointer is usually shaped like an arrow ⌕ , although it can change shape depending on where it is on the screen. How skilled you are in using a mouse depends on your ability to position the pointer. Most computer users place the mouse on a **mouse pad**, a flat piece of rubber that helps the mouse move smoothly. As you move the mouse on the mouse pad, the pointer on the screen moves in a corresponding direction.

You begin most Windows operations by positioning the pointer over a specific part of the screen. This is called **pointing**.

To move the pointer:

1. Position your right index finger over the left mouse button, as shown in Figure 1-2. Lightly grasp the sides of the mouse with your thumb and little fingers.

   TROUBLE? If you want to use the mouse with your left hand, ask your instructor or technical support person to help you use the Control Panel to swap the functions of the left and right mouse buttons. Be sure to find out how to change back to the right-handed mouse setting, so that you can reset the mouse each time you are finished in the lab.

2. Place the mouse on the mouse pad and then move the mouse. Watch the movement of the pointer.

   TROUBLE? If you run out of room to move your mouse, lift the mouse and place it in the middle of the mouse pad. Notice that the pointer does not move when the mouse is not in contact with the mouse pad.

When you position the mouse pointer over certain objects, such as the objects on the taskbar, a "tip" appears. These "tips" are called **ToolTips**, and they tell you the purpose or function of an object.

To view ToolTips:

1. Use the mouse to point to the **Start** button 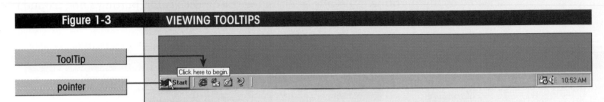. After a few seconds, you see the tip "Click here to begin," as shown in Figure 1-3.

Figure 1-3	VIEWING TOOLTIPS

ToolTip

pointer

2. Point to the time on the right end of the taskbar. Notice that today's date (or the date to which your computer's time clock is set) appears.

Clicking

Clicking is when you press a mouse button and immediately release it. Clicking sends a signal to your computer that you want to perform an action on the object you click. In Windows 98 you can click using both the left and right mouse buttons, but most actions are performed using the left mouse button. If you are told to click an object, click it with the left mouse button, unless instructed otherwise.

When you click the Start button, the Start menu appears. A **menu** is a list of options that helps you work with software. The **Start menu** provides you with access to programs, documents, and much more. Try clicking the Start button to open the Start menu.

To open the Start menu:

1. Point to the **Start** button.

2. Click the left mouse button. An arrow ▶ following an option on the Start menu indicates that you can view additional choices by navigating a **submenu**, a menu extending from the main menu. See Figure 1-4.

Figure 1-4	START MENU

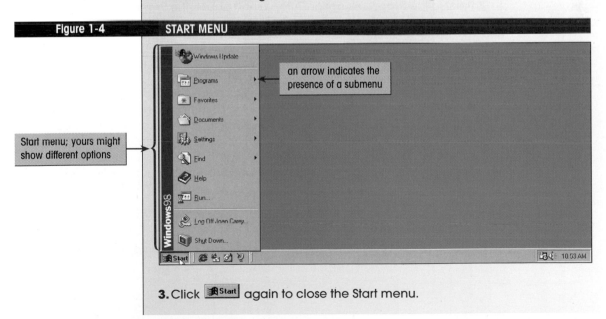

an arrow indicates the presence of a submenu

Start menu; yours might show different options

3. Click 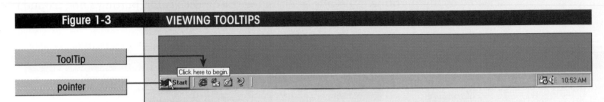 again to close the Start menu.

Next you'll learn how to open a submenu by selecting it.

Selecting

In Windows 98, pointing and clicking are often used to **select** an object, in other words, to choose it as the object you want to work with. Windows 98 shows you which object is selected by highlighting it, usually by changing the object's color, putting a box around it, or making the object appear to be pushed in, as shown in Figure 1-5.

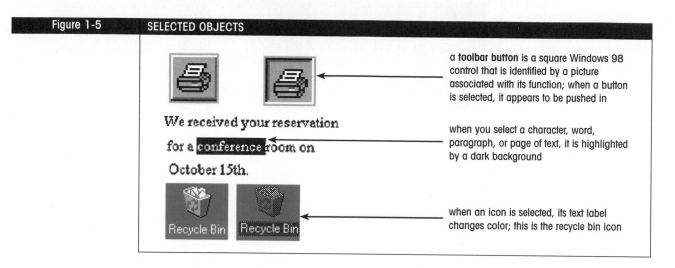

Figure 1-5   SELECTED OBJECTS

a **toolbar button** is a square Windows 98 control that is identified by a picture associated with its function; when a button is selected, it appears to be pushed in

We received your reservation for a conference room on October 15th.

when you select a character, word, paragraph, or page of text, it is highlighted by a dark background

Recycle Bin   Recycle Bin

when an icon is selected, its text label changes color; this is the recycle bin icon

In Windows 98, depending on your computer's settings, some objects are selected when you simply point to them, others when you click them. Practice selecting the Programs option on the Start menu to open the Programs submenu.

To select an option on a menu:

1. Click the **Start** button ![Start] and notice how it appears to be pushed in, indicating it is selected.

2. Point to the **Programs** option. After a short pause, the Programs submenu opens, and the Programs option is highlighted to indicate it is selected. See Figure 1-6.

   TROUBLE? If a submenu other than the Programs menu opens, you selected the wrong option. Move the mouse so that the pointer points to Programs.

   TROUBLE? If the Programs option doesn't appear, your Start menu might have too many options to fit on the screen. If that is the case, a small arrow appears at the top or bottom of the Start menu. Click first the top and then the bottom arrow to view additional Start menu options until you locate the Programs menu option, and then point to it.

Figure 1-6   **PROGRAMS SUBMENU**

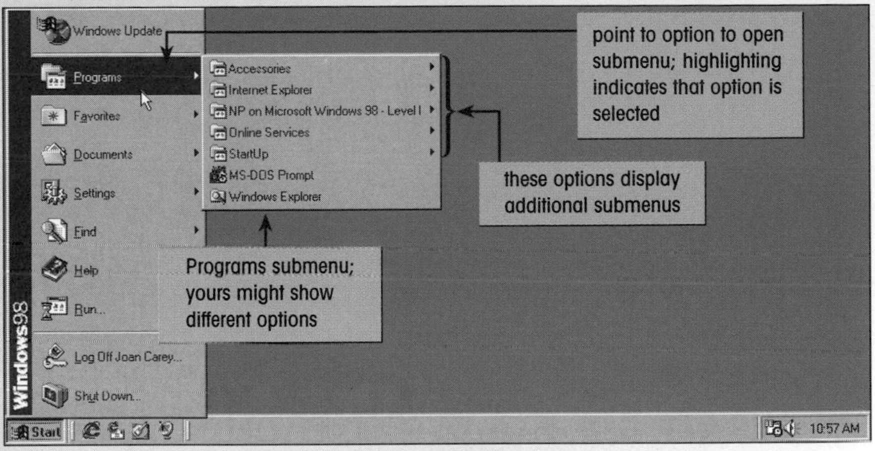

3. Now close the Start menu by clicking [Start] again.

You return to the desktop.

Right-Clicking

Pointing devices were originally designed with a single button, so the term "clicking" had only one meaning: you pressed that button. Innovations in technology, however, led to the addition of a second and even a third button (and more recently, options such as a wheel) that expanded the pointing device's capability. More recent software—especially that designed for Windows 98—takes advantage of additional buttons, especially the right button. However, the term "clicking" continues to refer to the left button; clicking an object with the *right* button is called **right-clicking**.

In Windows 98, right-clicking both selects an object and opens its **shortcut menu**, a list of options directly related to the object you right-clicked. You can right-click practically any object—the Start button, a desktop icon, the taskbar, and even the desktop itself—to view options associated with that object. For example, the first desktop shown in Figure 1-7 illustrates what happens when you click the Start button with the left mouse button to open the Start menu. Clicking the Start button with the right button, however, opens the Start button's shortcut menu, as shown in the second desktop.

| Figure 1-7 | CLICKING WITH THE LEFT AND RIGHT MOUSE BUTTONS |

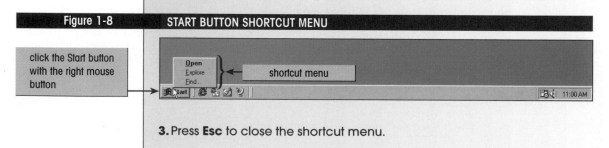

clicking Start button
with left mouse button
opens Start menu

click with left
mouse button

clicking Start button
with right mouse
button opens
shortcut menu

click with right
mouse button

Try using right-clicking to open the shortcut menu for the Start button.

To right-click an object:

1. Position the pointer over the Start button.

2. Right-click the **Start** button ![Start]. The shortcut menu that opens offers a list of options available to the Start button.

    TROUBLE? If you are using a trackball or a mouse with three buttons or a wheel, make sure you click the button on the far right, not the one in the middle.

    TROUBLE? If your menu looks slightly different from the one in Figure 1-8, don't worry. Computers with different software often have different options.

| Figure 1-8 | START BUTTON SHORTCUT MENU |

click the Start button
with the right mouse
button

Open
Explore
Find...

shortcut menu

Start   11:00 AM

3. Press **Esc** to close the shortcut menu.

You again return to the desktop.

Starting **and Closing a Program**

The software you use is sometimes referred to as a **program** or an **application**. To use a program, such as a word-processing program, you must first start it. With Windows 98 you start a program by clicking the Start button.

The Reference Window below explains how to start a program. Don't do the steps in the Reference Window now; they are for your later reference.

REFERENCE WINDOW   **RW**

Starting a Program
- Click the Start button, and point to Programs.
- If necessary, point to the submenu option that contains your program, then click the name of the program you want to run.

Windows 98 includes an easy-to-use word-processing program called WordPad. Suppose you want to start the WordPad program and use it to write a letter or report. You open Windows 98 programs from the Start menu. Programs are usually located on the Programs submenu or on one of its submenus. To start WordPad, for example, you navigate the Programs and Accessories submenus.

To start the WordPad program from the Start menu:

1. Click the **Start** button ![Start] to open the Start menu.

2. Point to **Programs**. The Programs submenu appears.

3. Point to **Accessories**. Another submenu appears. Figure 1-9 shows the open menus.

   TROUBLE? If a different menu opens, you might have moved the mouse diagonally so that a different submenu opened. Move the pointer to the right across the Programs option, and then move it up or down to point to Accessories. Once you're more comfortable moving the mouse, you'll find that you can eliminate this problem by moving the mouse quickly.

Figure 1-9	START MENU

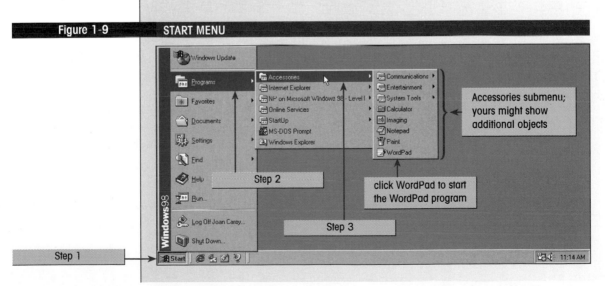

4. Click **WordPad**. The WordPad program opens, as shown in Figure 1-10. If the WordPad window does not fill the entire screen, don't worry. You will learn how to manipulate windows in Session 1.2.

| Figure 1-10 | THE WORDPAD PROGRAM |

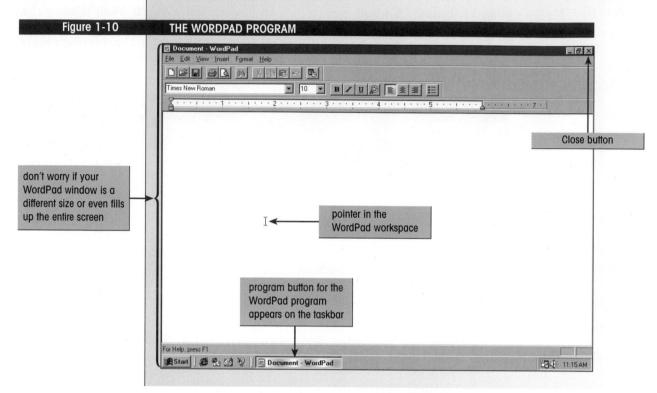

When a program is started, it is said to be **running**. A program button appears on the taskbar. **Program buttons** give you access to the programs running on the desktop.

When you are finished using a program, the easiest way to close it is to click the Close button ⊠.

To exit the WordPad program:

1. Click the **Close** button ⊠. See Figure 1-10. You return to the Windows 98 desktop.

Running Multiple Programs

One of the most useful features of Windows 98 is its ability to run multiple programs at the same time. This feature, known as **multitasking**, allows you to work on more than one project at a time and to switch quickly between projects. For example, you can start WordPad and leave it running while you then start the Paint program.

To run WordPad and Paint at the same time:

1. Start WordPad, then click the **Start** button 🏁Start again.

2. Point to **Programs**, then point to **Accessories**.

3. Click **Paint**. The Paint program appears, as shown in Figure 1-11. Now two programs are running at the same time.

Figure 1-11	THE PAINT PROGRAM

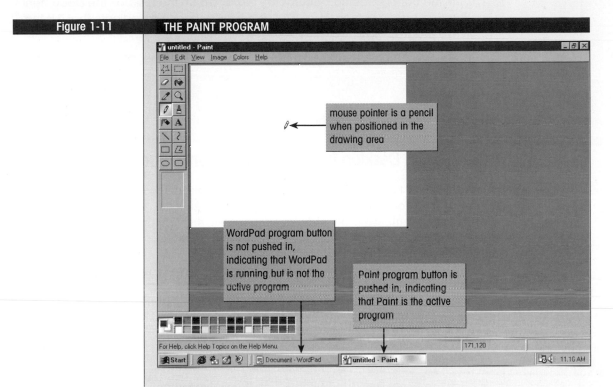

TROUBLE? If the Paint program does not fill the entire screen, don't worry. You will learn how to manipulate windows in Session 1.2.

What happened to WordPad? The WordPad program button is still on the taskbar, so even if you can't see it, WordPad is still running. You can imagine that it is stacked behind the Paint program, as shown in Figure 1-12.

Figure 1-12	PROJECTS STACKED ON A DESK

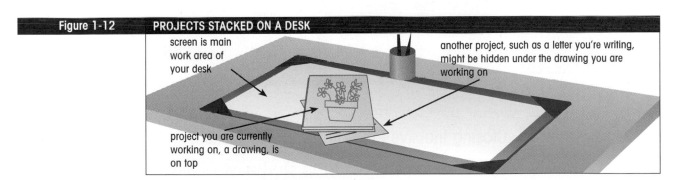

Switching Between Programs

Although Windows 98 allows you to run more than one program, only one program at a time is active. The **active** program is the program with which you are currently working. The easiest way to switch between programs is to use the buttons on the taskbar.

To switch between WordPad and Paint:

1. Click the button labeled **Document - WordPad** on the taskbar. The Document - WordPad button now looks as if it has been pushed in, to indicate that it is the active program, and WordPad moves to the front.

2. Next, click the button labeled **untitled - Paint** on the taskbar to switch to the Paint program.

The Paint program is again the active program.

Accessing the Desktop from the Quick Launch Toolbar

The Windows 98 taskbar, as you've seen, displays buttons for programs currently running. It also can contain **toolbars**, sets of buttons that give single-click access to programs or documents. In its default state, the Windows 98 taskbar displays the **Quick Launch toolbar**, which gives quick access to Web programs and to the desktop. Your taskbar might contain additional toolbars, or none at all.

When you are running more than one program but you want to return to the desktop, perhaps to use one of the desktop icons such as My Computer, you can do so by using one of the Quick Launch toolbar buttons. Clicking the Show Desktop button 🖉 returns you to the desktop. The open programs are not closed; they are simply inactive.

To return to the desktop:

1. Click the **Show Desktop** button 🖉 on the Quick Launch toolbar. The desktop appears, and both the Paint and WordPad programs are temporarily inactive. See Figure 1-13.

   TROUBLE? If the Quick Launch toolbar doesn't appear on your taskbar, right-click the taskbar, point to Toolbars, and then click Quick Launch and try Step 1 again.

| Figure 1-13 | ACCESSING THE DESKTOP |

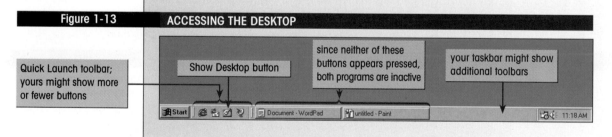

Quick Launch toolbar; yours might show more or fewer buttons

Show Desktop button

since neither of these buttons appears pressed, both programs are inactive

your taskbar might show additional toolbars

Closing Inactive Programs from the Taskbar

It is good practice to close each program when you are finished using it. Each program uses computer resources, such as memory, so Windows 98 works more efficiently when only the programs you need are open. You've already seen how to close an open program using the Close button ✖. You can also close a program, whether active or inactive, by using the shortcut menu associated with the program button on the taskbar.

To close WordPad and Paint using the program button shortcut menus:

1. Right-click the **untitled – Paint** button on the taskbar. To right-click something, remember that you click it with the right mouse button. The shortcut menu for that program button opens. See Figure 1-14.

| Figure 1-14 | PROGRAM BUTTON SHORTCUT MENU |

2. Click **Close**. The button labeled "untitled – Paint" disappears from the taskbar, and the Paint program closes.

3. Right-click the **Document – WordPad** button on the taskbar, and then click **Close**. The WordPad button disappears from the taskbar.

Shutting Down Windows 98

It is very important to shut down Windows 98 before you turn off the computer. If you turn off your computer without correctly shutting down, you might lose data and damage your files.

You should typically use the "Shut down" option when you want to turn off your computer. However, your school might prefer that you select the Log Off option on the Start menu. This option logs you out of Windows 98, leaves the computer turned on, and allows another user to log on without restarting the computer. Check with your instructor or technical support person for the preferred method at your school's computer lab.

To shut down Windows 98:

1. Click the **Start** button ![Start] on the taskbar to display the Start menu.

2. Click the **Shut Down** menu option. A box titled "Shut Down Windows" opens.

   TROUBLE? If you can't see the Shut Down menu option, your Start menu has more options than your screen can display. A small arrow appears at the bottom of the Start menu. Click this button until the Shut Down menu option appears, and then click Shut Down.

   TROUBLE? If you are supposed to log off rather than shut down, click the Log Off option instead and follow your school's logoff procedure.

3. Make sure the **Shut down** option is preceded by a small black bullet. See Figure 1-15.

   TROUBLE? If your Shut down option is not preceded by a small black bullet, point to the circle preceding the Shut down option and click it. A small black bullet appears in the circle, indicating that Windows 98 will perform the Shut down option. Your Shut Down Windows dialog box might show additional options, such as Stand by.

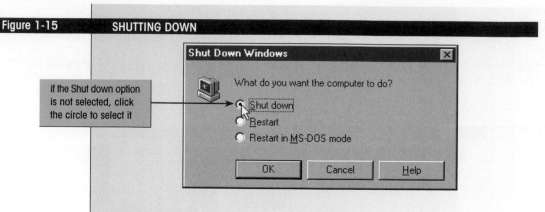

Figure 1-15   SHUTTING DOWN

if the Shut down option is not selected, click the circle to select it

Shut Down Windows

What do you want the computer to do?

○ Shut down
○ Restart
○ Restart in MS-DOS mode

[OK]   [Cancel]   [Help]

4. Click the **OK** button.

5. Click the **Yes** button if you are asked if you are sure you want to shut down.

6. Wait until you see a message indicating it is safe to turn off your computer. If your lab staff has requested you to switch off your computer after shutting down, do so now. Otherwise leave the computer running. Some computers turn themselves off automatically.

QUICK CHECK

1. What is the purpose of the taskbar?

2. The _____ feature of Windows 98 allows you to run more than one program at a time.

3. The _____ is a list of options that provides you with access to programs, documents, submenus, and more.

4. What should you do if you are trying to move the pointer to the left edge of your screen, but your mouse bumps into the keyboard?

5. Even if you can't see an open program on your desktop, the program might be running. How can you tell if a program is running?

6. Why is it good practice to close each program when you are finished using it?

7. Why should you shut down Windows 98 before you turn off your computer?

SESSION 1.2

In this session you will learn how to use many of the Windows 98 controls to manipulate windows and programs. You will also learn how to change the size and shape of a window; how to move a window; and how to use menus, dialog boxes, tabs, buttons, and lists to specify how you want a program to carry out a task.

Anatomy of a Window

When you run a program in Windows 98, it appears in a window. A **window** is a rectangular area of the screen that contains a program or data. Windows, spelled with an uppercase "W," is the name of the Microsoft operating system. The word "window" with a lowercase "w" refers to one of the rectangular areas on the screen. A window also contains controls for manipulating the window and for using the program. Figure 1-16 describes the controls you are likely to see in most windows.

Figure 1-16	WINDOW CONTROLS
CONTROL	**DESCRIPTION**
Menu bar	Contains the titles of menus, such as File, Edit, and Help
Pointer	Lets you manipulate window objects
Program button	Appears on the taskbar to indicate that a program is running on the desktop; appears pressed when program is active and not pressed when program is inactive
Sizing buttons	Let you enlarge, shrink, or close a window
Status bar	Provides you with messages relevant to the task you are performing
Title bar	Contains the window title and basic window control buttons
Toolbar	Contains buttons that provide you with shortcuts to common menu commands
Window title	Identifies the program and document contained in the window
Workspace	Part of the window you use to enter your work—to enter text, draw pictures, set up calculations, and so on

WordPad is a good example of a typical window, so try starting WordPad and identifying these controls in the WordPad window.

To look at window controls:

1. Make sure Windows 98 is running and you are at the Windows 98 desktop.

2. Start WordPad.

   TROUBLE? To start WordPad, click the Start button, point to Programs, point to Accessories, and then click WordPad.

3. On your screen, identify the controls labeled in Figure 1-17. Don't worry if your window fills the entire screen or is a different size. You'll learn to change window size shortly.

Figure 1-17 | **WORDPAD WINDOW CONTROLS**

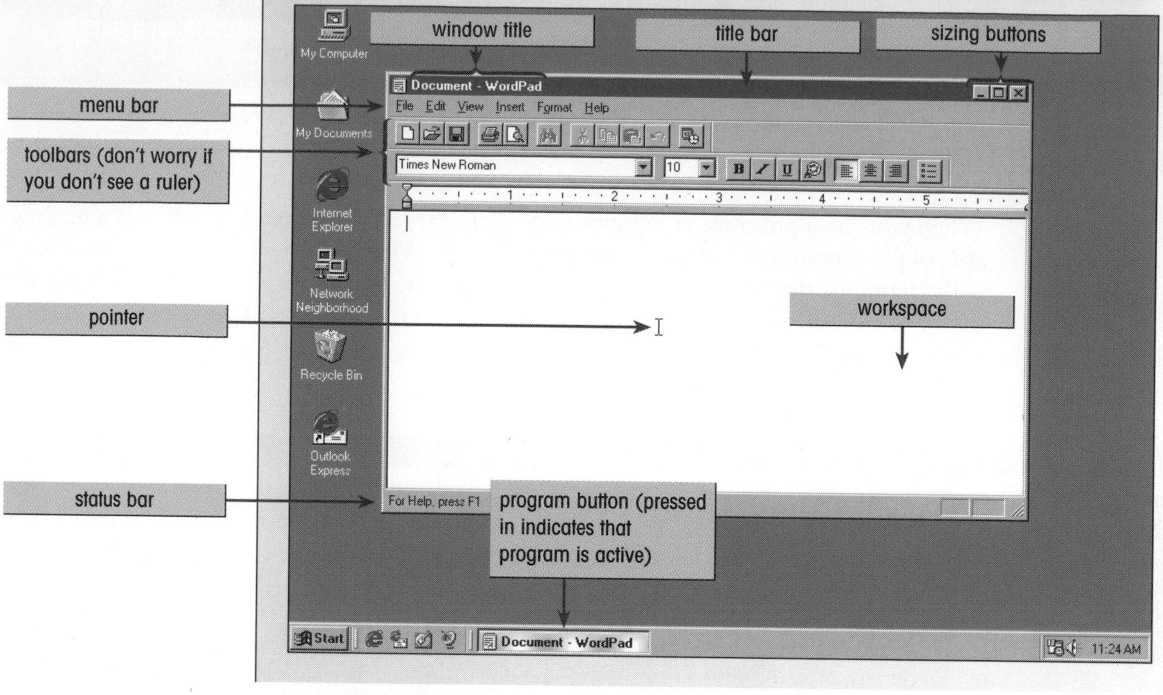

window title

title bar

sizing buttons

menu bar

toolbars (don't worry if you don't see a ruler)

pointer

status bar

workspace

program button (pressed in indicates that program is active)

Manipulating a Window

There are three buttons located on the right side of the title bar. You are already familiar with the Close button. The Minimize button hides the window so that only its program button is visible on the taskbar. The other button either maximizes the window or restores it to a predefined size. Figure 1-18 shows how these buttons work.

Minimizing a Window

The Minimize button ▬ hides a window so that only the button on the taskbar remains visible. You can use the Minimize button when you want to temporarily hide a window but keep the program running.

To minimize the WordPad window:

1. Click the **Minimize** button ▬. The WordPad window shrinks so that only the Document - WordPad button on the taskbar is visible.

   TROUBLE? If you accidentally clicked the Close button and closed the window, use the Start button to start WordPad again.

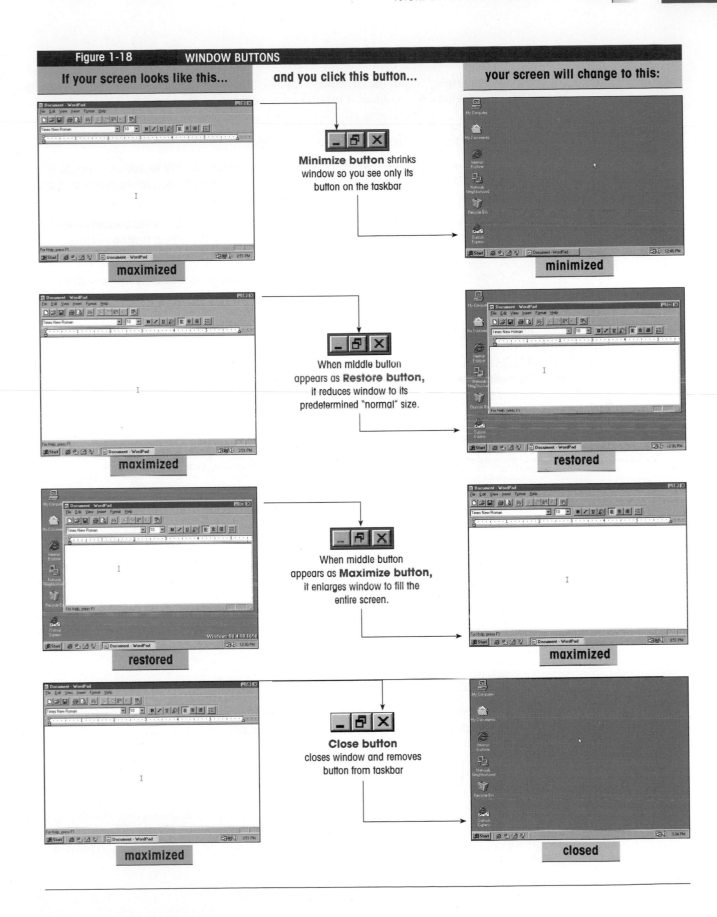

Figure 1-18   **WINDOW BUTTONS**

If your screen looks like this...   and you click this button...   your screen will change to this:

Minimize button shrinks window so you see only its button on the taskbar

maximized   minimized

When middle button appears as **Restore button**, it reduces window to its predetermined "normal" size.

maximized   restored

When middle button appears as **Maximize button**, it enlarges window to fill the entire screen.

restored   maximized

Close button closes window and removes button from taskbar

maximized   closed

Redisplaying a Window

You can redisplay a minimized window by clicking the program's button on the taskbar. When you redisplay a window, it becomes the active window.

> *To redisplay the WordPad window:*
>
> 1. Click the **Document - WordPad** button on the taskbar. The WordPad window is restored to its previous size. The Document - WordPad button looks pushed in as a visual clue that WordPad is now the active window.
>
> 2. The taskbar button provides another means of switching a window between its minimized and active state: click the **Document – WordPad** button on the taskbar again to minimize the window.
>
> 3. Click the **Document – WordPad** button once more to redisplay the window.

Maximizing a Window

The Maximize button enlarges a window so that it fills the entire screen. You will probably do most of your work using maximized windows because they allow you to see more of your program and data.

> *To maximize the WordPad window:*
>
> 1. Click the **Maximize** button ▣ on the WordPad title bar.
>
> **TROUBLE?** If the window is already maximized, it will fill the entire screen, and the Maximize button won't appear. Instead, you'll see the Restore button ▣. Skip Step 1.

Restoring a Window

The Restore button ▣ reduces the window so it is smaller than the entire screen. This is useful if you want to see more than one window at a time. Also, because of its smaller size, you can drag the window to another location on the screen or change its dimensions.

> *To restore a window:*
>
> 1. Click the **Restore** button ▣ on the WordPad title bar. Notice that once a window is restored, ▣ changes to the Maximize button ▣.

Moving a Window

You can use the mouse to move a window to a new position on the screen. When you hold down the mouse button while moving the mouse, you are said to be **dragging**. You can move objects on the screen by dragging them to a new location. If you want to move a window, you drag its title bar. You cannot move a maximized window.

To drag the WordPad window to a new location:

1. Position the mouse pointer on the WordPad window title bar.

2. While you hold down the left mouse button, move the mouse to drag the window. A rectangle representing the window moves as you move the mouse.

3. Position the rectangle anywhere on the screen, then release the left mouse button. The WordPad window appears in the new location.

4. Now drag the WordPad window to the upper-left corner of the screen.

Changing the Size of a Window

You can also use the mouse to change the size of a window. Notice the sizing handle at the lower-right corner of the window. The **sizing handle** provides a visible control for changing the size of a window.

To change the size of the WordPad window:

1. Position the pointer over the sizing handle . The pointer changes to a diagonal arrow .

2. While holding down the mouse button, drag the sizing handle down and to the right.

3. Release the mouse button. Now the window is larger.

4. Practice using the sizing handle to make the WordPad window larger or smaller, and then maximize the WordPad window.

You can also drag the window borders left, right, up, or down to change a window's size.

Using Program Menus

Most Windows programs use menus to provide an easy way for you to select program commands. The menu bar is typically located at the top of the program window and shows the titles of menus such as File, Edit, and Help.

Windows menus are relatively standardized—most Windows programs include similar menu options. It's easy to learn new programs, because you can make a pretty good guess about which menu contains the command you want.

Selecting Commands from a Menu

When you click any menu title, choices for that menu appear below the menu bar. These choices are referred to as **menu options** or **commands**. To select a menu option, you click it. For example, the File menu is a standard feature in most Windows programs and contains the options typically related to working with a file: creating, opening, saving, and printing a file or document.

To select the Print Preview menu option from the File menu:

1. Click **File** in the WordPad menu bar to display the File menu. See Figure 1-19.

TROUBLE? If you open a menu but decide not to select any of the menu options, you can close the menu by clicking its title again.

Figure 1-19	FILE MENU

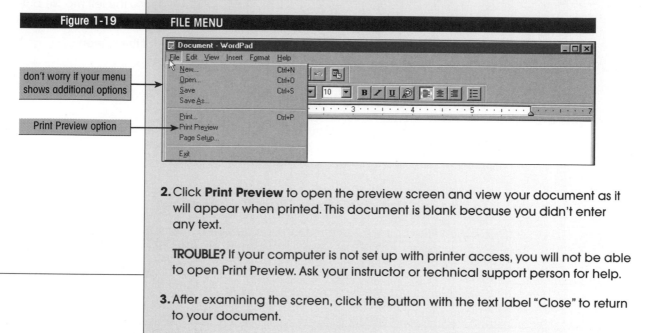

don't worry if your menu shows additional options

Print Preview option

2. Click **Print Preview** to open the preview screen and view your document as it will appear when printed. This document is blank because you didn't enter any text.

TROUBLE? If your computer is not set up with printer access, you will not be able to open Print Preview. Ask your instructor or technical support person for help.

3. After examining the screen, click the button with the text label "Close" to return to your document.

TROUBLE? If you close WordPad by mistake, restart it.

Not all menu options immediately carry out an action—some show submenus or ask you for more information about what you want to do. The menu gives you hints about what to expect when you select an option. These hints are sometimes referred to as **menu conventions**. Figure 1-20 describes the Windows 98 menu conventions.

Figure 1-20	MENU CONVENTIONS
CONVENTION	**DESCRIPTION**
Check mark	Indicates a toggle, or "on-off" switch (like a light switch) that is either checked (turned on) or not checked (turned off)
Ellipsis	Three dots that indicate you must make additional selections after you select that option. Options without dots do not require additional choices—they take effect as soon as you click them. If an option is followed by an ellipsis, a dialog box opens that allows you to enter specifications for how you want a task carried out
Triangular arrow	Indicates presence of a submenu. When you point at a menu option that has a triangular arrow, a submenu automatically appears
Grayed-out option	Option that is not available. For example, a graphics program might display the Text Toolbar option in gray if there is no text in the graphic to work with
Keyboard shortcut	A key or combination of keys that you can press to activate the menu option without actually opening the menu

Figure 1-21 shows examples of these menu conventions.

Figure 1-21	EXAMPLES OF MENU CONVENTIONS

check mark

grayed-out option

arrow indicating that
submenu will open

ellipsis

keyboard shortcut

submenu

The dialog box opens
when you choose an
option followed by
ellipsis. A **dialog box** lets
you enter specifications
for how you want a task
carried out.

View
✓ Tool Box   Ctrl+T
✓ Color Box   Ctrl+L
✓ Status Bar
✓ Text Toolbar
   Zoom   ▶
   View Bitmap Ctrl+F

Normal Size   Ctrl+PgUp
Large Size   Ctrl+PgDn
Custom...
Show Grid   Ctrl+I
✓ Show Thu...

Custom Zoom   ? ×
Current zoom: 100%   OK
Zoom to   Cancel
⦿ 100%   ○ 400%   ○ 800%
○ 200%   ○ 600%

Using Toolbars

A toolbar, as you've seen, contains buttons that provide quick access to important commands. Although you can usually perform all program commands using menus, the toolbar provides convenient one-click access to frequently used commands. For most Windows 98 functions, there is usually more than one way to accomplish a task. To simplify your introduction to Windows 98 in this tutorial, we will usually show you only one method for performing a task. As you become more accomplished at using Windows 98, you can explore alternate methods.

In Session 1.1 you learned that Windows 98 programs include ToolTips, which indicate the purpose and function of a tool. Now is a good time to explore the WordPad toolbar buttons by looking at their ToolTips.

To find out a toolbar button's function:

1. Position the pointer over any button on the toolbar, such as the Print Preview button. After a short pause, the name of the button appears in a box near the button, and a description of the button appears in the status bar just above the Start button. See Figure 1-22.

Figure 1-22	TOOLBAR BUTTON AIDS

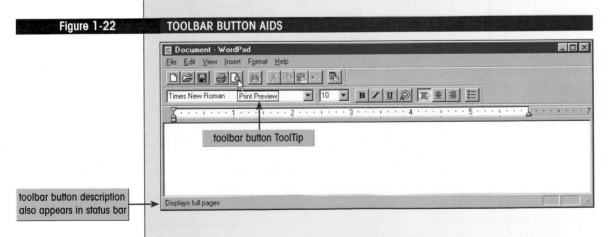

toolbar button ToolTip

toolbar button description
also appears in status bar

2. Move the pointer to each button on the toolbar to see its name and purpose.

You select a toolbar button by clicking it.

To select the Print Preview toolbar button:

1. Click the **Print Preview** button 🔍. The Print Preview screen appears. This is the same screen that appeared when you selected Print Preview from the File menu.

2. After examining the screen, click the button with the text label "Close" to return to your document.

Using List Boxes and Scroll Bars

As you might guess from the name, a **list box** displays a list of choices. In WordPad, date and time formats are shown in the Date/Time list box. List box controls usually include arrow buttons, a scroll bar, and a scroll box, as shown in Figure 1-23.

To use the Date/Time list box:

1. Click the **Date/Time** button 📋 to display the Date and Time dialog box. See Figure 1-23.

Figure 1-23   **LIST BOX**

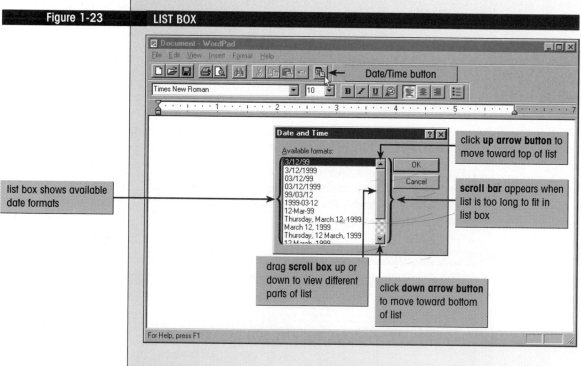

list box shows available date formats

click **up arrow button** to move toward top of list

scroll bar appears when list is too long to fit in list box

drag **scroll box** up or down to view different parts of list

click **down arrow button** to move toward bottom of list

2. To scroll down the list, click the **down arrow** button 🔽. See Figure 1-23.

3. Find the scroll box on your screen. See Figure 1-23.

4. Drag the **scroll box** to the top of the scroll bar. Notice how the list scrolls back to the beginning.

> **TROUBLE?** You learned how to drag when you learned to move a window. To drag the scroll box up, point to the scroll box, press and hold down the mouse button, and then move the mouse up.
>
> 5. Find a date format similar to "March 12, 1999." Click that date format to select it.
>
> 6. Click the **OK** button to close the Date and Time dialog box. This inserts the current date in your document.

You can access some list boxes directly from the toolbar. When a list box is on the toolbar, only the current option appears in the list box. A **list arrow** appears on the right of the box that you can click to view additional options.

> ### To use the Font Size list box:
>
> 1. Click the **list arrow** shown in Figure 1-24.

Figure 1-24	FONT SIZE LIST ARROW

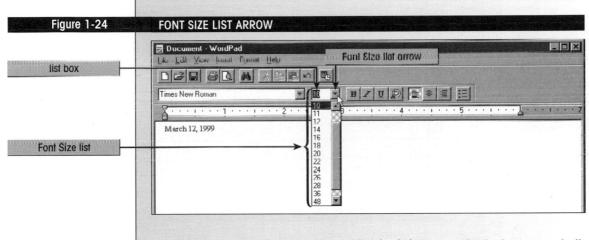

> 2. Click **18**. The list disappears, and the font size you selected appears in the list box.
>
> 3. Type a few characters to test the new font size.
>
> 4. Click the **Font Size** list arrow again.
>
> 5. Click **12**.
>
> 6. Type a few characters to test this type size.
>
> 7. Click the **Close** button ✖ to close WordPad.
>
> 8. When you see the message "Save changes to Document?" click the **No** button.

Using Dialog Box Controls

Recall that when you select a menu option or button followed by an ellipsis, a dialog box opens that allows you to provide more information about how a program should carry out a task. Some dialog boxes group different kinds of information into bordered rectangular areas called **panes**. Within these panes, you will usually find tabs, option buttons, check boxes, and other controls that the program uses to collect information about how you want it to perform a task. Figure 1-25 describes common dialog box controls.

Figure 1-25	DIALOG BOX CONTROLS
CONTROL	**DESCRIPTION**
Tabs	Modeled after the tabs on file folders, tab controls are often used as containers for other Windows 98 controls such as list boxes, radio buttons, and check boxes. Click the appropriate tab to view different pages of information or choices.
Option buttons	Also called **radio buttons**, option buttons allow you to select a single option from among one or more options.
Check boxes	Click a check box to select or deselect it; when it is selected, a check mark appears, indicating that the option is turned on; when deselected, the check box is blank and the option is off. When check boxes appear in groups, you can select or deselect as many as you want; they are not mutually exclusive, as option buttons are.
Spin boxes	Allow you to scroll easily through a set of numbers to choose the setting you want
Text boxes	Boxes into which you type additional information

Figure 1-26 displays examples of these controls.

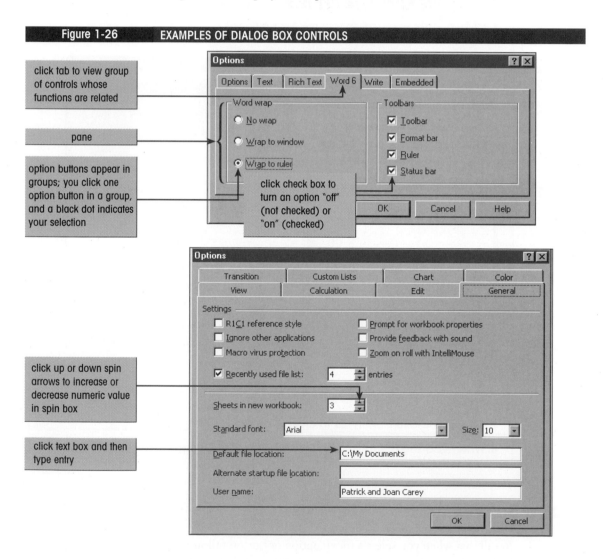

Figure 1-26	EXAMPLES OF DIALOG BOX CONTROLS

click tab to view group of controls whose functions are related

pane

option buttons appear in groups; you click one option button in a group, and a black dot indicates your selection

click check box to turn an option "off" (not checked) or "on" (checked)

click up or down spin arrows to increase or decrease numeric value in spin box

click text box and then type entry

Using Help

Windows 98 **Help** provides on-screen information about the program you are using. Help for the Windows 98 operating system is available by clicking the Start button on the taskbar, then selecting Help from the Start menu. If you want Help for a program, such as WordPad, you must first start the program, then click Help on the menu bar.

When you start Help, a Windows Help window opens, which gives you access to help files stored on your computer as well as help information stored on Microsoft's Web site. If you are not connected to the Web, you only have access to the help files stored on your computer.

To start Windows 98 Help:

1. Click the **Start** button.

2. Click **Help**. The Windows Help window opens to the Contents tab. See Figure 1-27.

   TROUBLE? If the Contents tab is not in front, click the Contents tab to view Help contents.

| Figure 1-27 | WINDOWS HELP WINDOW |

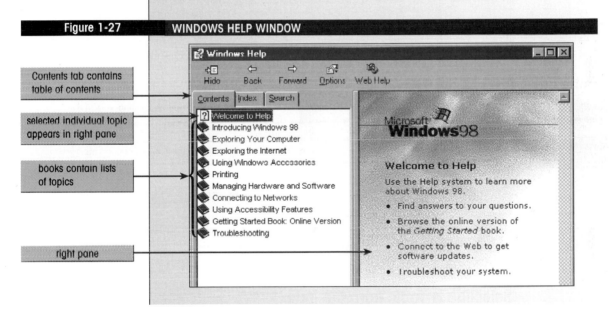

Help uses tabs for the three sections of Help: Contents, Index, and Search. The **Contents tab** groups Help topics into a series of books. You select a book 📖 by clicking it. The book opens, and a list of related topics appears from which you can choose. Individual topics are designated with the ❓ icon.

The **Index tab** displays an alphabetical list of all the Help topics from which you can choose. The **Search tab** allows you to search the entire set of Help topics for all topics that contain a word or words you specify.

Viewing Topics from the Contents Tab

You've already opened two of the Windows accessories, Paint and WordPad. Suppose you're wondering about the other accessory programs. You can use the Contents tab to find more information on a specific topic.

To use the Contents tab:

1. Click the **Using Windows Accessories** book icon 📖. A list of topics and related books appears below the book title. You decide to explore entertainment accessories.

2. Click the **Entertainment** book icon 📖.

3. Click the **CD Player** topic icon ？. Information about the CD Player accessory appears in the right pane, explaining how you can use the CD-ROM drive (if you have one) on your computer to play your favorite music CDs. See Figure 1-28.

Figure 1-28 — **LOCATING INFORMATION ABOUT CD PLAYER ACCESSORY**

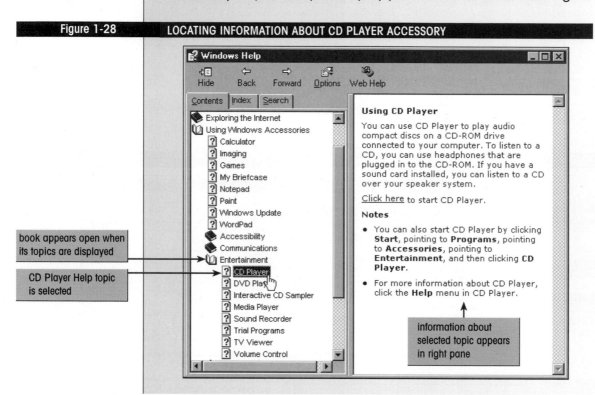

book appears open when its topics are displayed

CD Player Help topic is selected

information about selected topic appears in right pane

Selecting a Topic from the Index

The Index tab allows you to jump to a Help topic by selecting a topic from an indexed list. For example, you can use the Index tab to learn how to arrange the open windows on your desktop.

To find a Help topic using the Index tab:

1. Click the **Index** tab. A long list of indexed Help topics appears.

   TROUBLE? If this is the first time you've used Help on your computer, Windows 98 needs to set up the Index. This takes just a few moments. Wait until you see the list of index entries in the left pane, and then proceed to Step 2.

2. Drag the scroll box down to view additional topics.

3. You can quickly jump to any part of the list by typing the first few characters of a word or phrase in the box above the Index list. Click the box and then type **desktop** to display topics related to the Windows 98 desktop.

4. Click the topic **arranging windows on** and then click the **Display** button. When there is just one topic, it appears immediately in the right pane; otherwise, the Topics Found window opens, listing all topics indexed under the entry you're interested in. In this case, there are two choices.

5. Click **To minimize all open windows**, and then click the **Display** button. The information you requested appears in the right pane. See Figure 1-29. Notice in this topic that there is an underlined word: taskbar. You can click underlined words to view definitions or additional information.

Figure 1-29	USING THE INDEX TO LOCATE INFORMATION

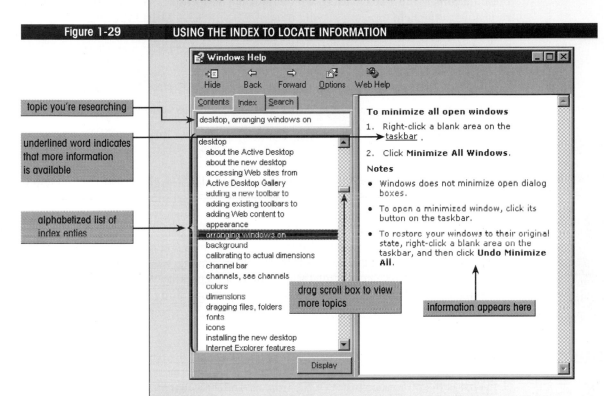

6. Click **taskbar**. A small box appears that defines the term "taskbar." See Figure 1-30

Figure 1-30	VIEWING ADDITIONAL INFORMATION

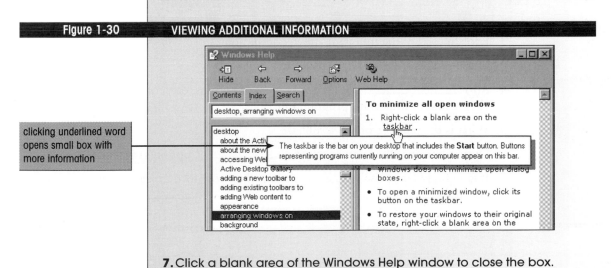

7. Click a blank area of the Windows Help window to close the box.

The third tab, the Search tab, works similarly to the Index tab, except that you type a word, and then the Help system searches for topics containing that word. You'll get a chance to experiment with the Search tab in the Tutorial Assignments.

Returning to a Previous Help Topic

You've looked at a few topics now. Suppose you want to return to the one you just saw. The Help window includes a toolbar of buttons that help you navigate the Help system. One of these buttons is the **Back** button, which returns you to topics you've already viewed. Try returning to the help topic on playing music CDs on your CD-ROM drive.

> ### To return to a help topic:
>
> **1.** Click the **Back** button. The Using CD Player topic appears.
>
> **2.** Click the **Close** button ☒ to close the Windows Help window.
>
> **3.** Log off or shut down Windows 98, depending on your lab's requirements.

Now that you know how Windows 98 Help works, don't forget to use it! Use Help when you need to perform a new task or when you forget how to complete a procedure.

You've finished the tutorial, and as you shut down Windows 98, Steve Laslow returns from class. You take a moment to tell him all you've learned: you know how to start and close programs and how to use multiple programs at the same time. You have learned how to work with windows and the controls they employ. Finally, you've learned how to get help when you need it. Steve congratulates you and comments that you are well on your way to mastering the fundamentals of using the Windows 98 operating system.

QUICK CHECK

1. What is the difference between the title bar and a toolbar?

2. Provide the name and purpose of each button:

   a. ▭   b. ▢   c. ▤   d. ☒

3. Explain each of the following menu conventions:

   a. Ellipsis...   b. Grayed-out   c. ▶   d. ✔

4. A(n) _____ consists of a group of buttons, each of which provides one-click access to important program functions.

5. What is the purpose of the scrollbar?

6. Option buttons allow you to select _____ option(s) at a time.

7. It is a good idea to use _____ when you need to learn how to perform new tasks.

TUTORIAL ASSIGNMENT

1. **Running Two Programs and Switching Between Them** In this tutorial you learned how to run more than one program at a time, using WordPad and Paint. You can run other programs at the same time, too. Complete the following steps and write out your answers to questions b through f:

   a. Start the computer. Enter your username and password if prompted to do so.
   b. Click the Start button. How many menu options are on the Start menu?
   c. Run the Calculator program located on the Accessories menu. How many program buttons are now on the taskbar (don't count toolbar buttons or items in the tray)?
   d. Run the Paint program and maximize the Paint window. How many programs are running now?
   e. Switch to Calculator. What are two visual clues that tell you that Calculator is the active program?
   f. Multiply 576 by 1457 using the Calculator accessory. What is the result?
   g. Close Calculator, then close Paint.

Explore

2. **WordPad Help** In Tutorial 1 you learned how to use Windows 98 Help. Just about every Windows 98 program has a help feature. Many computer users can learn to use a program just by using Help. To use Help, you start the program, then click the Help menu at the top of the screen. Try using WordPad Help:

   a. Start WordPad.
   b. Click Help on the WordPad menu bar, and then click Help Topics.
   c. Using WordPad Help, write out your answers to questions 1 through 4.
   1. How do you create a bulleted list?
   2. How do you set the margins in a document?
   3. How do you undo a mistake?
   4. How do you change the font style of a block of text?
   d. Close WordPad.

Explore

3. **The Search Tab** In addition to the Contents and Index tabs you worked with in this tutorial, Windows 98 Help also includes a Search tab. You may have heard that Windows 98 makes it possible to view television programs on your computer. You could browse through the Contents tab, although you might not know where to look to find information about television. You could also use the Index tab to search through the indexed entry. Or you could use the Search tab to find all Help topics that mention television.

   a. Start Windows 98 Help and use the Index tab to find information about television. How many topics are listed? What is their primary subject matter?
   b. Now use the Search tab to find information about television. Type "television" into the box on the Search tab, and then click the List Topics button.
   c. Write a paragraph comparing the two lists of topics. You don't have to view them all, but in your paragraph, indicate which tab seems to yield more information, and why. Close Help.

4. **Discover Windows 98** Windows 98 includes an online tour that helps you discover more about your computer and the Windows 98 operating system. You can use this tour to review what you learned in this tutorial and to pick up some new tips for using Windows 98. Complete the following steps and write out your answers to questions d–j.

   a. Click the Start button, point to Programs, point to Accessories, point to System Tools, and then click Welcome to Windows. If an error message appears at any point or if you can't locate this menu option, Welcome to Windows is probably not loaded on your computer. You will not be able to complete this assignment unless you have the Windows 98 CD. Check with your instructor.
   b. Click Discover Windows 98.
   c. Click Computer Essentials and follow the instructions on the screen to step through the tour.
   d. What is the "brain" of your computer, according to the tour information?
   e. What two devices do you use to communicate with your computer?

    f. What is the purpose of the ESC key?

    g. What is double-clicking?

    h. What is the purpose of the top section of the Start menu?

    i. What is another term for "submenu"?

    j. What function key opens the Help feature in most software?

PROJECTS

1. There are many types of pointing devices on the market today. Go to the library and research the types of devices that are available. Consider what devices are appropriate for these situations: desktop or laptop computers, connected or remote devices, and ergonomic or standard designs (look up the word "ergonomic").

    Use up-to-date computer books, trade computer magazines such as *PC Computing* and *PC Magazine*, or the Internet (if you know how) to locate information. Your instructor might suggest specific resources you can use. Write a one-page report describing the types of devices available, the differing needs of users, special features that make pointing devices more useful, price comparisons, and finally, an indication of what you would choose if you needed to buy a pointing device.

2. Using the resources available to you, either through your library or the Internet (if you know how), locate information about the release of Windows 98. Computing trade magazines are an excellent source of information about software. Read several articles about Windows 98 and then write a one-page essay that discusses the features that seem most important to the people who have evaluated the software. If you find reviews of the software, mention the features that reviewers had the strongest reaction to, pro or con.

3. **Upgrading** is the process of placing a more recent version of a product onto your computer. When Windows 98 first came out, people had to decide whether or not they wanted to upgrade their computers to Windows 98. Interview several people you know (at least three) who are well-informed Windows computer users. Ask them whether they are using Windows 98 or an older version of Windows. If they are using an older version, ask why they have chosen not to upgrade. If they are using Windows 98, ask them why they chose to upgrade. Ask such questions as:

    a. What features convinced you to upgrade or made you decide to wait?

    b. What role did the price of the upgrade play?

    c. Would you have had (or did you have) to purchase new hardware to make the upgrade? How did this affect your decision?

    d. If you did upgrade, are you happy with that decision? If you didn't, do you intend to upgrade in the near future? Why, or why not?

    Write a single-page essay summarizing what you learned from these interviews about making the decision to upgrade.

4. Choose a topic you'd like to research using the Windows 98 online Help system. Look for information on your topic using all three tabs: the Contents tab, the Index tab, and the Search tab. Once you've found all the information you can, compare the three methods (Contents, Index, Search) of looking for information. Write a paragraph that discusses which tab proved the most useful. Did you reach the same information topics using all three methods? In a second paragraph, summarize what you learned about your topic. Finally, in a third paragraph, indicate under what circumstances you'd use which tab.

LAB ASSIGNMENTS

Using a Keyboard To become an effective computer user, you must be familiar with your primary input device—the keyboard. See the Read This Before You Begin page for information on installing and starting the lab.

1. The Steps for the Using a Keyboard Lab provide you with a structured introduction to the keyboard layout and the function of special computer keys. Click the Steps button and begin the Steps. As you work through the Steps, answer all of the Quick Check questions that appear. When you complete the Steps, you will see a Summary Report that summarizes your performance on the Quick Checks. Follow the directions on the screen to print the Summary Report.

2. In Explore, start the typing tutor. You can develop your typing skills using the typing tutor in Explore. Take the typing test and print out your results.

3. In Explore, try to improve your typing speed by 10 words per minute. For example, if you currently type 20 words per minute, your goal will be 30 words per minute. Practice each typing lesson until you see a message that indicates that you can proceed to the next lesson. Create a Practice Record, as shown here, to keep track of how much you practice. When you have reached your goal, print out the results of a typing test to verify your results.

Practice Record

Name:

Section:

Start Date: Start Typing Speed: wpm

End Date: End Typing Speed: wpm

Lesson #:   Date Practiced/Time Practiced

Using a Mouse A mouse is a standard input device on most of today's computers. You need to know how to use a mouse to manipulate graphical user interfaces and to use the rest of the Labs. See the Read This Before You Begin page for information on installing and starting the lab.

1. The Steps for the Using a Mouse Lab show you how to click, double-click, and drag objects using the mouse. Click the Steps button and begin the Steps. As you work through the Steps, answer all of the Quick Check questions that appear. When you complete the Steps, you will see a Summary Report that summarizes your performance on the Quick Checks. Follow the directions on the screen to print the Summary Report.

2. In Explore, create a poster, to demonstrate your ability to use a mouse and to control a Windows program. To create a poster for an upcoming sports event, select a graphic, type the caption for the poster, then select a font, font styles, and a border. Print your completed poster.

QUICK | CHECK ANSWERS

Session 1.1

1. The taskbar contains buttons that give you access to tools and programs.

2. multitasking

3. Start menu

4. Lift the mouse up and move it to the right.

5. Its button appears on the taskbar.

6. To conserve computer resources such as memory.

7. To ensure you don't lose data and damage your files.

Session 1.2

1. The title bar identifies the window and contains window controls; toolbars contain buttons that provide you with shortcuts to common menu commands.

2. a. Minimize button shrinks window so you see button on taskbar

   b. Maximize button enlarges window to fill entire screen

   c. Restore button reduces window to predetermined size

   d. Close button closes window and removes button from taskbar

3. a. ellipsis indicates a dialog box will open

   b. grayed-out indicates option is not currently available

   c. arrow indicates a submenu will open

   d. check mark indicates a toggle option

4. toolbar

5. Scrollbars appear when the contents of a box or window are too long to fit; you drag the scroll box to view different parts of the contents.

6. one

7. online Help

WORKING WITH FILES

Creating, Saving, and Managing Files

OBJECTIVES

In this tutorial you will:

- Format a disk

- Enter, select, insert, and delete text

- Create and save a file

- Open, edit, and print a file

- Switch to Web style

- Create a Student Disk

- View the list of files on your disk and change view options

- Move, copy, delete, and rename a file

- Navigate Explorer windows

- Make a copy of your Student Disk

LABS

Using Files

CASE

Distance Education

You recently purchased a computer in order to gain new skills and stay competitive in the job market. Your friend Shannon suggests that you broaden your horizons by enrolling in a few distance education courses. **Distance education**, Shannon explains, is formalized learning that typically takes place using a computer, replacing normal classroom interaction with modern communications technology. Many distance education courses take advantage of the **Internet**, a vast structure of millions of computers located all over the world that are connected together so that they are able to share information. The **World Wide Web**, usually called the **Web**, is a popular service on the Internet that makes information readily accesssible. Educators can make their course material available on the Web.

Windows 98 makes it possible for your computer to display content in a way that is similar to the way it appears on the Web, and Shannon is eager to show you how. She suggests, however, that first you should get more comfortable with your computer—especially using programs and files. Shannon points out that most of the software installed on your computer was created especially for the Windows 98 operating system. This software is referred to as **Windows 98 applications** or **Windows 98 programs**. You can use software designed for older operating systems, but Windows 98 applications take better advantage of the features of the Windows 98 operating system.

You typically use Windows 98 applications to create files. A **file**, often referred to as a **document**, is a collection of data that has a name and is stored in a computer. Once you create a file, you can open it, edit its contents, print it, and save it again—usually using the same application program you used to create it.

Shannon suggests that you become familiar with how to perform these tasks in Windows 98 applications. Then she'll show you how to set up your computer so it incorporates the look and feel of the Web. Finally, you'll spend time learning how to organize your files.

SESSION 2.1

In Session 2.1 you will learn how to format a disk so it can store files. You will create, save, open, and print a file. You will find out how the insertion point differs from the mouse pointer, and you will learn the basic skills for Windows 98 text entry, such as inserting, deleting, and selecting. *For the steps of this tutorial you will need two blank 3½-inch disks.*

Formatting a Disk

Before you can save files on a disk, the disk must be formatted. When the computer **formats** a disk, the magnetic particles on the disk surface are arranged so data can be stored on the disk. Today, many disks are sold preformatted and can be used right out of the box. However, if you purchase an unformatted disk, or if you have an old disk you want to completely erase and reuse, you can format the disk using the Windows 98 Format command. This command is available through the **My Computer window**, a window that gives you access to the objects on your computer. You open My Computer by using its icon on the desktop. You'll learn more about the My Computer window later in this tutorial.

The following steps tell you how to format a 3½-inch high-density disk using drive A. Your instructor will tell you how to revise the instructions given in these steps if the procedure is different for your lab equipment.

Make sure you are using a blank disk before you perform these steps.

To format a disk:

1. Start Windows 98, if necessary.

2. Write your name on the label of a 3½-inch disk and insert your disk in drive A. See Figure 2-1.

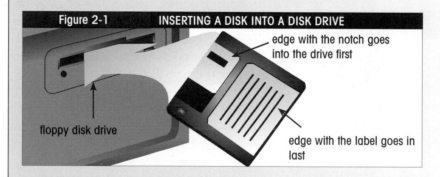

Figure 2-1   INSERTING A DISK INTO A DISK DRIVE

edge with the notch goes into the drive first

floppy disk drive

edge with the label goes in last

TROUBLE? If your disk does not fit in drive A, put it in drive B and substitute drive B for drive A in all of the steps for the rest of the tutorial.

3. Click the **My Computer** icon on the desktop. The icon is selected. Figure 2-2 shows the location of this icon on your desktop.

TROUBLE? If the My Computer window opens, skip Step 4. Your computer is using different settings, which you'll learn to change in Session 2.2.

4. Press **Enter** to open the My Computer window. See Figure 2-2 (don't worry if your window opens maximized).

TROUBLE? If you see a list instead of icons like those in Figure 2-2, click View, then click Large Icons. Don't worry if your toolbars don't exactly match those in Figure 2-2.

TROUBLE? If you see additional information or a graphic image on the left side of the My Computer window, Web view is enabled on your computer. Don't worry. You will learn how to enable and disable Web view in Session 2.2.

Figure 2-2	MY COMPUTER WINDOW

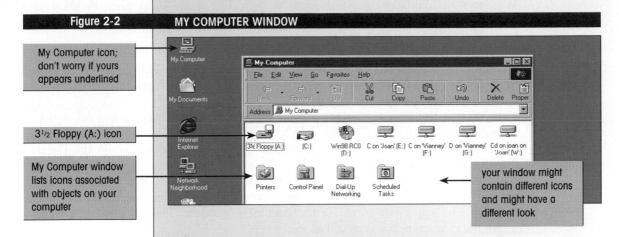

My Computer icon; don't worry if yours appears underlined

3½ Floppy (A:) icon

My Computer window lists icons associated with objects on your computer

your window might contain different icons and might have a different look

5. Right-click the **3½ Floppy (A:)** icon to open its shortcut menu.

6. Click **Format** on the shortcut menu. The Format dialog box opens.

7. Click the **Full** option button to perform a full format. Make sure the other dialog box settings on your screen match those in Figure 2-3.

Figure 2-3	FORMAT DIALOG BOX

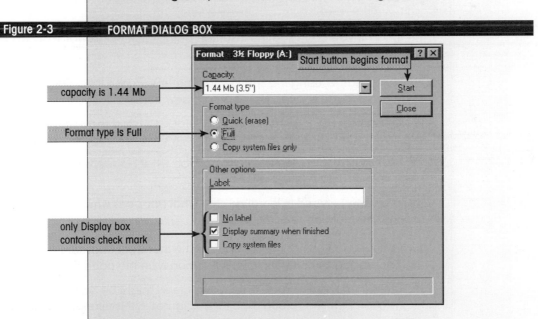

capacity is 1.44 Mb

Format type Is Full

only Display box contains check mark

Start button begins format

8. On the right side of the dialog box is a Start button. Click this **Start** button to begin formatting the disk. A series of blue boxes at the bottom of the Format window shows you how the format is progressing. When the format is complete, the Format Results dialog box appears.

9. Click the **Close** button, and then close any open windows on the desktop.

TROUBLE? To close the windows, click each Close button ⊠.

Working with Text

To accomplish many computing tasks, you need to type text in documents and text boxes. Windows 98 facilitates basic text entry by providing a text-entry area, by showing you where your text will appear on the screen, by helping you move around on the screen, and by providing insert and delete functions.

When you type sentences of text, do not press the Enter key when you reach the right margin of the page. Most software contains a feature called **word wrap**, which automatically continues your text on the next line. Therefore, you should press Enter only when you have completed a paragraph.

If you type the wrong character, press the Backspace key to back up and delete the character. You can also use the Delete key. What's the difference between the Backspace and the Delete keys? The Backspace key deletes the character to the left, while the Delete key deletes the character to the right.

Now you will type some text using WordPad, to practice what you've learned about text entry. When you first start WordPad, notice the flashing vertical bar, called the **insertion point**, in the upper-left corner of the document window. The insertion point indicates where the characters you type will appear.

To type text in WordPad:

1. Start WordPad and locate the insertion point.

   TROUBLE? If the WordPad window does not fill the screen, click the Maximize button ▣.

   TROUBLE? If you can't find the insertion point, click in the WordPad workspace area.

2. Type your name, using the Shift key to type uppercase letters and using the Spacebar to type spaces, just as on a typewriter.

3. Press the **Enter** key to end the current paragraph and move the insertion point down to the next line.

4. As you type the following sentences, watch what happens when the insertion point reaches the right edge of the page:

   This is a sample typed in WordPad. See what happens when the insertion point reaches the right edge of the page.

   TROUBLE? If you make a mistake, delete the incorrect character(s) by pressing the Backspace key on your keyboard. Then type the correct character(s).

   TROUBLE? If your text doesn't wrap, your screen might be set up to display more information than the screen used for the figures in this tutorial. Type the sentences again until text wraps automatically.

The Insertion Point Versus the Pointer

The insertion point is not the same as the mouse pointer. When the mouse pointer is in the text-entry area, it is called the **I-beam pointer** and looks like I. Figure 2-4 explains the difference between the insertion point and the I-beam pointer.

Figure 2-4	THE INSERTION POINT VS. THE POINTER

The best food in
town is at Joe's.

the insertion point shows your typing position on the screen—it moves as you type and usually blinks when you pause

The best food in
town is at Joe's.

the mouse pointer moves freely around on the screen as you move the mouse; when the mouse pointer is positioned in a text entry area, it looks like an I-Beam: I

The best food in
town is at Joe's.

when you move the I-beam pointer to a position on the screen where text has been typed, and you click the mouse, the insertion point moves to that location

To enter text, you move the I-beam pointer to the location where you want to type, and then click. The insertion point jumps to the location you clicked and, depending on the program you are using, may blink to indicate the program is ready for you to type. When you enter text, the insertion point moves as you type.

To move the insertion point:

1. Check the locations of the insertion point and the I-beam pointer. The insertion point should be at the end of the sentence you typed in the last set of steps.

   TROUBLE? If you don't see the I-beam pointer, move your mouse until you see it.

2. Use the mouse to move the I-beam pointer to the word "sample," then click the mouse button. The insertion point jumps to the location of the I-beam pointer.

3. Move the I-beam pointer to a blank area near the bottom of the workspace, and click. Notice the insertion point does not jump to the location of the I-beam pointer. Instead the insertion point jumps to the end of the last sentence. The insertion point can move only within existing text. It cannot be moved out of the existing text area.

Selecting Text

Many text operations are performed on a **block** of text, which is one or more consecutive characters, words, sentences, or paragraphs. Once you select a block of text, you can delete it, move it, replace it, underline it, and so on. As you select a block of text, the computer highlights it. If you want to remove the highlighting, just click in the margin of your document.

If you want to delete the phrase "See what happens" in the text you just typed and replace it with the phrase "You can watch word wrap in action," you do not have to delete the first phrase one character at a time. Instead, you can highlight the entire phrase and then type the replacement phrase.

To select and replace a block of text:

1. Move the I-beam pointer just to the left of the word "See."

2. While holding down the mouse button, drag the I-beam pointer over the text to the end of the word "happens." The phrase "See what happens" should now be highlighted. See Figure 2-5.

TROUBLE? If the space to the right of the word "happens" is also selected, don't worry. Your computer is set up to select spaces in addition to words. After completing Step 4, simply press the Spacebar to type an extra space if required.

| Figure 2-5 | HIGHLIGHTING TEXT |

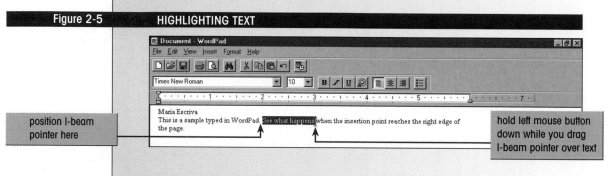

position I-beam pointer here

hold left mouse button down while you drag I-beam pointer over text

3. Release the mouse button.

TROUBLE? If the phrase is not highlighted correctly, repeat Steps 1 through 3.

4. Type **You can watch word wrap in action**

The text you typed replaces the highlighted text. Notice you did not need to delete the highlighted text before you typed the replacement text.

Inserting a Character

Windows 98 programs usually operate in **insert mode**—when you type a new character, all characters to the right of the insertion point are pushed over to make room.

Suppose you want to insert the word "sentence" before the word "typed" in your practice sentences.

To insert text:

1. Move the I-beam pointer just before the word "typed," then click to position the insertion point.

2. Type **sentence**

3. Press the **Spacebar**.

Notice how the letters in the first line are pushed to the right to make room for the new characters. When a word gets pushed past the right margin, the **word-wrap** feature moves it down to the beginning of the next line.

Saving a File

Using Files

As you type text, it is held temporarily in the computer's memory. For permanent storage, you need to save your work on a disk. In the computer lab, you will probably save your work on a floppy disk in drive A.

When you save a file, you must give it a name. Windows 98 allows you to use up to 255 characters in a filename, although usually the operating system requires some of those characters for designating file location and file type. So, while it is unlikely you would need that many characters, you should be aware that the full 255 characters might not always be available. You may use spaces and certain punctuation symbols in your filenames. You cannot use the symbols \ / ? : * " < > | in a filename, but other symbols such as & ; - and $ are allowed. Furthermore, filenames for files used by older Windows 3.1 or DOS applications (pre-1995 operating systems) must be eight characters or less. Thus when you save a file with a long filename in Windows 98, Windows 98 also creates an eight-character filename that can be used by older applications. The eight-character filename is created from the first six nonspace characters in the long filename, with the addition of a tilde (~) and a number. For example, the filename Car Sales for 1999 would be converted to Carsal~1.

Most filenames have an extension. An **extension** is a suffix, usually of three characters, separated from the filename by a period. In the filename Car Sales for 1999.doc, a period separates the filename from the file extension. The file extension "doc" helps categorize the file by type or by the software that created it. Files created with Microsoft Word software have a .doc extension, such as Resume.doc (pronounced "Resume dot doc"). In general you will not add an extension to your filenames, because the application software automatically does this for you.

Windows 98 keeps track of file extensions, but does not always display them. The steps in these tutorials refer to files using the filename, but not its extension. So if you see the filename Practice Text in the steps, but "Practice Text.doc" on your screen, don't worry—these refer to the same file. Also don't worry if you don't use consistent lowercase and uppercase letters when saving files. Usually the operating system doesn't distinguish between them. Be aware, however, that some programs are "case-sensitive"—they check for case in filenames.

Now you can save the document you typed.

To save a document:

1. Click the **Save** button [💾] on the toolbar. Figure 2-6 shows the location of this button and the Save As dialog box that appears after you click it.

Figure 2-6	SAVING A FILE

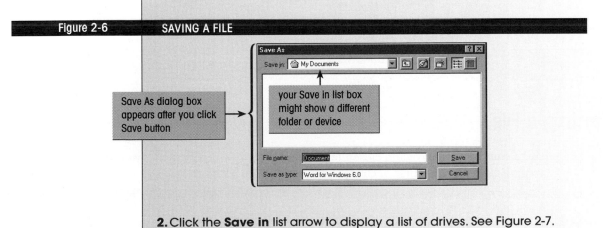

Save As dialog box appears after you click Save button →

your Save in list box might show a different folder or device

2. Click the **Save in** list arrow to display a list of drives. See Figure 2-7.

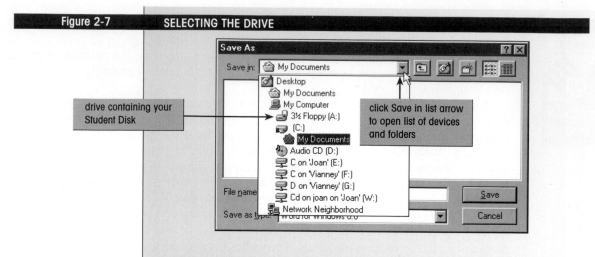

Figure 2-7   SELECTING THE DRIVE

3. Click **3½ Floppy (A:)**, and select the text in the File name box.

   TROUBLE? To select the text, move the I-beam pointer to the beginning of the word "Document." While you hold down the mouse button, drag the I-beam pointer to the end of the word.

4. Type **Practice Text** in the File name box.

5. Click the **Save** button in the lower-right corner of the dialog box. Your file is saved on your Student Disk, and the document title, "Practice Text," appears on the WordPad title bar.

What if you try to close WordPad before you save your file? Windows 98 will display a message—"Save changes to Document?" If you answer "Yes," Windows will display the Save As dialog box so you can give the document a name. If you answer "No," Windows 98 will close WordPad without saving the document. Any changes you made to the document would be lost, so when you are asked if you want to save a file, answer Yes, unless you are absolutely sure you don't need to keep the work you just did.

After you save a file, you can work on another document or close WordPad. Since you have already saved your Practice Text document, you'll continue this tutorial by closing WordPad.

To close WordPad:

1. Click the **Close** button ☒ to close the WordPad window.

Opening a File

Suppose you save and close the Practice Text file, then later you want to revise it. To revise a file you must first open it. When you **open** a file, its contents are copied into the computer's memory. If you revise the file, you need to save the changes before you close the application or work on a different file. If you close a revised file without saving your changes, you will lose them.

Typically, you use one of two methods to open a file. You could select the file from the Documents list or the My Computer window, or you could start an application program and then use the Open button to open the file. Each method has advantages and disadvantages.

The first method for opening the Practice Text file simply requires you to select the file from the Documents list or from the My Computer window. With this method the document, not the application program, is central to the task; hence, this method is sometimes referred to as **document-centric**. You only need to remember the name of your document or file—you do not need to remember which application you used to create the document.

The Documents list contains the names of the last 15 documents used. You access this list from the Start menu. When you have your own computer, the Documents list is very handy. In a computer lab, however, the files other students use quickly replace yours on the list.

If your file is not in the Documents list, you can open the file by selecting it from the My Computer window. Windows 98 starts an application program you can use to revise the file, then automatically opens the file. The advantage of this method is its simplicity. The disadvantage is Windows 98 might not start the application you expect. For example, when you select Practice Text, you might expect Windows 98 to start WordPad because you used WordPad to create it. Depending on the software installed on your computer system, however, Windows 98 might start the Microsoft Word application instead. Usually this is not a problem. Although the application might not be the one you expect, you can still use it to revise your file.

To open the Practice Text file by selecting it from My Computer:

1. From the desktop, open the **My Computer** window.

2. Click the **3½ Floppy (A:)** icon in the My Computer window.

   TROUBLE? If the 3½ Floppy (A:) window opens, skip Step 3.

3. Press **Enter**. The 3½ Floppy (A:) window opens.

4. Click the **Practice Text** file icon.

   TROUBLE? If the Practice Text document appears in a word-processing window, skip Step 5.

5. Press **Enter**. Windows 98 starts an application program, then automatically opens the Practice Text file. You could make revisions to the document at this point, but instead, you'll close all the windows on your desktop so you can try the other method for opening files.

   TROUBLE? If Windows 98 starts Microsoft Word or another word-processing program instead of WordPad, don't worry. You can use Microsoft Word to revise the Practice Text document.

6. Close all open windows on the desktop.

The second method for opening the Practice Text file requires you to open WordPad, then use the Open button to select the Practice Text file. The advantage of this method is you can specify the application program you want to use—WordPad, in this case. This method, however, involves more steps than the method you tried previously.

To start WordPad and open the Practice Text file using the Open button:

1. Start WordPad and maximize the WordPad window.

2. Click the **Open** button 📂 on the toolbar.

3. Click the **Look in** list arrow to display a list of drives.

4. Click **3½ Floppy (A:)** from the list.

5. Click **Practice Text** to make sure it is highlighted. See Figure 2-8.

Figure 2-8 | SELECTING THE FILE

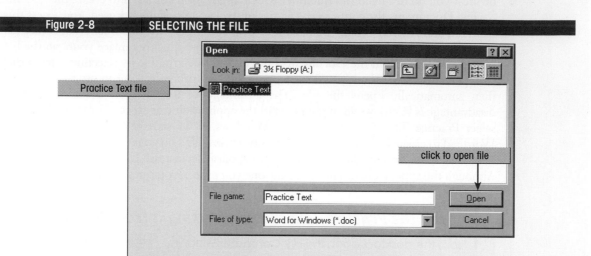

Practice Text file

click to open file

6. Click the **Open** button in the lower-right corner of the dialog box. Your document should appear in the WordPad work area.

Printing a File

Now that the Practice Text file is open, you can print it. It is a good idea to use Print Preview before you send your document to the printer. **Print Preview** shows on the screen exactly how your document will appear on paper. You can check your page layout so you don't waste paper printing a document that is not quite the way you want it. Your instructor might supply you with additional instructions for printing in your school's computer lab.

To preview, then print, the Practice Text file:

1. Click the **Print Preview** button 🔍 on the toolbar.

   TROUBLE? If an error message appears, printing capabilities might not be set up on your computer. Ask your instructor or lab assistant for help, or skip this set of steps.

2. Look at your print preview. Before you print the document and use paper, you should make sure the font, margins, and other document features look the way you want them to.

   TROUBLE? If you can't read the document text on screen, click the Zoom In button.

3. Click the **Print** button. A Print dialog box appears. Study Figure 2-9 to familiarize yourself with the controls in the Print dialog box.

Figure 2-9   PRINTING A FILE

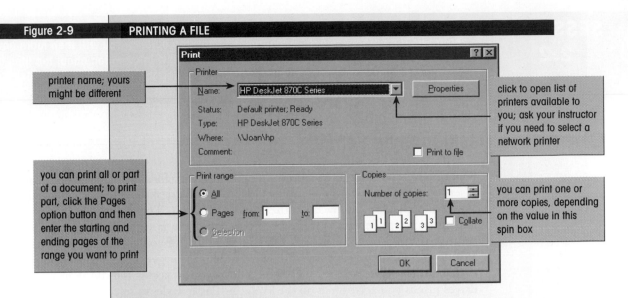

printer name; yours might be different

click to open list of printers available to you; ask your instructor if you need to select a network printer

you can print all or part of a document; to print part, click the Pages option button and then enter the starting and ending pages of the range you want to print

you can print one or more copies, depending on the value in this spin box

4. Make sure your screen shows the Print range set to "All" and the number of copies set to "1."

5. Click the **OK** button to print your document.

TROUBLE? If your document does not print, make sure the printer has paper and the printer online light is on. If your document still doesn't print, ask your instructor or lab assistant for help.

6. Close WordPad.

TROUBLE? If you see the message "Save changes to Document?" click the No button.

You've now learned how to create, save, open, and print word-processed files—essential skills for students in distance education courses that rely on word-processed reports transmitted across the Internet. Shannon assures you that the techniques you've just learned apply to most Windows 98 programs.

QUICK CHECK

1. A(n) _____ is a collection of data that has a name and is stored on a disk or other storage medium.

2. _____ erases all the data on a disk and arranges the magnetic particles on the disk surface so the disk can store data.

3. True or False: When you move the mouse pointer over a text entry area, the pointer shape changes to an I-bar.

4. What shows you where each character you type will appear?

5. _____ automatically moves text down to the beginning of the next line when you reach the right margin.

6. How do you select a block of text?

7. In the filename New Equipment.doc, doc is a(n) _____.

SESSION 2.2

In this session you will learn how to change settings in the My Computer window to control its appearance and the appearance of desktop objects. You will then learn how to use My Computer to manage the files on your disk; view information about the files on your disk; organize the files into folders; and move, delete, copy, and rename files. *For this session you will use a second blank 3½-inch disk.*

Changing Desktop Style Settings

Shannon tells you that in Windows 98 you work with files by manipulating icons that represent them. These icons appear in many places: the desktop, the My Computer windows, the 3½ Floppy (A:) window, and other similar windows. The techniques you use to manipulate these icons depend on whether your computer is using Classic-style or Web-style settings or a customized hybrid. **Classic style** allows you to use the same techniques in Windows 98 that are used in Windows 95, the previous version of the Windows operating system. **Web style**, on the other hand, allows you to access files on your computer's hard drives just as you access files on the Web. In Classic style, to select an item you click it, and to open an item you click it and then press Enter. In Web style, to select an item you point to it, and to open an item you click it.

Thus, if you wanted to open your Practice Text document from the My Computer window, in Classic style you would click its icon and press Enter, but in Web style you would simply click its icon.

Switching to Web Style

By default, Windows 98 starts using a combination of Classic and Web style settings, but it uses Classic click settings. Your computer might have been set differently. If you have your own computer, you can choose which style you want to use. If you want to minimize the number of mouse actions for a given task, or if you want to explore your computer in the same way you explore the Web, you'll probably want to use Web style. On the other hand, if you are used to Classic style settings, you might want to continue using them. Shannon suggests that you use Web style because you'll be able to use the same techniques on the Web, and you'll be more at ease with your distance learning courses. The next set of steps shows you how to switch to Web style, and the rest of the tutorial assumes that you're using Web-style settings.

To switch styles:

1. Click the **Start** button [Start] and then point to **Settings**.

2. Click **Folder Options**. The Folder Options dialog box opens.

   TROUBLE? If you can't open the Folder Options dialog box, or you can't make any changes to it, you probably don't have permission to change these settings. If your computer is set to use Classic style and you can't change this setting, you will notice a few differences in subsequent steps in this tutorial. The TROUBLE? paragraphs will help to ensure that you learn the proper techniques for the settings you are using.

3. On the General tab, click the **Web style** option button. See Figure 2-10.

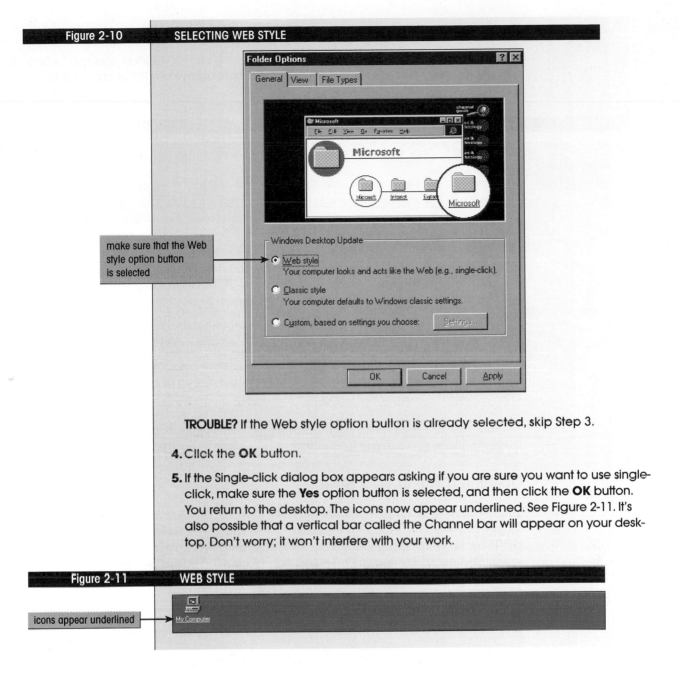

Figure 2-10   SELECTING WEB STYLE

make sure that the Web style option button is selected

TROUBLE? If the Web style option button is already selected, skip Step 3.

4. Click the **OK** button.

5. If the Single-click dialog box appears asking if you are sure you want to use single-click, make sure the **Yes** option button is selected, and then click the **OK** button. You return to the desktop. The icons now appear underlined. See Figure 2-11. It's also possible that a vertical bar called the Channel bar will appear on your desktop. Don't worry; it won't interfere with your work.

Figure 2-11   WEB STYLE

icons appear underlined

You are now using Web-style settings.

Selecting an Icon in Web Style

In Web style, you select an icon representing a device, folder, or file by pointing to the icon long enough for it to become highlighted. This technique is sometimes called **hovering**. The pointer changes from ↕ to ⬚ when you point to the icon. Try selecting the My Computer icon in Web style.

To select the My Computer icon in Web style:

1. Position the pointer over the My Computer icon on the desktop and notice how the pointer changes from ↖ to ☝ and the color of the text label changes to show it is selected. See Figure 2-12.

Figure 2-12 SELECTING AN ICON IN WEB STYLE

pointer when you point at icon in Web style

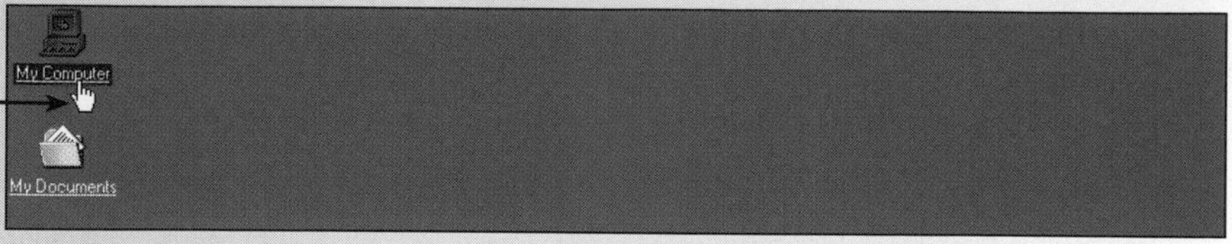

TROUBLE? If the My Computer icon is not selected when you point to it, you might not be holding the mouse steadily. You need to steadily "hover" the pointer over the object long enough for the object to become highlighted. Simply passing the mouse over an object will not select it.

TROUBLE? If in Web style you click the My Computer icon instead of simply pointing at it, the My Computer window will open. Close the window and repeat Step 1.

TROUBLE? If you were unable to switch to Web style because you didn't have permission, you'll need to click the My Computer icon to select it.

Note that the Web style selection technique only applies to icons on the desktop and icons in windows such as My Computer.

Opening a File in Web Style

You saw in Session 2.1 that you can open the Practice Text document directly from the 3½ Floppy (A:) window. The steps in Session 2.1 assumed you were using Classic style. Now you'll try opening the Practice Text document using Web style. You open an object by simply clicking it. Try opening your Practice Text file in Web style.

To open the Practice Text file in Web style:

1. Click the **My Computer** icon. The My Computer window opens.

   TROUBLE? If you were unable to switch to Web style, you'll need to press Enter after Steps 1, 2, and 3.

2. Click the **3½ Floppy (A:)** icon. The 3½ Floppy (A:) window opens.
3. Click the **Practice Text** icon. Your word-processing software starts and the Practice Text file opens.
4. Close all open windows.

Now that you've practiced working with icons in Web style, you'll learn other tasks you can perform with these icons to manage your files.

Creating Your Student Disk

For the rest of this session, you must create a Student Disk that contains some practice files. *You can use the disk you formatted in the previous session.*

If you are using your own computer, the NP on Microsoft Windows 98 menu selection will not be available. Before you proceed, you must go to your school's computer lab and find a computer that has the NP on Microsoft Windows 98 program installed. If you cannot get the files from the lab, ask your instructor or lab assistant for help. Once you have made your own Student Disk, you can use it to complete this tutorial on any computer you choose.

To add the practice files to your Student Disk:

1. Write "Disk 1 - Windows 98 Tutorial 2 Student Disk" on the label of your formatted disk (the same disk you used to save your Practice Text file).

2. Place the disk in drive A.

3. Click the **Start** button ![Start].

4. Point to **Programs**.

5. Point to **NP on Microsoft Windows 98 – Level I**.

   TROUBLE? If NP on Microsoft Windows 98 - Level I is not listed ask your instructor or lab assistant for help.

6. Click **Disk 1 (Tutorial 2)**. A message box opens, asking you to place your disk in drive A.

7. Click the **OK** button. Wait while the program copies the practice files to your formatted disk. When all the files have been copied, the program closes.

Your Student Disk now contains practice files you will use throughout the rest of this tutorial.

My Computer

The My Computer icon, as you have seen, represents your computer, its storage devices, printers, and other objects. The My Computer icon opens into the My Computer window, which contains an icon for each of the storage devices on your computer. On most computer systems, the My Computer window also contains the Control Panel and Printers folders, which help you add printers, control peripheral devices, and customize your Windows 98 work environment. Depending on the services your computer is running, you might see additional folders such as Dial-Up Networking (for some Internet connections) or Scheduled Tasks (for scheduling programs provided with Windows 98) that help you keep your computer running smoothly). Figure 2-13 shows how the My Computer window relates to your computer's hardware.

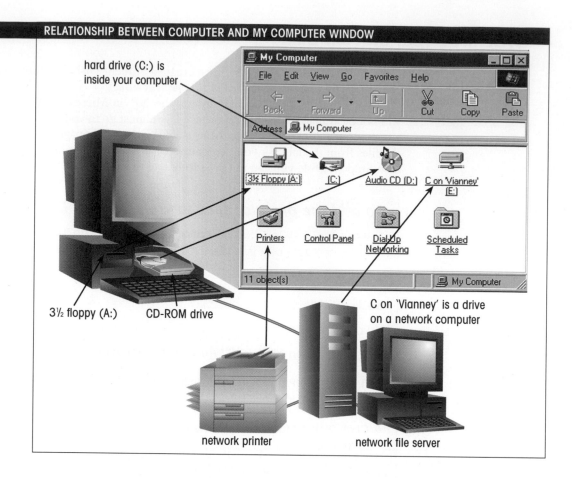

Figure 2-13 · **RELATIONSHIP BETWEEN COMPUTER AND MY COMPUTER WINDOW**

hard drive (C:) is inside your computer

3½ floppy (A:) CD-ROM drive

C on 'Vianney' is a drive on a network computer

network printer network file server

The first floppy drive on a computer is designated as drive A (if you add a second drive it is usually designated as drive B), and the first hard drive is designated drive C (if you add additional hard drives they are usually designated D, E, and so on).

You can use the My Computer window to keep track of where your files are stored and to organize your files. In this section of the tutorial you will move and delete files on your Student Disk in drive A. If you use your own computer at home or work, you will probably store your files on drive C instead of drive A. However, in a school lab environment you usually don't know which computer you will use, so you need to carry your files with you on a floppy disk that you use in drive A. In this session, therefore, you will learn how to work with the files on drive A. Most of what you learn will also work on your home or work computer when you use drive C (or other drives).

Now you'll open the My Computer window.

To open the My Computer window and explore the contents of your Student Disk:

1. Open the My Computer window.

2. Click the **3½ Floppy (A:)** icon. A window appears showing the contents of drive A; maximize this window if necessary. See Figure 2-14.

   TROUBLE? If you are using Classic style, click Settings, click the 3½ Floppy (A:) icon and then press Enter. Your window might look different from Figure 2-14; for example, you might see only files, and not the additional information on the left side of the window.

TROUBLE? If you see a list of filenames instead of icons, click View, then click Large Icons.

Figure 2-14	CONTENTS OF STUDENT DISK

icons show contents of drive A

three-letter file extensions might appear on your screen for some or all files

Changing My Computer View Options

Windows 98 offers several different options that control how toolbars, icons, and buttons appear in the My Computer window. You can choose to hide or display these options, depending on the task you are performing. To make the My Computer window on your computer look the same as it does in the figures in this book, you need to ensure four things: that only the Address and Standard toolbars are visible and Text Labels is enabled, that Web view is disabled, that Large Icons view is enabled, and that file extensions are hidden.

Controlling the Toolbar Display

The My Computer window, in addition to featuring a Standard toolbar, allows you to display the same toolbars that can appear on the Windows 98 taskbar, such as the Address toolbar or the Links toolbar. These toolbars make it easy to access the Web from the My Computer window. In this tutorial, however, you need to see only the Address and Standard toolbars. You can hide one or all of the My Computer toolbars, and you can determine how they are displayed, with or without text labels. Displaying the toolbars without text labels takes up less room on your screen, but it is not as easy to identify the button's function.

To display only the Address and Standard toolbars and to hide text labels:

1. Click **View**, point to **Toolbars**, and then examine the Toolbars submenu. The Standard Buttons, Address Bar, and Text Labels options should be preceded by a check mark. The Links option should not be checked.

2. If the Standard Buttons option *is not checked*, click it.

3. If necessary, reopen the Toolbars submenu, and then repeat Step 2 with the Address Bar and Text Labels options.

4. Open the Toolbars submenu once again, and if the Links option *is checked*, click it to disable it.

5. Click **View** and then point to **Toolbars** one last time and verify that your Toolbars submenu and the toolbar display look like Figure 2-15.

TROUBLE? If the checkmarks are distributed differently than in Figure 2-15, repeat Steps 1–5 until the correct options are checked.

TROUBLE? If your toolbars are not displayed as shown in Figure 2-15 (for example, both the Standard and Address toolbars might be on the same line, or the Standard toolbar might be above the Address toolbar), you can easily rearrange them. To move a toolbar, drag the vertical bar at the far left of the toolbar. By dragging that vertical bar, you can drag the toolbar left, right, up, or down.

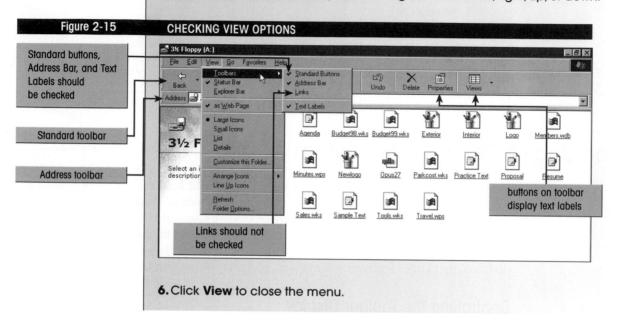

Figure 2-15   CHECKING VIEW OPTIONS

Standard buttons, Address Bar, and Text Labels should be checked

Standard toolbar

Address toolbar

Links should not be checked

buttons on toolbar display text labels

6. Click **View** to close the menu.

Web View

The My Computer window also can be viewed in **Web view**, which allows you to display and customize the My Computer window as a document you would see on the Web. Web view is automatically enabled when you switch to Web style; in its default appearance Web view shows information about the open folder or selected file, along with a decorated background. There are many advantages to Web view, including the ability to place information, graphics, and Web content in a folder window. Shannon says you'll find this feature useful once you've started your distance education courses. For now, however, you don't need to customize Web view, so you'll disable it.

To disable Web view:

1. Click **View**.

2. If the option "as Web Page" is preceded by a check mark, click **as Web Page** to disable Web view.

3. Click **View** again and ensure that as Web Page is not checked.

TROUBLE? If as Web Page is checked, repeat Steps 1 and 2.

4. Click **View** again to close the View menu.

Changing the Icon Display

Windows 98 provides four ways to view the contents of a disk—large icons, small icons, list, or details. The default view, Large Icons view, displays a large icon and title for each file. The icon provides a visual cue to the type and contents of the file, as Figure 2-16 illustrates.

Figure 2-16	TYPICAL ICONS AS THEY APPEAR IN MY COMPUTER

FILE AND FOLDER ICONS

	Text documents that you can open using the Notepad accessory are represented by notepad icons.
	Graphic image documents that you can open using the Paint accessory are represented by drawing instruments.
	Word-processed documents that you can open using the WordPad accessory are represented by a formatted notepad icon, unless your computer designates a different word-processing program to open files created with WordPad.
	Word-processed documents that you can open using a program such as Microsoft Word are represented by formatted document icons.
	Files created by programs that Windows does not recognize are represented by the Windows logo.
	A folder icon represents folders.
	Certain folders created by Windows 98 have a special icon design related to the folder's purpose.

PROGRAM ICONS

	Icons for programs usually depict an object related to the function of the program. For example, an icon that looks like a calculator represents the Calculator accessory.
	Non-windows programs are represented by the icon of a blank window.

Large Icons view helps you quickly identify a file and its type, but what if you want more information about a set of files? Details view shows more information than the large icon, small icon, and list views. Details view shows the file icon, the filename, the file size, the application you used to create the file, and the date/time the file was created or last modified.

To view a detailed list of files:

1. Click **View** and then click **Details** to display details for the files on your disk, as shown in Figure 2-17. Your files might be in a different order.

2. Look at the file sizes. Do you see that Exterior and Interior are the largest files?

3. Look at the dates and times the files were modified. Which is the oldest file?

Figure 2-17   DETAILS VIEW

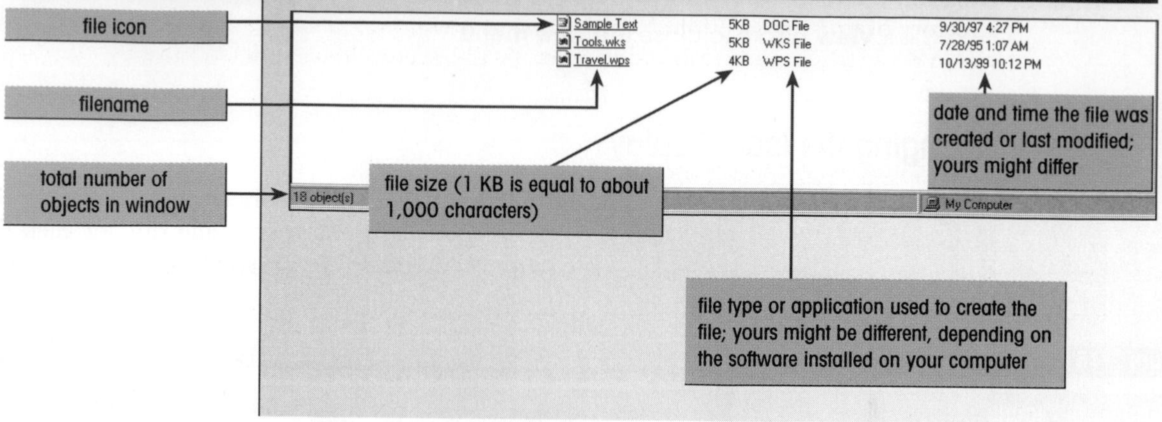

file icon

filename

total number of
objects in window

Sample Text	5KB	DOC File	9/30/97 4:27 PM
Tools.wks	5KB	WKS File	7/28/95 1:07 AM
Travel.wps	4KB	WPS File	10/13/99 10:12 PM

18 object(s)

file size (1 KB is equal to about
1,000 characters)

date and time the file was
created or last modified;
yours might differ

My Computer

file type or application used to create the
file; yours might be different, depending on
the software installed on your computer

Now that you have looked at the file details, switch back to Large Icon view.

To switch to Large Icon view:

1. Click **View** and then click **Large Icons** to return to the large icon display.

Hiding File Extensions

You have the option to show or hide file extensions for file types that Windows recognizes. Showing them takes up more room but gives more information about the file. In this tutorial, however, you don't need to see file extensions, so you'll hide them. They might already be hidden on your computer.

To hide file extensions:

1. Click **View** and then click **Folder Options**. Note this is the same dialog box you saw when switching to Web style. It is accessible from the Start menu and the My Computer window.

2. Click the **View** tab.

3. Make sure the **Hide file extensions for known file types** check box is checked. If it is not, click it to insert a check mark.

4. Click the **OK** button.

The only file extensions that now appear are those whose file type Windows doesn't recognize.

Folders and Directories

A list of related files located in the same place is referred to as a **directory**. The main directory of a disk is sometimes called the **root directory**, or the **top-level directory**. The root directory is created when you format a disk, and it is designated by a letter—usually A for your floppy disk and C for your hard disk. All of the files on your Student Disk are currently in the root directory of your floppy disk.

If too many files are stored in a directory, the directory list becomes very long and difficult to manage. You can divide a directory into **folders**, into which you group similar files. The directory of files for each folder then becomes much shorter and easier to manage. A folder within a folder is called a **subfolder**. Now, you'll create a folder called Practice to hold your documents.

To create a Practice folder:

1. Click **File**, and then point to **New** to display the submenu.

2. Click **Folder**. A folder icon with the label "New Folder" appears.

3. Type **Practice** as the name of the folder.

   TROUBLE? If nothing happens when you type the folder name, it's possible that the folder name is no longer selected. Right-click the Practice folder, click Rename, and then repeat Step 3.

4. Press the **Enter** key.

When you first create a folder, it doesn't contain any files. In the next set of steps, you will move a file from the root directory to the Practice folder.

Moving and Copying a File

You can move a file from one directory to another, or from one disk to another. When you move a file, it is copied to the new location you specify, and then the version in the old location is erased. The move feature is handy for organizing or reorganizing the files on your disk by moving them into appropriate folders. The easiest way to move a file is to hold down the right mouse button and drag the file from the old location to the new location. A menu appears and you select Move Here.

REFERENCE WINDOW   **RW**

Moving a File
- Locate the file in the My Computer window.
- Hold down the right mouse button while you drag the file icon to its new folder or disk location.
- Click Move Here.

Suppose you want to move the Minutes file from the root directory to the Practice folder. Depending on your computer's settings, this file appears either as Minutes or Minutes.wps. In the following steps, the file is referred to as Minutes.

To move the Minutes file to the Practice folder:

1. Point to the **Minutes** icon.

2. Press and hold the right mouse button while you drag the Minutes icon to the Practice folder. See Figure 2-18.

TROUBLE? If you release the mouse button by mistake before dragging the Minutes icon to the Practice folder, the Minutes shortcut menu opens. Press Esc and then repeat Steps 1 and 2.

Figure 2-18   **MOVING A FILE**

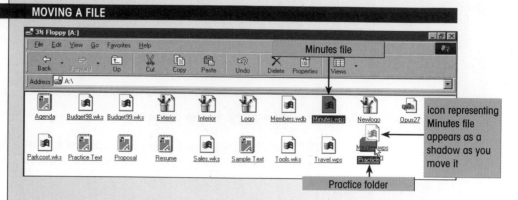

3. Release the right mouse button. A menu appears.

4. Click **Move Here**. The Minutes icon disappears from the window showing the files in the root directory.

Anything you do to an icon in the My Computer window is actually done to the file represented by that icon. If you move an icon, the file is moved; if you delete an icon, the file is deleted.

You can also copy a file from one folder to another, or from one disk to another. When you copy a file, you create an exact duplicate of an existing file in whatever disk or folder you specify. To copy a file from one folder to another on your floppy disk, you use the same procedure as for moving a file, except that you select Copy Here from the menu.

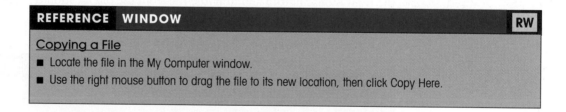

REFERENCE WINDOW   **RW**

Copying a File
- Locate the file in the My Computer window.
- Use the right mouse button to drag the file to its new location, then click Copy Here.

Try copying the Resume file into the Practice folder.

To copy the Resume file into the Practice folder:

1. Using the right mouse button, drag the Resume file into the Practice folder.

2. Click **Copy Here**. Notice this time the file icon does not disappear, because you didn't actually move it, you only copied it.

After you move or copy a file, it is a good idea to make sure it was moved to the correct location. You can easily verify that a file is in its new folder by displaying the folder contents.

To verify that the Minutes file was moved and the Resume file was copied to the Practice folder:

1. Click the **Practice** folder icon. The Practice window appears, and it contains two files—Minutes, which you moved, and Resume, which you copied.

   TROUBLE? If you are using Classic style, click Settings, click the Practice folder icon and then press Enter to open the Practice window.

Navigating Explorer Windows

The title bar of the open window on your computer, "Practice," identifies the name of the folder you just opened. Before you opened the Practice folder, you were viewing the contents of your floppy disk, so the window's title bar, 3½ Floppy (A:) (or possibly just A:/, depending on how your computer is set up), identified the drive containing your disk, drive A. Before you opened that window you were viewing the My Computer window. Windows that show the objects on your computer are called **Explorer windows** because they allow you to explore the contents of your computer's devices and folders.

You've seen that to navigate through the devices and folders on your computer, you open My Computer and then click the icons representing the objects you want to explore. But what if you want to move back to a previous Explorer window? The Standard toolbar, which stays the same regardless of which Explorer window is open, includes buttons that help you navigate through your Explorer windows. Figure 2-19 summarizes the navigation buttons on the Standard toolbar.

Figure 2-19		NAVIGATIONAL BUTTONS
BUTTON	**ICON**	**DESCRIPTION**
Back	⬅	Returns you to the Explorer window you were most recently viewing. This button is active only when you have viewed more than one Explorer window in the current session.
Forward	➡	Reverses the effect of the Back button.
Up	🔼	Moves you up one level on the hierarchy of your computer's objects; for example, moves you from a folder Explorer window to the drive containing the folder.

Try returning to the 3½ Floppy (A:) window using the Back button.

To navigate Explorer windows:

1. Click the **Back** button ⬅ to return to the 3½ Floppy (A:) window.

2. Click the **Forward** button ➡ to reverse the effect of the Back button and return to the Practice window.

3. Click the **Up** button 🔼 to move up one level. You again return to the 3½ Floppy (A:) window because the Practice folder is contained within the 3½ Floppy (A:) drive.

Deleting a File

You delete a file or folder by deleting its icon. However, be careful when you delete a folder, because you also delete all the files it contains! When you delete a file from a *hard drive* on your computer, the filename is deleted from the directory but the file contents are held in the Recycle Bin. The **Recycle Bin** is an area on your hard drive that holds deleted files until you remove them permanently; an icon on the desktop allows you easy access to the Recycle Bin. If you change your mind and want to retrieve a file deleted from your hard drive, you can recover it by using the Recycle Bin.

When you delete a file from a *floppy disk*, it does not go into the Recycle Bin. Instead, it is deleted as soon as its icon disappears.

Try deleting the file named Agenda from your Student Disk. Because this file is on the floppy disk and not on the hard disk, it will not go into the Recycle Bin, and if you change your mind you won't be able to recover it.

To delete the file Agenda:

1. Right-click the icon for the file Agenda.

2. Click **Delete**.

3. If a message appears asking, "Are you sure you want to delete Agenda?", click **Yes**. The file is deleted and the Agenda icon no longer appears.

Renaming a File

Sometimes you decide to give a file a different name to clarify the file's contents. You can easily rename a file by using the Rename option on the file's shortcut menu or by using the file's label. The same rules apply for renaming a file as applied for naming a file, and you are limited in the number and type of characters you can use.

When you rename a file when file extensions are showing, make sure to include the extension in the new name. If you don't, Windows warns you it might not be able to identify the file type with the new name. Since you set up View options to hide file extensions, this should not be an issue unless you are trying to rename a file whose type Windows doesn't recognize.

Practice using this feature by renaming the Logo file to give it a more descriptive filename.

To rename Logo:

1. Right-click the **Logo** icon.

2. Click **Rename**. After a moment, a box appears around the label.

3. Type **Corporate Logo Draft** as the new filename.

4. Press the **Enter** key. The file now appears with the new name.

5. Click the **Up** button 🔼 to move up one level to the My Computer window.

You can also edit an existing filename when you use the Rename command. Click to place the cursor at the location you want to edit, and then use the text-editing skills you learned with WordPad to edit the filename.

Copying an Entire Floppy Disk

You can have trouble accessing the data on your floppy disk if the disk is damaged, is exposed to magnetic fields, or picks up a computer virus. To avoid losing all your data, it is a good idea to make a copy of your floppy disk.

If you wanted to make a copy of an audio cassette, your cassette player would need two cassette drives. You might wonder, therefore, how your computer can make a copy of your disk if you have only one disk drive. Figure 2-20 illustrates how the computer uses only one disk drive to make a copy of a disk.

REFERENCE WINDOW `RW`

<u>Copying a Disk</u>
- Insert the disk you want to copy in drive A.
- In My Computer, right-click the 3½ Floppy (A:) icon, and then click Copy Disk.
- Click Start to begin the copy process.
- When prompted, remove the disk you want to copy, place your second disk in drive A, then click OK.

Figure 2-20   **USING ONE DISK DRIVE TO COPY A DISK**

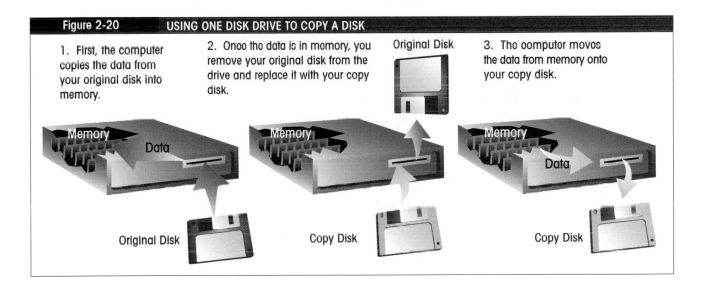

1. First, the computer copies the data from your original disk into memory.

2. Once the data is in memory, you remove your original disk from the drive and replace it with your copy disk.

3. The computer moves the data from memory onto your copy disk.

If you have an extra floppy disk, you can make a copy of your Student Disk now. If you change the files on your disk, make sure you copy the disk regularly to keep it updated.

To copy your Student Disk:

1. Write your name and "Windows 98 Disk 1 Student Disk Copy" on the label of your second disk. Make sure the disk is blank and formatted.

   TROUBLE? If you aren't sure the disk is blank, place it in the disk drive and open the 3½ Floppy (A:) window to view its contents. If the disk contains files you need, get a different disk. If it contains files you don't need, you could format the disk now, using the steps you learned at the beginning of this tutorial.

2. Make sure your Student Disk is in drive A and the My Computer window is open.

3. Right-click the **3½ Floppy (A:)** icon, and then click **Copy Disk**. The Copy Disk dialog box opens.

4. Click the **Start** button to begin the copy process.

5. When the message "Insert the disk you want to copy to (destination disk)..." appears, remove your Student Disk and insert your Windows 98 Disk 1 Student Disk Copy in drive A.

6. Click the **OK** button. When the copy is complete, you will see the message "Copy completed successfully." Click the **Close** button.

7. Close the My Computer window.

8. Remove your disk from the drive.

As you finish copying your disk, Shannon emphasizes the importance of making copies of your files frequently, so you won't risk losing important documents for your distance learning course. If your original Student Disk were damaged, you could use the copy you just made to access the files.

Keeping copies of your files is so important that Windows 98 includes with it a program called **Backup** that automates the process of duplicating and storing data. In the Projects at the end of the tutorial you'll have an opportunity to explore the difference between what you just did in copying a disk and the way in which a program such as the Windows 98 Backup program helps you safeguard data.

QUICK CHECK

1. If you want to find out about the storage devices and printers connected to your computer, what window can you open?

2. If you have only one floppy disk drive on your computer, it is usually identified by the letter _____ .

3. The letter C is typically used for the _____ drive of a computer.

4. What information does Details view supply about a list of folders and files?

5. The main directory of a disk is referred to as the _____ directory.

6. True or False: You can divide a directory into folders.

7. If you have one floppy disk drive, but you have two disks, can you copy the files on one floppy disk to the other?

TUTORIAL ASSIGNMENT

1. **Opening, Editing, and Printing a Document** In this tutorial you learned how to create a document using WordPad. You also learned how to save, open, and print a document. Practice these skills by opening the document called Resume in the Practice folder of your Student Disk. This document is a resume for Jamie Woods. Make the changes shown in Figure 2-21, and then save the document in the Pratice folder with the name "Resume 2" using the Save As command. After you save your revisions, preview and then print the document. Close WordPad.

Figure 2-21

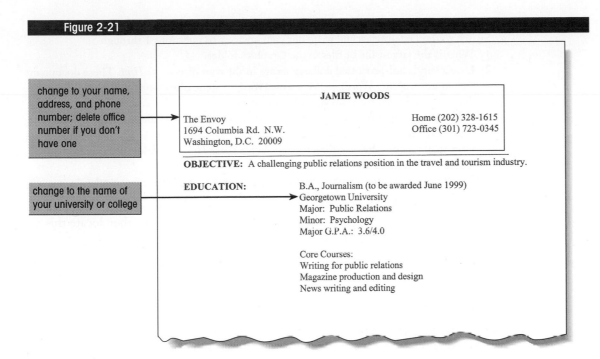

change to your name, address, and phone number; delete office number if you don't have one

change to the name of your university or college

JAMIE WOODS

The Envoy   Home (202) 328-1615
1694 Columbia Rd. N.W.   Office (301) 723-0345
Washington, D.C. 20009

OBJECTIVE: A challenging public relations position in the travel and tourism industry.

EDUCATION: B.A., Journalism (to be awarded June 1999)
                        Georgetown University
                        Major: Public Relations
                        Minor: Psychology
                        Major G.P.A.: 3.6/4.0

                        Core Courses:
                        Writing for public relations
                        Magazine production and design
                        News writing and editing

2. **Creating, Saving, and Printing a Letter**   Use WordPad to write a one-page letter to a relative or a friend. Save the document in the Practice folder on your Student Disk with the name "Letter." Use the Print Preview feature to look at the format of your finished letter, then print it, and be sure to sign it. Close WordPad.

3. **Managing Files and Folders**   Using the copy of the disk you made at the end of the tutorial, complete parts a through f below to practice your file management skills.

    a. Create a folder called Spreadsheets on your Student Disk.
    b. Move the files Parkcost, Budget98, Budget99, and Sales into the Spreadsheets folder.
    c. Create a folder called Park Project.
    d. Move the files Proposal, Members, Tools, Corporate Logo Draft, and Newlogo into the Park Project folder.
    e. Delete the file called Travel.
    f. Switch to the Details view and write out your answers to questions 1 through 5:
        1. What is the largest file or files in the Park Project folder?
        2. What is the newest file or files in the Spreadsheets folder?
        3. How many files (don't include folders) are in the root directory of your Student Disk?
        4. How are the Opus and Exterior icons different? Judging from the appearance of the icons, what would you guess these two files contain?
        5. Which file in the root directory has the most recent date?

4. **More Practice with Files and Folders**   For this assignment, you need a third blank disk. Complete parts a through g below to practice your file management skills.

    a. Write "Windows 98 Tutorial 2 Assignment 4" on the label of the blank disk, and then format the disk if necessary.
    b. Create a new Student Disk, using the Assignment 4 disk. Refer to the section "Creating Your Student Disk" in Session 2.2.
    c. Create three folders on the Assignment 4 Student Disk you just created: Documents, Budgets, and Graphics.
    d. Move the files Interior, Exterior, Logo, and Newlogo to the Graphics folder.
    e. Move the files Travel, Members, and Minutes to the Documents folder.

    f. Move Budget98 and Budget99 to the Budgets folder.

    g. Switch to the Details view and write out your answers to questions 1 through 5:

       1. What is the largest file or files in the Graphics folder?

       2. How many word-processed documents are in the root directory? *Hint*: These documents will appear with the WordPad, Microsoft Word, or some other word-processing icon, depending on what software you have installed.

       3. What is the newest file or files in the root directory (don't include folders)?

       4. How many files in all folders are 5 KB in size?

       5. How many files in the root directory are WKS files? *Hint*: Look in the Type column to identify WKS files.

       6. Do all the files in the Graphics folder have the same icon? What type are they?

5. **Finding a File**   The Help system includes a topic that discusses how to find files on a disk without looking through all the folders. Start Windows Help, then locate this topic, and answer questions a through c:

    a. To display the Find dialog box, you must click the _____ button, then point to _____ from the menu, and finally click _____ from the submenu.

    b. Do you need to type in the entire filename to find the file?

    c. How do you perform a case-sensitive search?

6. **Help with Files and Folders**   In Tutorial 2 you learned how to work with Windows 98 files and folders. What additional information on this topic does Windows 98 Help provide? Use the Start button to access Help. Use the Index tab to locate topics related to files and folders. Find at least two tips or procedures for working with files and folders that were not covered in the tutorial. Write out the tip in your own words and include the title of the Help screen that contains the information.

Explore ▶ 7. **Formatting Text**   You can use a word processor such as WordPad to **format** text, that is, to give it a specific look and feel by using bold, italics, and different fonts, and by applying other features. Using WordPad, type the title and words to one of your favorite songs and then save the document on your Student Disk (make sure you use your original Student Disk) with the name Song.

    a. Select the title, and then click the Center ▤, Bold **B**, and Italic *I* buttons on the toolbar.

    b. Click the Font list arrow and select a different font. Repeat this step several times with different fonts until you locate a font that matches the song.

    c. Experiment with formatting options until you find a look you like for your document. Save and print the final version.

PROJECTS

1. Formatting a floppy disk removes all the data on a disk. Answer the following questions using full sentences:

    a. What other method did you learn in this tutorial to remove data from a disk?

    b. If you wanted to remove all data from a disk, which method would you use? Why?

    c. What method would you use if you wanted to remove only one file? Why?

2. A friend who is new to computers is trying to learn how to enter text into WordPad. She has just finished typing her first paragraph when she notices a mistake in the first sentence. She can't remember how to fix a mistake, so she asks you for help. Write the set of steps she should try.

3. Computer users usually develop habits about how they access their files and programs. Take a minute to practice methods of opening a file, and then evaluate which method you would be likely to use and why.

   a. Using WordPad, create a document containing the words to a favorite poem, and save it on your Student Disk with the name Poem.
   b. Close WordPad and return to the desktop.
   c. Open the document using a *document-centric* approach.
   d. After a successful completion of part c, close the program and reopen the same document using another approach.
   e. Write the steps you used to complete parts c and d of this assignment. Then write a paragraph discussing which approach is most convenient when you are starting from the desktop, and indicate what habits you would develop if you owned your own computer and used it regularly.

Explore ▷ 4. The My Computer window gives you access to the objects on your computer. In this tutorial you used My Computer to access your floppy drive so you could view the contents of your Student Disk. The My Computer window gives you access to other objects too. Open My Computer and write a list of the objects you see, including folders. Then click each icon and write a two-sentence description of the contents of each window that opens.

Explore ▷ 5. In this tutorial you learned how to copy a disk to protect yourself in the event of data loss. If you had your own computer with an 80 MB hard drive that was being used to capacity, it would take many 1.44 MB floppy disks to copy the contents of the entire hard drive. Is copying a reasonable method to use for protecting the data on your hard disk? Why, or why not?

   a. As mentioned at the end of the tutorial, Windows 98 also includes an accessory called Backup that helps you safeguard your data. Backup doesn't just copy the data—it organizes it so that it takes up much less space than if you simply copied it. This program might not be installed on your computer, but if it is, try starting it (click the Start button, point to Programs, point to Accessories, point to System Tools, and then click Backup) and opening the Help files to learn what you can about how it functions. If it is not installed, skip part a.
   b. Look up the topic of backups in a computer concepts textbook or in computer trade magazines. You could also interview experienced computer owners to find out which method they use to protect their data. When you have finished researching the concept of the backup, write a single-page essay that explains the difference between copying and backing up files, and evaluates which method is preferable for backing up large amounts of data, and why.

LAB ASSIGNMENTS

Using Files

Using Files   In this Lab you manipulate a simulated computer to view what happens in memory and on disk when you create, save, open, revise, and delete files. Understanding what goes on "inside the box" will help you quickly grasp how to perform basic file operations with most application software. See the Read This Before You Begin page for instructions on starting the Using Files Course Lab.

1. Click the Steps button to learn how to use the simulated computer to view the contents of memory and disk when you perform basic file operations. As you proceed through the Steps, answer all of the Quick Check questions that appear. After you complete the Steps, you will see a Quick Check Summary Report. Follow the instructions on the screen to print this report.

2. Click the Explore button and use the simulated computer to perform the following tasks:

a. Create a document containing your name and the city in which you were born. Save this document as NAME.

b. Create another document containing two of your favorite foods. Save this document as FOODS.

c. Create another file containing your two favorite classes. Call this file CLASSES.

d. Open the FOOD file and add another one of your favorite foods. Save this file without changing its name.

e. Open the NAME file. Change this document so it contains your name and the name of your school. Save this as a new document called SCHOOL.

f. Write down how many files are on the simulated disk and the exact contents of each file.

g. Delete all the files.

3. In Explore, use the simulated computer to perform the following tasks.

a. Create a file called MUSIC that contains the name of your favorite CD.

b. Create another document that contains eight numbers and call this file LOTTERY.

c. You didn't win the lottery this week. Revise the contents of the LOTTERY file, but save the revision as LOTTERY2.

d. Revise the MUSIC file so it also contains the name of your favorite musician or composer, and save this file as MUSIC2.

e. Delete the MUSIC file.

f. Write down how many files are on the simulated disk and the exact contents of each file.

QUICK | CHECK ANSWERS

Session 2.1

1. file

2. Formatting

3. True

4. insertion point

5. Word wrap

6. Move the I-beam pointer to the left of the first word you want to select, then drag the I-beam pointer over the text to the end of the last word you want to select.

7. file extension

Session 2.2

1. My Computer

2. A

3. hard

4. file name, size, type, and date modified

5. root or top-level

6. True

7. yes

New Perspectives on

MICROSOFT®
ACCESS® 2000

Read This Before You Begin

To the Student

Data Disks

To complete the Level I tutorials, Review Assignments, and Case Problems, you need 6 Data Disks. Your instructor will either provide you with these Data Disks or ask you to make your own.

If you are making your own Data Disks, you will need 6 blank, formatted high-density disks. You will need to copy a set of folders from a file server or standalone computer or the Web onto your disks. Your instructor will tell you which computer, drive letter, and folders contain the files you need. You could also download the files by going to www.course.com, clicking Data Disk Files, and following the instructions on the screen.

The following list shows you which folders go on each of your disks, so that you will have enough disk space to complete all the tutorials, Review Assignments, and Case Problems:

Data Disk 1

Write this on the disk label:
Data Disk 1: Tutorial files

Put this folder from the Disk 1 folder on the disk:
Tutorial

Data Disk 2

Write this on the disk label:
Data Disk 2: Review Assignments files

Put this folder from the Disk 2 folder on the disk:
Review

Data Disk 3

Write this on the disk label:
Data Disk 3: Case Problem 1 files

Put this folder from the Disk 3 folder on the disk:
Cases

Data Disk 4

Write this on the disk label:
Data Disk 4: Case Problem 2

Put this folder from the Disk 4 folder on the disk:
Cases

Data Disk 5

Write this on the disk label:
Data Disk 5: Case Problem 3

Put this folder from the Disk 5 folder on the disk:
Cases

Data Disk 6

Write this on the disk label:
Data Disk 6: Case Problem 4

Put this folder from the Disk 6 folder on the disk:
Cases

When you begin each tutorial, be sure you are using the correct Data Disk. Refer to the "File Finder" Chart at the back of this text for more detailed information on which files are used in which tutorials. These Access Level I tutorials use the same files for Tutorials 1-4. If you are completing the Level II tutorials, you will need to create new Data Disks for those tutorials. See the inside front or inside back cover of this book for more information on Data Disk files, or ask your instructor or technical support person for assistance.

Course Labs

The Access Level I tutorials feature an interactive Course Lab to help you understand database concepts. There are Lab Assignments at the end of Tutorial 1 that relate to this Lab.

To start a Lab, click the **Start** button on the Windows taskbar, point to **Programs**, point to **Course Labs**, point to **New Perspectives Course Labs**, and click the name of the Lab you want to use.

Using Your Own Computer

If you are going to work through this book using your own computer, you need:

- **Computer System** Microsoft Windows 95, 98, NT, or higher must be installed on your computer. This book assumes a typical installation of Microsoft Access.

- **Data Disks** You will not be able to complete the tutorials or exercises in this book using your own computer until you have your Data Disks.

- **Course Labs** See your instructor or technical support person to obtain the Course Lab software for use on your own computer.

Visit Our World Wide Web Site

Additional materials designed especially for you are available on the World Wide Web.
Go to http://www.course.com.

To the Instructor

The Data Files and Course Labs are available on the Instructor's Resource Kit for this title. Follow the instructions in the Help file on the CD-ROM to install the programs to your network or standalone computer. For information on creating Data Disks or the Course Labs, see the "To the Student" section above.

You are granted a license to copy the Data Files and Course Labs to any computer or computer network used by students who have purchased this book.

OBJECTIVES

In this tutorial you will:

- Define the terms field, record, table, relational database, primary key, and foreign key

- Start and exit Access

- Open an existing database

- Identify the components of the Access and Database windows

- Open, navigate, and print a table

- Create, run, and print a query

- Create and print a form

- Use the Access Help system

- Create, preview, and print a report

- Compact a database

LAB

Databases

INTRODUCTION TO MICROSOFT ACCESS 2000

Viewing and Working with a Table Containing Customer Data

CASE

Valle Coffee

Ten years ago, Leonard Valle became the president of Algoman Imports, a small distributor of inexpensive coffee beans to supermarkets in western Michigan. At that time the company's growth had leveled off, so during his first three years Leonard took several dramatic, risky steps in an attempt to increase sales and profits. First, he changed the inexpensive coffee bean varieties that Algoman Imports had been distributing to a selection of gourmet varieties from Central and South America, Africa, and several island nations. Second, he purchased facilities and equipment so that the company could roast, grind, flavor, and package the coffee beans instead of buying them already roasted and packaged whole. Because the company could now control the quality of the finest gourmet coffees, Leonard stopped distributing to supermarkets and shifted sales to restaurants and offices throughout the area.

Within two years, company sales and profits soared; consequently, Leonard took over ownership of the company. He changed the company name to Valle Coffee, continued expanding into other markets and geographic areas (specifically, Ohio and Indiana), and expanded the company's line of coffee flavors and blends.

Part of Valle Coffee's success can be credited to its use of computers in all aspects of its business, including financial management, inventory control, shipping, receiving, production, and sales. Several months ago the company upgraded to Microsoft Windows and **Microsoft Access 2000** (or simply **Access**), a computer program used to enter, maintain, and retrieve related data in a format known as a database. Barbara Hennessey, office manager at Valle Coffee, and her staff use Access to maintain company data such as customer orders and billing, coffee supplier orders and payments, and advertising placements and payments. Barbara recently created a database named Restaurant to track the company's restaurant customers, their orders, and related data such as the products they order. She asks for your help in completing and maintaining this database.

SESSION 1.1

In this session, you will learn key database terms and concepts, start Access and open an existing database, identify components of the Access and Database windows, open and navigate a table, print a table, and exit Access.

Introduction to Database Concepts

Before you begin working on Barbara's database and using Access, you need to understand a few key terms and concepts associated with databases.

Organizing Data

Data is a valuable resource to any business. At Valle Coffee, for example, important data includes customers' names and addresses, and order dates and amounts. Organizing, storing, maintaining, retrieving, and sorting this type of data are critical activities that enable a business to find and use information effectively. Before storing data on a computer, however, you first must organize the data.

Your first step in organizing data is to identify the individual fields. A **field** is a single characteristic or attribute of a person, place, object, event, or idea. For example, some of the many fields that Valle Coffee tracks are customer number, customer name, customer address, customer phone number, order number, billing date, and invoice amount.

Next, you group related fields together into tables. A **table** is a collection of fields that describe a person, place, object, event, or idea. Figure 1-1 shows an example of a Customer table consisting of four fields: Customer #, Customer Name, Customer Address, and Phone Number.

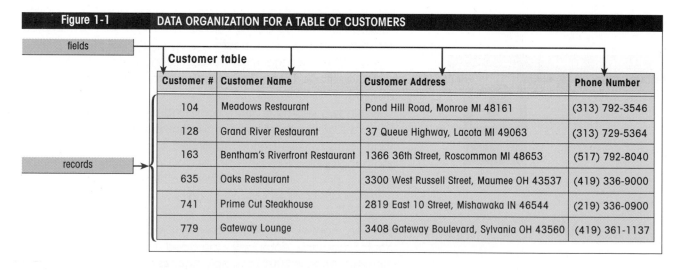

Figure 1-1   DATA ORGANIZATION FOR A TABLE OF CUSTOMERS

fields

Customer table

Customer #	Customer Name	Customer Address	Phone Number
104	Meadows Restaurant	Pond Hill Road, Monroe MI 48161	(313) 792-3546
128	Grand River Restaurant	37 Queue Highway, Lacota MI 49063	(313) 729-5364
163	Bentham's Riverfront Restaurant	1366 36th Street, Roscommon MI 48653	(517) 792-8040
635	Oaks Restaurant	3300 West Russell Street, Maumee OH 43537	(419) 336-9000
741	Prime Cut Steakhouse	2819 East 10 Street, Mishawaka IN 46544	(219) 336-0900
779	Gateway Lounge	3408 Gateway Boulevard, Sylvania OH 43560	(419) 361-1137

records

The specific value, or content, of a field is called the **field value**. In Figure 1-1, the first set of field values for Customer #, Customer Name, Customer Address, and Phone Number are, respectively, 104; Meadows Restaurant; Pond Hill Road, Monroe MI 48161; and (313) 792-3546. This set of field values is called a **record**. In the Customer table, the data for each customer is stored as a separate record. Six records are shown in Figure 1-1; each row of field values is a record.

Databases and Relationships

A collection of related tables is called a **database**, or a **relational database**. Valle Coffee's Restaurant database will contain two related tables: the Customer table, which Barbara has already created, and the Order table, which you will create in Tutorial 2. Sometimes you might want information about customers and the orders they placed. To obtain this information you must have a way to connect records in the Customer table to records in the Order table. You connect the records in the separate tables through a **common field** that appears in both tables. In the sample database shown in Figure 1-2, each record in the Customer table has a field named Customer #, which is also a field in the Order table. For example, Oaks Restaurant is the fourth customer in the Customer table and has a Customer # of 635. This same Customer # field value, 635, appears in three records in the Order table. Therefore, Oaks Restaurant is the customer that placed these three orders.

| Figure 1-2 | DATABASE RELATIONSHIP BETWEEN TABLES FOR CUSTOMERS AND ORDERS |

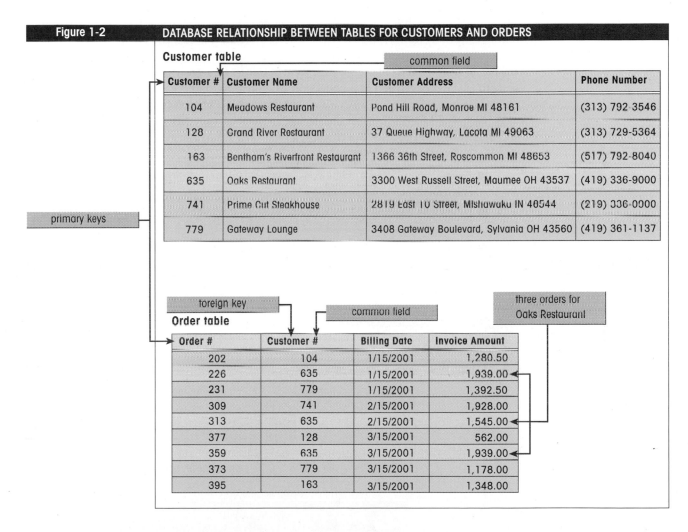

Customer table   common field

Customer #	Customer Name	Customer Address	Phone Number
104	Meadows Restaurant	Pond Hill Road, Monroe MI 48161	(313) 792-3546
128	Grand River Restaurant	37 Queue Highway, Lacota MI 49063	(313) 729-5364
163	Bentham's Riverfront Restaurant	1366 36th Street, Roscommon MI 48653	(517) 792-8040
635	Oaks Restaurant	3300 West Russell Street, Maumee OH 43537	(419) 336-9000
741	Prime Cut Steakhouse	2819 East 10 Street, Mishawaka IN 46544	(219) 336-0000
779	Gateway Lounge	3408 Gateway Boulevard, Sylvania OH 43560	(419) 361-1137

primary keys

foreign key   common field   three orders for Oaks Restaurant

Order table

Order #	Customer #	Billing Date	Invoice Amount
202	104	1/15/2001	1,280.50
226	635	1/15/2001	1,939.00
231	779	1/15/2001	1,392.50
309	741	2/15/2001	1,928.00
313	635	2/15/2001	1,545.00
377	128	3/15/2001	562.00
359	635	3/15/2001	1,939.00
373	779	3/15/2001	1,178.00
395	163	3/15/2001	1,348.00

Each Customer # in the Customer table must be unique, so that you can distinguish one customer from another and identify the customer's specific orders in the Order table. The Customer # field is referred to as the primary key of the Customer table. A **primary key** is a field, or a collection of fields, whose values uniquely identify each record in a table. In the Order table, Order # is the primary key.

When you include the primary key from one table as a field in a second table to form a relationship between the two tables, it is called a **foreign key** in the second table, as shown in Figure 1-2. For example, Customer # is the primary key in the Customer table and a foreign key in the Order table. Although the primary key Customer # has unique values in the Customer table, the same field as a foreign key in the Order table does not have unique values. The Customer # value 635, for example, appears three times in the Order table because the Oaks Restaurant placed three orders. Each foreign key value, however, must match one of the field values for the primary key in the other table. In the example shown in Figure 1-2, each Customer # value in the Order table must match a Customer # value in the Customer table. The two tables are related, enabling users to tie together the facts about customers with the facts about orders.

Relational Database Management Systems

To manage its databases, a company purchases a database management system. A **database management system** (**DBMS**) is a software program that lets you create databases and then manipulate data in them. Most of today's database management systems, including Access, are called relational database management systems. In a **relational database management system**, data is organized as a collection of tables. As stated earlier, a relationship between two tables in a relational DBMS is formed through a common field.

A relational DBMS controls the storage of databases on disk by carrying out data creation and manipulation requests. Specifically, a relational DBMS provides the following functions, which are illustrated in Figure 1-3:

- It allows you to create database structures containing fields, tables, and table relationships.
- It lets you easily add new records, change field values in existing records, and delete records.
- It contains a built-in query language, which lets you obtain immediate answers to the questions you ask about your data.
- It contains a built-in report generator, which lets you produce professional-looking, formatted reports from your data.
- It provides protection of databases through security, control, and recovery facilities.

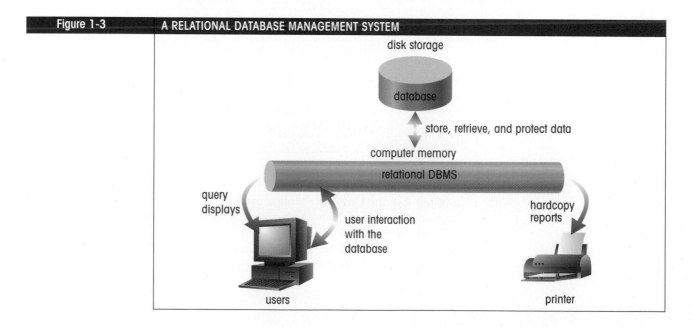

Figure 1-3   A RELATIONAL DATABASE MANAGEMENT SYSTEM

A company like Valle Coffee benefits from a relational DBMS because it allows several users working in different departments to share the same data. More than one user can enter data into a database, and more than one user can retrieve and analyze data that was entered by others. For example, Valle Coffee will keep only one copy of the Customer table, and all employees will be able to use it to meet their specific needs for customer information.

Finally, unlike other software programs, such as spreadsheets, a DBMS can handle massive amounts of data and can easily form relationships among multiple tables. Each Access database, for example, can be up to two gigabytes in size and can contain up to 32,768 objects (tables, queries, and so on).

Now that you've learned some database terms and concepts, you're ready to start Access and open the Restaurant database.

Starting Access

You start Access in the same way that you start other Windows programs—using the Start button on the taskbar.

To start Access:

1. Make sure Windows is running on your computer and the Windows desktop appears on your screen.

2. Click the **Start** button on the taskbar to display the Start menu, and then point to **Programs** to display the Programs menu.

3. Point to **Microsoft Access** on the Programs menu. See Figure 1-4.

| Figure 1-4 | STARTING MICROSOFT ACCESS |

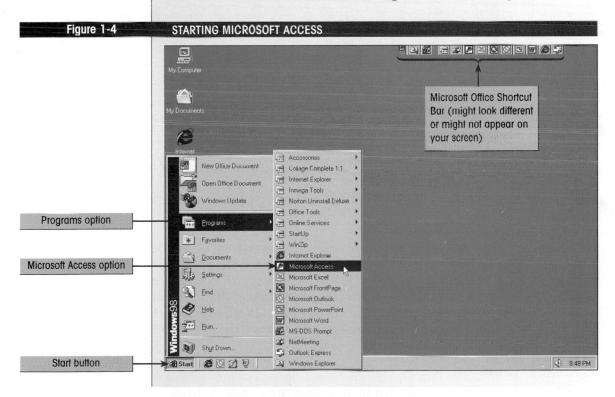

Microsoft Office Shortcut Bar (might look different or might not appear on your screen)

Programs option

Microsoft Access option

Start button

TROUBLE? Don't worry if your screen differs slightly from the figure. Although the figures in this book were created on a computer running Windows 98 in its default settings, the different Windows operating systems share the same basic user interface, and Microsoft Access runs equally well using Windows 95, Windows 98 in Web Style, Windows NT, or Windows 2000.

TROUBLE? If you don't see the Microsoft Access option on the Programs menu, ask your instructor or technical support person for help.

TROUBLE? The Office Shortcut Bar, which appears along the top border of the desktop in Figure 1-4, might look different on your screen, or it might not appear at all, depending on how your system is set up. Because these tutorials do not require you to use the Office Shortcut Bar, it has been omitted from the remaining figures in this text.

4. Click **Microsoft Access** to start Access. After a short pause, the Access copyright information appears in a message box and remains on the screen until the Access window is displayed. See Figure 1-5.

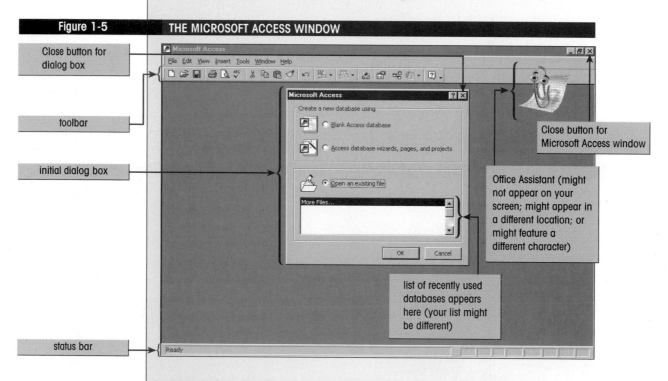

Figure 1-5   THE MICROSOFT ACCESS WINDOW

TROUBLE? Depending on how your system is set up, the Office Assistant (see Figure 1-5) might open when you start Access. If it opens, right-click the Office Assistant to display the shortcut menu, and then click Hide. You'll learn more about the Office Assistant later in this tutorial. If you've started Access immediately after installing it, you'll need to click the Start Using Microsoft Access option, which the Office Assistant displays, before hiding the Office Assistant.

When you start Access, the Access window contains a dialog box that allows you to create a new database or open an existing database. You can click the "Blank Access database" option button to create a new database on your own, or you can click the "Access database wizards, pages, and projects" option button and let a Wizard guide you through the steps for creating a database. In this case, you need to open an existing database.

Opening an Existing Database

To open an existing database, you can select the name of a database in the list of recently opened databases (if the list appears), or you can click the More Files option to open a database not listed. You need to open an existing database—the Restaurant database on your Data Disk.

To open the Restaurant database:

1. Make sure you have created your copy of the Access Data Disk, and then place your Data Disk in the appropriate disk drive.

   TROUBLE? If you don't have a Data Disk, you need to get one before you can proceed. Your instructor will either give you one or ask you to make your own. (See your instructor for information.) In either case, be sure that you have made a backup copy of your Data Disk before you begin working, so that the original Data Files will be available on the copied disk in case you need to start over because of an error or problem.

2. In the Microsoft Access dialog box, make sure the **Open an existing file** option button is selected. Also, if your dialog box contains a list of files, make sure the **More Files** option is selected.

3. Click the **OK** button to display the Open dialog box. See Figure 1-6.

Figure 1-6	OPEN DIALOG BOX

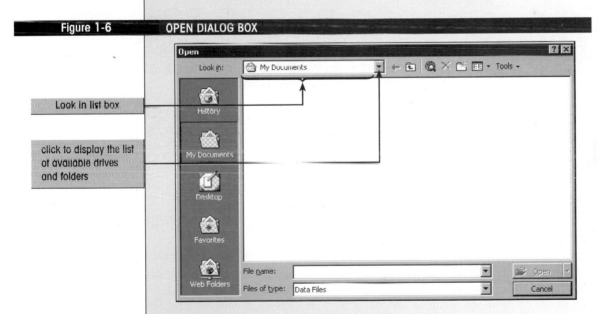

TROUBLE? The list of folders and files on your screen might be different from the list in Figure 1-6, which does not contain any items.

4. Click the **Look in** list arrow, and then click the drive that contains your Data Disk.

5. Click **Tutorial** in the list box (if necessary), and then click the **Open** button to display a list of the files in the Tutorial folder.

6. Click **Restaurant** in the list box, and then click the **Open** button. The Restaurant database opens in the Access window. See Figure 1-7.

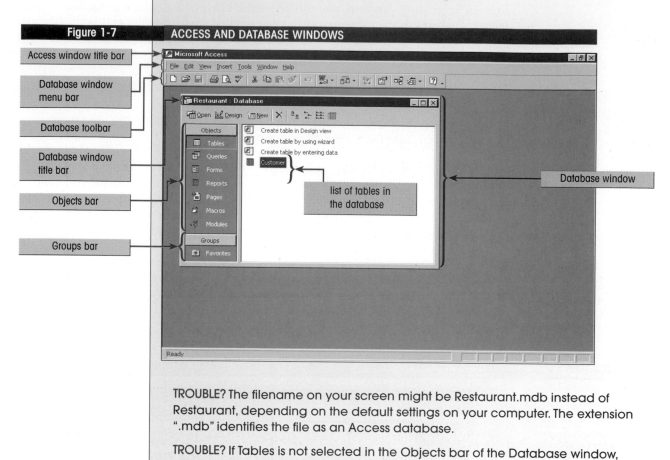

| Figure 1-7 | ACCESS AND DATABASE WINDOWS |

TROUBLE? The filename on your screen might be Restaurant.mdb instead of Restaurant, depending on the default settings on your computer. The extension ".mdb" identifies the file as an Access database.

TROUBLE? If Tables is not selected in the Objects bar of the Database window, click it to display the list of tables in the database.

Before you can begin working with the database, you need to become familiar with the components of the Access and Database windows.

The Access and Database Windows

The **Access window** is the program window that appears when you start the program. The **Database window** appears when you open a database; this window is the main control center for working with an open Access database. Except for the Access window title bar, all screen components now on your screen are associated with the Database window (see Figure 1-7). Most of these screen components—including the title bars, window sizing buttons, menu bar, toolbar, and status bar—are the same as the components in other Windows programs.

The Database window provides a variety of options for viewing and manipulating database objects. Each item in the **Objects bar** controls one of the major object groups—such as tables, queries, forms, and reports—in an Access database. The **Groups bar** allows you to organize different types of database objects into groups, with shortcuts to those objects, so that you can work with them more easily.

The Database window also provides a toolbar with buttons for quickly creating, opening, and managing objects, as well as shortcut options for some of these tasks.

Barbara has already created the Customer table in the Restaurant database. She asks you to open the Customer table and view its contents.

Opening an Access Table

As noted earlier, tables contain all the data in a database. Tables are the fundamental objects for your work in Access. To view, add, change, or delete data in a table, you first must open the table. You can open any Access object by using the Open button in the Database window.

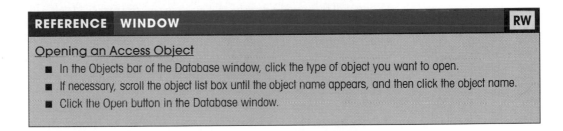

REFERENCE WINDOW   **RW**

Opening an Access Object
- In the Objects bar of the Database window, click the type of object you want to open.
- If necessary, scroll the object list box until the object name appears, and then click the object name.
- Click the Open button in the Database window.

You need to open the Customer table, which is the only table currently in the Restaurant database.

To open the Customer table:

1. If the Customer table is not highlighted, click **Customer** to select it.

2. Click the **Open** button in the Database window. The Customer table opens in Datasheet view on top of the Database and Access windows. See Figure 1-8.

Figure 1-8   **TABLE DISPLAYED IN DATASHEET VIEW**

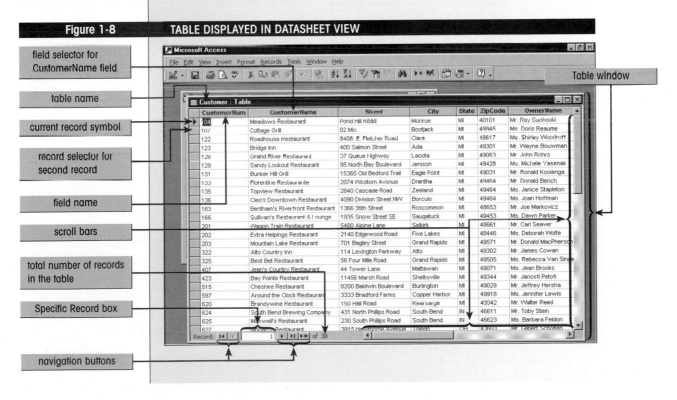

Datasheet view shows a table's contents as a **datasheet** in rows and columns, similar to a table or spreadsheet. Each row is a separate record in the table, and each column contains the field values for one field in the table. Each column is headed by a field name inside a field selector, and each row has a record selector to its left. Clicking a **field selector** or a **record selector** selects that entire column or row (respectively), which you can then manipulate. A field selector is also called a **column selector**, and a record selector is also called a **row selector**.

Navigating an Access Datasheet

When you first open a datasheet, Access selects the first field value in the first record. Notice that this field value is highlighted and that a darkened triangle symbol, called the current record symbol, appears in the record selector to the left of the first record. The **current record symbol** identifies the currently selected record. Clicking a record selector or field value in another row moves the current record symbol to that row. You can also move the pointer over the data on the screen and click one of the field values to position the insertion point.

The Customer table currently has nine fields and 38 records. To view fields or records not currently visible in the datasheet, you can use the horizontal and vertical scroll bars shown in Figure 1-8 to navigate through the data. The **navigation buttons**, also shown in Figure 1-8, provide another way to move vertically through the records. Figure 1-9 shows which record becomes the current record when you click each navigation button. The **Specific Record box**, which appears between the two sets of navigation buttons, displays the current record number. The total number of records in the table appears to the right of the navigation buttons.

Figure 1-9	NAVIGATION BUTTONS

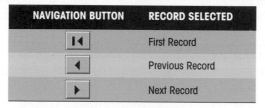

NAVIGATION BUTTON	RECORD SELECTED
|◄	First Record
◄	Previous Record
►	Next Record

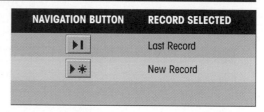

NAVIGATION BUTTON	RECORD SELECTED
►|	Last Record
►✳	New Record

Barbara suggests that you use the various navigation techniques to move through the Customer table and become familiar with its contents.

To navigate the Customer datasheet:

1. Click the right scroll arrow in the horizontal scroll bar a few times to scroll to the right and view the remaining fields in the Customer table.

2. Drag the scroll box in the horizontal scroll bar back to the left to return to the previous display of the datasheet.

3. Click the **Next Record** navigation button ![►]. The second record is now the current record, as indicated by the current record symbol in the second record selector. Also, notice that the second record's value for the CustomerNum field is highlighted, and "2" (for record number 2) appears in the Specific Record box.

4. Click the **Last Record** navigation button ![►|]. The last record in the table, record 38, is now the current record.

5. Click the **Previous Record** navigation button ◀ . Record 37 is now the current record.

6. Click the **First Record** navigation button ◄◄ . The first record is now the current record.

Next, Barbara asks you to print the Customer table so that you can refer to it as you continue working with the Restaurant database.

Printing a Table

In Access you can print a table using either the Print command on the File menu or the Print button on the toolbar. The Print command opens a dialog box in which you can specify print settings. The Print button prints the table using the current settings. You'll use the Print button to print the Customer table.

To print the Customer table:

1. Click the **Print** button on the Table Datasheet toolbar. Because all of the fields can't fit across one page, the table prints on two pages. You'll learn how to specify different print settings in later tutorials.

Now that you've viewed and printed the Customer table, you can exit Access.

Exiting Access

To exit Access, you simply click the Close button on the Access window title bar. When exiting, Access closes any open tables and the open database before closing the program.

To exit Access:

1. Click the **Close** button ☒ on the Access window title bar. The Customer table and the Restaurant database close, Access closes, and you return to the Windows desktop.

Now that you've become familiar with Access and the Restaurant database, you're ready to work with the data stored in the database.

Session 1.1 QUICK CHECK

1. A(n) _____ is a single characteristic of a person, place, object, event, or idea.

2. You connect the records in two separate tables through a(n) _____ that appears in both tables.

3. The _____, whose values uniquely identify each record in a table, is called a _____ when it is placed in a second table to form a relationship between the two tables.

4. In a table, the rows are called _____, and the columns are called _____.

5. The _____ identifies the selected record in an Access table.

6. Describe the two methods for navigating through a table.

SESSION 1.2

In this session, you will create and print a query; create and print a form; use the Help system; and create, preview, and print a report.

Kim Carpenter, the director of marketing at Valle Coffee, wants a list of all restaurant customers so that her staff can call customers to check on their satisfaction with Valle Coffee's services and products. She doesn't want the list to include all the fields in the Customer table (such as Street and ZipCode). To produce this list for Kim, you need to create a query using the Customer table.

Creating and Printing a Query

A **query** is a question you ask about the data stored in a database. In response to a query, Access displays the specific records and fields that answer your question. When you create a query, you tell Access which fields you need and what criteria Access should use to select the records. Then Access displays only the information you want, so you don't have to navigate through the entire database for the information.

You can design your own queries or use an Access **Query Wizard**, which guides you through the steps to create a query. The Simple Query Wizard allows you to select records and fields quickly, and is an appropriate choice for producing the customer list Kim wants.

To start the Simple Query Wizard:

1. Insert your Data Disk in the appropriate disk drive.

2. Start Access, make sure the **Open an existing file** option button is selected and the **More Files** option is selected, and then click the **OK** button to display the Open dialog box.

3. Click the **Look in** list arrow, click the drive that contains your Data Disk, click **Tutorial** in the list box, and then click the **Open** button to display the list of files in the Tutorial folder.

4. Click **Restaurant** in the list box, and then click the **Open** button.

5. Click **Queries** in the Objects bar of the Database window to display the Queries list. The Queries list box does not contain any queries yet.

You need to use the Simple Query Wizard to create the query for Kim. You can choose this Wizard either by clicking the New button, which opens a dialog box from which you can choose among several different Wizards to create your query, or by double-clicking the "Create query by using wizard" option, which automatically starts the Simple Query Wizard.

6. Double-click **Create query by using wizard**. The first Simple Query Wizard dialog box opens. See Figure 1-10.

Figure 1-10	FIRST SIMPLE QUERY WIZARD DIALOG BOX

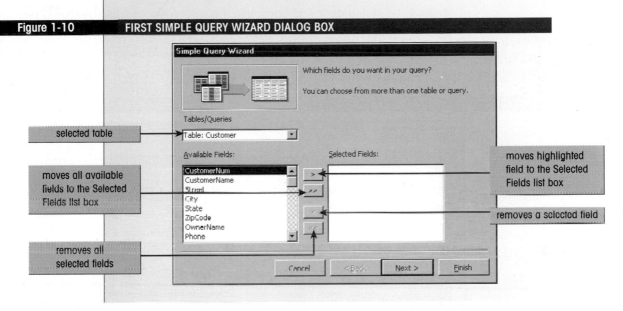

Because Customer is the only object currently in the Restaurant database, it is listed in the Tables/Queries box. You could click the Tables/Queries list arrow to choose another table or a query on which to base the query you're creating. The Available Fields list box lists the fields in the selected table (in this case, Customer). You need to select fields from this list to include them in the query. To select fields one at a time, click a field and then click the ⟩ button. The selected field moves from the Available Fields list box on the left to the Selected Fields list box on the right. To select all the fields, click the ⟩⟩ button. If you change your mind or make a mistake, you can remove a field by clicking it in the Selected Fields list box and then clicking the ⟨ button. To remove all selected fields, click the ⟨⟨ button.

Each Wizard dialog box contains buttons on the bottom that allow you to move to the previous dialog box (Back button), move to the next dialog box (Next button), or cancel the creation process (Cancel button) and return to the Database window. You can also finish creating the object (Finish button) and accept the Wizard's defaults for the remaining options.

Kim wants her list to include data from only the following fields: CustomerNum, CustomerName, City, State, OwnerName, and Phone. You need to select these fields to be included in the query.

To create the query using the Simple Query Wizard:

1. Click **CustomerNum** in the Available Fields list box (if necessary), and then click the ⟩ button. The CustomerNum field moves to the Selected Fields list box.

2. Repeat Step 1 for the fields **CustomerName**, **City**, **State**, **OwnerName**, and **Phone**, and then click the **Next** button. The second, and final, Simple Query Wizard dialog box opens and asks you to choose a name for your query. This name will appear in the Queries list in the Database window. You'll change the suggested name (Customer Query) to "Customer List."

3. Click at the end of the highlighted name, use the Backspace key to delete the word "Query," and then type **List**. Now you can view the query results.

4. Click the **Finish** button to complete the query. Access displays the query results in Datasheet view.

5. Click the **Maximize** button 🔲 on the Query window to maximize the window. See Figure 1-11.

| Figure 1-11 | QUERY RESULTS |

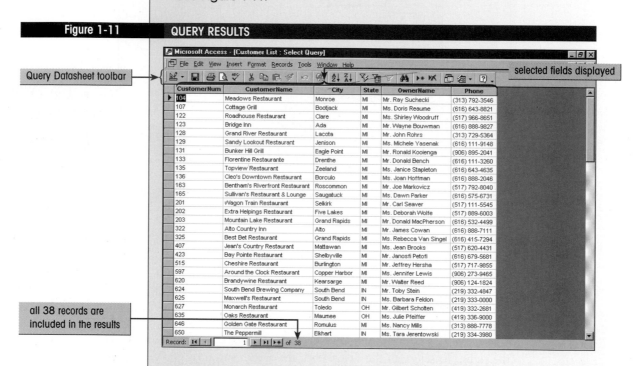

The datasheet displays the six selected fields for each record in the Customer table. The fields are shown in the order you selected them, from left to right.

The records are currently listed in order by the primary key field (CustomerNum). Kim prefers the records to be listed in order by state so that her staff members can focus on all records for the customers in a particular state. To display the records in the order Kim wants, you need to sort the query results by the State field.

To sort the query results:

1. Click to position the insertion point anywhere in the State column. This establishes the State column as the current field.

2. Click the **Sort Ascending** button ⬆ on the Query Datasheet toolbar. Now the records are sorted in ascending alphabetical order by the values in the State field. All the records for Indiana are listed first, followed by the records for Michigan and then Ohio.

Kim asks for a printed copy of the query results so that she can bring the customer list to a meeting with her staff members. To print the query results, you can use the Print button on the Query Datasheet toolbar.

To print the query results:

1. Click the **Print** button 🖨 on the Query Datasheet toolbar to print one copy of the query results with the current settings.

2. Click the **Close** button ❎ on the menu bar to close the query.

A dialog box opens and asks if you want to save changes to the design of the query. This box opens because you changed the sort order of the query results.

3. Click the **Yes** button to save the query design changes and return to the Database window. Notice that the Customer List query now appears in the Queries list box. In addition, because you maximized the Query window, now the Database window is also maximized. You need to restore the window.

4. Click the **Restore** button 🗗 on the menu bar to restore the Database window.

The query results are not stored in the database; however, the query design is stored as part of the database with the name you specified. You can re-create the query results at any time by running the query again. You'll learn more about creating and running queries in Tutorial 3.

After Kim leaves for her staff meeting, Barbara asks you to create a form for the Customer table so that her staff members can use the form to enter and work with data easily in the table.

Creating and Printing a Form

A **form** is an object you use to maintain, view, and print records in a database. Although you can perform these same functions with tables and queries, forms can present data in customized and useful ways.

In Access, you can design your own forms or use a Form Wizard to create forms for you automatically. A **Form Wizard** is an Access tool that asks you a series of questions, and then creates a form based on your answers. The quickest way to create a form is to use an **AutoForm Wizard**, which places all the fields from a selected table (or query) on a form automatically, without asking you any questions, and then displays the form on the screen.

Barbara wants a form for the Customer table that will show all the fields for one record at a time, with fields listed one below another. This type of form will make it easier for her staff to focus on all the data for a particular customer. You'll use the AutoForm: Columnar Wizard to create the form.

To create the form using an AutoForm Wizard:

1. Click **Forms** in the Objects bar of the Database window to display the Forms list. The Forms list box does not contain any forms yet.

2. Click the **New** button in the Database window to open the New Form dialog box. See Figure 1-12.

Figure 1-12	NEW FORM DIALOG BOX

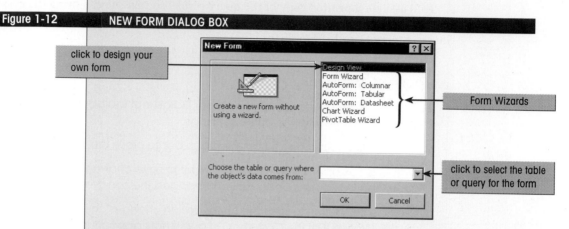

click to design your own form

Form Wizards

click to select the table or query for the form

The top list box provides options for designing your own form or creating a form using one of the Form Wizards. In the bottom list box, you choose the table or query that will supply the data for the form.

3. Click **AutoForm: Columnar** to select this AutoForm Wizard.

4. Click the list arrow for choosing the table or query on which to base the form, and then click **Customer**.

5. Click the **OK** button. The AutoForm Wizard creates the form and displays it in Form view. See Figure 1-13.

Figure 1-13	FORM CREATED BY THE AUTOFORM: COLUMNAR WIZARD

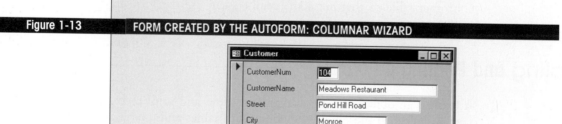

TROUBLE? The background of your form might look different from the one shown in Figure 1-13, depending on your computer's settings. If so, don't worry. You will learn how to change the form's style later in this text. For now, continue with the tutorial.

The form displays one record at a time in the Customer table. Access displays the field values for the first record in the table and selects the first field value (CustomerNum).

Each field name appears on a separate line and on the same line as its field value, which appears in a box. The widths of the boxes are different to accommodate the different sizes of the displayed field values; for example, compare the small box for the State field value with the larger box for the CustomerName field value. The AutoForm: Columnar Wizard automatically placed the field names and values on the form and supplied the background style.

Also, notice that the Form window contains navigation buttons, similar to those available in Datasheet view, which you can use to display different records in the form.

Barbara asks you to print the data for the Embers Restaurant, which is the last record in the table. After printing this record in the form, you'll save the form with the name "Customer Data" in the Restaurant database. Then the form will be available for later use. You'll learn more about creating and customizing forms in Tutorial 4.

To print the form with data for the last record, and then save and close the form:

1. Click the **Last Record** navigation button ⏭. The last record in the table, record 38 for Embers Restaurant, is now the current record.

2. Click **File** on the menu bar, and then click **Print**. The Print dialog box opens.

3. Click the **Selected Record(s)** option button, and then click the **OK** button to print only the current record in the form.

4. Click the **Save** button 💾 on the Form View toolbar. The Save As dialog box opens.

5. In the Form Name text box, click at the end of the highlighted word "Customer," press the **spacebar**, type **Data**, and then press the **Enter** key. Access saves the form as Customer Data in your Restaurant database and closes the dialog box.

6. Click the **Close** button ⊠ on the Form window title bar to close the form and return to the Database window. Note that the Customer Data form is now listed in the Forms list box.

Kim returns from her staff meeting with another request. She wants the same customer list you produced earlier when you created the Customer List query, but she'd like the information presented in a more readable format. She suggests you use the Access Help system to learn about formatting data in reports.

Getting Help

The Access Help system provides the same options as the Help system in other Windows programs—the Help Contents, the Answer Wizard, and the Help Index—which are available from the Microsoft Access Help window. The Access Help system also provides additional ways to get help as you work—the Office Assistant and the What's This? command. You'll learn how to use the Office Assistant next in this section. The What's This? command provides context-sensitive Help information. When you choose this command from the Help menu, the pointer changes to the Help pointer ⃟?, which you can then use to click any object or option on the screen to see a description of the object or option.

Finding Information with the Office Assistant

The Office Assistant is an interactive guide to finding information in the Help system. You can ask the Office Assistant a question, and then it will search the Help system to find an answer.

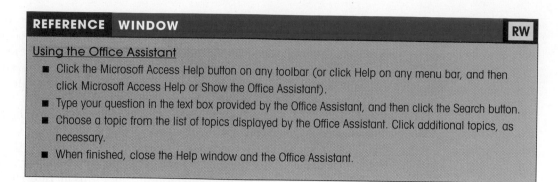

REFERENCE WINDOW   RW

Using the Office Assistant

■ Click the Microsoft Access Help button on any toolbar (or click Help on any menu bar, and then click Microsoft Access Help or Show the Office Assistant).
■ Type your question in the text box provided by the Office Assistant, and then click the Search button.
■ Choose a topic from the list of topics displayed by the Office Assistant. Click additional topics, as necessary.
■ When finished, close the Help window and the Office Assistant.

You'll use the Office Assistant to get Help about creating reports in Access. Because you chose to hide the Office Assistant earlier in this tutorial, you need to redisplay it first.

To get Help about reports:

1. Click the **Microsoft Access Help** button 🔲 on the Database toolbar. The Office Assistant appears and displays a text box in which you can type your question. See Figure 1-14.

Figure 1-14   USING THE OFFICE ASSISTANT

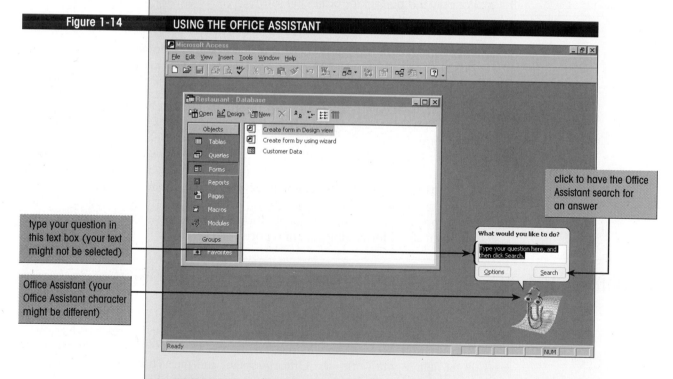

TROUBLE? If the Microsoft Access Help window opens instead of the Office Assistant, click the Close button 🔲 to close the Help window, click Help on the menu bar, and then click Show the Office Assistant. If you don't see the text box and the Search button, click the Office Assistant.

TROUBLE? Your Office Assistant might appear in a different location on your screen. You can click and drag the Office Assistant to move it to another location, if you want.

You need to find information about creating reports in Access. To do so, you can simply begin to type your question.

2. Type **How do I create a report?** and then click the **Search** button. The Office Assistant displays a list of relevant topics. See Figure 1-15.

Figure 1-15	LIST OF RELATED TOPICS

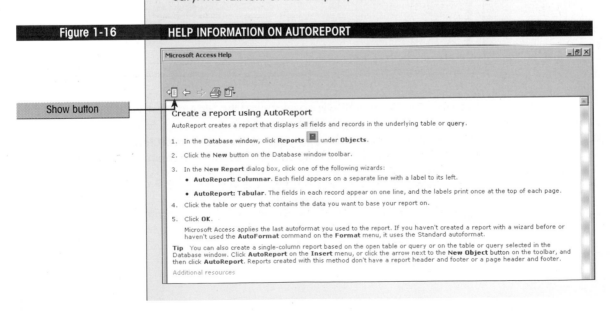

3. In the list of topics, click **Create a report**. The Office Assistant opens the topic in the Microsoft Access Help window, which opens on the left or right side of your screen. To see more of the Help window, you can maximize it.

4. Click the **Maximize** button 🗖 on the Microsoft Access Help window.

5. After reading the displayed text, click the topic **Create a report by using AutoReport** in the Help window. The Help window for using AutoReport opens. Because the Office Assistant might block the text in the Help window, you'll hide it again.

6. Right-click the **Office Assistant** to display the shortcut menu, click **Hide**, and then click anywhere in the Help window to redisplay the entire window, if necessary. The full text of the Help topic is now visible. See Figure 1-16.

Figure 1-16	HELP INFORMATION ON AUTOREPORT

Microsoft Access Help   _|5|×|

Show button

Create a report using AutoReport

AutoReport creates a report that displays all fields and records in the underlying table or query.

1. In the Database window, click **Reports** 🖼 under **Objects**.

2. Click the **New** button on the Database window toolbar.

3. In the **New Report** dialog box, click one of the following wizards:

 • **AutoReport: Columnar**. Each field appears on a separate line with a label to its left.

 • **AutoReport: Tabular**. The fields in each record appear on one line, and the labels print once at the top of each page.

4. Click the table or query that contains the data you want to base your report on.

5. Click **OK**.

 Microsoft Access applies the last autoformat you used to the report. If you haven't created a report with a wizard before or haven't used the **AutoFormat** command on the **Format** menu, it uses the Standard autoformat.

 Tip   You can also create a single-column report based on the open table or query or on the table or query selected in the Database window. Click **AutoReport** on the **Insert** menu, or click the arrow next to the **New Object** button on the toolbar, and then click **AutoReport**. Reports created with this method don't have a report header and footer or a page header and footer.

Additional resources

> **TROUBLE?** If the Microsoft Access Help window minimizes when you hide the Office Assistant, click the Microsoft Access Help program button on the taskbar to restore the window.
>
> 7. Read the information displayed in the Help window. Note that the AutoReport feature is similar to the AutoForm feature you used earlier. You'll use the AutoReport: Columnar Wizard to create the report for Kim.

As mentioned earlier, the Help system in Access provides different ways to find information, including the Contents, Answer Wizard, and Index features. To gain access to these features, you need to use the Show button in the Microsoft Access Help window (see Figure 1-16).

To display the additional Help features:

1. Click the **Show** button [icon] on the toolbar in the Microsoft Access Help window. The Contents, Answer Wizard, and Index tabs appear in the left frame of the window. See Figure 1-17.

| Figure 1-17 | ADDITIONAL HELP FEATURES |

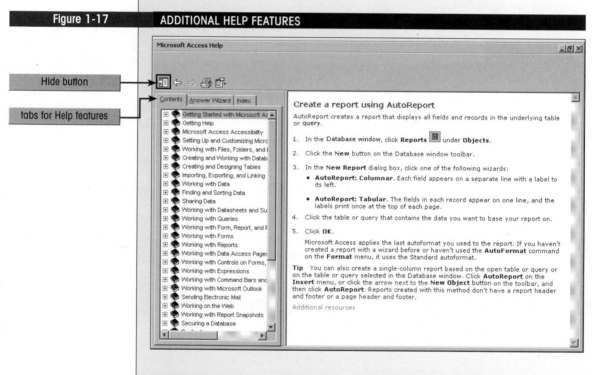

Hide button

tabs for Help features

Note that the Show button is now labeled the Hide button, which you could click to remove the display of the tabs. You'll have a chance to use some of these additional Help tools in the exercises at the end of this tutorial. For now, you can close the Microsoft Access Help window and create the report for Kim.

2. Click the **Close** button [X] on the Microsoft Access Help window title bar to exit Help and return to the Database window.

Creating, Previewing, and Printing a Report

A **report** is a formatted printout (or screen display) of the contents of one or more tables in a database. Although you can print data from tables, queries, and forms, reports provide you with the greatest flexibility for formatting printed output.

Kim wants a report showing the same information contained in the Customer List query that you created earlier. However, she wants the data for each customer to be grouped together, with one customer record below another, as shown in the report sketch in Figure 1-18. You'll use the AutoReport: Columnar Wizard to produce the report for Kim.

Figure 1-18	SKETCH OF KIM'S REPORT

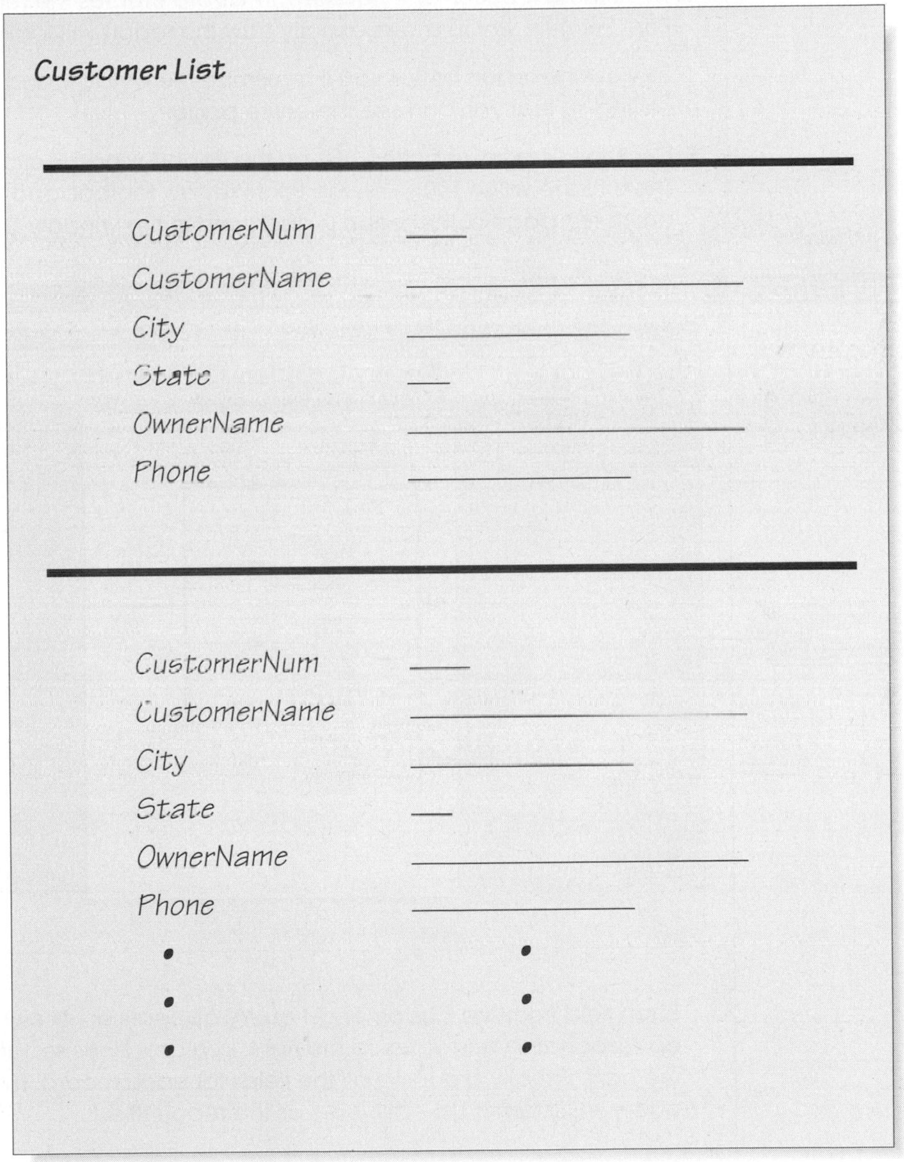

Customer List

CustomerNum   ____
CustomerName   _____
City   _____
State   ___
OwnerName   _____
Phone   _____

CustomerNum   ____
CustomerName   _____
City   _____
State   ___
OwnerName   _____
Phone   _____
                •   •
                •   •
                •   •

To create the report using the AutoReport: Columnar Wizard:

1. Click **Reports** in the Objects bar of the Database window, and then click the **New** button in the Database window to open the New Report dialog box, which is similar to the New Form dialog box you saw earlier.

2. Click **AutoReport: Columnar** to select this Wizard for creating the report.

   Because Kim wants the same data as in the Customer List query, you need to choose that query as the basis for the report.

3. Click the list arrow for choosing the table or query on which to base the report, and then click **Customer List**.

4. Click the **OK** button. The AutoReport Wizard creates the report and displays it in Print Preview, which shows exactly how the report will look when printed.

   To view the report better, you'll maximize the window and change the Zoom setting so that you can see the entire page.

5. Click the **Maximize** button ▣ on the Report window, click the **Zoom** list arrow (next to the value 100%) on the Print Preview toolbar, and then click **Fit**. The entire first page of the report is displayed in the window. See Figure 1-19.

Figure 1-19	FIRST PAGE OF THE REPORT IN PRINT PREVIEW

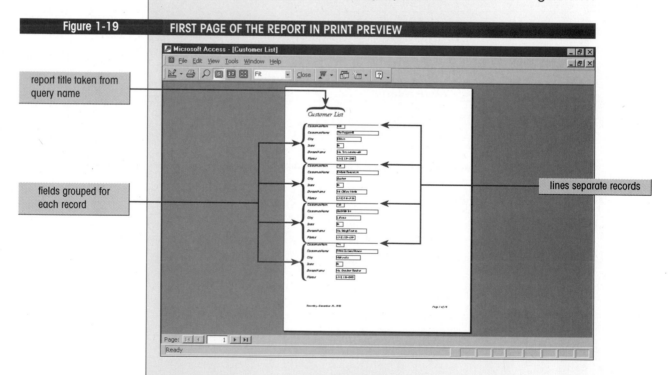

report title taken from query name

fields grouped for each record

lines separate records

Each field from the Customer List query appears on its own line, with the corresponding field value to the right, in a box. Lines separate one record from the next, visually grouping all the fields for each record. The name of the query—Customer List—appears as the report title.

TROUBLE? The background of your report might look different from the one shown in Figure 1-19, depending on your computer's settings. If so, don't worry. You will learn how to change the report's style later in this text.

The report spans multiple pages. Kim asks you to print just the first page of the report so that she can review its format. After printing the report page, you'll close the report without saving it because you can easily re-create it at any time. In general, it's best to save an object—report, form, or query—only if you anticipate using the object frequently or if it is time-consuming to create, because these objects use considerable storage space on your disk. You'll learn more about creating and customizing reports in Tutorial 4.

To print the first report page, and then close the report:

1. Click **File** on the menu bar, and then click **Print**. The Print dialog box opens. You need to change the print settings to print only the first page of the report.

2. In the Print Range section, click the **Pages** option button, type **1** in the From text box, press the **Tab** key, and then type **1** in the To text box.

3. Click the **OK** button to print the first page of the report. Now you can close the report.

4. Click the **Close** button ⊠ on the menu bar. *Do not* click the Close button on the Print Preview toolbar.

   TROUBLE? If you clicked the Close button on the Print Preview toolbar, you switched to Design view. Simply click the Close button ⊠ on the menu bar, and then continue with the tutorial.

   A dialog box opens and asks if you want to save the changes to the report design.

5. Click the **No** button to close the report without saving it.

When you work in an Access database and create and manipulate objects, such as queries, forms, and reports, the size of your database increases. To free up disk space and make a database a more manageable size, Access provides a way for you to compact a database.

Compacting a Database

Whenever you open an Access database and work in it, the size of the database increases. Likewise, when you delete records or database objects—such as queries, forms, and reports—the space occupied by the deleted records or objects on disk does not become available for other records or objects. To make the space available, you must compact the database. **Compacting** a database rearranges the data and objects in a database to make its size smaller. Unlike making a copy of a database file, which you do to protect your database against loss or damage, you compact a database to make it smaller, thereby making more space available on your disk.

Compacting and Repairing a Database

When you compact a database, Access repairs the database at the same time. In many cases, Access detects that a database is damaged when you try to open it and gives you the option to compact and repair it at that time. If you think your database might be damaged because it is behaving unpredictably, you can use the "Compact and Repair Database" option to fix it. With your database file open, choose the Database Utilities option from the Tools menu, and then choose the Compact and Repair Database option.

Compacting a Database Automatically

Access also allows you to set an option for your database file so that every time you close the database, it will be compacted automatically.

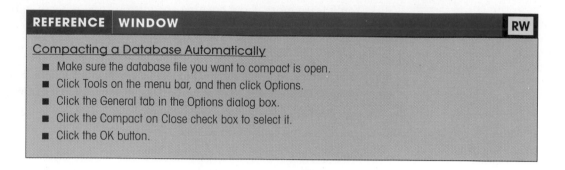

REFERENCE WINDOW   RW

Compacting a Database Automatically
- Make sure the database file you want to compact is open.
- Click Tools on the menu bar, and then click Options.
- Click the General tab in the Options dialog box.
- Click the Compact on Close check box to select it.
- Click the OK button.

You'll set the compact option now for the Restaurant database. Then, every time you subsequently open and close the Restaurant database, Access will compact the database file for you. After setting this option, you'll exit Access.

To set the option for compacting the Restaurant database:

1. Make sure the Restaurant Database window is open on your screen.

2. Click **Tools** on the menu bar, and then click **Options**. The Options dialog box opens.

3. Click the **General** tab in the dialog box, and then click the **Compact on Close** check box to select it. See Figure 1-20.

Figure 1-20   GENERAL TAB OF THE OPTIONS DIALOG BOX

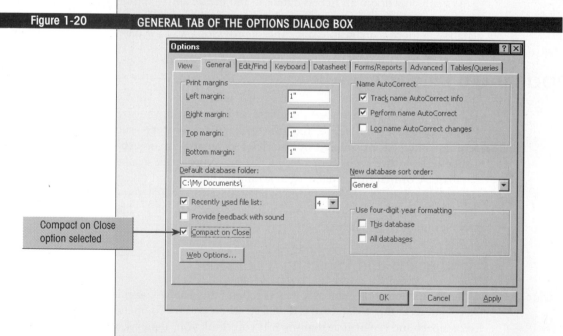

4. Click the **OK** button to set the option. Now you can exit Access.

5. Click the **Close** button ⊠ on the Access window title bar to exit Access. When you exit, Access closes the Restaurant database file and compacts it automatically.

Backing Up and Restoring a Database

As noted earlier, you make a backup copy of a database file to protect your database against loss or damage. You can make the backup copy using one of several methods: Windows Explorer, My Computer, Microsoft Backup, or other backup software. If you back up your database file to a floppy disk, and the file size exceeds the size of the disk, you cannot use Windows Explorer or My Computer; you must use Microsoft Backup or some other backup software so that you can copy the file over more than one disk.

To restore a database file that you have backed up, choose the same method you used to make the backup copy. For example, if you used the Microsoft Backup tool (which is one of the System Tool Accessories available from the Programs menu), you must choose the Restore option for this tool to copy the database file to your database folder. If the existing database file and the backup copy have the same name, restoring the backup copy might replace the existing file. If you want to save the existing file, rename it before you restore it.

With the Customer table in place, Barbara can continue to build the Restaurant database and use it to store, manipulate, and retrieve important data for Valle Coffee. In the following tutorials, you'll help Barbara complete and maintain the database, and you'll use it to meet the specific information needs of other Valle Coffee employees.

Session 1.2 QUICK CHECK

1. A(n) _____ is a question you ask about the data stored in a database.

2. Unless you specify otherwise, the records resulting from a query are listed in order by the _____.

3. The quickest way to create a form is to use a(n) _____.

4. Describe the form created by the AutoForm: Columnar Wizard.

5. Describe how you use the Office Assistant to get Help.

6. After creating a report, the AutoReport Wizard displays the report in _____.

REVIEW ASSIGNMENTS

In the Review Assignments, you'll work with the **Customer** database, which is similar to the database you worked with in the tutorial. Complete the following:

1. Make sure your Data Disk is in the disk drive.

2. Start Access and open the **Customer** database, which is located in the Review folder on your Data Disk.

Explore

3. In the Microsoft Access Help window, display and then click the Contents tab. (*Hint:* Click any topic displayed in the Office Assistant list box to open the Microsoft Access Help window.) Double-click the topic "Creating and working with Databases." Click the topic "Databases: What they are and how they work," and then click the related graphic for the topic. Read the displayed information. When finished, close the window to return to the Contents tab. Repeat this procedure for the similarly worded topics for tables, queries, forms, and reports. When finished reading all the topics, close the Microsoft Access Help window.

Explore

4. Use the Office Assistant to ask the following question: "How do I rename a table?" Choose the topic "Rename a database object" and read the displayed information. Close the Microsoft Access Help window and hide the Office Assistant. Then, in the **Customer** database, rename the **Table1** table as **Customers**.

5. Open the **Customers** table.

Explore

6. In the Microsoft Access Help window, display and then click the Index tab. (*Hint*: Click any topic displayed in the Office Assistant list box to open the Help window.) Type the keyword "print" in the Type keywords text box, and then click the Search button. Click the topic "Print a report." Read the displayed information, click the button for more information at the end of the first paragraph (>>), and then read the information. Close the Microsoft Access Help window. Print the **Customers** table datasheet in landscape orientation. Close the **Customers** table.

7. Use the Simple Query Wizard to create a query that includes the City, CustomerName, OwnerName, and Phone fields (in that order) from the **Customers** table. Name the query **Customer Phone List**. Sort the query results in ascending order by City. Print the query results, and then close and save the query.

8. Use the AutoForm: Columnar Wizard to create a form for the **Customers** table.

Explore

9. Use context-sensitive Help to find out how to move to a particular record and display it in the form. Click the What's This? command from the Help menu, and then use the Help pointer to click the number 1 in the Specific Record box at the bottom of the form. Read the displayed information. Click to close the Help box, and then use the Specific Record box to move to record 28 (for The Peppermill) in the **Customers** table.

10. Print the form for the current record (28), save the form as **Customer Info**, and then close the form.

Explore

11. Use the AutoReport: Tabular Wizard to create a report based on the **Customers** table. Print the first page of the report, and then close and save the report as **Customers**.

12. Set the option for compacting the **Customer** database on close.

13. Exit Access.

CASE PROBLEMS

Case 1. Ashbrook Mall Information Desk   Ashbrook Mall is a large, modern mall located in Phoenix, Arizona. The Mall Operations Office is responsible for everything that happens within the mall and anything that affects the mall's operation. Among the independent operations groups that report to the Mall Operations Office are the Maintenance Group, the Mall Security Office, and the Information Desk. You will be helping the Information Desk personnel.

One important service provided by the Information Desk is to maintain a catalog of current job openings at stores within the mall. Sam Bullard, the director of the Mall Operations Office, recently created an Access database named **MallJobs** to store this information. You'll help Sam complete and maintain this database. Complete the following:

1. Make sure your Data Disk is in the disk drive.

2. Start Access and open the **MallJobs** database, which is located in the Cases folder on your Data Disk.

3. Open the **Store** table, print the table datasheet, and then close the table.

4. Use the Simple Query Wizard to create a query that includes the StoreName, Contact, and Extension fields (in that order) from the **Store** table. Name the query **Contact List**. Print the query results, and then close the query.

Explore 5. Use the AutoForm: Tabular Wizard to create a form for the **Store** table. Print the form, save it as **Store Info**, and then close it.

Explore 6. Use the AutoReport: Columnar Wizard to create a report based on the **Store** table. Maximize the Report window and change the Zoom setting to Fit. Use the Two Pages button on the Print Preview toolbar to view both pages of the report in Print Preview. Print the first page of the report, and then close and save it as **Stores**.

7. Set the option for compacting the **MallJobs** database on close.

8. Exit Access.

Case 2. Professional Litigation User Services   Professional Litigation User Services (PLUS) is a company that creates all types of visual aids for judicial proceedings. Clients are usually private law firms, although the District Attorney's office has occasionally contracted for its services. PLUS creates graphs, maps, timetables, and charts, both for computerized presentations and in large-size form for presentation to juries. PLUS also creates videos, animations, presentation packages, and slide shows—in short, anything of a visual nature that can be used in a judicial proceeding to make, clarify, or support a point.

Raj Jawahir, a new employee at PLUS, is responsible for tracking the daily payments received from the firm's clients. He created an Access database named **Payments**, and needs your help in working with this database. Complete the following:

1. Make sure your Data Disk is in the disk drive.

2. Start Access and open the **Payments** database, which is located in the Cases folder on your Data Disk.

3. Open the **Firm** table, print the table datasheet, and then close the table.

4. Use the Simple Query Wizard to create a query that includes the FirmName, PLUSAcctRep, and Extension fields (in that order) from the **Firm** table. Name the query **AcctRep List**.

Explore 5. Sort the query results in descending order by the PLUSAcctRep field. (*Hint*: Use a toolbar button.)

Explore 6. Use the Office Assistant to ask the following question: "How do I select multiple records?" Click the topic "Selecting fields and records in Datasheet view." Hide the Office Assistant, read the displayed information, and then close the Help window. Select the first 10 records in the datasheet (all the records with the value "Tyler, Olivia" in the PLUSAcctRep field), and then print just the selected records. Close the query, and save your changes to the design.

7. Use the AutoForm: Columnar Wizard to create a form for the **Firm** table. Move to record 25, and then print the form for the current record only. Save the form as **Firm Info** and then close the form.

8. Use the AutoReport: Columnar Wizard to create a report based on the **Firm** table. Maximize the Report window and change the Zoom setting to Fit.

Explore 9. Use the View menu to view all eight pages of the report at the same time in Print Preview.

10. Print just the first page of the report, and then close and save the report as **Firms**.

11. Set the option for compacting the **Payments** database on close.

12. Exit Access.

Case 3. Best Friends   Best Friends is a not-for-profit organization that trains hearing and service dogs for people with disabilities. Established in 1989 in Boise, Idaho, by Noah and Sheila Warnick, Best Friends is modeled after Paws With A Cause®, the original and largest provider of hearing and service dogs in the United States. Like Paws With A Cause® and other such organizations, Best Friends strives to provide "Dignity Through Independence."

To raise funds for Best Friends, Noah and Sheila periodically conduct walk-a-thons. The events have become so popular that Noah and Sheila created an Access database named **Walks** to track walker and pledge data. You'll help them complete and maintain the **Walks** database. Complete the following:

1. Make sure your Data Disk is in the disk drive.

2. Start Access and open the **Walks** database, which is located in the Cases folder on your Data Disk.

3. Open the **Walker** table, print the table datasheet, and then close the table.

Explore   4. Use the Simple Query Wizard to create a query that includes all the fields in the **Walker** table *except* the Phone field. (*Hint*: Use the `>>` and `<` buttons to select the necessary fields.) In the second Simple Query Wizard dialog box, make sure the Detail option button is selected. (This second dialog box opens because the table contains numeric values.) Name the query **Walker Distance**.

Explore   5. Sort the results in descending order by the Distance field. (*Hint*: Use a toolbar button.) Print the query results, and then close and save the query.

6. Use the AutoForm: Columnar Wizard to create a form for the **Walker** table. Move to record 16, and then print the form for the current record only. Save the form as **Walker Info**, and then close it.

7. Use the AutoReport: Columnar Wizard to create a report based on the **Walker** table. Maximize the Report window and change the Zoom setting to Fit.

Explore   8. Use the View menu to view all six pages of the report at the same time in Print Preview.

9. Print just the first page of the report, and then close and save the report as **Walkers**.

10. Set the option for compacting the **Walks** database on close.

11. Exit Access.

Case 4. Lopez Lexus Dealerships   Maria and Hector Lopez own a chain of Lexus dealerships throughout Texas. They have used a computer in their business for several years to handle payroll and typical accounting functions. Because of the dealership's phenomenal expansion, both in the number of car locations and the number of cars handled, they created an Access database named **Lexus** to track their car inventory. You'll help them work with and maintain this database. Complete the following:

1. Make sure your Data Disk is in the disk drive.

2. Start Access and open the **Lexus** database, which is located in the Cases folder on your Data Disk.

3. Open the **Cars** table.

Explore   4. Print the **Cars** table datasheet in landscape orientation, and then close the table.

Explore   5. Use the Simple Query Wizard to create a query that includes the Model, Class, Year, LocationCode, Cost, and SellingPrice fields (in that order) from the **Cars** table. In the second Simple Query Wizard dialog box, make sure the Detail option button is selected. (This second dialog box opens because the table contains numeric values.) Name the query **Cost vs Selling**.

Explore   6. Sort the query results in descending order by SellingPrice. (*Hint*: Use a toolbar button.)

7. Print the query results, and then close and save the query.

8. Use the AutoForm: Columnar Wizard to create a form for the **Cars** table. Move to record 3, and then print the form for the current record only. Save the form as **Car Info**, and then close it.

Explore   9. Use the AutoReport: Tabular Wizard to create a report based on the **Cars** table. Maximize the Report window and change the Zoom setting to Fit. Use the Two Pages button on the Print Preview toolbar to view both pages of the report in Print Preview. Print the first page of the report in landscape orientation, and then close and save the report as **Cars**.

10. Set the option for compacting the **Lexus** database on close.

11. Exit Access.

INTERNET ASSIGNMENTS

The purpose of the Internet Assignments is to challenge you to find information on the Internet that you can use to create effective documents. The actual assignments are updated and maintained on the Course Technology Web site. Log on to the Internet and use your Web browser to go to the Student Online Companion to accompany this text at **www.course.com/NewPerspectives/office2000**. Click the Access link, and then click the link for Tutorial 1.

LAB ASSIGNMENTS

Databases

These Lab Assignments are designed to accompany the interactive Course Lab called Databases. To start the Databases Lab, click the Start button on the Windows taskbar, point to Programs, point to Course Labs, point to New Perspectives Applications, and then click Databases. If you do not see Course Labs on your Programs menu, see your instructor or technical support person.

Databases   This Databases Lab demonstrates the essential concepts of file and database management systems. You will use the Lab to search, sort, and report the data contained in a file of classic books.

1. Click the Steps button to review basic database terminology and to learn how to manipulate the classic books database. As you proceed through the Steps, answer all of the Quick Check questions that appear. After you complete the Steps, you will see a Quick Check summary report. Follow the instructions on the screen to print this report.

2. Click the Explore button. Make sure you can apply basic database terminology to describe the classic books database by answering the following questions:

   a. How many records does the file contain?

   b. How many fields does each record contain?

   c. What are the contents of the Catalog # field for the book written by Margaret Mitchell?

   d. What are the contents of the Title field for the record with Thoreau in the Author field?

   e. Which field has been used to sort the records?

3. In Explore, manipulate the database as necessary to answer the following questions:

   a. When the books are sorted by title, what is the first record in the file?

   b. Use the Search button to search for all the books in the West location. How many do you find?

   c. Use the Search button to search for all the books in the Main location that are checked in. What do you find?

4. Use the Report button to print out a report that groups the books by Status and sorts them by Title. On your report, circle the four field names. Draw a box around the summary statistics showing which books are currently checked in and which books are currently checked out.

QUICK | CHECK ANSWERS

Session 1.1

   1. field

   2. common field

   3. primary key; foreign key

   4. records; fields

   5. current record symbol

   6. Use the horizontal and vertical scroll bars to view fields or records not currently visible in the datasheet; use the navigation buttons to move vertically through the records.

Session 1.2

   1. query

   2. primary key

   3. AutoForm Wizard

   4. The form displays each field name on a separate line to the left of its field value, which appears in a box; the widths of the boxes represent the size of the fields.

   5. Click the Microsoft Access Help button on any toolbar (or choose Microsoft Access Help or Show the Office Assistant from the Help menu), type a question in the text box, click the Search button, and then choose a topic from the list displayed.

   6. Print Preview

OBJECTIVES

In this tutorial you will:

- Learn the guidelines for designing databases and Access tables

- Create and save a table

- Define fields and specify the primary key

- Add records to a table

- Modify the structure of a table

- Delete, move, and add fields

- Change field properties

- Copy records from another Access database

- Delete and change records

MAINTAINING A DATABASE

Creating, Modifying, and Updating an Order Table

Valle Coffee

The Restaurant database currently contains only one table—the Customer table—which stores data about Valle Coffee's restaurant customers. Barbara Hennessey also wants to track information about each order placed by each restaurant customer. This information includes the order's billing date and Invoice amount. Barbara asks you to create a second table in the Restaurant database, named Order, in which to store the order data.

Some of the order data Barbara needs is already stored in another Valle Coffee database. After creating the Order table and adding some records to it, you'll copy the records from the other database into the Order table. Then you'll maintain the Order table by modifying it and updating it to meet Barbara's specific data requirements.

SESSION 2.1

In this session, you will learn the guidelines for designing databases and Access tables. You'll also learn how to create a table, define the fields for a table, select the primary key for a table, save the table structure, and add records to a table datasheet.

Guidelines for Designing Databases

A database management system can be a useful tool, but only if you first carefully design the database so that it meets the needs of its users. In database design, you determine the fields, tables, and relationships needed to satisfy the data and processing requirements. When you design a database, you should follow these guidelines:

■ **Identify all the fields needed to produce the required information**. For example, Barbara needs information about customers and orders. Figure 2-1 shows the fields that satisfy those information requirements.

Figure 2-1	BARBARA'S DATA REQUIREMENTS

CustomerName   BillingDate
OrderNum   OwnerName
Street   InvoiceAmt
City   PlacedBy
State   Phone
ZipCode   FirstContact
CustomerNum

■ **Group related fields into tables.** For example, Barbara grouped the fields relating to customers into the Customer table. The other fields are grouped logically into the Order table, which you will create, as shown in Figure 2-2.

Figure 2-2	BARBARA'S FIELDS GROUPED INTO CUSTOMER AND ORDER TABLES

<u>Customer table</u>   <u>Order table</u>
CustomerNum   OrderNum
CustomerName   BillingDate
Street   PlacedBy
City   InvoiceAmt
State
ZipCode
OwnerName
Phone
FirstContact

■ **Determine each table's primary key.** Recall that a primary key uniquely identifies each record in a table. Although a primary key is not mandatory in Access, it's usually a good idea to include one in each table. Without a primary key, selecting the exact record you want can be a problem. For some tables, one of the fields, such as a Social Security number or credit card number, naturally serves the function of a primary key. For other tables, two or more fields might be needed to function as the primary key.

In these cases, the primary key is referred to as a **composite key**. For example, a school grade table would use a combination of student number and course code to serve as the primary key. For a third category of tables, no single field or combination of fields can uniquely identify a record in a table. In these cases, you need to add a field whose sole purpose is to serve as the primary key.

For Barbara's tables, CustomerNum is the primary key for the Customer table, and OrderNum will be the primary key for the Order table.

- **Include a common field in related tables.** You use the common field to connect one table logically with another table. For example, Barbara's Customer and Order tables will include the CustomerNum field as a common field. Recall that when you include the primary key from one table as a field in a second table to form a relationship, the field is called a foreign key in the second table; therefore, the CustomerNum field will be a foreign key in the Order table. With this common field, Barbara can find all orders placed by a customer; she can use the CustomerNum value for a customer and search the Order table for all orders with that CustomerNum value. Likewise, she can determine which customer placed a particular order by searching the Customer table to find the one record with the same CustomerNum value as the corresponding value in the Order table.

- **Avoid data redundancy.** Data redundancy occurs when you store the same data in more than one place. With the exception of common fields to connect tables, you should avoid redundancy because it wastes storage space and can cause inconsistencies, if, for instance, you type a field value one way in one table and a different way in the same table or in a second table. Figure 2-3 shows an example of incorrect database design that illustrates data redundancy in the Order table; the Customer Name field is redundant, and one value was entered incorrectly, in three different ways.

| Figure 2-3 | INCORRECT DATABASE DESIGN WITH DATA REDUNDANCY |

Customer table

Customer Number	Customer Name	Customer Address	Phone Number
104	Meadows Restaurant	Pond Hill Road, Monroe MI 48161	(313) 792-3546
128	Grand River Restaurant	37 Queue Highway, Lacota MI 49063	(313) 729-5364
163	Bentham's Riverfront Restaurant	1366 36th Street, Roscommon MI 48653	(517) 792-8040
635	Oaks Restaurant	3300 West Russell Street, Maumee OH 43537	(419) 336-9000
741	Prime Cut Steakhouse	2819 East 10 Street, Mishawaka IN 46544	(219) 336-0900
779	Gateway Lounge	3408 Gateway Boulevard, Sylvania OH 43560	(419) 361-1137

data redundancy

Order table

Order Number	Customer Number	Customer Name	Billing Date	Invoice Amount
202	104	Meadows Restaurant	01/15/2001	1,280.50
226	635	Oakes Restaurant	01/15/2001	1,939.00
231	779	Gateway Lounge	01/15/2001	1,392.50
309	741	Prime Cut Steakhouse	02/15/2001	1,928.00
313	635	Stokes Inn	02/15/2001	1,545.00
377	128	Grand River Restaurant	03/15/2001	562.00
359	635	Raks Restaurant	03/15/2001	1,939.00
373	779	Gateway Lounge	03/15/2001	1,178.00
395	163	Bentham's Riverfront Restaurant	03/15/2001	1,348.00

inconsistent data

■ **Determine the properties of each field.** You need to identify the **properties**, or characteristics, of each field so that the DBMS knows how to store, display, and process the field. These properties include the field's name, maximum number of characters or digits, description, valid values, and other field characteristics. You will learn more about field properties later in this tutorial.

The Order table you need to create will contain the fields shown in Figure 2-2. Before you create the table, you first need to learn some guidelines for designing Access tables.

Guidelines for Designing Access Tables

As just noted, the last step of database design is to determine the properties, such as the name and data type, of each field. Access has rules for naming fields, choosing data types, and defining other properties for fields.

Naming Fields and Objects

You must name each field, table, and other object in an Access database. Access then stores these items in the database, using the names you supply. It's best to choose a field or object name that describes the purpose or contents of the field or object, so that later you can easily remember what the name represents. For example, the two tables in the Restaurant database will be named Customer and Order, because these names suggest their contents.

The following rules apply to naming fields and objects:

■ A name can be up to 64 characters long.

■ A name can contain letters, numbers, spaces, and special characters, except for a period (.), exclamation mark (!), accent grave (`), and square brackets ([ ]).

■ A name cannot start with a space.

■ A table or query name must be unique within a database. A field name must be unique within a table, but it can be used again in another table.

In addition, experienced users of databases follow these tips for naming fields and objects:

■ Capitalize the first letter of each word in the name.

■ Avoid extremely long names because they are difficult to remember and reference.

■ Use standard abbreviations, such as Num for Number, Amt for Amount, and Qty for Quantity.

■ Do not use spaces in field names because these names will appear in column headings on datasheets and on labels on forms and reports. By not using spaces you'll be able to show more fields on these objects at one time.

Assigning Field Data Types

You must assign a data type for each field. The **data type** determines what field values you can enter for the field and what other properties the field will have. For example, the Order table will include a BillingDate field, so you will assign the date/time data type to this field because it will store date values. Then Access will allow you to enter and manipulate only dates or times as values in the BillingDate field.

Figure 2-4 lists the 10 data types available in Access, describes the field values allowed for each data type, explains when you should use each data type, and indicates the field size of each data type.

Figure 2-4	DATA TYPES FOR FIELDS	
DATA TYPE	**DESCRIPTION**	**FIELD SIZE**
Text	Allows field values containing letters, digits, spaces, and special characters. Use for names, addresses, descriptions, and fields containing digits that are not used in calculations.	0 to 255 characters; 50 characters default
Memo	Allows field values containing letters, digits, spaces, and special characters. Use for long comments and explanations.	1 to 64,000 characters; exact size is determined by entry
Number	Allows positive and negative numbers as field values. Numbers can contain digits, a decimal point, commas, a plus sign, and a minus sign. Use for fields that you will use in calculations, except calculations involving money.	1 to 15 digits
Date/Time	Allows field values containing valid dates and times from January 1, 100 to December 31, 9999. Dates can be entered in mm/dd/yy (month, day, year) format, several other date formats, or a variety of time formats such as 10:35 PM. You can perform calculations on dates and times, and you can sort them. For example, you can determine the number of days between two dates.	8 bytes
Currency	Allows field values similar to those for the number data type. Unlike calculations with number data type decimal values, calculations performed using the currency data type are not subject to round-off error.	Accurate to 15 digits on the left side of the decimal separator and to 4 digits on the right side
AutoNumber	Consists of integers with values controlled by Access. Access automatically inserts a value in the field as each new record is created. You can specify sequential numbering or random numbering. This guarantees a unique field value, so that such a field can serve as a table's primary key.	9 digits
Yes/No	Limits field values to yes and no, on and off, or true and false. Use for fields that indicate the presence or absence of a condition, such as whether an order has been filled, or if an employee is eligible for the company dental plan.	1 character
OLE Object	Allows field values that are created in other programs as objects, such as photographs, video images, graphics, drawings, sound recordings, voice-mail messages, spreadsheets, and word-processing documents. These objects can be linked or embedded.	1 gigabyte maximum; exact size depends on object size
Hyperlink	Consists of text used as a hyperlink address. A hyperlink address can have up to three parts: the text that appears in a field or control; the path to a file or page; and a location within the file or page. Hyperlinks help you to connect your application easily to the Internet or an intranet.	Up to 64,000 characters total for the three parts of a hyperlink data type
Lookup Wizard	Creates a field that lets you look up a value in another table or in a predefined list of values.	Same size as the primary key field used to perform the lookup

Assigning Field Sizes

The **field size** property defines a field value's maximum storage size for text, number, and AutoNumber fields only. The other data types have no field size property because their storage size is either a fixed, predetermined amount or is determined automatically by the field value itself, as shown in Figure 2-4. A text field has a default field size of 50 characters; you can also set its field size by entering a number in the range 1 to 255. For example, the OrderNum and CustomerNum fields in the Order table will be text fields with sizes of 3 each.

When you use the number data type to define a field, you should set the field's Field Size property based on the largest value that you expect to store in that field. Access processes smaller data sizes faster using less memory, so you can optimize your database's performance and its storage space by selecting the correct field size for each field. For example, it would be wasteful to use the Long Integer setting when defining a field that will only store whole numbers ranging from 0 to 255, because the Long Integer setting will use four bytes of storage space. A better choice would be the Byte setting, which uses one byte of storage space to store the same values. Other Field Size property settings for number fields are:

- **Byte**: Stores whole numbers (numbers with no fractions) from 0 to 255 in one byte
- **Integer**: Stores whole numbers from -32,768 to 32,767 in two bytes
- **Long Integer** (default): Stores whole numbers from -2,147,483,648 to 2,147,483,647 in four bytes
- **Single**: Stores positive and negative numbers to precisely seven decimal places and uses four bytes
- **Double**: Stores positive and negative numbers to precisely 15 decimal places and uses eight bytes
- **Replication ID**: Establishes a unique identifier for replication of tables, records, and other objects and uses 16 bytes
- **Decimal**: Stores positive and negative numbers to precisely 28 decimal places and uses 12 bytes

Barbara documented the design for the Order table by listing each field's name, data type, size (if applicable), and description, as shown in Figure 2-5. Note that Barbara assigned the text data type to the OrderNum field (the table's primary key), to the CustomerNum field (a foreign key to the Customer table), and to the PlacedBy field. BillingDate will have the date/time data type, and InvoiceAmt will have the currency data type.

Figure 2-5	DESIGN FOR THE ORDER TABLE			
Field Name	Data Type	Field Size	Description	
OrderNum	Text	3	primary key	
CustomerNum	Text	3	foreign key	
BillingDate	Date/Time			
PlacedBy	Text	25	person who placed order	
InvoiceAmt	Currency			

With Barbara's design, you are ready to create the Order table.

Creating a Table

Creating a table consists of naming the fields and defining the properties for the fields, specifying a primary key (and a foreign key, if applicable) for the table, and then saving the table structure. You will use Barbara's design (Figure 2-5) as a guide for creating the Order table. First, you need to open the Restaurant database.

To open the Restaurant database:

1. Place your Data Disk in the appropriate disk drive.

2. Start Access. The Access window opens with the initial dialog box.

3. Make sure that the **Open an existing file** option button and the **More Files** option are selected, and then click the **OK** button to display the Open dialog box.

4. Click the **Look in** list arrow, and then click the drive that contains your Data Disk.

5. Click **Tutorial** in the list box, and then click the **Open** button to display a list of the files in the Tutorial folder.

6. Click **Restaurant** in the list box, and then click the **Open** button. The Restaurant database opens in the Access window.

7. Make sure that **Tables** is selected in the Objects bar of the Database window.

The Customer table is listed in the Tables list box. Now you'll create the Order table in the Restaurant database.

To begin creating the Order table:

1. Click the **New** button in the Database window. The New Table dialog box opens. See Figure 2-6.

Figure 2-6	NEW TABLE DIALOG BOX

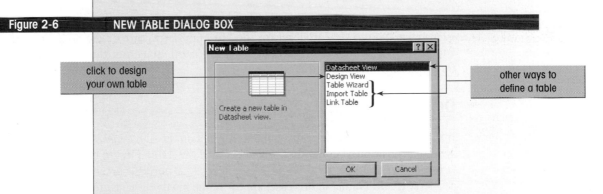

In Access, you can create a table from entered data (Datasheet View), define your own table (Design View), use a Wizard to automate the table creation process (Table Wizard), or use a Wizard to import or link data from another database or other data source (Import Table or Link Table). For the Order table, you will define your own table.

2. Click **Design View** in the list box, and then click the **OK** button. The Table window opens in Design view. See Figure 2-7.

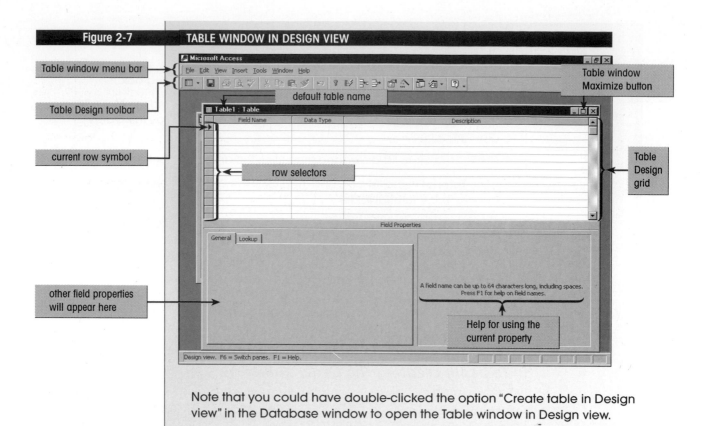

Figure 2-7   TABLE WINDOW IN DESIGN VIEW

- Table window menu bar
- Table Design toolbar
- current row symbol
- other field properties will appear here
- default table name
- Table window Maximize button
- Table Design grid
- row selectors
- Help for using the current property

Note that you could have double-clicked the option "Create table in Design view" in the Database window to open the Table window in Design view.

You use Design view to define or modify a table structure or the properties of the fields in a table. If you create a table without using a Wizard, you enter the fields and their properties for your table directly in this window.

Defining Fields

Initially, the default table name, Table1, appears on the Table window title bar, the current row symbol is positioned in the first row selector of the Table Design grid, and the insertion point is located in the first row's Field Name box. The purpose or characteristics of the current property (Field Name, in this case) appear in the lower-right section of the Table window. You can display more complete information about the current property by pressing the F1 key.

You enter values for the Field Name, Data Type, and Description field properties in the upper half of the Table window. You select values for all other field properties, most of which are optional, in the lower half of the window. These other properties will appear when you move to the first row's Data Type text box.

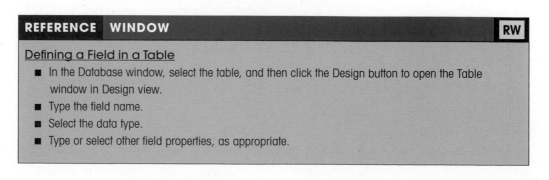

REFERENCE   WINDOW   RW

Defining a Field in a Table
- In the Database window, select the table, and then click the Design button to open the Table window in Design view.
- Type the field name.
- Select the data type.
- Type or select other field properties, as appropriate.

The first field you need to define is OrderNum.

To define the OrderNum field:

1. Type **OrderNum** in the first row's Field Name text box, and then press the **Tab** key (or press the **Enter** key) to advance to the Data Type text box. The default data type, Text, appears highlighted in the Data Type text box, which now also contains a list arrow, and field properties for a text field appear in the lower half of the window. See Figure 2-8.

Figure 2-8	TABLE WINDOW AFTER ENTERING THE FIRST FIELD NAME

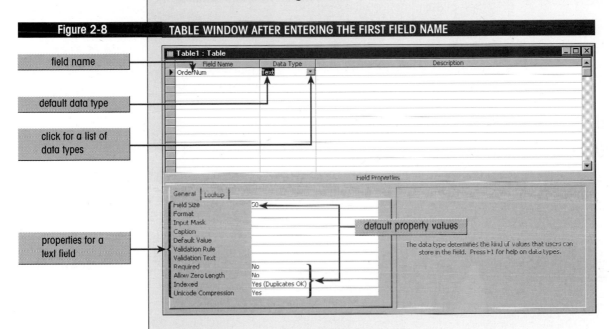

Notice that the lower-right section of the window now provides an explanation for the current property, Data Type.

TROUBLE? If you make a typing error, you can correct it by clicking the mouse to position the insertion point, and then using either the Backspace key to delete characters to the left of the insertion point or the Delete key to delete characters to the right of the insertion point. Then type the correct text.

Because order numbers will not be used for calculations, you will assign the text data type to the OrderNum field instead of the number data type, and then enter the Description property value as "primary key." You can use the Description property to enter an optional description for a field to explain its purpose or usage. A field's Description property can be up to 255 characters long, and its value appears in the status bar when you view the table datasheet.

2. Press the **Tab** key to accept Text as the field's data type and move to the Description text box, and then type **primary key** in the Description text box.

The Field Size property has a default value of 50, which you will change to a value of 3, because order numbers at Valle Coffee contain three digits. When you select or enter a value for a property, you *set* the property. The Required property has a default value of No, which means that a value does not need to be entered for the field. Because Barbara doesn't want an order entered without an order number, you will change the Required property to Yes. (Refer to the Access Help system for a complete description of all the properties available for the different data types.)

3. Select **50** in the Field Size text box either by dragging the pointer or double-clicking the mouse, and then type **3**.

4. Click the **Required** text box to position the insertion point there. A list arrow appears on the right side of the Required text box.

5. Click the **Required** list arrow. Access displays the Required list box. See Figure 2-9.

Figure 2-9	DEFINING THE ORDERNUM FIELD

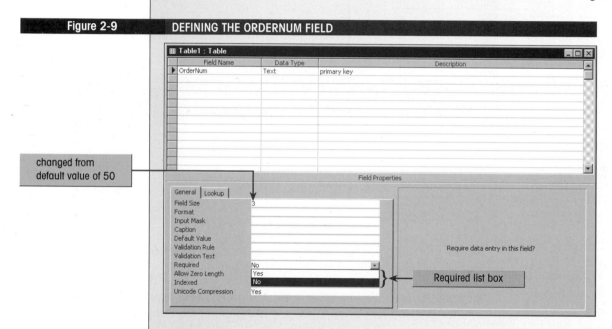

changed from default value of 50

Required list box

When you position the insertion point or select text in many Access text boxes, Access displays a list arrow, which you can click to display a list box with options. You can display the list arrow and the list box simultaneously if you click the text box near its right side.

6. Click **Yes** in the list box. The list box closes, and Yes is now the value for the Required property. The definition of the first field is complete.

Barbara's Order table design shows CustomerNum as the second field. You will define CustomerNum as a text field with a Description of "foreign key" and a Field Size of 3, because customer numbers at Valle Coffee contain three digits. Because it's possible that a record for an order might need to be entered for a customer not yet added to the database, Barbara asks you to leave the Required property at its default value of No.

To define the CustomerNum field:

1. Place the insertion point in the second row's Field Name text box, type **CustomerNum** in the text box, and then press the **Tab** key to advance to the Data Type text box.

   Customer numbers are not used in calculations, so you'll assign the text data type to the field, and then enter its Description value as "foreign key."

2. Press the **Tab** key to accept Text as the field's data type and to move to the Description text box, and then type **foreign key** in the Description text box.

   Next, you'll change the Field Size property to 3. Note that when defining the fields in a table, you can move between the top and bottom panes of the table window by pressing the F6 key.

3. Press the **F6** key to move to the bottom pane (Field Properties). The current entry for the Field Size property, 50, is highlighted.

4. Type **3** to set the Field Size property. You have completed the definition of the second field. See Figure 2-10.

| Figure 2-10 | TABLE WINDOW AFTER DEFINING THE FIRST TWO FIELDS |

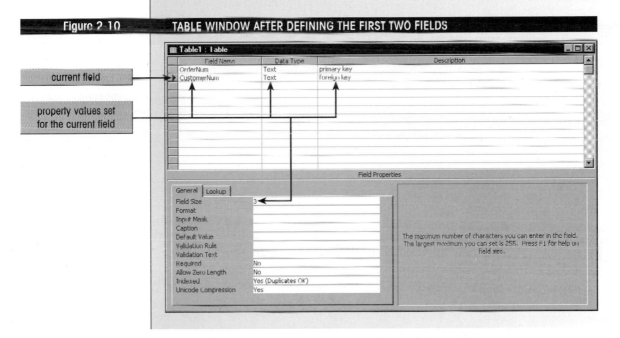

Using Barbara's Order table design in Figure 2-5, you can now complete the remaining field definitions: BillingDate with the date/time data type, PlacedBy with the text data type, and InvoiceAmt with the currency data type.

To define the BillingDate field:

1. Place the insertion point in the third row's Field Name text box, type **BillingDate** in the text box, and then press the **Tab** key to advance to the Data Type text box.

2. Click the **Data Type** list arrow, click **Date/Time** in the list box, and then press the **Tab** key to advance to the Description text box.

If you've assigned a descriptive field name and the field does not fulfill a special function (such as primary key), you usually do not enter a value for the optional Description property. BillingDate is a field that does not require a value for its Description property.

Barbara wants the values in the BillingDate field to be displayed in a format showing the month, day, and year as in the following example: 01/15/2001. You use the Format property to control the display of a field value.

3. In the Field Properties section, click the right side of the **Format** text box to display the list of predefined formats. As noted in the right section of the window, you can either choose a predefined format or enter a custom format.

TROUBLE? If you see a list arrow instead of a list of predefined formats, click the list arrow to display the list.

None of the predefined formats matches the layout Barbara wants for the BillingDate values. Therefore, you need to create a custom date format. Figure 2-11 shows some of the symbols available for custom date and time formats. (A complete description of all the custom formats is available in Help.)

Figure 2-11	SYMBOLS FOR SOME CUSTOM DATE FORMATS

SYMBOL	DESCRIPTION
/	date separator
d	day of the month in one or two numeric digits, as needed (1 to 31)
dd	day of the month in two numeric digits (01 to 31)
ddd	first three letters of the weekday (Sun to Sat)
dddd	full name of the weekday (Sunday to Saturday)
w	day of the week (1 to 7)
ww	week of the year (1 to 53)
m	month of the year in one or two numeric digits, as needed (1 to 12)
mm	month of the year in two numeric digits (01 to 12)
mmm	first three letters of the month (Jan to Dec)
mmmm	full name of the month (January to December)
yy	last two digits of the year (01 to 99)
yyyy	full year (0100 to 9999)

Barbara wants the dates to be displayed with a two-digit month (mm), a two-digit day (dd), and a four-digit year (yyyy). You'll enter this custom format now.

4. Click the **Format** list arrow to close the list of predefined formats, and then type **mm/dd/yyyy** in the Format text box. See Figure 2-12.

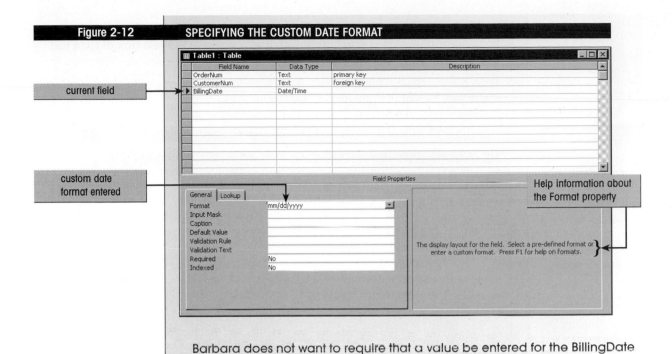

Figure 2-12	SPECIFYING THE CUSTOM DATE FORMAT

current field

custom date format entered

Help information about the Format property

Barbara does not want to require that a value be entered for the BillingDate field, so you have completed the definition of the field.

Now you're ready to finish the Order table design by defining the PlacedBy and InvoiceAmt fields.

To define the PlacedBy and InvoiceAmt fields:

1. Place the insertion point in the fourth row's Field Name text box.

2. Type **PlacedBy** in the Field Name text box, and then press the **Tab** key to advance to the Data Type text box.

   This field will contain names, so you'll assign the text data type to it. Also, Barbara wants to include the description "person who placed order" to clarify the contents of the field.

3. Press the **Tab** key to accept Text as the field's data type and to move to the Description text box, and then type **person who placed order** in the Description text box.

   Next, you'll change the Field Size property's default value of 50 to 25, which should be long enough to accommodate all names.

4. Press the **F6** key to move to and select 50 in the Field Size text box, and then type **25**.

   The definition of the PlacedBy field is complete. Next, you'll define the fifth and final field, InvoiceAmt. This field will contain dollar amounts, so you'll assign the currency data type to it.

5. Place the insertion point in the fifth row's Field Name text box.

6. Type **InvoiceAmt** in the Field Name text box, and then press the **Tab** key to advance to the Data Type text box.

You can select a value from the Data Type list box as you did for the BillingDate field. Alternatively, you can type the property value in the text box or type just the first character of the property value.

7. Type **c**. The value in the fifth row's Data Type text box changes to "currency," with the letters "urrency" highlighted. See Figure 2-13.

Figure 2-13   **SELECTING A VALUE FOR THE DATA TYPE PROPERTY**

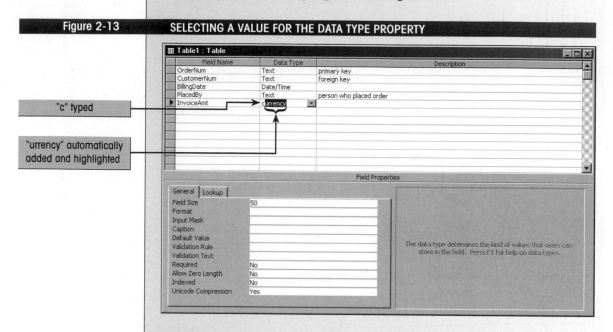

"c" typed

"urrency" automatically added and highlighted

8. Press the **Tab** key to advance to the Description text box. Access changes the value for the Data Type property to Currency.

In the Field Properties section, notice the default values for the Format, Decimal Places, and Default Value properties. For a field with a Format property value of Currency, two decimal places are provided when the Decimal Places property value is set to Auto. These properties, combined with the Default Value property of 0, specify that values in the InvoiceAmt field will initially appear as follows: $0.00. This is the format Barbara wants for the InvoiceAmt field, so you are finished defining the fields for the Order table.

Next, you need to specify the primary key for the Order table.

Specifying the Primary Key

Although Access does not require a table to have a primary key, including a primary key offers several advantages:

- A primary key uniquely identifies each record in a table.
- Access does not allow duplicate values in the primary key field. If a record already exists with an OrderNum value of 143, for example, Access prevents you from adding another record with this same value in the OrderNum field. Preventing duplicate values ensures the uniqueness of the primary key field.

- Access forces you to enter a value for the primary key field in every record in the table. This is known as **entity integrity**. If you do not enter a value for a field, you have actually given the field what is known as a **null value**. You cannot give a null value to the primary key field because entity integrity prevents Access from accepting and processing that record.

- Access stores records on disk in the same order as you enter them but displays them in order by the field values of the primary key. If you enter records in no specific order, you are ensured that you will later be able to work with them in a more meaningful, primary key sequence.

- Access responds faster to your requests for specific records based on the primary key.

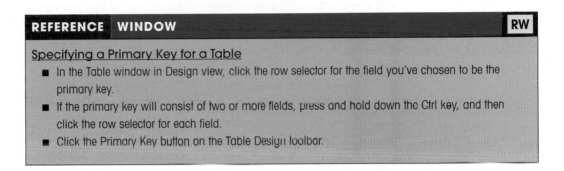

REFERENCE   WINDOW   `RW`

Specifying a Primary Key for a Table
- In the Table window in Design view, click the row selector for the field you've chosen to be the primary key.
- If the primary key will consist of two or more fields, press and hold down the Ctrl key, and then click the row selector for each field.
- Click the Primary Key button on the Table Design toolbar.

According to Barbara's design, you need to specify OrderNum as the primary key for the Order table.

To specify OrderNum as the primary key:

1. Position the pointer on the row selector for the OrderNum field until the pointer changes to ➡. See Figure 2-14.

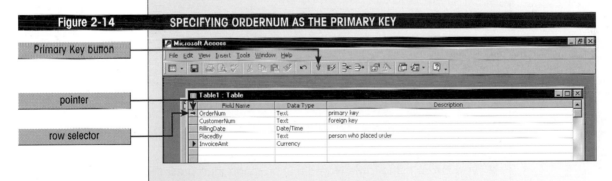

| Figure 2-14 | SPECIFYING ORDERNUM AS THE PRIMARY KEY |

2. Click the mouse button. The entire first row of the Table Design grid is highlighted.

3. Click the **Primary Key** button [ ] on the Table Design toolbar, and then click to the right of InvoiceAmt in the fifth row's Field Name text box to deselect the first row. A key symbol appears in the row selector for the first row, indicating that the OrderNum field is the table's primary key. See Figure 2-15.

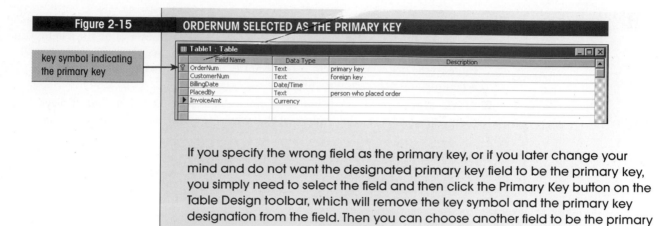

Figure 2-15 **ORDERNUM SELECTED AS THE PRIMARY KEY**

key symbol indicating
the primary key

Field Name	Data Type	Description
OrderNum	Text	primary key
CustomerNum	Text	foreign key
BillingDate	Date/Time	
PlacedBy	Text	person who placed order
InvoiceAmt	Currency	

If you specify the wrong field as the primary key, or if you later change your mind and do not want the designated primary key field to be the primary key, you simply need to select the field and then click the Primary Key button on the Table Design toolbar, which will remove the key symbol and the primary key designation from the field. Then you can choose another field to be the primary key, if necessary.

You've defined the fields for the Order table and specified its primary key, so you can now save the table structure.

Saving the Table Structure

The last step in creating a table is to name the table and save the table's structure on disk. Once the table is saved, you can use it to enter data in the table.

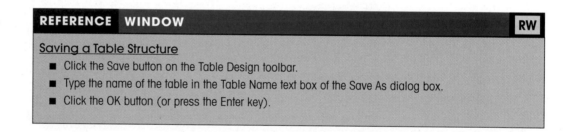

REFERENCE WINDOW   RW

Saving a Table Structure
- Click the Save button on the Table Design toolbar.
- Type the name of the table in the Table Name text box of the Save As dialog box.
- Click the OK button (or press the Enter key).

You need to save the table you've defined as "Order."

To name and save the Order table:

1. Click the **Save** button 🖫 on the Table Design toolbar. The Save As dialog box opens.

2. Type **Order** in the Table Name text box, and then press the **Enter** key. Access saves the table with the name Order in the Restaurant database on your Data Disk. Notice that Order appears instead of Table1 in the Table window title bar.

Next, Barbara asks you to add the two records shown in Figure 2-16 to the Order table. These two records contain data for orders that two customers recently placed with Valle Coffee.

Figure 2-16	RECORDS TO BE ADDED TO THE ORDER TABLE				
	OrderNum	CustomerNum	BillingDate	PlacedBy	InvoiceAmt
	323	624	02/15/2001	Isabelle Rouy	$1,986.00
	201	107	01/15/2001	Matt Gellman	$854.00

Adding Records to a Table

You can add records to an Access table in several ways. A table datasheet provides a simple way for you to add records. As you learned in Tutorial 1, a datasheet shows a table's contents in rows and columns. Each row is a separate record in the table, and each column contains the field values for one field in the table. To view a table datasheet, you first must change from Design view to Datasheet view.

You'll switch to Datasheet view and add the two records in the Order table datasheet.

To add the records in the Order table datasheet:

1. Click the **View** button for Datasheet view ![icon] on the Table Design toolbar. The Table window opens in Datasheet view. See Figure 2-17.

Figure 2-17	TABLE WINDOW IN DATASHEET VIEW

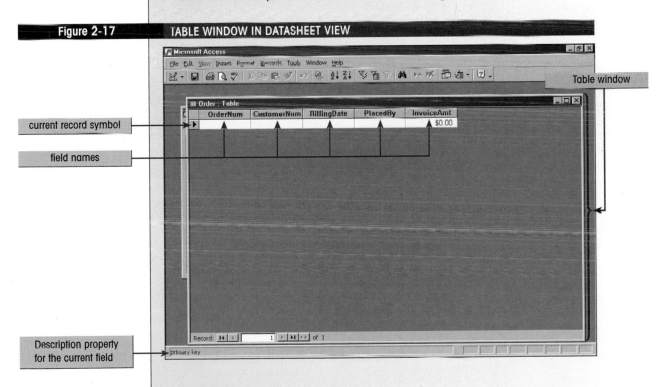

The table's five field names appear at the top of the datasheet. The current record symbol in the first row's record selector identifies the currently selected record, which contains no data until you enter the first record. The insertion point is located in the first row's OrderNum field, whose Description property appears in the status bar.

2. Type **323**, which is the first record's OrderNum field value, and then press the **Tab** key. Each time you press the Tab key, the insertion point moves to the right to the next field in the record. See Figure 2-18.

| Figure 2-18 | DATASHEET FOR ORDER TABLE AFTER ENTERING THE FIRST FIELD VALUE |

symbol for the record being edited

next new record symbol

field value entered

insertion point

current record

Order : Table

OrderNum	CustomerNum	BillingDate	PlacedBy	InvoiceAmt
323				$0.00
				$0.00

default value for InvoiceAmt field

Record: 1 of 1

TROUBLE? If you make a mistake when typing a value, use the Backspace key to delete characters to the left of the insertion point, or the Delete key to delete characters to the right of the insertion point. Then type the correct text. If you want to correct a value by replacing it entirely, double-click the value to select it, and then type the correct value.

The pencil symbol in the first row's record selector indicates that the record is being edited. The star symbol in the second row's record selector identifies the second row as the next one available for a new record. The InvoiceAmt column displays "$0.00," the default value for the field, as specified by the field's properties.

3. Type **624** and then press the **Tab** key. The insertion point moves to the right side of the BillingDate field.

Recall that you specified a custom format for the BillingDate field, mm/dd/yyyy. However, when you enter the digits for the year, you only need to enter the final two digits; you do not have to enter all four digits. For example, for a field value containing the year 1999, you only need to enter "99" and Access will store and automatically display the full four digits, as specified by the custom format.

4. Type **02/15/01** and then press the **Tab** key. Access displays the BillingDate field value as "02/15/2001" and the insertion point moves to the PlacedBy field.

5. Type **Isabelle Rouy** and then press the **Tab** key. The insertion point moves to the InvoiceAmt field, whose field value is highlighted.

Notice that field values for text fields are left-aligned in their boxes, and field values for date/time and currency fields are right-aligned in their boxes. If the default value of $0.00 is correct for the InvoiceAmt field, you can press the Tab key to accept the value and advance to the beginning of the next record. Otherwise, type the field value for the InvoiceAmt field. You do not need to type the dollar sign, commas, or decimal point (for whole dollar amounts) because Access adds these symbols automatically for you.

6. Type **1986** and then press the **Tab** key. Access displays $1,986.00 for the InvoiceAmt field, stores the first completed record in the Order table, removes the pencil symbol from the first row's record selector, advances the insertion point to the second row's OrderNum text box, and places the current record symbol in the second row's record selector.

Now you can enter the values for the second record.

7. Type **201** in the OrderNum field, press the **Tab** key to move to the CustomerNum field, type **107** in the CustomerNum field, and then press the **Tab** key. The insertion point moves to the right side of the BillingDate field.

8. Type **01/15/01** and then press the **Tab** key. The insertion point moves to the PlacedBy field.

9. Type **Matt Gellman** and then press the **Tab** key. The value in the InvoiceAmt field is now highlighted.

10. Type **854** and then press the **Tab** key. Access changes the InvoiceAmt field value to $854.00, saves the record in the Order table, and moves the insertion point to the beginning of the third row. See Figure 2-19.

Figure 2-19	ORDER TABLE DATASHEET AFTER ENTERING THE SECOND RECORD

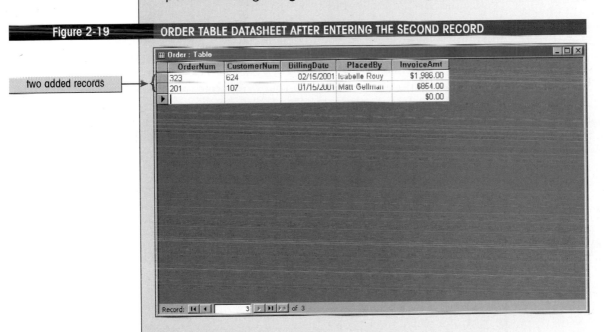

two added records

OrderNum	CustomerNum	BillingDate	PlacedBy	InvoiceAmt
323	624	02/15/2001	Isabelle Rouy	$1,986.00
201	107	01/15/2001	Matt Gellman	$854.00
				$0.00

Record: ◄◄ ◄ 3 ► ►► ►* of 3

Notice that "Record 3 of 3" appears around the navigation buttons, even though the table contains only two records. Access is anticipating that you will enter a new record, which would be the third of three records in the table. If you moved the insertion point to the second record, the display would change to "Record 2 of 2."

Even though the Order table contains only two records, Barbara asks you to print the table datasheet so that she can bring it with her to a staff meeting. She wants to show the table design to her staff members to make sure that it will meet their needs for tracking order data.

You'll use the Print button on the Table Datasheet toolbar to print one copy of the Order table with the current settings.

> ### To print the Order table:
>
> **1.** Click the **Print** button 🖨 on the Table Datasheet toolbar.
>
> Notice that the two records are currently listed in the order in which you entered them. However, once you close the table or change to another view, and then redisplay the table datasheet, the records will be listed in primary key order by the values in the OrderNum field.

You have created the Order table in the Restaurant database and added two records to the table, which Access saved automatically to the database on your Data Disk.

Saving a Database

Notice the Save button on the Table Datasheet toolbar. This Save button, unlike the Save buttons in other Windows programs, does not save the active document (database) to your disk. Instead, you use the Save button to save the design of a table, query, form, or report, or to save datasheet format changes. Access does not have a button or option you can use to save the active database.

Access saves the active database to your disk automatically, both on a periodic basis and whenever you close the database. This means that if your database is stored on a disk in drive A, you should never remove the disk while the database file is open. If you do remove the disk, Access will encounter problems when it tries to save the database, which might damage the database.

The Order table is now complete. In Session 2.2, you'll continue to work with the Order table by modifying its structure and entering and maintaining data in the table.

Session 2.1 QUICK CHECK

1. What guidelines should you follow when you design a database?

2. What is the purpose of the data type property for a field?

3. For which three types of fields can you assign a field size?

4. Why did you define the OrderNum field as a text field instead of a number field?

5. A(n) _____ value, which results when you do not enter a value for a field, is not permitted for a primary key.

6. What does a pencil symbol in a datasheet's row selector represent? A star symbol?

SESSION 2.2

In this session, you will modify the structure of a table by deleting, moving, and adding fields and changing field properties; copy records from another Access database; and update a database by deleting and changing records.

Modifying the Structure of an Access Table

Even a well-designed table might need to be modified. For example, the government at all levels and the competition place demands on a company to track more data and to modify the data it already tracks. Access allows you to modify a table's structure in Design view: you can add and delete fields, change the order of fields, and change the properties of the fields.

After meeting with her staff members and reviewing the structure of the Order table and the format of the field values in the datasheet, Barbara has several changes she wants you to make to the table. First, she has decided that it's not necessary to keep track of the name of the person who placed a particular order, so she wants you to delete the PlacedBy field. Also, she thinks that the InvoiceAmt field should remain a currency field, but she wants the dollar signs removed from the displayed field values in the datasheet. She also wants the BillingDate field moved to the end of the table. Finally, she wants you to add a yes/no field, named Paid, to the table to indicate whether or not the customer has paid for the order. The Paid field will be inserted between the CustomerNum and InvoiceAmt fields. Figure 2-20 shows Barbara's modified design for the Order table.

Figure 2-20	MODIFIED DESIGN FOR THE ORDER TABLE			

Field Name	Data Type	Field Size	Description
OrderNum	Text	3	primary key
CustomerNum	Text	3	foreign key
Paid	Yes/No		
InvoiceAmt	Currency		
BillingDate	Date/Time		

You'll begin modifying the table by deleting the PlacedBy field.

Deleting a Field

After you've defined a table structure and added records to the table, you can delete a field from the table structure. When you delete a field, you also delete all the values for the field from the table. Therefore, you should make sure that you need to delete a field and that you delete the correct field.

REFERENCE WINDOW	RW

Deleting a Field from a Table Structure
- In the Table window in Design view, right-click the row selector for the field you want to delete, to select the field and display the shortcut menu.
- Click Delete Rows on the shortcut menu.

You need to delete the PlacedBy field from the Order table structure.

To delete the PlacedBy field:

1. If you took a break after the previous session, make sure that Access is running and that the Order table of the Restaurant database is open.

2. Click the **View** button for Design view 🔲 on the Table Datasheet toolbar. The Table window for the Order table opens in Design view.

3. Position the pointer on the row selector for the PlacedBy field until the pointer changes to ➡.

4. Right-click to select the entire row for the field and display the shortcut menu, and then click **Delete Rows**.

   A dialog box opens asking you to confirm the deletion.

5. Click the **Yes** button to close the dialog box and to delete the field and its values from the table. See Figure 2-21.

Figure 2-21	TABLE STRUCTURE AFTER DELETING PLACEDBY FIELD

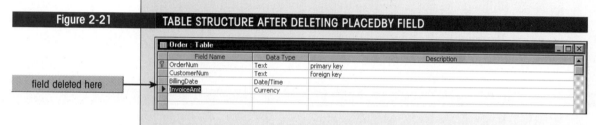

You have deleted the PlacedBy field in the Table window, but the change doesn't take place in the table on disk until you save the table structure. Because you have other modifications to make to the table, you'll wait until you finish them all before saving the modified table structure to disk.

Moving a Field

To move a field, you use the mouse to drag it to a new location in the Table window in Design view. Your next modification to the Order table structure is to move the BillingDate field to the end of the table, as Barbara requested.

To move the BillingDate field:

1. Click the **row selector** for the BillingDate field to select the entire row.

2. Place the pointer in the row selector for the BillingDate field, click the pointer ⬀, and then drag the pointer ⬀ to the row selector below the InvoiceAmt row selector. See Figure 2-22.

Figure 2-22	MOVING A FIELD IN THE TABLE STRUCTURE

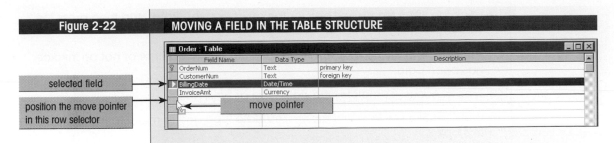

selected field

position the move pointer in this row selector

3. Release the mouse button. Access moves the BillingDate field below the InvoiceAmt field in the table structure.

TROUBLE? If the BillingDate field did not move, repeat Steps 1 through 3, making sure you firmly hold down the mouse button during the drag operation.

Adding a Field

Next, you need to add the Paid field to the table structure between the CustomerNum and InvoiceAmt fields. To add a new field between existing fields, you must insert a row. You begin by selecting the field that will be below the new field you want to insert.

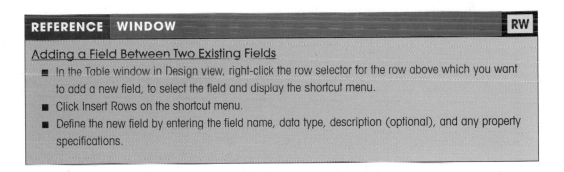

REFERENCE WINDOW   **RW**

Adding a Field Between Two Existing Fields

■ In the Table window in Design view, right-click the row selector for the row above which you want to add a new field, to select the field and display the shortcut menu.
■ Click Insert Rows on the shortcut menu.
■ Define the new field by entering the field name, data type, description (optional), and any property specifications.

To add the Paid field to the Order table:

1. Right-click the **row selector** for the InvoiceAmt field to select this field and display the shortcut menu, and then click **Insert Rows**. Access adds a new, blank row between the CustomerNum and InvoiceAmt fields. See Figure 2-23.

Figure 2-23	AFTER INSERTING A ROW IN THE TABLE STRUCTURE

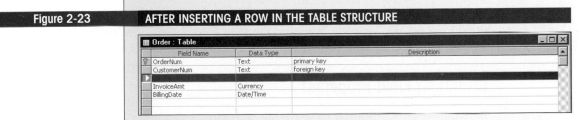

You'll define the Paid field in the new row for the Order table. Access will add this new field to the Order table structure between the CustomerNum and InvoiceAmt fields.

2. Click the **Field Name** text box for the new row, type **Paid**, and then press the **Tab** key.

The Paid field will be a yes/no field that will specify whether or not an invoice has been paid.

3. Type **y**. Access completes the data type as "yes/No."

4. Press the **Tab** key to select the yes/no data type and to move to the Description text box.

Notice that Access changes the value in the Data Type text box from "yes/No" to "Yes/No." Barbara wants the Paid field to have a Default Value property value of "No," so you need to set this property.

5. In the Field Properties section, click the **Default Value** text box, type **no**, and then click the **Description** text box for the Paid field. Notice that Access changes the Default Value property value from "no" to "No." See Figure 2-24.

Figure 2-24	PAID FIELD ADDED TO THE ORDER TABLE

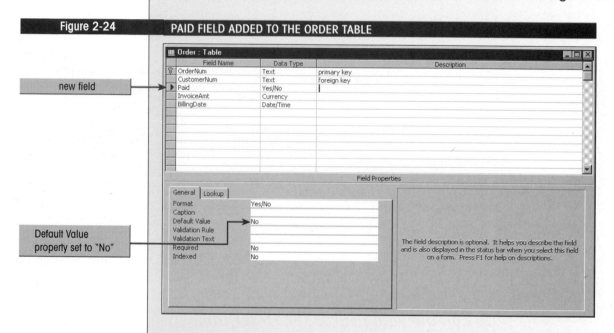

Because its field name clearly indicates its purpose, you do not need to enter a description for the Paid field.

You've completed adding the Paid field to the Order table in Design view. As with the other changes you've made, however, the Paid field is not added to the Order table in the Restaurant database until you save the changes to the table structure.

Changing Field Properties

Barbara's last modification to the table structure is to remove the dollar signs from the InvoiceAmt field values displayed in the datasheet—repeated dollar signs are unnecessary and they clutter the datasheet. As you learned earlier when defining the BillingDate field, you use the Format property to control the display of a field value.

To change the Format property of the InvoiceAmt field:

1. Click the **Description** text box for the InvoiceAmt field. The InvoiceAmt field is now the current field.

2. Click the right side of the **Format** text box to display the Format list box. See Figure 2-25.

| Figure 2-25 | FORMAT LIST BOX |

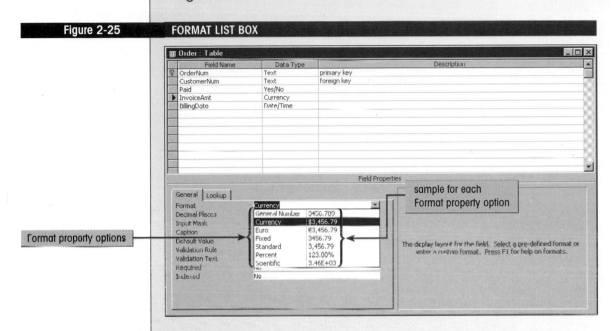

Format property options

sample for each Format property option

To the right of each Format property option is a field value whose appearance represents a sample of the option. The Standard option specifies the format Barbara wants for the InvoiceAmt field.

3. Click **Standard** in the Format list box to accept this option for the Format property.

Barbara wants you to add a third record to the Order table datasheet. Before you can add the record, you must save the modified table structure, and then switch to the Order table datasheet.

To save the modified table structure, and then switch to the datasheet:

1. Click the **Save** button on the Table Design toolbar. The modified table structure for the Order table is stored in the Restaurant database.

2. Click the **View** button for Datasheet view on the Table Design toolbar. The Order table datasheet opens. See Figure 2-26.

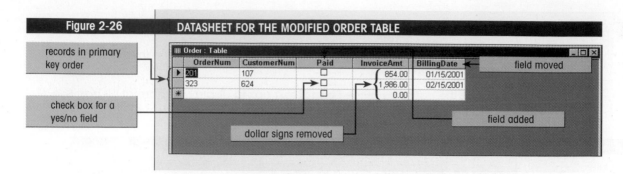

Figure 2-26 **DATASHEET FOR THE MODIFIED ORDER TABLE**

records in primary key order

check box for a yes/no field

field moved

field added

dollar signs removed

Notice that the PlacedBy field no longer appears in the datasheet, the BillingDate field is now the rightmost column, the InvoiceAmt field values do not contain dollar signs, and the Paid field appears between the CustomerNum and InvoiceAmt fields. The Paid column contains check boxes to represent the yes/no field values. Empty check boxes signify "No," which is the default value you assigned to the Paid field. A "Yes" value is indicated by a check mark in the check box. Also notice that the records appear in ascending order based on the value in the OrderNum field, the Order table's primary key, even though you did not enter the records in this order.

Barbara asks you to add a third record to the table. This record is for an order that has been paid.

To add the record to the modified Order table:

1. Click the **New Record** button ▶* on the Table Datasheet toolbar. The insertion point is located in the OrderNum field for the third row, which is the next row available for a new record.

2. Type **211**. The pencil symbol appears in the row selector for the third row, and the star appears in the row selector for the fourth row. Recall that these symbols represent a record being edited and the next available record, respectively.

3. Press the **Tab** key. The insertion point moves to the CustomerNum field.

4. Type **201** and then press the **Tab** key. The Paid field is now the current field.

   Recall that the default value for this field is "No," which means the check box is initially empty. For yes/no fields with check boxes, you press the Tab key to leave the check box unchecked; you press the spacebar or click the check box to add or remove a check mark in the check box. Because the invoice for this order has been paid, you need to insert a check mark in the check box.

5. Press the **spacebar**. A check mark appears in the check box.

6. Press the **Tab** key. The value in the InvoiceAmt field is now highlighted.

7. Type **703.5** and then press the **Tab** key. The insertion point moves to the BillingDate field.

8. Type **01/15/01** and then press the **Tab** key. Access saves the record in the Order table and moves the insertion point to the beginning of the fourth row. See Figure 2-27.

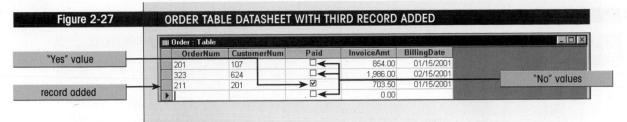

| Figure 2-27 | ORDER TABLE DATASHEET WITH THIRD RECORD ADDED |

"Yes" value

record added

"No" values

As you add records, Access places them at the end of the datasheet. If you switch to Design view, then return to the datasheet, or if you close the table and then open the datasheet, Access will display the records in primary key sequence.

You have modified the Order table structure and added one record. Instead of typing the remaining records in the Order table, Barbara suggests that you copy them from a table that already exists in another database, and then paste them into the Order table.

Copying Records from Another Access Database

You can copy and paste records from a table in the same database or in a different database only if the tables have the same structure—that is, the tables contain the same fields in the same order. Barbara's Valle database in the Tutorial folder on your Data Disk has a table named Restaurant Order that has the same table structure as the Order table. The records in the Restaurant Order table are the records Barbara wants you to copy into the Order table.

Other programs, such as Microsoft Word and Microsoft Excel, allow you to have two or more documents open at a time. However, you can have only one Access database open at a time. Therefore, you need to close the Restaurant database, open the Restaurant Order table in the Valle database, select and copy the table records, close the Valle database, reopen the Order table in the Restaurant database, and then paste the copied records.

To copy the records from the Restaurant Order table:

1. Click the **Close** button ⊠ on the Table window title bar to close the Order table, and then click the **Close** button ⊠ on the Database window title bar to close the Restaurant database.

2. Click the **Open** button 🖆 on the Database toolbar to display the Open dialog box.

3. If necessary, display the list of files on your Data Disk, and then open the **Tutorial** folder.

4. Open the database file named **Valle**. The Database window opens, showing the tables for the Valle database.

   Notice that the Valle database contains two tables: the Restaurant Customer table and the Restaurant Order table. The Restaurant Order table contains the records you need to copy.

5. Click **Restaurant Order** in the Tables list box, and then click the **Open** button in the Database window. The datasheet for the Restaurant Order table opens. See Figure 2-28. Note that this table contains a total of 102 records.

| Figure 2-28 | DATASHEET FOR THE VALLE DATABASE'S RESTAURANT ORDER TABLE |

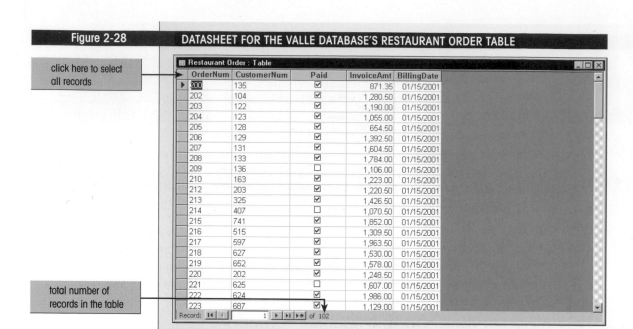

click here to select
all records

total number of
records in the table

Barbara wants you to copy all the records in the Restaurant Order table. You can select all records by clicking the row selector for the field name row.

6. Click the **row selector** for the field name row (see Figure 2-28). All the records in the table are now highlighted, which means that Access has selected all of them.

7. Click the **Copy** button on the Table Datasheet toolbar. All of the records are copied to the Windows Clipboard.

TROUBLE? If a Clipboard toolbar opens, click its Close button to close it, and then continue with Step 8.

8. Click the **Close** button ☒ on the Table window title bar. A dialog box opens asking if you want to save the data you copied on the Windows Clipboard.

9. Click the **Yes** button in the dialog box. The dialog box closes, and then the table closes.

10. Click the **Close** button ☒ on the Database window title bar to close the Valle database.

To finish copying and pasting the records, you must open the Order table and paste the copied records into the table.

To paste the copied records into the Order table:

1. Click **File** on the menu bar, and then click **Restaurant** in the list of recently opened databases. The Database window opens, showing the tables for the Restaurant database.

2. In the Tables list box, click **Order** (if necessary) and then click the **Open** button in the Database window. The datasheet for the Order table opens.

You must paste the records at the end of the table.

3. Click the **row selector** for row four, which is the next row available for a new record.

4. Click the **Paste** button 🖺 on the Table Datasheet toolbar. A dialog box opens, asking if you are sure you want to paste the records (102 in all).

5. Click the **Yes** button. All the records are pasted from the Windows Clipboard, and the pasted records remain highlighted. See Figure 2-29. Notice that the table now contains a total of 105 records—the three original records plus the 102 copied records.

Figure 2-29	TABLE AFTER COPYING AND PASTING RECORDS

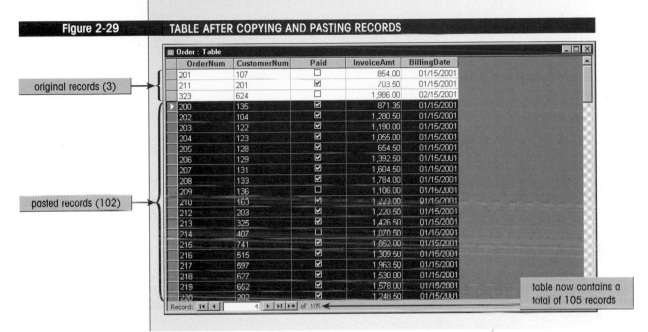

Using the Office Clipboard

When you copied records from the Valle database and pasted them into the Restaurant database, you used the Windows Clipboard. The **Windows Clipboard** is a temporary storage area for data that is cut or copied to it from any Windows program. The data is stored on the Clipboard until you either close Windows or cut or copy something else to the Clipboard.

When you need to copy multiple pieces of data from one program to another—or within the same program (such as Access)—you can use the Office Clipboard. The **Office Clipboard** lets you cut or copy up to 12 different items from any Office 2000 program so that you can paste these items into different locations later. For example, if you need to copy the records from Barbara's Valle database, and then open another database and copy additional records from it, you could copy each set of records to the Office Clipboard, open the Restaurant database, and then paste these two different sets of records in two actions. If you used the Windows Clipboard to copy the same records, you would only be able to paste the records from the second database, because the first set of records would be replaced by the second set of records when you performed the second copy operation.

The Office Clipboard appears automatically as a Clipboard toolbar as soon as you cut or copy two items to it. When the Clipboard toolbar opens, you will see a Copy button, Paste All button, and a Clear Clipboard button, along with icons that represent each item that you either cut or copied to the Clipboard. To paste an item in a new location, such as pasting records copied from one table to another, you select the location in which to paste the item, and then click the icon that contains the data to paste. In Access, the Paste All button is not available all the time, but you can still paste groups of items by inserting them individually.

You've completed copying and pasting the records between the two tables. Now that you have all the records in the Order table, Barbara examines the records to make sure they are correct. She finds one record that she wants you to delete and another record that needs changes to its field values.

Updating a Database

Updating, or **maintaining**, a database is the process of adding, changing, and deleting records in database tables to keep them current and accurate. You've already added records to the Order table. Now Barbara wants you to delete and change records.

Deleting Records

To delete a record, you need to select the record in Datasheet view, and then delete it using the Delete Record button on the Table Datasheet toolbar or the Delete Record option on the shortcut menu.

REFERENCE WINDOW | RW

Deleting a Record

- In the Table window in Datasheet view, click the row selector for the record you want to delete, and then click the Delete Record button on the Table Datasheet toolbar (or right-click the row selector for the record, and then click Delete Record on the shortcut menu).
- In the dialog box asking you to confirm the deletion, click the Yes button.

Barbara asks you to delete the record whose OrderNum is 200 because this record was entered in error; it represents an order from an office customer, not a restaurant customer, and therefore does not belong in the Restaurant database. The fourth record in the table has an OrderNum value of 200. This record is the one you need to delete.

To delete the record:

1. Right-click the **row selector** for row four. Access selects the fourth record and displays the shortcut menu. See Figure 2-30.

Figure 2-30 | **DELETING A RECORD**

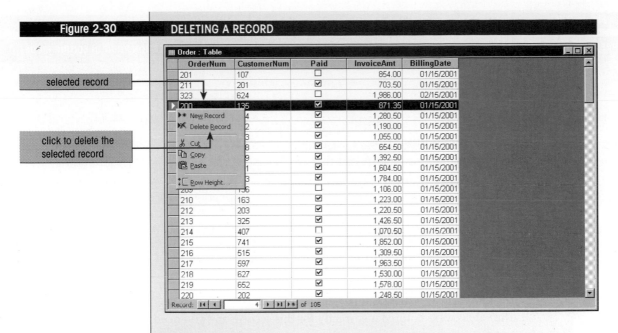

selected record

click to delete the
selected record

2. Click **Delete Record** on the shortcut menu. Access deletes the record and
opens a dialog box asking you to confirm the deletion.

TROUBLE? If you selected the wrong record for deletion, click the No button.
Access ends the deletion process and redisplays the deleted record. Repeat
Steps 1 and 2 to delete the correct record.

3. Click the **Yes** button to confirm the deletion and close the dialog box.

Barbara's final update to the Order table involves changes to field values in one of the records.

Changing Records

To change the field values in a record, you first must make the record the current record.
Then you position the insertion point in the field value to make minor changes or select the
field value to replace it entirely. In Tutorial 1, you used the mouse with the scroll bars and
the navigation buttons to navigate through the records in a datasheet. You can also use keystroke combinations and the F2 key to navigate a datasheet and to select field values.

The **F2 key** is a toggle that you use to switch between navigation mode and editing mode:

■ In **navigation mode**, Access selects an entire field value. If you type while you are
in navigation mode, your typed entry replaces the highlighted field value.

■ In **editing mode**, you can insert or delete characters in a field value based on the
location of the insertion point.

Figure 2-31 shows some of the navigation mode and editing mode keystroke techniques.

Figure 2-31	NAVIGATION MODE AND EDITING MODE KEYSTROKE TECHNIQUES	
PRESS	**TO MOVE THE SELECTION IN NAVIGATION MODE**	**TO MOVE THE INSERTION POINT IN EDITING MODE**
←	Left one field value at a time	Left one character at a time
→	Right one field value at a time	Right one character at a time
Home	Left to the first field value in the record	To the left of the first character in the field value
End	Right to the last field value in the record	To the right of the last character in the field value
↑ or ↓	Up or down one record at a time	Up or down one record at a time and switch to navigation mode
Tab or Enter	Right one field value at a time	Right one field value at a time and switch to navigation mode
Ctrl + Home	To the first field value in the first record	To the left of the first character in the field value
Ctrl + End	To the last field value in the last record	To the right of the last character in the field value

The record Barbara wants you to change has an OrderNum field value of 397. Some of the values were entered incorrectly for this record, and you need to enter the correct values.

To modify the record:

1. Make sure the OrderNum field value for the fourth record is still highlighted, indicating that the table is in navigation mode.

2. Press **Ctrl + End**. Access displays records from the end of the table and selects the last field value in the last record. This field value is for the BillingDate field.

3. Press the **Home** key. The first field value in the last record is now selected. This field value is for the OrderNum field.

4. Press the ↑ key. The OrderNum field value for the previous record is selected. This record is the one you need to change.

   Barbara wants you to change these field values in the record: OrderNum to 398, CustomerNum to 165, Paid to "Yes" (checked), and InvoiceAmt to 1426.50. You do not need to change the BillingDate.

5. Type **398**, press the **Tab** key, type **165**, press the **Tab** key, press the **spacebar** to insert a check mark in the Paid check box, press the **Tab** key, and then type **1426.5**. The changes to the record are complete.

6. Press the ↓ key to save the changes to the record and make the next record the current record. See Figure 2-32.

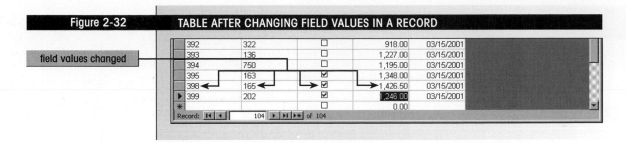

Figure 2-32   TABLE AFTER CHANGING FIELD VALUES IN A RECORD

field values changed

You've completed all of Barbara's updates to the Order table. Barbara asks you to print only the first page of data from the Order table datasheet so that she can show the revised table structure to her staff members. After you print the page, you can exit Access.

To print the first page of Order table data, and then exit Access:

1. Click **File** on the menu bar, and then click **Print** to open the Print dialog box.

2. In the Print Range section, click the **Pages** option button, type **1** in the From text box, press the **Tab** key, and then type **1** in the To text box.

3. Click the **OK** button to print the first page of data.

   Now you can exit Access.

4. Click the **Close** button [X] on the Access window title bar to close the Order table and the Restaurant database and to exit Access.

Barbara and her staff members approve of the revised table structure for the Order table. They are confident that the table will allow them to easily track order data for Valle Coffee's restaurant customers.

Session 2.2 QUICK CHECK

1. What is the effect of deleting a field from a table structure?

2. How do you insert a field between existing fields in a table structure?

3. A field with the _____ data type can appear in the table datasheet as a check box.

4. Which property do you use to control the display appearance of a field value?

5. Why must you close an open database when you want to copy records to it from a table in another database?

6. What is the difference between navigation mode and editing mode?

REVIEW ASSIGNMENTS

Barbara needs a database to track the coffee products offered by Valle Coffee. She asks you to create the database by completing the following:

1. Make sure your Data Disk is in the disk drive, and then start Access.

Explore ▶ 2. In the initial Microsoft Access dialog box, click the Blank Access database option button, and then click the OK button. In the File New Database dialog box, select the Review folder on your Data Disk, and then enter the name **Valle Products** for the database in the File name text box. Click the Create button to create the new database.

Explore ▶ 3. Display the Table window in Design view (if necessary), and then create a table using the table design shown in Figure 2-33.

Figure 2-33

Field Name	Data Type	Description	Field Size	Other Properties
ProductCode	Text	primary key	4	
CoffeeCode	Text	foreign key	4	
Price	Currency	price for this product		Format: Fixed Decimal Places: 2
Decaf	Text	D if decaf, Null if regular	1	Default Value: D
BackOrdered	Yes/No	back-ordered from supplier?		

4. Specify ProductCode as the primary key, and then save the table as **Product**.
5. Add the product records shown in Figure 2-34 to the **Product** table. (*Hint*: You must type the decimal point when entering the Price field values.)

Figure 2-34

ProductCode	CoffeeCode	Price	Decaf	BackOrdered
2316	JRUM	8.99		Yes
9754	HAZL	40.00	D	Yes
9309	COCO	9.99	D	No

6. Make the following changes to the structure of the **Product** table:
   a. Add a new field between the CoffeeCode and Price fields, using these properties:
      Field Name: WeightCode
      Data Type: Text
      Description: foreign key
      Field Size: 1
   b. Move the Decaf field so that it appears between the WeightCode and Price fields.
   c. Save the revised table structure.
7. Use the **Product** datasheet to update the database as follows:
   a. Enter these WeightCode values for the three records: A for ProductCode 2316, A for ProductCode 9309, and E for ProductCode 9754.
   b. Add a record to the **Product** datasheet with these field values:
      ProductCode: 9729
      CoffeeCode: COLS
      WeightCode: E
      Decaf: D
      Price: 39.75
      BackOrdered: Yes
8. Close the **Product** table, and then set the option for compacting the **Valle Products** database on close.

9. Barbara created a database with her name as the database name. The **Coffee Product** table in that database has the same format as the **Product** table you created. Copy all the records from the **Coffee Product** table in the **Barbara** database (located in the Review folder on your Data Disk) to the end of your **Product** table.

Explore 10. Because you added a number of records to the database, its size has increased. Compact the database manually using the Compact and Repair Database option.

11. Reopen the **Product** datasheet. The records now appear in primary key order by ProductCode. Then delete the record with the ProductCode 2372 from the **Product** table.

12. Delete the BackOrdered field from the **Product** table structure.

Explore 13. Use the Access Help system to learn how to resize datasheet columns to fit the data, and then resize all columns in the datasheet for the **Product** table so that each column fits its data. Scroll the datasheet to make sure all field values are fully displayed. For any field values that are not fully displayed, make sure the field values are visible on the screen, and then resize the appropriate columns again.

14. Print the first page of data from the **Product** table datasheet, and then save and close the table.

Explore 15. Create a table named **Weight**, based on the data shown in Figure 2-35, according to the following steps:

Figure 2-35

WeightCode	Weight/Size
A	1 lb pkg
B	6 lb case
C	24 ct 1.5 oz pkg
D	44 ct 1.25 oz pkg
E	44 ct 1.5 oz pkg
F	88 ct 1.25 oz pkg
G	88 ct 1.5 oz pkg

a. Select the Datasheet View option in the New Table dialog box.

b. Enter the seven records shown in Figure 2-35. (Do *not* enter the field names at this point.)

c. Switch to Design view, supply the table name, and then answer No if asked if you want to create a primary key.

d. Type the following field names and set the following properties:

WeightCode
Description: primary key
Field Size: 1
Weight/Size
Description: weight in pounds or size in packages (number and weight) per case
Field Size: 17

e. Specify the primary key, save the table structure changes, and then switch back to Datasheet view. If you receive any warning messages, answer Yes to continue.

f. Resize both datasheet columns to fit the data (use Access Help to learn how to resize datasheet columns, if necessary); then save, print, and close the datasheet.

Explore 16. Create a table named **Coffee** using the Import Table Wizard, which is available in the New Table dialog box. The table you need to import is named **Coffee.dbf** and is located in the Review folder on your Data Disk. This table has a dBASE 5 file type. (You'll need to change the entry in the Files of type list box to display the file in the list.) After importing the table, complete the following:

a. Change all field names to use the Valle Coffee convention of uppercase and lowercase letters, and then enter the following Description property values:

CoffeeCode: primary key
Decaf: is this coffee available in decaf?

    b. Change the Format property of the Decaf field to Yes/No.

    c. Specify the primary key, and then save the table structure changes.

    d. Switch to Datasheet view, and then resize all columns in the datasheet to fit the data. (Use Access Help to learn how to resize datasheet columns, if necessary.) Be sure to scroll through the table to make sure that all field values are fully displayed.

    e. Save, print, and then close the datasheet.

17. Close the **Valle Products** database, and then exit Access.

CASE PROBLEMS

Case 1. Ashbrook Mall Information Desk Sam Bullard, the director of the Mall Operations Office at Ashbrook Mall, uses the **MallJobs** database to maintain information about current job openings at stores in the mall. Sam asks you to help him maintain the database by completing the following:

1. Make sure your Data Disk is in the disk drive.
2. Start Access and open the **MallJobs** database located in the Cases folder on your Data Disk.
3. Create a table using the table design shown in Figure 2-36.

Figure 2-36

Field Name	Data Type	Description	Field Size
Job	Text	primary key	5
Store	Text	foreign key	3
Hours/Week	Text		20
Position	Text		35
ExperienceReq	Yes/No		

4. Specify Job as the primary key, and then save the table as **Job**.
5. Add the job records shown in Figure 2-37 to the **Job** table.

Figure 2-37

Job	Store	Hours/Week	Position	ExperienceReq
10037	TH	negotiable	Salesclerk	Yes
10053	BR	16-32	Server	No
10022	BE	35-45	Assistant Manager	Yes

6. Sam created a database named **Openings** that contains a table with job data named **Current Jobs**. The **Job** table you created has the same format as the **Current Jobs** table. Copy all the records from the **Current Jobs** table in the **Openings** database (located in the Cases folder on your Data Disk) to the end of your **Job** table.
7. Modify the structure of the **Job** table by completing the following:

    a. Delete the ExperienceReq field.

    b. Move the Hours/Week field so that it follows the Position field.

Explore 8. Use the Access Help system to learn how to resize datasheet columns to fit the data, and then switch to Datasheet view and resize all columns in the datasheet for the **Job** table.

9. Use the Job datasheet to update the database as follows:
   a. For Job 10048, change the Position value to Clerk, and change the Hours/Week value to 25-35.
   b. Add a record to the **Job** datasheet with the following field values:
      Job: 10034
      Store: JB
      Position: Salesclerk
      Hours/Week: negotiable
   c. Delete the record for Job 10031.
10. Switch to Design view, and then switch back to Datasheet view so that the records appear in primary key sequence by Job.
11. Print the **Job** table datasheet, and then save and close the table.
12. Close the **MallJobs** database, and then exit Access.

Case 2. Professional Litigation User Services (PLUS) Raj Jawahir is responsible for tracking the daily payments received from PLUS clients. You'll help him maintain the **Payments** database by completing the following:

1. Make sure your Data Disk is in the disk drive.
2. Start Access and open the **Payments** database located in the Cases folder on your Data Disk.

Explore

3. Create a table named **Payment** using the table design shown in Figure 2-38. (*Hint:* Make sure that you include spaces between the components of the custom format for the DatePaid field.)

Figure 2-38

Field Name	Data Type	Description	Field Size	Other Properties
Payment#	Text	primary key	5	
Firm#	Text	foreign key	4	
DatePaid	Date/Time			Format: mmm dd yyyy (custom format)
AmtPaid	Currency			Format: Standard

4. Add the payment records shown in Figure 2-39 to the **Payment** table.

Figure 2-39

Payment#	Firm#	DatePaid	AmtPaid
10031	1111	06/03/2001	2500.00
10002	1147	06/01/2001	1700.00
10015	1151	06/02/2001	2000.00

5. Modify the structure of the **Payment** table by completing the following:
   a. Add a new field between the Payment# and Firm# fields, using these properties:
      Field Name: Deposit#
      Data Type: Text
      Field Size: 3
   b. Move the DatePaid field so that it follows the AmtPaid field.
6. Use the **Payment** datasheet to update the database as follows:
   a. Enter these Deposit# values for the three records: 101 for Payment# 10002, 102 for Payment# 10015, and 103 for Payment# 10031.
   b. Add a record to the **Payment** datasheet with these field values:
      Payment#:   10105
      Deposit#:   117
      Firm#:   1103
      AmtPaid: 1,750.00
      DatePaid: 06/20/2001

7. Raj created a database named **PlusPays** that contains recent payments in the **Payment Records** table. The **Payment** table you created has the same format as the **Payment Records** table. Copy all the records from the **Payment Records** table in the **PlusPays** database (located in the Cases folder on your Data Disk) to the end of your **Payment** table.

Explore ▶ 8. Use the Access Help system to learn how to resize datasheet columns to fit the data, and then resize all columns in the datasheet for the **Payment** table.

9. For Payment# 10002, change the AmtPaid value to 1300.00.

10. Delete the record for Payment# 10096.

11. Print the first page of data from the **Payment** table datasheet, and then save and close the table.

12. Close the **Payments** database, and then exit Access.

Case 3. Best Friends Noah and Sheila Warnick continue to track information about participants in the walk-a-thons held to benefit Best Friends. Help them maintain the **Walks** database by completing the following:

1. Make sure your Data Disk is in the disk drive.

2. Start Access and open the **Walks** database located in the Cases folder on your Data Disk.

Explore ▶ 3. Create a table named **Pledge** using the Import Table Wizard. The table you need to import is named **Pledge.db** and is located in the Cases folder on your Data Disk. This table has a Paradox file type. (You'll need to change the entry in the Files of type list box to display the file in the list.) After importing the table, complete the following:

   a. Change all field names to use uppercase and lowercase letters, as appropriate, and then enter the following Description property values:

      PledgeNo: primary key
      WalkerID: foreign key
      PerMile: amount pledged per mile

   b. Specify the primary key, and then save the table structure changes.

   c. Switch to Datasheet view, and then resize all columns in the datasheet to fit the data. (Use Access Help to learn how to resize datasheet columns, if necessary.)

Explore ▶ 4. Modify the structure of the **Pledge** table by completing the following:

   a. Add a new field between the PaidAmt and PerMile fields, using these properties:

      Field Name: DatePaid
      Data Type: Date/Time
      Format: mm/dd/yyyy (custom format)

   b. Change the Data Type of both the PledgeAmt field and the PaidAmt field to Currency. For each of these fields, choose the Fixed format.

   c. Save the table structure. Answer Yes to any warning messages.

5. Use the **Pledge** datasheet to update the database as follows:

   a. Enter these DatePaid values for the five records: 09/15/2001 for PledgeNo 1, 09/01/2001 for PledgeNo 2, 08/25/2001 for PledgeNo 3, 09/20/2001 for PledgeNo 4, and 08/14/2001 for PledgeNo 5. Resize the DatePaid column to fit the data.

   b. Add a record to the **Pledge** datasheet with these field values:

      PledgeNo: 6
      Pledger: Gene Delsener
      WalkerID: 138
      PledgeAmt: 50
      PaidAmt: 50
      DatePaid: 09/18/2001
      PerMile: 0

   c. Enter the value 133 in the WalkerID field for PledgeNo 1.

   d. Change both the PledgeAmt value and the PaidAmt value for PledgeNo 3 to 25.00.

   e. Change the WalkerID value for PledgeNo 5 to 165.

6. Print the **Pledge** table datasheet, and then save and close the table.

7. Close the **Walks** database, and then exit Access.

Case 4. Lopez Lexus Dealerships   Maria and Hector Lopez use the **Lexus** database to track the car inventory in the chain of Lexus dealerships they own. You'll help them maintain the **Lexus** database by completing the following:

1. Make sure your Data Disk is in the disk drive.
2. Start Access and open the **Lexus** database located in the Cases folder on your Data Disk.
3. *Explore* Use the Import Spreadsheet Wizard to create a new table named **Locations**. The data you need to import is contained in the **Lopez** workbook, which is a Microsoft Excel file located in the Cases folder on your Data Disk.
   a. Select the Import Table option in the New Table dialog box.
   b. Change the entry in the Files of type list box to display the list of Excel workbook files in the Cases folder.
   c. Select the **Lopez** file and then click the Import button.
   d. In the Import Spreadsheet Wizard dialog boxes, choose the option for using column headings as field names; select the option for choosing your own primary key, and specify LocationCode as the primary key; and enter the table name (**Locations**). Otherwise, accept the Wizard's choices for all other options for the imported data.
4. *Explore* Use the Access Help system to learn how to resize datasheet columns to fit the data, and then open the **Locations** table and resize all columns in the datasheet.
5. Modify the structure of the **Locations** table by completing the following:
   a. For the LocationCode field, enter a Description property of "primary key," change the Field Size to 2, and change the Required property to Yes.
   b. For the LocationName field, change the Field Size to 25.
   c. For the ManagerName field, change the Field Size to 35.
   d. Save the table. If you receive any warning messages about lost data or integrity rules, click the Yes button.
6. Use the **Locations** datasheet to update the database as follows:
   a. For LocationCode A2, change the ManagerName value to Curran, Edward.
   b. Add a record to the **Locations** datasheet with these field values:
      LocationCode: H2
      LocationName: Houston
      ManagerName: Cohen, Molly
   c. Delete the record for LocationCode L2.
7. Print the **Locations** table datasheet, and then close the table.
8. *Explore* Use the Table Wizard to create a new table named **Managers** based on the sample **Employees** table, which is a sample table in the Business category, as follows:
   a. Add the following sample fields to your table (in the following order): SocialSecurityNumber, LastName, Region, DateHired, and Salary. Do *not* click the Next button yet.
   b. Click LastName in the "Fields in my new table" list, click the Rename Field button in the first Table Wizard dialog box, and then change the LastName field name to ManagerName. Click the Next button.
   c. Change the default table name to **Managers**. Select the option to create your own primary key, and then select an appropriate field as your primary key. (*Hint:* Select a field that will contain unique numbers, and then select the correct option button that represents your data.) Click the Next button, and then click the Finish button in the final Table Wizard dialog box.
   d. Enter the following data into the **Managers** table:
      Social Security Number: 789-00-8642
      ManagerName: Evans, Hannah
      Region: Austin
      DateHired: 05/31/96
      Salary: 52,000
   e. Resize all columns in the datasheet to fit the data.
9. Print the **Managers** table datasheet, and then save and close the table.
10. Close the **Lexus** database, and then exit Access.

INTERNET ASSIGNMENTS

The purpose of the Internet Assignments is to challenge you to find information on the Internet that you can use to create effective documents. The actual assignments are updated and maintained on the Course Technology Web site. Log on to the Internet and use your Web browser to go to the Student Online Companion to accompany this text at **www.course.com/NewPerspectives/office2000**. Click the Access link, and then click the link for Tutorial 2.

QUICK CHECK ANSWERS

Session 2.1

1. Identify all the fields needed to produce the required information, group related fields into tables, determine each table's primary key, include a common field in related tables, avoid data redundancy, and determine the properties of each field.
2. The data type determines what field values you can enter for the field and what other properties the field will have.
3. text, number, and AutoNumber fields
4. Order numbers will not be used for calculations.
5. null
6. the record being edited; the next row available for a new record

Session 2.2

1. The field and all its values are removed from the table.
2. In Design view, right-click the row selector for the row above which you want to insert the field, click Insert Rows on the shortcut menu, and then define the new field.
3. yes/no
4. Format property
5. Access allows you to have only one database open at a time.
6. In navigation mode, the entire field value is selected, and anything you type replaces the field value; in editing mode, you can insert or delete characters in a field value based on the location of the insertion point.

QUERYING A DATABASE

Retrieving Information About Restaurant Customers and Their Orders

OBJECTIVES

In this tutorial you will:

- Learn how to use the Query window in Design view

- Create, run, and save queries

- Define a relationship between two tables

- Sort data in a query

- Filter data in a query

- Specify an exact match condition in a query

- Change a datasheet's appearance

- Use a comparison operator to match a range of values

- Use the And and Or logical operators

- Perform calculations in a query using calculated fields, aggregate functions, and record group calculations

CASE

Valle Coffee

At a recent company meeting, Leonard Valle and other Valle Coffee employees discussed the importance of regularly monitoring the business activity of the company's restaurant customers. For example, Kim Carpenter and her marketing staff track customer activity to develop new strategies for promoting Valle Coffee products. Barbara Hennessey and her office staff need to track information about all the orders for which bills were sent out on a specific date, so that they can determine whether the bills have been paid. In addition, Leonard is interested in analyzing the payment history of restaurant customers to determine which customers pay their invoices in a timely manner, which customers have higher invoice amounts, and so on. All of these informational needs can be satisfied by queries that retrieve information from the Restaurant database.

SESSION 3.1

In this session, you will use the Query window in Design view to create, run, and save queries; define a one-to-many relationship between two tables; sort data with a toolbar button and in Design view; and filter data in a query datasheet.

Introduction to Queries

As you learned in Tutorial 1, a query is a question you ask about data stored in a database. For example, Kim might create a query to find records in the Customer table for only those customers location in a specific state. When you create a query, you tell Access which fields you need and what criteria Access should use to select the records.

Access provides powerful query capabilities that allow you to:

- display selected fields and records from a table
- sort records
- perform calculations
- generate data for forms, reports, and other queries
- update data in the tables in a database
- find and display data from two or more tables

Most questions about data are generalized queries in which you specify the fields and records you want Access to select. These common requests for information, such as "Which customers have unpaid bills?" or "Which type of coffee sells best in Ohio?" are called **select queries**. The answer to a select query is returned in the form of a datasheet.

More specialized, technical queries, such as finding duplicate records in a table, are best formulated using a Query Wizard. A Query Wizard prompts you for information by asking a series of questions and then creates the appropriate query based on your answers. In Tutorial 1, you used the Simple Query Wizard to display only some of the fields in the Customer table; Access provides other Query Wizards for more complex queries. For common, informational queries, it is easier for you to design your own query than to use a Query Wizard.

Kim wants you to create a query to display the customer number, customer name, city, owner name, and first contact information for each record in the Customer table. She needs this information for a market analysis her staff is completing on Valle Coffee's restaurant customers. You'll open the Query window to create the query for Kim.

Query Window

You use the Query window in Design view to create a query. In Design view you specify the data you want to view by constructing a query by example. Using **query by example (QBE)**, you give Access an example of the information you are requesting. Access then retrieves the information that precisely matches your example.

For Kim's query, you need to display data from the Customer table. You'll begin by starting Access, opening the Restaurant database, and displaying the Query window in Design view.

> ### To start Access, open the Restaurant database, and open the Query window in Design view:
>
> 1. Place your Data Disk in the appropriate disk drive.
>
> 2. Start Access and open the **Restaurant** database located in the Tutorial folder on your Data Disk. The Restaurant database is displayed in the Database window.

3. Click **Queries** in the Objects bar of the Database window, and then click the **New** button. The New Query dialog box opens. See Figure 3-1.

Figure 3-1	NEW QUERY DIALOG BOX

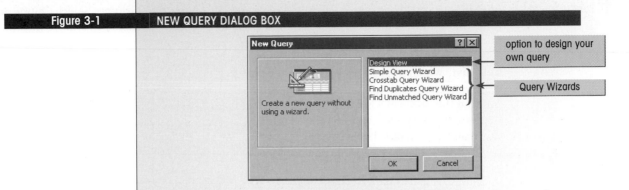

option to design your own query

Query Wizards

You'll design your own query instead of using a Query Wizard.

4. If necessary, click **Design View** in the list box.

5. Click the **OK** button. Access opens the Show Table dialog box on top of the Query window. (Note that you could also have double-clicked the option "Create query in Design view" from the Database window.) Notice that the title bar of the Query window shows that you are creating a select query.

   The query you are creating will retrieve data from the Customer table, so you need to add this table to the Select Query window.

6. Click **Customer** in the Tables list box (if necessary), click the **Add** button, and then click the **Close** button. Access places the Customer table's field list in the Select Query window and closes the Show Table dialog box.

   To display more of the fields you'll be using for creating queries, you'll maximize the Select Query window.

7. Click the **Maximize** button ☐ on the Select Query window title bar. See Figure 3-2.

Figure 3-2	SELECT QUERY WINDOW IN DESIGN VIEW

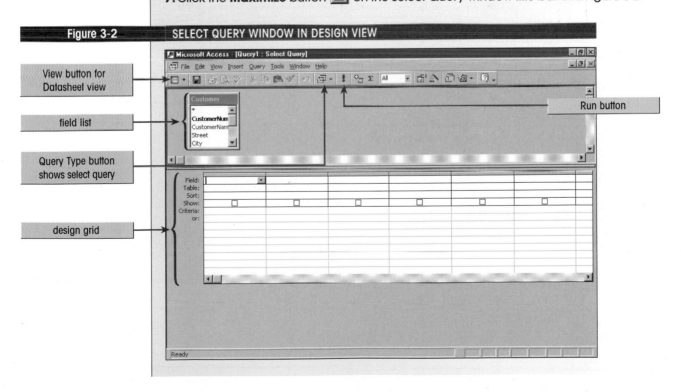

View button for Datasheet view

field list

Query Type button shows select query

design grid

Run button

In Design view, the Select Query window contains the standard title bar, menu bar, status bar, and the Query Design toolbar. On the toolbar, the Query Type button shows a select query; the icon on this button changes according to the type of query you are creating. The title bar on the Select Query window displays the query type, Select Query, and the default query name, Query1. You'll change the default query name to a more meaningful one later when you save the query.

The Select Query window in Design view contains a field list and the design grid. The **field list**, which appears in the upper-left area of the window, contains the fields for the table you are querying. The table name appears at the top of the list box, and the fields are listed in the order in which they appear in the table.

In the **design grid**, you include the fields and record selection criteria for the information you want to see. Each column in the design grid contains specifications about a field you will use in the query. You can choose a single field for your query by dragging its name from the field list to the design grid in the lower portion of the window. Alternatively, you can double-click a field name to place it in the next available design grid column.

When you are constructing a query, you can see the query results at any time by clicking the View button or the Run button on the Query Design toolbar. In response, Access displays the datasheet, which contains the set of fields and records that results from answering, or **running**, the query. The order of the fields in the datasheet is the same as the order of the fields in the design grid. Although the datasheet looks just like a table datasheet and appears in Datasheet view, a query datasheet is temporary, and its contents are based on the criteria you establish in the design grid. In contrast, a table datasheet shows the permanent data in a table. However, you can update data while viewing a query datasheet, just as you can when working in a table datasheet or a form.

If the query you are creating includes every field from the specified table, you can use one of the following three methods to transfer all the fields from the field list to the design grid:

- Click and drag each field individually from the field list to the design grid. Use this method if you want the fields in your query to appear in an order that is different from the order in the field list.

- Double-click the asterisk in the field list. Access places the table name followed by a period and an asterisk (as in "Customer.*") in the design grid, which signifies that the order of the fields will be the same in the query as it is in the field list. Use this method if you don't need to sort the query or specify conditions for the records you want to select. The advantage of using this method is that you do not need to change the query if you add or delete fields from the underlying table structure. Such changes are reflected automatically in the query.

- Double-click the field list title bar to highlight all the fields, and then click and drag one of the highlighted fields to the design grid. Access places each field in a separate column and arranges the fields in the order in which they appear in the field list. Use this method rather than the previous one if you need to sort your query or include record selection criteria.

Now you'll create and run Kim's query to display selected fields from the Customer table.

Creating **and Running a Query**

The default table datasheet displays all the fields in the table, in the same order as they appear in the table. In contrast, a query datasheet can display selected fields from a table, and the order of the fields can be different from that of the table.

Kim wants the CustomerNum, CustomerName, City, OwnerName, and FirstContact fields to appear in the query results. You'll add each of these fields to the design grid.

To select the fields for the query, and then run the query:

1. Drag **CustomerNum** from the Customer field list to the design grid's first column Field text box, and then release the mouse button. See Figure 3-3.

Figure 3-3	FIELD ADDED TO THE DESIGN GRID

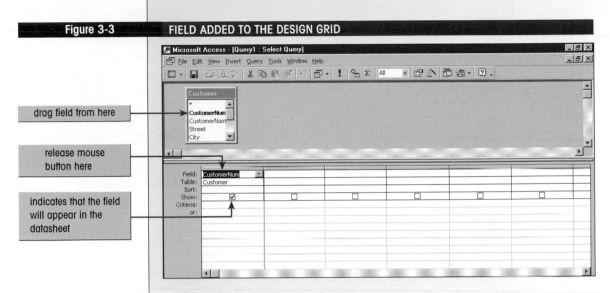

drag field from here

release mouse button here

indicates that the field will appear in the datasheet

In the design grid's first column, the field name CustomerNum appears in the Field text box, the table name Customer appears in the Table text box, and the check mark in the Show check box indicates that the field will be displayed in the datasheet when you run the query. Sometimes you might not want to display a field and its values in the query results. For example, if you are creating a query to show all customers located in Michigan, and you assign the name "Customers in Michigan" to the query, you do not need to include the State field value for each record in the query results—every State field value would be "MI" for Michigan. Even if you choose not to include a field in the display of the query results, you can still use the field as part of the query to select specific records or to specify a particular sequence for the records in the datasheet.

2. Double-click **CustomerName** in the Customer field list. Access adds this field to the second column of the design grid.

3. Scrolling the Customer field list as necessary, repeat Step 2 for the **City**, **OwnerName**, and **FirstContact** fields to add these fields to the design grid in that order.

Having selected the fields for Kim's query, you can now run the query.

TROUBLE? If you double-click the wrong field and accidentally add it to the design grid, you can remove the field from the grid. Select the field's column by clicking the pointer ↓ on the bar above the Field text box for the field you want to delete, click Edit on the menu bar, and then click Delete Columns.

4. Click the **Run** button on the Query Design toolbar. Access runs the query and displays the results in Datasheet view. See Figure 3-4.

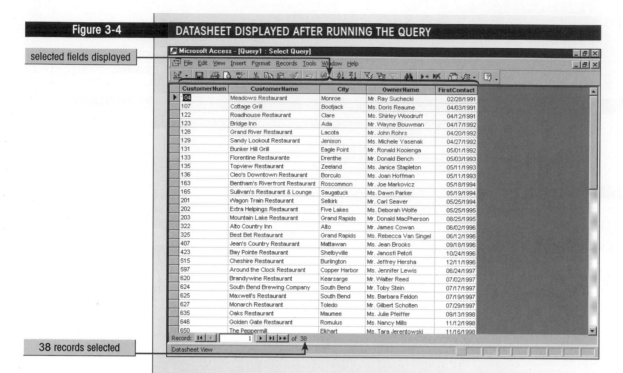

Figure 3-4   DATASHEET DISPLAYED AFTER RUNNING THE QUERY

selected fields displayed

38 records selected

The five fields you added to the design grid appear in the datasheet, and the records are displayed in primary key sequence by customer number. Access selected a total of 38 records for display in the datasheet.

Kim asks you to save the query as "Customer Analysis" so that she can easily retrieve the same data again.

5. Click the **Save** button on the Query Datasheet toolbar. The Save As dialog box opens.

6. Type **Customer Analysis** in the Query Name text box, and then press the **Enter** key. Access saves the query with the specified name in the Restaurant database on your Data Disk and displays the name in the title bar.

7. Click the **Close** button on the menu bar to close the query and return to the Database window. Note that the Customer Analysis query appears in the list of queries.

8. Click the **Restore** button on the menu bar to return the Database window to its original size.

Barbara also wants to view specific information in the Restaurant database. However, she needs to see data from both the Customer table and the Order table at the same time. To view data from two tables at the same time, you need to define a relationship between the tables.

Defining **Table Relationships**

One of the most powerful features of a relational database management system is its ability to define relationships between tables. You use a common field to relate one table to another. The process of relating tables is often called performing a **join**. When you join tables that have a common field, you can extract data from them as if they were one larger table. For example, you can join the Customer and Order tables by using the CustomerNum field in both tables as the common field. Then you can use a query, form, or report to extract selected data from each table, even though the data is contained in two separate tables, as shown in Figure 3-5. In the Orders query shown in Figure 3-5, the OrderNum, Paid, and InvoiceAmt columns are fields from the Order table, and the CustomerName and State columns are fields from the Customer table. The joining of records is based on the common field of CustomerNum. The Customer and Order tables have a type of relationship called a one-to-many relationship.

Figure 3-5	ONE-TO-MANY RELATIONSHIP AND SAMPLE QUERY

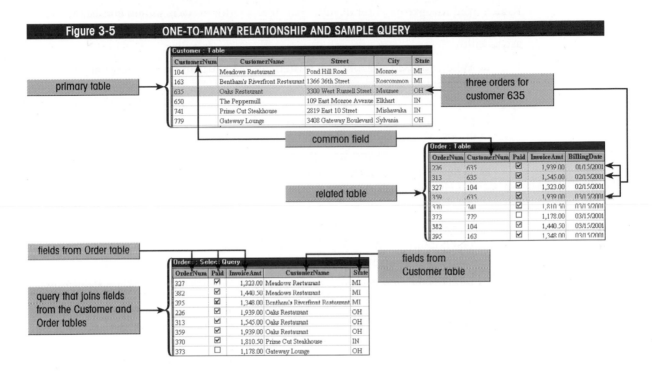

One-to-Many Relationships

A **one-to-many relationship** exists between two tables when one record in the first table matches zero, one, or many records in the second table, and when one record in the second table matches exactly one record in the first table. For example, as shown in Figure 3-5, customer 635 has three orders, customer 650 has zero orders, customers 163, 741, and 779 each have one order, and customer 104 has two orders. Every order has a single matching customer.

Access refers to the two tables that form a relationship as the primary table and the related table. The **primary table** is the "one" table in a one-to-many relationship; in Figure 3-5, the Customer table is the primary table because there is only one customer for each order. The **related table** is the "many" table; in Figure 3-5, the Order table is the related table because there can be many orders for each customer.

Because related data is stored in two tables, inconsistencies between the tables can occur. Consider the following scenarios:

■ Barbara adds an order to the Order table for customer 107, Cottage Grill. This order does not have a matching record in the Customer table. The data is inconsistent, and the order record is considered to be an **orphaned** record.

■ Barbara changes Oaks Restaurant from customer number 635 to 997 in the Customer table. Three orphaned records for customer 635 now exist in the Order table, and the database is inconsistent.

■ Barbara deletes the record for Meadows Restaurant, customer 104, in the Customer table because this customer is no longer a Valle Coffee customer. The database is again inconsistent; two records for customer 104 in the Order table have no matching record in the Customer table.

You can avoid these problems by specifying referential integrity between tables when you define their relationships.

Referential Integrity

Referential integrity is a set of rules that Access enforces to maintain consistency between related tables when you update data in a database. Specifically, the referential integrity rules are as follows:

■ When you add a record to a related table, a matching record must already exist in the primary table.

■ If you attempt to change the value of the primary key in the primary table, Access prevents this change if matching records exist in a related table. However, if you choose the **cascade updates** option, Access permits the change in value to the primary key and changes the appropriate foreign key values in the related table.

■ When you delete a record in the primary table, Access prevents the deletion if matching records exist in a related table. However, if you choose the **cascade deletes** option, Access deletes the record in the primary table and all records in related tables that have matching foreign key values.

Now you'll define a one-to-many relationship between the Customer and Order tables so that you can use fields from both tables to create a query that will retrieve the information Barbara wants.

Defining a Relationship Between Two Tables

When two tables have a common field, you can define a relationship between them in the Relationships window. The **Relationships window** illustrates the relationships among a database's tables. In this window you can view or change existing relationships, define new relationships between tables, and rearrange the layout of the tables.

You need to open the Relationships window and define the relationship between the Customer and Order tables. You'll define a one-to-many relationship between the two tables, with Customer as the primary table and Order as the related table, and with CustomerNum as the common field (the primary key in the Customer table and a foreign key in the Order table).

To define a one-to-many relationship between the two tables:

1. Click the **Relationships** button ⊞ on the Database toolbar. The Show Table dialog box opens on top of the Relationships window. See Figure 3-6.

Figure 3-6	SHOW TABLE DIALOG BOX

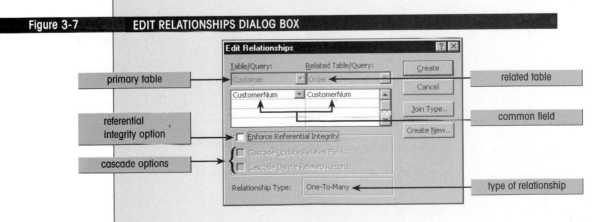

You must add each table participating in a relationship to the Relationships window.

2. Click **Customer** (If necessary) and then click the **Add** button. The Customer table is added to the Relationships window.

3. Click **Order** and then click the **Add** button. The Order table is added to the Relationships window.

4. Click the **Close** button in the Show Table dialog box to close it and reveal the entire Relationships window.

To form the relationship between the two tables, you drag the common field of CustomerNum from the primary table to the related table. Then Access opens the Edit Relationships dialog box, in which you select the relationship options for the two tables.

5. Click **CustomerNum** in the Customer table list, and drag it to **CustomerNum** in the Order table list. When you release the mouse button, the Edit Relationships dialog box opens. See Figure 3-7.

Figure 3-7	EDIT RELATIONSHIPS DIALOG BOX

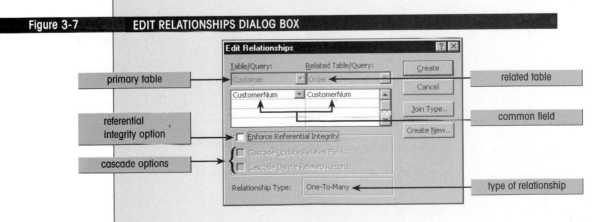

The primary table, related table, and common field appear at the top of the dialog box. The type of relationship, one-to-many, appears at the bottom of the dialog box. When you click the Enforce Referential Integrity check box, the two cascade options become available. If you select the Cascade Update Related Fields option, Access will change the appropriate foreign key values in the related table when you change a primary key value in the primary table. If you select the Cascade Delete Related Records option, when you delete a record in the primary table, Access will delete all records in the related table that have a matching foreign key value.

6. Click the **Enforce Referential Integrity** check box, click the **Cascade Update Related Fields** check box, and then click the **Cascade Delete Related Records** check box. You have now selected all the necessary relationship options.

7. Click the **Create** button to define the one-to-many relationship between the two tables and close the dialog box. The completed relationship appears in the Relationships window. See Figure 3-8.

Figure 3-8	DEFINED RELATIONSHIP IN THE RELATIONSHIPS WINDOW

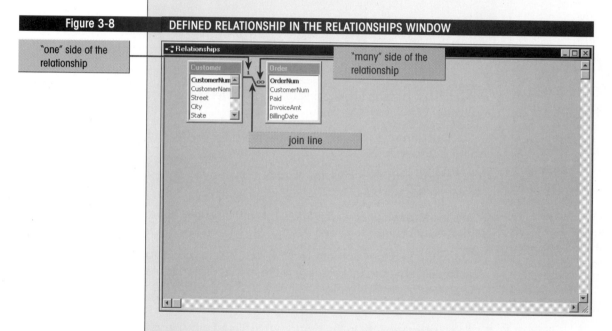

The **join line** connects the CustomerNum fields, which are common to the two tables. The common field joins the two tables, which have a one-to-many relationship. The "one" side of the relationship has the digit 1 at its end, and the "many" side of the relationship has the infinity symbol ∞ at its end. The two tables are still separate tables, but you can use the data in them as if they were one table.

8. Click the **Save** button 🖫 on the Relationship toolbar to save the layout in the Relationships window.

9. Click the **Close** button ✕ on the Relationships window title bar. The Relationships window closes, and you return to the Database window.

Now that you have joined the Customer and Order tables, you can create a query to produce the information Barbara wants. As part of her system for tracking payments received from restaurant customers, Barbara needs a query that displays the CustomerName, City, and State fields from the Customer table and the BillingDate, InvoiceAmt, and Paid fields from the Order table.

To create, run, and save the query using the Customer and Order tables:

1. With the Queries object selected in the Database window, double-click **Create query in Design view**. The Show Table dialog box opens on top of the Query window in Design view.

   You need to add both tables to the Query window.

2. Click **Customer** in the Tables list box (if necessary), click the **Add** button, click **Order**, click the **Add** button, and then click the **Close** button. The Customer and Order field lists appear in the Query window, and the Show Table dialog box closes. Note that the one-to-many relationship that exists between the two tables is shown in the Query window. Also, notice that the join line is thick at both ends; this signifies that you selected the option to enforce referential integrity. If you had not selected this option, the join line would be thin at both ends and neither the "1" nor the infinity symbol would appear, even though there is a one-to-many relationship between the two tables.

   You need to place the CustomerName, City, and State fields from the Customer field list into the design grid, and then place the BillingDate, InvoiceAmt, and Paid fields from the Order field list into the design grid.

3. Double-click **CustomerName** in the Customer field list to place CustomerName in the design grid's first column Field text box.

4. Repeat Step 3 to add the **City** and **State** fields from the Customer table, and then add the **BillingDate**, **InvoiceAmt**, and **Paid** fields (in that order) from the Order table, so that these fields are placed in the second through sixth columns of the design grid.

   The query specifications are complete, so you can now run the query.

5. Click the **Run** button [!] on the Query Design toolbar. Access runs the query and displays the results in the datasheet.

6. Click the **Maximize** button [□] on the Query window. See Figure 3-9.

Figure 3-9 | DATASHEET FOR THE QUERY BASED ON THE CUSTOMER AND ORDER TABLES

fields from the
Customer table

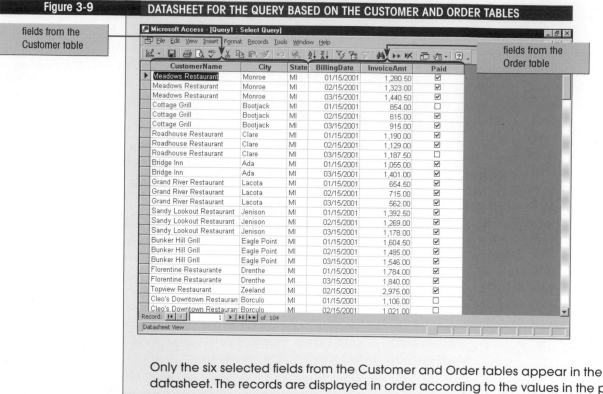

fields from the
Order table

Only the six selected fields from the Customer and Order tables appear in the datasheet. The records are displayed in order according to the values in the primary key field, CustomerNum, even though this field is not included in the query datasheet.

Barbara plans on frequently tracking the data retrieved by the query, so she asks you to save the query as "Customer Orders."

7. Click the **Save** button 🖫 on the Query Datasheet toolbar. The Save As dialog box opens.

8. Type **Customer Orders** in the Query Name text box, and then press the **Enter** key. Access saves the query with the specified name and displays the name in the Query window title bar.

Barbara decides she wants the records displayed in alphabetical order by customer name. Because your query displays data in order by the field value of CustomerNum, the primary key for the Customer table, you need to sort the records by CustomerName to display the data in the order Barbara wants.

Sorting Data in a Query

Sorting is the process of rearranging records in a specified order or sequence. Often you need to sort data before displaying or printing it, to meet a specific request. For example, Barbara might want to review order information arranged by the Paid field because she needs to know which orders are still unpaid. On the other hand, Leonard might want to view order information arranged by the InvoiceAmt totals for each customer, because he tracks company sales.

When you sort data in a database, you do not change the sequence of the records in the underlying tables. Only the records in the query datasheet are rearranged according to your specifications.

To sort records, you must select the **sort key**, which is the field used to determine the order of records in the datasheet. In this case, Barbara wants the data sorted by the customer name, so you need to specify the CustomerName field as the sort key. Sort keys can be text, number, date/time, currency, AutoNumber, yes/no, or Lookup Wizard fields, but not memo, OLE object, or hyperlink fields. You sort records in either ascending (increasing) or descending (decreasing) order. Figure 3-10 shows the results of each type of sort for different data types.

Figure 3-10	SORTING RESULTS FOR DIFFERENT DATA TYPES	
DATA TYPE	**ASCENDING SORT RESULTS**	**DESCENDING SORT RESULTS**
Text	A to Z	Z to A
Number	lowest to highest numeric value	highest to lowest numeric value
Date/Time	oldest to most recent date	most recent to oldest date
Currency	lowest to highest numeric value	highest to lowest numeric value
AutoNumber	lowest to highest numeric value	highest to lowest numeric value
Yes/No	yes (check mark in check box) then no values	no then yes values

Access provides several methods for sorting data in a table or query datasheet and in a form. One method, clicking the toolbar sort buttons, lets you sort the displayed records quickly.

Using a Toolbar Button to Sort Data

The **Sort Ascending** and **Sort Descending** buttons on the toolbar allow you to sort records immediately, based on the selected field. First you select the column on which you want to base the sort, and then you click the appropriate sort button on the toolbar to rearrange the records in either ascending or descending order. Unless you save the datasheet or form after you've sorted the records, the rearrangement of records is temporary.

Recall that in Tutorial 1 you used the Sort Ascending button to sort query results by the State field. You'll use this same button to sort the Customer Orders query results by the CustomerName field.

To sort the records using a toolbar sort button:

1. Click any visible CustomerName field value to establish this field as the current field.

2. Click the **Sort Ascending** button ![sort ascending icon] on the Query Datasheet toolbar. The records are rearranged in ascending order by customer name. See Figure 3-11.

Figure 3-11	SORTING RECORDS ON A SINGLE FIELD IN A DATASHEET

After viewing the query results, Barbara decides that she'd prefer to see the records arranged by the value in the Paid field, so that she can identify the paid invoices more easily. She wants to view all the unpaid invoices before the paid invoices (descending order for the Paid field, which is a yes/no field); plus, she wants to display the records within each group in increasing value of the InvoiceAmt field. To do this you need to sort using two fields.

Sorting Multiple Fields in Design View

Sort keys can be unique or nonunique. A sort key is **unique** if the value of the sort key field for each record is different. The CustomerNum field in the Customer table is an example of a unique sort key because each customer record has a different value in this field. A sort key is **nonunique** if more than one record can have the same value for the sort key field. For example, the Paid field in the Order table is a nonunique sort key because more than one record has the same Paid value.

When the sort key is nonunique, records with the same sort key value are grouped together, but they are not in a specific order within the group. To arrange these grouped records in a specific order, you can specify a **secondary sort key**, which is a second sort key field. The first sort key field is called the **primary sort key**. Note that the primary sort key is not the same as a table's primary key field. A table has at most one primary key, which must be unique, whereas any field in a table can serve as a primary sort key.

Access lets you select up to 10 different sort keys. When you use the toolbar sort buttons, the sort key fields must be in adjacent columns in the datasheet. You highlight the columns, and Access sorts first by the first column and then by each other highlighted column in order from left to right.

Barbara wants the records sorted first by the Paid field and then by the InvoiceAmt field. Although the two fields are adjacent, they are in the wrong order in your current query design. If you used a toolbar sort button, the InvoiceAmt field would be the primary sort key instead of the Paid field. You could move the InvoiceAmt field to the right of the Paid field in the query datasheet. However, you can specify only one type of sort—either ascending or descending—for selected columns in the query datasheet. This is not what Barbara wants; she wants the Paid field values to be sorted in descending order and the InvoiceAmt field values to be sorted in ascending order.

In this case, you need to specify the sort keys for the query in Design view. Any time you want to sort on multiple fields that are nonadjacent or in the wrong order, but you do not want to rearrange the columns in the query datasheet to accomplish the sort, you must specify the sort keys in Design view.

In the Query window in Design view, Access first uses the sort key that is leftmost in the design grid. Therefore, you must arrange the fields you want to sort from left to right in the design grid, with the primary sort key being the leftmost sort key field.

REFERENCE WINDOW   **RW**

Sorting a Query Datasheet
- In the query datasheet, select the field or adjacent fields on which you want to sort.
- Click the Sort Ascending button or the Sort Descending button on the Query Datasheet toolbar.

or

- In Design view, position the fields serving as sort keys from left (primary sort key) to right, and then select the sort order for each sort key.

To achieve the results Barbara wants, you need to switch to Design view, move the InvoiceAmt field to the right of the Paid field, and then specify the sort order for the two fields.

To select the two sort keys in Design view:

1. Click the **View** button for Design view on the Query Datasheet toolbar to open the query in Design view.

   First, you'll move the InvoiceAmt field to the right of the Paid field.

2. If necessary, click the right arrow in the design grid's horizontal scroll bar a few times to scroll to the right so that both the InvoiceAmt and Paid fields, as well as the next empty column, are completely visible.

3. Position the pointer above the InvoiceAmt field name until the pointer changes to ↓, and then click to select the field. See Figure 3-12.

Figure 3-12   **SELECTED INVOICEAMT FIELD**

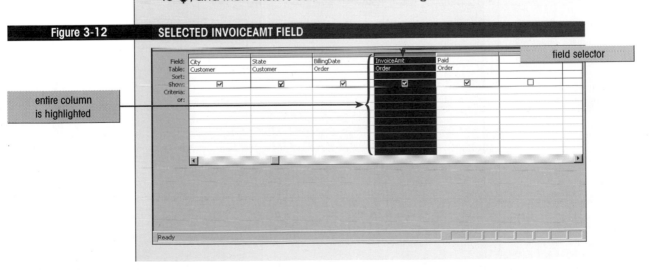

entire column is highlighted

field selector

4. Position the pointer in the field selector at the top of the highlighted column, and then click and drag the pointer to the right until the vertical line on the right of the Paid field is highlighted. See Figure 3-13.

Figure 3-13

DRAGGING THE FIELD IN THE DESIGN GRID

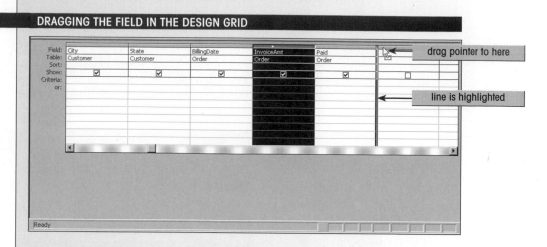

5. Release the mouse button. The InvoiceAmt field moves to the right of the Paid field.

The fields are now in the correct order for the sort. Next, you need to specify a descending sort order for the Paid field and an ascending sort order for the InvoiceAmt field.

6. Click the **Paid Sort** text box, click the **Sort** list arrow that appears, and then click **Descending**. You've selected a descending sort order for the Paid field, which will be the primary sort key. The Paid field is a yes/no field, and a descending sort order for this type of field displays all the no (unpaid) values before the yes (paid) values.

7. Click the **InvoiceAmt Sort** text box, click the **Sort** list arrow, click **Ascending**, and then click the **Criteria** text box for the InvoiceAmt field. You've selected an ascending sort order for the InvoiceAmt field, which will be the secondary sort key. See Figure 3-14.

Figure 3-14

SELECTING TWO SORT KEYS IN DESIGN VIEW

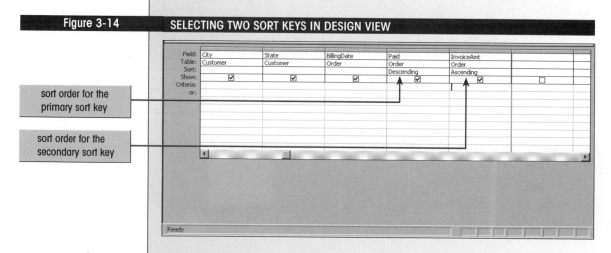

You have finished your query changes, so now you can run the query and then save the modified query with the same query name.

8. Click the **Run** button ! on the Query Design toolbar. Access runs the query and displays the query datasheet. The records appear in descending order, based on the values of the Paid field. Within groups of records with the same Paid field value, the records appear in ascending order by the values of the InvoiceAmt field. See Figure 3-15.

Figure 3-15	DATASHEET SORTED ON TWO FIELDS

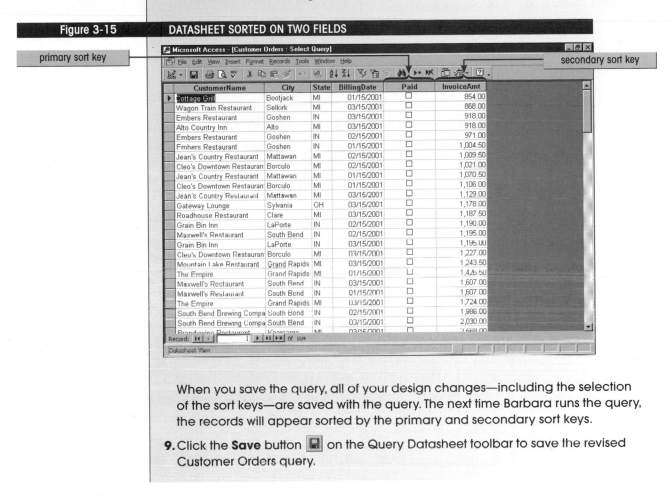

When you save the query, all of your design changes—including the selection of the sort keys—are saved with the query. The next time Barbara runs the query, the records will appear sorted by the primary and secondary sort keys.

9. Click the **Save** button 🖫 on the Query Datasheet toolbar to save the revised Customer Orders query.

Barbara wants to concentrate on the unpaid orders in the datasheet. Selecting only the unpaid orders is a temporary change that Barbara wants in the datasheet, so you do not need to switch to Design view and change the query. Instead, you can apply a filter.

Filtering Data

A **filter** is a set of restrictions you place on the records in an open datasheet or form to *temporarily* isolate a subset of the records. A filter lets you view different subsets of displayed records so that you can focus on only the data you need. Unless you save a query or form with a filter applied, an applied filter is not available the next time you run the query or open the form. The simplest technique for filtering records is Filter By Selection. **Filter By Selection** lets you select all or part of a field value in a datasheet or form, and then display only those records that contain the selected value in the field. Another technique for filtering records is to use **Filter By Form**, which changes your datasheet to display empty fields. Then you can select a value from the list arrow that appears when you click any blank field to apply a filter that selects only those records containing that value.

For Barbara's request, you need to select an unchecked box in the Paid field, which represents an unpaid order, and then use Filter By Selection to display only those query records with this same value.

To display the records using Filter By Selection:

1. Click any check box that is unchecked in the Paid column. When you click the check box, you select the field value, but you also change the check box from unchecked to checked. Because you've changed an unpaid order to a paid order, you need to click the same check box a second time.

2. Click the same check box a second time. The field value changes back to unchecked, which is now the selected field value.

3. Click the **Filter By Selection** button ![icon] on the Query Datasheet toolbar. Access displays the filtered results. Only the 25 query records that have an unchecked Paid field value appear in the datasheet; these records are the unpaid order records. Note that the status bar display (FLTR), the area next to the navigation buttons, and the selected Remove Filter button on the toolbar all indicate that the records have been filtered. See Figure 3-16.

Figure 3-16   USING FILTER BY SELECTION

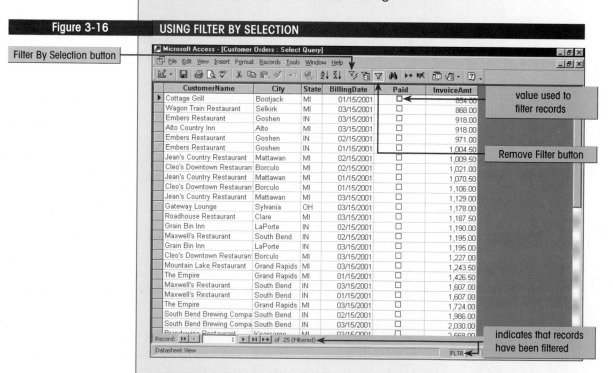

Barbara asks you to print the current datasheet so that she can give the printout to a staff member who is tracking unpaid orders.

4. Click the **Print** button 🖨 on the Query Datasheet toolbar to print the datasheet.

Now you can redisplay all the query records by clicking the Remove Filter button; this button works as a toggle to switch between the filtered and nonfiltered displays.

5. Click the **Remove Filter** button 🔽 on the Query Datasheet toolbar. Access redisplays all the records in the query datasheet.

6. Click the **Save** button 💾 on the Query Datasheet toolbar, and then click the **Close** button ✕ on the menu bar to save and close the query and return to the Database window.

7. Click the **Restore** button 🗗 on the menu bar to return the Database window to its original size.

The queries you've created will help Valle Coffee employees retrieve just the information they want to view. In the next session, you'll continue to create queries to meet their information needs.

Session 3.1 QUICK CHECK

1. What is a select query?

2. Describe the field list and the design grid in the Query window in Design view.

3. How are a table datasheet and a query datasheet similar? How are they different?

4. The _____ is the "one" table in a one-to-many relationship, and the _____ is the "many" table in the relationship.

5. _____ is a set of rules that Access enforces to maintain consistency between related tables when you update data in a database.

6. For a date/time field, what is ascending sort order?

7. When must you define multiple sort keys in Design view instead of in the query datasheet?

8. A(n) _____ is a set of restrictions you place on the records in an open datasheet or form to isolate a subset of records temporarily.

SESSION 3.2

In this session, you will specify an exact match condition in a query, change a datasheet's appearance, use a comparison operator to match a range of values, use the And and Or logical operators to define multiple selection criteria for queries, and perform calculations in queries.

Barbara wants to display customer and order information for all orders billed on 01/15/2001, so that she can see which orders have been paid. For this request, you need to create a query that displays selected fields from the Order and Customer tables and selected records that satisfy a condition.

Defining **Record Selection Criteria for Queries**

Just as you can display selected fields from a table in a query datasheet, you can display selected records. To tell Access which records you want to select, you must specify a condition as part of the query. A **condition** is a criterion, or rule, that determines which records are selected. To define a condition for a field, you place the condition in the field's Criteria text box in the design grid.

A condition usually consists of an operator, often a comparison operator, and a value. A **comparison operator** asks Access to compare the values of a database field to the condition value and to select all the records for which the relationship is true. For example, the condition >1000.00 for the InvoiceAmt field selects all records in the Order table having InvoiceAmt field values greater than 1000.00. Figure 3-17 shows the Access comparison operators.

Figure 3-17   ACCESS COMPARISON OPERATORS

OPERATOR	MEANING	EXAMPLE
=	equal to (optional; default operator)	="Hall"
<	less than	<#1/1/99#
<=	less than or equal to	<=100
>	greater than	>"C400"
>=	greater than or equal to	>=18.75
<>	not equal to	<>"Hall"
Between ... And...	between two values (inclusive)	Between 50 And 325
In ( )	in a list of values	In ("Hall", "Seeger")
Like	matches a pattern that includes wildcards	Like "706*"

Specifying an Exact Match

For Barbara's request, you need to create a query that will display only those records in the Order table with the value 01/15/2001 in the BillingDate field. This type of condition is called an **exact match** because the value in the specified field must match the condition exactly in order for the record to be included in the query results. You'll use the Simple Query Wizard to create the query, and then you'll specify the exact match condition.

To create the query using the Simple Query Wizard:

1. If you took a break after the previous session, make sure that Access is running, the Restaurant database is open, and the Queries object is selected in the Database window.

2. Double-click **Create query by using wizard**. Access opens the first Simple Query Wizard dialog box, in which you select the tables (or queries) and fields for the query.

3. Click the **Tables/Queries** list arrow, and then click **Table: Order**. The fields in the Order table appear in the Available Fields list box. See Figure 3-18.

Figure 3-18	FIRST SIMPLE QUERY WIZARD DIALOG BOX

Simple Query Wizard

Which fields do you want in your query?

You can choose from more than one table or query.

Tables/Queries

selected table → Table: Order ▼

Available Fields:

OrderNum
CustomerNum
Paid
InvoiceAmt
BillingDate

Selected Fields:

← move needed fields here

> >> < <<

Cancel   < Back   Next >   Finish

Except for the CustomerNum field, you will include all fields from the Order table in the query.

4. Click the ⟩⟩ button. All the fields from the Available Fields list box move to the Selected Fields list box.

5. Click **CustomerNum** in the Selected Fields list box, click the ⟨ button to move the CustomerNum field back to the Available Fields list box, and then click **BillingDate** in the Selected Fields list box.

Barbara also wants certain information from the Customer table included in the query results.

6. Click the **Tables/Queries** list arrow, and then click **Table: Customer**. The fields in the Customer table now appear in the Available Fields list box. Notice that the fields you selected from the Order table remain in the Selected Fields list box.

7. Click **CustomerName** in the Available Fields list box, and then click the ⟩ button to move CustomerName to the Selected Fields list box.

8. Repeat Step 7 to move the **State**, **OwnerName**, and **Phone** fields into the Selected Fields list box.

9. Click the **Next** button to open the second Simple Query Wizard dialog box, in which you choose whether the query will display records from the selected tables or a summary of those records. Summary options show calculations such as average, minimum, maximum, and so on. Barbara wants to view the details for the records, not a summary.

10. Make sure the **Detail (shows every field of every record)** option button is selected, and then click the **Next** button to open the last Simple Query Wizard dialog box, in which you choose a name for the query and complete the Wizard. You need to enter a condition for the query, so you'll want to modify the query's design.

11. Type **January Orders**, click the **Modify the query design** option button, and then click the **Finish** button. Access saves the query as January Orders and opens the query in Design view. See Figure 3-19.

Figure 3-19 | **QUERY IN DESIGN VIEW**

query name

indicates a one-to-many relationship

field lists

fields placed in the design grid (not all fields are visible on the screen at the same time)

January Orders : Select Query

Customer
*
CustomerNum
CustomerName
Street
City

1 ∞

Order
*
OrderNum
CustomerNum
Paid
InvoiceAmt

Field:	OrderNum	Paid	InvoiceAmt	BillingDate	CustomerName	State
Table:	Order	Order	Order	Order	Customer	Customer
Sort:						
Show:	☑	☑	☑	☑	☑	☑
Criteria:						
or:						

enter condition here

The field lists for the Customer and Order tables appear in the top portion of the window, and the join line indicating a one-to-many relationship connects the two tables. The selected fields appear in the design grid. Not all of the fields are visible in the grid; to see the other selected fields, you need to scroll to the right using the horizontal scroll bar.

To display the information Barbara wants, you need to enter the condition for the BillingDate field in its Criteria text box. Barbara wants to display only those records with a billing date of 01/15/2001.

To enter the exact match condition, and then run the query:

1. Click the **BillingDate Criteria** text box, type **1/15/01**, and then press the **Enter** key. The condition changes to #1/15/01#. (Note that you do not have to type the date as 01/15/2001; if you did, Access would still change the condition to #1/15/01#.)

   Access automatically placed number signs (#) before and after the condition. You must place date and time values inside number signs when using these values as selection criteria. If you omit the number signs, however, Access will include them automatically.

2. Click the **Run** button [!] on the Query Design toolbar. Access runs the query and displays the selected field values for only those records with a BillingDate field value of 01/15/2001. A total of 36 records are selected and displayed in the datasheet. See Figure 3-20.

Figure 3-20 | **DATASHEET DISPLAYING SELECTED FIELDS AND RECORDS**

click here to select all records

only records with a BillingDate value of 01/15/2001 are selected

36 records selected

January Orders : Select Query

OrderNum	Paid	InvoiceAmt	BillingDate	CustomerName	State	OwnerName
201	☐	854.00	01/15/2001	Cottage Grill	MI	Ms. Doris Reaum
202	☑	1,280.50	01/15/2001	Meadows Restaurant	MI	Mr. Ray Sucheck
203	☑	1,190.00	01/15/2001	Roadhouse Restaurant	MI	Ms. Shirley Woo
204	☑	1,055.00	01/15/2001	Bridge Inn	MI	Mr. Wayne Bouw
205	☑	654.50	01/15/2001	Grand River Restaurant	MI	Mr. John Rohrs
206	☑	1,392.50	01/15/2001	Sandy Lookout Restaurant	MI	Ms. Michele Yas
207	☑	1,604.50	01/15/2001	Bunker Hill Grill	MI	Mr. Ronald Kooie
208	☑	1,784.00	01/15/2001	Florentine Restaurante	MI	Mr. Donald Bench
209	☐	1,106.00	01/15/2001	Cleo's Downtown Restauran	MI	Ms. Joan Hoffma
210	☑	1,223.00	01/15/2001	Bentham's Riverfront Restau	MI	Mr. Joe Markovic
211	☑	703.50	01/15/2001	Wagon Train Restaurant	MI	Mr. Carl Seaver
212	☑	1,220.50	01/15/2001	Mountain Lake Restaurant	MI	Mr. Donald MacF
213	☑	1,426.50	01/15/2001	Best Bet Restaurant	MI	Ms. Rebecca Va

Record: 1 of 36

Barbara would like to see more fields and records on the screen at one time. She asks you to maximize the datasheet, change the datasheet's font size, and resize all the columns to their best fit.

Changing a Datasheet's Appearance

You can change the characteristics of a datasheet, including the font type and size of text in the datasheet, to improve its appearance or readability. You also can resize the datasheet columns to view more columns on the screen at the same time.

You'll maximize the datasheet, change the font size from the default 10 points to 8, and then resize the datasheet columns.

To change the font size and resize columns in the datasheet:

1. Click the **Maximize** button 🔲 on the Query window title bar.

2. Click the **record selector** to the left of the field names at the top of the datasheet (see Figure 3-20) to select the entire datasheet.

3. Click **Format** on the menu bar, and then click **Font** to open the Font dialog box.

4. Scroll the Size list box, click **8**, and then click the **OK** button. The font size for the entire datasheet changes to 8.

   Next you need to resize the columns to their best fit—that is, so each column is just wide enough to fit the longest value in the column.

5. Position the pointer in the OrderNum field selector. When the pointer changes to ↓, click to select the entire column and deselect all other columns.

6. Click the horizontal scroll right arrow until the Phone field is fully visible, and then position the pointer in the Phone field selector until the pointer changes to ↓.

7. Press and hold the **Shift** key, and then click the mouse button. All the columns are selected. Now you can resize all of them at once.

8. Position the pointer at the right edge of the Phone field selector until the pointer changes to ↔. See Figure 3-21.

| Figure 3-21 | PREPARING TO RESIZE ALL COLUMNS TO THEIR BEST FIT |

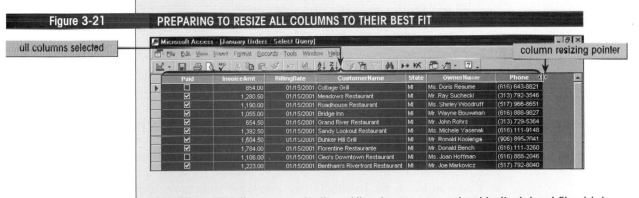

all columns selected

column resizing pointer

9. Double-click the mouse button. All columns are resized to their best fit, which makes each column just large enough to fit the longest *visible* field value in the column, including the field name at the top of the column. Scroll through the datasheet and resize individual columns as needed to display all field values completely.

10. If necessary, scroll to the left so that the OrderNum field is visible, and then click any field value box (except a Paid field value) to deselect all columns. See Figure 3-22.

Figure 3-22

DATASHEET AFTER CHANGING FONT SIZE AND COLUMN WIDTHS

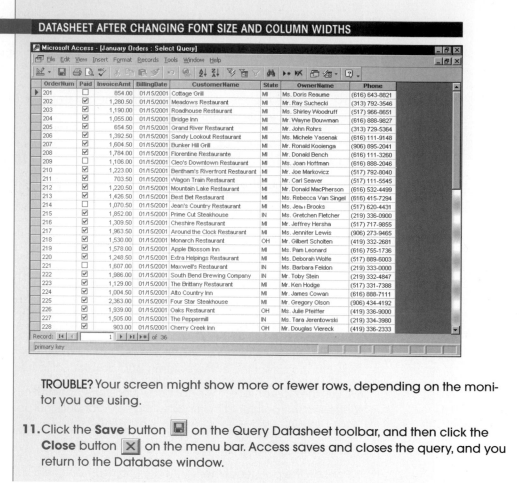

TROUBLE? Your screen might show more or fewer rows, depending on the monitor you are using.

11. Click the **Save** button 🖫 on the Query Datasheet toolbar, and then click the **Close** button ☒ on the menu bar. Access saves and closes the query, and you return to the Database window.

After viewing the query results, Barbara decides that she would like to see the same fields, but only for those records whose InvoiceAmt exceeds $2,000. She wants to note this information and pass it along to her staff members so that they can contact those customers with higher outstanding invoices. To create the query needed to produce these results, you need to use a comparison operator to match a range of values—in this case, any InvoiceAmt value greater than $2,000.

Using a Comparison Operator to Match a Range of Values

Once you create and save a query, you can click the Open button to run it again, or you can click the Design button to change its design. Because the design of the query you need to create next is similar to the January Orders query, you will change its design, run the query to test it, and then save the query with a new name, which keeps the January Orders query intact.

To change the January Orders query design to create a new query:

1. Click the **January Orders** query in the Database window (if necessary), and then click the **Design** button to open the January Orders query in Design view.

2. Click the **InvoiceAmt Criteria** text box, type **>2000**, and then press the **Tab** key. See Figure 3-23.

Figure 3-23	CHANGING A QUERY'S DESIGN TO CREATE A NEW QUERY

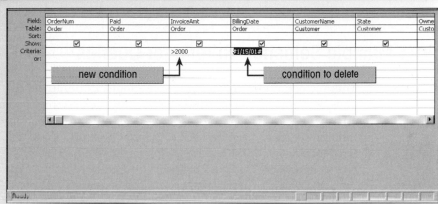

Barbara's new condition specifies that a record will be selected only if its InvoiceAmt field value exceeds 2000. Before you run the query, you need to delete the condition for the BillingDate field.

3. With the BillingDate field condition highlighted, press the **Delete** key. Now there is no condition for the BillingDate field.

4. Click the **Run** button on the Query Design toolbar. Access runs the query and displays the selected fields for only those records with an InvoiceAmt field value greater than 2000. A total of four records are selected. See Figure 3-24.

Figure 3-24	RUNNING THE MODIFIED QUERY

Of the records retrieved, Barbara notes that order numbers 365 and 387 have not yet been paid and the amount of each. She gives this information to her staff.

So that Barbara can display this information again, as necessary, you'll save the query as High Invoice Amounts.

5. Click **File** on the menu bar, and then click **Save As** to open the Save As dialog box.

6. In the text box for the new query name, type **High Invoice Amounts**. Notice that the As text box specifies that you are saving the data as a query.

7. Click the **OK** button to save the query using the new name. The new query name appears in the Query window title bar.

8. Click the **Close** button ⊠ on the menu bar. The Database window becomes the active window.

Leonard asks Barbara for a list of the orders billed on 01/15/2001 that are still unpaid. He wants to know which customers are slow in paying their invoices. To produce this data, you need to create a query containing two conditions—one for the order's billing date and another to indicate that the order is unpaid.

Defining Multiple Selection Criteria for Queries

Multiple conditions require you to use **logical operators** to combine two or more conditions. When you want a record selected only if two or more conditions are met, you need to use the **And logical operator**. In this case, Leonard wants to see only those records with a BillingDate field value of 01/15/2001 *and* a Paid field value of No. If you place conditions in separate fields in the *same* Criteria row of the design grid, all the conditions in that row must be met in order for a record to be included in the query results. However, if you place conditions in *different* Criteria rows, a record will be selected if at least one of the conditions is met. If none of the conditions is met, then Access does not select the record. When you place conditions in different Criteria rows, you are using the **Or logical operator**. Figure 3-25 illustrates the difference between the And and Or logical operators.

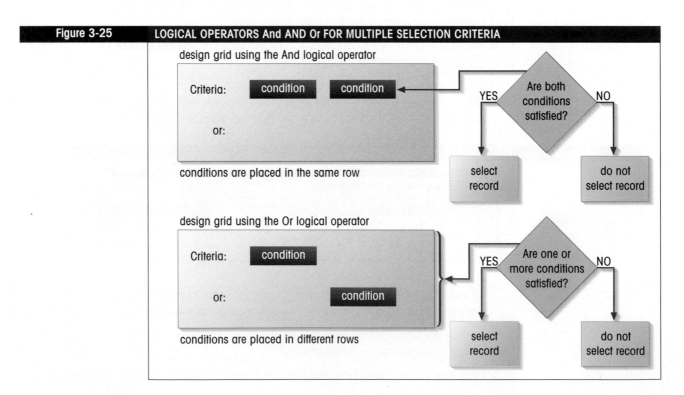

Figure 3-25   LOGICAL OPERATORS And AND Or FOR MULTIPLE SELECTION CRITERIA

The And Logical Operator

To create Leonard's query, you need to modify the existing January Orders query to show only the unpaid orders billed on 01/15/2001. For the modified query, you must add a second condition in the same Criteria row. The condition #1/15/01# for the BillingDate field finds records billed on the specified date, and the condition "No" in the Paid field finds records whose invoices have not been paid. Because the conditions appear in the same Criteria row, the query will select records only if both conditions are met.

After modifying the query, you'll save it and then rename it as "Unpaid January Orders," overwriting the January Orders query, which Barbara no longer needs.

To modify the January Orders query and use the And logical operator:

1. With the Queries object selected in the Database window, click **January Orders** (if necessary), and then click the **Design** button to open the query in Design view.

2. Click the **Paid Criteria** text box, type **no**, and then press the **Tab** key. See Figure 3-26.

Figure 3-26	QUERY TO FIND UNPAID JANUARY ORDERS

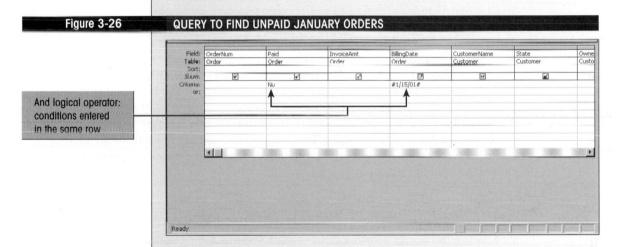

And logical operator: conditions entered in the same row

The condition for the BillingDate field is already entered, so you can run the query.

3. Click the **Run** button on the Query Design toolbar. Access runs the query and displays in the datasheet only those records that meet both conditions: a BillingDate field value of 01/15/2001 and a Paid field value of No. A total of six records are selected. See Figure 3-27.

Figure 3-27	RESULTS OF QUERY USING THE AND LOGICAL OPERATOR

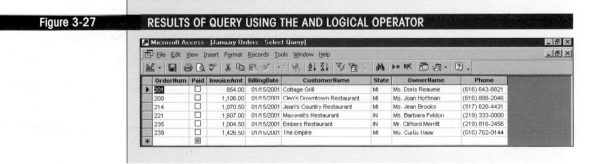

Now you can save the changes to the query and rename it.

4. Click the **Save** button 🖫 on the Query Datasheet toolbar, and then click the **Close** button ☒ on the menu bar.

5. Right-click **January Orders** in the Queries list box, and then click **Rename** on the shortcut menu.

6. Click to position the insertion point to the left of the word "January," type **Unpaid**, press the **spacebar**, and then press the **Enter** key. The query name is now Unpaid January Orders.

Leonard also wants to determine which restaurant customers are most valuable to Valle Coffee. Specifically, he wants to see a list of those customers who have been placing orders for many years or who place orders for a substantial amount of money, so that he can call the customers personally and thank them for their business. To create this query, you need to use the Or logical operator.

The Or Logical Operator

For Leonard's request, you need a query that selects records when either one of two conditions is satisfied or when both conditions are satisfied. That is, a record is selected if the FirstContact field value is less than 01/1/1994 (to find those customers who have been doing business with Valle Coffee the longest) *or* if the InvoiceAmt field value is greater than 2000 (to find those customers who spend more money). You will enter the condition for the FirstContact field in one Criteria row and the condition for the InvoiceAmt field in another Criteria row, thereby using the Or logical operator.

To display the information Leonard wants to view, you'll create a new query containing the CustomerName, OwnerName, Phone, and FirstContact fields from the Customer table and the InvoiceAmt field from the Order table. Then you'll specify the conditions using the Or logical operator.

To create the query and use the Or logical operator:

1. In the Database window, double-click **Create query in Design view**. The Show Table dialog box opens on top of the Query window in Design view.

2. Click **Customer** in the Tables list box (if necessary), click the **Add** button, click **Order**, click the **Add** button, and then click the **Close** button. The Customer and Order field lists appear in the Query window and the Show Table dialog box closes.

3. Double-click **CustomerName** in the Customer field list to add the CustomerName field to the design grid's first column Field text box.

4. Repeat Step 3 to add the **OwnerName**, **Phone**, and **FirstContact** fields from the Customer table, and then add the **InvoiceAmt** field from the Order table.

   Now you need to specify the first condition, <1/1/94, in the FirstContact field.

5. Click the **FirstContact Criteria** text box, type **<1/1/94** and then press the **Tab** key.

   Because you want records selected if either of the conditions for the FirstContact or InvoiceAmt fields is satisfied, you must enter the condition for the InvoiceAmt field in the "or" row of the design grid.

6. Press the ↓ key, and then type **>2000** in the "or" text box for InvoiceAmt. See Figure 3-28.

Figure 3-28 | **QUERY WINDOW WITH THE OR LOGICAL OPERATOR**

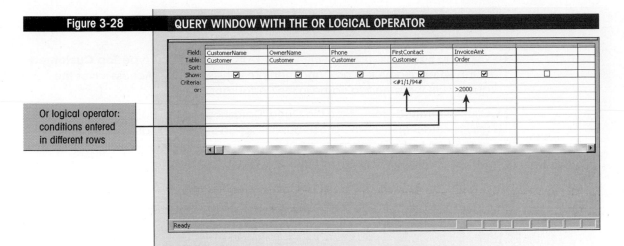

Or logical operator:
conditions entered
in different rows

The query specifications are complete, so now you can run the query.

7. Click the **Run** button ⚡ on the Query Design toolbar. Access runs the query
and displays only those records that meet either condition: a FirstContact field
value less than 01/1/1994 or an InvoiceAmt field value greater than 2000. A total
of 29 records are selected.

Leonard wants the list displayed in alphabetical order by CustomerName.

8. Click any visible CustomerName field value to establish this field as the current
field, and then click the **Sort Ascending** button ⯅↓ on the Query Datasheet
toolbar.

9. Resize all datasheet columns to their best fit. Be sure to scroll through the entire
datasheet to make sure that all values are completely displayed. Deselect all
columns when finished resizing, and then return to the top of the datasheet. See
Figure 3-29.

Figure 3-29 | **RESULTS OF QUERY USING THE OR LOGICAL OPERATOR**

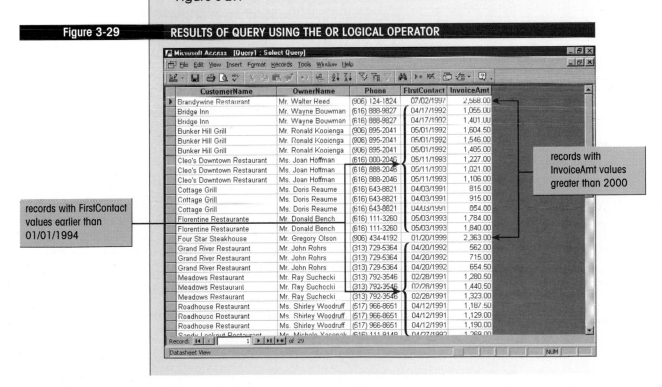

records with FirstContact
values earlier than
01/01/1994

records with
InvoiceAmt values
greater than 2000

Now you'll save the query as Top Customers, print the query results, and then close the query.

10. Click the **Save** button 🖫 on the Query Datasheet toolbar, type **Top Customers** in the Query Name text box, and then press the **Enter** key. Access saves the query with the specified name in the Restaurant database.

11. Click the **Print** button 🖨 on the Query Datasheet toolbar to print the query results, and then click the **Close** button ⊠ on the menu bar to close the query and return to the Database window.

Next, Leonard asks Barbara if the Restaurant database can be used to perform calculations. He is considering adding a 2% late charge to the unpaid invoices billed in January, and he wants to know exactly what these charges would be.

Performing Calculations

In addition to using queries to retrieve, sort, and filter data in a database, you can use a query to perform calculations. To perform a calculation, you define an **expression** containing a combination of database fields, constants, and operators. For numeric expressions, the data types of the database fields must be number, currency, or date/time; the constants are numbers such as .02 (for the 2% late charge); and the operators can be arithmetic operators (+ – * /) or other specialized operators. In complex expressions you can enclose calculations in parentheses to indicate which one should be performed first. In expressions without parentheses, Access calculates in the following order of precedence: multiplication and division before addition and subtraction. When operators have equal precedence, Access calculates them in order from left to right.

To perform a calculation in a query, you add a calculated field to the query. A **calculated field** is a field that displays the results of an expression. A calculated field appears in a query datasheet; however, it does not exist in a database. When you run a query that contains a calculated field, Access evaluates the expression defined by the calculated field and displays the resulting value in the datasheet.

Creating a Calculated Field

To produce the information Leonard wants, you need to open the Unpaid January Orders query and create a calculated field that will multiply each InvoiceAmt field value by .02 to account for the 2% late charge Leonard is considering.

To enter an expression for a calculated field, you can type it directly in a Field text box in the design grid. Alternatively, you can open the Zoom box or Expression Builder and use either one to enter the expression. The **Zoom box** is a large text box for entering text, expressions, or other values. **Expression Builder** is an Access tool that contains an expression box for entering the expression, buttons for common operators, and one or more lists of expression elements, such as table and field names. Unlike a Field text box, which is too small to show an entire expression at one time, the Zoom box and Expression Builder are large enough to display lengthy expressions. In most cases Expression Builder provides the easiest way to enter expressions.

Using Expression Builder
- Display the query in Design view.
- In the design grid, position the insertion point in the Field text box of the field for which you want to create an expression.
- Click the Build button on the Query Design toolbar.
- Use the expression elements and common operators to build the expression, or type the expression directly.
- Click the OK button.

You'll begin by opening the Unpaid January Orders query in Design view and modifying it to show only the information Leonard wants to view.

To modify the Unpaid January Orders query:

1. In the Database window, click **Unpaid January Orders**, and then click the **Design** button.

   Leonard wants to see only the OrderNum, CustomerName, and InvoiceAmt fields. So, you'll first delete the unnecessary fields, and then uncheck the Show boxes for the Paid and BillingDate fields. You need to keep these two fields in the query because they specify the conditions for the query; however, Leonard does not want them to appear in the query results.

2. Scroll the design grid to the right until the last three fields—State, OwnerName, and Phone—are visible.

3. Position the pointer on the State field until the pointer changes to ↓, click and hold down the mouse button, drag the mouse to the right to highlight the State, OwnerName, and Phone fields, and then release the mouse button.

4. Press the **Delete** key to delete the three selected fields.

5. Scroll the design grid back to the left, click the **Show** check box for the Paid field to remove the check mark, and then click the **Show** check box for the BillingDate field to remove the check mark.

   Next you'll move the InvoiceAmt field to the right of the CustomerName field so that the InvoiceAmt values will appear next to the calculated field values in the query results.

6. Make sure both the InvoiceAmt field and the empty field to the right of the CustomerName field are visible in the design grid.

7. Select the InvoiceAmt field, and then use the pointer ⬚ to drag the field to the right of the CustomerName field.

8. If necessary, scroll the design grid so that the empty field to the right of InvoiceAmt is visible, and then click anywhere in the design grid to deselect the InvoiceAmt field. See Figure 3-30.

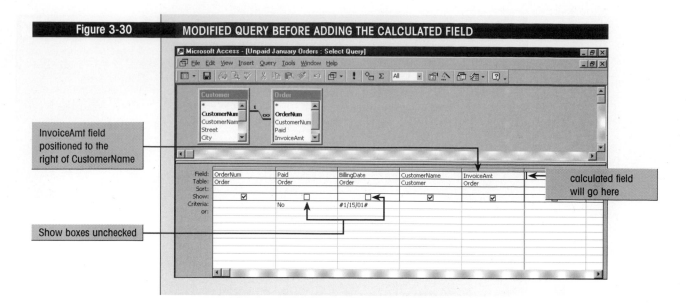

Figure 3-30 | **MODIFIED QUERY BEFORE ADDING THE CALCULATED FIELD**

Now you're ready to use Expression Builder to enter the calculated field in the Unpaid January Orders query.

To add the calculated field to the Unpaid January Orders query:

1. Position the insertion point in the Field text box to the right of the InvoiceAmt field, and then click the **Build** button on the Query Design toolbar. The Expression Builder dialog box opens. See Figure 3-31.

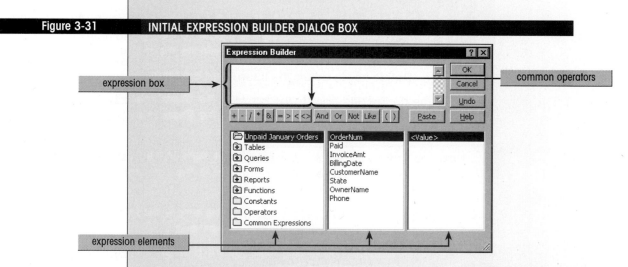

Figure 3-31 | **INITIAL EXPRESSION BUILDER DIALOG BOX**

You use the common operators and expression elements to help you build an expression. Note that the Unpaid January Orders query is already selected in the list box on the lower left; the fields included in the query are listed in the center box.

The expression for the calculated field will multiply the InvoiceAmt field values by the numeric constant .02 (which represents a 2% late charge). To include a field in the expression, you select the field and then click the Paste button. To include a numeric constant, you simply type the constant in the expression.

2. Click **InvoiceAmt** and then click the **Paste** button. [InvoiceAmt] appears in the expression box.

To include the multiplication operator in the expression, you click the asterisk (*) button.

3. Click the * button in the row of common operators, and then type **.02**. You have completed the entry of the expression. See Figure 3-32.

Figure 3-32   COMPLETED EXPRESSION FOR THE CALCULATED FIELD

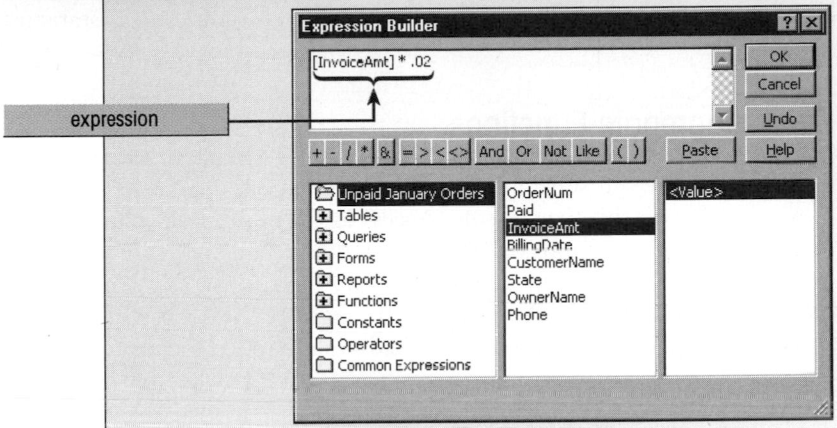

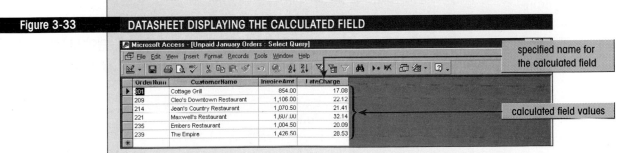

Note that you also could have typed the expression directly into the expression box, instead of clicking the field name and the operator.

4. Click the **OK** button. Access closes the Expression Builder dialog box and adds the expression to the design grid in the Field text box for the calculated field.

Next, you need to specify a name for the calculated field as it will appear in the query results.

5. Press the **Home** key to position the insertion point to the left of the expression.

You'll enter the name LateCharge, which is descriptive of the field's contents; then you'll run the query.

6. Type **LateCharge:**. *Make sure you include the colon following the field name.* The colon is needed to separate the field name from its expression.

Now you can run the query.

7. Click the **Run** button [!] on the Query Design toolbar. Access runs the query and displays the query datasheet, which contains the three specified fields and the calculated field with the name "LateCharge." See Figure 3-33.

Figure 3-33   DATASHEET DISPLAYING THE CALCULATED FIELD

> You'll save the query as Unpaid With Late Charge, and then close it.
>
> 8. Click **File** on the menu bar, click **Save As**, type **Unpaid With Late Charge**, press the **Enter** key, and then click the **Close** button ☒ on the menu bar. The Database window becomes the active window.

Barbara prepares a report of Valle Coffee's restaurant business for Leonard on a regular basis. The information in the report includes a summary of the restaurant orders. Barbara lists the total invoice amount for all orders, the average invoice amount, and the total number of orders. She asks you to create a query to determine these statistics from data in the Order table.

Using Aggregate Functions

You can calculate statistical information, such as totals and averages, on the records selected in a query. To do this, you use the Access aggregate functions. **Aggregate functions** perform arithmetic operations on selected records in a database. Figure 3-34 lists the most frequently used aggregate functions. Aggregate functions operate on the records that meet a query's selection criteria. You specify an aggregate function for a specific field, and the appropriate operation applies to that field's values for the selected records.

Figure 3-34	FREQUENTLY USED AGGREGATE FUNCTIONS	
AGGREGATE FUNCTION	**DETERMINES**	**DATA TYPES SUPPORTED**
Avg	Average of the field values for the selected records	AutoNumber, Currency, Date/Time, Number
Count	Number of records selected	AutoNumber, Currency, Date/Time, Memo, Number, OLE Object, Text, Yes/No
Max	Highest field value for the selected records	AutoNumber, Currency, Date/Time, Number, Text
Min	Lowest field value for the selected records	AutoNumber, Currency, Date/Time, Number, Text
Sum	Total of the field values for the selected records	AutoNumber, Currency, Date/TIme, Number

To display the total, average, and count of all the invoice amounts in the Order table, you will use the Sum, Avg, and Count aggregate functions for the InvoiceAmt field.

> ### To calculate the total, average, and count of all invoice amounts:
>
> 1. Double-click **Create query in Design view**. Access opens the Show Table dialog box on top of the Query window in Design view.
>
> 2. Click **Order**, click the **Add** button, and then click the **Close** button. The Order field list is added to the top of the Query window, and the dialog box closes.
>
> To perform the three calculations on the InvoiceAmt field, you need to add the field to the design grid three times.
>
> 3. Double-click **InvoiceAmt** in the Order field list three times to add three copies of the field to the design grid.

You need to select an aggregate function for each InvoiceAmt field. When you click the Totals button on the Query Design toolbar, a row labeled "Total" is added to the design grid. The Total row provides a list of the aggregate functions that you can select.

4. Click the **Totals** button [Σ] on the Query Design toolbar. A new row labeled "Total" appears between the Table and Sort rows in the design grid. See Figure 3-35.

Figure 3-35	TOTAL ROW INSERTED IN THE DESIGN GRID

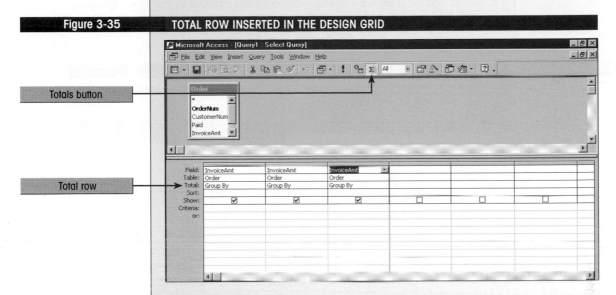

Totals button

Total row

In the Total row, you specify the aggregate function you want to use for a field.

5. Click the right side of the first column's **Total** text box, and then click **Sum**. This field will calculate the total of all the InvoiceAmt field values.

   When you run the query, Access automatically will assign a datasheet column name of "SumOfInvoiceAmt" for this field. You can change the datasheet column name to a more descriptive or readable name by entering the name you want in the Field text box. However, you must also keep the field name InvoiceAmt in the Field text box, because it identifies the field whose values will be summed. The Field text box will contain the datasheet column name you specify followed by the field name (InvoiceAmt) with a colon separating the two names.

6. Position the insertion point to the left of InvoiceAmt in the first column's Field text box, and then type **Total of Invoices:**. Be sure you include the colon at the end.

7. Click the right side of the second column's **Total** text box, and then click **Avg**. This field will calculate the average of all the InvoiceAmt field values.

8. Position the insertion point to the left of InvoiceAmt in the second column's Field text box, and then type **Average of Invoices:**.

9. Click the right side of the third column's **Total** text box, and then click **Count**. This field will calculate the total number of invoices (orders).

10. Position the insertion point to the left of InvoiceAmt in the third column's Field text box, and then type **Number of Invoices:**.

   The query design is complete, so you can run the query.

11. Click the **Run** button ⚡ on the Query Design toolbar. Access runs the query and displays one record containing the three aggregate function values. The single row of summary statistics represents calculations based on the 104 records selected in the query.

You need to resize the three columns to their best fit to see the column names.

12. Resize each column by double-clicking the ✛ pointer on the right edge of each column's field selector; then position the insertion point at the start of the field value in the first column. See Figure 3-36.

Figure 3-36	RESULTS OF THE QUERY USING AGGREGATE FUNCTIONS

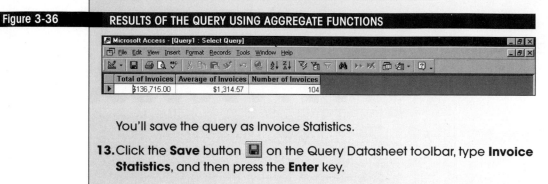

You'll save the query as Invoice Statistics.

13. Click the **Save** button 💾 on the Query Datasheet toolbar, type **Invoice Statistics**, and then press the **Enter** key.

Barbara's report to Leonard also includes the same invoice statistics (total, average, and count) for each month. Because Valle Coffee sends invoices to its restaurant customers once a month, each invoice in a month has the same billing date. Barbara asks you to display the invoice statistics for each different billing date in the Order table.

Using Record Group Calculations

In addition to calculating statistical information on all or selected records in selected tables, you can calculate statistics for groups of records. For example, you can determine the number of customers in each state or the total invoice amounts by billing date.

To create a query for Barbara's latest request, you can modify the current query by adding the BillingDate field and assigning the Group By operator to it. The **Group By operator** divides the selected records into groups based on the values in the specified field. Those records with the same value for the field are grouped together, and the datasheet displays one record for each group. Aggregate functions, which appear in the other columns of the design grid, provide statistical information for each group.

You need to modify the current query to add the Group By operator for the BillingDate field. This will display the statistical information grouped by billing date for the 104 selected records in the query.

To add the BillingDate field with the Group By operator, and then run the query:

1. Click the **View** button for Design view 📉 on the Query Datasheet toolbar to switch to Design view.

2. Scroll the Order field list, if necessary, and then double-click **BillingDate** to add the field to the design grid. Group By, which is the default option in the Total row, appears for the BillingDate field.

You've completed the query changes, so you can run the query.

3. Click the **Run** button 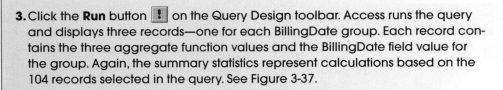 on the Query Design toolbar. Access runs the query and displays three records—one for each BillingDate group. Each record contains the three aggregate function values and the BillingDate field value for the group. Again, the summary statistics represent calculations based on the 104 records selected in the query. See Figure 3-37.

Figure 3-37	AGGREGATE FUNCTIONS GROUPED BY BILLINGDATE

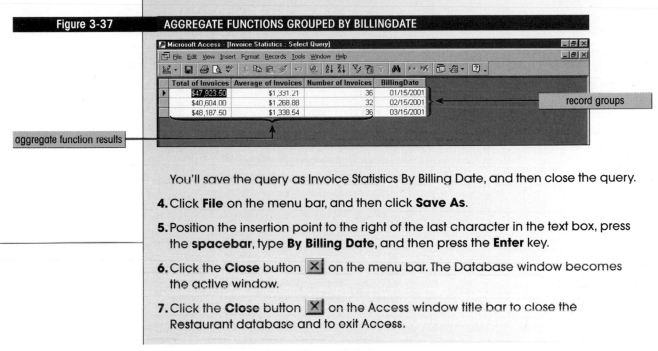

Total of Invoices	Average of Invoices	Number of Invoices	BillingDate
$47,923.50	$1,331.21	36	01/15/2001
$40,604.00	$1,268.88	32	02/15/2001
$48,187.50	$1,338.54	36	03/15/2001

aggregate function results

record groups

You'll save the query as Invoice Statistics By Billing Date, and then close the query.

4. Click **File** on the menu bar, and then click **Save As**.

5. Position the insertion point to the right of the last character in the text box, press the **spacebar**, type **By Billing Date**, and then press the **Enter** key.

6. Click the **Close** button ✕ on the menu bar. The Database window becomes the active window.

7. Click the **Close** button ✕ on the Access window title bar to close the Restaurant database and to exit Access.

The queries you've created and saved will help Leonard, Barbara, Kim, and other employees monitor and analyze the business activity of Valle Coffee's restaurant customers. Now any employee can run the queries at any time, modify them as needed, or use them as the basis for designing new queries to meet additional information requirements.

Session 3.2 QUICK CHECK

1. A(n) _____ is a criterion, or rule, that determines which records are selected for a query datasheet.

2. In the design grid, where do you place the conditions for two different fields when you use the And logical operator? The Or logical operator?

3. To perform a calculation in a query, you define a(n) _____ containing a combination of database fields, constants, and operators.

4. How does a calculated field differ from a table field?

5. What is an aggregate function?

6. The _____ operator divides selected records into groups based on the values in a field.

REVIEW ASSIGNMENTS

Barbara needs information from the **Valle Products** database, and she asks you to query the database by completing the following:

1. Make sure your Data Disk is in the disk drive, start Access, and then open the **Valle Products** database located in the Review folder on your Data Disk.

2. Create a select query based on the **Product** table. Display the ProductCode, WeightCode, and Price fields in the query results; sort in descending order based on the Price field values; and select only those records whose CoffeeCode value equals BRUM. (*Hint*: Do not display the CoffeeCode field values in the query results.) Save the query as **BRUM Coffee**, run the query, print the query datasheet, and then close the query.

Explore ▷ 3. Define a one-to-many relationship between the primary **Coffee** table and the related **Product** table, and then define a one-to-many relationship between the primary **Weight** table and the related **Product** table. (*Hint*: Add all three tables to the Relationships window, and then define the two relationships.) Select the referential integrity option and both cascade options for both relationships.

4. Create a select query based on the **Coffee**, **Product**, and **Weight** tables. Select the fields CoffeeType, CoffeeName, ProductCode, Decaf (from the **Product** table), Price, and Weight/Size, in that order. Sort in ascending order based on the CoffeeName field values. Select only those records whose CoffeeType equals "Flavored." (*Hint*: Do not display the CoffeeType field values in the query results.) Save the query as **Flavored Coffees**, and then run the query. Resize all columns in the datasheet to fit the data. Print the datasheet, and then save the query.

5. Use the Office Assistant to learn about Filter By Form. (*Hint:* Ask the Office Assistant the question, "How do I use Filter By Form," and then click the topic "Filter records by entering values in a blank view of your form or datasheet.") Read the topic, and then close the Microsoft Access Help window.

Explore ▷ 6. Use the Filter By Form button on the Query Datasheet toolbar to filter the records that have a Weight/Size of "1 lb pkg," and then apply the filter. Print the query datasheet.

Explore ▷ 7. Remove the filter to display all records, and then save and close the query.

Explore ▷ 8. Create a query based on the **Product** table that shows all products that do not have a WeightCode field value of A, and whose Price field value is greater than 50; display all fields except Decaf from the **Product** table. Save the query as **Pricing**, and then run the query.

Explore ▷ 9. Open the **Pricing** query in Design view. Create a calculated field named NewPrice that displays the results of increasing the Price values by 3%. Display the results in descending order by NewPrice. Save the query as **New Prices**, run the query, resize all columns in the datasheet to fit the data, print the query datasheet, and then save and close the query.

10. Open the **Flavored Coffees** query in Design view. Modify the query to display only those records with a CoffeeType field value of "Flavored" or with a Price field value greater than 50. Save the query as **Flavored Plus Higher Priced**, and then run the query. Resize all columns in the datasheet to fit the data, print the query datasheet, and then save and close the query.

Explore ▷ 11. Create a new query based on the **Product** table. Use the Min and Max aggregate functions to find the lowest and highest values in the Price field. Name the two aggregate fields Lowest Price and Highest Price, respectively. Save the query as **Lowest And Highest Prices**, run the query, and then print the query datasheet.

Explore ▶ 12. Open the **Lowest And Highest Prices** query in Design view. Use the Show Table button on the Query Design toolbar to open the Show Table dialog box, and then add the **Weight** table to the query. Modify the query so that the records are grouped by the Weight/Size field. Save the query as **Lowest And Highest Prices By Weight/Size**, run the query, print the query datasheet, and then close the query.

13. Close the **Valle Products** database, and then exit Access.

CASE PROBLEMS

Case 1. Ashbrook Mall Information Desk   Sam Bullard wants to view specific information about jobs available at the Ashbrook Mall. He asks you to query the **MallJobs** database by completing the following:

1. Make sure your Data Disk is in the disk drive, start Access, and then open the **MallJobs** database located in the Cases folder on your Data Disk.

2. Define a one-to-many relationship between the primary **Store** table and the related **Job** table. Select the referential integrity option and both cascade options for the relationship.

3. Create a select query based on the **Store** and **Job** tables. Display the StoreName, Location, Position, and Hours/Week fields, in that order. Sort in ascending order based on the StoreName field values. Run the query, save the query as **Store Jobs**, and then print the datasheet.

4. Use Filter By Selection to temporarily display only those records with a Location field value of A3 in the **Store Jobs** query datasheet. Print the datasheet and then remove the filter. Save and close the query.

5. Open the **Store Job**s query in Design view. Modify the query to display only those records with a Position value of Server. Run the query, save the query as **Server Jobs**, and then print the datasheet.

6. Open the **Server Jobs** query in Design view. Modify the query to display only those records with a Position value of Server and with an Hours/Week value of 20-25. Run the query, save it with the same name, print the datasheet, and then close the query.

7. Close the **MallJobs** database, and then exit Access.

Case 2. Professional Litigation User Services (PLUS)   Raj Jawahir is completing an analysis of the payment history of PLUS clients. To help him find the information he needs, you'll query the **Payments** database by completing the following:

1. Make sure your Data Disk is in the disk drive, start Access, and then open the **Payments** database located in the Cases folder on your Data Disk.

2. Define a one-to-many relationship between the primary **Firm** table and the related **Payment** table. Select the referential integrity option and both cascade options for the relationship.

3. Create a select query based on the **Firm** and **Payment** tables. Display the fields Firm# (from the **Firm** table), FirmName, AmtPaid, and DatePaid, in that order. Sort in descending order based on the AmtPaid field values. Select only those records whose AmtPaid is greater than 2500. Save the query as **Large Payments**, and then run the query. Print the datasheet and then close the query.

4. For all payments on 06/01/2001, display the Payment#, AmtPaid, DatePaid, and FirmName fields. Save the query as **June 1 Payments**, and then run the query. Switch to Design view, modify the query so that the DatePaid values do not appear in the query results, and then save the modified query. Run the query, print the query results, and then close the query.

Explore ▶ 5. For all firms that have Olivia Tyler as a PLUS account representative, display the FirmName, FirmContact, AmtPaid, and DatePaid fields. Save the query as **Tyler Accounts**, run the query, print the query results, and then close the query.

6. For all payments made on 06/10/2001 or 06/11/2001, display the fields DatePaid, AmtPaid, FirmName, and Firm# (from the **Firm** table). Display the results in ascending order by DatePaid and then in descending order by AmtPaid. Save the query as **Selected Dates**, run the query, print the query datasheet, and then close the query.

Explore ▶ 7. Use the **Payment** table to display the highest, lowest, total, average, and count of the AmtPaid field for all payments. Then do the following:
   a. Specify column names of HighestPayment, LowestPayment, TotalPayments, AveragePayment, and #Payments. Save the query as **Payment Statistics**, and then run the query. Resize all datasheet columns to their best fit, save the query, and then print the query results.
   b. Change the query to display the same statistics grouped by DatePaid. Save the query as **Payment Statistics By Date**, run the query, and then print the query results.
   c. Change the **Payment Statistics By Date** query to display the same statistics by DatePaid, then by Deposit#. Save the query as **Payment Statistics By Date By Deposit**, run the query, print the query results using landscape orientation, and then save and close the query.

8. Close the **Payments** database, and then exit Access.

Case 3. Best Friends   Noah and Sheila Warnick want to find specific information about the walk-a-thons they conduct for Best Friends. You'll help them find the information in the **Walks** database by completing the following:

1. Make sure your Data Disk is in the disk drive, start Access, and then open the **Walks** database located in the Cases folder on your Data Disk.

2. Define a one-to-many relationship between the primary **Walker** table and the related **Pledge** table. Select the referential integrity option and both cascade options for the relationship.

3. For all walkers with a PledgeAmt field value of greater than 30, display the WalkerID, LastName, PledgeNo, and PledgeAmt fields. Sort the query in ascending order by PledgeAmt. Save the query as **Large Pledges**, run the query, print the query datasheet, and then close the query.

4. For all walkers who pledged less than $15 or who pledged $5 per mile, display the Pledger, PledgeAmt, PerMile, LastName, FirstName, and Distance fields. Save the query as **Pledged Or Per Mile**, run the query, and then print the query datasheet. Change the query to select all walkers who pledged less than $15 and who pledged $5 per mile. Save the query as **Pledged And Per Mile**, and then run the query. Describe the results. Close the query.

Explore ▶ 5. For all pledges, display the WalkerID, Pledger, Distance, PerMile, and PledgeAmt fields. Save the query as **Difference**. Create a calculated field named CalcPledgeAmt that displays the results of multiplying the Distance and PerMile fields; then save the query. Create a second calculated field named Difference that displays the results of subtracting the CalcPledgeAmt field from the PledgeAmt field. Format the calculated fields as fixed. (*Hint*: Choose the Properties option on the shortcut menu for the selected field.) Display the results in ascending order by PledgeAmt. Save the modified query, and then run the query. Resize all datasheet columns to their best fit, print the query results, and then save and close the query.

6. Use the **Pledge** table to display the total, average, and count of the PledgeAmt field for all pledges. Then do the following:

    a. Specify column names of TotalPledge, AveragePledge, and #Pledges.

Explore

    b. Change properties so that the values in the TotalPledge and AveragePledge columns display two decimal places and the fixed format. (*Hint*: Choose the Properties option on the shortcut menu for the selected field.)

    c. Save the query as **Pledge Statistics**, run the query, resize all datasheet columns to their best fit, and then print the query datasheet. Save the query.

Explore

    d. Change the query to display the sum, average, and count of the PledgeAmt field for all pledges by LastName. (*Hint*: Use the Show Table button on the Query Design toolbar to add the **Walker** table to the query.) Save the query as **Pledge Statistics By Walker**, run the query, print the query datasheet, and then close the query.

7. Close the **Walks** database, and then exit Access.

Case 4. Lopez Lexus Dealerships   Maria and Hector Lopez want to analyze data about the cars and different locations for their Lexus dealerships. Help them query the **Lexus** database by completing the following:

1. Make sure your Data Disk is in the disk drive, start Access, and then open the **Lexus** database located in the Cases folder on your Data Disk.

2. Define a one-to-many relationship between the primary **Locations** table and the related **Cars** table. Select the referential integrity option and both cascade options for the relationship.

3. For all vehicles, display the Model, Class, Year, LocationCode, and SellingPrice fields. Save the query as **Car Info**, and then run the query. Resize all datasheet columns to their best fit. In Datasheet view, sort the query results in descending order by the SellingPrice field. Print the query datasheet, and then save and close the query.

4. For all vehicles manufactured in 2000, display the Model, Year, Cost, SellingPrice, and LocationName fields. Sort the query in ascending order by Cost. Save the query as **2000 Cars**, and then run the query. Modify the query to remove the display of the Year field values from the query results. Save the modified query, run the query, print the query datasheet, and then close the query.

Explore

5. For all vehicles located in Laredo or with a transmission of M5, display the Model, Year, Cost, SellingPrice, Transmission, LocationCode, and LocationName fields. Save the query as **Location Or Trans**, run the query, and then print the query datasheet using landscape orientation. Change the query to select all vehicles located in Laredo and with a transmission of M5. Save the query as **Location And Trans**, run the query, print the query datasheet in landscape orientation, and then close the query.

6. For all vehicles, display the Model, Class, Year, Cost, and SellingPrice fields. Save the query as **Profit**. Then create a calculated field named Profit that displays the difference between the vehicle's selling price and cost. Display the results in descending order by Profit. Save the query, run the query, print the query datasheet, and then close the query.

Explore

7. Use the **Cars** table to determine the total cost, average cost, total selling price, and average selling price of all vehicles. Use the Index tab in online Help to look up the word "caption"; then click the topic "Change a field name in a query." Read the displayed information, and then click and read the subtopic "Display new field names by changing the Caption property." Close the Help window. Set the Caption property of the four fields to Total Cost, Average Cost, Total Selling Price, and Average Selling Price, respectively. Save the query as **Car Statistics**, run the query, resize all datasheet columns to their best fit, print the query datasheet, and then save the query again. Revise the query

to show the car statistics grouped by LocationName. (*Hint*: Use the Show Table button on the Query Design toolbar to display the Show Table dialog box.) Set the Caption property of the LocationName field to Location. Save the revised query as **Car Statistics By Location**, run the query, print the query datasheet, and then close the query.

Explore ▶ 8. Use the Answer Wizard to ask the following question: "How do I create a Top Values query?" Click the topic "Display only the highest or lowest values in the query's results." Read the displayed information, and then close the Help window. Open the **Profit** query in Design view, and then modify the query to display only the top five values for the Profit field. Save the query as **Top Profit**, run the query, print the query datasheet, and then close the query.

9. Close the **Lexus** database, and then exit Access.

INTERNET ASSIGNMENTS

The purpose of the Internet Assignments is to challenge you to find information on the Internet that you can use to create effective documents. The actual assignments are updated and maintained on the Course Technology Web site. Log on to the Internet and use your Web browser to go to the Student Online Companion to accompany this text at **www.course.com/NewPerspectives/office2000**. Click the Access link, and then click the link for Tutorial 3.

QUICK CHECK ANSWERS

Session 3.1

1. a general query in which you specify the fields and records you want Access to select
2. The field list contains the table name at the top of the list box and the table's fields listed in the order in which they appear in the table; the design grid displays columns that contain specifications about a field you will use in the query.
3. A table datasheet and a query datasheet look the same, appearing in Datasheet view, and can be used to update data in a database. A table datasheet shows the permanent data in a table, whereas a query datasheet is temporary and its contents are based on the criteria you establish in the design grid.
4. primary table; related table
5. referential integrity
6. oldest to most recent date
7. when you want to perform different types of sorts (both ascending and descending, for example) on multiple fields, and when you want to sort on multiple fields that are nonadjacent or in the wrong order, but you do not want to rearrange the columns in the query datasheet to accomplish the sort
8. filter

Session 3.2

1. condition
2. in the same Criteria row; in different Criteria rows
3. expression
4. A calculated field appears in a query datasheet but does not exist in a database, as does a table field.
5. a function that performs an arithmetic operation on selected records in a database
6. Group By

In this tutorial you will:

- Create a form using the Form Wizard

- Change a form's AutoFormat

- Navigate a form and find data using a form

- Preview and print selected form records

- Maintain table data using a form

- Create a form with a main form and a subform

- Create a report using the Report Wizard

- Insert a picture in a report

- Preview and print a report

CREATING FORMS AND REPORTS

Creating an Order Data Form, a Customer Orders Form, and a Customers and Orders Report

CASE

Valle Coffee

Barbara Hennessey wants to continue to enhance the Restaurant database to make it easier for her office staff members and other Valle Coffee employees to find and maintain data. In particular, she wants the database to include a form for the Order table, similar to the Customer Data form, which is based on the Customer table. She also wants a form that shows data from both the Customer and Order tables at the same time, so that all the order information for each customer appears with the corresponding customer data, giving a complete picture of the restaurant customers and their orders.

In addition, Kim Carpenter would like a report showing customer and order data, so that her marketing staff members will have printed output to refer to when completing market analyses and planning strategies for selling to restaurant customers. She wants the information to be formatted attractively, perhaps including the Valle Coffee cup logo on the report for visual interest.

SESSION 4.1

In this session, you will create a form using the Form Wizard, change a form's AutoFormat, navigate a form, find data using a form, preview and print selected form records, and maintain table data using a form.

Creating a Form Using the Form Wizard

As you learned in Tutorial 1, a form is an object you use to maintain, view, and print records in a database. In Access, you can design your own forms or use Form Wizards to create them for you automatically.

Barbara asks you to create a new form that her staff can use to view and maintain data in the Order table. In Tutorial 1, you used the AutoForm Wizard—which creates a form automatically, using all the fields in the selected table or query—to create the Customer Data form. To create the form for the Order table, you'll use the Form Wizard. The **Form Wizard** allows you to choose some or all of the fields in the selected table or query, choose fields from other tables and queries, and display the chosen fields in any order on the form. You can also choose a style for the form.

> ### To open the Restaurant database and activate the Form Wizard:
>
> 1. Place your Data Disk in the appropriate disk drive.
>
> 2. Start Access and open the Restaurant database located in the Tutorial folder on your Data Disk. The Restaurant database is displayed in the Access window.
>
> 3. Click **Forms** in the Objects bar of the Database window. The Forms list includes the Customer Data form you created in Tutorial 1.
>
> 4. Click the **New** button in the Database window. The New Form dialog box opens.
>
> 5. Click **Form Wizard**, click the list arrow for choosing a table or query, click **Order** to select this table as the source for the form, and then click the **OK** button. The first Form Wizard dialog box opens. See Figure 4-1.

Figure 4-1	FIRST FORM WIZARD DIALOG BOX

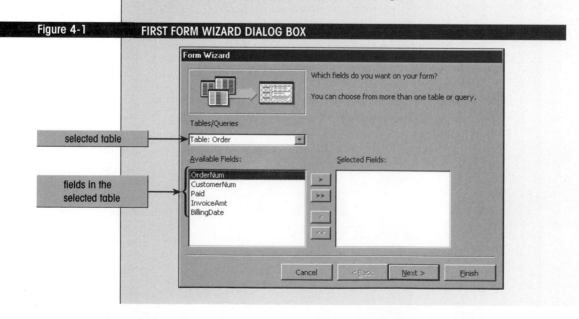

selected table

fields in the selected table

Barbara wants the form to display all the fields in the Order table, but in a different order. She would like the Paid field to appear at the bottom of the form so that it stands out more, making it easier to determine if an order has been paid.

To finish creating the form using the Form Wizard:

1. Click **OrderNum** in the Available Fields list box (if necessary), and then click the ▸ button to move the field to the Selected Fields list box.

2. Repeat Step 1 to select the **CustomerNum**, **InvoiceAmt**, **BillingDate**, and **Paid** fields, in that order.

3. Click the **Next** button to display the second Form Wizard dialog box, in which you select a layout for the form. See Figure 4-2.

Figure 4-2	CHOOSING A LAYOUT FOR THE FORM

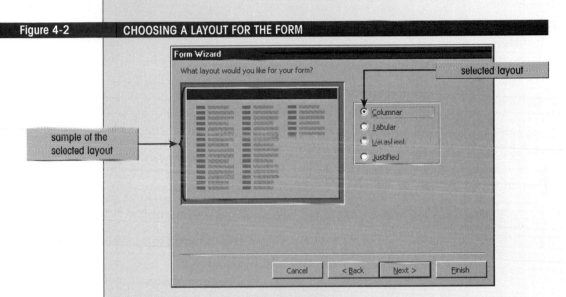

The layout choices are columnar, tabular, datasheet, and justified. A sample of the selected layout appears on the left side of the dialog box.

4. Click each of the option buttons and review the corresponding sample layout.

The tabular and datasheet layouts display the fields from multiple records at one time, whereas the columnar and justified layouts display the fields from one record at a time. Barbara thinks the columnar layout is the appropriate arrangement for displaying and updating data in the table, so you'll choose this layout.

5. Click the **Columnar** option button (if necessary), and then click the **Next** button. Access displays the third Form Wizard dialog box, in which you choose a style for the form. See Figure 4-3.

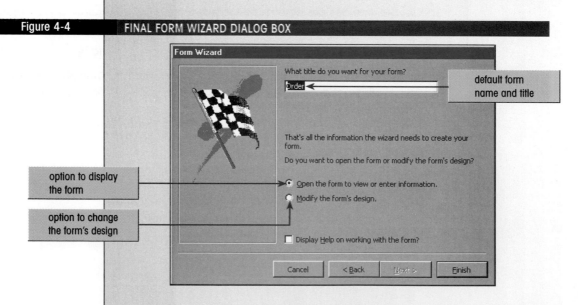

Figure 4-3 | CHOOSING A STYLE FOR THE FORM

Form Wizard

What style would you like?

sample of the selected style

Blends
Blueprint
Expedition
Industrial
International
Ricepaper
SandStone
Standard
Stone
Sumi Painting

Form Wizard styles

Label   Data

Cancel   < Back   Next >   Finish

A sample of the selected style appears in the box on the left. If you choose a style, which is called an **AutoFormat**, and decide you'd prefer a different one after the form is created, you can change it.

TROUBLE? Don't worry if a different form style is selected in your dialog box than the one shown in Figure 4-3. The dialog box displays the most recently used style, which might be different on your computer.

6. Click each of the styles and review the corresponding sample.

Barbara likes the Expedition style and asks you to use it for the form.

7. Click **Expedition** and then click the **Next** button. Access displays the final Form Wizard dialog box and shows the Order table's name as the default form name; "Order" is also the default title that will appear in the form's title bar. See Figure 4-4.

Figure 4-4 | FINAL FORM WIZARD DIALOG BOX

Form Wizard

What title do you want for your form?

Order

default form name and title

That's all the information the wizard needs to create your form.

Do you want to open the form or modify the form's design?

option to display the form

● Open the form to view or enter information.

option to change the form's design

○ Modify the form's design.

□ Display Help on working with the form?

Cancel   < Back   Next >   Finish

You'll use Order Data as the form name and, because you don't need to change the form's design at this point, you'll display the form.

8. Position the insertion point to the right of Order in the text box, press the **spacebar**, type **Data**, and then click the **Finish** button. The completed form is displayed in Form view. See Figure 4-5.

| Figure 4-5 | COMPLETED FORM FOR THE ORDER TABLE |

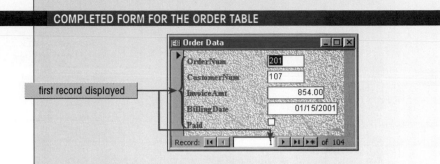

first record displayed

TROUBLE? If the navigation bar at the bottom of your Form window does not display all of the navigation buttons or the "of 104" text, drag the right edge of the Form window to the right so that all of the navigation bar is visible.

After viewing the form, Barbara decides that she doesn't like the form's style—the background makes the field names a bit difficult to read. She asks you to change the form's style.

Changing a Form's AutoFormat

You can change a form's appearance by choosing a different AutoFormat for the form. As you learned when you created the Order Data form, an **AutoFormat** is a predefined style for a form (or report). The AutoFormats available for a form are the ones you saw when you selected the form's style using the Form Wizard. To change an AutoFormat, you must switch to Design view.

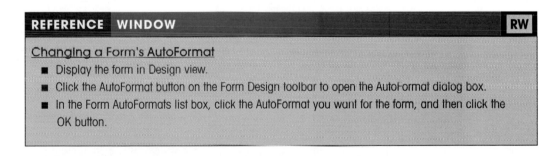

REFERENCE WINDOW   **RW**

Changing a Form's AutoFormat
- Display the form in Design view.
- Click the AutoFormat button on the Form Design toolbar to open the AutoFormat dialog box.
- In the Form AutoFormats list box, click the AutoFormat you want for the form, and then click the OK button.

To change the AutoFormat for the Order Data form:

1. Click the **View** button for Design view 🔳 on the Form View toolbar. The form is displayed in Design view. See Figure 4-6.

Figure 4-6   FORM DISPLAYED IN DESIGN VIEW

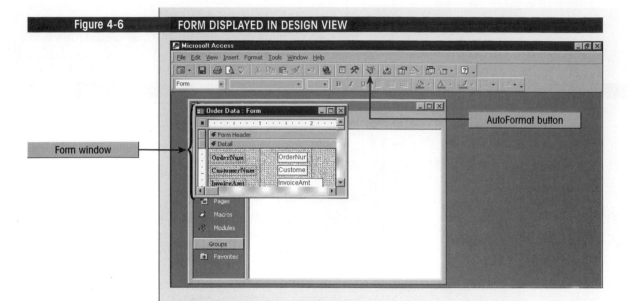

TROUBLE? If your screen displays any window other than those shown in Figure 4-6, click the Close button ☒ on the window's title bar to close it.

You use Design view to modify an existing form or to create a form from scratch. In this case, you need to change the AutoFormat for the Order Data form.

2. Click the **AutoFormat** button 🗃 on the Form Design toolbar. The AutoFormat dialog box opens.

3. Click the **Options** button to display the AutoFormat options. See Figure 4-7.

Figure 4-7   AUTOFORMAT DIALOG BOX

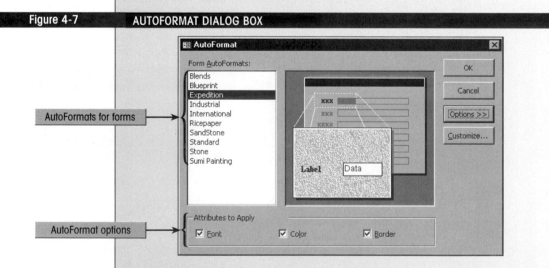

A sample of the selected AutoFormat appears to the right of the Form AutoFormats list box. The options at the bottom of the dialog box allow you to apply the selected AutoFormat or just its font, color, or border.

Barbara decides that she prefers the Standard AutoFormat, because its field names and field values are easy to read.

4. Click **Standard** in the Form AutoFormats list box, and then click the **OK** button. The AutoFormat dialog box closes, the Standard AutoFormat is applied to the form, and the Form window in Design view becomes the active window.

5. Click the **View** button for Form view 📧 on the Form Design toolbar. The form is displayed in Form view with the new AutoFormat. See Figure 4-8.

| Figure 4-8 | FORM DISPLAYED WITH THE NEW AUTOFORMAT |

You have finished modifying the format of the form and can now save it.

6. Click the **Save** button 🖫 on the Form View toolbar to save the modified form.

Barbara wants to view some data in the Order table, using the form. To view data, you need to navigate through the form.

Navigating a Form

To maintain and view data using a form, you must know how to move from field to field and from record to record. The mouse movement, selection, and placement techniques to navigate a form are the same techniques you've used to navigate a table datasheet and the Customer Data form you created in Tutorial 1. Also, the navigation mode and editing mode keystroke techniques are the same as those you used previously for datasheets (see Figure 2-31).

To navigate through the form:

1. Press the **Tab** key to move to the CustomerNum field value, and then press the **End** key to move to the Paid field. Because the Paid field is a yes/no field, its value is not highlighted; instead, a dashed box appears around the field name to indicate that it is the current field.

2. Press the **Home** key to move back to the OrderNum field value. The first record in the Order table still appears in the form.

3. Press **Ctrl + End** to move to the Paid field in record 104, which is the last record in the table. The record number for the current record appears between the navigation buttons at the bottom of the form.

4. Click the **Previous Record** navigation button ◀ to move to the Paid field in record 103.

5. Press the ↑ key twice to move to the InvoiceAmt field value in record 103.

6. Position the insertion point between the numbers "2" and "6" in the InvoiceAmt field value to switch to editing mode, press the **Home** key to move the insertion point to the beginning of the field value, and then press the **End** key to move the insertion point to the end of the field value.

7. Click the **First Record** navigation button [◄] to move to the InvoiceAmt field value in the first record. The entire field value is highlighted because you have switched from editing mode to navigation mode.

8. Click the **Next Record** navigation button [►] to move to the InvoiceAmt field value in record 2, which is the next record.

Barbara asks you to display the records for Jean's Country Restaurant, whose customer number is 407, because she wants to review the orders for this customer.

Finding Data Using a Form

The **Find** command allows you to search the data in a form and to display only those records you want to view. You choose a field to serve as the basis for the search by making that field the current field; then you enter the value you want Access to match in the Find and Replace dialog box. You can use the Find command for a form or datasheet, and you can activate the command from the Edit menu or by clicking the toolbar Find button.

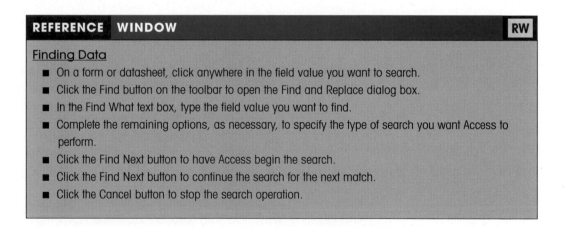

REFERENCE WINDOW   RW

Finding Data
- On a form or datasheet, click anywhere in the field value you want to search.
- Click the Find button on the toolbar to open the Find and Replace dialog box.
- In the Find What text box, type the field value you want to find.
- Complete the remaining options, as necessary, to specify the type of search you want Access to perform.
- Click the Find Next button to have Access begin the search.
- Click the Find Next button to continue the search for the next match.
- Click the Cancel button to stop the search operation.

You need to find all records in the Order table for Jean's Country Restaurant, whose customer number is 407.

To find the records using the Order Data form:

1. Position the insertion point in the CustomerNum field value box. This is the field for which you will find matching values.

2. Click the **Find** button [🔍] on the Form View toolbar. The Find and Replace dialog box opens. Note that the Look In list box shows the name of the field that Access will search (in this case, the CustomerNum field), and the Match list box indicates that Access will find values that match the entire entry in the field. You could choose to match only part of a field value.

3. If the Find and Replace dialog box covers any part of the form, move the dialog box by dragging its title bar. Move the Order Data form window as well, if necessary. See Figure 4-9.

| Figure 4-9 | FIND AND REPLACE DIALOG BOX |

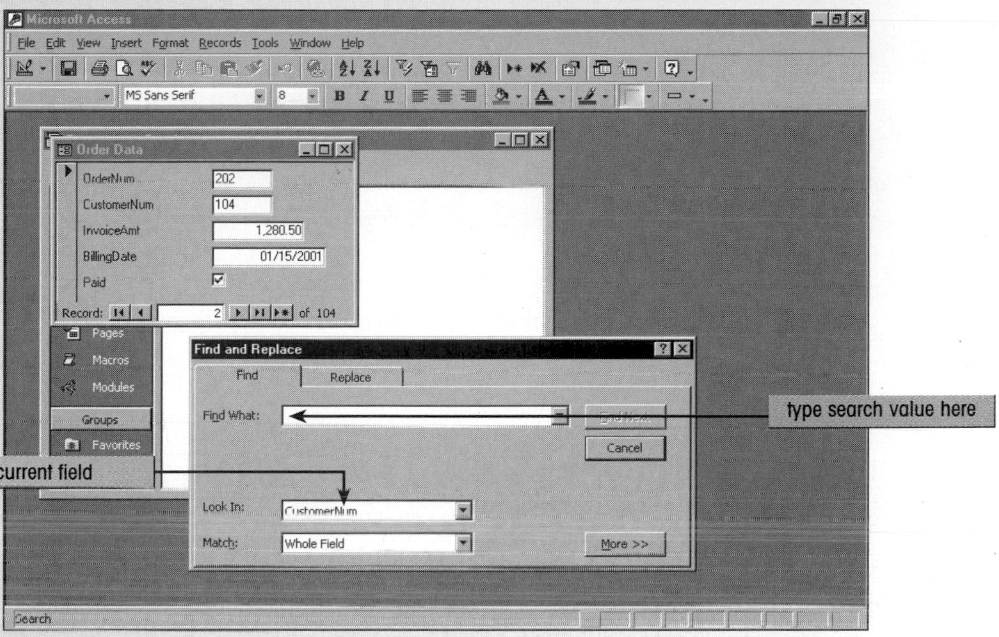

4. In the Find What text box, type **407** and then click the **Find Next** button. Access displays record 14, which is the first record for CustomerNum 407.

5. Click the **Find Next** button. Access displays record 51, which is the second record for CustomerNum 407.

6. Click the **Find Next** button. Access displays record 88, which is the third record for CustomerNum 407.

7. Click the **Find Next** button. Access displays a dialog box informing you that the search is finished.

8. Click the **OK** button to close the dialog box.

The search value you enter can be an exact value, such as the customer number 407 you just entered, or it can include wildcard characters. A **wildcard character** is a placeholder you use when you know only part of a value or when you want to start or end with a specific character or match a certain pattern. Figure 4-10 shows the wildcard characters you can use when finding data.

Figure 4-10	WILDCARD CHARACTERS	
WILDCARD CHARACTER	**PURPOSE**	**EXAMPLE**
*	Match any number of characters. It can be used as the first and/or last character in the character string.	th* finds *the, that, this, therefore,* and so on
?	Match any single alphabetic character.	a?t finds *act, aft, ant,* and *art*
[ ]	Match any single character within the brackets.	a[fr]t finds *aft* and *art* but not *act* and *ant*
!	Match any character not within brackets.	a[!fr]t finds *act* and *ant* but not *aft* and *art*
-	Match any one of a range of characters. The range must be in ascending order (a to z, not z to a).	a[d-p]t finds *aft* and *ant* but not *act* and *art*
#	Match any single numeric character.	#72 finds *072, 172, 272, 372,* and so on

To check if their orders have been paid, Barbara wants to view the order records for two customers: Cheshire Restaurant (CustomerNum 515) and Around the Clock Restaurant (CustomerNum 597). You'll use the * wildcard character to search for these customers' orders.

To find the records using the * wildcard character:

1. Double-click **407** in the Find What text box to select the entire value, and then type **5***.

   Access will match any field value in the CustomerNum field that starts with the digit 5.

2. Click the **Find Next** button. Access displays record 16, which is the first record for CustomerNum 515. Note that the Paid field value is checked, indicating that this order has been paid.

3. Click the **Find Next** button. Access displays record 17, which is the first record for CustomerNum 597.

4. Click the **Find Next** button. Access displays record 39, which is the second record for CustomerNum 597.

5. Click the **Find Next** button. Access displays record 68, which is the second record for CustomerNum 515.

6. Click the **Find Next** button. Access displays record 82, which is the third record for CustomerNum 515.

7. Click the **Find Next** button. Access displays a dialog box informing you that the search is finished.

8. Click the **OK** button to close the dialog box.

9. Click the **Cancel** button to close the Find and Replace dialog box.

All five orders have been paid, but Barbara wants to make sure Valle Coffee has a record of payment for order number 375. She asks you to print the data displayed on the form for record 82, which is for order number 375, so she can ask a staff member to look for the payment record for this order.

Previewing and Printing Selected Form Records

Access prints as many form records as can fit on a printed page. If only part of a form record fits on the bottom of a page, the remainder of the record prints on the next page. Access allows you to print all pages or a range of pages. In addition, you can print the currently selected form record.

Before printing record 82, you'll preview the form record to see how it will look when printed.

To preview the form and print the data for record 82:

1. Make sure record 82 is the current record in the Order Data form.

2. Click the **Print Preview** button 🔍 on the Form View toolbar. The Print Preview window opens, showing the form records for the Order table in miniature.

3. Click the **Maximize** button 🔲 on the form's title bar.

4. Click the **Zoom** button 🔍 on the Print Preview toolbar, and then use the vertical scroll bar to view the contents of the window. See Figure 4-11.

| Figure 4-11 | PRINT PREVIEW WINDOW DISPLAYING FORM RECORDS |

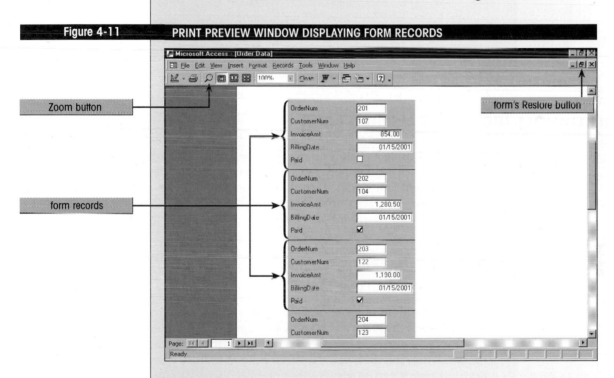

TROUBLE? The field labels in your form might be truncated so that all letters do not display correctly. This problem will not affect the steps; continue with Step 5.

Each record from the Order table appears in a separate form. Access places as many form records as will fit on each page.

5. Click the **Restore** button 🗗 on the Print Preview menu bar, and then click the **Close** button on the Print Preview toolbar to return to the table in Form view.

6. Click **File** on the menu bar, and then click **Print**. The Print dialog box opens.

7. Click the **Selected Record(s)** option button to print only the current form record (record 82).

8. Click the **OK** button to close the dialog box and to print the selected record.

Barbara has identified several updates she wants you to make to the Order table using the Order Data form, as shown in Figure 4-12.

Figure 4-12	UPDATES TO THE ORDER TABLE

Order Number	Update Action
319	Change InvoiceAmt to 1,175.00 Change Paid to Yes
392	Delete record
400	Add new record for CustomerNum 135, InvoiceAmt of 1,350.00, BillingDate of 03/15/2001, and Paid status of No

Maintaining Table Data Using a Form

Maintaining data using a form is often easier than using a datasheet, because you can concentrate on all the changes required to a single record at one time. You already know how to navigate a form and find specific records. Now you'll make the changes Barbara requested to the Order table, using the Order Data form.

First, you'll update the record for OrderNum 319.

To change the record using the Order Data form:

1. Make sure the Order Data form is displayed in Form view.

   The current record number appears between the sets of navigation buttons at the bottom of the form. If you know the number of the record you want to change, you can type the number and press the Enter key to go directly to the record. When she reviewed the order data to identify possible corrections, Barbara noted that 48 is the record number for order number 319.

2. Select the number **82** that appears between the navigation buttons, type **48**, and then press the **Enter** key. Record 48 (order number 319) is now the current record.

   You need to change the InvoiceAmt field value to 1,175.00 and the Paid field value to Yes for this record.

3. Position the insertion point between the numbers 9 and 5 in the InvoiceAmt field value, press the **Backspace** key, and then type **7**. Note that the pencil symbol appears in the top left of the form, indicating that the form is in editing mode.

4. Press the **Tab** key twice to move to the Paid field value, and then press the **spacebar** to insert a check mark in the check box. See Figure 4-13.

Figure 4-13	ORDER RECORD AFTER CHANGING FIELD VALUES

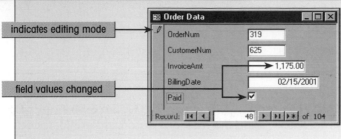

You have completed the changes for order number 319. Barbara's next update is to delete the record for order number 392. The customer who placed this order canceled it before the order was filled and processed.

To delete the record using the Order Data form:

1. Click anywhere in the OrderNum field value to make it the current field.

2. Click the **Find** button 🔍 on the Form View toolbar. The Find and Replace dialog box opens.

3. Type **392** in the Find What text box, click the **Find Next** button, and then click the **Cancel** button. The record for order number 392 is now the current record.

4. Click the **Delete Record** button 🗙 on the Form View toolbar. A dialog box opens, asking you to confirm the record deletion.

5. Click the **Yes** button. The dialog box closes, and the record for order number 392 is deleted from the table.

Barbara's final maintenance change is to add a record for a new order placed by Topview Restaurant.

To add the new record using the Order Data form:

1. Click the **New Record** button ▶* on the Form View toolbar. Record 104, the next record available for a new record, becomes the current record. All field value boxes are empty, and the insertion point is positioned at the beginning of the field value for OrderNum.

2. Refer to Figure 4-14 and enter the value shown for each field. Press the **Tab** key to move from field to field.

Figure 4-14   COMPLETED FORM FOR THE NEW RECORD

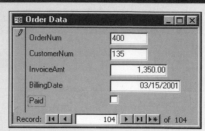

TROUBLE? Compare your screen with Figure 4-14. If any field value is wrong, correct it now, using the methods described earlier for editing field values.

3. After entering the value for BillingDate, press the **Tab** key twice (if necessary). Record 105, the next record available for a new record, becomes the current record, and the record for order number 400 is saved in the Order table.

You've completed Barbara's changes to the Order table, so you can close the Order Data form.

4. Click the **Close** button [X] on the form's title bar. The form closes and you return to the Database window. Notice that the Order Data form is listed in the Forms list box.

The Order Data form will enable Barbara and her staff to enter and maintain data easily in the Order table. In the next session, you'll create another form for working with data in both the Order and Customer tables at the same time. You'll also create a report showing data from both tables.

Session 4.1 QUICK CHECK

1. Describe the difference between creating a form using the AutoForm Wizard and creating a form using the Form Wizard.

2. What is an AutoFormat, and how do you change one for an existing form?

3. Which table record is displayed in a form when you press Ctrl + End while you are in navigation mode?

4. You can use the Find command to search for data in a form or _____.

5. Which wildcard character matches any single alphabetic character?

6. How many form records does Access print by default on a page?

SESSION 4.2

In this session, you will create a form with a main form and a subform, create a report using the Report Wizard, insert a picture in a report, and preview and print a report.

Barbara would like you to create a form so that she can view the data for each customer and all the orders for the customer at the same time. The type of form you need to create will include a main form and a subform.

Creating a Form with a Main Form and a Subform

To create a form based on two tables, you must first define a relationship between the two tables. In Tutorial 3, you defined a one-to-many relationship between the Customer (primary) and Order (related) tables, so you are ready to create the form based on both tables.

When you create a form containing data from two tables that have a one-to-many relationship, you actually create a main form for data from the primary table and a subform for data from the related table. Access uses the defined relationship between the tables to automatically join the tables through the common field that exists in both tables.

Barbara and her staff will use the form when contacting customers about the status of their order payments. Consequently, the main form will contain the customer number and name, owner name, and phone number; the subform will contain the order number, paid status, invoice amount, and billing date.

You'll use the Form Wizard to create the form.

To create the form using the Form Wizard:

1. If you took a break after the previous session, make sure that Access is running and the Restaurant database is open.

2. Make sure the Forms object is selected in the Database window, and then click the **New** button. The New Form dialog box opens.

   When creating a form based on two tables, you first choose the primary table and select the fields you want to include in the main form; then you choose the related table and select fields from it for the subform.

3. Click **Form Wizard**, click the list arrow for choosing a table or query, click **Customer** to select this table as the source for the main form, and then click the **OK** button. The first Form Wizard dialog box opens, in which you select fields in the order you want them to appear on the main form.

   Barbara wants the form to include only the CustomerNum, CustomerName, OwnerName, and Phone fields from the Customer table.

4. Click **CustomerNum** in the Available Fields list box (if necessary), and then click the [>] button to move the field to the Selected Fields list box.

5. Repeat Step 4 for the **CustomerName**, **OwnerName**, and **Phone** fields.

   The CustomerNum field will appear in the main form, so you do not have to include it in the subform. Otherwise, Barbara wants the subform to include all the fields from the Order table.

6. Click the **Tables/Queries** list arrow, and then click **Table: Order**. The fields from the Order table appear in the Available Fields list box. The quickest way to add the fields you want to include is to move all the fields to the Selected Fields list box, and then to remove the only field you don't want to include (CustomerNum).

7. Click the ⟩⟩ button to move all the fields from the Order table to the Selected Fields list box.

8. Click **Order.CustomerNum** in the Selected Fields list box, and then click the ⟨ button to move the field back to the Available Fields list box. Note that the table name (Order) is included in the field name to distinguish it from the same field (CustomerNum) in the Customer table.

9. Click the **Next** button. The next Form Wizard dialog box opens. See Figure 4-15.

Figure 4-15	CHOOSING A MAIN/SUBFORM FORMAT

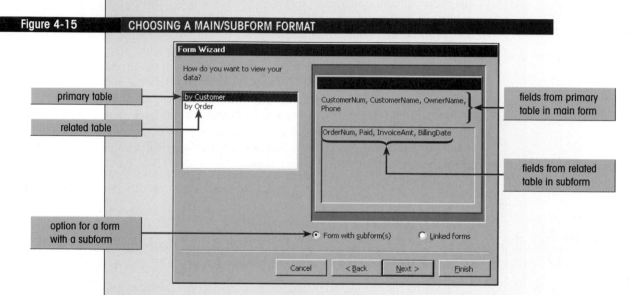

In this dialog box, the list box on the left shows the order in which you will view the selected data: first by data from the Customer table (primary table), then by data from the Order table (related table). The form will be displayed as shown in the right side of the dialog box, with the fields from the Customer table at the top in the main form, and the fields from the Order table at the bottom in the subform. The selected option button specifies a main form with a subform.

The default options shown in Figure 4-15 are correct for creating a form with Customer data in the main form and Order data in the subform.

To finish creating the form:

1. Click the **Next** button. The next Form Wizard dialog box opens, in which you choose the subform layout.

The tabular layout displays subform fields as a table, whereas the datasheet layout displays subform fields as a table datasheet. The layout choice is a matter of personal preference. You'll use the datasheet layout.

2. Click the **Datasheet** option button (if necessary), and then click the **Next** button. The next Form Wizard dialog box opens, in which you choose the form's style.

Barbara wants all forms to have the same style, so you will choose Standard, which is the same style you used to create the Order Data form earlier.

3. Click **Standard** (if necessary) and then click the **Next** button. The next Form Wizard dialog box opens, in which you choose names for the main form and the subform.

You will use Customer Orders as the main form name and Order Subform as the subform name.

4. Position the insertion point to the right of the last letter in the Form text box, press the **spacebar**, and then type **Orders**. The main form name is now Customer Orders. Note that the default subform name, Order Subform, is the name you want, so you don't need to change it.

You have answered all the Form Wizard questions.

5. Click the **Finish** button. After a few moments, the completed form is displayed in Form view.

Depending on your monitor's resolution, one or more of the columns in the subform might not be wide enough to display the field names entirely. If so, you need to resize the columns to their best fit.

6. Double-click the pointer ✛ at the right edge of each column in the subform. The columns are resized to their best fit and all field names are fully displayed. See Figure 4-16.

Figure 4-16   COMPLETED FORM

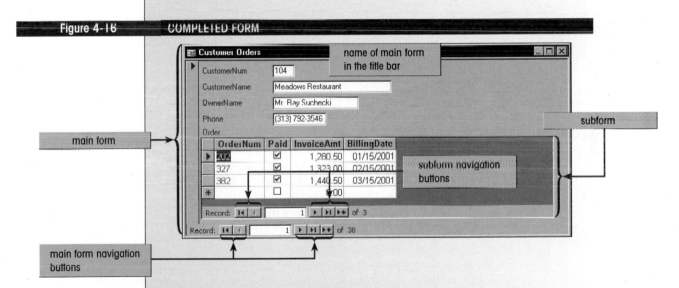

In the main form, Access displays the fields from the first record in the Customer table in columnar format. The records in the main form appear in primary key sequence by customer number. Customer 104 has three related records in the Order table; these records are shown in the subform in a datasheet format. The form shows that Meadows Restaurant has placed three orders with Valle Coffee, and each order has been paid.

Two sets of navigation buttons appear near the bottom of the form. You use the top set of navigation buttons to select records from the related table in the subform, and the bottom set to select records from the primary table in the main form.

You'll use the navigation buttons to view different records.

To navigate to different main form and subform records:

1. Click the **Last Record** navigation button ▶| in the main form. Record 38 in the Customer table for Embers Restaurant becomes the current record in the main form. The subform shows that this customer has placed three orders with Valle Coffee, all of which are unpaid.

2. Click the **Last Record** navigation button ▶| in the subform. Record 3 in the Order table becomes the current record in the subform.

3. Click the **Previous Record** navigation button ◀ in the main form. Record 37 in the Customer table for The Empire becomes the current record in the main form. This customer has placed two orders, both of which are unpaid.

   You have finished your work with the form, so you can close it.

4. Click the **Close** button ☒ on the form title bar. The form closes, and you return to the Database window. Notice that both the main form, Customer Orders, and the subform, Order Subform, appear in the Forms list box.

Kim would like a report showing data from both the Customer and Order tables so that all the pertinent information about restaurant customers and their orders is available in one place.

Creating a Report Using the Report Wizard

As you learned in Tutorial 1, a report is a formatted hardcopy of the contents of one or more tables in a database. In Access, you can create your own reports or use the Report Wizard to create them for you. Like the Form Wizard, the **Report Wizard** asks you a series of questions and then creates a report based on your answers. Whether you use the Report Wizard or design your own report, you can change the report's design after you create it.

Kim wants you to create a report that includes selected customer data from the Customer table and all the orders from the Order table for each customer. Kim has sketched a design of the report she wants (Figure 4-17). Like the Customer Orders form you just created, which includes a main form and a subform, the report will be based on both tables, which are joined in a one-to-many relationship through the common field of CustomerNum. As shown in the sketch in Figure 4-17, the selected customer data from the primary Customer table includes the customer number, name, city, state, owner name, and phone. Below the data for each customer, the report will include the order number, paid status, invoice amount, and billing date from the related Order table. The set of field values for each order is called a **detail record**.

| Figure 4-17 | REPORT SKETCH FOR THE CUSTOMERS AND ORDERS REPORT |

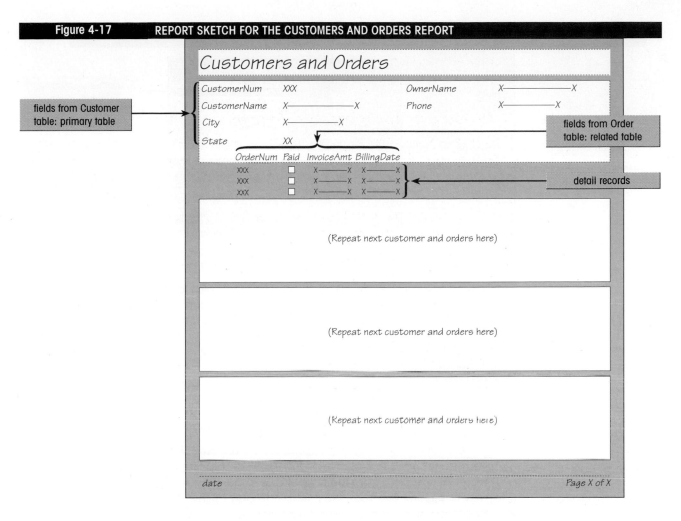

You'll use the Report Wizard to create the report according to the design in Kim's sketch.

To start the Report Wizard and select the fields to include in the report:

1. Click **Reports** in the Objects bar of the Database window to display the Reports list box. You have not yet created and saved any reports.

2. Click the **New** button in the Database window. The New Report dialog box opens.

   Although the data for the report exists in two tables (Customer and Order), you can choose only one table or query to be the data source for the report in the New Report dialog box. However, in the Report Wizard dialog boxes you can include data from other tables. You will select the primary Customer table in the New Report dialog box.

3. Click **Report Wizard**, click the list arrow for choosing a table or query, and then click **Customer**. See Figure 4-18.

Figure 4-18   COMPLETED NEW REPORT DIALOG BOX

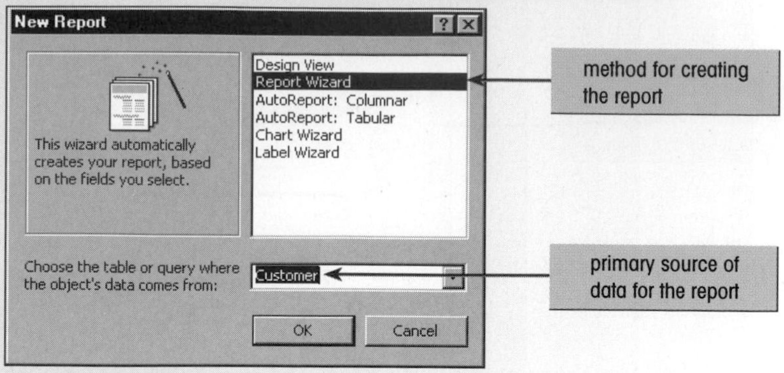

New Report

This wizard automatically creates your report, based on the fields you select.

Design View
Report Wizard
AutoReport: Columnar
AutoReport: Tabular
Chart Wizard
Label Wizard

method for creating the report

Choose the table or query where the object's data comes from:

Customer

primary source of data for the report

OK   Cancel

4. Click the **OK** button. The first Report Wizard dialog box opens.

   In the first Report Wizard dialog box, you select fields in the order you want them to appear on the report. Kim wants the CustomerNum, CustomerName, City, State, OwnerName, and Phone fields from the Customer table to appear on the report.

5. Click **CustomerNum** in the Available Fields list box (if necessary), and then click the ⟩ button. The field moves to the Selected Fields list box.

6. Repeat Step 5 for **CustomerName, City, State, OwnerName**, and **Phone**.

7. Click the **Tables/Queries** list arrow, and then click **Table: Order**. The fields from the Order table appear in the Available Fields list box.

   The CustomerNum field will appear on the report with the customer data, so you do not have to include it in the detail records for each order. Otherwise, Kim wants all the fields from the Order table to be included in the report. The easiest way to include the necessary fields is to add all the Order table fields to the Selected Fields list box, and then to remove the only field you don't want to include—CustomerNum.

8. Click the ⟩⟩ button to move all the fields from the Available Fields list box to the Selected Fields list box.

9. Click **Order.CustomerNum** in the Selected Fields list box, click the ⟨ button to move the selected field back to the Available Fields list box, and then click the **Next** button. The second Report Wizard dialog box opens. See Figure 4-19.

Figure 4-19   **CHOOSING A GROUPED OR UNGROUPED REPORT**

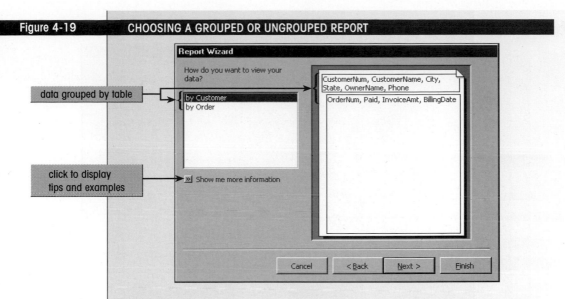

You can choose to arrange the selected data grouped by table, which is the default, or ungrouped. For a grouped report, the data from a record in the primary table appears as a group, followed by the joined records from the related table. For the report you are creating, data from a record in the Customer table appears in a group, followed by the records for the customer from the Order table. An example of an ungrouped report would be a report of records from the Customer and Order tables in order by OrderNum. Each order and its associated customer data would appear together; the data would not be grouped by table.

You can display tips and examples for the choices in the Report Wizard dialog box by clicking the "Show me more information" button [»].

To display tips about the options in the Report Wizard dialog box:

1. Click the [»] button. The Report Wizard Tips dialog box opens. Read the displayed information in the dialog box.

   You can display examples of different grouping methods by clicking the [»] button ("Show me examples").

2. Click the [»] button. The Report Wizard Examples dialog box opens. See Figure 4-20.

Figure 4-20   REPORT WIZARD EXAMPLES DIALOG BOX

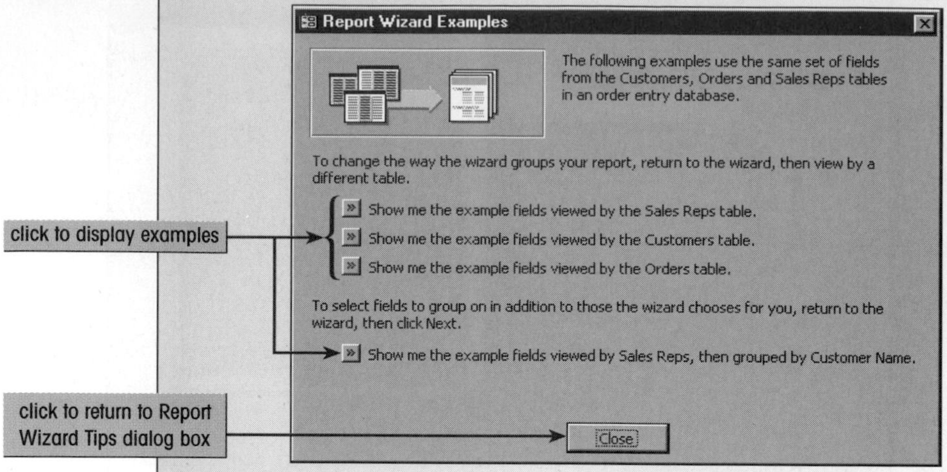

You can display examples of different grouping methods by clicking the ⟫ buttons.

3. Click each ⟫ button in turn, review the displayed example, and then click the **Close** button to return to the Report Wizard Examples dialog box.

4. Click the **Close** button to return to the Report Wizard Tips dialog box, and then click the **Close** button to return to the second Report Wizard dialog box.

The default options shown on your screen are correct for the report Kim wants, so you can continue responding to the Report Wizard questions.

To finish creating the report using the Report Wizard:

1. Click the **Next** button. The next Report Wizard dialog box opens, in which you choose additional grouping levels.

Two grouping levels are shown: one for a customer's data, and the other for a customer's orders. Grouping levels are useful for reports with multiple levels, such as those containing monthly, quarterly, and annual totals, or those containing city and country groups. Kim's report contains no further grouping levels, so you can accept the default options.

2. Click the **Next** button. The next Report Wizard dialog box opens, in which you choose the sort order for the detail records. See Figure 4-21.

Figure 4-21   **CHOOSING THE SORT ORDER FOR DETAIL RECORDS**

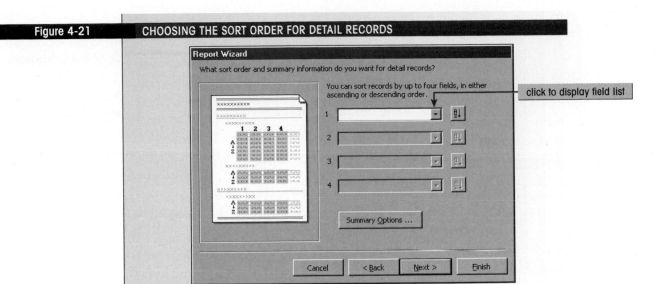

The records from the Order table for a customer represent the detail records for Kim's report. She wants these records to appear in increasing, or ascending, order by the value in the OrderNum field.

3. Click the **1** list arrow, click **OrderNum**, and then click the **Next** button. The next Report Wizard dialog box opens, in which you choose a layout and page orientation for the report. See Figure 4-22.

Figure 4-22   **CHOOSING THE REPORT LAYOUT AND PAGE ORIENTATION**

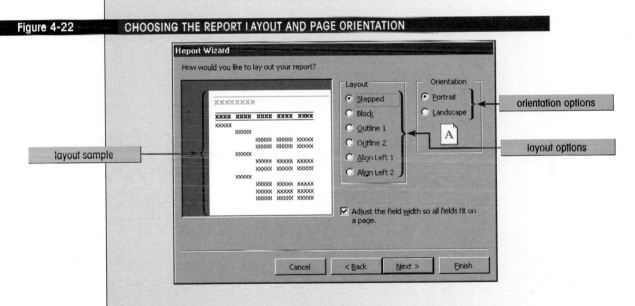

A sample of each layout appears in the box on the left.

4. Click each layout option and examine each sample that appears. You'll use the Outline 2 layout option because it resembles the layout shown in Kim's sketch of the report.

5. Click the **Outline 2** option button, and then click the **Next** button. The next Report Wizard dialog box opens, in which you choose a style for the report.

A sample of the selected style, or AutoFormat, appears in the box on the left. You can always choose a different AutoFormat after you create the report, just as you can when creating a form. Kim likes the appearance of the Corporate AutoFormat, so you'll choose this one for your report.

6. Click **Corporate** (if necessary) and then click the **Next** button. The last Report Wizard dialog box opens, in which you choose a report name, which also serves as the printed title on the report.

According to Kim's sketch, the report title you need to specify is "Customers and Orders."

7. Type **Customers and Orders** and then click the **Finish** button. The Report Wizard creates the report based on your answers and saves it as an object in your database. Then Access opens the Customers and Orders report in Print Preview.

To view the report better, you need to maximize the report window.

8. Click the **Maximize** button 🗖 on the Customers and Orders title bar.

To view the entire page, you need to change the Zoom setting.

9. Click the **Zoom** list arrow on the Print Preview toolbar, and then click **Fit**. The first page of the report is displayed in Print Preview. See Figure 4-23.

| Figure 4-23 | REPORT DISPLAYED IN PRINT PREVIEW |

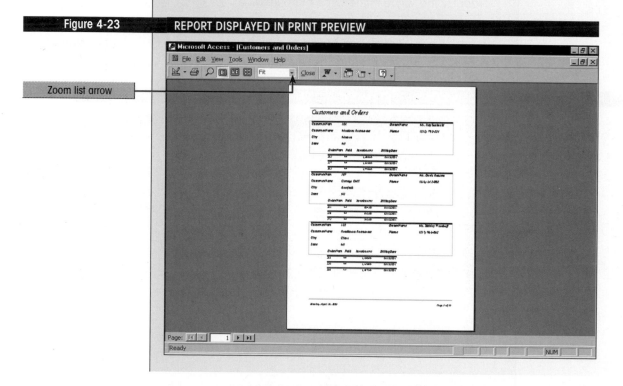

Zoom list arrow

When a report is displayed in Print Preview, you can use the pointer to toggle between a full-page display and a close-up display of the report. Kim asks you to check the report to see if any adjustments need to be made. To do so, you need to view a close-up display of the report.

To view a close-up display of the report and make any necessary corrections:

1. Click the pointer 🔍 at the top center of the report. The display changes to show the report close up. See Figure 4-24. The last digit in each phone number might not be visible in the report on your screen. To fix this, you first need to display the report in Design view.

Figure 4-24	CLOSE-UP VIEW OF THE REPORT

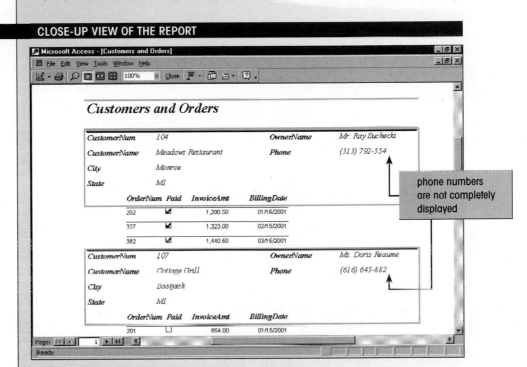

TROUBLE? Scroll your screen as necessary so that it matches the screen in Figure 4-24.

TROUBLE? If the phone numbers on your report are displayed correctly, follow the remaining steps so you will know how to make corrections, even though you will not need to resize the field.

2. Click the **View** button for Design view 🔲 on the Print Preview toolbar. Access displays the report in Design view. See Figure 4-25.

Figure 4-25   REPORT DISPLAYED IN DESIGN VIEW

label control for
the Phone field

text box control for
the Phone field

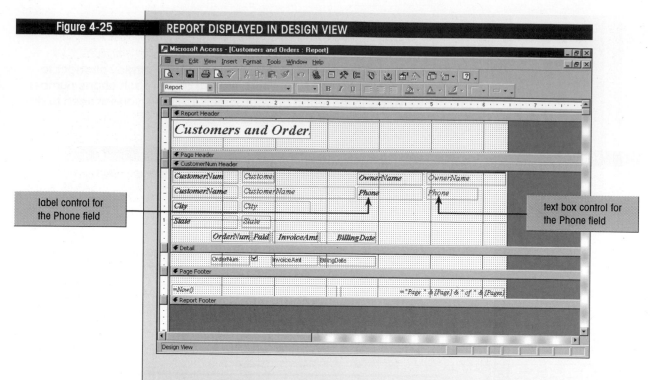

TROUBLE? If your screen displays any window other than those shown in Figure 4-25, click the Close button ☒ on the window's title bar to close it.

You use the Report window in Design view to modify existing reports and to create custom reports.

Each item on a report in Design view is called a **control**. For example, the Phone field consists of two controls: the label "Phone," which appears on the report to identify the field value, and the Phone text box, in which the actual field value appears. You need to widen the text box control for the Phone field so that the entire field value is visible in the report.

3. Click the text box control for the Phone field to select it. Notice that small black boxes appear on the border around the control. These boxes, which are called **handles**, indicate that the control is selected and can be manipulated.

4. Position the pointer on the center right handle of the Phone text box control until the pointer changes to ↔. See Figure 4-26.

| Figure 4-26 | RESIZING THE PHONE TEXT BOX CONTROL |

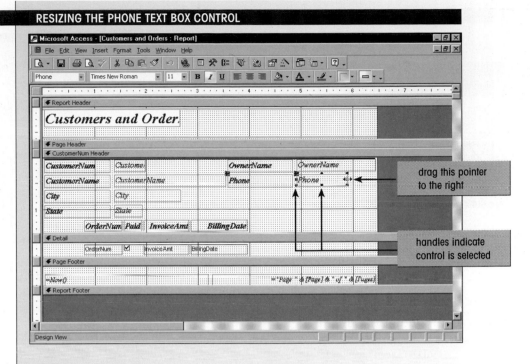

5. Click and drag the pointer to the right until the right edge of the control is aligned with the 6 inch mark on the horizontal ruler, and then release the mouse button.

Now you need to switch back to Print Preview and make sure that the complete value for the Phone field is visible.

6. Click the **View** button for Print Preview ▣ on the Report Design toolbar. The report appears in Print Preview. Notice that the Phone field values are now completely displayed.

7. Click **File** on the menu bar, and then click **Save** to save the modified report.

Kim decides that she wants the report to include the Valle Coffee cup logo to the right of the report title, for visual interest. You can add the logo to the report by inserting a picture of the coffee cup.

Inserting a Picture in a Report

In Access, you can insert a picture or other graphic image in a report or form to enhance the appearance of the report or form. Sources of graphic images include Microsoft Paint, other drawing programs, and scanners. The file containing the picture you need to insert is named ValleCup, and is located in the Tutorial folder on your Data Disk.

To insert the picture in the report:

1. Click the **Close** button on the Print Preview toolbar to display the report in Design view. See Figure 4-27.

Figure 4-27   INSERTING A PICTURE IN DESIGN VIEW

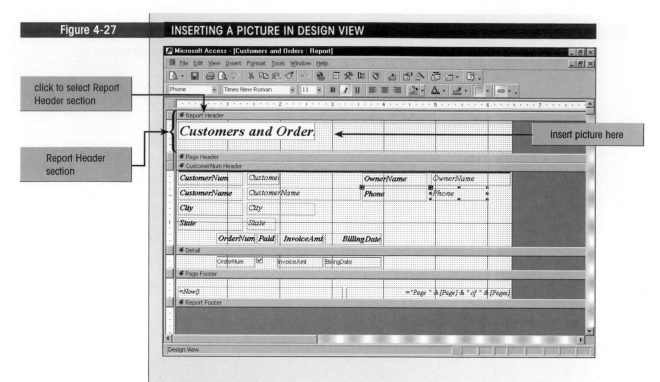

Kim wants the picture to appear on the first page of the report only; therefore, you need to insert the picture in the Report Header section (see Figure 4-27). Any text or graphics placed in this section appear once at the beginning of the report.

2. Click the **Report Header** bar to select this section of the report. The bar is high-lighted to indicate that the section is selected.

3. Click **Insert** on the menu bar, and then click **Picture**. The Insert Picture dialog box opens. See Figure 4-28.

Figure 4-28   INSERT PICTURE DIALOG BOX

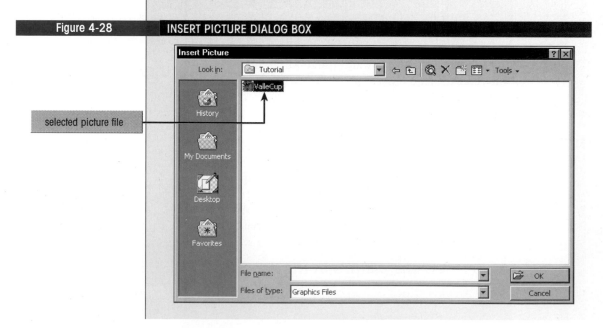

4. If necessary, open the Tutorial folder on your Data Disk, click **ValleCup** to select the picture of the Valle Coffee cup, and then click the **OK** button. The picture is inserted at the far left of the Report Header section, covering some of the report title text. See Figure 4-29.

Figure 4-29	PICTURE INSERTED IN REPORT

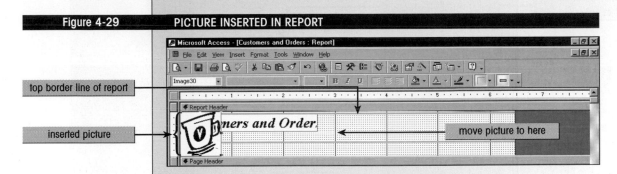

top border line of report →

inserted picture →

move picture to here

Notice that handles appear on the border around the picture, indicating that the picture is selected and can be manipulated.

Kim wants the picture to appear to the right of the report title, so you need to move the picture using the mouse.

5. Position the pointer on the picture until the pointer changes to 👆, and then click and drag the mouse to move the picture to the right so that its left edge aligns with the 3-inch mark on the horizontal ruler and its top edge is just below the top border line above the report title (see Figure 4-29).

6. Release the mouse button. The picture appears in the new position. See Figure 4-30.

Figure 4-30	REPOSITIONED PICTURE IN THE REPORT

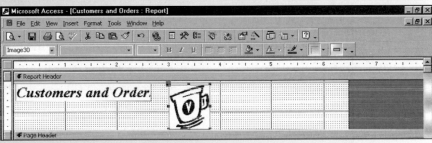

TROUBLE? If your picture is in a different location from the one shown in Figure 4-30, use the pointer 👆 to reposition the picture until it is in approximately the same position shown in the figure. Be sure that the top edge of the picture is below the top border line of the report.

7. Click the **View** button for Print Preview 🔍 on the Report Design toolbar to view the report in Print Preview. The report now includes the inserted picture. If necessary, click the **Zoom** button 🔍 on the Print Preview toolbar to display the entire report page. See Figure 4-31.

Figure 4-31   **PRINT PREVIEW OF REPORT WITH PICTURE**

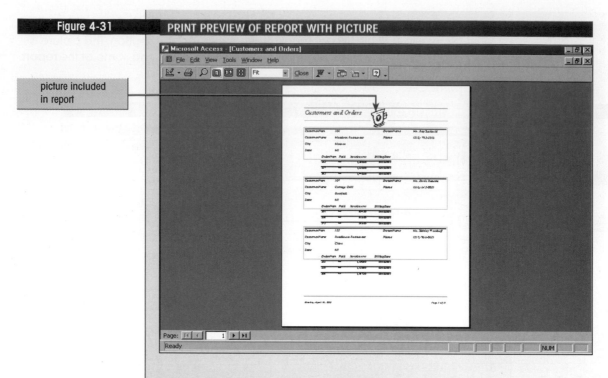

picture included
in report

8. Click **File** on the menu bar, and then click **Save** to save the changes you made
to the report.

The report is now complete. You'll print a hardcopy of just the first page of the report so
that Kim can review the report layout and the inserted picture.

To print page 1 of the report:

1. Click **File** on the menu bar, and then click **Print**. The Print dialog box opens.

2. In the Print Range section, click the **Pages** option button. The insertion point now
appears in the From text box so that you can specify the range of pages to print.

3. Type **1** in the From text box, press the **Tab** key to move to the To text box, and
then type **1**. These settings specify that only page 1 of the report will be printed.

4. Click the **OK** button. The Print dialog box closes, and the first page of the report
is printed. See Figure 4-32.

Figure 4-32   FIRST PAGE OF THE CUSTOMERS AND ORDERS REPORT

inserted picture

report title

fields from Customer table

fields from Order table

page footer

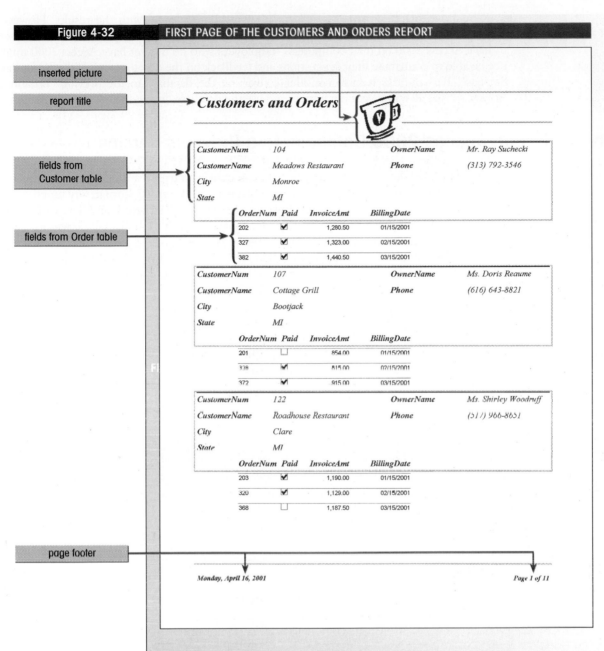

Customers and Orders

CustomerNum	104	OwnerName	Mr. Ray Suchecki
CustomerName	Meadows Restaurant	Phone	(313) 792-3546
City	Monroe		
State	MI		

OrderNum	Paid	InvoiceAmt	BillingDate
202	✔	1,280.50	01/15/2001
327	✔	1,323.00	02/15/2001
382	✔	1,440.50	03/15/2001

CustomerNum	107	OwnerName	Ms. Doris Reaume
CustomerName	Cottage Grill	Phone	(616) 643-8821
City	Bootjack		
State	MI		

OrderNum	Paid	InvoiceAmt	BillingDate
201	☐	854.00	01/15/2001
328	✔	815.00	02/15/2001
372	✔	915.00	03/15/2001

CustomerNum	122	OwnerName	Ms. Shirley Woodruff
CustomerName	Roadhouse Restaurant	Phone	(517) 966-8651
City	Clare		
State	MI		

OrderNum	Paid	InvoiceAmt	BillingDate
203	✔	1,190.00	01/15/2001
320	✔	1,129.00	02/15/2001
368	☐	1,187.50	03/15/2001

Monday, April 16, 2001   *Page 1 of 11*

TROUBLE? Depending on the printer you're using, the total number of pages in your report might be fewer or greater than the total indicated in the figure.

Kim approves of the report layout and contents, so you can close the report.

5. Click the **Close** button ☒ on the menu bar.

TROUBLE? If you click the Close button on the Print Preview toolbar by mistake, Access redisplays the report in Design view. Click the Close button ☒ on the menu bar.

6. Click the **Close** button ☒ on the Access title bar to close the database and exit Access.

Kim shows her report to Barbara, and they are both pleased with the results. However, Barbara wants to consider the fact that Valle Coffee is in the process of upgrading all of its users to have Access 2000 on their computers—employees who do not yet have Access 2000 might not be able to contribute their suggestions and feedback on the development of the Restaurant database. Barbara asks Kim to consider converting the database to the previous version of Access, so that all employees can inspect and use the database during the conversion period.

Converting an Access 2000 Database to a Previous Version

Access 2000 includes a new feature that lets you convert a database to the previous version, Access 97. When you convert an Access 2000 database to Access 97 format, any functionality that is specific to Access 2000 is lost. However, the database's structure and data will be useable in the converted database. To convert a database, open it in the Database window, click Tools on the menu bar, point to Database Utilities, point to Convert Database, and then click To Prior Access Database Version. The Convert Database Into dialog box will open, in which you can specify a filename and location for the converted database. After you click the Save button, Access 2000 will convert the database and save it as an Access 97 database, so that Access 97 users will be able to open the database as if it were created in Access 97.

If you try to open an Access 97 database in Access 2000, the Convert/Open Database dialog box will open and offer you two options: convert the database to Access 2000 format, or open the database in Access 97 format. When you are sharing a database with Access 97 users, you should select the "open" option so the database will be usable with both Access versions. Kim and Barbara might decide to convert and use the Restaurant database in Access 97 format while all database users are being upgraded to Access 2000. When every employee has Access 2000, the database can be opened and used in Access 2000 format only.

Barbara is satisfied that the forms you created—the Order Data form and the Customer Orders form—will make it easier to enter, view, and update data in the Restaurant database. The Customers and Orders report presents important information about Valle Coffee's restaurant customers in an attractive and professional format, which will help Kim and her staff in their sales and marketing efforts.

Session 4.2 QUICK | CHECK

1. How are a related table and a primary table associated with a form that contains a main form and a subform?

2. Describe how you use the navigation buttons to move through a form containing a main form and a subform.

3. When you use the Report Wizard, the report name is also used as the

   _____ .

4. Each item on a report in Design view is called a(n) _____ .

5. To insert a picture in a report, the report must be displayed in _____ .

6. Any text or graphics placed in the _____ section of a report will appear only on the first page of the report.

7. Describe one advantage and one disadvantage of converting an Access 2000 database to Access 97 format.

REVIEW ASSIGNMENTS

Barbara wants to enhance the **Valle Products** database with forms and reports, and she asks you to complete the following:

1. Make sure your Data Disk is in the disk drive, start Access, and then open the **Valle Products** database located in the Review folder on your Data Disk.

2. Use the Form Wizard to create a form based on the **Product** table. Select all fields for the form, the Columnar layout, the SandStone style, and the title **Product Data** for the form.

3. Using the form you created in the previous step, print the fifth form record, change the AutoFormat to Sumi Painting, save the changed form, and then print the fifth form record again.

4. Use the **Product Data** form to update the **Product** table as follows:
   a. Navigate to the record with the ProductCode 2410. Change the field values for WeightCode to A, Decaf to D, and Price to 8.99 for this record.
   b. Use the Find command to move to the record with the ProductCode 4306, and then delete the record.
   c. Add a new record with the following field values:
      ProductCode: 2306
      CoffeeCode: AMAR
      WeightCode: A
      Decaf: Null
      Price: 7.99
   d. Print only this form record, and then save and close the form.

Explore ▶ 5. Use the AutoForm: Columnar Wizard to create a form based on the **New Prices** query. Save the form as **New Prices**, and then close the form.

6. Use the Form Wizard to create a form containing a main form and a subform. Select the CoffeeName and CoffeeType fields from the **Coffee** table for the main form, and select all fields except CoffeeCode from the **Product** table for the subform. Use the Datasheet layout and the Sumi Painting style. Specify the title **Coffee Products** for the main form and the title **Product Subform** for the subform. Resize all columns in the subform to their best fit. Print the eighth main form record and its subform records. Close the form.

Explore ▶ 7. Use the Report Wizard to create a report based on the primary **Coffee** table and the related **Product** table. Select all fields from the **Coffee** table except Decaf, and select all fields from the **Product** table except CoffeeCode. In the third Report Wizard dialog box, specify the CoffeeType field as an additional grouping level. Sort the detail records by ProductCode. Choose the Align Left 2 layout and the Formal style for the report. Specify the title **Valle Coffee Products** for the report.

8. Insert the ValleCup picture, which is located in the Review folder on your Data Disk, in the Report Header section of the **Valle Coffee Products** report. Position the picture so that its left edge aligns with the 4-inch mark on the horizontal ruler and its top edge is just below the top border line of the report.

9. Print only the first page of the report, and then close and save the modified report.

10. Close the **Valle Products** database, and then exit Access.

CASE PROBLEMS

Case 1. Ashbrook Mall Information Desk   Sam Bullard wants the **MallJobs** database to include forms and reports that will help him track and distribute information about jobs available at the Ashbrook Mall. You'll create the necessary forms and reports by completing the following:

1. Make sure your Data Disk is in the disk drive, start Access, and then open the **MallJobs** database located in the Cases folder on your Data Disk.

2. Use the Form Wizard to create a form based on the **Store** table. Select all fields for the form, the Columnar layout, and the Blends style. Specify the title **Store Data** for the form.

3. Change the AutoFormat for the **Store Data** form to Standard.

4. Use the Find command to move to the record with the Store value of TH, and then change the Contact field value for this record to Sarah Pedicini.

5. Use the **Store Data** form to add a new record with the following field values:
   Store: PW
   StoreName: Pet World
   Location: B2
   Contact: Ryan Shevlin
   Extension: 2311

   Print only this form record, and then save and close the form.

6. Use the Form Wizard to create a form containing a main form and a subform. Select all the fields from the **Store** table for the main form, and select all fields except Store from the **Job** table for the subform. Use the Tabular layout and the Standard style. Specify the title **Jobs By Store** for the main form and the title **Job Subform** for the subform.

7. Print the ninth main form record and its subform records, and then close the **Jobs By Store** form.

8. Use the Report Wizard to create a report based on the primary **Store** table and the related **Job** table. Select all the fields from the **Store** table, and select all the fields from the **Job** table except Store. Sort the detail records by Job. Choose the Align Left 2 layout and Landscape orientation for the report. Choose the Casual style. Specify the title **Available Jobs** for the report, and then print and close the report.

9. Close the **MallJobs** database, and then exit Access.

Case 2. Professional Litigation User Services   Raj Jawahir continues his work with the **Payments** database to track and analyze the payment history of PLUS clients. To help him, you'll enhance the **Payments** database by completing the following:

1. Make sure your Data Disk is in the disk drive, start Access, and then open the **Payments** database located in the Cases folder on your Data Disk.

2. Use the Form Wizard to create a form containing a main form and a subform. Select the Firm# and FirmName fields from the **Firm** table for the main form, and select all fields except Firm# from the **Payment** table for the subform. Use the Datasheet layout and the Industrial style. Specify the title **Firm Payments** for the main form and the title **Payment Subform** for the subform. Resize all columns in the subform to their best fit. Print the first main form record and its displayed subform records.

3. For the form you just created, change the AutoFormat to SandStone, save the changed form, and then print the first main form record and its displayed subform records.

4. Navigate to the second record in the subform for the first main record, and then change the AmtPaid field value to 1,800.00.

5. Use the Find command to move to the record with the Firm# 1142, and delete the record. Answer Yes to any warning messages about deleting the record.

Explore 6. Use the appropriate wildcard character to find all records with the abbreviation "DA" (for District Attorney) anywhere in the firm name. (*Hint*: You must enter the wildcard character before and after the text you are searching for.) How many records did you find? Close the **Firm Payments** form.

Explore 7. Use the Report Wizard to create a report based on the primary **Firm** table and the related **Payment** table. Select all fields from the **Firm** table except Extension, and select all fields from the **Payment** table except Firm#. In the third Report Wizard dialog box, specify the PLUSAcctRep field as an additional grouping level. Sort the detail records by AmtPaid in *descending* order. Choose the Block layout, Landscape orientation, and the Bold style for the report. Specify the title **Payments By Firms** for the report.

8. Insert the PLUS picture, which is located in the Cases folder on your Data Disk, in the Report Header section of the **Payments By Firms** report. Leave the picture in its original position at the left edge of the report header.

Explore 9. Use the Office Assistant to ask the following question: "How do I move an object behind another?" Click the topic "Move a text box or other control in front of or behind other controls." Read the information and then close the Help window. Make sure the PLUS picture is still selected, and then move it behind the Payments By Firms title.

Explore 10. Use the Office Assistant to ask the following question: "How do I change the background color of an object?" Click the topic "Change the background color of a control or section." Read the information and then close the Help window and hide the Office Assistant. Select the Payments By Firms title object, and then change its background color to Transparent.

11. Display the report in Print Preview. Print just the first page of the report, and then close and save the report.

12. Close the **Payments** database, and then exit Access.

Case 3. Best Friends Noah and Sheila Warnick want to create forms and reports for the **Walks** database. You'll help them create these database objects by completing the following:

1. Make sure your Data Disk is in the disk drive, start Access, and then open the **Walks** database located in the Cases folder on your Data Disk.

2. Use the Form Wizard to create a form based on the **Walker** table. Select all fields for the form, the Columnar layout, and the Blueprint style. Specify the title **Walker Data** for the form.

3. Use the **Walker Data** form to update the **Walker** table as follows:

   a. For the record with the WalkerID 175, change the LastName to Petr and the Distance to 2.0.
   b. Add a new record with the following values:
      WalkerID: 225
      LastName: Bethel
      FirstName: Martha
      Phone: 711-0825
      Distance: 2.7
   c. Print just this form record.
   d. Delete the record with the WalkerID field value of 187.

4. Change the AutoFormat of the **Walker Data** form to Expedition, save the changed form, and then use the form to print the last record in the **Walker** table. Close the form.

5. Use the Form Wizard to create a form containing a main form and a subform. Select all the fields from the **Walker** table for the main form, and select the Pledger, PledgeAmt, PaidAmt, and DatePaid fields from the **Pledge** table for the subform. Use the Tabular layout and the Expedition style. Specify the title **Walkers And Pledges** for the main form and the title **Pledge Subform** for the subform. Close the form.

   Explore

6. Open the **Pledge Subform** in Design view. In the Form Header section, reduce the width of the PledgeAmt, PaidAmt, and DatePaid controls so that the control boxes are just slightly wider than the field names. (*Hint*: Select each control and use the pointer ↔ on the middle right handle to resize each control.) Repeat this procedure to resize the same controls in the Detail section of the form. Then, use the pointer ✋ to move these same controls—in both the Form Header section and the Detail section—to the left, so that the right edge of the DatePaid control (in each section) aligns approximately with the 3½-inch mark on the horizontal ruler. Close and save the **Pledge Subform**. Then, open the **Walkers And Pledges** form in Form view. Use the navigation buttons to find the first main form record that contains values in the subform. If any field values in the subform are not fully visible because of the resizing, close the **Walkers And Pledges** form, open the **Pledge Subform** in Design view, and make any necessary adjustments so that all four fields in the subform appear in the **Walkers And Pledges** form, and so that all field values are fully visible in the subform. Then reopen the form and display the first main form record with values in the subform.

7. Print the current main form record and its subform records, and then close the **Walkers And Pledges** form.

8. Use the Report Wizard to create a report based on the primary **Walker** table and the related **Pledge** table. Select all fields from the **Walker** table, and select all fields from the **Pledge** table except WalkerID. Sort the detail records by PledgeNo. Choose the Align Left 2 layout and Landscape orientation for the report. Choose the Formal style. Specify the title **Walk-A-Thon Walkers And Pledges** for the report.

   Explore

9. View both pages of the report in Print Preview. (*Hint*: Use a toolbar button.) Print the entire report, and then close it.

10. Close the **Walks** database, and then exit Access.

Case 4. Lopez Lexus Dealerships   Maria and Hector Lopez want to create forms and reports that will help them track and analyze data about the cars and different locations for their Lexus dealerships. Help them enhance the **Lexus** database by completing the following:

1. Make sure your Data Disk is in the disk drive, start Access, and then open the **Lexus** database located in the Cases folder on your Data Disk.

2. Use the Form Wizard to create a form containing a main form and a subform. Select all the fields from the **Locations** table for the main form, and select the VehicleID, Model, Class, Year, Cost, and SellingPrice fields from the **Cars** table for the subform. Use the Datasheet layout and the Standard style. Specify the title **Locations And Cars** for the main form and the title **Cars Subform** for the subform. Resize all columns in the subform to their best fit. Print the first main form record and its displayed subform records.

3. For the form you just created, change the AutoFormat to International, save the changed form, and then print the first main form record and its displayed subform records.

4. Navigate to the third record in the subform for the seventh main record, and then change the SellingPrice field value to $49,875.00.

5. Use the Find command to move to the record with the LocationCode P1, and delete the record. Answer Yes to any warning messages about deleting the record.

6. Use the appropriate wildcard character to find all records with a LocationCode value that begins with the letter "H." How many records did you find? Close the form.

Explore ▸ 7. Use the Report Wizard to create a report based on the primary **Locations** table and the related **Cars** table. Select all fields from the **Locations** table, and select all fields from the **Cars** table except Manufacturer, Transmission, and LocationCode. Specify two sort fields for the detail records: first, the Year field in ascending order, then the SellingPrice field in descending order. Choose the Outline 1 layout and Landscape orientation for the report. Choose the Compact style. Specify the title **Dealership Locations And Cars** for the report.

Explore ▸ 8. View the first two pages of the report in Print Preview at the same time. (*Hint*: Use a toolbar button.) Print the first two report pages, and then close the report.

9. Close the **Lexus** database, and then exit Access.

INTERNET ASSIGNMENTS

The purpose of the Internet Assignments is to challenge you to find information on the Internet that you can use to create effective documents. The actual assignments are updated and maintained on the Course Technology Web site. Log on to the Internet and use your Web browser to go to the Student Online Companion to accompany this text at **www.course.com/NewPerspectives/office2000**. Click the Access link, and then click the link for Tutorial 4.

QUICK CHECK ANSWERS

Session 4.1

1. The AutoForm Wizard creates a form automatically using all the fields in the selected table or query; the Form Wizard allows you to choose some or all of the fields in the selected table or query, choose fields from other tables and queries, and display fields in any order on the form.

2. An AutoFormat is a predefined style for a form (or report). To change a form's AutoFormat, display the form in Design view, click the AutoFormat button on the Form Design toolbar, click the new AutoFormat in the Form AutoFormats list box, and then click the OK button.

3. the last record in the table

4. datasheet

5. the question mark (?)

6. as many form records as can fit on a printed page

Session 4.2

1. The main form displays the data from the primary table, and the subform displays the data from the related table.

2. You use the top set of navigation buttons to select and move through records from the related table in the subform, and the bottom set to select and move through records from the primary table in the main form.

3. report title

4. control

5. Design view

6. Report Header

7. One advantage is that users of the database who do not have Access 2000 can inspect and use the converted database; a disadvantage is that the converted database will not include functionality that is specific to Access 2000.

New Perspectives on

MICROSOFT®
ACCESS 2000

Read This Before You Begin

To the Student

Data Disks

To complete the Level II tutorials, Review Assignments, and Case Problems, you will need either 7 Data Disks or access to your computer's hard drive or a personal network drive. Your instructor will either provide you with these Data Disk files or ask you to make your own.

Because the files you work with can be very large and contain links to one another, and it often takes much longer for your computer to access the files off of your floppy drive, it is recommended that you work off of your hard drive or personal network drive. If you do not have access to do so, and need to make your own Data Disks, you will need 7 blank, formatted high-density disks. You will need to copy a set of folders from a file server or standalone computer or the Web onto your disks. Your instructor will tell you which computer, drive letter, and folders contain the files you need. You could also download the files by going to www.course.com, clicking Data Disk Files, and following the instructions on the screen.

The following list shows you which folders go on each of your disks, so that you will have enough disk space to complete all the tutorials, Review Assignments, and Case Problems:

Data Disk 1
Write this on the disk label
Level II (Tutorials 5-7)
Data Disk 1: Tutorial files
Put the contents of this
folder on the disk
Disk 1

Data Disk 2
Write this on the disk label
Level II (Tutorials 5-7)
Data Disk 2: Review
Assignments
Put the contents of this
folder on the disk
Disk 2

Data Disk 3
Write this on the disk label
Level II (Tutorials 5-7)
Data Disk 3: Case Problem 1
Put the contents of this
folder on the disk
Disk 3

Data Disk 4
Write this on the disk label
Level II (Tutorials 5-7)
Data Disk 4: Case Problem 2
Put the contents of this
folder on the disk
Disk 4

Data Disk 5
Write this on the disk label
Level II (Tutorials 5-7)
Data Disk 5: Case Problem 3
Put the contents of this
folder on the disk
Disk 5

Data Disk 6
Write this on the disk label
Level II (Tutorials 5-7)
Data Disk 6: Case Problem 4
Put the contents of this
folder on the disk
Disk 6

Data Disk 7
Write this on the disk label
Level II (Tutorials 5-7)
Data Disk 7: Case Problem 5
Put the contents of this
folder on the disk
Disk 7

When you begin each tutorial, be sure you are using the correct Data Disk. Refer to the "File Finder" Chart at the back of this text for more detailed information on which files are used in which tutorials. These Access Level II tutorials use the same files for Tutorials 5-7. If you are completing the Level III tutorials (Tutorials 8 and up), you will need to create new data disks for those tutorials. See the inside back cover of this book for more information on Data Disk files, or ask your instructor or technical support person for assistance.

Course Labs

The Access Level II tutorials features an interactive Course Lab to help you understand Internet concepts. There are Lab Assignments at the end of Tutorial 7 that relate to this Lab.

To start a Lab, click the **Start** button on the Windows taskbar, point to **Programs**, point to **Course Labs**, point to **New Perspectives Course Labs**, and click the name of the Lab you want to use.

Using Your Own Computer

If you are going to work through this book using your own computer, you need:

- **Computer System** Microsoft Windows 95, 98, NT, or higher must be installed on your computer. This book assumes a typical installation of Microsoft Access.

- **Data Disks** You will not be able to complete the tutorials or exercises in this book using your own computer until you have your Data Disks. It is highly recommended that you work off of your computer's hard drive or your personal network drive.

- **Course Labs** See your instructor or technical support person to obtain the Course Lab software for use on your own computer.

Visit Our World Wide Web Site

Additional materials designed especially for you are available on the World Wide Web. Go to http://www.course.com.

To the Instructor

The Data Files and Course Labs are available on the Instructor's Resource Kit for this title. Follow the instructions in the Help file on the CD-ROM to install the programs to your network or standalone computer. For information on creating Data Disks or the Course Labs, see the "To the Student" section above.

You are granted a license to copy the Data Files and Course Labs to any computer or computer network used by students who have purchased this book.

OBJECTIVES

In this tutorial you will:

- Create a Lookup Wizard field in a table
- Display related table records in a subdatasheet
- Create an input mask for a table field
- Define multiple selection criteria in a query
- Use the In, Like, and Not operators in a query
- Use both the And and Or logical operators in the same query
- Create a parameter query
- Design and create a custom form
- Select, move, and delete controls
- Add form headers and footers
- Add a picture to a form
- Use Control Wizards to create a multi-page form
- Use a filter to select and sort records in a form

CREATING
MORE ADVANCED QUERIES AND CUSTOM FORMS

Making the Dining Database Easier to Use

CASE

Valle Coffee

Ten years ago Leonard Valle became president of Algoman Imports, a small distributor of inexpensive coffee beans to supermarkets in western Michigan. Since that time, Leonard has transformed the company into a popular distributor of gourmet coffees to restaurants and offices. He took over company ownership, changed the company name to Valle Coffee, and expanded its market area to include Indiana and Ohio.

Leonard has incorporated the use of computers in all aspects of the business, including financial management, inventory, production, and sales. The company has developed the Dining database of customer information and uses **Microsoft Access 2000** (or simply **Access**) to manage it.

The Dining database contains tables, queries, forms, and reports that Barbara Hennessey, office manager, and Kim Carpenter, director of marketing, use to keep track of customer orders and billing and marketing information.

Leonard, Kim, and Barbara are pleased with the information they are able to get from the Dining database. They are interested in taking better advantage of the power of Access to make the database easier to use and to create more sophisticated queries and custom forms. For example, Kim wants to obtain lists of customers in certain area codes, and Barbara needs a list of unpaid invoices for customers in Indiana or Ohio. Barbara also wants to change the design of the Order table and the Customer table. For the Order table, she wants to make it easier to enter the CustomerNum value for an Order record. For the Customer table, she wants to improve the appearance of Phone field values and to learn more about subdatasheets. In this tutorial, you'll make the necessary modifications and customizations to the Dining database.

SESSION 5.1

In this session, you will change the CustomerNum field in the Order table to a Lookup Wizard field, display related Order table records as a subdatasheet in the Customer table, and create an input mask for the Phone field in the Customer table. You will also create a pattern match query, a list-of-values query, and a query selecting nonmatching values. Finally, you will construct complex selection criteria using the And with Or operators, and you'll create a parameter query.

Creating a Lookup Wizard Field

The Order table in the Dining database contains information about orders placed by Valle Coffee's customers. Barbara wants to make it easier for her staff members to enter data in the table. In particular, it would be easier for them if they did not have to remember the correct customer number of the customer who placed the order. So, Barbara wants to change the CustomerNum field in the Order table to a Lookup Wizard field. A **Lookup Wizard field** allows the user to select a value from a list of possible values. For the CustomerNum field, the user will be able to select a customer number using the list of customer names in the Customer table, rather than having to remember the correct customer number. The CustomerNum field in the Order table will store the customer number, but the customer name will appear in Datasheet view. This makes it easier for the user and guarantees that the customer number entered is valid.

Barbara asks you to change the CustomerNum field in the Order table to a Lookup Wizard field. You begin by opening the Order table in Design view.

To open the Order table in Design view:

1. Make sure you have created your copy of the Access Data Disk, and then place your Data Disk in the appropriate disk drive.

   TROUBLE? If you don't have a Data Disk, you need to get one before you can proceed. Your instructor will either give you one or ask you to make your own. (See your instructor for information.) In either case, be sure you have made a copy of your Data Disk before you begin, so that the original Data Disk files will be available on the copied disk in case you need to start over because of an error or problem.

   TROUBLE? If you are not sure which disk drive to use for your Data Disk, read the "Read This Before You Begin" page on page WD 5.02 or ask your instructor for help.

2. Start Access and open the **Dining** database located in the Tutorial folder on your Data Disk. The Dining database is displayed in the Access window.

3. Make sure that Tables is selected in the Objects bar of the Database window, click **Order**, and then click the **Design** button to open the Order table in Design view. See Figure 5-1.

Figure 5-1	ORDER TABLE IN DESIGN VIEW

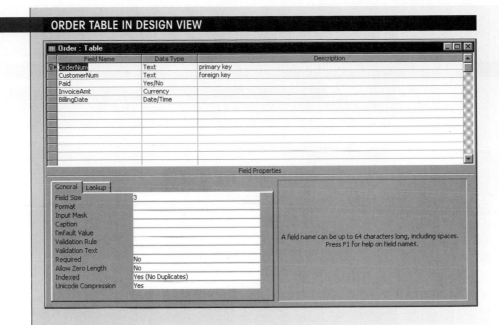

Now you can change the data type of the CustomerNum field to Lookup Wizard.

To change the CustomerNum field to a Lookup Wizard field:

1. Click the **Data Type** text box for the CustomerNum field, click the **Data Type** list arrow, and then click **Lookup Wizard**. The first Lookup Wizard dialog box opens. See Figure 5-2.

Figure 5-2	FIRST LOOKUP WIZARD DIALOG BOX

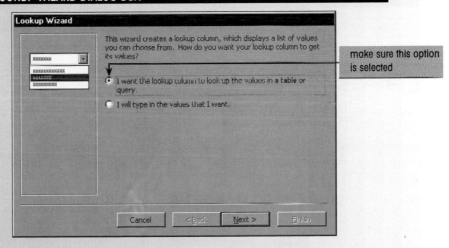

make sure this option is selected

This dialog box lets you specify a list of values that are allowed for the CustomerNum value in a record in the Order table. You can specify a table or query from which the value is selected, or you can enter a new list of values. You want the CustomerNum value to come from the Customer table.

2. Make sure the option for looking up the values in a table or query is selected, and then click the **Next** button to display the next Lookup Wizard dialog box.

3. Make sure Customer is selected, and then click the **Next** button to display the next Lookup Wizard dialog box. See Figure 5-3.

Figure 5-3	SELECTING THE CUSTOMER TABLE FIELDS

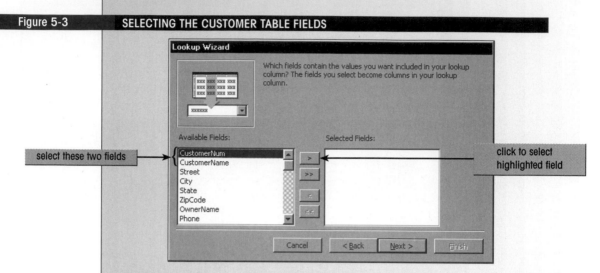

select these two fields

click to select
highlighted field

This dialog box lets you select the necessary fields from the Customer table. You need to select the CustomerNum field because it is the common field that links the Customer and Order tables. You also must select the CustomerName field because Barbara wants the user to be able to select from a list of customer names when entering a new order record.

4. Click the [>] button to select the CustomerNum field from the Customer table so that it will be included in the lookup column. Click the [>] button to select the CustomerName field, and then click the **Next** button. See Figure 5-4.

Figure 5-4	ADJUSTING THE WIDTH OF THE LOOKUP FIELD

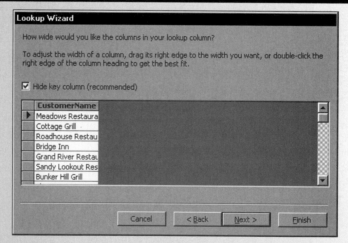

In this dialog box you can adjust the width of the CustomerName column, which will appear when a user enters a CustomerNum for the order in the Order table. The user can select a CustomerName, and the correct CustomerNum will be entered automatically. The selected "Hide key column" option means that the list of CustomerNum values will not appear in the datasheet.

5. Place the pointer on the right edge of the CustomerName field column heading. When the pointer changes to a ✛ shape, double-click to resize the column to fit the data.

6. Scroll down the list of CustomerNames and, if necessary, repeat Step 5 to make the column wider. Then click the **Next** button.

In this dialog box, you can specify the caption that will appear for the field in Datasheet view. The default value is the field name, CustomerNum. Because the field will show customer names in Datasheet view, you will change the caption to CustomerName.

7. Type **CustomerName** in the text box, and then click the **Finish** button.

To create the Lookup Wizard field, Access must save the table design and create the necessary relationship so that Access can enter the correct CustomerNum value when the user selects a customer name. Access displays a dialog box asking you to confirm saving the table.

8. Click the **Yes** button. Access creates the Lookup Wizard field, and you return to the Order table in Design view. See Figure 5-5.

| Figure 5-5 | LOOKUP WIZARD FIELD DEFINED |

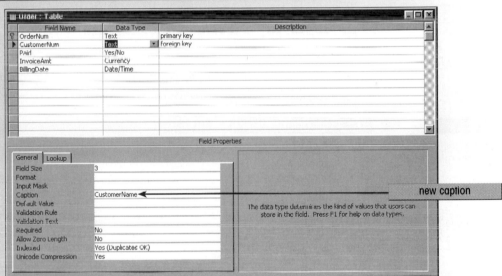

The Data Type value for the CustomerNum field still says Text, because this field contains text data. However, Access will now use the CustomerNum field value to look up and display customer names from the Customer table.

Barbara asks you to enter a new record in the Order table (Figure 5-6). To do so you need to switch to Datasheet view.

Figure 5-6 THE NEW ORDER TABLE RECORD

OrderNum	CustomerName	Paid	InvoiceAmt	BillingDate
401	Roadhouse Restaurant	No	1,100.00	3/15/2001

To enter the new Order table record:

1. Click the **View** button for Datasheet view 🔲 on the Table Design toolbar to open the table in Datasheet view. Notice that the customer names, instead of the customer numbers, now appear in the second column, as specified by the Lookup Wizard field.

   You need to widen the CustomerName column to display the complete field values.

2. Place the pointer on the right edge of the CustomerName column heading. When the pointer changes to a ↔ shape, double-click to resize the column to fit the data.

3. Click the **New Record** button ▶* on the Table Datasheet toolbar. Record 105, the next record available for a new record, becomes the current record.

4. In the OrderNum field, type **401**, and then press the **Tab** key to move to the CustomerNum field, which has the caption CustomerName. A list arrow now appears at the right of the CustomerName field text box.

5. Click the list arrow to display the list of CustomerName field values from the Customer table. See Figure 5-7.

Figure 5-7 LIST OF CUSTOMERNAME FIELD VALUES

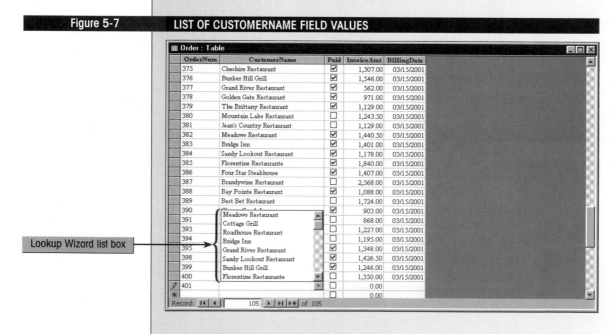

Lookup Wizard list box

6. Click **Roadhouse Restaurant** to select this field value. The list box closes and Roadhouse Restaurant appears in the CustomerName text box. However, it is the value 122, which is the CustomerNum field value for Roadhouse Restaurant, that is stored in the CustomerNum field for this order.

7. Refer to Figure 5-6 and enter the remaining field values for the new order record.

8. Click the **Close** button ☒ on the Table window title bar to close the Order table.

9. Click the **Yes** button when you're asked if you want to save your changes.

Barbara has noticed that a plus symbol recently appeared to the left of the CustomerNum field in the Customer table datasheet and asks what function it serves. You investigate and find that defining the one-to-many relationship between the Customer and Order tables caused the plus symbol to appear.

Displaying **Related Records in a Subdatasheet**

In the Dining database, there's a one-to-many relationship between the Customer and Order tables. The Customer table is the primary, or "one," table, and the Order table is the related, or "many," table. You need to open the Relationships window to see this one-to-many relationship between the Customer and Order tables.

To view table relationships in the Relationships window:

1. Click the **Relationships** button 🔡 on the Database toolbar. The Relationships window opens. See Figure 5-8.

| Figure 5-8 | DEFINED TABLE RELATIONSHIPS IN THE RELATIONSHIPS WINDOW |

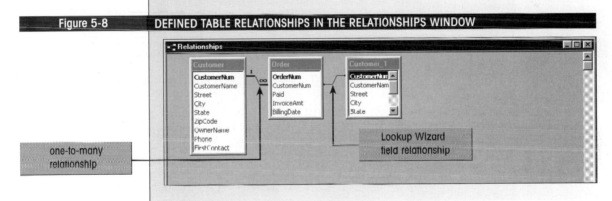

one-to-many relationship

Lookup Wizard field relationship

Two relationships appear in the Relationships window for the Dining database. The leftmost relationship is the one-to-many relationship between the Customer and Order tables. The join line connects the CustomerNum fields, which are common to the two tables. The "one" side of the relationship has the digit 1 at its end, and the "many" side of the relationship has the infinity symbol ∞ at its end. The Lookup Wizard added the rightmost relationship so that the correct CustomerNum field value can be stored in the Order table when a value for the CustomerName field is selected. The table name of Customer_1 is an alias for the Customer table to distinguish the two copies in the Relationships window.

For tables such as the Customer and Order tables that have one-to-many relationships, you can display records from the related table—the Order table in this case—as a **subdatasheet** in the primary table's datasheet—the Customer tables in this case. You'll open the Customer table to display the subdatasheet after closing the Relationships window.

To close the Relationships window and display Order table records in a subdatasheet:

1. Click the **Close** button ⊠ on the Relationships window title bar. The Relationships window closes.

2. Click **Customer** in the Tables list box, and then click the **Open** button. The Customer table opens in Datasheet view, and a column of plus symbols appears to the left of the CustomerNum column. See Figure 5-9.

Figure 5-9   CUSTOMER TABLE DATASHEET WITH SUBDATASHEET NOT EXPANDED

expand indicator →

	CustomerNum	CustomerName	Street	City	State	Zip	OwnerName	
+	104	Meadows Restaurant	Pond Hill Road	Monroe	MI	48161	Mr. Ray Suchecki	313
+	107	Cottage Grill	82 Mix	Bootjack	MI	49945	Ms. Doris Reaume	616
+	122	Roadhouse Restaurant	8408 E. Fletcher Road	Clare	MI	48617	Ms. Shirley Woodruff	517
+	123	Bridge Inn	400 Salmon Street	Ada	MI	49301	Mr. Wayne Bouwman	616
+	128	Grand River Restaurant	37 Queue Highway	Lacota	MI	49063	Mr. John Rohrs	313
+	129	Sandy Lookout Restaurant	95 North Bay Boulevard	Jenison	MI	49428	Ms. Michele Yasenak	616
+	131	Bunker Hill Grill	15365 Old Bedford Trail	Eagle Point	MI	49031	Mr. Ronald Kooienga	906
+	133	Florentine Restaurante	2874 Western Avenue	Drenthe	MI	49464	Mr. Donald Bench	616
+	135	Topview Restaurant	2840 Cascade Road	Zeeland	MI	49464	Ms. Janice Stapleton	616
+	136	Cleo's Downtown Restaurant	4090 Division Street NW	Borculo	MI	49464	Ms. Joan Hoffman	616
+	163	Bentham's Riverfront Restaurant	1366 36th Street	Roscommon	MI	48653	Mr. Joe Markovicz	517
+	165	Sullivan's Restaurant & Lounge	1935 Snow Street SE	Saugatuck	MI	49453	Ms. Dawn Parker	616
+	201	Wagon Train Restaurant	5480 Alpine Lane	Selkirk	MI	48661	Mr. Carl Seaver	517
+	202	Extra Helpings Restaurant	2140 Edgewood Road	Five Lakes	MI	48446	Ms. Deborah Wolfe	517
+	203	Mountain Lake Restaurant	701 Bagley Street	Grand Rapids	MI	49571	Mr. Donald MacPherson	616
+	322	Alto Country Inn	114 Lexington Parkway	Alto	MI	49302	Mr. James Cowan	616
+	325	Best Bet Restaurant	56 Four Mile Road	Grand Rapids	MI	49505	Ms. Rebecca Van Singel	616
+	407	Jean's Country Restaurant	44 Tower Lane	Mattawan	MI	49071	Ms. Jean Brooks	517
+	423	Bay Pointe Restaurant	11456 Marsh Road	Shelbyville	MI	49344	Mr. Janosfi Petofi	616
+	515	Cheshire Restaurant	8200 Baldwin Boulevard	Burlington	MI	49029	Mr. Jeffrey Hersha	517
+	597	Around the Clock Restaurant	3333 Bradford Farms	Copper Harbor	MI	49918	Ms. Jennifer Lewis	906
+	620	Brandywine Restaurant	150 Hall Road	Kearsarge	MI	49942	Mr. Walter Reed	906
+	624	South Bend Brewing Company	431 North Phillips Road	South Bend	IN	46611	Mr. Toby Stein	219
+	625	Maxwell's Restaurant	230 South Phillips Road	South Bend	IN	46623	Ms. Barbara Feldon	219
+	627	Monarch Restaurant	3915 Hawthorne Avenue	Toledo	OH	43603	Mr. Gilbert Scholten	415

Record: ◄ ◄ 1 ► ►I ►* of 38

TROUBLE? If the column of plus symbols does not appear, click Insert on the menu bar, click Subdatasheet, click Order, and then click the OK button.

When you first open a table (or query) datasheet, its subdatasheet is not expanded. To display the subdatasheet for a customer, you need to click the expand indicator in the row for that customer.

3. Click the expand indicator ⊞ for Cottage Grill, which is CustomerNum 107. The subdatasheet for Customer 107 opens. See Figure 5-10.

Figure 5-10   ORDER SUBDATASHEET EXPANDED

collapse indicator →

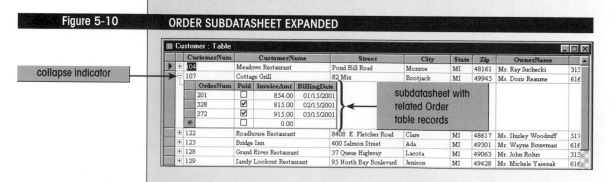

subdatasheet with related Order table records

With the subdatasheet displayed, you can navigate and update the sub-datasheet just as you can a normal datasheet. Barbara now understands the subdatasheet feature and doesn't have any updates, so you'll collapse the subdatasheet.

4. Click the collapse indicator ⊟ for Cottage Grill. The subdatasheet for customer 107 closes.

5. If necessary, scroll to the right until you can see the Phone field values.

Barbara asks you to change the appearance of the Phone field to a standard telephone number format.

Using the Input Mask Wizard

The Phone field in the Customer table is a 10-digit number that's difficult to read because it's displayed without any of the special formatting characters usually associated with a telephone number. For example, the Phone field value for Cottage Grill, which is displayed as 6166438821, would be more readable if it were displayed in any one of the following formats: 616-643-8821, 616.643.8821, 616/643-8821, or (616) 643-8821. Barbara asks you to use the 616-643-8821 style for the Phone field.

Barbara wants the hyphens to appear as literal display characters, which means that hyphens should appear, with blanks to fill in with digits, whenever Phone field values are entered. Thus, you need to create an input mask. An **input mask** is a predefined format you use to enter data in a field. An easy way to create an input mask is to use the **Input Mask Wizard**, which is an Access tool that guides you in creating a predefined format for a field. You must use the Input Mask Wizard in Design view.

To use the Input Mask Wizard for the Phone field:

1. Click the **View** button for Design view 🖼 on the Table Datasheet toolbar to display the Customer table in Design view.

2. Click the **Field Name** text box for the Phone field to make it the current field and to display its Field Properties options.

3. Click the **Input Mask** text box. A Build button 🔳 appears to the right of the Input Mask text box.

4. Click the **Build** button 🔳 next to the Input Mask text box, and then click the **Yes** button to save the table. The first Input Mask Wizard dialog box opens. See Figure 5-11.

Figure 5-11 INPUT MASK WIZARD DIALOG BOX

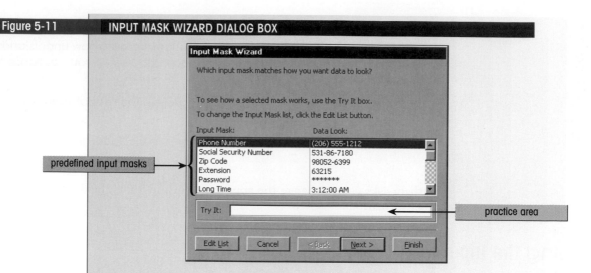

predefined input masks

practice area

TROUBLE? If a dialog box opens and tells you that this feature is not installed, insert your Office 2000 CD into the correct drive, and then click the OK button. If you do not have an Office 2000 CD, ask your instructor or technical support person for help.

You can scroll the Input Mask list box, select the input mask you want, and then enter representative values to practice using the input mask.

5. If necessary, click **Phone Number** in the Input Mask list box to select it.

6. Click the far left side of the Try It text box. (___) ___-____ appears in the Try It text box. The underscores are placeholder characters that are replaced as you type a phone number.

7. Type **9876543210** to practice entering a sample phone number. The input mask makes the typed value appear as (987) 654-3210.

8. Click the **Next** button. The next Input Mask Wizard dialog box opens, in which you can change the input mask and placeholder character. Because it's easier to change an input mask after the Input Mask Wizard has finished, you'll accept all Wizard defaults.

9. Click the **Finish** button. The Input Mask Wizard creates the default phone number input mask, placing it in the Input Mask text box for the Phone field. See Figure 5-12.

Figure 5-12 INPUT MASK CREATED BY THE INPUT MASK WIZARD

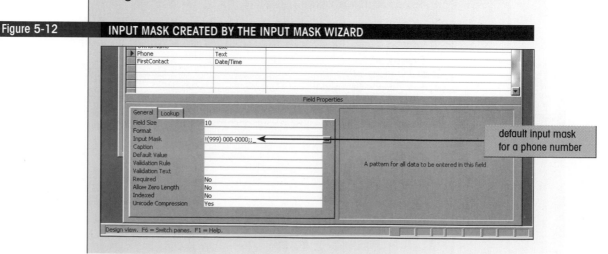

default input mask for a phone number

The characters preceding the first semicolon represent the input mask. The symbols in the default phone number input mask of !(999) 000-0000;;_ have the meanings shown in Figure 5-13.

Figure 5-13	INPUT MASK CHARACTERS
INPUT MASK CHARACTER	**DESCRIPTION**
!	Causes the input mask to display from right to left, rather than the default of left to right. Characters typed into the mask always fill in from left to right.
9	Digit or space can be entered. Entry is not required.
0	Digit only can be entered. Entry is required.
;;	The character between the first and second semicolon determines whether to store the literal display characters, such as the hyphen and parentheses, in the database. If left blank or given a value of 1, it does not store the literal characters. If given a value of 0, it stores the literal characters.
_	Placeholder character because it follows the second semicolon.
'	Literal display character
-	Literal display character

Now you'll change the default input mask to the format Barbara requested.

To view and change the input mask for the Phone field:

1. Click the **View** button for Datasheet view 🖩 on the Table Design toolbar, and then click the **Yes** button when asked if you want to save the table changes. The Customer table opens in Datasheet view.

2. If necessary, scroll the table to the right until the Phone field is visible. The Phone field values now have the format specified by the input mask.

3. Click the **View** button for Design view 🗹 on the Table Datasheet toolbar to display the Customer table in Design view.

   The input mask has changed from !(999) 000-0000;;_ to !\(999") "000\-0000;;_. The backslash character (\) causes the character that follows to be displayed as a literal character. Also, characters enclosed in quotation marks are displayed as literal characters.

4. Change the input mask to **!999\-000\-0000;;_** in the Input Mask text box for the Phone field.

5. Click 🖩 on the Table Design toolbar, and then click the **Yes** button to save the table changes. Access displays the Customer table in Datasheet view.

6. Scroll the table to the right until the Phone field is visible. The Phone field values now have the format Barbara requested. See Figure 5-14.

| Figure 5-14 | AFTER CHANGING THE PHONE FIELD INPUT MASK |

Customer : Table

	CustomerName	Street	City	State	Zip	OwnerName	Phone	First
	Meadows Restaurant	Pond Hill Road	Monroe	MI	48161	Mr. Ray Suchecki	313-792-3546	02
	Cottage Grill	82 Mix	Bootjack	MI	49945	Ms. Doris Reaume	616-643-8821	04
	Roadhouse Restaurant	8408 E. Fletcher Road	Clare	MI	48617	Ms. Shirley Woodruff	517-966-8651	04
	Bridge Inn	400 Salmon Street	Ada	MI	49301	Mr. Wayne Bouwman	616-888-9827	04
	Grand River Restaurant	37 Queue Highway	Lacota	MI	49063	Mr. John Rohrs	313-729-5364	04
	Sandy Lookout Restaurant	95 North Bay Boulevard	Jenison	MI	49428	Ms. Michele Yasenak	616-111-9148	04
	Bunker Hill Grill	15365 Old Bedford Trail	Eagle Point	MI	49031	Mr. Ronald Kooienga	906-895-2041	05
	Florentine Restaurante	2874 Western Avenue	Drenthe	MI	49464	Mr. Donald Bench	616-111-3260	05
	Topview Restaurant	2840 Cascade Road	Zeeland	MI	49464	Ms. Janice Stapleton	616-643-4635	05
	Cleo's Downtown Restaurant	4090 Division Street NW	Borculo	MI	49464	Ms. Joan Hoffman	616-888-2046	05
	Bentham's Riverfront Restaurant	1366 36th Street	Roscommon	MI	48653	Mr. Joe Markovicz	517-792-8040	05

Phone field with
input mask

7. Click the **Close** button [X] on the table's title bar. The table closes and you return to the Database window.

You are now ready to create the queries that Barbara and Kim requested. You are already familiar with queries that use an exact match or a range of values (using the > comparison operator) to select records. Access provides many other operators for creating select queries. These operators allow you to create more complicated queries that are difficult or impossible to create with exact match or range of values selection criteria.

Barbara and Kim created a list of questions they want to answer using the Dining database:

■ Which customers are located in the 313 area code?

■ What is the customer information for customers 123, 135, and 202?

■ What is the customer information for all customers *except* customers 123, 135, and 202?

■ What are the customer numbers, customer names, order numbers, and invoice amounts for unpaid invoices for customers in Indiana or Ohio?

■ What are the customer names, amounts overdue, and potential late charges for customers with overdue January invoices in a particular state? For this query, the user specifies the state.

You will create the necessary queries to answer these questions. To do so you'll use the Query window in Design view.

Using a Pattern Match in a Query

Kim wants to view the records for all customers in the 313 area code. She will be traveling in that area next week and wants to contact those customers. To answer Kim's question, you can create a query that uses a pattern match. A **pattern match** selects records that have a value for the selected field matching the pattern of the simple condition value, in this case, to select customers with 313 area codes. You do this using the Like comparison operator.

The **Like comparison operator** selects records by matching field values to a specific pattern that includes one or more wildcard characters—asterisk (*), question mark (?), and number symbol (#). The asterisk represents any string of characters, the question mark represents any single character, and the number symbol represents any single digit. Using a pattern match is similar to using an exact match, except that a pattern match includes wildcard characters.

To create the query, you must first place the Customer table field list in the Query window in Design view.

To create the pattern match query in Design view:

1. Click **Queries** in the Objects bar of the Database window, and then click the **New** button. The New Query dialog box opens.

2. Click **Design View** in the list box (if necessary), and then click the **OK** button. The Show Table dialog box opens on top of the Query window.

3. Click **Customer** in the Tables list box, click the **Add** button, and then click the **Close** button. Access places the Customer table field list in the Query window.

4. Double-click the title bar of the Customer field list to highlight all the fields, and then drag one of the highlighted fields to the design grid. Access places each field in a separate column in the design grid, in the same order that the fields appear in the table. See Figure 5-15.

Figure 5-15	ADDING THE FIELDS FOR THE QUERY

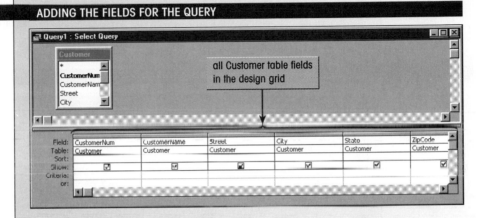

You will now enter the pattern match condition Like "313*" for the Phone field. Access will select records that have a Phone field value containing 313 in positions one through three. The asterisk (*) wildcard character specifies that any characters can appear in the remaining positions of the field value.

To select records that match the specified pattern:

1. Scroll the design grid until the Phone field is visible.

2. Click the **Phone Criteria** text box, and then type **Like "313*"**. See Figure 5-16. (Note that if you omit the Like operator, Access will automatically add it when you run the query.)

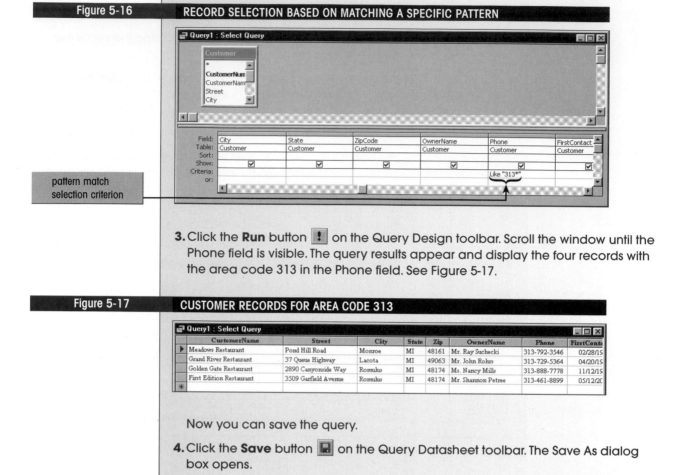

Figure 5-16 — RECORD SELECTION BASED ON MATCHING A SPECIFIC PATTERN

pattern match selection criterion

3. Click the **Run** button ! on the Query Design toolbar. Scroll the window until the Phone field is visible. The query results appear and display the four records with the area code 313 in the Phone field. See Figure 5-17.

Figure 5-17 — CUSTOMER RECORDS FOR AREA CODE 313

CustomerName	Street	City	State	Zip	OwnerName	Phone	FirstConta
Meadows Restaurant	Pond Hill Road	Monroe	MI	48161	Mr. Ray Suchecki	313-792-3546	02/28/19
Grand River Restaurant	37 Queue Highway	Lacota	MI	49063	Mr. John Rohrs	313-729-5364	04/20/19
Golden Gate Restaurant	2890 Canyonside Way	Romulus	MI	48174	Ms. Nancy Mills	313-888-7778	11/12/19
First Edition Restaurant	3509 Garfield Avenue	Romulus	MI	48174	Mr. Shannon Petree	313-461-8899	05/12/20

Now you can save the query.

4. Click the **Save** button on the Query Datasheet toolbar. The Save As dialog box opens.

5. Type **313 Area Code** in the Query Name text box, and then press the **Enter** key. Access saves the query in the Dining database on your Data Disk.

Next, Kim asks you to create a query that will display the customer information for customers 123, 135, and 202. She wants to assign these customers to a particular salesperson, and she would like a printout of the customer data to give to the salesperson. To produce the results Kim wants, you'll create a query using a list-of-values match.

Using a List-of-Values Match in a Query

A **list-of-values match** selects records whose value for the selected field matches one of two or more simple condition values. You could accomplish this by including several Or conditions in the design grid, but Access also provides the In comparison operator that works as shorthand. The **In comparison operator** allows you to define a condition with two or more values. If a record's field value matches one value from the list of values, then Access selects that record for inclusion in the query results.

To display the information Kim requested, you want records selected if the CustomerNum field value is equal to 123, 135, or 202. These are the values you will use with the In comparison operator.

To create the query using a list-of-values match:

1. Click the **View** button for Design view ![icon] on the Query Datasheet toolbar to display the Query window in Design view.

   First you need to delete the condition for the previous query you created.

2. Click the **Phone Criteria** text box, press the **F2** key to highlight the entire condition, and then press the **Delete** key to remove the condition.

   Now you can enter the criteria for the new query using the In comparison operator. When you use this operator, you must enclose the list of values you want to match within parentheses and separate the values with commas. In addition, for Text data types you must enclose each value in quotation marks, but you don't use the quotation marks for Number data type fields.

3. Scroll the design grid to the left to display the CustomerNum column, click the **CustomerNum Criteria** text box, and then type **In ("123","135","202")**. See Figure 5-18.

Figure 5-18	RECORD SELECTION BASED ON MATCHING FIELD VALUES TO A LIST OF VALUES

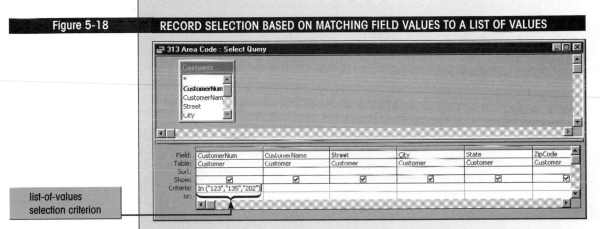

list-of-values
selection criterion

4. Click the **Run** button ![icon] on the Query Design toolbar. Access runs the query and displays the results, which show the three records with 123, 135, or 202 in the CustomerNum field.

   Now you can print the query results for Kim. Also, because Kim won't need to display this information again, you don't have to save this query.

5. Click the **Print** button ![icon] on the Query Datasheet toolbar. Access prints the query results.

Kim wants to assign the remaining customers to other salespersons in her group. She needs a list of all the customers except customers 123, 135, and 202 to help her plan the assignments. You can create this query by modifying the previous one to include a non-matching value.

Using a Nonmatching Value in a Query

A **nonmatching value** selects records whose value for the selected field does not match the simple condition value. You create the selection criterion using the Not logical operator. The **Not logical operator** negates a criterion. For example, if you enter Not = "MI" in the Criteria text box for the State field in the Customer table, the query results will show the records for which the State field value is not MI; that is, all customers not located in Michigan.

To create Kim's query, you will combine the Not operator with the In operator to select customer records whose CustomerNum field value is not in the list ("123","135","202").

To create the query using a nonmatching value:

1. Click the **View** button for Design view 🖾 on the Query Datasheet toolbar to switch back to Design view.

2. If necessary, position the insertion point immediately to the left of the word "In" in the Criteria text box for the CustomerNum field.

3. Type **Not** and then press the **spacebar**. Access will select a record only if the CustomerNum field value is not in the list ("123","135","202"). See Figure 5-19.

| Figure 5-19 | RECORD SELECTION BASED ON NOT MATCHING A LIST OF VALUES |

negation operator with list-of-values selection criterion

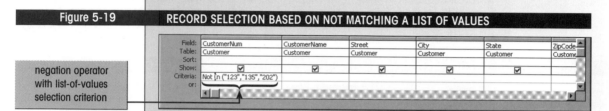

TROUBLE? Your screen might show only part of the criterion in the CustomerNum Criteria text box.

4. Click the **Run** button ❗ on the Query Design toolbar. Access runs the query and displays only those records with a CustomerNum field value that is not 123, 135, or 202. A total of 35 records are included in the query results. See Figure 5-20.

| Figure 5-20 | RESULTS OF QUERY USING NONMATCHING VALUES |

customers 123, 135, and 202 not selected

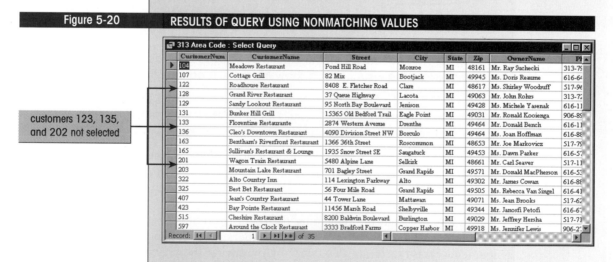

5. Click the **Print** button 🖨 on the Query Datasheet toolbar to print the query results.

Now you can close the query without saving it, because Kim will not need to run this query again.

6. Click the **Close** button ❌ on the Query window to close it, and then click the **No** button when asked if you want to save the query.

You are now ready to create the query to answer Barbara's question about unpaid invoices in Indiana or Ohio.

Using Both the And and Or Operators in the Same Query

Barbara wants to see the customer numbers, customer names, order numbers, and invoice amounts for unpaid invoices for customers in Indiana or Ohio. To create this query, you need to use both the And and Or logical operators to create two compound conditions. That is, you will create conditions that select records for customers who are located in Indiana *and* who have unpaid invoices *or* customers who are located in Ohio *and* who have unpaid invoices. Because you want the customer names shown with the invoice information in the query results, you will use fields from both the Customer and Order tables.

> ### To add the fields to the query design:
>
> 1. With Queries selected in the Objects bar of the Database window, click the **New** button. The New Query dialog box opens.
>
> 2. Click **Design View** (if necessary), and then click the **OK** button. The Show Table dialog box opens on top of the Query window in Design view.
>
> 3. Double-click **Customer** to add the Customer table to the Query window.
>
> 4. Double-click **Order** to add the Order table to the Query window, and then click the **Close** button to close the Show Table dialog box.
>
> 5. Double-click **CustomerNum**, double-click **CustomerName**, and then double-click **State** in the Customer field list to add these fields to the design grid.
>
> 6. Double-click **OrderNum**, double-click **Paid**, and then double-click **InvoiceAmt** in the Order field list to add these fields to the design grid.

You've selected all the fields to include in the query. Now you're ready to add the selection criteria, which will include both the And and Or logical operators.

> ### To specify the criteria using the And logical operator with the Or logical operator:
>
> 1. Click the **State Criteria** text box, and then type **="IN"**.
>
>   Kim wants to view data for customers in Indiana or Ohio, so you need to enter the Or condition for the State field.
>
> 2. Press the ↓ key, and then type **="OH"**.
>
>   Now, for each of the existing conditions, you need to enter the And condition that selects only those records for customers who have not paid their invoices.
>
> 3. Scroll right (if necessary) to display the Paid field, click the **Paid Criteria** text box, and then type **=No**.
>
> 4. Press the ↓ key, and then type **=No**.
>
>   When you save this query, you'll specify a name that indicates the data is for unpaid invoices. Therefore, you don't have to display the Paid field values in the query results.

5. Click the **Show** check box for the Paid field to remove the check mark. The query definition is now complete. See Figure 5-21.

Figure 5-21   **AND WITH OR CONDITIONS IN THE DESIGN GRID**

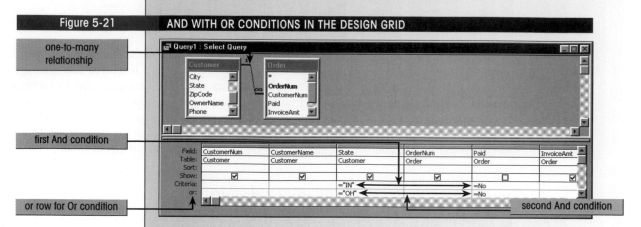

one-to-many relationship

first And condition

or row for Or condition

second And condition

6. Click the **Run** button on the Query Design toolbar. Access runs the query and displays the results. See Figure 5-22.

Figure 5-22   **RESULTS OF QUERY USING AND WITH OR**

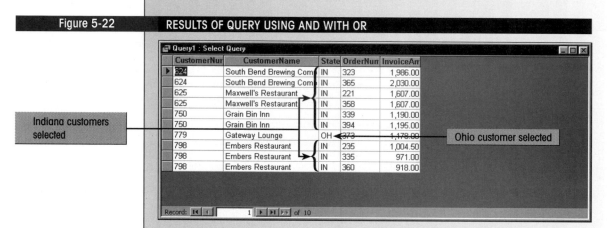

Indiana customers selected

Ohio customer selected

The query results show the records for customers in Indiana or Ohio that have unpaid invoices. Because you unchecked the Show box for the Paid field, it does not appear in the query results. Next, because some column headings and field values are not fully displayed, you'll change the font to Times New Roman 8 from the default, Arial 10.

7. Click **Format** on the menu bar, click **Font** to open the Font dialog box, scroll the Font list box, click **Times New Roman**, scroll the Size list box, click **8**, and then click the **OK** button. The font size for the entire query datasheet changes to Times New Roman 8.

Next, you'll save the query with a name indicating that the query selects unpaid invoices.

8. Click the **Save** button on the Query Datasheet toolbar, type **IN and OH Unpaid Invoices** in the Query Name text box, and then press the **Enter** key to save the query.

9. Click the **Close** button on the Query window.

Creating a Parameter Query

Barbara's final query asks for the customer name, amount overdue, and late charge for customers with overdue January invoices in a particular state. For this query, she wants to be able to specify the state, such as MI (Michigan), IN (Indiana), or OH (Ohio).

To create this query, you will modify the existing Unpaid With Late Charge query. You could create a simple condition using an exact match for the State field, which you would need to change in Design view every time you run the query. Instead, you will create a parameter query. A **parameter query** is a query that prompts you for information when the query runs. In this case, you want to create a query that prompts you to select the customers' state from the table. You enter the prompt in the Criteria text box for the State field.

When Access runs the query, it will display a dialog box and prompt you to enter the state. Access then creates the query results just as if you had changed the criteria in Design view.

REFERENCE WINDOW   RW

Creating a Parameter Query
- Create a select query that includes all the fields that will appear in the query results. Also choose the sort keys and set the criteria that do not change when you run the query.
- Decide on the fields that will have prompts when you run the query. In the Criteria text box for each of those fields, type the prompt you want to appear in a message box when you run the query, and enclose the prompt in brackets.

Now you can open the Unpaid With Late Charge query in Design view and change its design to create the parameter query.

To create the parameter query based on an existing query:

1. Make sure that Queries is selected in the Objects bar of the Database window, click **Unpaid With Late Charge**, and then click the **Design** button to display the query in Design view.

   Now you need to add the State field to the query design and enter a prompt in the Criteria box for the State field.

2. Scroll the design grid to the right to display the first blank column.

3. Double-click **State** in the Customer field list to add this field in the next available column in the design grid.

   Next you must enter the criteria for the parameter query. In this case, Kim wants the query to prompt users to enter the state for the customer information they want to view. So, you need to enter the prompt in the Criteria text box for the State field. The text of the prompt must be enclosed within brackets.

4. Click the **State Criteria** text box, and then type [**Enter the state:**]. See Figure 5-23.

Figure 5-23   SPECIFYING THE PROMPT FOR THE PARAMETER QUERY

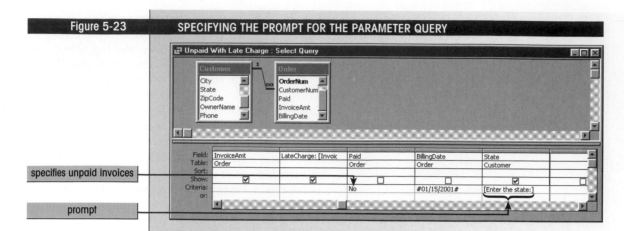

specifies unpaid invoices

prompt

TROUBLE? Depending on your system settings, the year in the BillingDate Criteria text box might contain only two digits.

5. Click the **Run** button ![run] on the Query Design toolbar. Access runs the query and displays a dialog box prompting you for the name of the state. See Figure 5-24.

Figure 5-24   ENTER PARAMETER VALUE DIALOG BOX

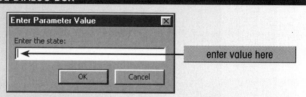

enter value here

The text you specified in the Criteria text box of the State field appears above a text box, in which you must type a State field value. You must enter the value so that it matches the spelling of a State field value in the table, but the value you enter can be either lowercase or uppercase.

6. To see the January unpaid invoices for customers in Indiana, type **IN**, and then press the **Enter** key. Access displays the data for the customers in Indiana who have unpaid January invoices (in this case, only two customers). See Figure 5-25.

Figure 5-25   RESULTS OF THE PARAMETER QUERY

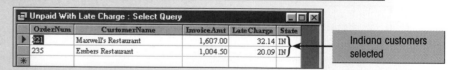

Indiana customers selected

Barbara plans to run this query frequently to monitor the payment activity of the restaurant customers, so she asks you to save it with a new name (to keep the original query intact).

7. Click **File** on the menu bar, and then click **Save As**. The Save As dialog box opens.

8. Position the insertion point immediately to the right of the "e" in Charge, press the **spacebar**, type **Parameter**, and then press the **Enter** key.

9. Click the **Close** button ![X] on the Query window.

The Lookup Wizard field you specified and the input mask and queries you created will make the Dining database easier to use. In the next session, you will create a custom form for the database, which will help Valle Coffee's employees enter and maintain data more easily.

Session 5.1 QUICK CHECK

1. What is a Lookup Wizard field?

2. What is a subdatasheet?

3. A(n) _____ is a predefined format you use to enter data in a field.

4. Which comparison operator is used to select records based on a specific pattern?

5. What is the purpose of the asterisk (*) in a pattern match query?

6. When do you use the In comparison operator?

7. How do you negate a selection criterion?

8. When do you use a parameter query?

SESSION 5.2

In this session, you will create a custom form for customer information. You will work in Design view to add form controls, create a form header with a title and a picture, and add color to the background of the form.

Creating a Custom Form

Barbara has been using the Customer Orders form to enter and view information about Valle Coffee's customers and their orders. She likes having all the information on a single form, but she would prefer to have the fields rearranged and a picture added to the form. To make the form easier to read, she wants to have the customer and order information on separate pages, like the tabs in a dialog box. She asks you to create a new form to display the information in this way. Because this form is significantly different from the Customer Orders form, you will create a new custom form.

To create a custom form, you can modify an existing form or design and create a form from scratch. In either case, you create a custom form in the Form window in Design view. You can design a custom form to match a paper form, to display some fields side by side and others top to bottom, to highlight certain sections with color, or to add special buttons and list boxes. A multi-page form displays the form on more than one page on a single screen. Each page is labeled with a tab and, by clicking a tab, you can display the information on that page.

Designing a Custom Form

Whether the custom form you want to create is simple or complex, it is always best to plan the form's content and appearance first. Figure 5-26 shows Barbara's design for the custom form she wants you to create.

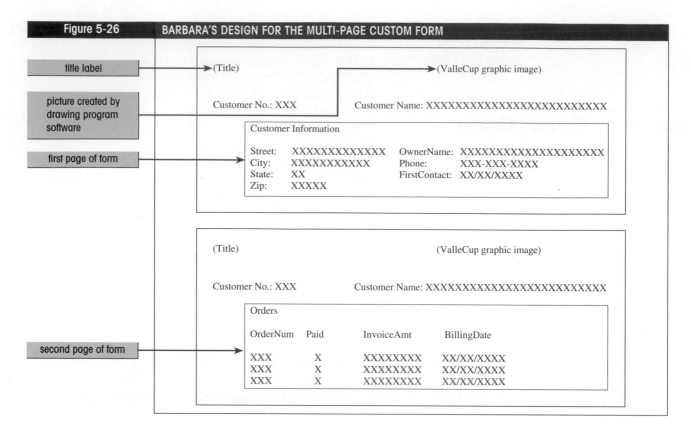

Figure 5-26   BARBARA'S DESIGN FOR THE MULTI-PAGE CUSTOM FORM

Notice that the top of the form displays a title and picture. Below these items are the CustomerNum and CustomerName fields. Also, notice that Barbara's form contains two pages. The first page, labeled "Customer Information," displays the address and contact information for the customer. The second page, labeled "Orders," displays order information for the customer. Each field value from the Customer table will appear in a text box and will be preceded by a label. The label will be the value of the field's Caption property (if any) or the field name. The locations and lengths of each field value are indicated by a series of Xs in Barbara's form design. For example, the three Xs that follow the CustomerNum field label indicate that the field value will be three characters long. The Order table fields appear in a subform on the second page.

With the design for the custom form in place, you are ready to create it. You could use an AutoForm Wizard or the Form Wizard to create a basic form and then customize it in Design view. However, you would need to make many modifications to a basic form to create the form Barbara wants, so you will create the entire form directly in Design view.

The Form Window in Design View

You use the Form window in Design view to create and modify forms. To create Barbara's custom form, you'll create a blank form based on the Customer table and then add the Order table fields in a subform.

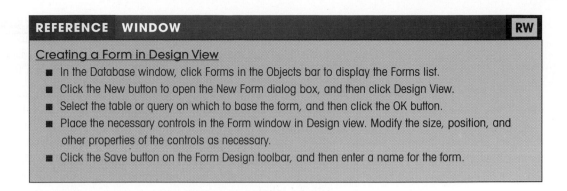

REFERENCE   WINDOW   **RW**

<u>Creating a Form in Design View</u>
- In the Database window, click Forms in the Objects bar to display the Forms list.
- Click the New button to open the New Form dialog box, and then click Design View.
- Select the table or query on which to base the form, and then click the OK button.
- Place the necessary controls in the Form window in Design view. Modify the size, position, and other properties of the controls as necessary.
- Click the Save button on the Form Design toolbar, and then enter a name for the form.

To create a blank form in Design view:

1. If you took a break after the previous session, make sure that Access is running, and that the Dining database from the Tutorial folder on your Data Disk is open. Make sure that Forms is selected in the Objects bar of the Database window.

2. Click the **New** button. The New Form dialog box opens.

3. Click **Design View** (if necessary), click the list arrow for choosing a table or query, click **Customer**, and then click the **OK** button. Access opens the Form window in Design view.

4. Click the **Maximize** button 🔲 on the Form window to maximize the window. See Figure 5-27.

Figure 5-27	FORM WINDOW IN DESIGN VIEW

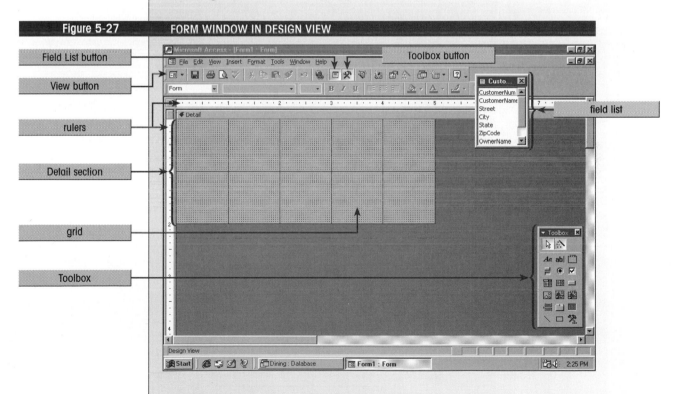

Field List button

View button

rulers

Detail section

grid

Toolbox

Toolbox button

field list

TROUBLE? If the rulers, grid, or toolbox do not appear, click View on the menu bar, and then click Ruler, Grid, or Toolbox to display the missing component. If the grid is still invisible, see your instructor or technical support person for assistance. If the Toolbox is not positioned as in Figure 5-27, click the Toolbox window's title bar and then drag it to the position shown.

The Form window in Design view contains the tools necessary to create a custom form. You create the form by placing objects on the blank form in the window. Each object—such as a text box, list box, rectangle, or command button—that you place on a form is called a **control**. There are three kinds of controls that you can place on a form:

- A **bound control** is linked, or bound, to a field in the underlying table or query. You use a bound control to display table field values.

- An **unbound control** is not linked to a field in the underlying table or query. You use an unbound control to display text, such as a form title or instructions, to display lines and rectangles, or to display graphics and pictures from other software programs. An unbound control that displays text is called a **label**.

- A **calculated control** displays a value calculated from data from one or more fields.

To create a bound control, you use the Field List button on the Form Design toolbar to display a list of fields available from the underlying table or query. Then you drag fields from the field list box to the Form window and place the bound controls where you want them to appear on the form.

To place other controls on a form, you use the buttons on the toolbox. The **toolbox** is a specialized toolbar containing buttons that represent the tools you use to place controls on a form or a report. ScreenTips are available for each button. If you want to show or hide the toolbox, click the Toolbox button on the Form Design toolbar. The buttons available on the toolbox are described in Figure 5-28.

Figure 5-28		SUMMARY OF BUTTONS AVAILABLE ON THE TOOLBOX FOR A FORM OR REPORT	
BUTTON	BUTTON NAME	PURPOSE ON A FORM OR A REPORT	CONTROL WIZARD AVAILABLE
	Bound Object Frame	Display a frame for enclosing a bound OLE object stored in an Access database table	Yes
	Check Box	Display a check box control bound to a Yes/No field	Yes
	Combo Box	Display a control that combines the features of a list box and a text box; you can type in the text box or select an entry in the list box to add a value to an underlying field	Yes
	Command Button	Display a control button you can use to link to an action, such as finding a record, printing a record, or applying a form filter	Yes
	Control Wizards	Activate Control Wizards for certain other toolbox tools	No
	Image	Display a graphic image	Yes
	Label	Display text, such as title or instructions; an unbound control	No
	Line	Display a line	No
	List Box	Display a control that contains a scrollable list of values	Yes
	More Controls	Display a list of all available controls	No
	Option Button	Display an option button control bound to a yes/no field	Yes
	Option Group	Display a group frame containing toggle buttons, options buttons, or check boxes	Yes
	Page Break	Begin a new screen on a form or a new page on a report	No
	Rectangle	Display a rectangle	No

Figure 5-28	**SUMMARY OF BUTTONS AVAILABLE ON THE TOOLBOX FOR A FORM OR REPORT (CONTINUED)**		
BUTTON	**BUTTON NAME**	**PURPOSE ON A FORM OR A REPORT**	**CONTROL WIZARD AVAILABLE**
	Select Objects	Select, move, size, and edit controls	No
	Subform/Subreport	Display data from more than one table	Yes
	Tab Control	Display a tab control with multiple pages	No
abl	Text Box	Display a label attached to a text box that contains a bound control or a calculated control	No
	Toggle Button	Display a toggle button control bound to a yes/no field	Yes
	Unbound Object Frame	Display a frame for enclosing an unbound OLE object, such as a Microsoft Excel worksheet	Yes

The Form window in Design view also contains a Detail section, which appears as a light gray rectangle, in which you place the fields, labels, and values for your form. You can change the size of the Detail section by dragging its edges. The grid consists of the dots that appear in the Detail section to help you position controls precisely on a form.

The rulers at the top and at the left edge of the Detail section define the horizontal and vertical dimensions of the form and serve as a guide for placing controls on the form.

Your first task is to add bound controls to the Detail section for the CustomerNum and CustomerName fields from the Customer table.

Adding Fields to a Form

When you add a bound control to a form, Access adds a field-value text box and, to its left, a label. The text box displays the field values from the table or query, and the label identifies the values. To create a bound control, you display the field list by clicking the Field List button on the Form Design toolbar. Then you select one or more fields from the field list box and drag them to the form. You select a single field by clicking the field. You select two or more fields by holding down the Ctrl key and clicking each field, and you select all fields by double-clicking the field list title bar.

You will add bound controls to the Detail section for two of the fields in the field list. Because you will not need the toolbox for a while, you can close it.

To add bound controls for the CustomerNum and CustomerName fields:

1. Click the **Close** button ▨ on the toolbox to close it.

2. If necessary, click the **Field List** button ▤ on the Form Design toolbar to display the field list.

3. Click **CustomerNum** in the field list, press and hold down the **Ctrl** key, click **CustomerName** in the field list, and then release the **Ctrl** key. Both fields are selected.

4. Click the highlighted fields and then drag them to the form's Detail section. Release the mouse button when the pointer is positioned at the 1-inch mark on the horizontal ruler and just below the top of the Detail section. Access adds two bound controls—one for the CustomerNum field and one for the CustomerName field—in the Detail section of the form. See Figure 5-29.

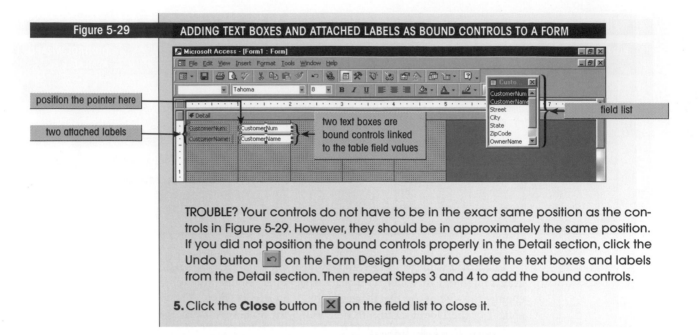

| Figure 5-29 | ADDING TEXT BOXES AND ATTACHED LABELS AS BOUND CONTROLS TO A FORM |

TROUBLE? Your controls do not have to be in the exact same position as the controls in Figure 5-29. However, they should be in approximately the same position. If you did not position the bound controls properly in the Detail section, click the Undo button 🔄 on the Form Design toolbar to delete the text boxes and labels from the Detail section. Then repeat Steps 3 and 4 to add the bound controls.

5. Click the **Close** button ☒ on the field list to close it.

Working on a form in Design view might seem awkward at first. With practice you will become comfortable with creating a custom form. Remember that you can always click the Undo button immediately after you make an error or undesired form adjustment.

Comparing the form's Detail section with Barbara's design, notice that you need to arrange the text boxes so that they appear next to each other. To do so you must select and move the controls.

Selecting and Moving Controls

Two text boxes now appear in the form's Detail section, one below the other. Each text box is a bound control linked to a field in the underlying table and has a label box attached to its left. This means that if you move the text box, the label will move with it. Each text box and each label is an object on the form and appears with square boxes on the corners and edges. These boxes are called **handles**. Handles appear around an object when it is selected, and they allow you to move or resize the control.

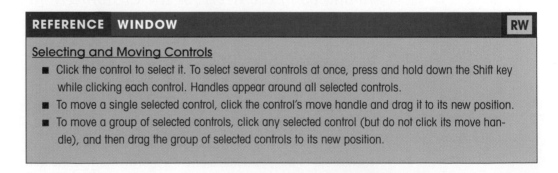

REFERENCE WINDOW   RW

Selecting and Moving Controls
- Click the control to select it. To select several controls at once, press and hold down the Shift key while clicking each control. Handles appear around all selected controls.
- To move a single selected control, click the control's move handle and drag it to its new position.
- To move a group of selected controls, click any selected control (but do not click its move handle), and then drag the group of selected controls to its new position.

To move a single bound control, you must first select just that control. All the controls on your form are currently selected and will move together if you move any one of them. You first need to deselect all the bound controls and then select the CustomerName control to move it to the right of the CustomerNum control. The CustomerName control consists of the CustomerName field-value text box and the corresponding label to its left.

To select the CustomerName bound control:

1. Click the gray area outside the Detail section to deselect the selected controls.

2. Click the **CustomerName** field-value text box to select it. Move handles, which are the larger handles, appear on the upper-left corner of the field-value text box and its attached label box. Sizing handles appear, but only on the field-value text box. See Figure 5-30.

Figure 5-30	SELECTING A SINGLE BOUND CONTROL

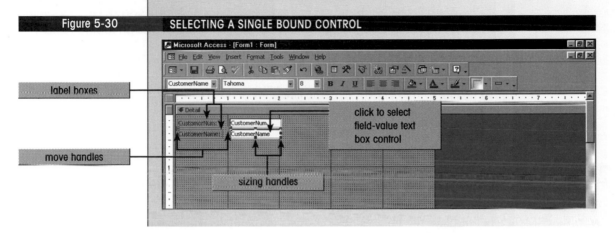

You can move a field-value text box and its attached label box together. To move them, place the pointer anywhere on the border of the field-value text box, but not on a move handle or a sizing handle. When the pointer changes to a ✋ shape, you can drag the field-value text box and its attached label box to the new location. As you move the boxes, their outline moves to show you the changing position.

You can also move either the field-value text box or its label box individually. If you want to move the field-value text box but not its label box, for example, place the pointer on the text box's move handle. When the pointer changes to a ☝ shape, drag the field-value text box to the new location. You use the label box's move handle in a similar way to move just the label box.

To arrange the text boxes to match Barbara's design, you must move the CustomerName control up and to the right.

To move the CustomerName control:

1. Place the pointer on the CustomerName control, but not on a move handle or a sizing handle. When the pointer changes to a ✋ shape, click and drag the control up and to the right. An outline of the control appears as you change its position, to guide you in the move operation. Use the grid dots in the Detail section to help you position the control as shown in Figure 5-31.

Figure 5-31   MOVING THE CUSTOMERNAME CONTROL

TROUBLE? Your control does not have to be in the exact same position as the control in Figure 5-31. However, it should be in approximately the same position, and it should be aligned with the CustomerNum control. If you did not place the control correctly, click the Undo button on the Form Design toolbar, and then repeat Step 1.

According to Barbara's design, the labels for the two controls should be "Customer No.:" and "Customer Name:" (respectively). To modify the text of the labels, you need to change each label's caption.

Changing a Label's Caption

The text in a label is defined by the field name or by the field's Caption property. By default, a label displays the field name as it exists in the underlying table or query. If you want the label to display different text, you need to change the label's Caption property value.

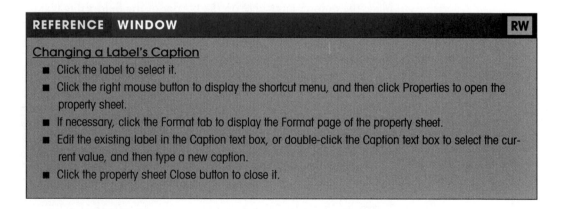

REFERENCE WINDOW   **RW**

Changing a Label's Caption
- Click the label to select it.
- Click the right mouse button to display the shortcut menu, and then click Properties to open the property sheet.
- If necessary, click the Format tab to display the Format page of the property sheet.
- Edit the existing label in the Caption text box, or double-click the Caption text box to select the current value, and then type a new caption.
- Click the property sheet Close button to close it.

You need to change the Caption property of the two labels on your form to "Customer No.:" and "Customer Name:".

To change the Caption property value for the two labels:

1. Click the **CustomerNum** label box to select it.

2. Click the right mouse button to display the shortcut menu, and then click **Properties**. The property sheet for the CustomerNum label opens.

3. If necessary, click the property sheet title bar and drag the property sheet down until the CustomerNum and CustomerName label boxes are visible.

4. If necessary, click the **Format** tab to display the Format page of the property sheet.

5. Position the insertion point between the "r" and the "N" in CustomerNum: in the Caption text box, and then press the **spacebar**.

   TROUBLE? If you do not see the Caption text box on your Format page, then you selected the wrong control in Step 1. Click the CustomerNum label box to change to the property sheet for this control, and then repeat Step 5.

6. Position the insertion point between the "m" in Num and the colon following it, press the **Backspace** key twice, and then type **o.** (including the period). The value should now be Customer No.:. See Figure 5-32.

Figure 5-32	CHANGING THE CAPTION PROPERTY FOR THE LABEL

TROUBLE? Some of the property values on your screen (such as the Left and Top margin values) might be different from those shown in Figure 5-32, if your controls are in slightly different positions from those in the figure.

7. Click the **CustomerName** label box to select it. The property sheet now displays the properties for the CustomerName label, and the CustomerNum label in the Detail section now displays Customer No.:.

8. Position the insertion point between the "r" and "N" in CustomerName, and then press the **spacebar**. The label should now be Customer Name:.

9. Click the **Close** button X on the property sheet to close it.

When you create a form, you should periodically check your progress by displaying the form in Form view. You might see adjustments you want to make on your form in Design view. Next, you'll save the current form design and then view the form in Form view.

To save the form and switch to Form view:

1. Click the **Save** button on the Form Design toolbar. The Save As dialog box opens.

2. Type **Customer Information Multi-page**, and then press the **Enter** key. Access saves the form design.

3. Click the **View** button for Form view 🖩 on the Form Design toolbar. Access closes the Form window in Design view and displays the form in Form view. See Figure 5-33.

Figure 5-33	FORM WINDOW IN FORM VIEW

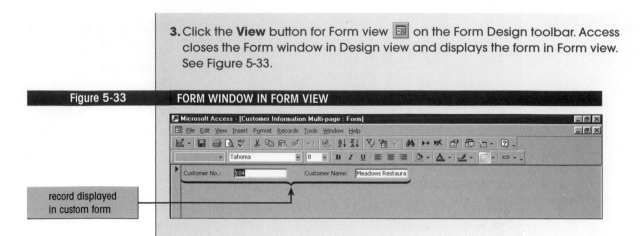

record displayed
in custom form

Access displays the CustomerNum and CustomerName field values for the first record in the Customer table (Meadows Restaurant). You can use the navigation buttons to view other records from the table in the form.

The form displayed in Form view reveals some adjustments you need to make to the form design. The CustomerNum field-value text box is too large for the field value, and the CustomerName field-value text box is too small for the field value. So you will resize both text boxes.

Resizing Controls

A selected control displays seven sizing handles, one on each side of the control and one at each corner except the upper-left corner. The upper-left corner displays the move handle. Positioning the pointer over a sizing handle changes the pointer to a two-headed arrow; the direction in which the arrows are pointing indicates the direction in which you can resize the selected control. When you drag a sizing handle, you resize the control. Thin lines appear, which guide you as you resize the control.

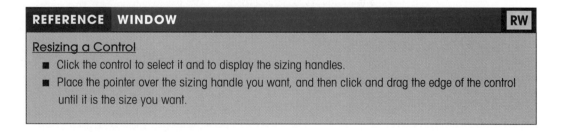

REFERENCE WINDOW   RW

Resizing a Control
- Click the control to select it and to display the sizing handles.
- Place the pointer over the sizing handle you want, and then click and drag the edge of the control until it is the size you want.

You'll begin by resizing the CustomerNum text box, which is much larger than necessary to display the three-digit customer number. Then you'll resize the CustomerName text box to make it large enough to display the complete customer name.

To resize the two text boxes:

1. Click the **View** button for Design view 🖾 on the Form View toolbar to return to the Form window in Design view.

2. Click the **CustomerNum** text box to select it.

3. Place the pointer on the middle-right handle. When the pointer changes to a ←→ shape, click and drag the right border horizontally to the left until the text box is approximately the size of the text box shown in Figure 5-34.

TROUBLE? If you change the vertical size of the box by mistake, just click the Undo button 🔄 on the Form Design toolbar, and then repeat Step 3.

Now you will move the CustomerName control to its correct position, and then resize the CustomerName text box.

4. Click the **CustomerName** text box to select the bound control. Place the pointer on the CustomerName text box, but not on a move handle or a sizing handle. When the pointer changes to a 🖐 shape, click and drag the control to the left until its left edge is at the 2-inch mark on the horizontal ruler. Release the mouse button.

5. Place the pointer on the middle-right handle of the CustomerName text box control. When the pointer changes to a ←→ shape, click and drag the right border horizontally to the right until the right edge of the text box is at the 4¾-inch mark on the horizontal ruler. Release the mouse button. See Figure 5-34.

| Figure 5-34 | CUSTOMERNUM AND CUSTOMERNAME TEXT BOXES MOVED AND RESIZED |

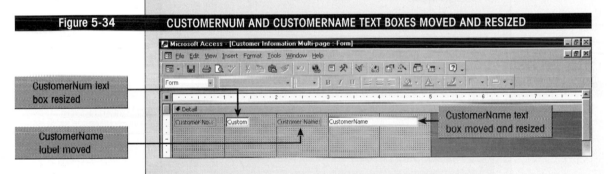

CustomerNum text box resized

CustomerName label moved

CustomerName text box moved and resized

6. Click the **View** button for Form view 📧 on the Form Design toolbar to view the controls on the form. Notice that the text boxes are now the appropriate size for displaying the field values.

Now you will add the title and picture to the top of the form.

Using Form Headers and Form Footers

The Form Header and Form Footer sections allow you to add titles, instructions, command buttons, and other information to the top and bottom of your form, respectively. Controls placed in the Form Header or Form Footer sections remain on the screen whenever the form is displayed; they do not change when the contents of the Detail section change. To add either a header or footer to your form, you must first add both the Form Header and Form Footer sections as a pair to the Form window in Design view. If your form needs one of these sections but not the other, you can remove a section by setting its height to zero, which is the same method you would use to remove any section from a form.

According to Barbara's design, your form must include a Form Header section that will contain the form title and a picture of the Valle Coffee cup logo. You need to add this section to your form.

To add Form Header and Form Footer sections to the form:

1. Click the **View** button for Design view 🔲 on the Form View toolbar to switch to Design view.

2. Click **View** on the menu bar, and then click **Form Header/Footer**. Access inserts a Form Header section above the Detail section and a Form Footer section below the Detail section. See Figure 5-35.

Figure 5-35   ADDING THE FORM HEADER AND FORM FOOTER SECTIONS

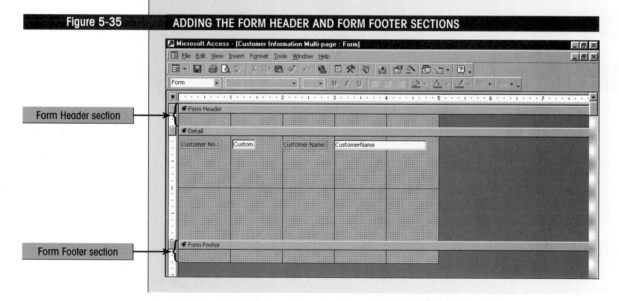

You do not need a Form Footer section in this form, so you'll remove it by making its height zero.

To remove the Form Footer section:

1. Place the pointer at the bottom edge of the Form Footer section. When the pointer changes to a ⬍ shape, click and drag the bottom edge of the section up until it disappears. Even though the words Form Footer remain, the area defining the section is set to zero, and the section will not appear in the form.

You can now add the title to the Form Header section, using the Label tool on the toolbox.

Adding a Label to a Form

The form design shows a title at the top of the form. You can add a title or other text to a form by using the Label tool on the toolbox.

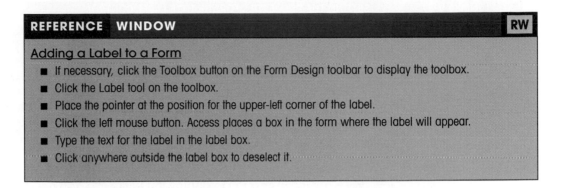

REFERENCE WINDOW   **RW**

Adding a Label to a Form
- If necessary, click the Toolbox button on the Form Design toolbar to display the toolbox.
- Click the Label tool on the toolbox.
- Place the pointer at the position for the upper-left corner of the label.
- Click the left mouse button. Access places a box in the form where the label will appear.
- Type the text for the label in the label box.
- Click anywhere outside the label box to deselect it.

You'll begin by placing a label box for the title in the Form Header section.

To place a label on the form:

1. Click the **Toolbox** button 🛠 on the Form Design toolbar to display the toolbox.

2. Click the **Label** tool 🔤 on the toolbox.

3. Move the pointer to the Form Header section. The pointer changes to a $^+$A shape.

4. Position the center of the + portion of the pointer on the grid dot in the upper-left corner of the Form Header section. This will be the upper-left corner of the label.

5. Click the left mouse button. Access inserts a small label box in the Form Header section and places the insertion point in the label box.

6. Type **Valle Coffee Customer Information** in the label box, and then click anywhere outside of the label box to deselect it. See Figure 5-36.

| Figure 5-36 | LABEL PLACED IN THE FORM HEADER SECTION |

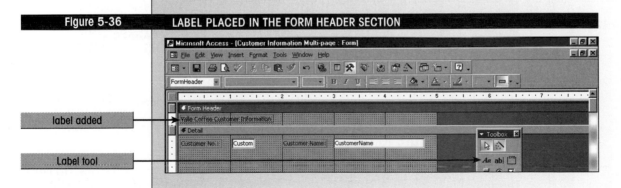

Barbara wants the title to be prominent on the form, so you will change the format of the text in the label to increase its font size and change the font weight to bold. You do this by using the buttons on the Formatting toolbar.

To change the font size and weight for the title:

1. Click the title label control to select it.

2. Click the **Font Size** list arrow on the Formatting toolbar, and then click **14**.

3. Click the **Bold** button **B** on the Formatting toolbar. See Figure 5-37.

| Figure 5-37 | SETTING THE PROPERTIES FOR THE TITLE LABEL CONTROL |

The label control now displays the title in 14-point bold. However, the label control is not large enough to display the entire title. You need to resize the label control so that it is large enough to display all the text.

4. Click **Format** on the menu bar, point to **Size**, and then click **To Fit**. The label control is resized to display the entire title. The Form Header automatically increases in size to accommodate the new label size. See Figure 5-38.

| Figure 5-38 | TITLE LABEL CONTROL RESIZED TO FIT |

Barbara also wants the Valle Coffee logo, which is a picture of a coffee cup, to appear at the top of the form. You will now add the picture to the Form Header section.

Adding a Picture to a Form

Access has the ability to use files and data created by other software programs. To enhance the appearance of a form or report, for example, you can include a picture or other graphic image on the form or report. To do so you use the Image tool on the toolbox.

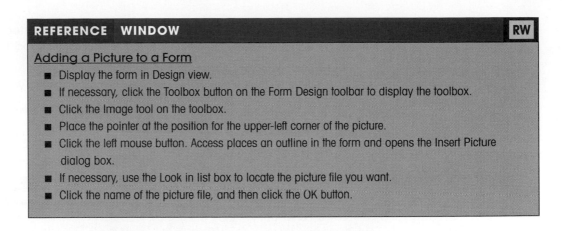

Adding a Picture to a Form
- Display the form in Design view.
- If necessary, click the Toolbox button on the Form Design toolbar to display the toolbox.
- Click the Image tool on the toolbox.
- Place the pointer at the position for the upper-left corner of the picture.
- Click the left mouse button. Access places an outline in the form and opens the Insert Picture dialog box.
- If necessary, use the Look in list box to locate the picture file you want.
- Click the name of the picture file, and then click the OK button.

In this case, the Valle Coffee logo was created in a drawing program and saved in a file named ValleCup. Now you'll add this picture to the top right of the form.

To place the picture on the form:

1. Click the **Image** tool on the toolbox.

2. Move the pointer to the Form Header section. The pointer changes to a shape.

3. Using the ruler as a guide, position the + portion of the pointer slightly below tho top of the Form Header section, approximately ¼-inch from the right edge of the title label control. (See Figure 5-38 for the correct position.) This will be the upper-left corner of the picture.

4. Click the left mouse button. Access places an outline in the Form Header section and opens the Insert Picture dialog box. See Figure 5-39.

Figure 5-39 INSERT PICTURE DIALOG BOX

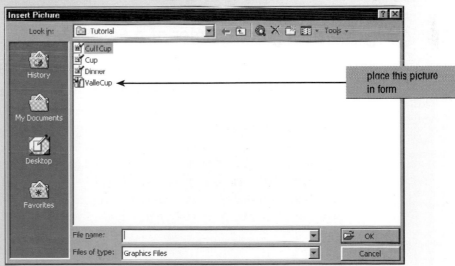

5. Make sure Tutorial appears in the Look in list box, click **ValleCup** to select the picture file, and then click the **OK** button.

The Insert Picture dialog box closes, and the picture is inserted in the form. The Form Header section automatically enlarges to accommodate the size of the image.

Now, you'll view the form with the new header after saving your form changes.

6. Click the **Save** button 🖫 on the Form Design toolbar to save the form.

7. Click the **View** button for Form view 🖽 on the Form Design toolbar to view the form. See Figure 5-40.

Figure 5-40	VIEWING THE FORM WITH THE NEW HEADER

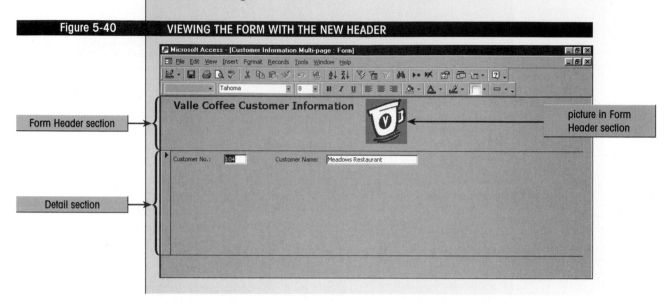

Form Header section

picture in Form Header section

Detail section

Barbara views the form and confirms that the title and picture are correctly placed, formatted, and sized. However, she would like the background color of the form to be dark gray to match the background color of the picture, so that the picture will blend in better with the form.

Changing **the Background Color of a Form Object**

You can change the background color of a form or of a specific section or object on the form by using tools available in Design view.

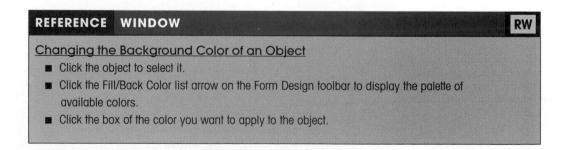

REFERENCE   WINDOW   RW

Changing the Background Color of an Object
- Click the object to select it.
- Click the Fill/Back Color list arrow on the Form Design toolbar to display the palette of available colors.
- Click the box of the color you want to apply to the object.

You need to change the background color of the Form Header section and the Detail section of the form to match the background color of the picture. This will cause the picture to blend in with the form.

To change the background color of the Detail and Form Header sections:

1. Click the **View** button for Design view 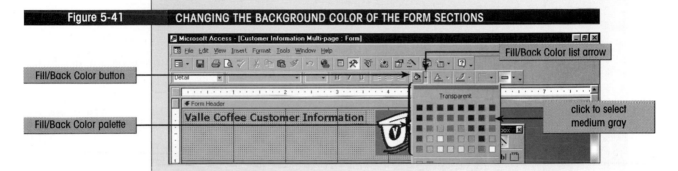 on the Form View toolbar to switch to Design view.

2. Click an empty area of the Detail section. This makes the Detail section the selected control.

3. Click the list arrow for the **Fill/Back Color** button 🖌 on the Form Design toolbar. Access displays the palette of available colors. See Figure 5-41.

Figure 5-41   CHANGING THE BACKGROUND COLOR OF THE FORM SECTIONS

4. Click the medium gray box in the color palette at the right end of the second row (see Figure 5-41). The background of the Detail section changes to the medium gray color.

   Now you need to apply the same color to the Form Header section. To do so, you do not have to redisplay the color palette; once you select a color from the palette, it remains in effect so that you can apply the color to other objects by simply clicking the Fill/Back Color button.

5. Click an empty area of the Form Header section. This makes the Form Header section the selected control.

6. Click the **Fill/Back Color** button 🖌 (not the list arrow) on the Form Design toolbar. The Form Header section now appears with the medium gray background.

   Now you can save the form and view your changes in Form View.

7. Click the **Save** button 💾 (not the list arrow) on the Form Design toolbar to save the form.

8. Click the **View** button for Form view 📧 on the Form Design toolbar to view the form. See Figure 5-42.

Figure 5-42   FORM WITH NEW BACKGROUND COLOR

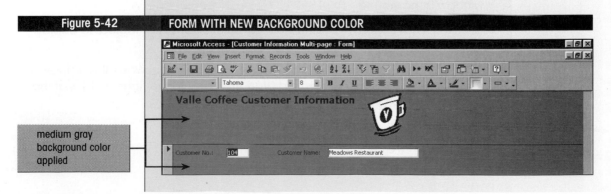

medium gray background color applied

In the next session, you will add two pages to the form: one to display the customer address and contact information, and another to display the order information.

Session 5.2 QUICK CHECK

1. What is the difference between a bound control and an unbound control?

2. How do you move a control and its label together?

3. How do you change a label name?

4. How do you resize a control?

5. What is the Form Header section?

6. How do you insert a picture, created using another software program, in a form?

SESSION 5.3

In this session, you will create a multi-page form and use Control Wizards to add a sub-form. You will also use the custom form to filter the data and save the filter as a query.

Creating a Multi-page Form Using Tab Controls

You can create a multi-page form in two ways: by inserting a page break control in the form or by using a tab control. If you insert a page break control in a form, the user can move between pages using the Page Up and Page Down keys on the keyboard. If you use a tab control, the control appears with tabs at the top, with one tab for each page. The user can switch between pages by clicking the tabs.

Barbara wants to include a tab control with two pages on the Valle Coffee Customer Information Multi-page form. The first page of the tab control will contain customer information, such as the address, owner name, and other fields from the Customer table. The second page of the tab control will contain a subform with order information for that customer.

First you will resize the Detail section of the form to make room for the tab control.

To resize the Detail section:

1. If you took a break after the previous session, make sure that Access is running, that the Dining database from the Tutorial folder on your Data Disk is open, and that the Customer Information Multi-page form is open in Form view and the window is maximized.

2. Click the **View** button for Design view 🖾 on the Form View toolbar to display the form in Design view.

3. Place the pointer on the right edge of the Detail section. When the pointer changes to a ↔ shape, click and drag the edge to the right until it is at the 5½-inch mark on the horizontal ruler.

Now you can place the tab control on the form.

To place the tab control on the form:

1. Click the **Tab Control** tool ⊞ on the toolbox.

2. Position the + portion of the pointer at the left edge of the Detail section, approximately ½-inch below the top of the Detail section, and then click the left mouse button. (Refer to Figure 5-43 for the correct position for the tab control.) Access places a tab control in the Detail section.

   Now you will resize the tab control so that it is large enough to display the remaining fields for the form.

3. Scroll down the Form window (if necessary) until the tab control is completely visible, click the right-middle handle of the tab control, and then drag it to the right until it is three grid dots from the right edge of the form. See Figure 5-43.

Figure 5-43	TAB CONTROL PLACED IN THE DETAIL SECTION AND RESIZED

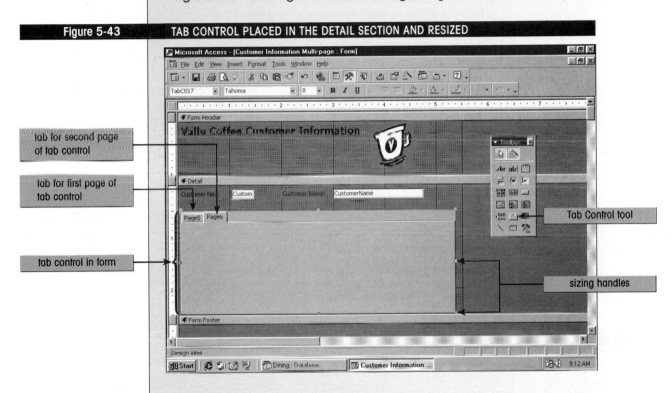

TROUBLE? The page tabs on your screen might show different page numbers in the labels, depending on how you completed the previous steps. This will not affect the form. Just continue with the tutorial.

The top of the tab control displays two tabs. Each tab indicates a separate page on the form. On the first page, you will place the controls for the fields from the Customer table. On the second page, you will place a subform displaying the fields from the Order table for that customer. The user can move between the two pages by clicking the tabs.

To add the fields to the tab control:

1. Click the **Field List** button ▤ on the Form Design toolbar to display the field list.

2. Click the **Street** field in the field list, scroll to the end of the field list, press and hold down the **Shift** key, click the **FirstContact** field, and then release the **Shift** key. All the fields in the list, except CustomerNum and CustomerName, should be selected.

3. Drag the selected fields to the tab control and release the mouse button when the pointer is approximately at the 1-inch mark on the horizontal ruler.

4. Click the **Close** button ⊠ on the field list to close it.

5. Click a blank area of the tab control to deselect the text boxes and their labels.

   Now you need to move and resize the text boxes to match Barbara's form design.

6. Click the **Street text box** to select it, and then place the pointer on its move handle in the upper-left corner. When the pointer changes to a 🖑 shape, click and drag the **Street text box** to the left, to the ¾-inch mark (approximately) on the horizontal ruler. Refer to Figure 5-44 to help you position the text box.

7. Place the pointer on the middle-right handle of the Street text box. When the pointer changes to a ←→ shape, click and drag the right border to the right until the text box is approximately the size of the text box shown in Figure 5-44.

   Now that you've positioned the Street text box, you can position the Street label automatically by selecting both controls and then using the Align command on the Format menu.

8. Press and hold down the **Shift** key, click the **Street label box** (both the Street label box and Street field-name text box should be selected), release the **Shift** key, click **Format** on the menu bar, point to **Align**, and then click **Top**. The two controls are now aligned on their top edges.

9. Move and resize the text boxes for the remaining fields. Use Figure 5-44 as a guide for positioning and sizing the text boxes. Be sure to use the Align command on the Format menu to position pairs of text boxes, aligning controls on their top or left edges.

| Figure 5-44 | CUSTOMER FIELDS PLACED IN THE TAB CONTROL |

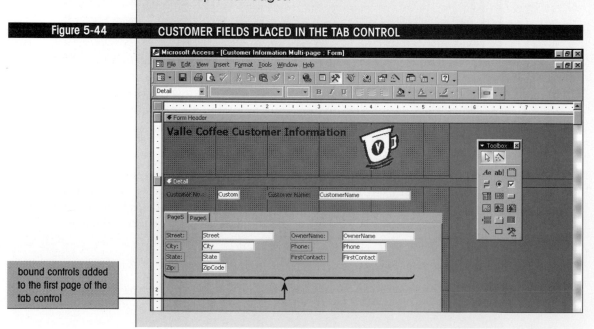

bound controls added to the first page of the tab control

TROUBLE? Your controls do not have to be in the exact same position as the controls in Figure 5-44. However, they should be in approximately the same position. If you did not place the controls correctly, move and resize them now.

Notice that the label boxes on the form are left-justified; that is, they are aligned on their left edges. Barbara thinks that the form will look better if these labels are right-justified, or aligned on their right edges. To align them, you will select all the labels in a column and use the shortcut menu.

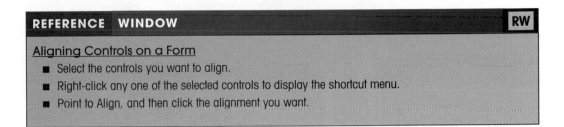

REFERENCE WINDOW   RW

Aligning Controls on a Form
- Select the controls you want to align.
- Right-click any one of the selected controls to display the shortcut menu.
- Point to Align, and then click the alignment you want.

To select and align all the label boxes on the right:

1. Click the **Street label box** to select it.

2. Press and hold down the **Shift** key while you click each of the remaining label boxes below the Street label so that all four are selected, and then release the **Shift** key.

3. Right-click any one of the selected label boxes to display the shortcut menu.

4. Point to **Align**, and then click **Right**. Access aligns the label boxes on their right edges. See Figure 5-45.

| Figure 5-45 | ALIGNING THE LABEL BOXES |

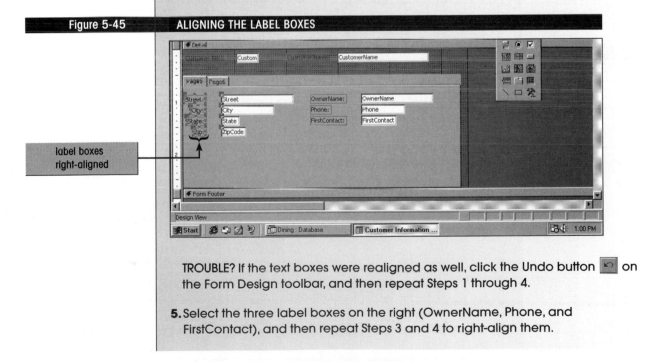

label boxes right-aligned

TROUBLE? If the text boxes were realigned as well, click the Undo button 🔄 on the Form Design toolbar, and then repeat Steps 1 through 4.

5. Select the three label boxes on the right (OwnerName, Phone, and FirstContact), and then repeat Steps 3 and 4 to right-align them.

6. Click the **Save** button 🖫 on the Form Design toolbar to save the form.

7. Click the **View** button for Form view 🖼 on the Form Design toolbar to view the form. See Figure 5-46.

| Figure 5-46 | FIRST RECORD IN FORM VIEW |

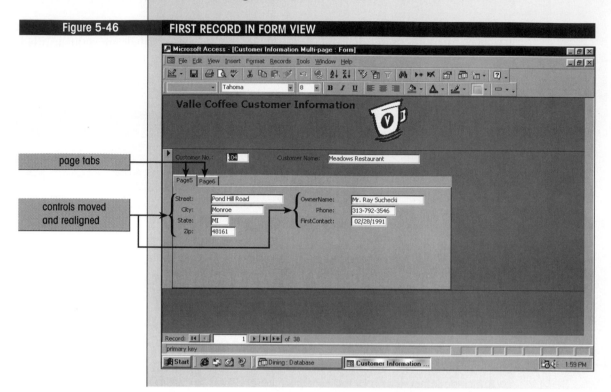

You are now ready to add the Order table fields as a subform on the second page of the form.

Adding a Subform Using Control Wizards

You use the Subform/Subreport button on the toolbox to add a subform to a form. If you want help in defining the subform, you can first select one of the Access Control Wizards. A **Control Wizard** asks you a series of questions and then creates a control on a form or report based on your answers. Access offers Control Wizards for the Combo Box, List Box, Option Group, Command Button, and Subform/Subreport tools, among others.

You will use the Subform/Subreport Wizard to add the subform for the Order table records. This subform will appear on the second page of the form.

To add the subform to the form:

1. Click the **View** button for Design view 🖎 on the Form View toolbar to switch to Design view.

2. Make sure the **Control Wizards** tool 🖎 on the toolbox is selected.

3. Click the tab for the second page (the tab on the right) to select that page.

4. Click the **Subform/Subreport** tool 🖼 on the toolbox.

5. Position the + portion of the pointer near the upper-left corner of the tab control, and then click the left mouse button. Access places a subform control in the tab control and opens the first SubForm Wizard dialog box.

You can use an existing table, query, or form as the source for a new subform. You'll use the Order table as the basis for the new subform.

To use the SubForm Wizard to add the subform to the form:

1. Make sure the Use existing Tables and Queries option button is selected, and then click the **Next** button. Access opens the next SubForm Wizard dialog box. See Figure 5-47.

| Figure 5-47 | SELECTING THE TABLE AND FIELDS FOR THE SUBFORM |

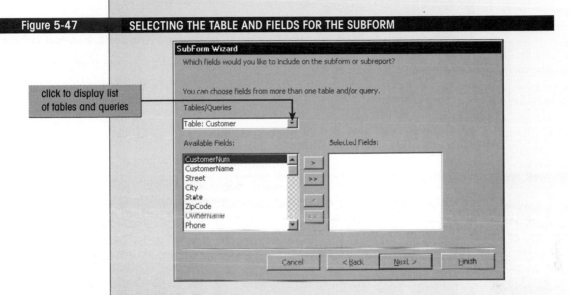

This dialog box allows you to select the table or query on which the subform is based and to select the fields from that table or query.

2. Click the **Tables/Queries** list arrow to display the list of tables and queries in the Dining database, and then click **Table: Order**. The Available Fields list box shows the fields in the Order table.

3. Click the >> button to move all available fields to the Selected Fields list box, and then click the **Next** button. See Figure 5-48.

| Figure 5-48 | SELECTING THE LINKING FIELD |

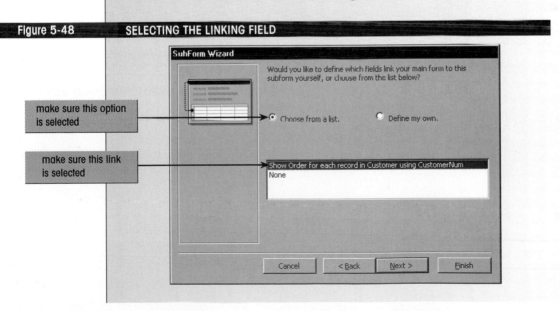

This dialog box allows you to select the link between the Customer table and the Order table. CustomerNum, as the common field between the two tables, links the two tables. Also, CustomerNum is the means by which a record in the main form, which displays data from the Customer table, is synchronized to records in the subform, which displays data from the Order table.

4. Make sure the Choose from a list option button is selected and that the first link is highlighted, and then click the **Next** button. The next SubForm Wizard dialog box allows you to specify a name for the subform.

5. Type **Customer Information Subform** and then click the **Finish** button. A subform object, which is where the Order records will appear, is inserted in the tab control.

TROUBLE? If your form is no longer maximized, click the Maximize button 🔲 on the form to maximize it.

6. Click the **View** button for Form view 🖳 on the Form Design toolbar to view the form. See Figure 5-49.

| Figure 5-49 | VIEWING THE FORM WITH THE TAB CONTROL |

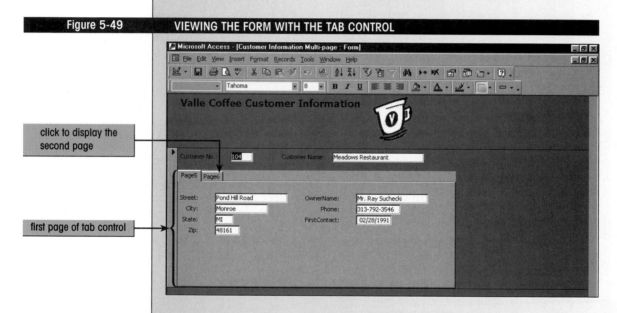

The tab control shows the customer information on the current page. You can view the order information for the customer by clicking the second page.

7. Click the page tab on the right to display the order information. See Figure 5-50.

| Figure 5-50 | VIEWING THE SUBFORM ON THE TAB CONTROL |

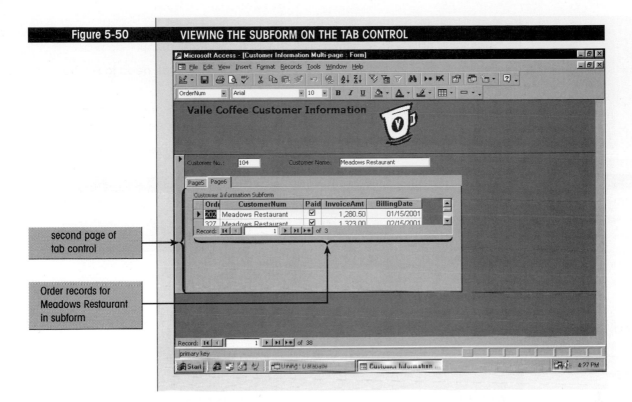

second page of tab control

Order records for Meadows Restaurant in subform

After viewing the form, Barbara identifies several modifications she'd like you to make. The subform is not properly sized, and the column headings in the subform are not displayed completely. She wants you to resize the subform and its columns so that the columns are entirely visible. She also wants you to delete the CustomerNum field from the subform, because the labels at the top of the form already provide both the customer number and the customer name. Finally, she asks you to delete the Customer Information Subform label and edit the labels for the tabs in the tab control so that they indicate the contents of each page.

You can resize the subform and edit the labels in Design view. Then you can delete the CustomerNum field from the subform and resize the Order columns in Form view. You will begin by resizing the subform and editing the labels for the tabs.

To resize the subform, delete its label, and edit the labels for the tabs:

1. Click the **View** button for Design view 🔲 on the Form View toolbar.

2. If necessary, scroll down until the bottom of the subform is visible. If necessary, click the right tab to select it.

   If you click a tab, you select the tab control, and sizing handles appear on the edges of the tab control. If you want to select a subform positioned in a tab control, you should click the right or bottom edge of the subform; sizing handles disappear from the tab control and appear on the subform, indicating that it's selected.

3. Select the subform, and then place the pointer on the middle-bottom sizing handle of the subform. When the pointer changes to a ↕ shape, click and drag the edge of the subform to the 2¼-inch mark on the vertical ruler.

4. Right-click the label for the subform control (make sure the subform no longer has sizing handles), and then click **Cut** on the shortcut menu.

Now you can change the labels on the tabs. To do so, you need to set the Caption property for each tab.

5. Right-click the subform page tab (not the subform itself), and then click **Properties** on the shortcut menu to open the property sheet.

6. Click the **Format** tab, and then type **Orders** in the Caption text box. See Figure 5-51.

Figure 5-51   SETTING THE CAPTION PROPERTY VALUE FOR THE PAGE TABS

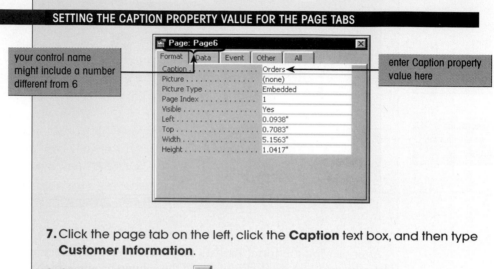

your control name might include a number different from 6

enter Caption property value here

---

7. Click the page tab on the left, click the **Caption** text box, and then type **Customer Information**.

8. Click the **Close** button ⊠ on the property sheet to close it.

Now you can view the form, resize the columns in the Orders subform, and delete the CustomerNum field from the subform.

To view the form and resize the columns and delete the CustomerNum field in the Orders subform:

1. Click the **View** button for Form view 📧. The first customer record, for Meadows Restaurant, is displayed in the form.

2. Click the **Orders** tab. The second page of the multi-page form displays the Order records for Meadows Restaurant.

Now you can resize the columns in the Order subform.

3. Place the pointer on the column heading for the OrderNum field in the subform. When the pointer changes to a ↓ shape, click and drag the pointer to the right to highlight all the columns in the subform.

4. Place the pointer on the line between any two columns. When the pointer changes to a ↔ shape, double-click to resize all the columns.

Next, you'll delete, or hide, the CustomerNum field from the subform.

5. Right-click **CustomerNum** in the subform, and then click **Hide Columns** on the shortcut menu. The CustomerNum column is hidden in the subform. See Figure 5-52.

Figure 5-52	ORDER FIELDS AFTER RESIZING

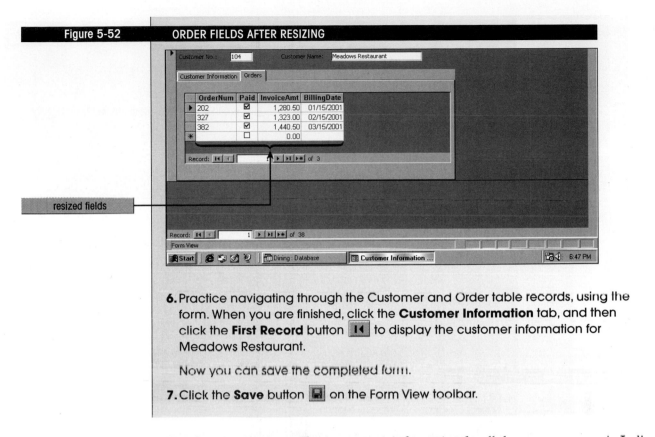

resized fields

6. Practice navigating through the Customer and Order table records, using the form. When you are finished, click the **Customer Information** tab, and then click the **First Record** button to display the customer information for Meadows Restaurant.

Now you can save the completed form.

7. Click the **Save** button on the Form View toolbar.

Kim has a new request. She wants to see information for all the new customers in Indiana or Ohio. She defines a new customer as one whose first contact date was in 2001 or later. She'd like to view this information using the Customer Information Multi-page form. To produce the results she wants, you need to use a filter with the form.

Using a Filter with a Form

Recall that a **filter** is a set of criteria that describes the records you want to see, in a datasheet or a form, and their sequence. A filter is like a query, but it applies only to the current datasheet or form. If you want to use a filter at another time, you can save the filter as a query.

Access provides four filter tools that allow you to specify and apply filters: Filter By Selection, Filter By Form, Filter For Input, and Advanced Filter/Sort. With Filter By Selection, Filter By Form, and Filter For Input, you specify the record selection criteria directly in the form. Filter By Selection finds records that match a particular field value. Filter By Form and Filter For Input find records that match multiple selection criteria, using the same Access logical and comparison operators that you use in queries. After applying a filter by selection or by form or for input, you can rearrange the records using the Sort Ascending or Sort Descending toolbar buttons, if necessary.

Advanced Filter/Sort allows you to specify multiple selection criteria and to specify a sort order for the selected records in the Advanced Filter/Sort window, in the same way you specify record selection criteria and sort orders for a query in Design view.

To produce the results Kim wants, you'll use Filter By Form.

Using Filter By Form

Because the Customer Information Multi-page form already shows all the customer information, you can use Filter By Form to display information for only the new customers in Indiana or Ohio.

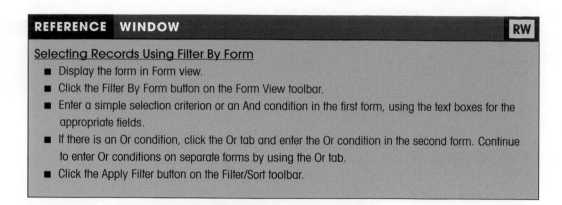

REFERENCE WINDOW   **RW**

Selecting Records Using Filter By Form
- Display the form in Form view.
- Click the Filter By Form button on the Form View toolbar.
- Enter a simple selection criterion or an And condition in the first form, using the text boxes for the appropriate fields.
- If there is an Or condition, click the Or tab and enter the Or condition in the second form. Continue to enter Or conditions on separate forms by using the Or tab.
- Click the Apply Filter button on the Filter/Sort toolbar.

The multiple selection criteria you will enter are: Indiana *and* first contact after 12/31/2000 *or* Ohio *and* first contact after 12/31/2000.

To select the records using Filter By Form:

1. Click the **Filter By Form** button 🔳 on the Form View toolbar. Access displays a blank form. See Figure 5-53.

Figure 5-53	BLANK FORM FOR FILTER BY FORM

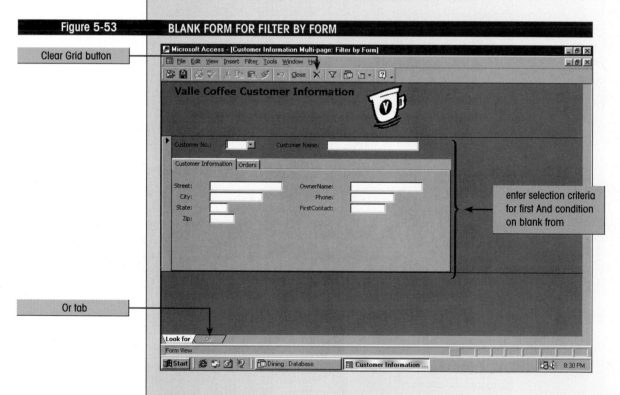

In this blank form, you specify multiple selection criteria by entering conditions in the text boxes for the fields in a record. If you enter criteria in more than one field, you create the equivalent of an And condition—Access will select any record that matches all the criteria. To create an Or condition, you enter the criteria for the first part of the condition in the field on the first (Look for) blank form, and then click the Or tab to display a new blank form. You enter the criteria for the second part of the condition in the same field on this new blank form. Access selects any record that matches all the criteria on the Look for form *or* all the criteria on the Or form.

2. Click the **State** text box, click the list arrow, and then click **IN**. Access adds the criterion "IN" to the State text box.

3. Click the **FirstContact** text box, and then type **>#12/31/2000#**. The number signs (#) indicate a date. If you omit them, Access adds them automatically.

You have now specified the logical operator (And) and the comparison operator (>) for the condition "Indiana and after 12/31/2000." To add the rest of the criteria, you need to display the Or form.

4. Click the **Or** tab to display a second blank form. The insertion point is in the text box for the FirstContact field. Also, notice that a third tab, which is also labeled "Or," is now available in case you need to specify another Or condition.

5. Type **>#12/31/2000#**.

6. Click the **State** text box, click the list arrow, and then click **OH**. The form now contains the equivalent of the second And condition: "Ohio and after 12/31/2000." See Figure 5-54.

Figure 5-54	COMPLETED FILTER BY FORM

Apply Filter button

second And
condition entered
on Or tab

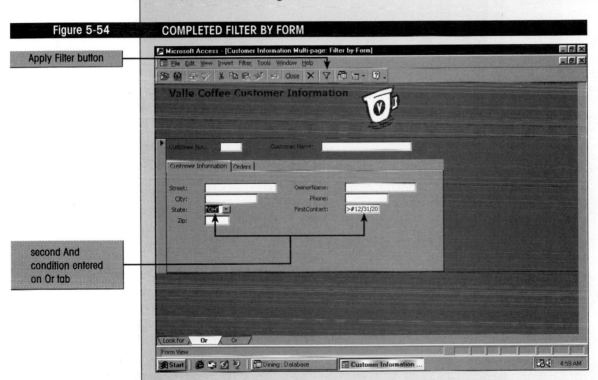

Combined with the Look for form, you now have the Or condition, and the Filter By Form conditions are complete.

7. Click the **Apply Filter** button on the Filter/Sort toolbar. Access applies the filter and displays the first record that matches the selection criteria (the Gateway Lounge in Ohio, first contacted on 3/5/2001). The bottom of the screen shows that the filter selected two records. See Figure 5-55.

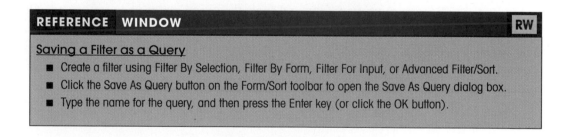

Figure 5-55   FIRST RECORD THAT MATCHES THE SELECTION CRITERIA

Remove Filter button

indicates filter applied

8. Click the **Next Record** button ▶ to display the second selected record (the Embers Restaurant in Indiana, first contacted on 12/28/2001).

Now that you have defined the filter, you can save it as a query, so that Kim can easily view this information again in the future.

Saving a Filter as a Query

By saving a filter as a query, you can reuse the filter in the future by opening the saved query.

REFERENCE   WINDOW   **RW**

Saving a Filter as a Query

■ Create a filter using Filter By Selection, Filter By Form, Filter For Input, or Advanced Filter/Sort.
■ Click the Save As Query button on the Form/Sort toolbar to open the Save As Query dialog box.
■ Type the name for the query, and then press the Enter key (or click the OK button).

You'll save the filter you just created as a query named "New Customers in Indiana and Ohio."

To save the filter as a query:

1. Click the **Filter By Form** button 🖼 on the Form View toolbar. Access displays the form with the selection criteria.

2. Click the **Save As Query** button 🖫 on the Filter/Sort toolbar. The Save As Query dialog box opens.

3. Type **New Customers in Indiana and Ohio** in the Query Name text box, and then press the **Enter** key. Access saves the filter as a query and closes the dialog box.

   Now you can clear the selection criteria, close the Filter by Form window, and return to Form view.

4. Click the **Clear Grid** button ⊠ on the Filter/Sort toolbar. Access removes the selection criteria from the forms.

5. Click the **Close** button ⊠ on the menu bar to close the Filter by Form window and return to Form view. The filter is still in effect in this window, so you need to remove it.

6. Click the **Remove Filter** button ⊽ on the Form View toolbar. The bottom of the screen shows that there are 38 available records.

Next, to check that the filter was saved as a query, you'll close the Form window and view the list of queries on the Queries tab.

To close the Form window and view the query list:

1. Click the **Close** button ⊠ on the menu bar.

2. Click **Queries** in the Objects bar of the Database window to display the Queries list. The query "New Customers in Indiana and Ohio" is now listed.

The next time Kim wants to view the records selected by this query, she can apply the query to the form. If she simply runs the query, she will see the selected records, but they will not be shown in the Customer Information Multi-page form. Instead, she can open the form and apply the saved query to select the records she wants to view in the form.

Applying a Filter that Was Saved as a Query

To see how to apply a query as a filter to a form, you will open the Customer Information Multi-page form and apply the New Customers in Indiana and Ohio query as a filter.

REFERENCE WINDOW   **RW**

Applying a Filter that Was Saved as a Query

- Open the form to which you want to apply the filter.
- Click the Filter By Form button on the Form View toolbar.
- Click the Load from Query button on the Filter/Sort toolbar.
- Select the query you want to apply. Access loads the saved query into the Filter grid.
- Click the Apply Filter button on the Filter/Sort toolbar.

To apply the filter that you saved as a query:

1. Click **Forms** in the Objects bar of the Database window, and then double-click **Customer Information Multi-page** to display this form in Form view.

2. Click the **Filter By Form** button 🗐 on the Form View toolbar.

3. Click the **Load from Query** button 🖉 on the Filter/Sort toolbar. Access opens the Applicable Filter dialog box. See Figure 5-56.

| Figure 5-56 | APPLICABLE FILTER DIALOG BOX |

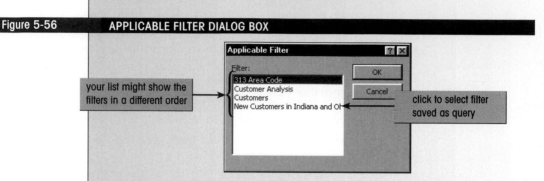

your list might show the filters in a different order

click to select filter saved as query

4. Click **New Customers in Indiana and Ohio** in the Filter list box, and then click the **OK** button. Access loads the saved query into the Filter grid.

5. Click the **Apply Filter** button 🔽 on the Filter/Sort toolbar. Access applies the filter and displays the first record in the form.

6. Click the **Close** button ⊠ on the menu bar to close the form and return to the Database window.

   You can now close the Dining database and exit Access.

7. Click ⊠ on the Access window to close the database and to exit Access.

The new queries and forms that you created will make it much easier for Leonard, Barbara, and Kim to enter, retrieve, and view information in the Dining database.

Session 5.3 QUICK CHECK

1. Describe how you would use a Control Wizard to add a tab control to a form.

2. How do you right-align a group of labels?

3. What is the purpose of Filter By Form?

4. How do you reuse a filter in the future?

5. What is the difference between opening a query and applying a query to a form?

REVIEW ASSIGNMENTS

The **Products** database in the Review folder on your Data Disk contains information about Valle Coffee products. The **Coffee** table in the database contains records of the various types of coffee that Valle Coffee sells. The **Product** table contains pricing information, and the **Weight** table contains packaging information. The database contains several other objects, including queries, forms, and reports. Barbara wants you to make a change to the design of the **Product** table, create some new queries, and create a custom form. Complete the following:

1. Make sure your Data Disk is in the appropriate disk drive, start Access, and then open the **Products** database located in the Review folder on your Data Disk.

2. Open the **Product** table in Design view. Change the WeightCode field data type to Lookup Wizard. Look up values in the **Weight** table, select all fields from the **Weight** table, and accept all other Lookup Wizard default choices.

3. Create a query to find all records in the **Coffee** table where the CoffeeName field begins with "Colombian." Include all fields in the query results. Run the query, save it as **Colombian Coffees**, and then close the query.

4. Create a query to find all records in the **Product** table where the WeightCode value is A, B, or G. Use a list-of-values match for the selection criterion. Include all fields in the query results. Save the query as **A/B/G Weight Codes**, run the query, and then print the query results. Keep the query open.

5. Modify the previous query to find all records in the **Product** table where the WeightCode is not A, B, or G. Save the query as **Not A/B/G Weight Codes**, run the query, print the query results, and then close the query.

6. Create a query to select all the records from the **Coffee** table for Decaffeinated coffees that are African or Special Import. Display the CoffeeName and CoffeeType fields in the query results. Save the query as **Decaf Africans and Special Imports**, run the query, print the query results, and then close the query.

7. Create a parameter query to select the **Product** table records for a WeightCode that the user specifies. Include all fields in the query results. Save the query as **Weight Code Parameter**. Run the query and enter the WeightCode A. Print the query results, and then close the query.

8. Create a custom form based on the **Special Imports** query. Use the design in Figure 5-57 as a guide. Use the Fill/Back Color button to change the background color of the Price field-value text box to light blue (bottom row, third from the right on the palette). Save the form as **Special Imports**. Open the form and print the first record.

Figure 5-57

```
                        Valle Coffee Special Imports
        Coffee Name: XXXXXXXXXXXXXX              Price: $XXX.XX
        Product Code: XXXX                       Weight/Size: XXXXXXXXXXXXXX
```

9. Use Filter By Form with the **Special Imports** form to select all records where the CoffeeName field value starts with "Hawaiian" or "Yemen" and the price is over $50.00. Apply the filter. How many records are selected? Print the first selected record. Save the filter as a query named **Expensive Hawaiian and Yemen Products**. Close the form.

10. Using Figure 5-58 as a guide, create a multi-page form based on the **Coffee** and **Product** tables.

Figure 5-58

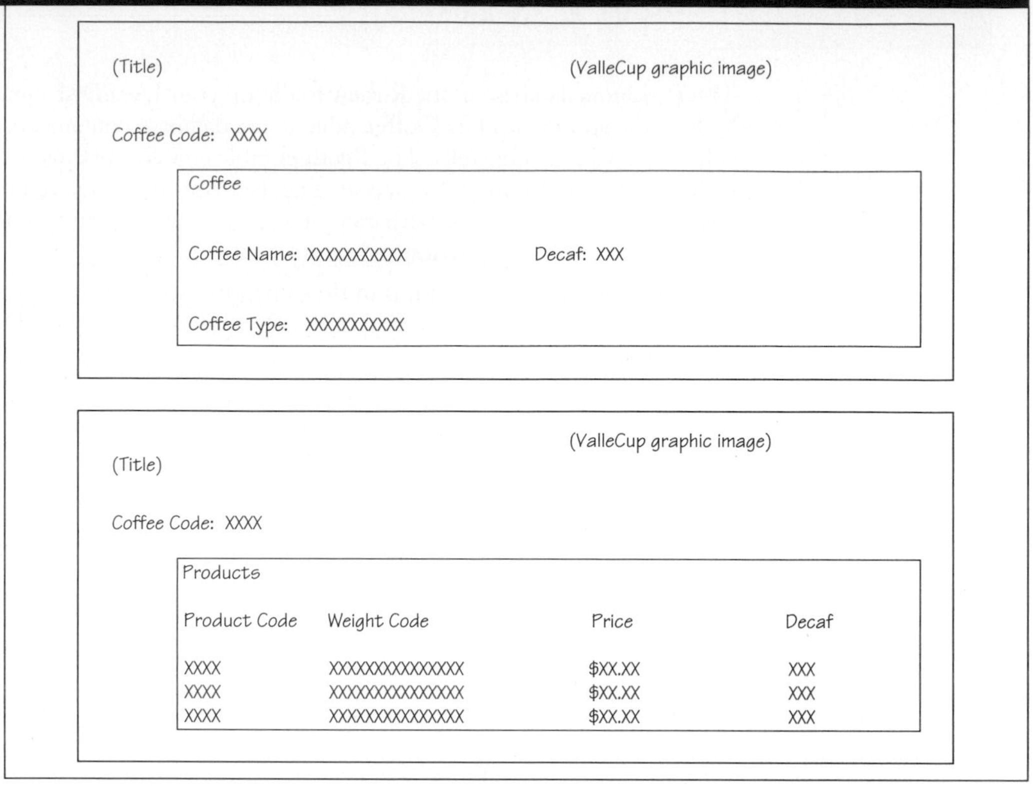

a. Place the CoffeeCode field at the top of the Detail section. Change the caption for the CoffeeCode control to Coffee Code.

b. Insert a Form Header section in the form. Place a title label in the Form Header section. Enter the title Valle Coffee Products.

c. Place the **ValleCup** picture in the Form Header section to the right of the title. The file containing this picture is located in the Review folder on your Data Disk.

d. Place a tab control below the Coffee Code label in the Detail section. On the first page of the tab control, place the remaining fields from the **Coffee** table.

e. On the second page of the tab control, place a subform based on the **Product** table. Save the subform as **Product Subform Tab Control**.

> **Explore**

f. Change the Caption property for each tab and for the necessary fields on the first page. Then change the Caption property for the necessary fields on the subform.

g. Save the form as **Coffee Multi-page**.

h. View the form, resize the subform columns to their best fit, print both pages for the last record, and then close the form.

> **Explore**

11. Open the **Coffee Multi-page** form and then save it as **Enhanced Coffee Multi-page**. Make the following changes to the form design and save the changes:

a. Use the Font/Fore Color button to change the color of the text in the title label to red.

b. Add a Form Footer section. In the center of the Form Footer section, place a label with the text "Valle Gourmet Coffees are the Midwest's favorite." Change the font to 12-point italic, make the color of the text red, and then size the title label to fit.

c. Print both pages for the first record, and then save and close the form.

12. Close the **Products** database, and then exit Access.

CASE PROBLEMS

Case 1. Ashbrook Mall Information Desk   The Mall Operations Office is responsible for everything that happens in the Ashbrook Mall in Phoenix, Arizona. To maintain a catalog of job openings at the mall stores, Sam Bullard, director of the Mall Operations Office, has created an Access database named **Ashbrook**. Sam asks you to create several new queries and a new form for this database. You'll do so by completing the following:

1. Make sure your Data Disk is in the appropriate disk drive, start Access, and then open the **Ashbrook** database located in the Cases folder on your Data Disk.

2. Open the **Job** table in Design view. Change the Store field data type to Lookup Wizard. Look up values in the **Store** table, select the Store and Store Name fields from the **Store** table, and accept all other Lookup Wizard default choices. View the **Store** table datasheet, resize the Store column to its best fit, save the table, and then close the table.

3. Create a query to find all records in the **Store** table where the Location field begins with "B". Include all fields from the **Store** table in the query results. Save the query as **B Locations**, run the query, print the query results, and then close the query.

4. Create a query to find all records in the **Job** table where the Position value is Clerk, Salesclerk, or Stock Clerk. Use a list-of-values match for the selection criterion. Display the Position and Hours/Week fields in the query results. Save the query as **Clerk-Type Positions**, run the query, and then print the query results. Keep the query open.

5. Modify the previous query to find all records in the **Job** table where the Position value is not any of: Clerk, Salesclerk, or Stock Clerk. Save the query as **Not Clerk-Type Positions**, run the query, print the query results, and then close the query.

6. Create a query to select all the records for jobs where the Position value is Clerk and the Location value is A3 or B5. Display the Job, StoreName, and Contact fields in the query results. Save the query as **Clerk and Location A3/B5**, run the query, print the query results, and then close the query.

7. Create a parameter query to select the **Job** table records for a Location that the user specifies. Include all the fields from the **Job** table and the Location and Contact fields from the **Store** table in the query results. Save the query as **Job Location Parameter**. Run the query and enter the Location B5. Print the query results, and then close the query.

8. Create a custom form based on the **Store Jobs** query. Display all fields in the form. Use your own design for the form. Save the form as **Store Jobs**. Open the form and print the first record.

9. Use Filter By Form with the **Store Jobs** form to select all records where the Position value is Clerk or the StoreName value is Pinson Shoes. Apply the filter. How many records are selected? Print the first record. Save the filter as a query named **Clerks or Shoe Stores**, and then close the form.

10. Create a multi-page custom form named **Job Information Multi-page** based on the **Job** and **Store** tables by completing the following:

    a. Place the Position field in the Detail section of the form.
    b. On the first page of the tab control, display the other fields from the **Job** table. Make sure all the field-value text boxes are left-aligned, all labels are right-aligned, and each field-value text box is an appropriate size. Change the Caption property for the first tab to Job Information.
    c. On the second page of the tab control, display the Store information in a subform named **Store Subform**. Resize the subform, change the Caption property for the second tab to Store Information, delete the subform label, and then resize the subform columns to their best fit in Form view.

Explore

    d. Insert a Form Header section in the form. Place a title label in the Form Header section. Enter the title Ashbrook Mall Job Openings. Change the title label font to bold MS Sans Serif 14, use the Font/Fore Color button to change the color of the text in the title label to orange (row 3, column 2 on the palette), and then size the title label to fit.

Explore

    e. Select the title label and use the Special Effect button on the Form Design toolbar to apply the raised special effect to it.

    f. View the form, and then print both pages for the first record.

11. Close the form, and then close the **Ashbrook** database.

Case 2. Professional Litigation User Services   Professional Litigation User Services (PLUS) creates all types of visual aids for judicial proceedings. To track daily payments received from the firm's clients, Raj Jawahir has created the **FirmPays** database. To make the database easier to use, Raj wants several new queries and forms created, which you'll do by completing the following:

1. Make sure your Data Disk is in the appropriate disk drive, start Access, and then open the **FirmPays** database located in the Cases folder on your Data Disk.

2. Open the **Payment** table in Design view. Change the Firm# field data type to Lookup Wizard. Look up values in the **Firm** table, select the Firm# and FirmName fields from the **Firm** table, and accept all other Lookup Wizard default choices. Resize the Firm# column in the datasheet to its best fit.

3. Use the Input Mask Wizard to add an input mask to the DatePaid field in the **Payment** table. Select the Short Date input mask, and then click the Finish button. Modify the default Short Date input mask by changing the slashes to hyphens (there are two slashes to change). Test the input mask to make sure it contains hyphens by typing over one of the existing dates in Datasheet view, being sure not to change the date, and then close the table.

4. Create a query to find all records in the **Firm** table where the PLUSAcctRep field begins with "Tyler". Display all fields in the query results. Save the query as **Tyler Accounts**, run the query, print the query results, and then close the query.

5. Create a query to find all records in the **Payment** table where the Firm# value is 1111, 1115, or 1152. Use a list-of-values match for the selection criterion. Display the Payment#, Firm#, AmtPaid, and DatePaid fields in the query results. Save the query as **Firms 1111/1115/1152**, run the query, and then print the query results. Keep the query open.

6. Modify the previous query to find all records in the **Payment** table where the Firm# value is not any of: 1111, 1115, or 1152. Save the query as **Not Firms 1111/1115/1152**, run the query, print the query results, and then close the query.

7. Modify the **June 2 Payments** query to select all the records where the PLUSAcctRep field is Abelson, David or Martinez, Nancy. Display all the fields in the query results. Save the query as **Abelson or Martinez**, run the query, print the query results, and then close the query.

8. Create a parameter query to select the **Payment** table records for a Deposit# that the user specifies. Select only records where the AmtPaid is greater than $1,500.00. Include all the fields in the query results. Save the query as **Deposits Parameter**. Run the query and enter the Deposit# 102. Print the query results, and then close the query.

9. Create a custom form based on the **Payment Statistics by Date** query. Display all fields in the form. Use your own design for the form. Save the form as **Payment Statistics by Date**. Open the form, print the first record, and then close the form.

Explore

10. Create a custom form based on the **Payment Statistics by Date by Deposit** query. Display all fields in the form. Use your own design for the form. Change the Deposit# label and text box format so that the label and field value are displayed with 12-point bold text on a red background. Open the form and print the first record. Save the form as **Payment Statistics by Date by Deposit**.

11. Use Filter By Form with the **Payment Statistics by Date by Deposit** form to select all deposits made after June 10 where the Highest Payment was greater than $1,800.00 or the Average Payment was greater than $1,200.00. Apply the filter. How many records are selected? Print the first selected record. Save the filter as a query named **Highest and Average Payments**. Close the form.

Explore 12. Use the Office Assistant to ask the following question: "How do I add a calculated field to a subform?" Click the topic "Create a calculated control on a form or report." Read the information and then close the Help window and hide the Office Assistant. Open the **Firm Payments** form in Design view and save it as **Firm Payments Coffee Cost**. Add a calculated field named CoffeeCost to the Detail section of the subform that displays the results of multiplying the AmtPaid field by 0.6 (60%). Position the calculated field to the right of the DatePaid field. Set the calculated field's Name property to Coffee Cost, its Format property to Standard, and its Decimal Places property to 2. View the form, resize the calculated field in the subform if necessary, print the first form record, and then save and close the form.

13. Create a multi-page custom form named **Firm Multi-page** based on the **Firm** and **Payment** tables, by completing the following:

   a. Place a title label at the top of the form. Enter the title Firms. Change the title label font to bold MS Sans Serif 24, and then resize the title label to fit.

   b. Place the Firm# and FirmName fields in the Detail section of the form.

Explore c. Change the Firm# and FirmName label and text box formats so that the label and field values are displayed with MS Sans Serif 12-point bold text in red letters. Make sure each control box is an appropriate size.

   d. On the first page of the tab control, display the other fields from the **Firm** table. Make sure all the field-value text boxes are left-aligned, all labels are right-aligned, and each field-value text box is an appropriate size. Change the Caption property for the first tab to Firm Information.

   e. On the second page of the tab control, display the Payment information in a subform named **Firm Multi-page Subform**. Resize the subform, change the Caption property for the second tab to Payment Information, delete the subform label, and then resize the subform columns to their best fit in Form view.

   f. View the form, print both pages for the first record, and then save and close the form.

Explore 14. Open the **Firm Multi-page** form and save it as **Enhanced Firm Multi-page**. Make the following changes to the form design and save the changes:

   a. Change the background color of all sections of the form (except the subform) to light blue (row 5, column 5 on the palette).

   b. Use the Line/Border Width button to place a border (weight 2) around the title label.

   c. Use the Font/Fore Color button to change the color of the title label to red.

   d. Print both pages of the finished form for the first record, save your changes, and then close the form.

15. Close the **FirmPays** database, and then exit Access.

Case 3. Best Friends   Best Friends is a not-for-profit organization that trains hearing and service dogs for people with disabilities. To raise funds, Best Friends periodically sponsors walk-a-thons. These fundraisers have been so popular that Noah and Sheila Warnick, the founders of Best Friends, have created the **Pledges** database to keep track of walkers and their pledges. The **Pledges** database has been a useful tool for Noah and Sheila. Now, they need several new queries and forms to provide them with better information. You'll help them create these queries and forms by completing the following:

1. Make sure your Data Disk is in the appropriate disk drive, start Access, and then open the **Pledges** database located in the Cases folder on your Data Disk.

2. Open the **Pledge** table in Design view. Change the WalkerID field data type to Lookup Wizard. Look up values in the **Walker** table, select the WalkerID, LastName, and FirstName fields from the **Walker** table, and accept all other Lookup Wizard default choices. Resize the WalkerID column in the datasheet to its best fit.

3. Use the Input Mask Wizard to add an input mask to the Phone field in the **Walker** table. Select the Phone Number input mask, and then click the Finish button. Modify the default input mask by changing it to 000\-0000;;_. Test the input mask by typing over one of the existing Phone field values, being sure not to change the value, and then close the table.

4. Create a query to find all records in the **Walker** table where the Distance value is 2.4, 2.7, or 2.8. Use a list-of-values match for the selection criterion. Display all fields in the query results. Save the query as **Specific Distances**, run the query, and then print the query results. Keep the query open.

5. Modify the previous query to find all records in the **Walker** table where the Distance value is not 2.4, 2.7, or 2.8. Save the query as **Not Specific Distances**, run the query, print the query results, and then close the query.

6. Modify the **Pledge Statistics by Walker** query to select all records where the TotalPledge is greater than 20 and the AveragePledge is greater than 10 or the #Pledges is greater than 1. Display all the fields in the query results. Save the query as **Pledge Statistics by Walker Modified**, run the query, print the query results, and then close the query.

7. Create a parameter query to select the **Walker** table records for a Distance that the user specifies. Display the LastName, FirstName, and Distance fields in the query results. Save the query as **Distance Parameter**. Run the query and enter the Distance 2.3. Print the query results, and then close the query.

8. Create a custom form based on the **Walker** table. Display all fields in the form. Use your own design for the form. Save the form as **Walker**. Open the form, print the first record, and then close the form.

Explore ▶ 9. Create a custom form based on the **Difference** query. Display all fields in the form. Use your own design for the form. Change the Pledger label and text box format so that the label and field value are displayed with 12-point bold blue text on a yellow background. Save the form as **Difference**, view the form, print the first form record, and then close the form.

Explore ▶ 10. Use the Office Assistant to ask the following question: "How do I add a calculated field to a form?" Click the topic "Create a calculated control on a form or report." Read the information and then close the Help window and hide the Office Assistant. Open the **Difference** form in Design view and save it as **Difference Modified**. Add a calculated field to the form that displays the results of calculating the percentage of the PledgeAmt field value represented by the Difference field value. (*Hint*: Set the Format property for the calculated field to an appropriate value.) View the form, print the first form record, and then save and close the form.

11. Use Filter By Form with the **Difference** form to select all records where the PledgeAmt is less than $10.00. Apply the filter. How many records are selected? Print the first selected record. Save the filter as a query named **Small Pledges**, and then close the form.

12. Create a multi-page custom form named **Walker Information Multi-page** based on the **Walker** and **Pledge** tables, by completing the following:

   a. Place the WalkerID, LastName, and FirstName fields in the Detail section of the form.
   b. On the first page of a tab control, display the other fields from the **Walker** table. Make sure each field-value text box is an appropriate size. Change the Caption property for the first tab to Walker.
   c. On the second page of the tab control, display the Pledge information in a subform named **Multi-page Subform**. Resize the subform, change the Caption property for the second tab to Pledges, delete the subform label, and then resize the subform columns to their best fit in Form view.
   d. View the form, print both pages for the tenth record, and then save and close the form.

Explore ▶ 13. Open the **Walker Information Multi-page** form and save it as **Enhanced Walker Information Multi-page**. Make the following changes to the form design and save the changes:
   a. Change the background color of all sections of the form (except the subform) to light yellow.
   b. Use the Line/Border Width button to place a border (weight 2) around the WalkerID, LastName, and FirstName field-value text boxes. Change the font size and weight for these field-value text boxes so that they stand out more on the form. Resize the field-value text box controls, if necessary.
   c. Use the Font/Fore Color button to change the color of the LastName and FirstName field values to red.
   d. Use the Special Effect button on the Form Design toolbar to display the **Multi-page Subform** subform with a shadow.
   e. View the form, print the Pledges page for the tenth record, and then save and close the form.

14. Close the **Pledges** database, and then exit Access.

Case 4. Lopez Lexus Dealerships   Maria and Hector Lopez own a chain of Lexus dealerships throughout Texas. To keep track of the cars at their various dealerships, they have created the **Lopez** database. Maria and Hector want you to create several queries and forms to make the **Lopez** database easier to use. To create the queries and forms, complete the following:

1. Make sure your Data Disk is in the appropriate disk drive, start Access, and then open the **Lopez** database located in the Cases folder on your Data Disk.

2. Open the **Car** table in Design view. Change the LocationCode field data type to Lookup Wizard. Look up values in the **Location** table, select the LocationCode and LocationName fields from the **Location** table, and accept all other Lookup Wizard default choices. Resize the LocCode (Caption property value for the LocationCode field) column in the datasheet to its best fit, and then save and close the table.

3. Create a query to find all records in the **Car** table where the Class value is S1, S3, or S4. Use a list-of-values match for the selection criterion. Display all fields in the query results. Save the query as **Class S1/S3/S4**, run the query, and then print the query results. Keep the query open.

4. Modify the previous query to find all records in the **Car** table where the Class value is not any of: S1, S3, or S4. Save the query as **Not Class S1/S3/S4**, run the query, print the query results, and then close the query.

5. Create a query to select all **Car** records for cars with five-speed manual transmissions (Transmission field value M5) in Location E1 or L1. Display the Model, Class, Year, and Selling Price fields in the query results. Save the query as **Trans M5 For Location E1/L1**, run the query, print the query results, and then close the query.

6. Create a parameter query to select the **Car** table records for a Transmission that the user specifies. Include all the fields in the query results. Save the query as **Transmission Parameter**. Run the query and enter the Transmission A4. Print the query results, and then close the query.

7. Create a custom form based on the **Car** table. Display all fields in the form. Use your own design for the form. Save the form as **Car Data**. Open the form, print the first record, and then close the form.

Explore ▶ 8. Create a custom form based on the **2000 Cars** query. Display all fields in the form. Use your own design for the form, but place the title "2000 Lexus Automobiles" in the Form Header section. Change the Model label and field-value text box format so that the label and field value are displayed with 12-point bold text on a light blue background. Save the form as **2000 Cars**, and then print the first form record.

9. Use Filter By Form with the **2000 Cars** form to select all records for cars over $50,000 in selling price or located in Houston. Apply the filter. Print the first record. How many records are selected? Save the filter as a query named **2000 Cars Filter**, and then close the form.

10. Create a multi-page custom form named **Location Information Multi-page** based on the **Location** and **Car** tables, by completing the following:

   a. Place the LocationName field in the Detail section of the form.

   b. On the first page of a tab control, display the other fields from the **Location** table. Make sure each field-value text box is an appropriate size. Change the Caption property for the first tab to Location Information.

   c. On the second page of the tab control, display the Car information in a subform named **Multi-page Subform**. Resize the subform, change the Caption property for the second tab to Car Information, delete the subform label, and then resize the subform columns to their best fit in Form view.

   d. View the form, print both pages for the first record, and then save and close the form.

Explore ▶   11. Open the **Location Information Multi-page** form and save it as **Enhanced Location Information Multi-page**. Make the following changes to the form design and save the changes:

   a. Change the background color of all sections of the form (except the subform) to light blue.

   b. Use the Line/Border Width button to place a border (weight 2) around the LocationName label and field-value text box. Change the font size and weight for these controls so that they stand out more on the form. Resize these controls, if necessary.

   c. Use the Font/Fore Color button to change the color of the ManagerName value to red.

   d. Use the Raised Special Effect button on the Form Design toolbar to change the display of the **Multi-page Subform** subform.

   e. Print both pages of the finished form for the first record, and then save and close the form.

12. Close the **Lopez** database, and then exit Access.

Case 5. eACH Internet Auction Site Chris and Pat Aquino own a successful ISP (Internet service provider) and want to expand their business to host an Internet auction site. The auction site will let sellers offer items for sale, such as antiques, first-edition books, vintage dolls, coins, art, stamps, glass bottles, autographs, and sports memorabilia. After a seller posts an item for sale, it is sold at the auction site by accepting bids from buyers. Before people can sell items and bid on items, they must register with the auction site. Each item will be listed by subcategory within a general category, making it easy for bidders to find items of interest to them. For example, the general category of antiques might consist of several subcategories, including ancient world, musical instruments, and general.

Chris and Pat have registered their Web site name of eACH, which stands for *e*lectronic *A*uction *C*ollectibles *H*ost. Now they need to create a database that keeps track of the registered people, the items for sale, and the bids received for those items by the Web site. Because the process of creating a complete database—all fields, tables, relationships, queries, forms, and other database objects—for eACH is an enormous undertaking, you'll start with just a few of the database components, and then you will create additional ones in subsequent tutorials.

Complete the following steps to create the database and its initial objects:

1. Read the appendix entitled "Relational Databases and Database Design" at the end of this book.

2. Use your Web browser to gather information about other Internet auction sites so that you are familiar with common rules and requirements, categories and subcategories, fields and their attributes, and entities. (*Hint*: Yahoo (www.yahoo.com) lists the names of several auction sites, and eBay (www.ebay.com) is a popular Internet auction site.)

3. The initial database structure includes the following relations and fields.

   a. The **Category** relation includes a unique category number and a category (the category name or description).

   b. The **Subcategory** relation includes a unique subcategory number, subcategory (the subcategory name or description), and a category number.

c. The **Registrant** relation includes a unique registrant number, last name, first name, middle initial, phone number, e-mail address, an optional user ID, and a password. Each person registers once, and then can sell items and bid on items.

d. The **Item** relation includes a unique item number, the registrant who's the seller of the item, the subcategory number, a title (a short item description), a description (a fuller item description), a quantity (the number of identical items being sold separately, if there's more than one), a minimum bid amount in whole dollars, a duration (the number of days bids will be accepted for the item), an optional reserve price amount in whole dollars (the lowest sale price acceptable to the seller; this is not made available to bidders), and the date and time bidding started on the item.

4. Based on Step 3, draw an entity-relationship diagram showing the entities (relations) and the relationships between the entities.

5. Based on Steps 3 and 4, create on paper the initial database design for the eACH system. For each relation, identify all primary and foreign keys. For each field, determine its attributes, such as data type, field size, and validation rules.

6. Create the database structure using Access. Use a database name of **eACH**, and place the database in the Cases folder on your Data Disk. Create the tables with their fields. Be sure to set each field's properties correctly, select a primary key for each table, and then define the relationships between appropriate tables.

7. For each table, create a form that you'll use to view, add, edit, and delete records in that table.

8. For tables that have a one-to-many relationship, create a form with a main form for the primary table and a subform for the related table.

9. Design test data for each table in the database. You can research Internet auction sites to collect realistic values for categories, subcategories, and other fields, if necessary. Be sure your test data covers common situations. For example, there should be at least two sellers with multiple items for sale; one seller should be selling items in the same subcategory, and another seller should be selling items in different subcategories. There should be at least one seller who has no items for sale. Each table should contain at least 10 records. Include your name as one of the registrants, and include at least two items that you're selling.

10. Add the test data to your tables using the forms you created in Steps 7 and 8.

11. Open each table datasheet, resize all datasheet columns to their best fit, and then print each datasheet.

12. Set the option for compacting the **eACH** database on close.

13. Use the Input Mask Wizard to add an appropriate input mask to one field in any table. Print the table's datasheet after adding the input mask.

14. Create, test, save, and print one parameter query.

15. Close the **eACH** database, and then exit Access.

INTERNET ASSIGNMENTS

The purpose of the Internet Assignments is to challenge you to find information on the Internet that you can use to create effective documents. The actual assignments are updated and maintained on the Course Technology Web site. Log on to the Internet and use your Web browser to go to the Student Online Companion to accompany this text at **www.course.com/NewPerspectives/office2000**. Click the Access link, and then click the link for Tutorial 5.

Quick Check Answers

Session 5.1

1. A Lookup Wizard field lets you select a value from a list of possible values, making data entry easier.

2. If two tables have a one-to-many relationship, when you display the primary table in Datasheet view, you can use a subdatasheet to display and edit the records from the related table.

3. input mask

4. Like

5. The asterisk is a wildcard that represents any string of characters in a pattern match query.

6. Use the In comparison operator to define a condition with two or more values.

7. Use the Not logical operator to negate a condition.

8. Use a parameter query when you want the user to be prompted to enter the selection criteria when the query runs.

Session 5.2

1. A bound control is linked to a field in the underlying table or query; an unbound control is not.

2. Position the pointer anywhere on the border of the control, and then drag the control and its attached label box.

3. Right-click the label, click Properties on the shortcut menu, click the Format tab, edit the existing label in the Caption text box or double-click it to select the current value, and then type a new caption.

4. Select the control, position the pointer on a sizing handle, and then click and drag the pointer.

5. The Form Header section lets you add titles, instructions, command buttons, and other information to the top of your form.

6. Open the form in Design view, click the Image button on the toolbar, position the pointer at the location for the upper-left corner of the picture, click the left mouse button, select the picture file, and then click OK.

Session 5.3

1. Open the form in Design view, click the Tab Control tool on the toolbox, position the pointer in the form at the location for the upper-left corner of the tab control, and then click the left mouse button.

2. Click a label, press and hold down the Shift key and click the other labels, click Format on the menu bar, point to Align, and then click Right.

3 Filter By Form finds records that match multiple selection criteria using the same Access logical and comparison operators that you use in queries.

4. Save the filter as a query, and then apply the query to a form.

5. Opening a query runs the query and displays the results in Datasheet view. Applying a query to a form opens the query and displays the results in a form.

In this tutorial you will:

- Design and create a custom report

- Assign a conditional value to a calculated field

- Modify report controls and properties

- Sort and group data

- Calculate group and overall totals

- Hide duplicate values

- Embed and link objects in a report

- Export Access data to other programs

CUSTOMIZING
REPORTS AND INTEGRATING ACCESS WITH OTHER PROGRAMS

Creating a Custom Invoices Report and a Report with an Embedded Chart and a Linked Document

CASE

Valle Coffee

At a recent staff meeting, Leonard Valle indicated that he would like new reports created for the Dining database. In the first report, he wants to see a printed list of all orders placed by Valle Coffee customers. He also wants monthly subtotals of billing amounts and a grand total for all billing amounts. The second report Leonard needs is a customer report with an embedded chart that graphically summarizes monthly billing activity. He can use both of these reports to monitor customer orders and monthly billing.

In this tutorial, you will create the reports for Leonard. In building the reports, you will use many of the Access report customization features—such as grouping data, calculating totals, and adding lines to separate report sections. These features will enhance Leonard's reports and make them easier to read.

You will also integrate Access with other programs to include the chart that Leonard requested to summarize monthly billing activity graphically. Finally, you will link a report to a word-processing document that describes the report's contents, and you'll export the records from an Access table to a spreadsheet for further analysis.

SESSION 6.1

In this session, you will create a custom report. You will modify a query and add a calculated field to the query. Finally, you will add, move, resize, and align controls in the report and change their captions.

Creating a Custom Report

A **report** is a formatted hard copy of the contents of one or more tables from a database. Although you can format and print data using datasheets, queries, and forms, reports allow you greater flexibility and provide a more professional, custom appearance. For example, Valle Coffee can customize its reports to print billing statements and mailing labels.

An Access report is divided into sections. Each report can have seven different sections, which are described in Figure 6-1.

Figure 6-1	DESCRIPTIONS OF ACCESS REPORT SECTIONS
REPORT SECTION	**DESCRIPTION**
Report Header	Appears once at the beginning of a report. Use it for report titles, company logos, report introductions, and cover pages.
Page Header	Appears at the top of each page of a report. Use it for column headings, report titles, page numbers, and report dates. If your report has a Report Header section, it precedes the first Page Header section.
Group Header	Appears once at the beginning of a new group of records. Use it to print the group name and the field value that all records in the group have in common. A report can have up to 10 grouping levels.
Detail	Appears once for each record in the underlying table or query. Use it to print selected fields from the table or query and to print calculated values.
Group Footer	Appears once at the end of a group of records. It is usually used to print totals for the group.
Report Footer	Appears once at the end of the report. Use it for report totals and other summary information.
Page Footer	Appears at the bottom of each page of a report. Use it for page numbers and brief explanations of symbols or abbreviations. If your report has a Report Footer section, it precedes the Page Footer section on the last page of the report.

You don't have to include all seven sections in a report. When you design your report, you determine which sections to include and what information to place in each section. Figure 6-2 shows a sample report produced from the Dining database.

Figure 6-2 SAMPLE REPORT SHOWING THE SEVEN SECTIONS OF A REPORT

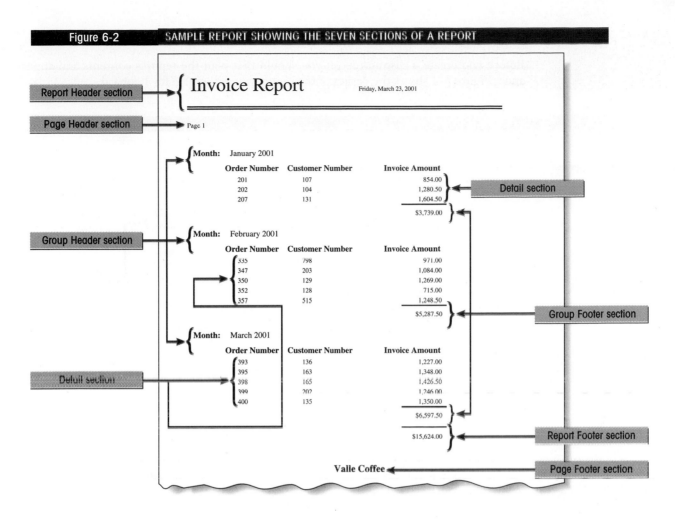

The first report you need to create will list the records for all orders in the Order table. Leonard wants the report to group the invoices by the value in the BillingDate field. The report should also contain the following four sections:

- A Page Header section will show the report title, current date, page number, and column headings for each field.
- A Detail section will list the billing date, order number, customer name, invoice amount, and an indication of whether the invoice has been paid. Records in each group will appear in ascending order by customer name.
- A Group Footer section will print subtotals of the InvoiceAmt field for each BillingDate group.
- A Report Footer section will print the grand total of the InvoiceAmt field.

From your work with AutoReport and the Report Wizard, you know that, by default, Access places the report title in the Report Header section and the date and page number in the Page Footer section. Leonard prefers the report title, date, and page number to appear at the top of each page, so you need to place this information in the Page Header section.

You could use the Report Wizard to create the report, and then modify the report to match the report design. However, because you need to make several customizations, you will create the report in Design view. If you modify a report created by AutoReport or the Report Wizard, or if you design and create your own report, you produce a **custom report**. You should create a custom report whenever AutoReport or the Report Wizard cannot automatically create the specific report you need.

Designing a Custom Report

Before you create a custom report, you should first plan the report's contents and appearance. Figure 6-3 shows the design of the report you will create for Leonard.

Figure 6-3	DESIGN FOR THE CUSTOM REPORT

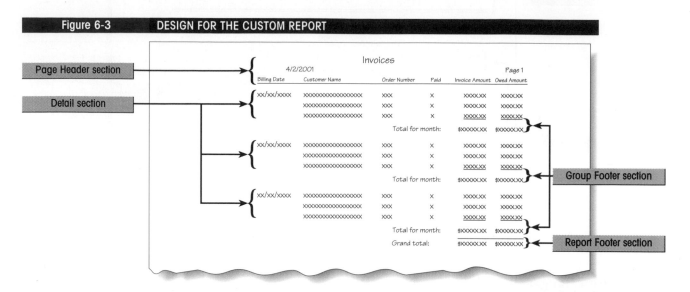

The Page Header section contains the report title, Invoices. Descriptive column headings, which are underlined, appear at the bottom of the Page Header section; the current date and page number appear between the report title and column heading lines.

In the Detail section, the locations and lengths of the field values are indicated by a series of Xs. For example, the three Xs below the Order Number field indicate that the field value will be three characters long.

The subtotals for each group will appear in the Group Footer section, and overall totals will appear in the Report Footer section. Totals will appear for the InvoiceAmt field from the Order table and for the OwedAmt field, which is a calculated field based on the InvoiceAmt and Paid field values.

The data for a report can come from either a single table or from a query based on one or more tables. Your report will contain data from the Customer and Order tables. The High Invoice Amounts query contains the fields you need. You will modify the query by removing the selection criterion, deleting unnecessary fields, and adding the calculated field; then you'll use the query as the basis for your report.

To modify the query:

1. Place your Data Disk in the appropriate disk drive.

2. Start Access and open the **Dining** database located in the Tutorial folder on your Data Disk.

3. Click **Queries** in the Objects bar of the Database window, scroll to the left (if necessary), right-click **High Invoice Amounts**, and then click **Design View** on the shortcut menu. The query is displayed in Design view. See Figure 6-4.

| Figure 6-4 | QUERY IN DESIGN VIEW |

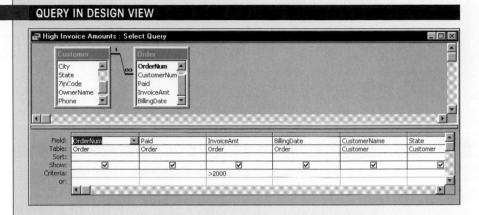

Next, you need to delete the condition for the InvoiceAmt field, because Leonard's report will include all records from the Order table.

4. Click the **InvoiceAmt Criteria** text box, press the **F2** key to select the criterion, and then press the **Delete** key.

The query design also contains the State, OwnerName, and Phone fields, which you do not need for this query, so you can delete them.

5. Scroll the design grid to the right until the State, OwnerName, and Phone fields are visible.

6. Position the pointer on the State field until the pointer changes to a ⬇ shape, click and drag the mouse to the right until all three fields—State, OwnerName, and Phone—are selected.

7. Click the **Cut** button on the Query Design toolbar to remove the three fields.

The query now selects the OrderNum, Paid, InvoiceAmt, BillingDate, and CustomerName fields for all records in the Customer and Order tables. You are now ready to add the calculated field to the query design.

Assigning a Conditional Value to a Calculated Field

You can create a calculated field on a form or report, but then you wouldn't be able to calculate subtotals by month and a grand total for the calculated field. However, you can calculate totals on a form or report for any field, including calculated fields, from a table or query that's used as the basis for the form or report. Because Leonard wants subtotals and a grand total for the OwedAmt field on his report, you'll need to add the OwedAmt calculated field to the query.

Leonard wants the OwedAmt field to show a blank value for a paid order and the value of the InvoiceAmt field for an unpaid order. To permit the OwedAmt field to be one of two values based on a condition, you'll use the IIf function for the calculated field. The **IIf function** lets you assign one value to a calculated field or control if a condition is true, and a second value if the condition is false. Because the Paid field is a yes/no field, the format of the IIf function you'll use is: *IIf([Paid],Null,[InvoiceAmt])*. You interpret this function as: If the Paid field value is true (Yes), then make the calculated field value null (blank); otherwise, make the calculated field value the same as the InvoiceAmt field value.

To add the OwedAmt calculated field to the query:

1. Right-click the **Field** text box to the right of the CustomerName field, and then click **Zoom** on the shortcut menu. The Zoom dialog box opens.

   The **Zoom dialog box** has a large text box for entering text, expressions, and other values.

2. Type **OwedAmt: IIf((Paid),Null,(InvoiceAmt))**. See Figure 6-5.

Figure 6-5	CALCULATED FIELD IN THE ZOOM DIALOG BOX

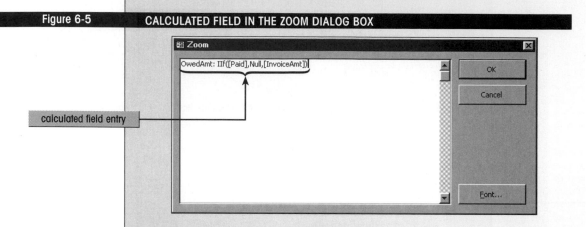

calculated field entry

TROUBLE? If your calculated field is different from Figure 6-5, correct it until it matches.

3. Click the **OK** button to close the Zoom dialog box.

   To keep the original query intact, you'll save this query as "Invoice Amounts."

4. Click **File** on the menu bar, and then click **Save As**. The Save As dialog box opens.

5. Position the insertion point to the left of the query name, use the Delete key to delete the word "High" and the space following it, and then click the **OK** button. Access saves the modified query.

   TROUBLE? If you receive an error message when you try to save the query, make sure that the expression that you entered in Step 2 matches the one shown in Figure 6-5, correct any errors, and then repeat Steps 4 and 5 to save the query.

   Next, you'll run the query to verify the results.

6. Click the **Run** button ![Run button] on the Query Design toolbar. The query datasheet appears and displays the five fields from the Customer and Order tables and the calculated field, OwedAmt. See Figure 6-6.

Figure 6-6	DATASHEET DISPLAYING THE CALCULATED FIELD

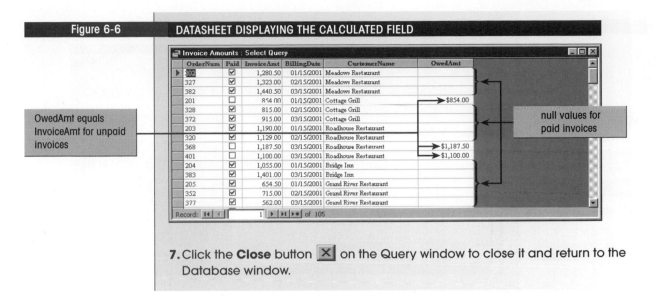

OwedAmt equals InvoiceAmt for unpaid invoices

null values for paid invoices

7. Click the **Close** button ☒ on the Query window to close it and return to the Database window.

You are now ready to create the report. To do so, you need to display a blank report in Design view.

Report Window in Design View

The Report window in Design view is similar to the Form window in Design view, which you used in Tutorial 5 to customize forms.

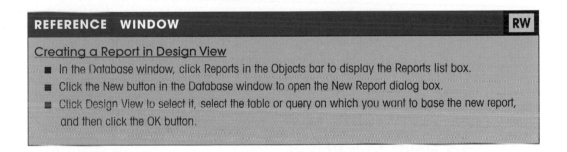

REFERENCE WINDOW   RW

Creating a Report in Design View
- In the Database window, click Reports in the Objects bar to display the Reports list box.
- Click the New button in the Database window to open the New Report dialog box.
- Click Design View to select it, select the table or query on which you want to base the new report, and then click the OK button.

The report you are creating will be based on the Invoice Amounts query that you just modified. To begin, you need to create a blank report in Design view.

To create a blank report in Design view:

1. Click **Reports** in the Objects bar of the Database window to open the Reports list box, and then click the **New** button in the Database window to open the New Report dialog box.

2. Click **Design View** (if necessary), and then click the **list arrow** to display the list of tables and queries in the Dining database.

3. Click **Invoice Amounts** to select this query as the basis for your report, and then click the **OK** button. The Report window in Design view opens and displays a blank report.

4. Click the **Maximize** button ☐ on the Report window. See Figure 6-7.

| Figure 6-7 | REPORT WINDOW IN DESIGN VIEW |

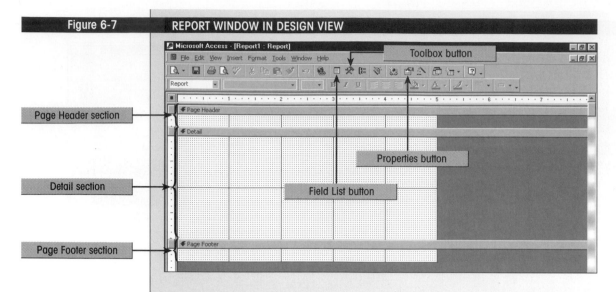

TROUBLE? If the rulers or grid do not appear, click View on the menu bar, and then click Ruler or Grid to display the missing component. A check mark appears to the left of these components when they are displayed in the Report window. If the grid is still not displayed, see your instructor or technical support person for assistance. If the toolbox is open, click the Close button ☒ on the toolbox to close it. If the field list is open, click the Close button ☒ on the field list to close it.

Notice that the Report window in Design view has many of the same components as the Form window in Design view. For example, the Report Design toolbar includes a Properties button, a Field List button, and a Toolbox button. Both windows also have horizontal and vertical rulers, a grid, and a Formatting toolbar.

Unlike the Form window in Design view, which initially displays only the Detail section on a blank form, the Report window also displays a Page Header section and a Page Footer section. Reports often contain these sections, so Access automatically includes them in a blank report.

Adding Fields to a Report

Your first task is to add bound controls to the Detail section for all the fields from the Invoice Amounts query. Recall that a bound control displays field values from the table or query on which a form or report is based. You add bound controls to a report in the same way that you add them to a form.

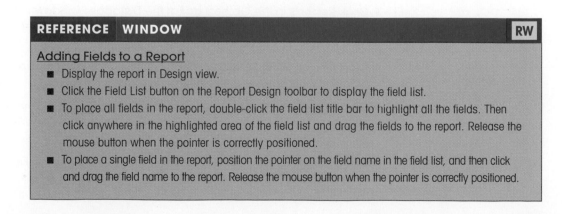

REFERENCE WINDOW   **RW**

Adding Fields to a Report
- Display the report in Design view.
- Click the Field List button on the Report Design toolbar to display the field list.
- To place all fields in the report, double-click the field list title bar to highlight all the fields. Then click anywhere in the highlighted area of the field list and drag the fields to the report. Release the mouse button when the pointer is correctly positioned.
- To place a single field in the report, position the pointer on the field name in the field list, and then click and drag the field name to the report. Release the mouse button when the pointer is correctly positioned.

You need to add a bound control for each field in the Invoice Amounts query. You can add all these bound controls at once by dragging them as a group from the field list to the Detail section.

To add bound controls for all the fields in the field list:

1. Click the **Field List** button ⊞ on the Report Design toolbar. The field list opens. See Figure 6-8.

Figure 6-8	FIELD LIST

2. Double-click the field list title bar to highlight all the fields in the Invoice Amounts field list.

3. Click anywhere in the highlighted area of the field list (but not on the title bar), and then drag the fields to the Detail section. Release the mouse button when the pointer 🖰 is positioned at the top of the Detail section and at the 1¼-inch mark on the horizontal ruler. Bound controls are added for the six selected fields. Each bound control consists of a text box and an attached label. The attached labels are positioned to the left of the text boxes, except for the label for the Paid check box. See Figure 6-9. Notice that the text boxes are aligned at the 1¼-inch mark.

Figure 6-9	ADDING BOUND CONTROLS TO THE REPORT

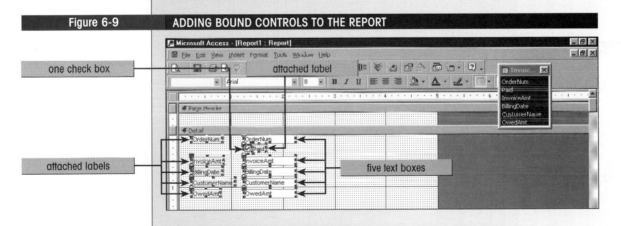

TROUBLE? If you did not position the bound controls properly in the Detail section, click the Undo button ↶ on the Report Design toolbar, and then repeat Step 3.

Performing operations in the Report window in Design view will become easier with practice. Remember, you can always click the Undo button immediately after you make a report design change that produces unsatisfactory results. You can also click the Print Preview button at any time to view your progress on the report.

Working with Controls

Five text boxes and one check box now appear in a column in the Detail section. Each of these boxes is a bound control linked to a field in the underlying query and has an attached label box. The label boxes appear to the left of the text boxes and to the right of the check box. The labels identify the contents of the text boxes and the check box, which will display the field values from the database. According to Leonard's plan for the report (see Figure 6-3), you need to move all the label boxes to the Page Header section, where they will serve as column headings for the field values. You then need to reposition the label boxes, text boxes, and the check box so that they are aligned properly. Before you begin working with the controls in the Report window, you'll close the field list because you no longer need it.

To close the field list and then move all the label boxes to the Page Header section:

1. Click the **Close** button ☒ on the field list to close it.

2. Click anywhere in the Page Header section to deselect the five text boxes, the check box, and their attached label boxes.

3. While pressing and holding down the **Shift** key, click each of the six label boxes in the Detail section, and then release the **Shift** key. This action selects all the label boxes in preparation for cutting them from the Detail section and pasting them in the Page Header section.

4. Position the pointer in any one of the selected label boxes. The pointer changes to a 🖐 shape.

5. Click the right mouse button to display the shortcut menu.

6. Click **Cut** on the shortcut menu to delete the label boxes from the Detail section. See Figure 6-10.

Figure 6-10   **LABEL BOXES CUT FROM THE DETAIL SECTION**

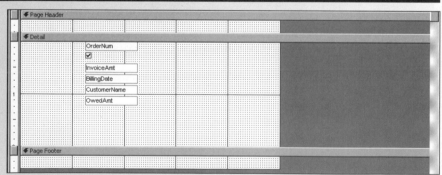

TROUBLE? If you inadvertently selected the text boxes and/or the check box in addition to the label boxes, click the Undo button 🔄 on the Report Design toolbar, and then repeat Steps 2 through 6, being careful to select only the label boxes.

7. Click anywhere in the Page Header section, click the right mouse button in the Page Header section to open the shortcut menu, and then click **Paste**. Access pastes all the label boxes into the Page Header section and automatically resizes the section to display the label boxes. See Figure 6-11.

| Figure 6-11 | LABEL BOXES PASTED IN THE PAGE HEADER SECTION |

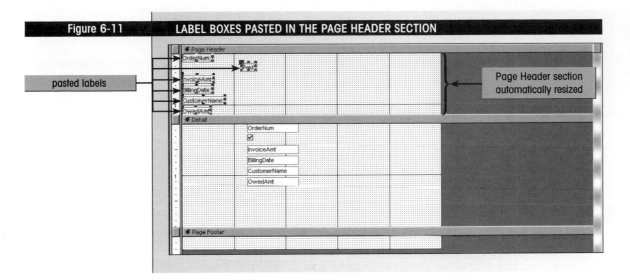

pasted labels

Cutting and pasting the label boxes has unlinked them from their attached text boxes and check box. You can now select and move either a label box or a text box (or check box), but not both at once.

Moving and Resizing Controls

You can move or resize any individual control or multiple selected controls in the Report window. When you select a control, a move handle appears in the top-left corner of the control. This handle is the one you use to reposition the control. A selected control also displays sizing handles around its border, which you can use to resize a control in different directions.

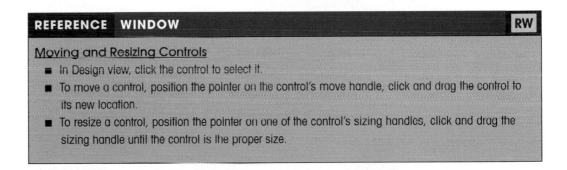

REFERENCE WINDOW   **RW**

Moving and Resizing Controls
- In Design view, click the control to select it.
- To move a control, position the pointer on the control's move handle, click and drag the control to its new location.
- To resize a control, position the pointer on one of the control's sizing handles, click and drag the sizing handle until the control is the proper size.

You need to reposition the text boxes, check box, and label boxes to match the report's design. You'll begin by repositioning the text boxes and check box in the Detail section, which should appear in a row beginning with the BillingDate field. You will also resize the text boxes so the contents will be displayed completely.

To move the text boxes and check box and resize the text boxes:

1. Click the **BillingDate text box** in the Detail section, position the pointer on the move handle in the upper-left corner of the text box so it changes to a ✥ shape, and then drag the text box to the upper-left corner of the Detail section.

Now you will resize the BillingDate text box so it is just large enough to display a date.

2. Position the pointer on the middle-right sizing handle of the BillingDate text box. When the pointer changes to a ↔ shape, click and drag the right border to the left, to the .625-inch mark (approximately) on the horizontal ruler.

3. Refer to Figure 6-12 and use the procedures in Steps 1 and 2 to move the other five controls and resize the remaining text boxes in the Detail section to match the figure as closely as possible. Note that you need to increase the size of the CustomerName text box and decrease the size of the OrderNum, InvoiceAmt, and OwedAmt text boxes. See Figure 6-12.

| Figure 6-12 | AFTER MOVING AND RESIZING THE CONTROLS IN THE DETAIL SECTION |

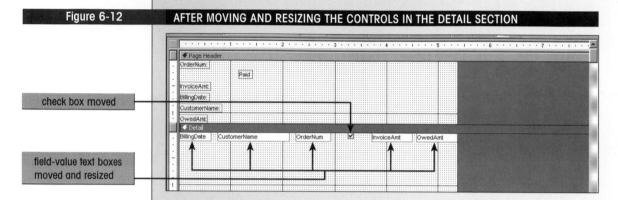

After repositioning and resizing the OwedAmt text box, you might need to change the form's width to match the figure.

4. If you need to change the form's width, position the pointer on the right edge of the Detail section. When the pointer changes to a ✛ shape, click and drag the right edge to the right to align with the right edge of the OwedAmt text box.

The Detail section is now much taller than necessary to display these controls. The extra space below the text boxes and check box will show as white space between records in the printed report. The report will be more readable and require fewer pages if the records in the Detail section are printed without a large space between them. You can resize the Detail section so that the records will be printed closer together.

To resize the Detail section:

1. If necessary, scroll down to display the bottom edge of the Detail section.

2. Position the pointer on the bottom edge of the Detail section. When the pointer changes to a ✛ shape, click and drag the bottom edge up to align with the bottom of the controls. If necessary, scroll up to display the top of the report. See Figure 6-13.

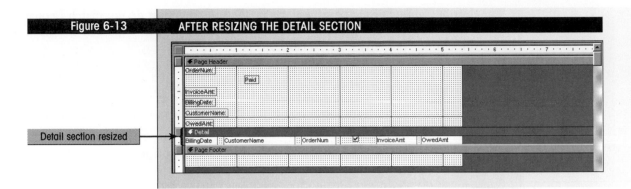

Figure 6-13   **AFTER RESIZING THE DETAIL SECTION**

Detail section resized

You've made many modifications to the report design and should save the report before proceeding.

To save the Report design:

1. Click the **Save** button 🔲 on the Report Design toolbar. The Save As dialog box opens.

2. Type **Invoices** in the Report Name text box, and then press the **Enter** key. The dialog box closes and Access saves the report in the Dining database.

The report design shows column headings different from the text currently displayed in the label boxes in the Page Header section. Next, you need to change the text of the labels by changing each label's Caption property.

Changing the Caption Property

Each label has a Caption property that controls the text that is displayed in the label. The default Caption property value for a bound control is the field name followed by a colon. Other controls, such as buttons and tab controls, have Caption properties as well. You can change the value of a Caption property for an object by using the property sheet for that object. You should change the Caption property value for an object if the default value is difficult to read or understand.

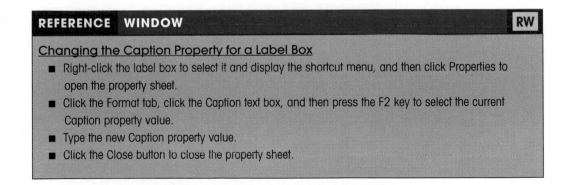

REFERENCE   WINDOW   **RW**

<u>Changing the Caption Property for a Label Box</u>
- Right-click the label box to select it and display the shortcut menu, and then click Properties to open the property sheet.
- Click the Format tab, click the Caption text box, and then press the F2 key to select the current Caption property value.
- Type the new Caption property value.
- Click the Close button to close the property sheet.

The default Caption property values for the labels in the report do not match Leonard's report design. For example, the label OrderNum: should be Order Number. You need to change the Caption property for each label except the Paid label.

To change the Caption property for the labels:

1. Right-click the **OrderNum label box** in the Page Header section, and then click **Properties** to open the property sheet for the OrderNum label.

2. If necessary, click the **Format** tab to display the Format page of the property sheet. The current Caption property value, OrderNum:, is selected. You need to insert a space between "Order" and "Num," delete the colon following the text, and then type the letters "ber".

3. Position the insertion point to the right of the letter "r," press the **spacebar**, press the **End** key to position the insertion point to the right of the colon, press the **Backspace** key to delete it, and then type **ber**. See Figure 6-14.

Figure 6-14	CHANGING THE CAPTION PROPERTY VALUE

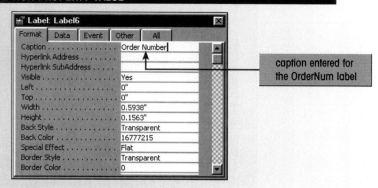

caption entered for the OrderNum label

TROUBLE? The property sheet title bar on your screen might have a title other than the one shown in Figure 6-14. This causes no problems.

4. Click the **InvoiceAmt label box** to select it. The property sheet changes to show the properties for the InvoiceAmt label.

5. Edit the text of the Caption property so that it displays the value **Invoice Amount**.

6. Repeat Steps 4 and 5 for the BillingDate, CustomerName, and OwedAmt label boxes. Change them to **Billing Date**, **Customer Name**, and **Owed Amount**, respectively.

7. Click the **Close** button ![X] on the property sheet to close it.

Next, you need to resize the Order Number, Invoice Amount, and Owed Amount label boxes so that the captions fit. You can resize all three boxes at the same time.

To resize the label boxes:

1. Click an empty area of the grid to deselect any selected label boxes.

2. While pressing and holding down the **Shift** key, click the **Order Number label box**, click the **Invoice Amount label box**, and the **Owed Amount label box** to select all three controls, and then release the **Shift** key.

> **3.** Click **Format** on the menu bar, point to **Size**, and then click **To Fit**. Access resizes all three label boxes to fit the captions.

Now you need to align the label boxes with the corresponding text boxes in the Detail section.

Aligning Controls

You can align controls in a report or form using the **Align** command, which provides options for aligning controls in different ways. For example, if you select objects in a column, you can use the Align Left option to align the left edges of the objects. Similarly, if you select objects in a row, you can use the Align Top option to align the top edges of the objects. The Align Right and Align Bottom options work in the same way. A fifth option, Align To Grid, aligns selected objects with the grid dots in the Report window. You will use the Align Right, Align Left, and Align Top options to align the labels in the Page Header section with their corresponding text boxes in the Detail section. Recall that the labels will serve as column headings in the report, so they must be aligned correctly with the text boxes, which will display the field values from the database.

To align the labels in the Page Header section with the text boxes in the Detail section:

1. Click an empty area of the grid to deselect the selected label boxes.

2. Click the **Owed Amount label** to select it. Position the pointer on the Owed Amount label. When the pointer changes to a 🖑 shape, click and drag the Owed Amount label to the right, above the Owed Amount text box.

3. Press and hold down the **Shift** key, click the **OwedAmt text box** to select it, and then release the **Shift** key. Both the label box and the text box are selected. You can now align them on their right edges.

4. Click **Format** on the menu bar, point to **Align**, and then click **Right** to right-align the label with the text box. See Figure 6-15.

| Figure 6-15 | AFTER ALIGNING THE OWED AMOUNT LABEL AND OWEDAMT TEXT BOX |

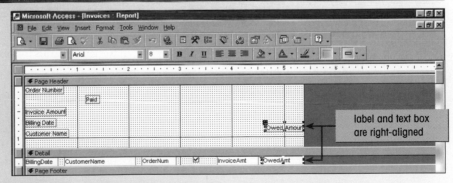

5. Repeat Steps 1 through 4 for the Invoice Amount label and InvoiceAmt text box to right-align them.

6. Left-align the four remaining labels with their respective text boxes by clicking **Left** (instead of Right) on the Format menu's Align command.

7. Click an empty area of the Page Header section to deselect all objects, click the **Billing Date label** to select it, press and hold down the **Shift** key, click the remaining labels, and then release the **Shift** key. All of the labels are now selected.

8. Click **Format** on the menu bar, point to **Align**, and then click **Top** to top-align the labels.

9. Position the pointer on any of the selected labels. When the pointer changes to a 🖐 shape, click and drag the labels up or down as necessary until they are positioned like the labels in Figure 6-16.

| Figure 6-16 | LABELS BOXES ALIGNED ABOVE TEXT BOXES AND CHECK BOX |

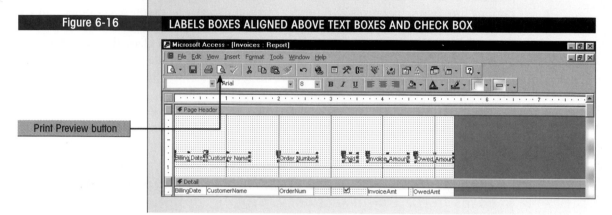

Print Preview button

There's too much space between the labels and the bottom of the Page Header section, so you'll resize the Page Header section. Then you'll save the modified report and preview it to see what it will look like when printed.

To resize the Page Header section and then save and preview the report:

1. Position the pointer on the bottom edge of the Page Header section. When the pointer changes to a ╪ shape, click and drag the bottom edge up, leaving two lines of grid dots visible below the labels to visually separate the labels from the field values when the report is printed.

2. Click the **Save** button 🖫 on the Report Design toolbar.

3. Click the **Print Preview** button 🔍 on the Report Design toolbar. Access displays the report in Print Preview.

4. Scroll the Print Preview window so that you can see more of the report on the screen. See Figure 6-17.

| Figure 6-17 | REPORT DISPLAYED IN PRINT PREVIEW |

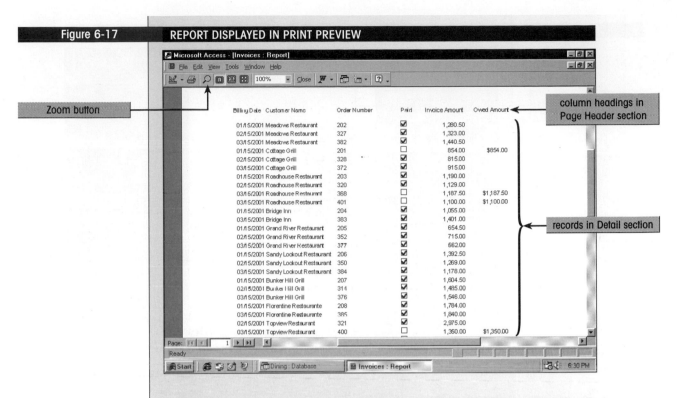

TROUBLE? If your report shows a larger gap between the records in the Detail section, you need to reduce the height of the Detail section. The bottom of the Detail section should align with the bottom of the text boxes in that section. Click the Close button on the Print Preview toolbar to return to Design view, and then drag the bottom of the Detail section up until it aligns with the bottom of the text boxes in that section. Then redisplay the report in Print Preview.

You can use the Zoom button to view the entire page on the screen, which will give you a sense of how the final printed page will look.

5. Click the **Zoom** button 🔍 on the Print Preview toolbar. Access displays the full report page on the screen. See Figure 6-18.

| Figure 6-18 | FULL REPORT PAGE DISPLAYED |

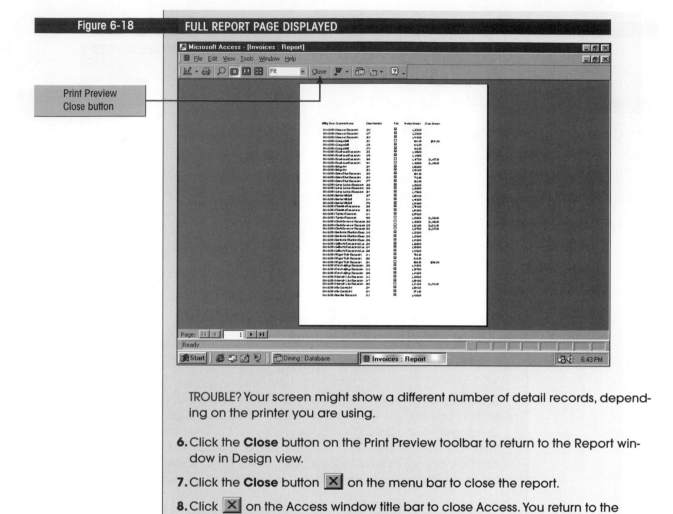

Print Preview
Close button

TROUBLE? Your screen might show a different number of detail records, depending on the printer you are using.

6. Click the **Close** button on the Print Preview toolbar to return to the Report window in Design view.

7. Click the **Close** button ✕ on the menu bar to close the report.

8. Click ✕ on the Access window title bar to close Access. You return to the Windows desktop.

You have completed the Detail section of the report and started to work on the Page Header section. In the next session, you will complete the report according to Leonard's design.

Session 6.1 QUICK CHECK

1. The _____ function lets you assign one value to a calculated field if a condition is true and a second value if the condition is false.

2. Describe the seven sections in an Access report.

3. What is a custom report?

4. What does the Report window in Design view have in common with the Form window in Design view? How do the two windows differ?

5. What is the Caption property for an object, and when would you change it?

6. How do you left-align objects in a column?

7. What is the purpose of the Zoom button in Print Preview?

SESSION 6.2

In this session, you will complete the Invoices report. You will insert a title, the date, and page number, and a line in the Page Header section. You will also add Group Header and Group Footer sections and specify the grouping and sorting fields for the records. Finally, you will add group subtotals to the Group Footer section and a grand total to the Report Footer section.

Adding the Date to a Report

According to Leonard's design, the report must include the date in the Page Header section. To add the date to a report, you insert the Date function in a text box. The **Date function** is a type of calculated control that prints the current date on a report. The format of the Date function is =Date(). The equals sign (=) indicates that this is a calculated control; Date is the name of the function; and the parentheses () indicate a function rather than simple text.

REFERENCE WINDOW RW

Adding the Date to a Report
- Display the Report in Design view.
- Click the Text Box tool on the toolbox.
- Position the pointer where you want the date to appear, and then click to place the text box in the report.
- Click the text box, type =Date( ), and then press the Enter key.

You need to insert the Date function in the Page Header section so that the current date will be printed on each page of the report.

To add the Date function to the Page Header section:

1. Make sure your Data Disk is in the appropriate drive and Access is running. Open the **Dining** database from the Tutorial folder on your Data Disk, and then open the **Invoices** report in Design view. If necessary, maximize the Report window.

2. If necessary, click the **Toolbox** button ✕ on the Report Design toolbar to display the toolbox.

   TROUBLE? If the toolbox is in the way of your report design, drag the toolbox to the far right side of the Report window.

3. Click the **Text Box** tool 🔲 on the toolbox.

4. Position the pointer in the Page Header section. The pointer changes to a ⁺🔲 shape.

5. When the pointer's plus symbol (+) is positioned in the Page Header section at approximately the ¾-inch mark on the horizontal ruler and the ⅜-inch mark on the vertical ruler (see Figure 6-19), click the mouse button. Access adds a text box with an attached label box to its left. Inside the text box is the description Unbound. Recall that an unbound control is a control that is not linked to a database table field.

6. Click the **Unbound text box** to position the insertion point and remove the word "Unbound," and then type **=Date()** and press the **Enter** key. See Figure 6-19.

Figure 6-19   ADDING THE CURRENT DATE TO THE REPORT

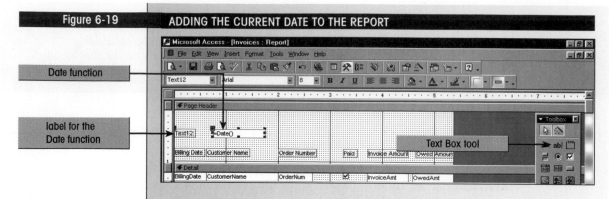

Date function

label for the
Date function

Text Box tool

TROUBLE? If your text box and attached label box are too close together, resize and reposition the text box using Figure 6-19 as a guide. Also, the attached label box on your screen might have a caption, such as "Text6," other than the one shown, depending on the exact way you completed previous steps. This causes no problem.

7. Click the **Print Preview** button 🔍 on the Report Design toolbar. Access displays the report in Print Preview.

8. If necessary, click the **Zoom** button 🔍 on the Print Preview toolbar, and then scroll up to see the date in the Page Header. See Figure 6-20.

Figure 6-20   REPORT WITH DATE IN PAGE HEADER SECTION

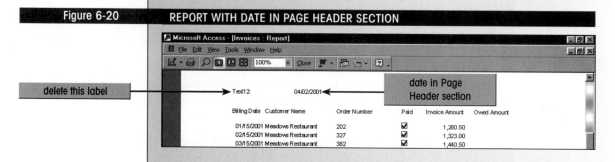

delete this label

date in Page
Header section

TROUBLE? Your date might appear with a two-digit year instead of the four-digit year shown in Figure 6-20 and with a different date format, depending on your computer's date settings.

When Access prints your report, the current date appears instead of the Date function you entered in the Unbound text box. Notice that the label for the date is unnecessary, so you can delete the label box. To make the date more prominent in the Page Header, you'll increase the font size of the text in the Date text box to 10 and then move the text box to the left edge of the Page Header section.

To delete the Date label box and modify the Date text box:

1. Click the **Close** button on the Print Preview toolbar to return to Design view.

2. Position the pointer on the Date label box, which is located in the upper left of the Page Header section.

3. Click the right mouse button to select the label box and open the shortcut menu, and then click **Cut** to delete the label.

4. Click the **Date text box**, and then drag its move handle to the left edge of the Page Header section.

5. Click the **Font Size** list arrow on the Formatting toolbar, and then click **10** to change the font size of the Date text box.

   Next, you'll save your changes, which you should do frequently when you plan to make further changes to your report design.

6. Click the **Save** button 🖫 on the Report Design toolbar.

You are now ready to add page numbers to the Page Header section.

Adding Page Numbers to a Report

You can instruct Access to print the page number in a report by including an expression in the Page Header or Page Footer section. You can type the expression in an unbound control, just as you did for the Date function, or you can use the Page Numbers option on the Insert menu. The inserted page number expression automatically prints the correct page number on each page of a report.

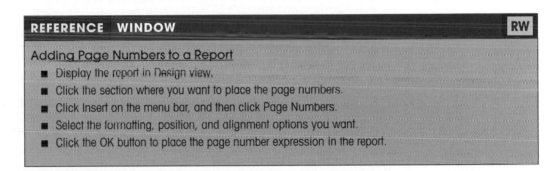

REFERENCE WINDOW   **RW**

Adding Page Numbers to a Report
- Display the report in Design view.
- Click the section where you want to place the page numbers.
- Click Insert on the menu bar, and then click Page Numbers.
- Select the formatting, position, and alignment options you want.
- Click the OK button to place the page number expression in the report.

Leonard wants the page number to be printed at the right side of the Page Header section on the same line with the date. You'll use the Page Numbers option to insert the page number in the report.

To add page numbers in the Page Header section:

1. Click an empty area of the Page Header section to deselect the Date text box.

2. Click **Insert** on the menu bar, and then click **Page Numbers**. The Page Numbers dialog box opens.

   The Format options allow you to specify the format of the page number. Leonard wants the page numbers to appear as Page 1, Page 2, etc. This is the Page N format option. The Position options allow you to place the page numbers at the top of the page in the Page Header section or at the bottom of the page in the Page Footer section. Leonard's design shows the page numbers at the top of the page.

3. Make sure that the Page N option button is selected in the Format section and that the Top of Page (Header) option button is selected in the Position section.

   The report design shows the page numbers at the right side of the page. You can specify this placement in the Alignment list box.

4. Click the **Alignment** list arrow, and then click **Right**.

5. Make sure that the Show Number on First Page check box is checked so that the page number prints on the first page as well as on all other pages. See Figure 6-21.

Figure 6-21   COMPLETED PAGE NUMBERS DIALOG BOX

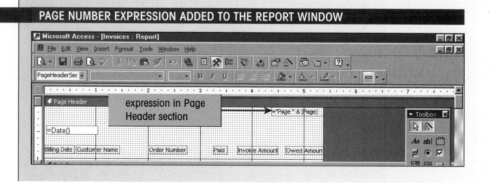

click to select format

click to select position on page

indicates page number will be printed on all pages

click to display alignment options

---

6. Click the **OK** button. Access adds a text box in the upper-right corner of the Page Header section. See Figure 6-22. The expression ="Page " & (Page) in the text box means that the report will show the word "Page " followed by the page number when the report is printed.

Figure 6-22   PAGE NUMBER EXPRESSION ADDED TO THE REPORT WINDOW

Microsoft Access - [Invoices : Report]

expression in Page Header section

=Date()

Billing Date | Customer Name | Order Number | Paid | Invoice Amount | Owed Amount

---

Leonard wants the text of the page number to be the same size as the text of the date. So, you need to change the font size of the Page Number text box to 10. To duplicate the formatting of the Date text box, you can use the Format Painter. The **Format Painter** allows you to copy the format of an object and apply it to other objects in the report. This makes it easy to create several objects with the same font style and size, the same color, and the same special effect applied.

Leonard's report design also shows the page number aligned on its bottom edge with the date in the Page Header section.

To use the Format Painter to format the Page Number text box and to align controls:

1. Click the **Date text box** to select it.

2. Click the **Format Painter** button on the Report Design toolbar.

3. Click the **Page Number text box**. The Format Painter automatically formats the Page Number text box like the Date text box (with a font size of 10). The label ="Page " & (Page) is larger than the text box. Also, notice that the letter "g" in the second word "Page" is not completely visible, so you need to resize the text box to fit.

4. Click the **Page Number text box**, click **Format** on the menu bar, point to **Size**, and then click **To Fit**. Access resizes the text box. The page number expression still does not fit the text box, but the actual page number will fit when the report is printed.

You'll now align the Date and Page Number text boxes on their bottom edges.

5. Hold down the **Shift** key, click the **Date text box**, release the **Shift** key, click **Format** on the menu bar, point to **Align**, and then click **Bottom**. Both text boxes now are aligned on their bottom edges.

6. Click the **Print Preview** button [image] on the Report Design toolbar. Access displays the report in Print Preview. See Figure 6-23.

Figure 6-23	COMPLETED PAGE HEADER SECTION

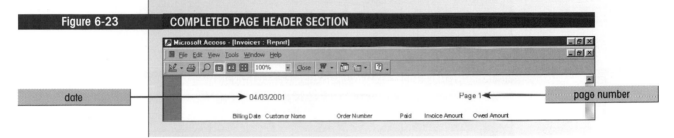

Now you are ready to add the title to the Page Header section.

Adding a Title to a Report

The report design includes the title Invoices, which you'll add to the Page Header section. To make the report title stand out, Leonard asks you to increase the report title font size from 8, the default, to 14.

To add the title to the Page Header section:

1. Click the **Close** button on the Print Preview toolbar to return to Design view.

2. Click the **Label** tool [Aa] on the toolbox.

3. Position the pointer in the Page Header section. The pointer changes to a ^+A shape.

4. Click the left mouse button when the pointer's plus symbol (+) is positioned at the ¼-inch mark on the vertical ruler and at the 2-inch mark on the horizontal ruler. Access places a very narrow text box in the Page Header section. When you start typing in this text box, it will expand to accommodate the text.

5. Type **Invoices** and then press the **Enter** key. See Figure 6-24.

Figure 6-24	ADDING A LABEL FOR THE REPORT TITLE

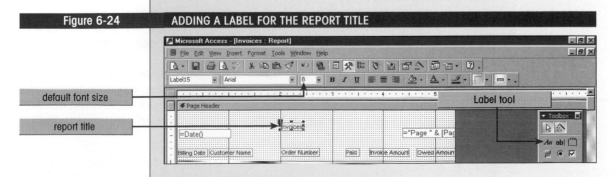

The label is still selected, so you can increase the report title font size.

6. Click the **Font Size** list arrow on the Formatting toolbar, and then click **14**. The font size of the report title changes from 8 to 14. The text box is now too small to display the entire report title. You need to resize the text box in the Page Header section.

7. Click **Format** on the menu bar, point to **Size**, and then click **To Fit** to resize the report title text box.

Leonard wants to see how the report looks, so you'll switch to Print Preview to check the report against his design.

8. Click the **Print Preview** button 🔍 on the Report Design toolbar. The report displays in Print Preview.

9. If necessary, scroll the Print Preview window so that you can see more of the report on the screen. See Figure 6-25.

| Figure 6-25 | REPORT TITLE DISPLAYED IN PAGE HEADER SECTION |

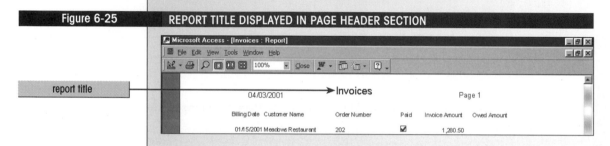

report title →

To make your report look more like the report design, you will reposition the column heading labels to just below the date and page number, and you'll decrease the height of the Page Header section to reduce the white space below it.

To move the labels and decrease the Page Header section height:

1. Click the **Close** button on the Print Preview toolbar to return to Design view.

2. Click an empty area of the Page Header section to deselect any selected objects.

3. While pressing and holding down the **Shift** key, click each of the six label boxes (for the report's column headings) in the Page Header section to select them, and then release the **Shift** key.

4. Position the pointer on one of the selected labels, and when the pointer changes to a ✋ shape, click and drag the label boxes up so that they are positioned just below the date and page number. Release the mouse button when the labels are positioned two rows of grid dots below the date and page number (see Figure 6-26).

TROUBLE? If the label boxes do not move, the Page Number text box or Date text box is probably selected along with the label boxes. Repeat Steps 2 through 4.

5. Position the pointer at the bottom edge of the Page Header section. When the pointer changes to a ✛ shape, click and drag the bottom edge up to reduce the height of the Page Header section. Release the mouse button when the bottom of the Page Header section is positioned two rows of grid dots below the label boxes. See Figure 6-26.

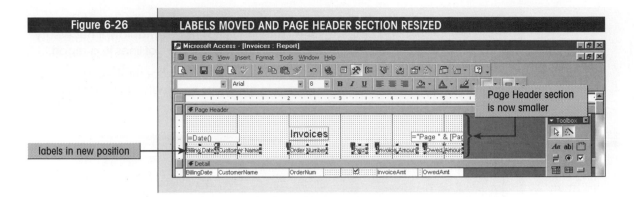

Figure 6-26   LABELS MOVED AND PAGE HEADER SECTION RESIZED

Now you can add a line beneath the column headings to separate them from the text boxes in the Detail section.

Adding Lines to a Report

You can use lines in a report to improve the report's readability and to group related information together. The Line tool on the toolbox allows you to add a line to a report or form.

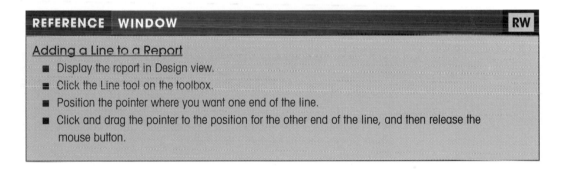

REFERENCE WINDOW   **RW**

Adding a Line to a Report
- Display the report in Design view.
- Click the Line tool on the toolbox.
- Position the pointer where you want one end of the line.
- Click and drag the pointer to the position for the other end of the line, and then release the mouse button.

You will add a horizontal line to the bottom of the Page Header section to visually separate it from the Detail section when the report is printed.

To add a line to the report:

1. Click the **Line** tool on the toolbox.

2. Position the pointer in the Page Header section. The pointer changes to a shape.

3. Position the pointer's plus symbol (+) at the left edge of the Page Header section, just below the column headings.

4. Click and drag a horizontal line from left to right, ending at the right edge of the Page Header section, and then release the mouse button.

   TROUBLE? If the line is not straight, click the Undo button on the Report Design toolbar, and then repeat Steps 1 through 4.

   Leonard wants the line to stand out more, so he asks you to increase the line's thickness.

5. With the line still selected, click the **Properties** button 🖽 on the Report Design toolbar to open the property sheet, and then click the **Format** tab, if necessary. The Border Width property controls the width, or thickness, of lines in a report.

6. Click the right side of the **Border Width** text box in the property sheet to display the list of border width options, and then click **3 pt**. The line's width increases. See Figure 6-27.

Figure 6-27	CHANGING THE WIDTH OF THE LINE

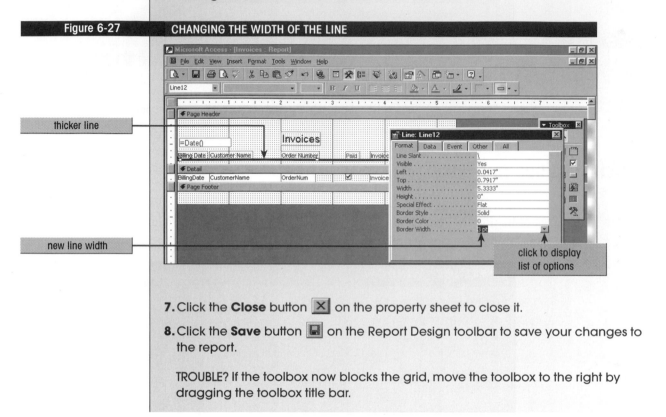

thicker line

new line width

click to display
list of options

7. Click the **Close** button ☒ on the property sheet to close it.

8. Click the **Save** button 🖫 on the Report Design toolbar to save your changes to the report.

TROUBLE? If the toolbox now blocks the grid, move the toolbox to the right by dragging the toolbox title bar.

Leonard wants to be able to find OwedAmt field values over $1500 and over $2000 more easily on the report.

Defining Conditional Formatting Rules

One way to make OwedAmt field values easier to spot on the report is to use conditional formatting for the OwedAmt field-value text box in the Detail section. **Conditional formatting** allows you to change the format of a report or form control based on the control's value. For example, you can change the OwedAmt field's font style or color when its value is over $2000 and change to a different font style or color when its value is between $1500 and $2000; the defined font style or color for the control is used for all other values.

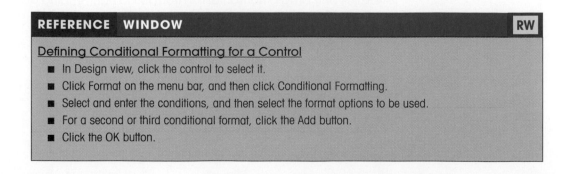

REFERENCE WINDOW	RW

Defining Conditional Formatting for a Control
- In Design view, click the control to select it.
- Click Format on the menu bar, and then click Conditional Formatting.
- Select and enter the conditions, and then select the format options to be used.
- For a second or third conditional format, click the Add button.
- Click the OK button.

You will use bold and italics for OwedAmt field values over $2000 and will use bold for values between $1500 and $2000.

To define conditional formatting for the OwedAmt field:

1. Click the **OwedAmt text box** in the Detail section, click **Format** on the menu bar, and then click **Conditional Formatting**. The Conditional Formatting dialog box opens. See Figure 6-28.

Figure 6-28	CONDITIONAL FORMATTING DIALOG BOX

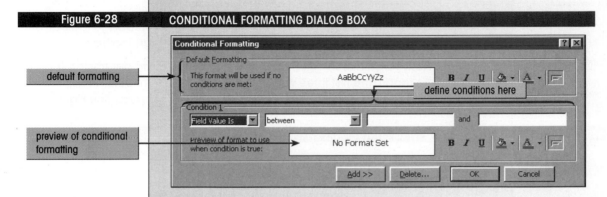

First, you'll define the conditional formatting for OwedAmt field values between $1500 and $2000.

2. Make sure that the list box immediately under "Condition 1" displays "Field Value Is" and that the second box displays "between."

3. Click in the third box, type **1500**, press the **Tab** key, and then type **2000**. The condition will be true for all OwedAmt field values between $1500 and $2000.

   Now you need to select the format that will be used for the first condition.

4. Click the **Bold** button **B** in the Condition 1 section, and then click the **Add** button. The first condition and its format are defined, and the Conditional Formatting dialog box expands for the entry of a second condition. See Figure 6-29.

Figure 6-29	AFTER DEFINING THE FIRST CONDITIONAL FORMAT

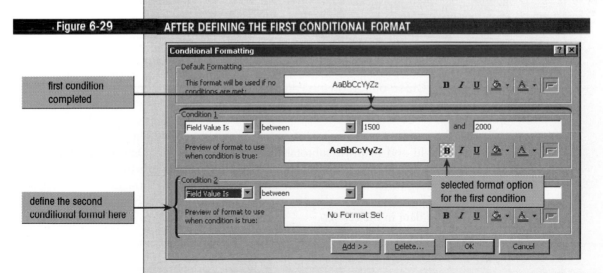

Next, you'll define the conditional formatting for OwedAmt field values over $2000.

5. In the Condition 2 section, click the **list arrow** for the second box, click **greater than**, press the **Tab** key, and then type **2000**. The condition will be true for all OwedAmt field values greater than $2000.

6. In the Condition 2 section, click the **Bold** button **B**, and then click the **Italic** button **I**. The second condition and its format are defined.

   You've finished defining the conditional formats for the OwedAmt field. Next, you'll accept the conditional formats, save your work, and then show Leonard how the report looks.

7. Click the **OK** button, click the **Save** button 💾 on the Report Design toolbar, and then click the **Print Preview** button 🔍 on the Report Design toolbar.

8. Click the **Next Page** button ▶ in the horizontal scroll bar to display the second page of the report. The first three values in the Owed Amount column use the default format, and the other five values use conditional formats. See Figure 6-30.

Figure 6-30	PRINT PREVIEWING CONDITIONAL FORMATS

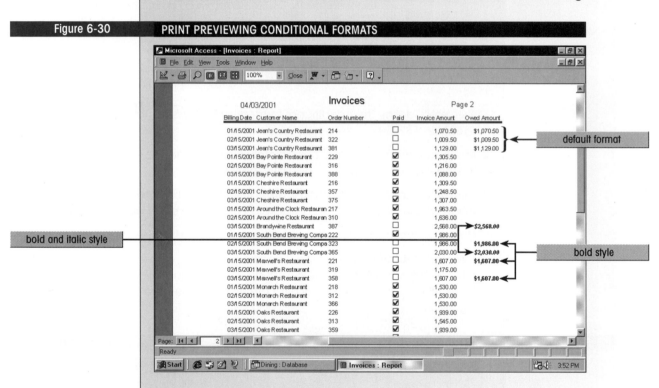

9. Click the **Close** button on the Print Preview toolbar to return to Design view.

Leonard would like the report to print records in ascending order based on the BillingDate field and to print subtotals for each set of BillingDate field values. He also wants the records for each BillingDate group to be printed with the unpaid invoices first and in descending order by InvoiceAmt. That way, he can review the monthly billings more easily and monitor the invoices that have not been paid. To make these changes, you need to sort and group data in the report.

Sorting and Grouping Data in a Report

Access allows you to organize the records in a report by sorting the records using one or more sort keys. Each sort key can also be a grouping field. If you specify a sort key as a grouping field, you can include a Group Header section and a Group Footer section for the group. A Group Header section will typically include the name of the group, and a Group Footer section will typically include a count or subtotal for records in that group.

You use the Sorting and Grouping button on the Report Design toolbar to select sort keys and grouping fields for a report. Each report can have up to 10 sort fields, and any of the sort fields can also be grouping fields.

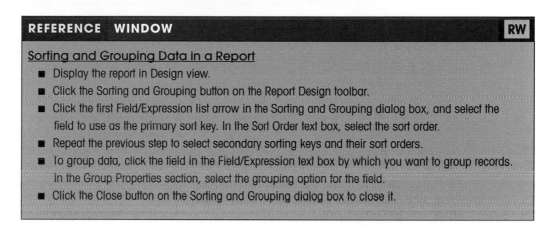

REFERENCE WINDOW   RW

Sorting and Grouping Data in a Report
- Display the report in Design view.
- Click the Sorting and Grouping button on the Report Design toolbar.
- Click the first Field/Expression list arrow in the Sorting and Grouping dialog box, and select the field to use as the primary sort key. In the Sort Order text box, select the sort order.
- Repeat the previous step to select secondary sorting keys and their sort orders.
- To group data, click the field in the Field/Expression text box by which you want to group records. In the Group Properties section, select the grouping option for the field.
- Click the Close button on the Sorting and Grouping dialog box to close it.

Because Leonard wants records listed in ascending order based on the BillingDate field and subtotals printed for each BillingDate group, you need to specify the BillingDate field as both the primary sort key and the grouping field. Leonard also wants unpaid invoices listed first and all invoices to be sorted in descending order by InvoiceAmt. So, you need to specify the Paid field as the secondary sort key and the InvoiceAmt field as the tertiary (third) sort key.

To select the sort keys and group field:

1. Click the **Sorting and Grouping** button 📑 on the Report Design toolbar. The Sorting and Grouping dialog box opens.

   The top section of the Sorting and Grouping dialog box allows you to specify the sort keys for the records in the Detail section. For each sort key, the bottom section of the dialog box allows you to designate the sort key as a grouping field and to specify whether you want a Group Header section, a Group Footer section, and other options for the group.

2. Click the **list arrow** in the first **Field/Expression** text box to display the list of available fields, and then click **BillingDate**. Ascending is the default sort order in the Sort Order text box, so you do not need to change this setting.

   You can now designate BillingDate as a grouping field and specify that you want a Group Footer section for this group. This section will contain the subtotals for the invoices by BillingDate.

3. Click the right side of the **Group Footer** text box, and then click **Yes**. Access adds a Group Footer section named BillingDate Footer to the Report window. See Figure 6-31.

Figure 6-31	ADDING A GROUP FOOTER SECTION

symbol indicates
grouping field

Group Footer
section added

grouping options

sort order

primary sort key

creates Group
Footer section

Notice the symbol placed next to the Field/Expression text box for BillingDate. This symbol indicates that BillingDate has been designated as a grouping field.

You can now specify the second and third sort keys and their sort orders.

4. Click the right side of the second **Field/Expression** text box to display the list of fields, and then click **Paid**. For a yes/no field, the default sort order, Ascending, displays Yes values before No values. Therefore, you need to change the sort order for the Paid field to Descending so that unpaid (No) invoices are listed first.

5. Click the right side of the second **Sort Order** text box, and then click **Descending**.

6. Click the right side of the third **Field/Expression** text box, and then click **InvoiceAmt**.

7. Click the right side of the third **Sort Order** text box, and then click **Descending**. See Figure 6-32.

Figure 6-32	COMPLETED SORTING AND GROUPING DIALOG BOX

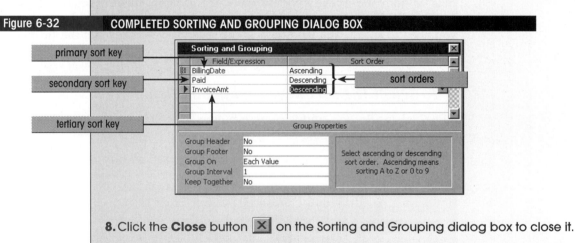

primary sort key

secondary sort key

tertiary sort key

sort orders

8. Click the **Close** button ⊠ on the Sorting and Grouping dialog box to close it.

You are now ready to calculate the group totals and overall totals for the InvoiceAmt field values.

Calculating Group Totals and Overall Totals

When you print a report, anything contained in the Report Footer section appears once at the end of the report. This section is often used to display overall totals. Leonard wants the report to print overall totals based on the InvoiceAmt field. To include information in the Report Footer, you must first add both a Report Header section and a Report Footer section to the report.

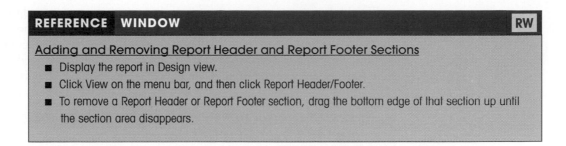

REFERENCE WINDOW   RW

Adding and Removing Report Header and Report Footer Sections
- Display the report in Design view.
- Click View on the menu bar, and then click Report Header/Footer.
- To remove a Report Header or Report Footer section, drag the bottom edge of that section up until the section area disappears.

Before adding totals to the report, you need to add Report Header and Report Footer sections.

To add Report Header and Report Footer sections:

1. Click **View** on the menu bar, and then click **Report Header/Footer**. Access places a Report Header section at the top of the Report window and a Report Footer section at the bottom. See Figure 6-33.

Figure 6-33   REPORT HEADER AND REPORT FOOTER SECTIONS ADDED

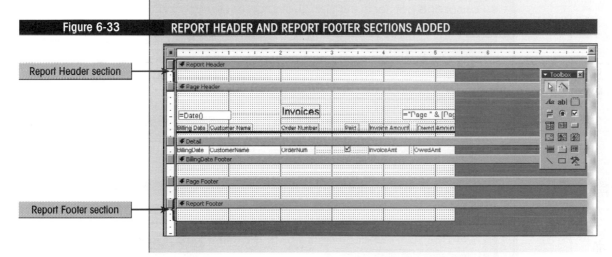

Report Header section

Report Footer section

Leonard wants the report to print subtotals for each BillingDate group, as well as an overall total, based on the InvoiceAmt field. To calculate these totals for the InvoiceAmt field, you use the **Sum function**. You place the Sum function in a Group Footer section to print each group's total and in the Report Footer section to print the overall total. The format for the Sum function is =Sum([*fieldname*]). To create the appropriate text boxes in the footer sections, you use the Text Box tool on the toolbox.

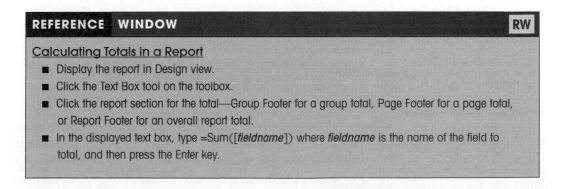

REFERENCE WINDOW   RW

Calculating Totals in a Report
- Display the report in Design view.
- Click the Text Box tool on the toolbox.
- Click the report section for the total—Group Footer for a group total, Page Footer for a page total, or Report Footer for an overall report total.
- In the displayed text box, type =Sum([*fieldname*]) where *fieldname* is the name of the field to total, and then press the Enter key.

To add the group totals and overall total to your report, you need to increase the size of the BillingDate Footer and Report Footer sections to make room for the control that will contain the Sum function. Because you will not use the Report Header section and the Page Footer section, you can also decrease their sizes to zero now. Then you need to add text boxes for the Sum function in both the BillingDate Footer section and the Report Footer section.

To resize the sections and add text boxes for the InvoiceAmt group and overall totals:

1. Position the pointer on the bottom edge of the BillingDate Footer section. When the pointer changes to a ✛ shape, click and drag the bottom edge down until six rows of grid dots are visible in the BillingDate Footer section.

2. Use the ✛ pointer to decrease the height of the Report Header and Page Footer sections to 0, and to increase the height of the Report Footer section to six rows of grid dots. The new height of the Report Footer section will allow sufficient room to place the totals in this section.

3. Click the **Text Box** tool ⓐⓑⓛ on the toolbox.

4. Position the pointer in the BillingDate Footer section, and click the left mouse button when the pointer's plus symbol (+) is positioned in the second row of grid dots and vertically aligned with the left edge of the InvoiceAmt text box (see Figure 6-34). Access adds a text box with an attached label box to its left.

5. Click ⓐⓑⓛ on the toolbox.

6. Position the pointer in the Report Footer section, and click the left mouse button when the pointer's plus symbol (+) is positioned in the second row of grid dots and vertically aligned with the left edge of the InvoiceAmt text box. Access adds a text box with an attached label box to its left. See Figure 6-34.

| Figure 6-34 | ADDING TEXT BOXES IN THE FOOTER SECTIONS |

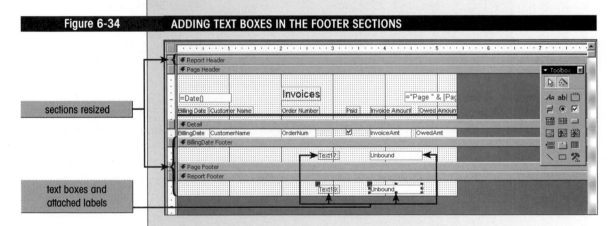

Now enter the Caption values for the identifying labels.

7. Right-click the label box in the BillingDate Footer section, and then click **Properties** on the shortcut menu to open the property sheet. The Format tab is selected and the Caption text box is highlighted.

8. Type **Total for month:**.

9. If the property sheet blocks the label box in the Report Footer section, drag the property sheet title bar to unblock the label box. Click the label box in the Report Footer section, click the **Caption** text box, press the **F2** key to select the existing caption, and then type **Grand total:**.

10. Click the **Close** button ☒ on the property sheet to close it.

> **TROUBLE?** If the toolbox now blocks the grid, move the toolbox to the right by dragging the toolbox title bar.

The text box labels are not big enough to display the label values, so you need to resize them now.

To resize the text box labels:

1. Press and hold down the **Shift** key, click the label box in the BillingDate Footer section, and then release the **Shift** key. Both total label boxes are now selected.

2. Click **Format** on the menu bar, point to **Size**, and then click **To Fit**. Access resizes the label boxes to display the entire labels.

You can now add the Sum function to the two footer section text boxes. Leonard wants the totals displayed as currency, with dollar signs and two digits after the decimal point. You can specify this format in the Format property for the text boxes.

To add the Sum function to calculate group and overall totals:

1. Click the **Unbound text box** in the BillingDate Footer section to select it, click the text box again to position the insertion point in it, type **=Sum((InvoiceAmt))**, and then press the **Enter** key.

2. Click the text box in the Report Footer section to select it, click the text box again to position the insertion point in it, type **=Sum((InvoiceAmt))**, and then press the **Enter** key.

You can now resize the text boxes so that the totals will line up with the InvoiceAmt values in the Detail section.

3. Select both the text box in the BillingDate Footer section and the text box in the Report Footer section, and then click the middle-right sizing handle of either text box and drag it to the left until the right edge of each box is two grid dots to the right of the InvoiceAmt text box in the Detail section. Refer to Figure 6-35 to help you position the right edge.

| Figure 6-35 | ADDING A GROUP TOTAL AND OVERALL TOTAL |

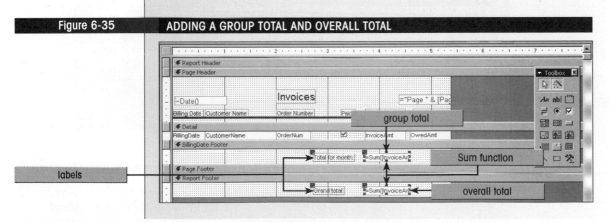

TROUBLE? If your labels and text boxes are not sized and positioned like those in Figure 6-35, resize or move them now. To resize a label or text box, click the box to select it and use the sizing handles to change the size. To move a label or text box, click the box to select it and use the move handle to change the position.

Now you can format the text boxes as Currency so that the total amounts will include dollar signs and two decimal places.

4. Right-click the **InvoiceAmt text box** in the BillingDate Footer section, and then click **Properties** to open the property sheet. "Multiple selection" appears in the property sheet's title bar, because both footer text boxes were selected when you opened the property sheet.

5. Click the **Format** tab (if necessary), click the **Format** list arrow, scroll the list of available formats, and then click **Currency**.

6. Click the **Close** button ⊠ on the property sheet to close it.

TROUBLE? If the toolbox now blocks the grid, move the toolbox to the right by dragging the toolbox title bar.

You can now add the Sum function for the OwedAmt field to the two footer sections. You'll save time by copying the existing footer text boxes and moving and modifying the copied text boxes.

To copy and modify the footer text boxes:

1. Click an empty area of the Report Footer section to deselect any selected controls.

2. Right-click the **InvoiceAmt text box** in the BillingDate Footer section, and then click **Copy** on the shortcut menu.

3. Right-click an empty area of the BillingDate Footer section, click **Paste** on the shortcut menu, right-click an empty area of the Report Footer section, and then click **Paste** on the shortcut menu. Copies of the label and text boxes now appear in the upper-left corners of both footer sections. See Figure 6-36.

| Figure 6-36 | AFTER PASTING LABELS AND TEXT BOXES TO THE FOOTER SECTIONS |

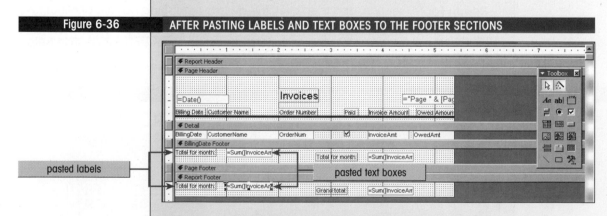

pasted labels

pasted text boxes

Because the InvoiceAmt labels already identify the group and overall totals, you can now delete the two labels.

4. Select both pasted labels, and then click the **Cut** button ✂ on the Report Design toolbar. Both pasted labels are now deleted from the footer sections.

Next, you'll change the Sum function for both pasted text boxes.

5. Select both pasted text boxes, right-click one of the selected text boxes, and then click **Properties** on the shortcut menu. The property sheet opens, once again with "Multiple selection" appearing in its title bar.

6. Click the **Data** tab on the property sheet, select **Invoice** in the Control Source text box, and then type **Owed**. The Control Source text box now contains =Sum((OwedAmt)).

7. Click the **Close** button on the property sheet to close it and, if necessary, move the toolbox to the right by dragging the toolbox title bar.

You can now move the selected text boxes into position at the right side of the two footer sections.

8. Position the pointer on one of the selected text boxes, and when the pointer changes to a 🖐 shape, click and drag the text boxes to the right so that they are positioned one grid dot to the right of the InvoiceAmt text boxes. See Figure 6-37.

| Figure 6-37 | AFTER MOVING THE PASTED TEXT BOXES TO THE RIGHT |

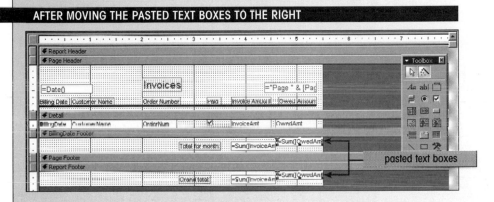

Next, you'll align each OwedAmt text box in the footer sections with the bottom edges of the other controls in the footer sections.

To align the OwedAmt footer text boxes with the other footer controls:

1. Click an empty area of the Report Footer section to deselect any selected controls.

2. Select both the **InvoiceAmt text box** and the **OwedAmt text box** in the BillingDate Footer section, click **Format** on the menu bar, point to **Align**, and then click **Bottom**. The controls in the BillingDate Footer section are now aligned on their bottom edges.

3. Repeat Steps 1 and 2 for the InvoiceAmt text box and the OwedAmt text box in the Report Footer section.

You've made a number of changes to the report design, so you should save these changes.

4. Click the **Save** button 💾 on the Report Design toolbar to save your changes to the report.

Leonard wants lines above both the group totals and the overall totals, to visually separate the total amounts from the values in the Detail section. So, you'll add lines above each Sum function.

To add lines above the totals:

1. Click the **Line** tool on the toolbox.

2. Position the pointer in the BillingDate Footer section. The pointer changes to a ⁺‿ shape.

3. Position the pointer's plus symbol (+) in the first row of grid dots and vertically align it with the left edge of the InvoiceAmt text box in the BillingDate Footer section.

4. Click and drag the pointer to the right until the right end of the horizontal line is above the right edge of the OwedAmt text box (see Figure 6-38).

5. Repeat Steps 1 through 4 to add a line above the Sum functions in the Report Footer section. See Figure 6-38.

| Figure 6-38 | ADDING LINES ABOVE THE GROUP AND OVERALL TOTALS |

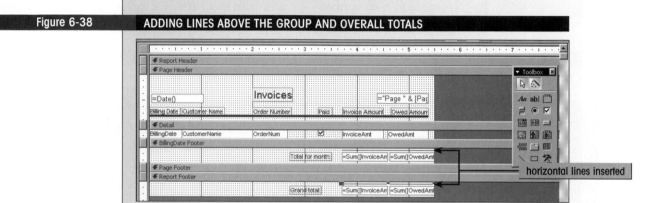

6. Click the **Print Preview** button on the Report Design toolbar. Access displays the first page of the report.

7. Click the **Last Page** button in the horizontal scroll bar to display the last page of the report. If necessary, scroll down to see the last BillingDate group subtotal and the overall total at the bottom of the report. See Figure 6-39.

| Figure 6-39 | GROUP AND OVERALL TOTALS IN THE REPORT |

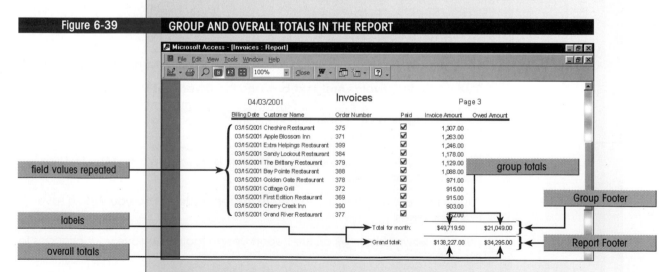

TROUBLE? Your report might display a different number of detail lines, depending on your printer settings.

After viewing the report, Leonard decides that the Detail section would be more readable if the BillingDate was printed only once for each group.

Hiding Duplicate Values in a Report

Your next change is to display the BillingDate value only in the first record in a group. Within a group, all BillingDate field values are the same, so if you display only the first one, you simplify the report and make it easier to read.

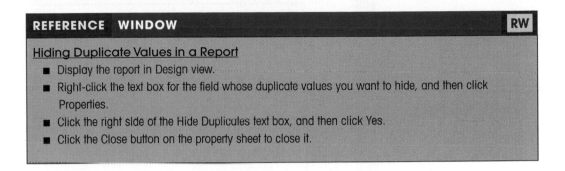

REFERENCE WINDOW   **RW**

Hiding Duplicate Values in a Report
- Display the report in Design view.
- Right-click the text box for the field whose duplicate values you want to hide, and then click Properties.
- Click the right side of the Hide Duplicates text box, and then click Yes.
- Click the Close button on the property sheet to close it.

To hide the duplicate BillingDate values:

1. Click the **Close** button on the Print Preview toolbar to return to Design view.

2. Right-click the **BillingDate text box** in the Detail section, and then click **Properties** to open the property sheet.

3. Click the **Format** tab (if necessary), click the right side of the **Hide Duplicates** text box, and then click **Yes**. See Figure 6-40.

| Figure 6-40 | HIDING THE DUPLICATE FIELD VALUES |

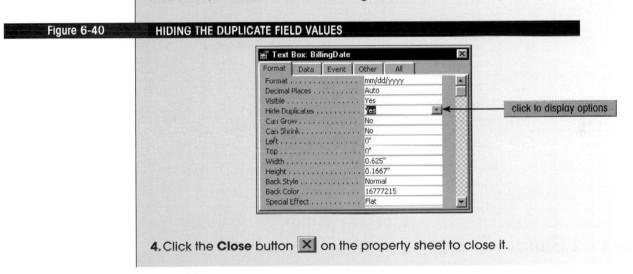

4. Click the **Close** button ⊠ on the property sheet to close it.

The report is finished. You can now preview the report pages, and then save and print the report.

To view, save, and print the report:

1. Click the **Print Preview** button ⬚ on the Report Design toolbar. Access displays the first page of the report. See Figure 6-41.

Figure 6-41   THE BEGINNING OF THE REPORT IN PRINT PREVIEW

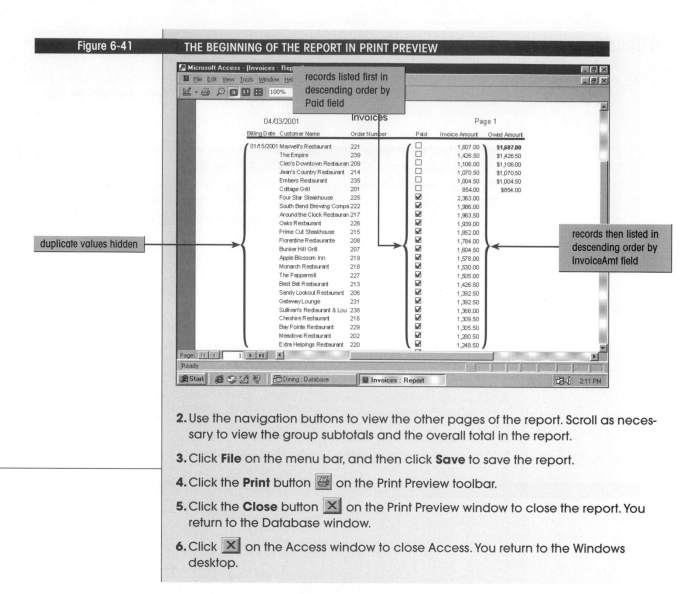

2. Use the navigation buttons to view the other pages of the report. Scroll as necessary to view the group subtotals and the overall total in the report.

3. Click **File** on the menu bar, and then click **Save** to save the report.

4. Click the **Print** button on the Print Preview toolbar.

5. Click the **Close** button on the Print Preview window to close the report. You return to the Database window.

6. Click on the Access window to close Access. You return to the Windows desktop.

Leonard is very pleased with the report and feels that it will help him keep better track of outstanding invoices. In the next session, you'll use integration techniques to create another report for Leonard.

Session 6.2 QUICK CHECK

1. What is a grouping field?

2. When do you use the Text Box tool?

3. What do you type in a text box to tell Access to print the current date?

4. How do you insert a page number in a Page Header section?

5. What is the maximum number of conditional formats you can define for a control?

6. What is the function of the Sorting and Grouping button?

7. How do you calculate group totals and overall totals?

8. Why might you want to hide duplicate values in a report that includes groups?

SESSION 6.3	In this session, you will integrate Access with other Office 2000 programs. You will create an embedded chart in a report and place a linked Word document in the Detail section, and then edit the chart and the document. Then you'll export Access data to an Excel worksheet.

Integrating Access with Other Programs

Leonard is so pleased with the report that you created for him that he immediately thinks of another report that would be helpful to him. He asks if you can create a report with a graph showing the total amounts for the invoices for each month.

When you create a report or form in Access, you might want to include more than just the formatted listing of records. For example, you might want to include objects such as a long text passage, a graphic image, or a chart summarizing the data. You also might want to include a graphic image or other object as a field value in a table record. Access does not allow you to create long text passages easily, nor does Access have the capability to create graphic images or charts. Instead, you can create these objects using other programs and then place them in a report or form using the appropriate integration method.

When you integrate information between programs, the program containing the original information, or **object**, is called the **source** program, and the program in which you place the same information is called the **destination** program.

Access offers three ways for you to integrate objects created by other programs:

- **Importing**. When you import an object, you include the contents of a file in the form, report, or field. In Tutorial 5, for example, you imported a graphic image created in Microsoft Paint, a drawing program. Once an object is imported, it has no relation to the program in which it was created; it is simply an object in the form, report, or field.

- **Embedding**. When you embed an object, you preserve its connection to the source program, which enables you to edit the object, if necessary, using the features of the source program. You can edit the object by double-clicking it, which starts the source program. Any changes you make to the object are reflected *only* in the form, report, or field in which it is embedded; the changes do not affect the original object in the file from which it was embedded. Likewise, if you start the source program outside Access and make any changes to the original object, these changes are not reflected in the embedded object.

- **Linking**. When you link an object to a form, report, or field, you preserve its connection to the original file. You can edit a linked object by double-clicking it, which starts the source program. Any changes you make to the object are reflected in both the original file created in the source program and the linked file in the destination program. You can also start the source program outside Access and edit the object's original file. These changes would also be reflected in the original file and in the linked object in the Access form, report, or field.

In general, you import an object when you simply want a copy of the object in your form, report, or field and you don't intend to make any changes to the object. You embed or link an object when you want a copy of the object in your form, report, or field and you intend to edit the object. You embed the object if you do not want your edits to affect any other copies of the object in other programs. You link the object when you want your edits to be reflected in both the original object and the linked object.

Integrating objects among programs is made possible through the features of **object linking and embedding (OLE)**. Not all programs support OLE, although most do. If you have difficulty linking or embedding objects between programs, it is possible that the program you are using does not support OLE.

The design for Leonard's report, shown in Figure 6-42, includes an embedded chart showing the totals of invoices in the report by month, and a linked text document in the Detail section. To include the chart you will use the Access Chart Wizard. The text document is a Microsoft Word file that you will link to the report. In that way, any changes made to the original Word document will appear in the report.

Figure 6-42	DESIGN FOR THE INVOICE TOTALS BY MONTH REPORT

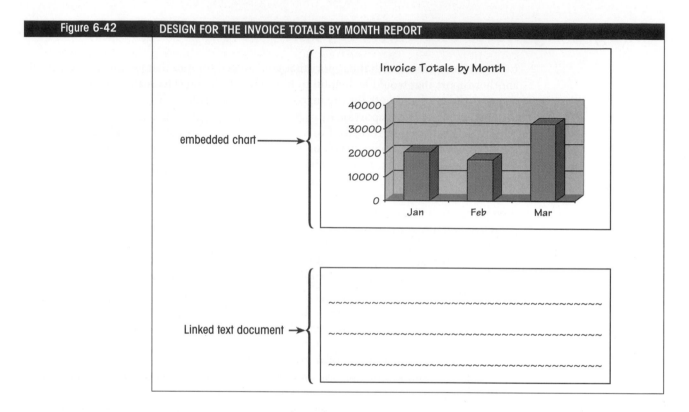

Embedding a Chart in a Report

Access provides the Chart Wizard to assist you in embedding a chart in a form or report. The chart itself is actually created by another program, Microsoft Graph, and is automatically embedded by the Chart Wizard. After embedding a chart in a report, you can edit it using the Microsoft Graph program.

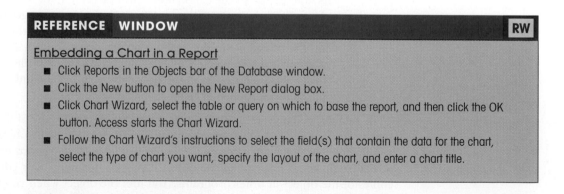

REFERENCE WINDOW   RW

Embedding a Chart in a Report
- Click Reports in the Objects bar of the Database window.
- Click the New button to open the New Report dialog box.
- Click Chart Wizard, select the table or query on which to base the report, and then click the OK button. Access starts the Chart Wizard.
- Follow the Chart Wizard's instructions to select the field(s) that contain the data for the chart, select the type of chart you want, specify the layout of the chart, and enter a chart title.

The Order table in the Dining database contains all the information necessary for the chart Leonard wants to include in his report, so you will base the report on the Order table.

To start the Chart Wizard to create a report with an embedded chart:

1. Make sure that Access is running and the **Dining** database from the Tutorial folder on your Data Disk is open. If necessary, maximize the Database window.

2. Click **Reports** in the Objects bar of the Database window, and then click the **New** button to open the New Report dialog box.

3. Click **Chart Wizard** to select it, click the **list arrow** for choosing the table or query on which to base the report, scroll down the list and click **Order**, and then click the **OK** button. Access starts the Chart Wizard and opens the first Chart Wizard dialog box.

   TROUBLE? If a dialog box opens and tells you that the Chart Wizard feature is not currently installed, insert your Office 2000 CD in the correct drive, and then click the Yes button. If you do not have an Office 2000 CD, ask your instructor or technical support person for help.

This first Chart Wizard dialog box allows you to select the fields that contain the data for the chart. Leonard wants the chart to show the totals of the InvoiceAmt field by BillingDate, so you need to select these two fields.

To create a report with an embedded chart:

1. Click **InvoiceAmt** in the Available Fields list box, and then click the ⊳ button to move the InvoiceAmt field to the Fields for Chart list.

2. Click **BillingDate** in the Available Fields list box, and then click the ⊳ button to move the BillingDate field to the Fields for Chart list.

3. Click the **Next** button. Access displays the next Chart Wizard dialog box, which allows you to select the type of chart you want.

   According to Leonard's design, the data should be represented by columns. A column chart is appropriate for showing the variation of a quantity (total of invoices) over a period of time (month). A 3-D chart adds perspective to the chart. So, you'll select a 3-D Column Chart for the report.

4. Click the **3-D Column Chart** button (second button in the first row) to select the 3-D Column Chart type. See Figure 6-43.

Figure 6-43	SELECTING THE TYPE OF CHART

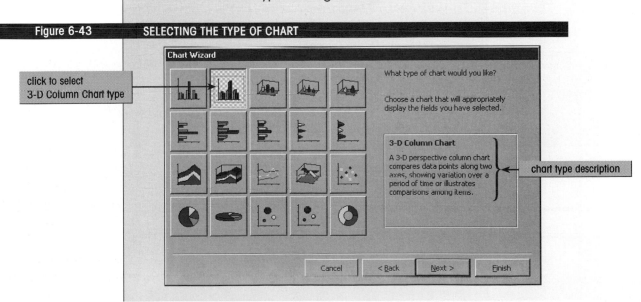

The box on the right displays a brief description of the selected chart type.

5. Click the **Next** button. Access displays the next Chart Wizard dialog box, which allows you to modify the layout of the chart. You'll use the default layout and modify it later, if necessary, after seeing how the chart appears in the report.

6. Click the **Next** button to display the final dialog box, in which you enter the title that will appear at the top of the chart.

7. Type **Invoice Totals by Month** in the text box, make sure the options for displaying a legend and opening the report are selected and that the option for displaying Help is not, and then click the **Finish** button. Access creates the report and displays it, with the embedded chart, in the Print Preview window.

8. Click the **Maximize** button 🔲 on the Report window, and then scroll the window until the entire chart is visible. See Figure 6-44.

| Figure 6-44 | COMPLETED CHART IN PRINT PREVIEW |

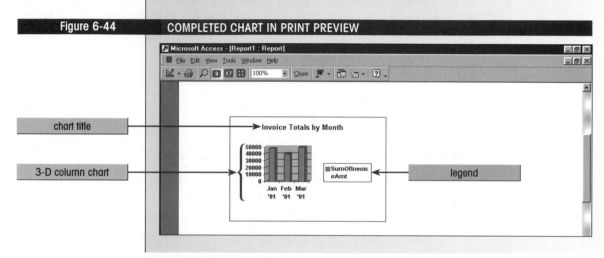

After viewing the chart, Leonard decides that it needs some modification. He'd like the chart to be larger and centered on the page. Also, he thinks that the legend is unnecessary, because the chart title is descriptive enough, and therefore it can be deleted. You can make these changes by switching to Design view, resizing the Detail section and the chart, and then starting Microsoft Graph so that you can edit the chart.

To switch to Design view and start Microsoft Graph:

1. Click the **Close** button on the Print Preview toolbar to display the Report window in Design view. The chart appears in the Detail section of the report.

    TROUBLE? If the chart appears with the incorrect legend and different columns, this is a minor Access display error and will not affect the final chart in the printed report.

2. If the toolbox is open, click its **Close** button ❌ to close it.

3. Move the pointer to the bottom of the Detail section. When the pointer changes to a ╪ shape, click and drag the bottom of the Detail section down until the bottom is at the 4-inch mark on the vertical ruler. Release the mouse button.

    TROUBLE? If you did not position the bottom of the Detail section correctly, simply click and drag the bottom of the Detail section up or down as necessary. Then continue with the steps.

4. Click the chart object. Sizing handles appear on the sides and corners of the chart.

5. Position the pointer on the lower-right corner of the chart. When the pointer changes to a ↖ shape, click and drag the lower-right corner down to the 3½-inch mark on the vertical ruler, and to the right to the 5¼-inch mark on the horizontal ruler. Release the mouse button, and then scroll up (if necessary). See Figure 6-45.

Figure 6-45	CHART AFTER RESIZING IN REPORT WINDOW

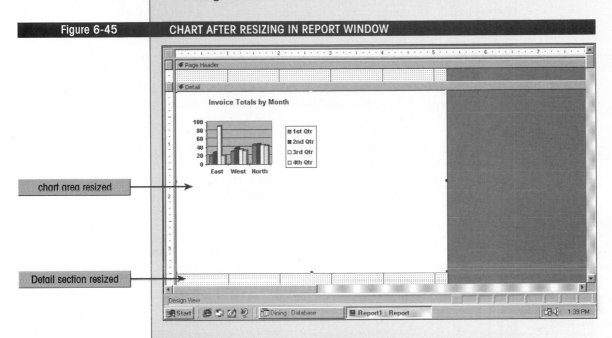

chart area resized

Detail section resized

6. Right-click the chart object, point to **Chart Object**, and then click **Edit**. Microsoft Graph starts and displays the chart. See Figure 6-46.

Figure 6-46	CHART WITH MICROSOFT GRAPH ACTIVE

Microsoft Graph menu bar

Microsoft Graph toolbar

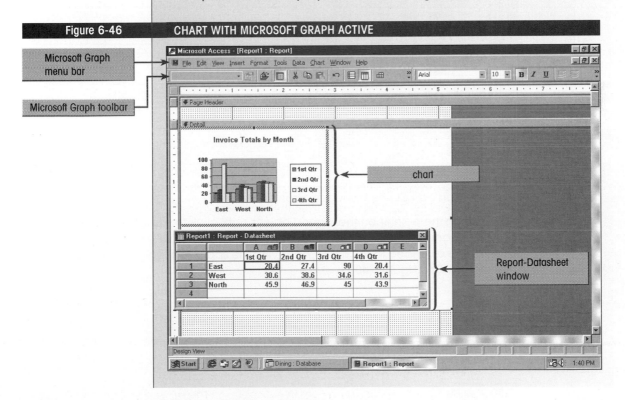

chart

Report-Datasheet window

Microsoft Graph is the source program, the program in which the original chart was created by the Chart Wizard. Because the chart is embedded in the report, editing the chart object starts Graph and allows you to edit the chart using the Microsoft Graph menu bar and toolbar. In addition to the selected chart, the Report window contains one smaller window: Report - Datasheet. The Report - Datasheet window displays the data on which the chart is based. You will not need the Report - Datasheet window. All of your changes will be made in the Report - Chart window and in the Report window in Design view.

After you close the Report - Datasheet window, you need to enlarge the chart. Then you'll delete the legend.

To enlarge the chart and delete the legend:

1. Click the **Close** button ☒ on the Report - Datasheet window to close it.

2. Position the pointer on the lower-right corner of the chart. When the pointer changes to a ↖ shape, click and drag the lower-right corner down to the 3½-inch mark on the vertical ruler, and to the right to the 5¼-inch mark on the horizontal ruler. Release the mouse button. See Figure 6-47.

| Figure 6-47 | CHART AFTER RESIZING |

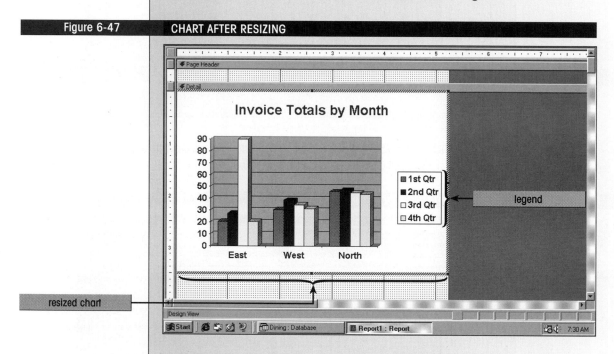

Now you can delete the legend from the chart.

3. Position the pointer on the legend object, right-click to display the shortcut menu, and then click **Clear** to remove the legend from the chart. The column chart is extended to the right, occupying the space occupied previously by the legend. See Figure 6-48.

Figure 6-48	MODIFIED CHART

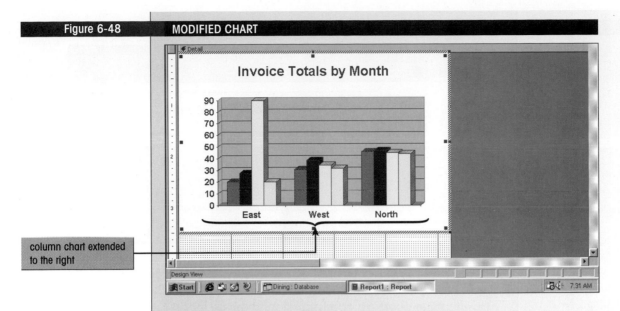

column chart extended to the right

You've finished your Microsoft Graph changes to the chart, so you'll return to the Report window in Design view to center the chart in the report page.

4. Click anywhere in the Page Header section. Microsoft Graph closes, and the edited chart appears in the Report window. See Figure 6-49.

Figure 6-49	EDITED CHART IN THE REPORT WINDOW

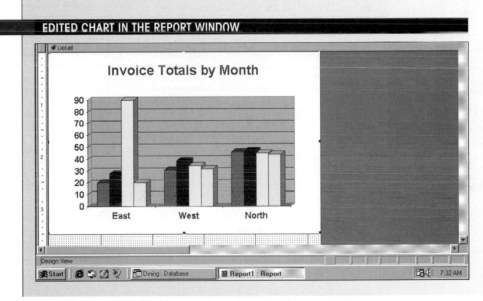

The chart is now larger, and the box in which it appears in the Detail section is the same size as the chart. Next, you need to center the chart in the report page.

To center the chart in the report page and preview the chart:

1. Position the pointer on the chart object. When the pointer changes to a 🖑 shape, click and drag the chart object to the right until its left edge is at the 1-inch mark on the horizontal ruler, and then release the mouse button.

2. Click the **Print Preview** button 🔍 on the Report Design toolbar. Access displays the first page of the report. Notice that the correct chart is displayed. Scroll to see more of the chart. See Figure 6-50.

Figure 6-50   **CHART REPORT IN PRINT PREVIEW**

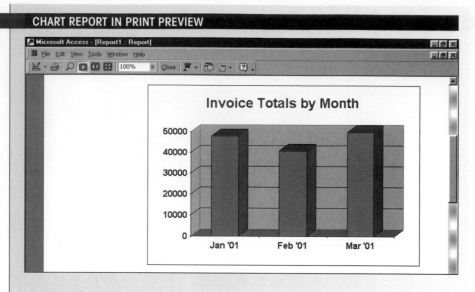

Now that the chart is properly positioned on the report page, you are ready to place the text document in the Detail section. Because you've made many changes to the report design, you'll save it first.

To save the report:

1. Click **File** on the menu bar, and then click **Save**. The Save As dialog box opens.
2. Type **Invoice Totals by Month**, and then press the **Enter** key to save the report.

Linking a Word Document in a Report

The report design in Figure 6-42 shows some text below the chart. This text explains the contents of the chart. You can add text to an Access report by creating a label control, but a label control is not designed to hold a large amount of text. It is inconvenient to enter and edit more than a short label in a label control. Instead, you can create a larger text document using a word-processing program, such as Microsoft Word, and then insert the document as a linked object in the report.

In the past, Barbara Hennessey has created similar reports for Leonard using Microsoft Word and drawing the chart by hand. She has already created a text document that you can include in your report. You will insert this Word document as a linked object in the Detail section of your report. That way, if Barbara later changes the document in Word, the changes will be reflected automatically in the Detail section of the Invoice Totals by Month report.

REFERENCE   WINDOW   **RW**

<u>Inserting a Linked Object in a Report</u>

- Display the report in Design view.
- Click the Unbound Object Frame tool on the toolbox.
- Position the pointer at the upper-left corner of the area where the linked object will be placed, click and drag the pointer to the lower-right corner of the area for the linked object, and then release the mouse button.
- Click the Create from File option button in the Insert Object dialog box.
- In the File text box, enter the name of the file containing the object, or click the Browse button and use the Browse dialog box to locate and select the file.
- Click the Link check box to select it.
- Click the OK button.

The Word document contains several lines of text. To make room for it in the Detail section, you need to resize the Detail section.

To resize the Detail section:

1. Click the **Close** button on the Print Preview toolbar to return to Design view.
2. Scroll down until the bottom of the Detail section is visible. Position the pointer at the bottom of the Detail section. When the pointer changes to a ✚ shape, click and drag the bottom of the Detail section down until the bottom is at the 5-inch mark on the vertical ruler. Release the mouse button.

You are now ready to insert the linked text document.

To insert the linked text document:

1. Click the **Toolbox** button 🛠 on the Report Design toolbar to display the toolbox. If necessary, drag the toolbox to the right of the grid.
2. Click the **Unbound Object Frame** tool 🖽 on the toolbox.
3. Position the pointer's plus symbol (+) at the 3¾-inch mark on the vertical ruler and the 1-inch mark on the horizontal ruler. Click and drag the pointer to the 4¾-inch mark on the vertical ruler and the 4½-inch mark on the horizontal ruler. Release the mouse button. Access inserts an unbound object frame in the Detail section and opens the Insert Object dialog box.

   The Word document is a file stored on your Data Disk, so you need to create the linked object from a file.
4. Click the **Create from File** option button to select it. The dialog box changes to display the File text box, the Browse button, and the Link check box. See Figure 6-51.

Figure 6-51   **INSERT OBJECT DIALOG BOX**

click to create an
object from a file

click to locate the file

your path might
be different

click to create a link

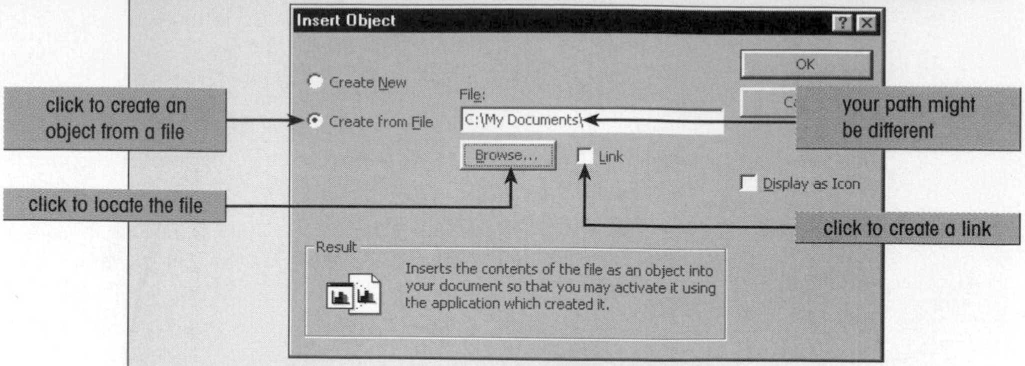

5. Click the **Browse** button to open the Browse dialog box. If necessary, use the Look in list box to display the contents of the Tutorial folder on your Data Disk.

6. In the files list box, click **ChartTxt** to select the Word document file, and then click the **OK** button. The Browse dialog box closes.

   Next, you must indicate that you want to link to the document file rather than embed it in the report.

7. Click the **Link** check box to select it, and then click the **OK** button. The Insert Object dialog box closes, and the document is placed in the Detail section. See Figure 6-52.

Figure 6-52   **LINKED TEXT DOCUMENT IN THE DETAIL SECTION**

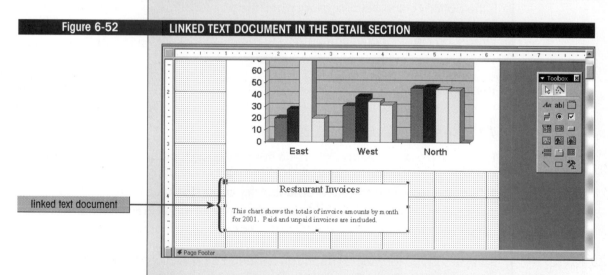

linked text document

TROUBLE? If the document on your screen extends further to the right than shown in Figure 6-52, use its middle-right sizing handle to drag its right border to the left, to the 4½-inch mark on the horizontal ruler. If the grid extends beyond the right edge of the chart, drag the grid to the left until it's at the right edge of the chart.

8. Click the **Print Preview** button on the Report Design toolbar, and then click the **Zoom** button on the Print Preview toolbar to view the entire report page. See Figure 6-53.

Figure 6-53   **INSERTED REPORT IN PRINT PREVIEW**

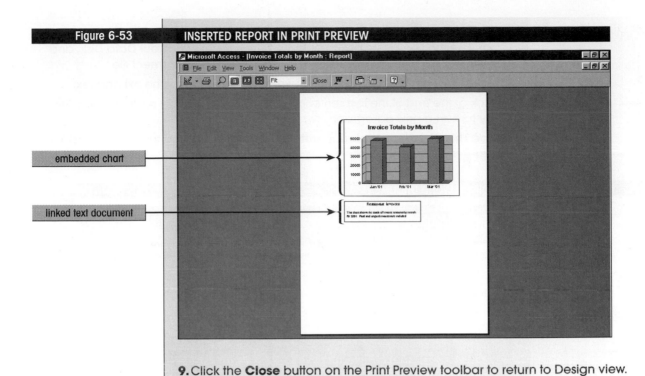

embedded chart

linked text document

9. Click the **Close** button on the Print Preview toolbar to return to Design view.

Because you checked the Link check box, the text document is *linked* to the original Word document. Any changes made to the original document will be reflected automatically in the text document in your Access report. If you had not checked the Link check box, the text document would be *embedded*.

Barbara wants to make a change to the ChartTxt document. She wants to add a sentence indicating that the chart is updated monthly. Because the report object is linked to the Word document, you'll make this change to the original document using the Word program, and then view the results in the Report window in Access.

To edit the original document in Word:

1. Click the **Start** button on the taskbar, point to **Programs**, and then click **Microsoft Word**. The Word 2000 program starts and the Word window opens. See Figure 6-54.

Figure 6-54   **WORD WINDOW**

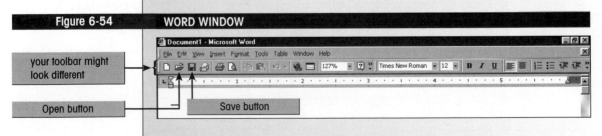

your toolbar might look different

Open button

Save button

TROUBLE? If you cannot locate Microsoft Word on the Programs menu, it might be located in another program group on your computer. Try looking through program groups to find it. If you cannot locate Microsoft Word anywhere, ask your instructor or technical support person for assistance. If the Microsoft Word program is not installed on your computer, click the Access window to close the Programs menu and then skip Steps 2 through 7.

2. Click the **Open** button 🖼 on the Standard toolbar to display the Open dialog box. Use the Look in list box to open the Tutorial folder on your Data Disk, and then double-click **ChartTxt** in the file list to open the document file.

You'll add the new sentence in its own paragraph, below the existing text.

3. Click at the end of the last sentence in the document, and then press the **Enter** key to start a new paragraph.

4. Type **This chart is updated monthly.** (Make sure that you type the period.) See Figure 6-55.

Figure 6-55	MODIFIED WORD DOCUMENT

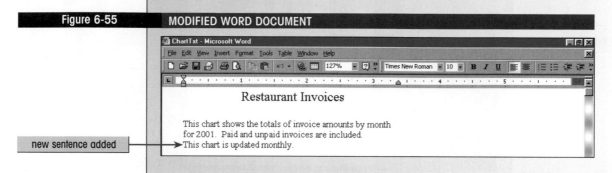

new sentence added

TROUBLE? If you make a typing error, use the Backspace key to erase the incorrect text and then retype the text correctly.

5. Click the **Save** button 🖫 on the Standard toolbar to save the modified document, and then click the **Close** button ☒ on the Word window title bar to exit Word. The Word window closes, and the Access Report window in Design view becomes active.

6. If necessary, scroll down to see the text object.

The text object in the Detail section does not yet reflect the change you made in the original Word document. If you were to close the Report window and return to the Database window and then reopen the report, Access would update the link and the report would show the new sentence you added. Access automatically updates any links to linked objects whenever a form or report is opened. However, you can also update a link manually to see a change reflected.

To update the link manually:

1. Click **Edit** on the menu bar, and then click **OLE/DDE Links** to open the Links dialog box, which allows you to select the linked object or objects to be updated.

2. Click **ChartTxt.doc** in the Links list box to select this file. See Figure 6-56.

| Figure 6-56 | UPDATING THE LINK MANUALLY |

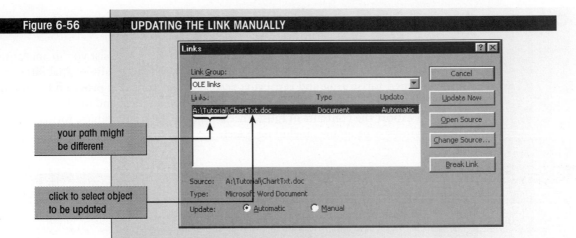

your path might be different

click to select object to be updated

3. Click the **Update Now** button. Access updates the link to the ChartTxt document on your Data Disk and updates the object in the Detail section.

4. Click the **Close** button to close the Links dialog box and to view the updated report. See Figure 6-57.

| Figure 6-57 | REPORT WITH THE MODIFIED TEXT IN THE DETAIL SECTION |

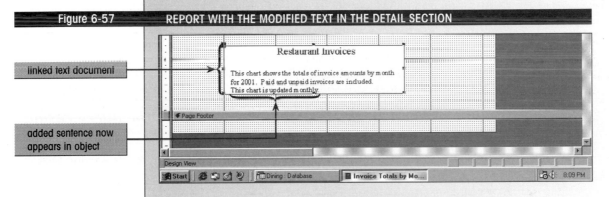

linked text document

added sentence now appears in object

The report is now complete. You can save the report design, print the report for Leonard, and then close the Report window.

To save, print, and close the report:

1. Click the **Save** button 🖫 on the Report Design toolbar.

2. Click the **Print** button 🖨 on the Report Design toolbar to print the report.

3. Click the **Close** button ☒ on the menu bar to close it and return to the Database window.

Leonard views the printed report and is pleased with the results. Being able to integrate Access data with other programs—Graph and Word in this instance—makes it easier to analyze the data. Leonard has one more integration task for you to complete. He wants to perform some more detailed analysis on invoice data. To do so, he wants to work with the data in a Microsoft Excel worksheet.

Exporting an Access Query as an Excel Worksheet

A spreadsheet program, such as Microsoft Excel, is designed to assist you in analyzing data. Although a database management program provides some data analysis capabilities, it is primarily designed for storing and retrieving records. A spreadsheet program has many more powerful tools for analyzing data to create budgets, projections, and models.

You can export the contents of most Access objects, including tables, forms, and reports, to other Windows programs, including Excel.

REFERENCE WINDOW   **RW**

Exporting an Access Table or Query to Excel
- Open the table you want to export in Datasheet view, or run the query to view the query results.
- Click Tools on the menu bar, point to Office Links, and then click Analyze It with MS Excel.

Like many business managers, Leonard uses a spreadsheet program as a planning and budgeting tool for his business. He would like to use the invoice information from past months to help him project future sales. He asks you to transfer the results of the Invoice Statistics by Billing Date query to an Excel worksheet so that he can use the results to create the necessary projections. Recall that when Access runs a query, the query results are a temporary display of the records in one or more tables. After you run the Invoice Statistics by Billing Date query, you can export the query results directly to Excel.

To open and run the query, and then export the query results to Excel:

1. Click **Queries** in the Objects bar of the Database window to display the Queries list box.

2. Right-click **Invoice Statistics by Billing Date**, and then click **Open** to run the query. Access displays the query results.

3. Click **Tools** on the menu bar, point to **Office Links**, and then click **Analyze It with MS Excel**. Access automatically starts Excel and places the query results in the worksheet. See Figure 6-58.

Figure 6-58   **QUERY RESULTS IN THE EXCEL WORKSHEET**

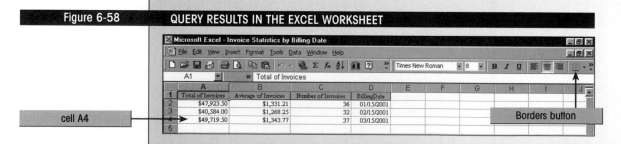

cell A4

Borders button

Notice that each field value is placed in a single cell in the worksheet. The field names are entered in the first row of cells in the worksheet. You can now use this data just as you would any other data in an Excel worksheet.

Leonard wants to see the total of the invoice amounts, so he asks you to create a grand total for the data in column A. You'll first create a line to separate the grand total amount from the other invoice amounts.

To create the grand total amount:

1. Click cell **A4** to select the first cell in the last row of data in column A (see Figure 6-58).

2. Click the list arrow for the **Borders** button [ ] on the Formatting toolbar to display the list of border options, and then click the **Thick Bottom Border** button (the second choice in row two). See Figure 6-59. Access places a heavy border on the bottom of cell A4.

Figure 6-59	ADDING A BOTTOM BORDER TO THE CELL

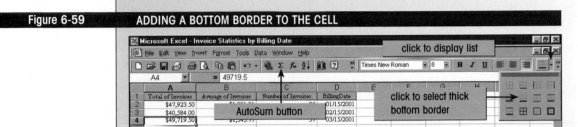

TROUBLE? If the Borders button is not visible on your Formatting toolbar, click the More Buttons button [ ] on the Formatting toolbar and then click the Borders button [ ].

TROUBLE? Your Borders button might look different from the one shown in Figure 6-59 and might be in a different position on the Formatting toolbar.

3. Click cell **A5** to select it, and then click the **AutoSum** button [Σ] on the Standard toolbar. Excel automatically creates the formula to sum the contents of the cells above cell A5. See Figure 6-60.

Figure 6-60	FORMULA TO SUM THE CONTENTS OF CELLS A2 THROUGH A4

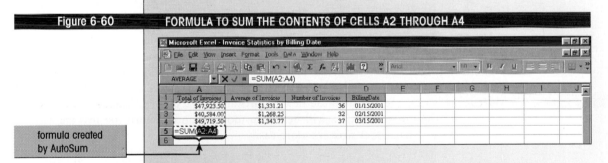

4. Press the **Enter** key to enter the formula. Excel displays the sum of the contents of cells A2 through A4 in cell A5. See Figure 6-61.

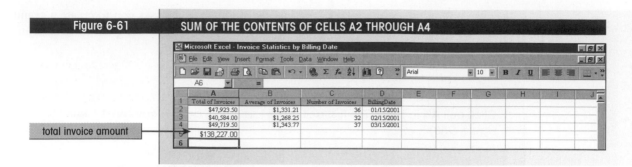

Figure 6-61   SUM OF THE CONTENTS OF CELLS A2 THROUGH A4

total invoice amount

Leonard plans on doing more work with the data in Excel later. For now, you can save the worksheet, close Excel, and return to the Database window in Access.

Saving the Worksheet and Exiting Excel

When you exported the Invoice Statistics by Billing Date query results to Excel, the worksheet was automatically saved with the name Invoice Statistics by Billing Date. Because you have made changes to the worksheet, you need to save them now before exiting Excel. Then you can exit Access.

To save the worksheet, exit Excel, and then exit Access:

1. Click the **Save** button 🖫 on the Standard toolbar.

   TROUBLE? If Excel opens a dialog box indicating that this worksheet was created by a previous version, click the Yes button to save the worksheet.

2. Click the **Close** button ☒ on the Excel window title bar to exit Excel and return to the Database window in Access.

3. Click the **Close** button ☒ on the Access window to close Access. You return to the Windows desktop.

When you exported the query results to Excel, Access placed a copy of the query results in the worksheet. The query results are not linked or embedded in the Excel worksheet, so any later changes made to the Access data will not be reflected in the Excel worksheet. Similarly, any changes made in the worksheet will not affect the Access data.

Leonard is very pleased with the new reports and the Excel worksheet you created. The reports and the integrated data will help him monitor and analyze the invoice activity of Valle Coffee's restaurant customers more easily.

Session 6.3 QUICK CHECK

1. Why might you want to embed or link an object in an Access report?
2. What is the difference between embedding and linking?
3. What is OLE?
4. When you insert an object in a report or form using the Insert Object dialog box, how do you specify that the object is to be linked rather than embedded?
5. If you modify a linked object, in what program do you make the changes?
6. What are two ways to update links to linked objects in a report?
7. How do you export a table or the results of a query to Excel?

REVIEW ASSIGNMENTS

Barbara wants you to make several changes to the **Products** database. She asks you to create a report based on the **Coffee** table. The report will contain Report Header, Page Header, Detail, and Page Footer sections. Barbara wants the records to be grouped on the value in the CoffeeType field, and she wants you to add a CoffeeType Header section. Barbara would also like you to embed a chart in a new report. The chart should be a pie chart showing the distribution of CoffeeType values. Finally, Barbara asks you to create an Excel worksheet based on the query results from the **Pricing** query.

1. Make sure your Data Disk is in the appropriate disk drive, start Access, and then open the **Products** database located in the Review folder on your Data Disk.
2. Create a new report based on the **Coffee** table. Save the report as **Coffee Types**. Figure 6-62 shows the completed report. Refer to the figure as a guide as you complete Steps 3 through 11.
3. Include the following sections in your report: Report Header, Page Header, Detail, and Page Footer.

Figure 6-62

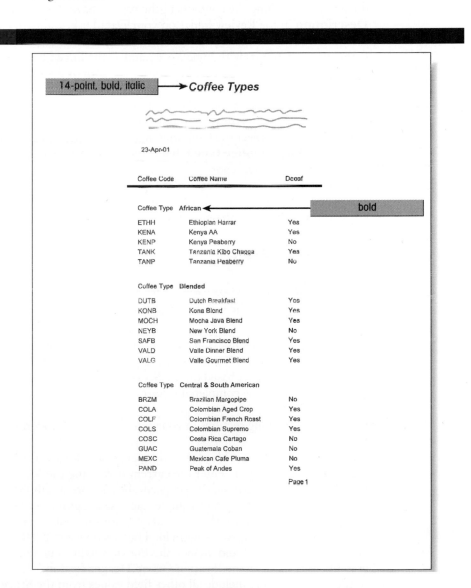

4. At the top of the Report Header section, enter and format the report title. In the Page Header section, enter the current date using the Medium Date format. (*Hint*: Set the Format property on the property sheet's Format tab.) Position the column heading labels below the date. Add a single line (use a 3 pt border for the line) below the column headings and change the necessary captions to match the figure.

5. Specify CoffeeType as the grouping field. Sort the records in ascending order by CoffeeName.

Explore ▶ 6. Create a Group Header section for the CoffeeType grouping field. Place the CoffeeType field value in the CoffeeType Header section, keep the entire group together, and bold the CoffeeType field-value text box.

7. In the Detail section, include all other field values from the **Coffee** table.

Explore ▶ 8. In the Detail section, use the IIf function to add a calculated field, whose value is "Yes" when the Decaf field value is true, and whose value is "No" otherwise. (*Hint*: A calculated control on a form or report must begin with an equals sign (=), followed by the IIf function.) Move the Decaf field to the right, set its Visible property to No, and then align the calculated field with the Decaf label in the Page Header section.

9. In the Page Footer section, include a right-aligned page number.

Explore ▶ 10. Use a word-processing program, such as Word, WordPad, or Notepad, to create a short document describing the contents of the report. Save the document as **Coffee Report Description** in the Review folder on your Data Disk, and then close your word processor. Link the document to your report, placing it in the Report Header section. Compare your results with Figure 6-62 and, if the linked text document is too wide, select and resize it. If necessary, decrease the width of the grid.

11. Print the entire report, and then save and close it.

Explore ▶ 12. Use the Chart Wizard to create a new report based on the **Coffee** table. Create a column chart showing the distribution of CoffeeType values. Select CoffeeType as the only field in the chart, select the Column Chart chart type, and use a title of Coffee Types. Save the report as **CoffeeType Chart**, and then preview it and print it in the correct orientation. Close the report.

13. Run the **Pricing** query and export the query results to Excel. Save the Excel worksheet and overwrite the current version, print the worksheet, and then exit Excel.

14. Close the **Products** database, and then exit Access.

CASE PROBLEMS

Case 1. Ashbrook Mall Information Desk   Sam Bullard needs a custom report for the **Ashbrook** database, and he wants to export the data in the **Store** table to an Excel worksheet. You will create the necessary report and worksheet by completing the following:

1. Make sure your Data Disk is in the appropriate disk drive, start Access, and then open the **Ashbrook** database located in the Cases folder on your Data Disk.

2. Create a custom report based on the **Store Jobs** query. Save the report as **Store Jobs**. Figure 6-63 shows the completed report. Refer to the figure as you complete Steps 3 through 10.

3. Include the following sections in your report: Report Header, Page Header, Detail, and Page Footer.

4. At the top of the Report Header section, enter and format the report title. At the top of the Page Header section, enter the current date using the Medium Date format. (*Hint*: Set the Format property on the property sheet's Format tab.) Position the column heading labels below the date. Add a single line (use a 3 pt border for the line) below the column headings and change the necessary captions to match the figure.

Explore ▶ 5. Specify Position as the grouping field. There is no sorting field. Create a Position Group Header section and include the Position field value in the section. Apply the gray fill/back color to the Position Group Header section.

6. In the Detail section, include all other field values from the **Store Jobs** query.

7. In the Page Footer section, include a page number centered at the bottom of the page.

 Explore

8. Use a word-processing program, such as Word, WordPad, or Notepad, to create a short document describing the contents of the report. Save the document in the Cases folder on your Data Disk as **Store Jobs Report Description**, and then close your word processor. Link the document to your report, placing it in the Report Header section. Change the Border Style property of the linked object to transparent. Compare your results with Figure 6-63 and, if the linked object is too wide, select and resize it. If necessary, decrease the width of the grid.

Explore

9. Use the Special Effect button on the Report Design toolbar to create a Shadowed special effect for the report title in the Report Header section.

10. Print the report, and then save and close it.

Figure 6-63

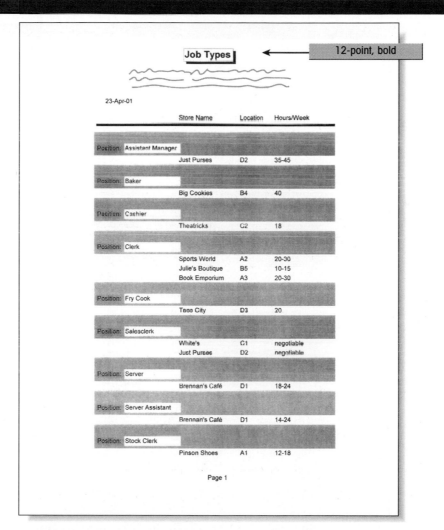

Explore

11. Drag and drop the **Store** table data from Access to export it to Excel. (*Hint*: Make sure Tables is selected in the Objects bar of the Database window, but do not open the **Store** table. Start Excel, right-click an unoccupied area on the taskbar, click Tile Windows Horizontally, and then drag the **Store** table from the Tables list of the Database window to cell A1 in the Excel worksheet.) Save the Excel worksheet as **Ashbrook Stores** in the Cases folder on your Data Disk, print the worksheet, and then exit Excel. Maximize the Access window.

12. Close the **Ashbrook** database, and then exit Access.

Case 2. Professional Litigation User Services   Raj Jawahir wants you to create a custom report for the **FirmPays** database. The report will be based on the results of a query you will create using the **Firm** and **Payment** tables. Raj also asks you to export the Payment data to Excel for analysis. You will create the query, report, and worksheet by completing the following:

1. Make sure your Data Disk is in the appropriate disk drive, start Access, and then open the **FirmPays** database located in the Cases folder on your Data Disk.

2. Create a new query based on the **Firm** and **Payment** tables. Select the Firm#, FirmName, and PLUSAcctRep fields from the **Firm** table, and all fields except Firm# from the **Payment** table. Save the query as **Account Representatives**, and then close it.

3. Create a custom report based on the **Account Representatives** query. Save the report as **Payments By Account Representative**. Figure 6-64 shows the completed report. Refer to the figure as a guide as you complete Steps 4 through 14.

Figure 6-64

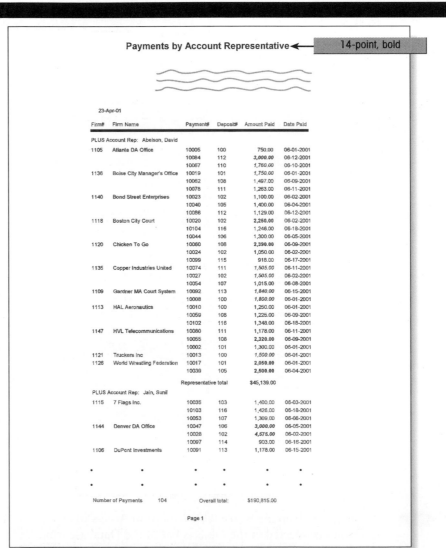

4. Include the following sections in your report: Report Header, Page Header, Detail, Page Footer, and Report Footer.

5. In the Report Header section, enter and format the report title.

6. At the top of the Page Header section, enter the current date using the Medium Date format. (*Hint*: Set the Format property on the property sheet's Format tab.) Position the column headings below the date. Add a single line (use a 4 pt border for the line) below the column headings and change the necessary captions to match the figure.

Explore

7. Specify PLUSAcctRep as the grouping field. Sort the records in ascending order by FirmName. Create a PLUSAcctRep Group Header section and a PLUSAcctRep Group Footer section. In the PLUSAcctRep Header section, include the PLUSAcctRep field value; use a Caption value for the label of PLUS Account Rep:.

8. In the Detail section, include all other field values from the **Account Representatives** query. Hide duplicate values for the Firm# and FirmName fields. Define conditional formatting rules for the AmtPaid field—use bold and italic for values over 2500, use bold for values between 2000.01 and 2500, and use italic for values between 1500 and 2000.

9. In the Page Footer section, include a centered page number.

10. In the PLUSAcctRep Footer section, include a subtotal of the AmtPaid field values. Format the field-value text box as currency, if necessary.

11. In the Report Footer section, include a grand total of the AmtPaid field values. Format the field-value text box as currency, if necessary.

Explore

12. In the Report Footer section, include a count of the Payment# values. Use the expression =Count([Payment#]) and enter the label shown in the figure.

Explore

13. Use a word-processing program, such as Word, WordPad, or NotePad, to create a short document describing the contents of the report. Save the document in the Cases folder on your Data Disk as **Account Representatives Report Description**, and then close your word processor. Link the document to your report, placing it in the Report Header section. Compare your results with Figure 6-64 and, if the linked text document is too wide, select and resize it. If necessary, decrease the width of the grid.

14. Print the report, and then save and close it.

Explore

15. Drag and drop the **Account Representatives** query from Access to export it to Excel. (*Hint*: Make sure the Queries object is selected in the Database window, but do not open the **Account Representatives** query. Start Excel, right-click an unoccupied area on the taskbar, click Tile Windows Horizontally, and then drag the **Account Representatives** query from the Queries list to cell A1 in the Excel worksheet.) Save the Excel workbook as **PLUS Account Representatives** in the Cases folder on your Data Disk.

Explore

16. Modify the worksheet to calculate the average payment amount. (*Hint*: Place the formula in cell F106, and then click the Paste Function button on the toolbar.) Place an appropriate label in cell E106. Save and print the modified worksheet, and then exit Excel.

Explore

17. Create a custom report named **Firm with Subreport** based on the **Firm** and **Payment** tables, by completing the following:

   a. Use the Report Wizard to create a report based on the **Firm** table. Include all fields from the table; select no grouping levels or sort fields; use the Tabular layout, Portrait orientation, and Corporate style; and use a title of **Firm with Subreport**.

   b. In Design view for the **Firm with Subreport** report, increase the height of the Detail section to the .875-inch mark on the vertical ruler, and then use the Subform/Subreport tool on the toolbox to add a subreport. Include all fields from the **Payment** table and accept all other defaults.

   c. Delete the subreport label, view the report in Print Preview, save the report, print the first page, and then save and close the report.

18. Close the **FirmPays** database, and then exit Access.

Case 3. Best Friends   Noah Warnick asks you to create a custom report for the **Pledges** database so that he can keep better track of the participants in their walk-a-thons. The report will be based on the **Walker** table. Also, Sheila Warnick needs to analyze the pledges and asks you to create a worksheet based on the **Pledge Statistics by Walker** query. You'll create the report and worksheet by completing the following:

1. Make sure your Data Disk is in the appropriate disk drive, start Access, and then open the **Pledges** database located in the Cases folder on your Data Disk.

2. Create a custom report based on the **Walker** table. Figure 6-65 shows the completed report. Save the report as **Walkers**. Refer to the figure as you complete Steps 3 through 11.

Figure 6-65

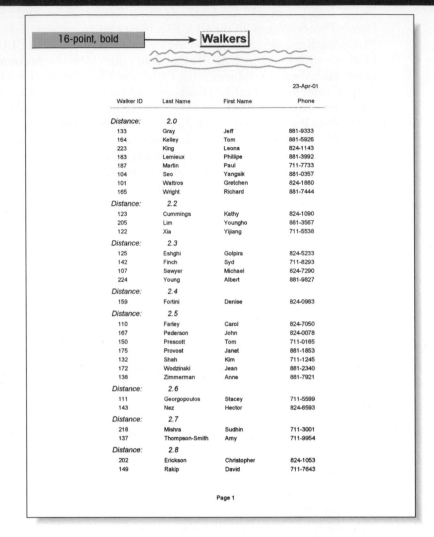

3. Include the following sections in your report: Report Header, Page Header, Detail, and Page Footer.

4. At the top of the Report Header section, enter and format the report title.

Explore 5. Use the Special Effect button on the Report Design toolbar to apply the Raised special effect to the title label in the Report Header section.

6. At the top right of the Page Header section, enter the current date using the Medium Date format. (*Hint*: Set the Format property on the property sheet's Format tab.) Position the column heading labels below the date. Add a single line below the column headings and change the necessary captions to match the figure.

Explore 7. Specify Distance as the grouping field. Sort the records in ascending order by LastName. Add the Distance Group Header section, include the Distance field value and the label "Distance:" in the section, and keep the entire group together. Format the Distance field value and label as 10-point italic.

8. In the Detail section, include all other field values from the **Walker** table.

9. In the Page Footer section, include a page number at the center of the page.

Explore 10. Use a word-processing program, such as Word, WordPad, or Notepad, to create a short document describing the contents of the report. Save the document as **Walkers Report Description** in the Cases folder on your Data Disk, and then close your word processor. Link the document to your report and place it in the Report Header section. Compare your results with Figure 6-65 and, if the linked text document is too wide, select and resize it.

11. Print the report, and then save and close it.

12. Run the **Pledge Statistics by Walker** query and export the query results to Excel. Save the Excel worksheet (and overwrite the current version if necessary), print the worksheet, and then exit Excel.

13. Close the **Pledges** database, and then exit Access.

Case 4. Lopez Lexus Dealerships   Maria and Hector Lopez need two new custom reports for the **Lopez** database. Hector asks you to create a report based on the **Car** table by modifying a report you will create using the Report Wizard. Maria asks you to create a custom report based on the **Car** table. The Car records will be grouped by Model, and you will include subtotals and totals for the Cost and SellingPrice fields. They also ask you to create an Excel chart based on the query results from the **Cost vs Selling** query. Complete the following:

1. Make sure your Data Disk is in the appropriate disk drive, start Access, and then open the **Lopez** database located in the Cases folder on your Data Disk.

Explore
2. Use the Report Wizard to create a report based on the **Car** table. Select all the fields from the table in the order in which they are stored in the table. Do not select a grouping field or a sort field, use the block layout and Portrait orientation, select the Corporate style, and enter **Cars by Year** as the report title. Then customize the report by completing Steps 3 through 5.

3. Move the day/date (Now()) and page number text fields to the Report Header section. Adjust the font size and widths in the column headings so that the entire labels are visible. Finally, remove the Page Footer section.

4. Preview and then print the entire report.

5. Save and close the report.

6. Create a blank report based on the **Car** table.

Explore
7. Sketch a design for the report based on the requirements described in Steps 8 through 14, and then create the report following these steps. Save the report as **Cars By Model And Year**.

8. Include the following sections in your report: Page Header, Detail, Group Footer, and Report Footer.

9. At the top of the Page Header section, enter the report title **Cars by Model and Year** as 14-point, bold text. Enter the current date and the page number in appropriate locations in this section. Below these elements, add a row of column headings with these labels: Manufacturer, Model, Year, Cost, and Selling Price. Add a single horizontal line below the column headings.

10. In the Detail section, include the field values for Manufacturer, Model, Year, Cost, and Selling Price. Hide duplicate values for the Manufacturer field.

11. In the Group Footer section, print the group total for the Cost and Selling Price fields. (If necessary, change their formats to currency.) Select Model as the primary sort key and as the grouping field. Select Year as the secondary sort key, but do not use it as a grouping field. Choose ascending sort order for the sort keys.

Explore
12. Use a word-processing program, such as Word, WordPad, or Notepad, to create a short document describing the contents of the report. Save the document as **Cars Report Description** in the Cases folder on your Data Disk, and then close your word processor. Link the document to your report and place it in the Report Header section. If the linked text document is too wide, select and resize it. Change the Line/Border Color property for the linked object to transparent.

13. In the Report Footer section, print the overall totals for the Cost and SellingPrice fields. (If necessary, change their formats to currency.)

14. Print the entire report, and then save and close it.

Explore

15. Use the Chart Wizard to create a pie chart report based on the Model field in the **Car** table. Each wedge in the pie should represent the count of cars of each model. Insert percents as labels for each wedge. (*Hint*: While using Microsoft Graph for the chart, click Chart on the menu bar, click Chart Options, and then click the Data Labels tab.) Title the report Model Pie Chart, and then save the report as **Model Pie Chart**. Print the report, and then close it.

16. Run the **Cost vs Selling** query and export the query results to Excel. Save the Excel worksheet (and overwrite the current version if necessary), print the worksheet, and then exit Excel.

Explore

17. Hector has pictures of some of the cars available for sale. He asks you to include these pictures with the appropriate records in the **Car** table. You'll embed the pictures as OLE objects in a new field by doing the following:
    a. Open the **Car** table in Design view.
    b. Create a new field named Picture. Select OLE Object as the data type for the new field.
    c. Save the table design and switch to Datasheet view.
    d. Click the Picture field for the record for VehicleID 3N4TA (record 1). Click Insert on the menu bar, and then click Object to open the Insert Object dialog box.
    e. Click the Create from File option button, and then click the Browse button. Open the file **3N4TA.bmp** from the Cases folder on your Data Disk. Click the OK button in the Insert Object dialog box to insert the object in the field. Notice that the value Bitmap Image appears in the Picture field for the first record.
    f. Repeat Steps d and e to enter field values for VehicleID 79XBF (record 3) and VehicleID AAEAF (record 6). The filenames are **79XBF.bmp** and **AAEAF.bmp**, respectively.
    g. Double-click the Picture field value for the first record to view the picture. Access automatically opens the Paint application to display the picture. (Maximize the Paint window, if necessary.) When you are done viewing the picture, close the Paint window.
    h. Repeat Step g to view the picture for record 3 and then for record 6.
    i. Close the **Car** table.

18. Close the **Lopez** database, and then exit Access.

Case 5. eACH Internet Auction Site   Chris and Pat Aquino want you to continue your development of their Internet auction site for collectibles. Their auction site is now a proven success with tens of thousands of bids placed daily. However, their costs have increased because they've had to install additional servers and high-speed communication lines to support the growing traffic at eACH. Offsetting their costs is the income they earn from eACH—a seller is charged $2 to post an item, and the seller is charged an additional 3% of the final sale price. The number of items for sale vary dramatically each day, so Chris and Pat want you to design and then create a custom report to project income from the **eACH** database; the basis for the report will be a query you'll need to create. Because they want to analyze projected income, they additionally ask you to export the query to an Excel worksheet. You will create the necessary query, report, and worksheet by completing the following:

1. Make sure your Data Disk that contains the **eACH** database is in the appropriate drive, start Access, and then open the **eACH** database in the Cases folder on your Data Disk.

2. Create a select query based on all four tables in the database. Display the subcategory name from the **Subcategory** table; the category name from the **Category** table; the title from the **Item** table; the seller's last name and first name from the **Registrant** table; and the minimum bid from the Item table, in that order. Create a calculated field named ProjectedIncome that displays the results of adding $2 to 3% of the minimum bid. Format the calculated field as standard with two decimal places. Sort the query in descending order by ProjectedIncome. Save the query as **Projected Income**, run the query, print the query in landscape orientation, save the query, and then close the query.

3. Design a custom report that includes at least the following features:
   a. Use the **Projected Income** query as the basis for the report.
   b. Include in a Page Header section the report title, the current date, the page number, and column headings.
   c. Include in a Group Header section, the subcategory name and category name, using an ascending order sort for both fields.
   d. Include in a Detail section, the title, seller's first name and last name, the minimum bid, and the ProjectedIncome field. Hide duplicate values for the title.
   e. Include in a Group Footer section, an appropriate label and totals by subcategory for the minimum bid and ProjectedIncome field.
   f. Include in a Report Footer section, an appropriate label and totals for the minimum bid and ProjectedIncome field.
4. Based on your Step 3 design, create, test, and print the custom report. Save the report as **Projected Income Based on Minimum Bid**. You might need to add records to your tables and modify existing records to have enough data with a sufficient level of variety to test your report features.
5. Run the **Projected Income** query and export the query results to Excel. Modify the worksheet to calculate the total of minimum bid and ProjectedIncome columns. Place an appropriate label in the same row as the total values, and add border lines above the total values. Print the Excel worksheet in landscape orientation, save the worksheet and overwrite the current version, exit Excel, and then close the query.
6. Close the **eACH** database, and then exit Access.

INTERNET ASSIGNMENTS

The purpose of the Internet Assignments is to challenge you to find information on the Internet that you can use to create effective documents. The actual assignments are updated and maintained on the Course Technology Web site. Log on to the Internet and use your Web browser to go to the Student Online Companion to accompany this text at **www.course.com/NewPerspectives/office2000**. Click the Access link, and then click the link for Tutorial 6.

QUICK CHECK ANSWERS

Session 6.1

1. IIf
2. The Report Header section appears once at the beginning of a report. The Page Header section appears at the top of each page of a report. The Group Header section appears once at the beginning of a new group of records. The Detail section appears once for each record in the underlying table or query. The Group Footer section appears once at the end of a group of records. The Report Footer section appears once at the end of a report. The Page Footer section appears at the bottom of each page of a report.
3. A custom report is a report you make by modifying a report created by AutoReport or the Report Wizard, or by creating a report from scratch in Design view.
4. The Report window in Design view has many of the same components as the Form window in Design view, including a Properties button, a Field List button, and a Toolbox button on the toolbar. Both windows also have horizontal and vertical rulers, a grid, and a Formatting toolbar. Unlike the Form window in Design view, which initially displays only the Detail section on a blank form, the Report window also displays a Page Header section and a Page Footer section.

5. The Caption property for an object determines the text displayed for the object. You change the Caption property value for an object when the default value is difficult to read or understand.

6. Click an object, hold down the Shift key and click the other objects, release the Shift key, click Format on the menu bar, point to Align, and then click Left.

7. Clicking the Zoom button changes the size of the page displayed in Print Preview.

Session 6.2

1. A grouping field is a field from the underlying table or query by which records are grouped in a report.

2. Use the Text Box tool to create a text box in a form or report.

3. Type =Date() in the text box.

4. Click Insert on the menu bar; click Page Numbers; specify the format, position, and alignment of the page number; and then click OK.

5. three

6. The Sorting and Grouping button opens the Sorting and Grouping dialog box, which allows you to specify sorting and grouping fields for a report.

7. Place a text box in the Group Footer or Report Footer section. In the text box, enter the expression =Sum([*fieldname*]), where *fieldname* is the name of the field you want to total.

8. Hiding duplicate values makes the report easier to read; duplicate values clutter the report.

Session 6.3

1. You embed or link objects in an Access report to include objects created by other programs, including objects that you cannot create in Access (for example, charts).

2. An embedded object preserves its connection to the program in which it was created. Any changes you make to the object are reflected in the Access embedded file, not in the original file. A linked object preserves its connection to the original source file. Any changes you make in the object are reflected in both the linked file in Access and the original file.

3. OLE stands for object linking and embedding; a program that supports OLE can create objects that can be embedded or linked in another program.

4. Insert the object from a file and select the Link check box.

5. You use the source program in which the object was originally created.

6. Each linked object is updated automatically when the report is opened. To update links manually, click Edit on the menu bar, click OLE/DDE Links, select the link (or links) to update, click Update Now, and then click Close.

7. Select the table or query in the Database window and open the table or query in Datasheet view, click Tools on the menu bar, point to Office Links, and then click Analyze It with MS Excel.

In this tutorial you will:

- Export an Access table to an HTML document

- View an HTML document using a browser

- Use a Wizard to create a data access page for an Access table

- Update a data access page using a Web browser

- Sort and filter data access page records

- Create a custom data access page

- Import an HTML document as an Access table

- Add hyperlink fields to an Access table

- Create hyperlinks to Office documents and Web pages

WORKING
WITH HTML DOCUMENTS, DATA ACCESS PAGES, AND HYPERLINK FIELDS

Creating Web-Enabled Information for Valle Coffee

CASE

Valle Coffee

Leonard Valle, Barbara Hennessey, and Kim Carpenter are pleased with the design and contents of the Dining database. Their work has been made much easier because they are able to obtain the information they need from the database quickly. Barbara feels that others in the company would benefit from gaining access to the Dining database. Leonard asks whether the database can be made available to employees over the company network. That way, employees could obtain company information using their desktop computers rather than using paper forms.

Kim mentions that most employees, such as the customer representatives in the marketing department, do not need access to the entire database, nor should they be able to make changes to the database objects. She proposes publishing the necessary Access data on the company's internal network as Web pages.

In this tutorial, you will use Access to make objects in the Dining database available to employees on their internal network.

SESSION 7.1

In this session, you will export an Access table to an HTML document and then view the HTML document using a Web browser. Then, you'll use a Wizard to create a data access page for an Access table, and use your Web browser to update the data access page and sort and filter records. Finally, you'll create a custom data access page.

Using the Web

The **World Wide Web** (also called **WWW** or simply the **Web**) is a vast collection of linked documents that reside on computers around the world. These computers are linked together in a public worldwide network called the **Internet**. A computer that publishes documents on the Web must be running special server software. A computer running server software is called a **Web server**, and it has an Internet address called a **Uniform Resource Locator (URL)**. If your computer has a telephone connection, such as a modem, and you have an account with an **Internet service provider (ISP)**, which is a company that offers connections to the Internet, you can connect your computer to any Web server and view the Web documents published there. You view the documents using a program called a **Web browser**. Popular Web browsers include Microsoft Internet Explorer and Netscape Navigator.

A Web page contains the necessary instructions for your Web browser to display its text and graphics. These instructions, called **tags**, describe how text is formatted, position graphic images, and set the background color and other visual characteristics of the Web page. Certain tags, called **hyperlinks**, link one Web page to another. When you click hyperlink text, the linked page opens. Hyperlinks connect Web pages throughout the Internet, and these connections form the Web. Hyperlinks are the primary means of navigation in the Web.

You can create a page by typing the necessary instructions, using **Hypertext Markup Language (HTML)**, into a word-processing document and saving the document on a disk. Some programs, such as Access, have built-in tools that convert objects to HTML documents for viewing on the Web. Figure 7-1 illustrates the process of creating a Web page using Access and viewing it with a Web browser.

Figure 7-1	CREATING AND VIEWING A WEB PAGE

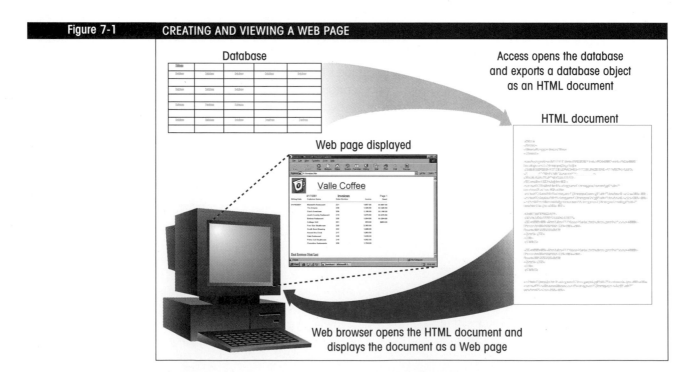

Figure 7-2 shows a Web page and the HTML document that creates it.

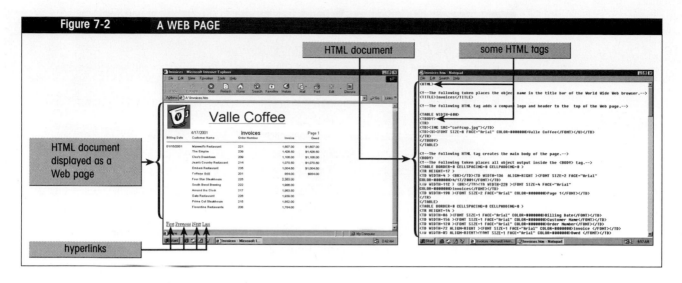

Figure 7-2   A WEB PAGE

The HTML document in Figure 7-2 contains the necessary information to create a Web page that displays one page of the Invoices report. The words enclosed in angle brackets (<>) are HTML tags. The Web page shows how this document looks when viewed using a Web browser. Notice the words First, Previous, Next, and Last at the bottom of the Web page. These are hyperlinks to other Web pages, in this case to other pages of the Invoices report. Hyperlinks usually appear in a different color from other text on a Web page and are often underlined to indicate that they are hyperlinks.

Web pages that are created from an Access database can be either static or dynamic. A **static Web page** reflects the state of the database when the page was created. Subsequent changes to the database records are not reflected in the static Web page that you created. A **dynamic Web page** is updated automatically each time the page is viewed and reflects the current state of the database at that time. When you use a browser to open a Web page created from an Access database, you cannot make changes to the database using a static Web page, but you can change database data for certain types of dynamic Web pages. You'll work with both static and dynamic Web pages in this tutorial.

To publish information in the Dining database to Valle Coffee's intranet as Web pages, you must convert Access objects to HTML format. After you have created the HTML documents, you can place them on the company Web server where they can be viewed on any computer on the network using a Web browser. Of course, Valle Coffee does not want its private database to be available worldwide, so your documents will be placed on a Web server dedicated to the company's private network. Private networks, called **intranets**, are common in companies, educational institutions, and other organizations. Data can be shared on an intranet in much the same way as on the Internet, but access to it is restricted to members of the organization.

Exporting an Access Table to an HTML Document

Leonard has asked you to create an HTML document for the Customer table. He wants this data to be available to customer representatives working outside the office. The customer representatives will access the company's intranet from laptop computers connected to telephone lines. Leonard wants you to create static Web pages because the customer representatives need to view them only once a month to complete their monthly status reports. Barbara will update these static Web pages monthly.

Creating the necessary HTML document is not as difficult as it might appear at first. You will use the Export command on the File menu, which converts database objects to HTML documents automatically.

REFERENCE WINDOW   RW

Exporting an Access Object to an HTML Document
- In the Database window, click the object (table, query, form, or report) you want to export.
- Click File on the menu bar, and then click Export.
- Enter the filename in the File name text box, and then select the location where you want to save the file.
- Click the Save as type list arrow, and then click HTML Documents.
- Click the Save formatted check box (if using a template), and then click the Save button.
- Select the template (if necessary), and then click the OK button.

To complete the following steps, you need to use Access and a Web browser. The steps in this tutorial are written for Internet Explorer, the Web browser used at Valle Coffee. If you use Netscape Navigator or another browser, the steps you need to complete will be slightly different.

You can now export the Customer table as an HTML document.

To export the Customer table as an HTML document:

1. Place your Data Disk in the appropriate disk drive, start Access, and then open the **Dining** database located in the Tutorial folder on your Data Disk.

2. Click **Tables** in the Objects bar of the Database window, click **Customer**, click **File** on the menu bar, and then click **Export**. The Export dialog box opens.

   This dialog box lets you specify the filename for the exported file and its type and location. You'll save the file as an HTML document in the Tutorial folder on your Data Disk.

3. Make sure the Save in list box displays the Tutorial folder on your Data Disk.

4. Click the **Save as type** list arrow, click **HTML Documents**, and then click the **Save formatted** check box. See Figure 7-3.

| Figure 7-3 | EXPORT DIALOG BOX |

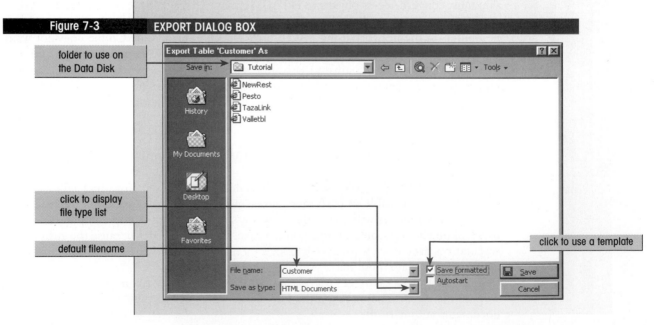

folder to use on the Data Disk

click to display file type list

default filename

click to use a template

When you select the Save formatted option, the HTML Output Options dialog box opens next so you can specify the location of an HTML template. A **template** is a file that contains HTML instructions for creating a Web page with both text and graphics, together with special instructions that tell Access where to place the Access data on the Web page. Barbara used Microsoft Word to create an HTML template, named Valletbl, that you can use. This template will automatically include the coffee cup logo and Valle Coffee company name in all Web pages created with it.

5. Click the **Save** button. The HTML Output Options dialog box opens. You need to locate Barbara's template file on your Data Disk.

6. If there's already an entry in the HTML Template text box, press the **Delete** key to remove the entry.

7. Click the **Browse** button. The HTML Template to Use dialog box opens. If necessary, use the Look in list box to display the contents of the Tutorial folder on your Data Disk, click **Valletbl**, and then click the **OK** button. Access closes the HTML Template to Use dialog box, and returns to the HTML Output Options dialog box and displays the location and filename for the HTML template. See Figure 7-4.

Figure 7-4	HTML OUTPUT OPTIONS DIALOG BOX

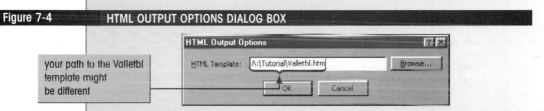

your path to the Valletbl template might be different

TROUBLE? If Valletbl does not appear in the Tutorial folder on your Data Disk when you open the HTML Template to Use dialog box, click the Cancel button to return to the HTML Output Options dialog box. If your Data Disk is in drive A, type A:\Tutorial\Valletbl.htm in the HTML Template text box to specify the template file manually.

8. Click the **OK** button. The HTML Output Options dialog box closes, and the HTML document named Customer is saved on your Data Disk.

Now you can view the Web page.

Viewing an HTML Document Using Internet Explorer

Leonard asks to see the Web page you have created. You can view the HTML document that you created using any Web browser. You'll view it using Microsoft Internet Explorer next.

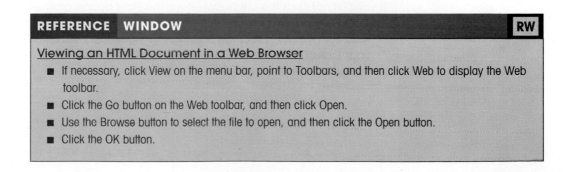

REFERENCE WINDOW   **RW**

Viewing an HTML Document in a Web Browser

- If necessary, click View on the menu bar, point to Toolbars, and then click Web to display the Web toolbar.
- Click the Go button on the Web toolbar, and then click Open.
- Use the Browse button to select the file to open, and then click the Open button.
- Click the OK button.

You can now view the Customer table Web page.

To view the Customer table Web page:

1. Click **View** on the menu bar, point to **Toolbars**, and then click **Web**. Access displays the Web toolbar. See Figure 7-5.

Figure 7-5	DISPLAYING THE WEB TOOLBAR

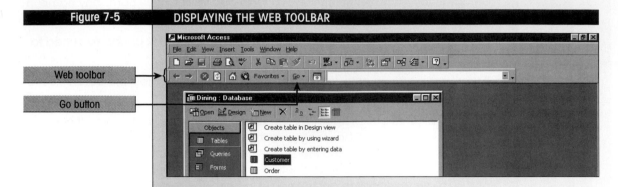

Web toolbar

Go button

2. Click the **Go** button on the Web toolbar, and then click **Open** in the list that opens. Access opens the Open Internet Address dialog box, in which you can specify the URL of the Internet site or the name of the HTML document you want to view.

3. Click the **Browse** button. Access opens the Browse dialog box. If necessary, use the Look in list box to display the contents of the Tutorial folder on your Data Disk, click **Customer**, and then click the **Open** button. Access returns to the Open Internet Address dialog box and displays the address for the HTML document. See Figure 7-6.

Figure 7-6	OPEN INTERNET ADDRESS DIALOG BOX

your path to the
Customer Web page
might be different

4. Click the **OK** button. Internet Explorer starts, and the Customer Web page opens in the Internet Explorer window. See Figure 7-7.

TROUBLE? If a dialog box opens and tells you that an unexpected error has occurred, click the OK button, click the Start button on the taskbar, point to Programs, click Internet Explorer, and then type A:\Tutorial\Customer.html in the Address bar and press the Enter key. (If necessary, substitute the correct path for your Data Files.)

Figure 7-7	CUSTOMER TABLE IN THE INTERNET EXPLORER WINDOW

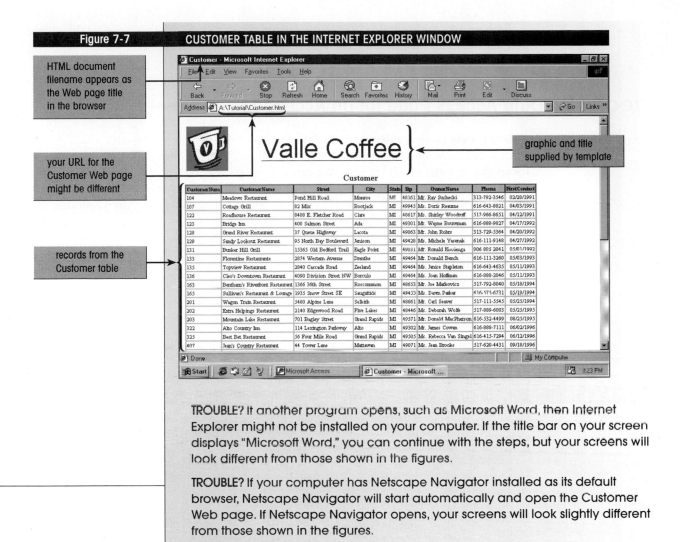

HTML document filename appears as the Web page title in the browser

your URL for the Customer Web page might be different

records from the Customer table

graphic and title supplied by template

TROUBLE? If another program opens, such as Microsoft Word, then Internet Explorer might not be installed on your computer. If the title bar on your screen displays "Microsoft Word," you can continue with the steps, but your screens will look different from those shown in the figures.

TROUBLE? If your computer has Netscape Navigator installed as its default browser, Netscape Navigator will start automatically and open the Customer Web page. If Netscape Navigator opens, your screens will look slightly different from those shown in the figures.

TROUBLE? If a Web browser is not installed on your computer, ask your instructor or technical support person for help.

Changes that Valle Coffee employees make to the Dining database will not appear in the Customer Web page that you created, because it is a static page—that is, it reflects the state of the Customer table in the Dining database at the time you created it. To create the data used by the customer representatives, Barbara will have to export the Customer Web page monthly.

Because a static Web page is not linked to the Customer table on which it is based, you cannot use your browser to make changes to its data. Before closing the Customer Web page, you'll try to change one of its field values.

To attempt to change a field value, and then close the browser:

1. Double-click **MI** in the State column for the first record (Meadows Restaurant), and then type **OH**. The value of MI remains highlighted and unchanged, because the Customer Web page is a static page.

2. Click the **Close** button ☒ on the Internet Explorer window to close it.

3. Click the **Microsoft Access** program button on the taskbar to return to Access.

Barbara asks if it's possible to create a dynamic Web page for the Customer table that she and her staff can update using their browsers. To accomplish this task for Barbara, you'll need to create a data access page.

Creating a Data Access Page for an Access Table

A **data access page** is a dynamic HTML document that you can open with a Web browser to view or update current data in an Access database. Unlike other database objects, such as forms and reports, which are stored in the Access database, data access pages are stored outside the database as separate HTML documents. You can create a data access page in Design view or by using a Wizard. To create the data access page for the Customer table, you'll use the AutoPage: Columnar Wizard.

To create the data access page using the AutoPage: Columnar Wizard:

1. Click **Pages** in the Objects bar of the Database window to display the Pages list. The Pages list box does not contain any pages yet.

2. Click the **New** button in the Database window to open the New Data Access Page dialog box. See Figure 7-8.

| Figure 7-8 | NEW DATA ACCESS PAGE DIALOG BOX |

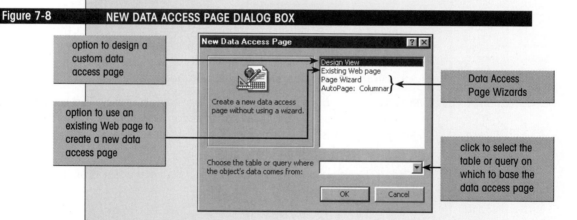

The top list box provides options for designing your own data access page or creating a data access page using an existing Web page or one of the Data Access Page Wizards. In the bottom list box, you choose the table or query that will supply the data for the data access page.

3. Click **AutoPage: Columnar**, click the list arrow for choosing the table or query on which to base the data access page, click **Customer**, and then click the **OK** button. The AutoPage: Columnar Wizard creates the data access page and opens it in Page view. See Figure 7-9.

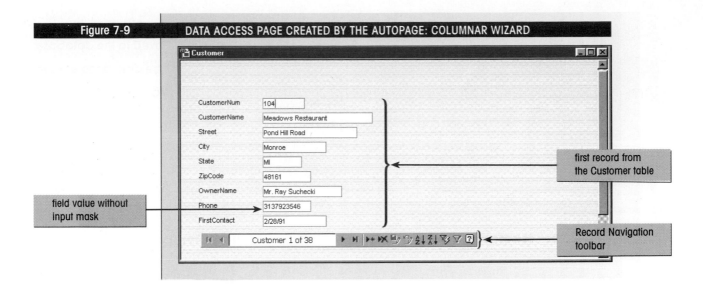

Figure 7-9 DATA ACCESS PAGE CREATED BY THE AUTOPAGE: COLUMNAR WIZARD

The data access page, which has an appearance similar to a form, displays one record's field values from the Customer table at a time. Each field value has its familiar formatting, except for the Phone field, which is not using the input mask you created for it in Tutorial 5.

The **Record Navigation toolbar**, which appears below the record, allows you to move between records in the table, add and delete records, edit and undo entries, sort and filter data, and request Help. No ScreenTips exist for the buttons on the Record Navigation toolbar, but 11 of the 13 buttons are familiar because you've seen them on other Access toolbars. Only the Save Record button and the Undo button are new buttons on the Record Navigation toolbar.

Barbara wants to make sure that she can update the Customer table using the data access page that you created. You can use a data access page to update data in Page view or with a Web browser, so you'll show Barbara how to use both update methods. First, you'll save the data access page and then you'll update a field value in Page view.

To save the data access page, and then update a field value in Page view:

1. Click the **Save** button on the Page View toolbar. The Save As Data Access Page dialog box opens.

2. Type **Customer Page** in the File name box. If necessary, use the Save in list box to display the contents of the Tutorial folder on your Data Disk, and then click the **Save** button. Access saves the data access page as Customer Page on your Data Disk, even though Customer, which is the Title property value for the data access page, still appears on the Page view title bar.

3. Double-click **MI** in the State field text box, type **OH**, and then press the **Tab** key. The value of the State field is now OH.

   Next, you'll close the data access page.

4. Click the **Close** button on the Customer window title bar. A message opens and warns you that your change to the State field will be discarded because you didn't save it. You can save changes to a record automatically by navigating to another record, or explicitly by clicking the Save Record button on the Record Navigation toolbar. You'll cancel the message, and then explicitly save your change.

5. Click the **Cancel** button, and then click the **Save Record** button 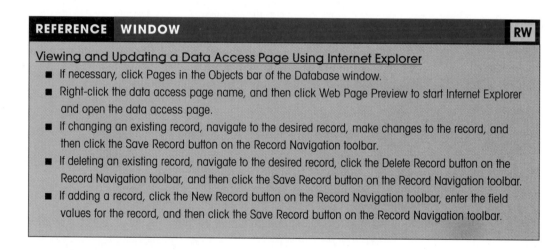 on the Record Navigation toolbar. Your change to the record is saved to the database.

You've completed working in Page view, so you can close the data access page.

6. Click the **Close** button ☒ on the Customer window title bar. The data access page closes, and you return to the Database window. Notice that the Customer Page data access page is listed in the Pages list box.

Next, you'll view the data access page with your browser. Then you'll show Barbara how to update data in a data access page using a browser; you'll change the State field value for the first record back to MI.

Updating a Data Access Page Using Internet Explorer

A data access page can be viewed using any Web browser software. However, if you want to update a data access page, you must use the latest version of Microsoft Internet Explorer, version 5, or another browser that supports data access pages.

REFERENCE WINDOW   **RW**

Viewing and Updating a Data Access Page Using Internet Explorer
- If necessary, click Pages in the Objects bar of the Database window.
- Right-click the data access page name, and then click Web Page Preview to start Internet Explorer and open the data access page.
- If changing an existing record, navigate to the desired record, make changes to the record, and then click the Save Record button on the Record Navigation toolbar.
- If deleting an existing record, navigate to the desired record, click the Delete Record button on the Record Navigation toolbar, and then click the Save Record button on the Record Navigation toolbar.
- If adding a record, click the New Record button on the Record Navigation toolbar, enter the field values for the record, and then click the Save Record button on the Record Navigation toolbar.

You can now view and update the data access page.

To view and update the data access page using Internet Explorer:

1. Right-click **Customer Page** in the Pages list box, and then click **Web Page Preview**. Internet Explorer starts and opens the Customer Page data access page. See Figure 7-10.

Figure 7-10	DATA ACCESS PAGE IN THE INTERNET EXPLORER WINDOW

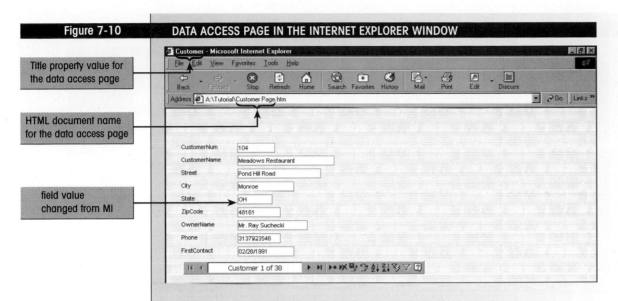

Title property value for the data access page

HTML document name for the data access page

field value changed from MI

You'll change the State field value for the first record back to MI.

2. Double-click **OH** in the State field text box, type **MI**, press the **Tab** key, and then click the **Save Record** button ![icon] on the Record Navigation toolbar. The value of the State field is changed to MI in the database.

Barbara asks about the other buttons on the Record Navigation toolbar. Next, you'll show her how to sort and filter data access page records.

Sorting and Filtering Data Access Page Records

The sort and filter buttons on the Record Navigation toolbar work the same for data access pages as they do for forms. You'll show Barbara how to sort and filter data access page records based on the values of the State field.

To sort and filter data access page records:

1. Click the **State text box**, and then click the **Sort Descending** button ![icon] on the Record Navigation toolbar. Access rearranges the records in descending order by state—records for Ohio (OH) first, followed by records for Michigan (MI), and then for Indiana (IN).

You can now filter records, selecting just the customers from Ohio.

2. Click the **State text box**, and then click the **Filter By Selection** button ![icon] on the Record Navigation toolbar. Access filters the customer records, selecting the first of the four records that have a state field value of OH. See Figure 7-11.

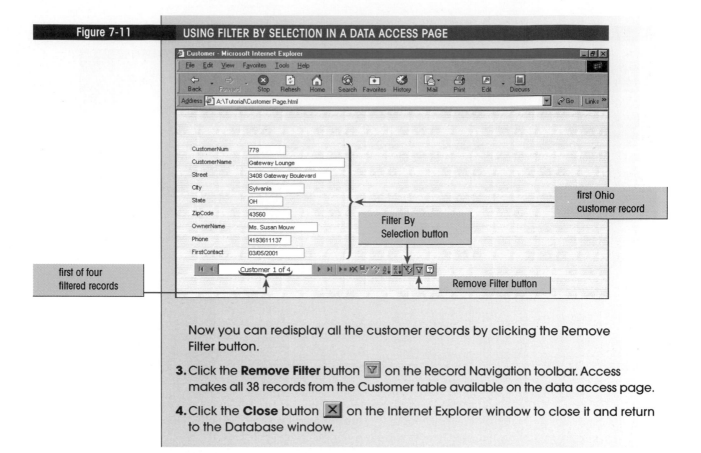

Figure 7-11   **USING FILTER BY SELECTION IN A DATA ACCESS PAGE**

Now you can redisplay all the customer records by clicking the Remove Filter button.

3. Click the **Remove Filter** button 🔽 on the Record Navigation toolbar. Access makes all 38 records from the Customer table available on the data access page.

4. Click the **Close** button ☒ on the Internet Explorer window to close it and return to the Database window.

When visiting clients at their restaurants, the customer representatives frequently need access to current information about customers and their orders at the same time. Barbara asks if it's possible to create a data access page that the customer representatives can use to view, but not update, current Dining database information about customers and their orders. To do this, you'll create a custom data access page in Design view.

Creating a Custom Data Access Page

Every data access page is a dynamic HTML document. When you open a data access page, you are viewing current data from the Access database that produced the data access page. If a single table or query is the basis for the data access page, then you can use the data access page to update the data in the database. However, if two or more related tables are the basis for the data access page, then you can only view the data; updates to the database are not permitted. To create a data access page that the customer representatives can view but not update, you'll create a data access page that includes data selected from the Customer table and from the related Order table.

Just as with forms and reports, you could use a Wizard to create a basic data access page and then customize it in Design view, or you could create a data access page from scratch in Design view. To create the data access page with the customer and order information for Barbara, you'll design the entire data access page in Design view.

Creating a Blank Data Access Page in Design View

You use the Page window in Design view to create and modify data access pages. To create Barbara's data access page, you'll create a blank data access page and then add fields and controls to it.

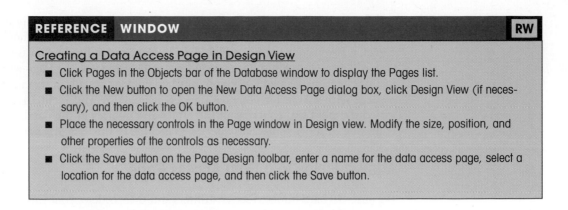

Creating a Data Access Page in Design View

■ Click Pages in the Objects bar of the Database window to display the Pages list.

■ Click the New button to open the New Data Access Page dialog box, click Design View (if necessary), and then click the OK button.

■ Place the necessary controls in the Page window in Design view. Modify the size, position, and other properties of the controls as necessary.

■ Click the Save button on the Page Design toolbar, enter a name for the data access page, select a location for the data access page, and then click the Save button.

To create the data access page, you must first create a blank data access page in the Page window in Design view.

To create a blank data access page in Design view:

1. Click the **New** button in the Database window. The New Data Access Page dialog box opens.

2. Click **Design View** in the list box (if necessary), and then click the **OK** button. Access displays the Page window in Design view.

3. Click the **Maximize** button ▢ on the Data Access Page title bar. See Figure 7-12.

Figure 7-12	PAGE WINDOW IN DESIGN VIEW

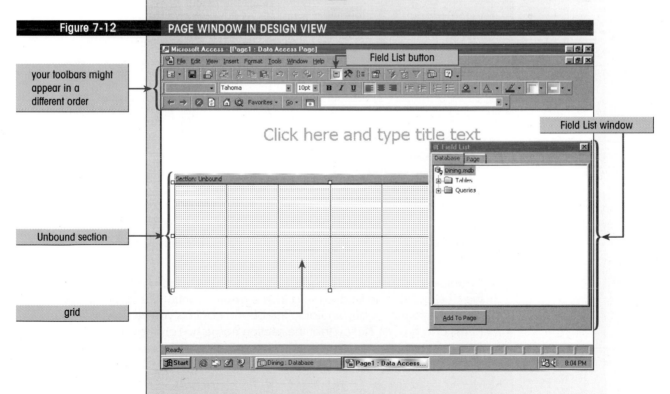

TROUBLE? If the grid is not displayed, click View on the menu bar, and then click Grid. If the Field List window is not displayed, click the Field List button ▤ on the Page Design toolbar. If any other window or toolbar is open, click its Close button ☒.

The Page window in Design view has many of the same components as the Form and Report windows in Design view. For example, these windows include a Formatting toolbar, a grid, a Properties button, a Field List button, and a Toolbox button.

Unlike the Form and Report windows in Design view, the Page window initially contains just one section, named Unbound, until you place controls in it, and a message that you can replace with a title for your data access page. Also, the Field List window, which is also called the field list, contains all the tables and queries in the database; you can select fields from one or more tables and queries to include in the data access page.

Adding Fields to a Data Access Page

Because Barbara wants to see customers and their orders, your first task is to use the field list to add fields for the Customer table to the grid.

To add fields to the grid from the field list for the Customer table:

1. Click ⊞ next to Tables in the field list, and then click ⊞ next to Customer in the field list. The fields from the Customer table and a folder for related tables are now visible in the field list. See Figure 7-13.

Figure 7-13   **FIELDS AND RELATED TABLES FOLDER FOR THE CUSTOMER TABLE**

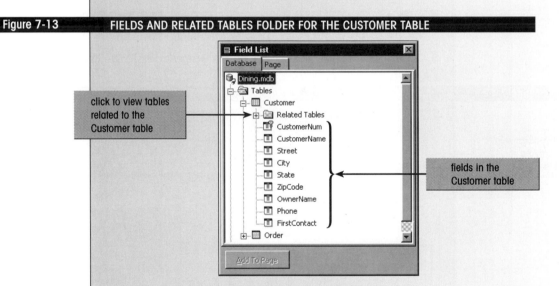

click to view tables related to the Customer table

fields in the Customer table

Barbara wants you to include only the CustomerName, City, and State fields from the Customer table in the data access page.

2. Double-click **CustomerName** in the field list. Access adds a bound control for the CustomerName field to the grid. The bound control consists of a text box and an attached label, similar to the bound controls you've used previously for forms and reports. Notice that the section name has changed to Header: Customer; this section is referred to as the Customer Header section. Below the Customer Header section, Access adds the Customer Navigation section, which contains the Record Navigation toolbar.

3. Repeat Step 2 to select the **City** and **State** fields, in that order.

Barbara wants you to include all the fields from the Order table in the data access page.

4. Click ➕ next to Related Tables in the field list to display the tables that are related to the Customer table.

Barbara asks why the Order table appears twice as a related table. To help answer her question, you'll show Barbara the multiple relationships between the two tables in the Relationships window and then print a copy of the Dining database relationships for her.

Printing Database Relationships

You need to open the Relationships window to view and print the relationships between tables in the Dining database.

To view and print the Dining database relationships:

1. Click the **Dining : Database** program button on the taskbar to return to the Database window.

2. Click the **Relationships** button ⚏ on the Database toolbar. The Relationships window opens. See Figure 7-14.

| Figure 7-14 | TWO TABLE RELATIONSHIPS IN THE RELATIONSHIPS WINDOW |

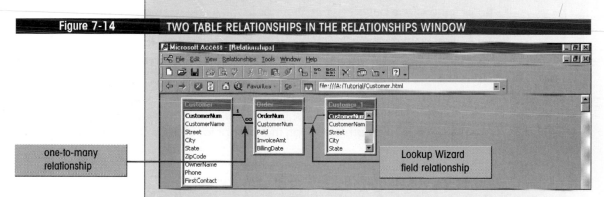

Two relationships appear in the Relationships window for the Dining database. The leftmost relationship is the one-to-many relationship between the Customer and Order tables. The Lookup Wizard, which you used in Tutorial 5, added the rightmost relationship so that the correct CustomerNum field value can be stored in the Order table when a value for the CustomerName field is selected. The table name of Customer_1 is an alias for the Customer table, which allows you to distinguish between the two copies of it in the Relationships window.

You can use the Relationships window to answer Barbara's question. The Order table appears twice as a related table in the Page window's field list because it participates in two relationships with the Customer table.

Next, you'll print a copy of the database relationships so that Barbara can use it as a reference.

3. Click **File** on the menu bar, and then click **Print Relationships**. The Relationships window opens in Print Preview. See Figure 7-15.

| Figure 7-15 | THE RELATIONSHIPS WINDOW IN PRINT PREVIEW |

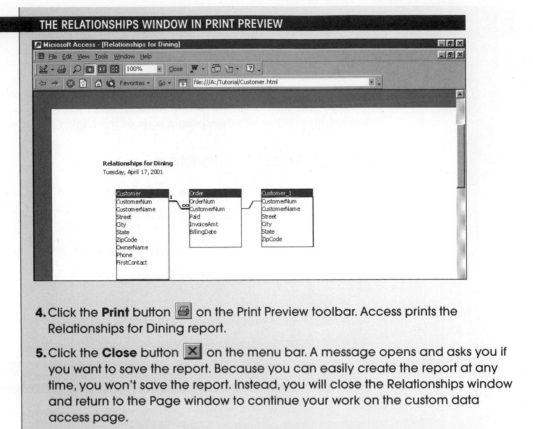

4. Click the **Print** button 🖨 on the Print Preview toolbar. Access prints the Relationships for Dining report.

5. Click the **Close** button ✕ on the menu bar. A message opens and asks you if you want to save the report. Because you can easily create the report at any time, you won't save the report. Instead, you will close the Relationships window and return to the Page window to continue your work on the custom data access page.

6. Click the **No** button to close the report without saving changes, click ✕ on the menu bar to close the Relationships window, and then click the **Page1 : Data Access Page** program button on the taskbar to return to the Page window.

You'll continue creating the custom data access page.

Adding Fields and a Title to a Data Access Page

Because Barbara wants to see customers and their orders, your next task is to use the field list to add fields for the Order table to the grid.

To add fields to the grid from the field list for the Order table:

1. Drag the first Order table from the field list to the middle bottom of the Customer Header section, until a thick blue line appears with arrows on its ends. See Figure 7-16.

Figure 7-16   ADDING THE ORDER TABLE FIELDS TO THE GRID

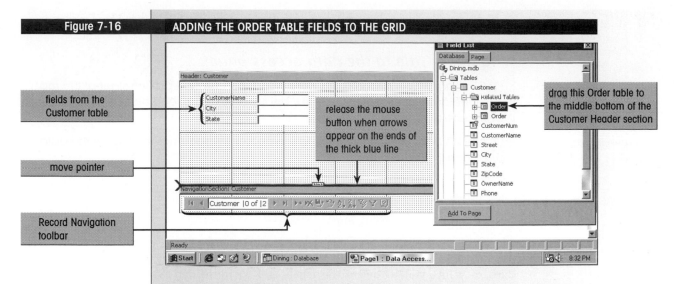

2. Release the mouse button, and then scroll down the Page Design window. All fields from the Order table are added to the grid in a new Order Header section, and a new Order Navigation section is added above the Customer Navigation section. See Figure 7-17.

Figure 7-17   DATA ACCESS PAGE AFTER ADDING ALL FIELDS TO THE GRID

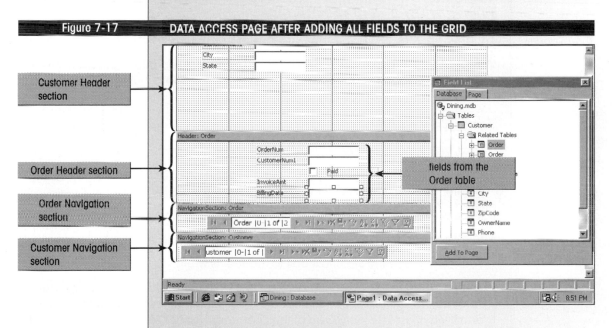

You're done with the field list, so you can close it.

3. Click the **Close** button ☒ on the Field List window to close it, and then scroll up to the top of the Page Design window.

Notice that an Expand button ⊞ now appears in the Customer Header section. When you view the data access page in Page view or with your browser, the Customer Header and Customer Navigation sections will be displayed, but the Order Header and Order Navigation sections will be hidden. Each customer record has an Expand button, and clicking this button opens a band that contains the orders for the customer. At the same time, the Expand button changes to a Collapse button ⊟, which you can click to collapse or hide the customer's orders. The Expand and Collapse buttons provide the same features as do the expand and collapse indicators you used with subdatasheets in Tutorial 5.

Next, you'll add a title to the data access page above the Customer Header section.

To add a title to the data access page:

1. Click anywhere on the **Click here and type title text** placeholder at the top of the data access page. The text disappears and is replaced by a large insertion point.

2. Type **Customers and Orders**. Your typed entry becomes the title for the data access page.

Next, you'll modify the controls in the Customer Header section.

Moving and Resizing Controls on a Data Access Page

Barbara wants you to delete the labels and to move and resize the text boxes in the Customer Header section. She feels that the field values without labels are self-explanatory, and she'd prefer to view as many customers as possible at one time.

To delete the labels, and then to move and resize the text boxes in the Customer Header section:

1. Right-click the **CustomerName label**, and then click **Cut** on the shortcut menu.

2. Repeat Step 1 to delete the **City** and **State** labels. After deleting the City label, the Office Clipboard starts automatically. Click the **Close** button ☒ on the Office Clipboard to close it.

   TROUBLE? If the Office Assistant opens, right-click it, and then click Hide to close it.

   Next, you'll move and resize the three text boxes.

3. Click the **CustomerName text box** (the top text box), and then use the ✛ pointer to drag the text box into position. See Figure 7-18.

4. Repeat Step 3 for the two remaining text boxes. See Figure 7-18.

5. Click an empty area of the Customer Header section to deselect all controls.

   You'll now resize the State text box to reduce its width.

6. Click the **State text box** (the rightmost text box) in the Customer Header section, use the ↔ pointer on the middle-right handle to resize the State text box, and then click an empty area of the Customer Header section. See Figure 7-18.

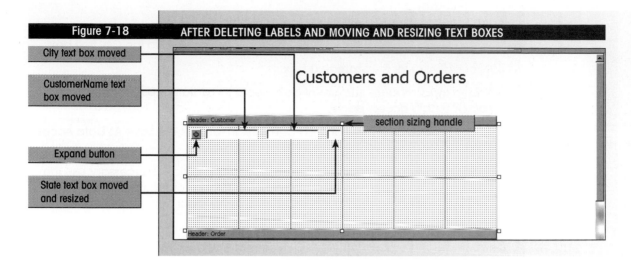

Figure 7-18 **AFTER DELETING LABELS AND MOVING AND RESIZING TEXT BOXES**

City text box moved

CustomerName text box moved

Expand button

State text box moved and resized

section sizing handle

Customers and Orders

Next, you'll finish your changes to the Customer Header section by reducing the section's height and applying a special effect to the text boxes.

Resizing a Section and Applying a Special Effect

Barbara prefers a different special effect for the three text boxes in the Customer Header section, and she asks you to reduce the height of the section.

To resize the Customer Header section, and then change the special effects for the text boxes:

1. Position the pointer on the middle-bottom handle of the Customer Header section and, when the pointer changes to a ↕ shape, drag the bottom up, until it's just below the text boxes. See Figure 7-19.

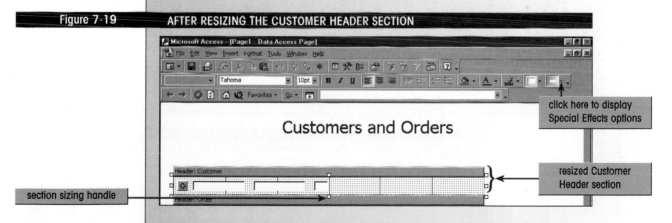

Figure 7-19 **AFTER RESIZING THE CUSTOMER HEADER SECTION**

click here to display Special Effects options

resized Customer Header section

section sizing handle

Customers and Orders

Next, you'll change the special effect for each of the text boxes.

2. Click the **CustomerName text box**, click the list arrow for the **Special Effect** button ▣ on the Page Design toolbar, and then click the **Special Effect: Ridged** button ▣. The ridged special effect is applied to the CustomerName text box.

TROUBLE? If the Special Effect button does not appear on the Page Design toolbar, click the More Buttons button ▸ on the Page Design toolbar, and then click the Special Effect button on the button palette.

3. Click the **City text box**, and then click the **Special Effect** button 🔲 on the Page Design toolbar. The ridged special effect is applied to the City text box.

4. Repeat Step 3 for the **State text box**.

You've made a large number of changes to the data access page, so you'll save the data access page.

5. Click the **Save** button 🔲 on the Page Design toolbar. The Save As Data Access Page dialog box opens.

6. Type **Customers and Orders Page** in the File name box. If necessary, use the Save in list box to display the contents of the Tutorial folder on your Data Disk, and then click the **Save** button. Access saves the data access page as Customers and Orders Page on your Data Disk.

Next, you'll modify the controls in the Order Header section.

Adding and Modifying a Caption Section

Barbara wants the text boxes in the Order Header section to be placed across, rather than down, the page. Also, she wants the labels in the Order Header section placed above the text boxes; this means you'll need to add the Order Caption section to the grid. A **Caption section** on a data access page is used to display captions, or headings, for columns of data. The Order Caption section will be displayed above the Order Header section and will appear only when the Order Header section is displayed.

To add the Order Caption section to the grid:

1. Click the **Sorting and Grouping** button 📋 on the Page Design toolbar. The Sorting and Grouping dialog box opens.

   TROUBLE? If the Sorting and Grouping button does not appear on the Page Design toolbar, click the More Buttons button 🔳 on the Page Design toolbar, and then click the Sorting and Grouping button on the button palette.

2. Click **Order** to make it the current field. See Figure 7-20.

| Figure 7-20 | SORTING AND GROUPING DIALOG BOX |

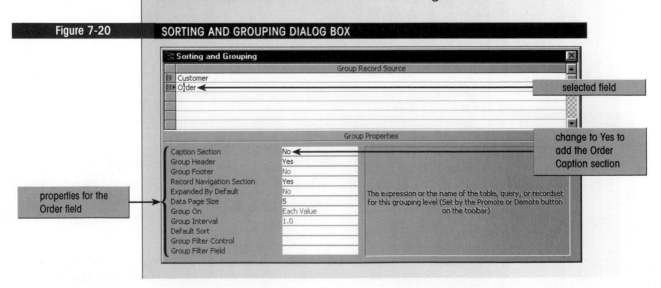

3. Click the right side of the **Caption Section** text box, and then click **Yes**. The Order Caption section is added to the grid between the Customer Header and Order Header sections.

4. Click the **Close** button ☒ on the Sorting and Grouping dialog box to close it.

Next, you'll cut the labels from the Order Header section and then paste, move, and resize them in the Order Caption section.

To cut and paste the labels, and then move and resize them in the Order Caption section:

1. Right-click the **OrderNum label** in the Order Header section, and then click **Cut** on the shortcut menu. The OrderNum label is deleted from the Order Header section.

2. Right-click anywhere in an empty area of the Order Caption section, and then click **Paste** on the shortcut menu. The OrderNum label is added to the upper-left corner of the Order Caption section.

3. Resize and move the **OrderNum label**. See Figure 7-21.

4. Repeat Steps 1 through 3 for the **CustomerNum1**, **Paid**, **InvoiceAmt**, and **BillingDate** labels.

5. Click in the **CustomerNum1 label box** to position the insertion point in it, and then change the name of the CustomerNum1 label to **CustomerNum**. See Figure 7-21.

| Figure 7-21 | AFTER MOVING AND RESIZING LABELS IN THE ORDER CAPTION SECTION |

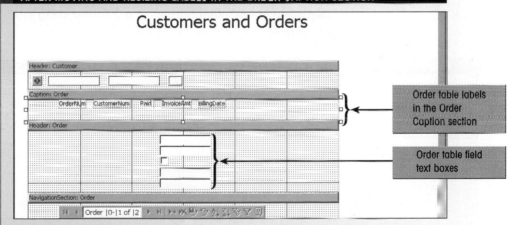

You can now resize the Order Caption section to reduce its height.

6. Click anywhere in an empty area of the Order Caption section. Sizing handles appear on the edges of the section.

7. Position the pointer on the middle-bottom handle of the Order Caption section and, when the pointer changes to a ↕ shape, drag the bottom up to the bottom of the labels. When you release the mouse button, the Order Caption section is resized to match the height of the label boxes.

Next, you'll position the Order table field text boxes in a row at the top of the Order Header section and resize the text boxes as necessary.

To move and resize the field text boxes in the Order Header section:

1. Resize and move the **OrderNum text box**. See Figure 7-22.

2. Repeat Step 1 for the **CustomerNum**, **Paid**, **InvoiceAmt**, and **BillingDate** text boxes. Click the page title to deselect any controls and sections. See Figure 7-22.

Figure 7-22	AFTER MOVING AND RESIZING TEXT BOXES IN THE ORDER HEADER SECTION

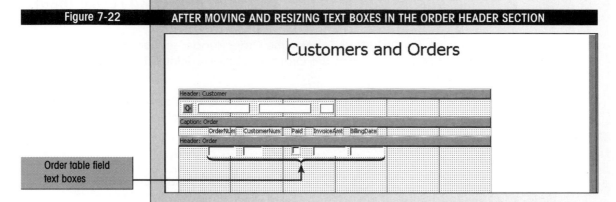

Order table field text boxes

You can now resize the Order Header section to reduce its height.

3. Click anywhere in an empty area of the Order Header section. Sizing handles appear on the edges of the section.

4. Position the pointer on the middle-bottom handle of the Order Header section and, when the pointer changes to a ↕ shape, drag the bottom up to the bottom of the text boxes. See Figure 7-23.

Figure 7-23	COMPLETED DATA ACCESS PAGE

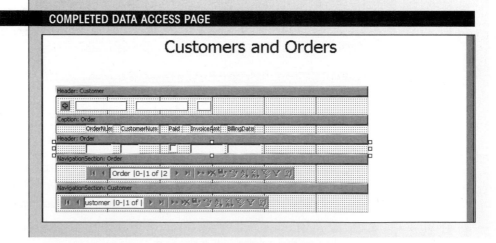

Next, you'll select a theme for the data access page.

Selecting a Theme

Before viewing the completed form, Barbara wants to know if you can easily change the overall style of the data access form. You can select a **theme**, which is a predefined style for a data access page, to make the change that Barbara wants.

To select a theme for a data access page:

1. Click **Format** on the menu bar, and then click **Theme**. The Theme dialog box opens. See Figure 7-24.

Figure 7-24	THEME DIALOG BOX

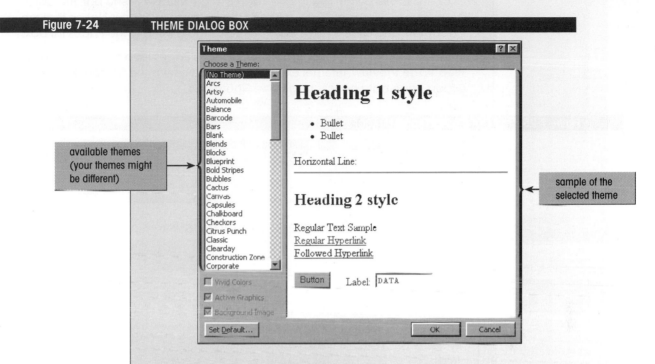

TROUBLE? If a dialog box opens and tells you that the Theme feature is not currently installed, insert your Microsoft Office 2000 CD in the correct drive, and then click the OK button. If you do not have an Office 2000 CD, ask your instructor or technical support person for help.

A sample of the selected theme appears in the box on the right.

2. Click several of the styles in the Choose a Theme list box, and review the corresponding sample.

TROUBLE? If one of the themes you select displays an Install button instead of a sample, choose another theme from the list box.

3. Click **Construction Zone** in the Choose a Theme list box, and then click the **OK** button. The selected theme is applied to the data access page.

TROUBLE? If an Install button appears in the sample box for the Construction Zone theme, choose another theme that's already installed on your system.

Next, you'll save and view the completed data access page.

Saving and Viewing a Data Access Page

Barbara wants to view the completed data access page, but first you'll save the changes you made to it.

To save and view the completed data access page:

1. Click the **Save** button 🖫 on the Page Design toolbar.

2. Click the **Close** button ☒ on the Page Design window menu bar. The data access page closes and you return to the Database window. Notice that the Customers and Orders Page data access page is listed in the Pages list box.

3. Right-click **Customers and Orders Page** in the Pages list box, and then click **Web Page Preview**. Internet Explorer starts and opens the Customers and Orders Page data access page. See Figure 7-25.

Figure 7-25	COMPLETED DATA ACCESS PAGE

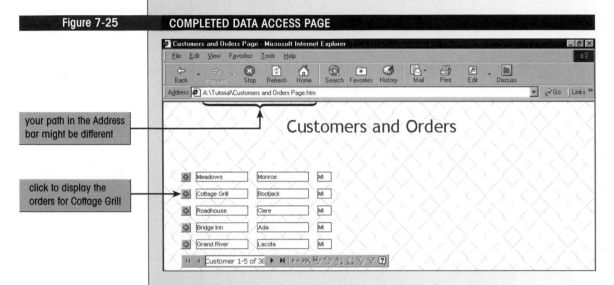

your path in the Address bar might be different

click to display the orders for Cottage Grill

Next, you show Barbara how to view a customer's orders.

4. Click the **Expand** button 🞐 to the left of Cottage Grill (the second record). The three orders for Cottage Grill are displayed between Cottage Grill and the next customer record, the Record Navigation toolbar for orders appears, and the Expand button changes to the Collapse button. See Figure 7-26.

Figure 7-26	DISPLAYING THE ORDERS FOR COTTAGE GRILL

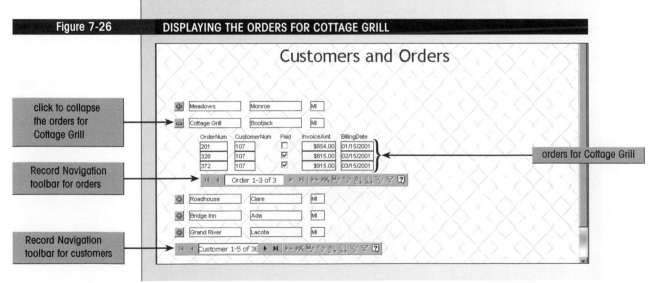

click to collapse the orders for Cottage Grill

orders for Cottage Grill

Record Navigation toolbar for orders

Record Navigation toolbar for customers

The Customers and Orders Page data access page is a grouped data access page. A **grouped data access page** is a data access page that uses two or more group levels to display information from general categories to specific details. For the Customers and Orders Page data access page, the first group level is data from the Customer table, and the second group level is data from the Order table. Data from the Customer table represents the general category, and data from the Order table represents the specific details. You can view data on grouped data access pages, but you can't add, change, or delete data. However, like all data access pages, grouped data access pages are dynamic—they reflect the current state of the database at the time you open them.

You'll try to change the value for the Cottage Grill's State field to show Barbara that you can't update a grouped data access page.

5. Double-click **MI** in the State column for the second record (Cottage Grill), and then type **OH**. The value of MI remains highlighted and unchanged, because you can't update the grouped data access page.

6. Click the **Collapse** button ⊟ to the left of Cottage Grill. The three orders for Cottage Grill and the Record Navigation toolbar for orders are no longer displayed, and the Collapse button changes back to the Expand button.

You've completed your work with the data access page, so you can close it and the Dining database.

7. Click the **Close** button ⊠ on the Internet Explorer window title bar. Internet Explorer closes, and you return to the Database window.

8. Click **View** on the menu bar, point to **Toolbars**, and then click **Web** to close the Web toolbar.

9. Click ⊠ on the Access window title bar to close the Dining database and to exit Access.

Leonard and Barbara are pleased with the HTML documents and the data access pages that you created. Your work will make it easy to distribute important Dining database information on the company's intranet. In the next session, you will continue to work with HTML documents to further enhance the database.

Session 7.1 QUICK | CHECK

1. What is the World Wide Web?

2. What is the purpose of a Web browser?

3. What is HTML?

4. What is a hyperlink?

5. What is an HTML template?

6. What is a data access page?

7. What is a theme?

8. What is a grouped data access page?

SESSION 7.2

In this session, you will import data from an HTML document into an Access table. You will add a hyperlink field to a table and enter hyperlink values that link records to Word documents. You will also add a hyperlink field to a table and enter hyperlink values that link records to HTML documents.

Importing an HTML Document as an Access Table

Kim Carpenter, the marketing manager, is an active user of the Web. She recently discovered a site published by the Upper Midwest Tourism Office. One of the pages at that site lists restaurants that have opened recently in Valle Coffee's customer area. Each of these new restaurants is a potential customer for Valle Coffee. Kim asks whether you can import the restaurant information from that page into an Access table. With the data in an Access table, she will be able to create queries, forms, and reports based on the data.

Access can import data from an HTML document as a database object. Provided that the data is formatted as a table or as a list in the HTML document, Access can import it directly into a database table.

REFERENCE WINDOW   **RW**

Importing an HTML Document as an Access Table
- Click File on the menu bar, point to Get External Data, and then click Import.
- Click the Files of type list arrow, and then click HTML Documents.
- Use the Look in list box to select the HTML document to import.
- Click the Import button to open the first Import HTML Wizard dialog box.
- Complete the Wizard dialog boxes to specify whether the first row of data should be used for column headings; to specify whether records should be imported to a new table or appended to an existing table; to specify the field names, data types, and indexing options for the fields; to specify a primary key; and to enter the table name.
- Click the OK button to confirm that the data has been imported.

Kim saved the HTML document containing the new restaurant information in the Tutorial folder on your Data Disk with the filename NewRest. You will use the Access Import HTML Wizard to import the data into a new table in the Dining database. First, you'll begin by viewing the HTML document using Internet Explorer.

To view the NewRest HTML document:

1. Make sure that Access is running, that the **Dining** database from the Tutorial folder on your Data Disk is open, that the Database window is maximized, and that the Web toolbar is displayed.

2. Click the **Go** button on the Web toolbar, and then click **Open**. The Open Internet Address dialog box opens. You need to find the file that Kim saved.

3. Click the **Browse** button. The Browse dialog box opens.

4. Make sure the Look in list box displays the Tutorial folder on your Data Disk, click **NewRest**, and then click the **Open** button to select the file and return to the Open Internet Address dialog box.

5. Click the **OK** button. Internet Explorer starts and opens the NewRest HTML document. See Figure 7-27.

| Figure 7-27 | NEWREST HTML DOCUMENT |

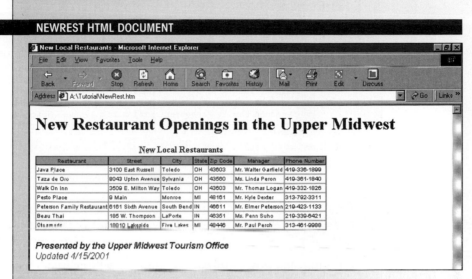

The data in this HTML document is stored in a table, which makes it a good candidate for importing into an Access table. You are finished viewing the HTML document, so you can close Internet Explorer.

6. Click the **Close** button ☒ on the Internet Explorer window to close it.

7. Click the **Dining : Database** program button on the taskbar to return to Access.

Now you will import the NewRest HTML document as an Access database table using the Import HTML Wizard.

To import the HTML document as an Access table:

1. Click **File** on the menu bar, point to **Get External Data**, and then click **Import**. The Import dialog box opens.

2. If necessary, click the **Files of type** list arrow, and then click **HTML Documents**.

3. Make sure the Look in list box displays the Tutorial folder on your Data Disk, and then click **NewRest** to select it.

4. Click the **Import** button. Access opens the first Import HTML Wizard dialog box. This dialog box displays the first few rows of data read from the HTML document. See Figure 7-28.

Figure 7-28   **FIRST IMPORT HTML WIZARD DIALOG BOX**

click to select first row
as column headings

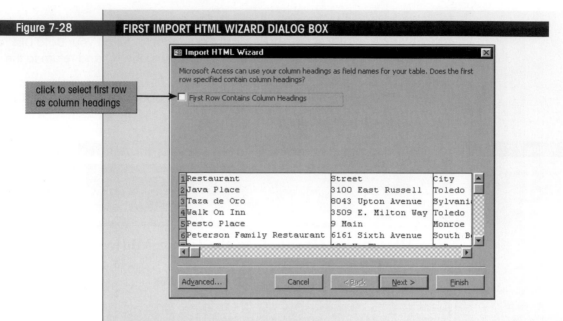

Access allows you to specify that the first row of data contains column headings (field names). Because the first row of this data contains column headings, you will specify that the first row should be used as field names in the new table.

5. Click the **First Row Contains Column Headings** check box. The first row of data changes to column headings.

6. Click the **Next** button. Access opens the next Import HTML Wizard dialog box, which allows you to import the records to a new table or append them to an existing table. Because the structure of this table is not the same as the structure of any existing tables in the Dining database, you will create a new table.

7. Make sure the **In a New Table** option button is selected, and then click the **Next** button to open the next dialog box. See Figure 7-29.

Figure 7-29   **SPECIFYING FIELD NAMES, DATA TYPES, AND INDEXING OPTIONS**

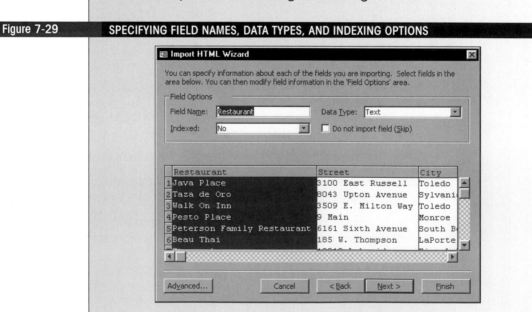

You use this dialog box to change the field name, data type, and indexing option for each of the fields in the new table. If you do not make any choices, Access will assign an appropriate field name, data type, and indexing option for each field. You can also choose not to import selected fields.

You will change the name of the Zip Code field to ZipCode and the name of the Phone Number field to PhoneNumber, to be consistent with the field naming style in other Dining database tables.

To finish importing the HTML document as an Access table:

1. Scroll the field list to the right to display the Zip Code and Phone Number fields. Click the **Zip Code** field to select it, and then delete the space between Zip and Code in the Field Name text box.

2. Click the **Phone Number** field to select it, and then delete the space between Phone and Number in the Field Name text box. See Figure 7-30.

Figure 7-30	AFTER CHANGING THE ZIPCODE AND PHONENUMBER FIELD NAMES

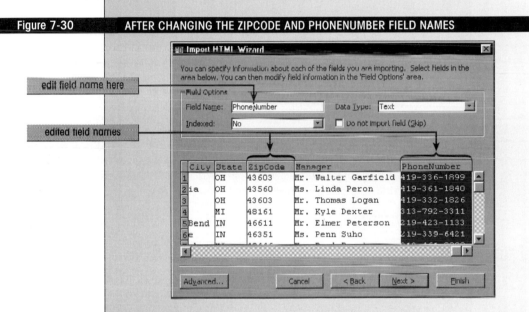

3. Click the **Next** button. The next dialog box allows you to specify a primary key field for the table or let Access add an AutoNumber field as a primary key field. See Figure 7-31.

Figure 7-31   SPECIFYING THE PRIMARY KEY FIELD

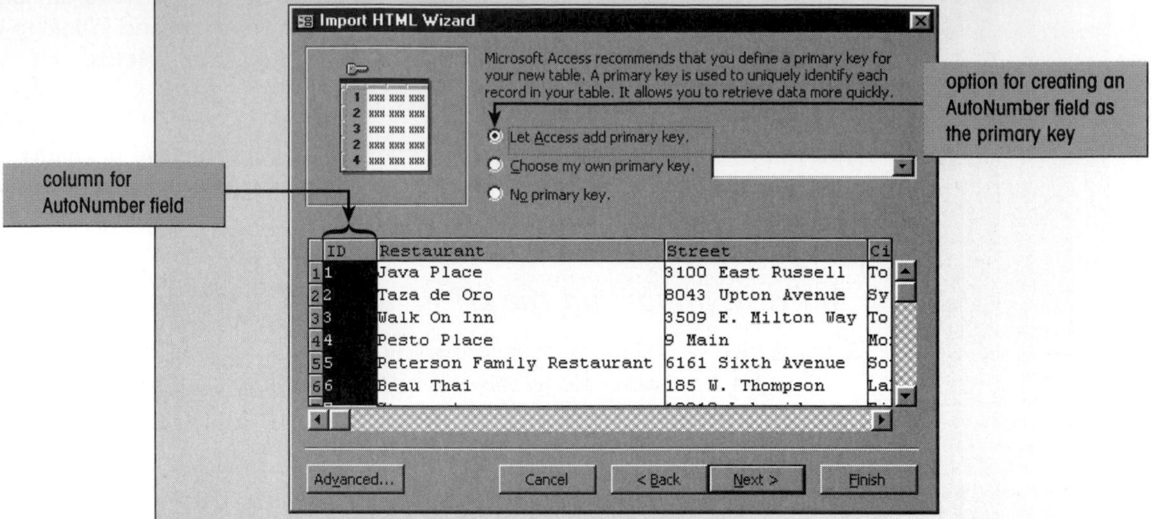

option for creating an AutoNumber field as the primary key

column for AutoNumber field

Because the table does not contain a field that would be appropriate as a primary key, you'll let Access assign a primary key field. Access will create a field with the AutoNumber data type as the primary key field for the new table.

4. Make sure the **Let Access add primary key** option button is selected, and then click the **Next** button to open the final dialog box. This dialog box allows you to enter the name of the new table.

5. In the Import to Table text box, type **Potential Customers**, and then click the **Finish** button. Access imports the HTML document and saves its data in a table named Potential Customers. When the Wizard is finished creating the file, it opens a dialog box confirming that it has finished.

6. Click the **OK** button to end the importing process and return to the Database window.

The HTML document has been imported and its data has been saved in a new table named Potential Customers. This table is now listed in the Tables list box of the Database window. Kim asks you to view the data and then print a copy of the records for her.

To view the Potential Customers table and print its records:

1. Right-click **Potential Customers** in the tables list, and then click **Open** on the shortcut menu. Access opens the Potential Customers table in Datasheet view. See Figure 7-32.

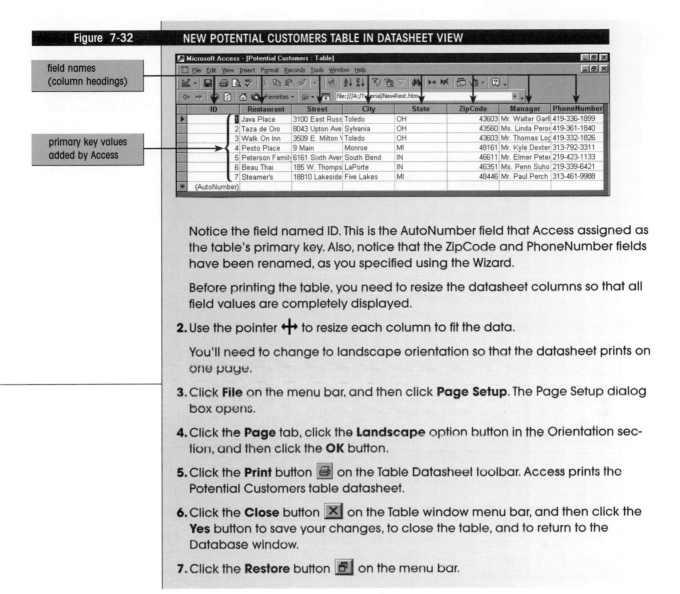

Figure 7-32   NEW POTENTIAL CUSTOMERS TABLE IN DATASHEET VIEW

field names
(column headings)

primary key values
added by Access

Notice the field named ID. This is the AutoNumber field that Access assigned as the table's primary key. Also, notice that the ZipCode and PhoneNumber fields have been renamed, as you specified using the Wizard.

Before printing the table, you need to resize the datasheet columns so that all field values are completely displayed.

2. Use the pointer ↔ to resize each column to fit the data.

You'll need to change to landscape orientation so that the datasheet prints on one page.

3. Click **File** on the menu bar, and then click **Page Setup**. The Page Setup dialog box opens.

4. Click the **Page** tab, click the **Landscape** option button in the Orientation section, and then click the **OK** button.

5. Click the **Print** button 🖨 on the Table Datasheet toolbar. Access prints the Potential Customers table datasheet.

6. Click the **Close** button ☒ on the Table window menu bar, and then click the **Yes** button to save your changes, to close the table, and to return to the Database window.

7. Click the **Restore** button 🗗 on the menu bar.

Kim reviews and approves the printed output. In the future, when the Upper Midwest Tourism Office publishes new lists of recently opened restaurants, she can add them to the Potential Customers table.

Creating **Hyperlinks to Documents in Other Office 2000 Programs**

Kim used the Potential Customers datasheet that you printed and gave to her to set up meetings with the new restaurants' managers. She visited several of the restaurants and returned with notes about the visits. Kim saved her field notes in Word documents. Now she would like some way of connecting these notes with the corresponding records in the Potential Customers table. This would allow her to review her notes when she views the records in the table.

Each restaurant's set of notes is a separate Word document. For example, Kim created a Word document named Java to mark her notes on the new Java Place restaurant. Similarly, her notes on Taza de Oro are in a file named Taza, and the file for Peterson Family Restaurant is named Peterson. To connect Kim's notes with the corresponding records in the Potential Customers table, you need to create a hyperlink field in the table.

Creating a Hyperlink Field

Access allows you to create a hyperlink field in a table. The field value in a hyperlink field is a hyperlink to another object. These objects can be database objects (such as tables or forms), a Word document, a named range in an Excel worksheet, or even a World Wide Web page. When you click a hyperlink field value, the associated program starts and opens the linked object.

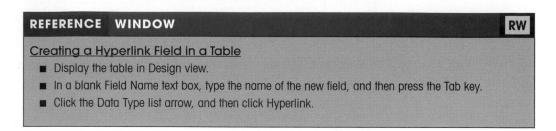

REFERENCE WINDOW   RW

Creating a Hyperlink Field in a Table
- Display the table in Design view.
- In a blank Field Name text box, type the name of the new field, and then press the Tab key.
- Click the Data Type list arrow, and then click Hyperlink.

You will create a hyperlink field in the Potential Customers table. The hyperlink field value will be a hyperlink to one of Kim's Word documents. When Kim clicks a hyperlink, Word will start and open the document that contains her notes.

To add a hyperlink field to the table:

1. In the Database window Tables list, right-click **Potential Customers**, and then click **Design View** on the shortcut menu. The table is displayed in Design view.

2. Scroll down the field list to display a blank row (if necessary), click the **Field Name** text box in the empty row, type **FieldNotes**, and then press the **Tab** key.

3. Click the **Data Type** list arrow, and then click **Hyperlink**. See Figure 7-33.

Figure 7-33   ADDING A HYPERLINK FIELD TO A TABLE

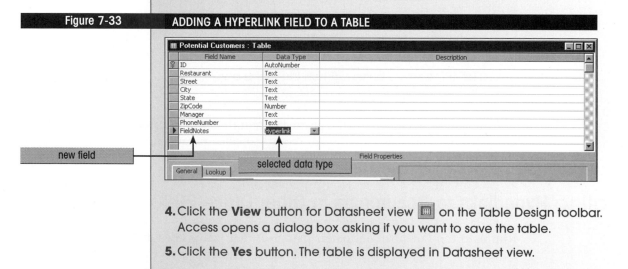

4. Click the **View** button for Datasheet view 🗔 on the Table Design toolbar. Access opens a dialog box asking if you want to save the table.

5. Click the **Yes** button. The table is displayed in Datasheet view.

Now you can add the hyperlink field values to the Potential Customers table. These field values will be hyperlinks to the Word documents Kim created.

Entering a Hyperlink Field Value

When you add a field value in a hyperlink field, you can enter the name of an object, such as a table, form, worksheet, or document, or you can enter a URL to a Web page. You can type the field value directly into the field, or you can use the Insert Hyperlink dialog box to enter it.

REFERENCE WINDOW   RW

Entering a Hyperlink Field Value in a Table
- In Datasheet view, click the hyperlink field for the appropriate record.
- Click the Insert Hyperlink button on the Table Datasheet toolbar.
- Select the file, URL, or object by clicking the appropriate button.
- Change the Text to display text box value, if necessary.
- Click the OK button.

You will use the Insert Hyperlink dialog box to enter the necessary hyperlink field values.

To enter field values in the hyperlink field:

1. In Datasheet view, scroll the table to the right until the new FieldNotes field is visible, and then click the **FieldNotes** text box for the Java Place record (record 1).

2. Click the **Insert Hyperlink** button on the Table Datasheet toolbar. The Insert Hyperlink dialog box opens. See Figure 7-34.

Figure 7-34	INSERT HYPERLINK DIALOG BOX

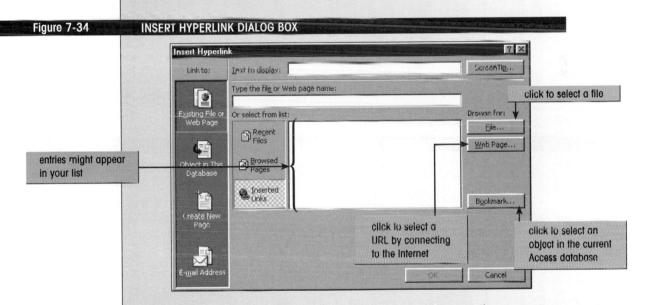

In the Insert Hyperlink dialog box, you can type the link, select the link from the list box, or select the link by using one of the three buttons. Click the File button to select a file as the link, click the Web Page button to select a URL for a Web page as the link by connecting to the Internet, or click the Bookmark button to select an object in the current Access database as the link.

3. Click the **File** button. The Link to File dialog box opens.

4. Make sure the Look in list box displays the contents of the Tutorial folder on your Data Disk, click **Java**, and then click the **OK** button. The Link to File dialog box closes, and the name of the Java file appears in the two text boxes in the Insert Hyperlink dialog box. The Text to display text box shows what will be displayed as a field value in the database hyperlink field. The second text box shows the filename of the link; that is, it shows which file will be opened when you click the hyperlink field.

You'll change the value of the Text to display text box to Java Place so that it is more descriptive.

5. Select **.doc** in the Text to display text box, press the **spacebar**, and then type **Place**. See Figure 7-35.

Figure 7-35   ENTERING A HYPERLINK FIELD VALUE

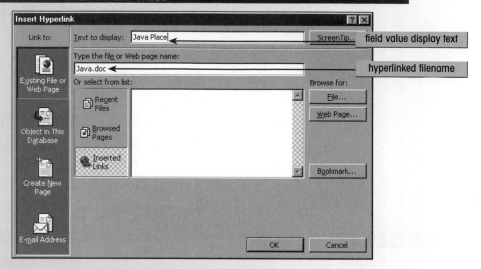

field value display text

hyperlinked filename

6. Click the **OK** button to close the Insert Hyperlink dialog box. The display text for the hyperlink field value appears in the FieldNotes field for the first record. See Figure 7-36.

Figure 7-36   AFTER ENTERING HYPERLINK FIELD VALUE

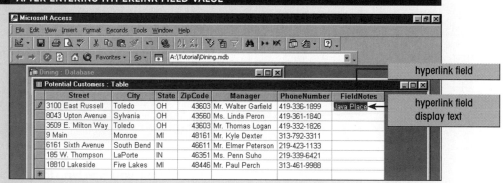

hyperlink field

hyperlink field display text

TROUBLE? If you selected the wrong hyperlink value, right-click the hyperlink field value, point to Hyperlink on the shortcut menu, click Edit Hyperlink, and then repeat Steps 3 through 6.

7. Use the same procedure to enter hyperlink field values for the records for Taza de Oro (record 2) and Peterson Family Restaurant (record 5). Select **Taza** as the filename and type **Taza de Oro** as the display text value for the Taza de Oro record; select **Peterson** as the filename and type **Peterson Family Restaurant** as the display text value for the Peterson record. When you are finished, the Datasheet window should look like Figure 7-37.

| Figure 7-37 | HYPERLINK FIELD VALUES ENTERED FOR THE THREE RECORDS |

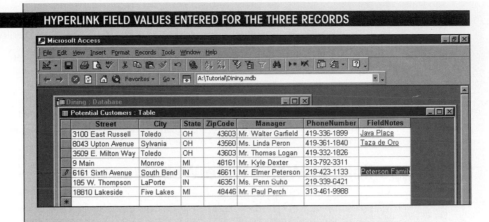

Notice that the hyperlink field values have a different appearance from the other field values. The hyperlink field values are shown in a different color and are underlined. This indicates that they are hyperlinks.

Kim wants to test one of the new hyperlink fields in the Potential Customers table. You'll use the hyperlinks to view her corresponding notes.

Using a Hyperlink

When you click a hyperlink field value, its associated program starts and opens the linked object. When you click a value in the FieldNotes field, for example, Word will start and open the linked document.

To use a hyperlink to open a Word document:

1. Click the **Peterson Family Restaurant** FieldNotes hyperlink. Word starts and opens the Peterson document, which contains Kim's field notes for Peterson Family Restaurant. See Figure 7-38.

| Figure 7-38 | FIELD NOTES FOR PETERSON FAMILY RESTAURANT IN THE PETERSON DOCUMENT |

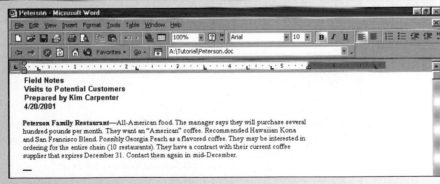

TROUBLE? If Word is not installed on your computer, another program, such as WordPad, might start and open the field notes. The specific program that starts and opens the field notes is not important. Simply continue with the steps.

2. Click the **Close** button  on the Word program window to close the document and exit Word.

3. Click the **Potential Customers** program button on the taskbar to return to the datasheet. Notice that the Peterson Family Restaurant hyperlink changed color to purple, which indicates that you followed this hyperlink.

Kim reviews the notes and is satisfied that she can now link her field notes with the Potential Customers data. She asks you to add one more hyperlink field to the Potential Customers table. This new field will contain hyperlinks to World Wide Web pages.

Creating Hyperlinks to World Wide Web Pages

When Kim visited the potential new customers, she learned that some of the restaurants maintain World Wide Web sites. Kim wants you to add an additional hyperlink field to the Potential Customers table that includes a hyperlink to each restaurant's Web site. For each restaurant, the field value for the hyperlink will be the URL for its Web site. Usually, when you create a hyperlink to a Web site, you use the URL of the site's home page, which is the first page that opens when you link to the site. When you click a field value for a record, the Web browser on your computer starts and opens the home page for that site.

Before you can enter the field values, you must add a new hyperlink field to the Potential Customers table.

To add a new hyperlink field:

1. Click the **View** button for Design view ☒ on the Table Datasheet toolbar.

2. Scroll down the field list to the first blank row (if necessary), click the Field Name text box in the blank row, type **HomePage**, and then press the **Tab** key.

3. Type **h** and then press the **Tab** key. See Figure 7-39.

Figure 7-39	HOMEPAGE HYPERLINK FIELD DEFINED

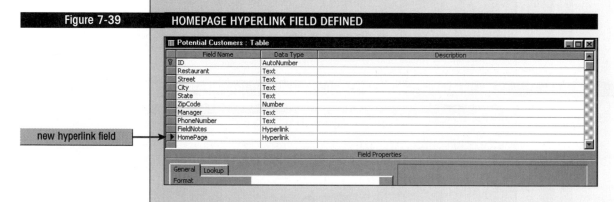

4. Click the **View** button for Datasheet view ▦ on the Table Design toolbar, and then click the **Yes** button to save and return to the table datasheet.

You can now enter the URLs for the restaurants' home pages. You will not enter actual URLs; instead you will simulate using URLs by entering the names of appropriate HTML documents that are stored on your Data Disk.

To enter the field values for hyperlinks to HTML documents:

1. Scroll right until the new HomePage field is visible, and then click the **HomePage** text box for the Taza de Oro record (record 2).

2. Click the **Insert Hyperlink** button on the Table Datasheet toolbar. The Insert Hyperlink dialog box opens.

3. Click the **File** button. The Link to File dialog box opens.

4. Make sure the Look in list box displays the contents of the Tutorial folder on your Data Disk, click **TazaLink**, and then click the **OK** button. The Link to File dialog box closes, and the name of the TazaLink file appears in both text boxes in the Insert Hyperlink dialog box. See Figure 7-40.

Figure 7-40	ENTERING A HYPERLINK FIELD VALUE FOR THE HTML DOCUMENT

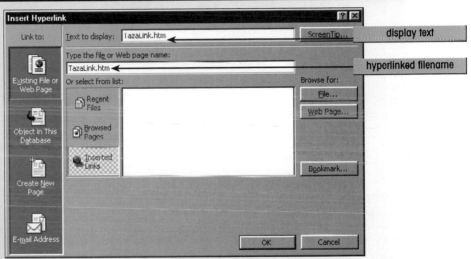

Because you want the display text for the hyperlink field to be the same as the hyperlinked filename, you will not change the entry in the Text to display text box.

5. Click the **OK** button to close the Insert Hyperlink dialog box. The hyperlink field value appears in the HomePage field for the second record. See Figure 7-41.

Figure 7-41	HYPERLINK FIELD VALUE ENTERED FOR THE RESTAURANT'S HOME PAGE

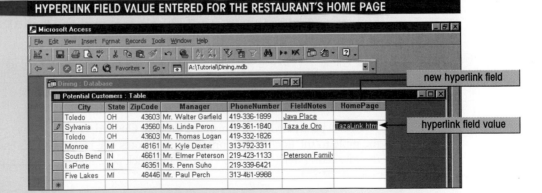

6. Use the same procedure to enter a hyperlink field value for the record for Pesto Place (record 4). Select the HTML document named **Pesto** as the file to link to.

You can now view the restaurants' home pages by clicking the hyperlinks in the HomePage field.

To view the home pages:

1. Click **Pesto.htm** in the HomePage field for record 4. Internet Explorer starts and opens the HTML document for Pesto Place's home page. See Figure 7-42.

Figure 7-42   HOME PAGE FOR PESTO PLACE

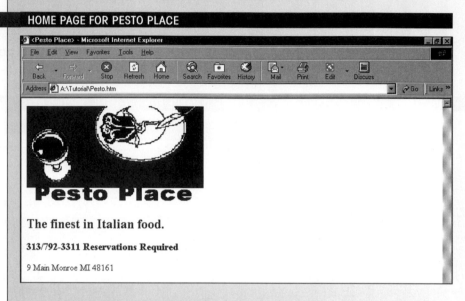

2. Click the **Close** button ☒ on the Internet Explorer window title bar to close it.

3. Click the **Potential Customers** program button on the taskbar to return to the datasheet.

4. Click **TazaLink.htm** in the HomePage field for record 2. Internet Explorer starts and opens the HTML document for Taza de Oro's home page.

5. Click ☒ on the Internet Explorer window title bar to close it.

6. Click the **Potential Customers** program button on the taskbar to return to the datasheet.

   You can now close the Dining database and exit Access. First you'll close the Web toolbar.

7. Click **View** on the menu bar, point to **Toolbars**, and then click **Web**. Access closes the Web toolbar.

8. Click ☒ on the Access window title bar to close the Dining database and to exit Access. You return to the Windows desktop.

Kim is pleased with the finished Potential Customers table. She is certain that the links from the table to the documents containing her notes will make it much easier for her and others in the marketing department to identify and track potential new customers for Valle Coffee.

Session 7.2 QUICK CHECK

1. What types of HTML formats can Access import as table data?

2. What data type is the primary key when you let Access assign a primary key with the Import HTML Wizard?

3. What does the field value of a hyperlink field represent?

4. In the Insert Hyperlink dialog box, what are your three choices for the hyperlink field value?

5. Which program starts when you click a URL value for a hyperlink field?

6. How do you view a hyperlink that is named in a hyperlink field?

REVIEW ASSIGNMENTS

Barbara wants you to export to the company intranet two objects from the **Products** database. She wants to make the **Product** table data and the **Coffee Types** report available to company employees on the company's intranet. She also wants you to create two data access pages, import an HTML document of coffee importers as a new table, and then create a hyperlink field that's linked to Web pages. She asks you to do the following:

1. Make sure your Data Disk is in the appropriate disk drive, start Access, open the **Products** database located in the Review folder on your Data Disk, and then open the Web toolbar.

2. Export the **Product** table to an HTML document in the Review folder on your Data Disk, using the HTML template named **Valletbl**, which is located in the Review folder on your Data Disk. Use Internet Explorer to open the **Product** HTML document, print the first page, and then close Internet Explorer.

Explore   3. Export the **Coffee Types** report to an HTML document in the Review folder on your Data Disk, using the HTML template named **Vallerpt**, which is located in the Review folder on your Data Disk. Use Internet Explorer to open the **Coffee Types** HTML document. Then scroll to the bottom of the document; use the First, Previous, Next, and Last buttons to navigate through the Web page; print the first page of the report; and then close Internet Explorer.

4. Use the AutoPage: Columnar Wizard to create a data access page based on the **Pricing** query. Save the data access page in the Review folder on your Data Disk as **Pricing Query**, sort the data access page in descending order based on the ProductCode field, move to the second record, print this record, and then close the data access page.

5. Create a custom data access page named **Coffee Products** based on the **Coffee** and **Product** tables. Use the design in Figure 7-43 as a guide.

Figure 7-43

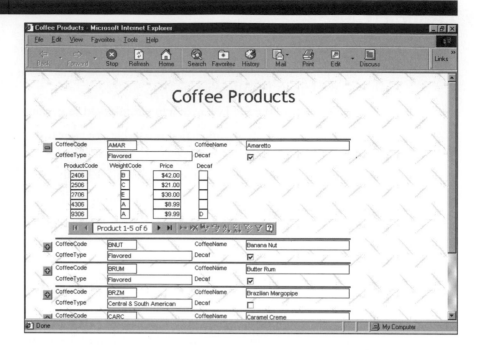

a. Place the four fields from the **Coffee** table in the Coffee Header section.

b. Place the ProductCode, WeightCode, Price, and Decaf fields from the **Product** table in the Product Header section. Change the name of the Decaf1 label to Decaf.

c. Select the Industrial theme.

Explore

d. Move and resize the fields in the Coffee Header section.

Explore

e. Add a line above the CoffeeCode and CoffeeName fields in the Coffee Header section, and then reduce the height of the section. (*Hint*: Use the Line tool on the toolbox.)

f. Create a Product Caption section, cut and paste the labels from the Product Header section to the Product Caption section, move and resize the labels and text boxes in the Product Caption and Product Header sections, and then reduce the height of both sections.

g. Use Coffee Products as the title for the data access page.

h. Save the data access page as **Coffee Products**.

i. Close the data access page, use the Web Page Preview command to view the data access page, expand the third record (Butter Rum), print the Web page, and then close Internet Explorer.

6. The **Importer** HTML document in the Review folder on your Data Disk contains a table of coffee importers in the local area. Use the following instructions to import the **Importer** HTML document into the **Products** database as a new table:

a. Choose the option for using the column headings as field names in the table.

b. Let Access assign the primary key.

c. Name the new table **Coffee Importer**.

d. Open the **Coffee Importer** table, resize all datasheet columns to fit the data, and then print the table.

e. Save and close the table.

7. Some of the coffee importers have home pages on the Web. Two of the HTML documents for the home pages are stored in the Review folder on your Data Disk. These files are called **Wwfoods** (the home page for World-Wide Foods) and **Johnson** (the home page for Johnson Restaurant Supply). Add a hyperlink field, named Home Page, to the **Coffee Importer** table. Add hyperlink values for World-Wide Foods (record 3) and Johnson Restaurant Supply (record 5).

8. View the World-Wide Foods home page, and then print the page. View the Johnson Restaurant Supply home page, and then print the page.

9. Close the Web toolbar, close the **Products** database, and then exit Access.

CASE PROBLEMS

Case 1. Ashbrook Mall Information Desk Sam Bullard wants to use the mall's computer intranet to publicize job openings at the mall. He wants you to export the **Job** table and **Store Jobs** report to the intranet as Web pages. He also wants you to create two data access pages, import an HTML document of minimum allowable wages as a new table, and then create a hyperlink field that's linked to Word documents. He asks you to make the following changes to the **Ashbrook** database:

1. Make sure your Data Disk is in the appropriate disk drive, start Access, open the **Ashbrook** database located in the Cases folder on your Data Disk, and then open the Web toolbar.

2. Export the **Job** table to an HTML document in the Cases folder on your Data Disk, using the HTML template named **Jobtbl**, which is located in the Cases folder on your Data Disk. Use Internet Explorer to open the **Job** HTML document, print the page, and then close Internet Explorer.

Explore 3. Export the **Store Jobs** report to an HTML document in the Cases folder on your Data Disk, using the HTML template named **Jobrpt**, which is located in the Cases folder on your Data Disk. Use Internet Explorer to open the **Store Jobs** HTML document, print the page, and then close Internet Explorer.

Explore 4. Use the Page Wizard to create a data access page based on the **Job** table, as follows:

   a. Select all fields from the **Job** table; remove Store as a grouping level, do not select a sort field; and then use Job Page as the title, opening the page when you finish.
   b. Use the data access page to add a new record to the **Job** table with the following values. Job: 10011, Store: BC, Hours/Week: 20–30, and Position: Clerk. Save the record.
   c. Close the data access page, saving it as **Job Page** in the Cases folder on your Data Disk.
   d. Open the **Job** table datasheet, print the datasheet, and then close the table.

5. Create a custom data access page named **Available Jobs** based on the **Store** and **Job** tables. Use the design in Figure 7-44 as a guide.

Figure 7-44

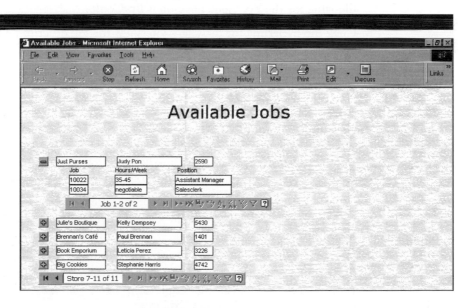

a. Place the StoreName, Contact, and Extension fields from the **Store** table in the Store Header section.

b. Place the Job, Hours/Week, and Position fields from the **Job** table (use the first **Job** table in the Related Tables folder) in the Job Header section. Change the name of the Job1 label to Job.

c. Select the Sumi Painting theme.

d. In the Store Header section, delete all the labels, move and resize the text boxes as shown in Figure 7-44, and then reduce the height of the section.

e. Create a Job Caption section, cut and paste the labels from the Job Header section to the Job Caption section, move and resize the labels and text boxes in the Job Caption and Job Header sections, and then reduce the height of both sections.

f. Use Available Jobs as the title for the data access page.

Explore

g. Change to a descending sort order based on the StoreName field, and change the default page size to 6 (from 5). (*Hint*: Set the Default Sort and Data Page Size properties for the Store group in the Sorting and Grouping dialog box.)

h. Save the data access page as **Available Jobs** in the Cases folder on your Data Disk.

i. Close the data access page, use the Web Page Preview command to view the data access page, navigate to the second Store page, expand the first record (Just Purses), print the Web page, and then close Internet Explorer.

6. The **Wages** HTML document in the Cases folder on your Data Disk contains information about the minimum allowable wages for positions offered by Ashbrook Mall stores. Import the **Wages** HTML document into the Ashbrook database as a new table, as follows:

a. Choose the option for using the column headings as field names in the table.

b. Let Access assign the primary key.

c. Name the new table **Minimum Wage**.

d. Open the **Minimum Wage** table, resize all datasheet columns to fit the data, and then print the table.

e. Save and close the table.

7. Sam Bullard has created Word documents containing details about various mall jobs in the Cases folder on your Data Disk. Add a hyperlink field, named JobDescription, to the **Minimum Wage** table. Add hyperlink field values for the Baker, Cashier, Clerk, and Fry Cook records. The filenames are the names for the positions; for example, the filename for the Fry Cook position is FryCook.

8. Click the hyperlink for the Clerk job. View the job description in the Word document, print the description, and then close Word.

9. Close the Web toolbar, close the **Ashbrook** database, and then exit Access.

Case 2. Professional Litigation User Services   Raj Jawahir wants you to integrate the **FirmPays** database with the company intranet. He wants to export the **Firm** table and the **Payments By Account Representative** report to the intranet as Web pages. He also wants you to create a data access page, import an HTML document of new legal firms opening in the area, create a hyperlink field that's linked to Web pages, and then link to a table in another database. He asks you to complete the following:

1. Make sure your Data Disk is in the appropriate disk drive, start Access, open the **FirmPays** database located in the Cases folder on your Data Disk, and then open the Web toolbar.

2. Export the **Firm** table to an HTML document in the Cases folder on your Data Disk, using the HTML template named **PLUStbl**, which is located in the Cases folder on your Data Disk. Use Internet Explorer to open the **Firm** HTML document, print the page, and then close Internet Explorer.

Explore ▶ 3. Export the **Payments By Account Representative** report to an HTML document in the Cases folder on your Data Disk, using the HTML template named **PLUSrpt**, which is located in the Cases folder on your Data Disk. Use Internet Explorer to open the **Payments By Account Representative** HTML document. Then scroll to the bottom of the document; use the First, Previous, Next, and Last buttons to navigate through the Web page; print the last page of the report; and then close Internet Explorer.

4. Use the AutoPage: Columnar Wizard to create a data access page based on the **Payment** table, and then do the following:

   a. Use the data access page to add a new record to the **Payment** table with the following values. Payment#: 10106, Deposit#: 117, Firm#: 1104, AmtPaid: 850.00, and DatePaid: 6/20/2001. Save the record.

   b. Filter the data access page, selecting all records with a DatePaid value of 06/20/2001. Print the first filtered record.

   c. Close the data access page, saving it as **Payment** in the Cases folder on your Data Disk.

5. The local bar association maintains a Web site that lists the new legal firms opening in the area. The **NewFirms** HTML document in the Cases folder on your Data Disk contains this data. Import the **NewFirms** HTML document into the **FirmPays** database as a new table, as follows:

   a. Choose the option for using the column headings as field names in the table.

   b. Change the field name Prospects to Prospect.

   c. Let Access assign the primary key.

   d. Name the new table **Prospect**.

   e. Open the **Prospect** table, resize all datasheet columns to fit the data, and then print the table.

   f. Save and close the table.

6. The firm Dupont Investments has a Web site that it uses to advertise its practice. The firm's home page HTML document is named **Dupont** and is stored in the Cases folder on your Data Disk. Add a hyperlink field to the **Prospect** table. Name the field WebSite. Then create a hyperlink for the Dupont Investments record that opens the Dupont HTML document on your Data Disk.

7. Click the hyperlink for the Dupont Investments record, view the Dupont home page, print the page, and then close Internet Explorer. Close the table.

Explore ▶ 8. Raj has a table in another database that he wants to access using the **FirmPays** database. You'll need to link to that table.

   a. Use the Office Assistant to ask the following question: "How do I link to a table?" Choose the topic "Link data," and then choose the first topic under "Import database objects." Read the information and then close the Help window and hide the Office Assistant.

   b. Link to the **Service** table in the **Services** database, which is located in the Cases folder on your Data Disk.

   c. Open the **Service** table, print the datasheet, and then close the table.

   d. Next, learn how to delete the link to the **Service** table. Use the Office Assistant to ask the following question: "How do I link to a table?" Choose the topic "Link data," and then choose the second topic under "Manage linked tables." Read the information and then close the Help window and hide the Office Assistant.

   e. Delete the link to the **Service** table.

9. Print the database relationships in the **FirmPays** database.

10. Close the Web toolbar, close the **FirmPays** database, and then exit Access.

Case 3. Best Friends   Noah and Sheila Warnick want you to export some of the **Pledges** database data on the office intranet. Specifically, they want to export the **Walker** table and the **Walkers** report as Web pages. They also want you to create a data access page, import an HTML document that contains local mall information, and then create a hyperlink field that's linked to Web pages. They ask you to complete the following:

1. Make sure your Data Disk is in the appropriate disk drive, start Access, open the **Pledges** database located in the Cases folder on your Data Disk, and then open the Web toolbar.

2. Export the **Walker** table to an HTML document in the Cases folder on your Data Disk, using the HTML template named **Walktbl**, which is located in the Cases folder on your Data Disk. Use Internet Explorer to open the **Walker** HTML document, print the page, and then close Internet Explorer.

Explore   3. Export the **Walkers** report to an HTML document in the Cases folder on your Data Disk, using the HTML template named **Walkrpt**, which is located in the Cases folder on your Data Disk. Use Internet Explorer to open the **Walkers** HTML document, print the report, and then close Internet Explorer.

4. Use the AutoPage: Columnar Wizard to create a data access page based on the **Walker** table, and then do the following:

   a. Use the data access page to add a new record to the **Walker** table with the following values. WalkerID: 226, LastName: Cunningham, FirstName: Carie, Phone: 881-3117, and Distance: 2. Save the record.

   b. Close the data access page, saving it as **Walker Page**.

   c. Open the **Walker Page** data access page in Design view.

Explore   d. Change to an ascending sort order based on the LastName field, followed by an ascending sort order based on the FirstName field. (*Hint*: Set the Default Sort property for the Walker group in the Sorting and Grouping dialog box.)

Explore   e. Draw one rectangle around the five labels and text boxes in the Walker Header section. (*Hint*: Use the Rectangle tool on the toolbox.)

   f. Change the theme to Rice Paper.

   g. Save and close the data access page, use the Web Page Preview command to view the data access page, print the first Web page, and then close Internet Explorer.

5. Noah is interested in contacting several local malls to hold "mall walk" events as fundraisers. The **Malls** HTML document, which is stored in the Cases folder on your Data Disk, is from a Web site that publishes a list of local malls and their managers. Import the **Malls** HTML document into the **Pledges** database as a new table, as follows:

   a. Choose the option for using the column headings as field names in the table.

   b. Let Access assign the primary key.

   c. Name the new table **Mall**.

   d. Open the **Mall** table, resize all datasheet columns to fit the data, and then print the table.

   e. Save and close the table.

6. The file **Southgat** is the HTML document from a Web site for the Southgate Mall. Add a hyperlink field to the **Mall** table. Name the field HomePage. Add a hyperlink for the Southgate Mall record to the **Southgat** HTML document in the Cases folder on your Data Disk.

7. Click the hyperlink for the Southgate Mall record, view the Southgate Mall home page, print the page, and then close Internet Explorer.

8. Close the Web toolbar, close the **Pledges** database, and then exit Access.

Case 4. Lopez Lexus Dealerships   Maria and Hector Lopez have established an intranet for their dealerships. They want you to export some of the **Lopez** database data as HTML documents for their dealers to view. They also want you to create two data access pages, import an HTML document of fuel mileage data for Lexus models as a new table, and then create a hyperlink field that's linked to Word documents. They ask you to make the following changes to the **Lopez** database:

1. Make sure your Data Disk is in the appropriate disk drive, start Access, open the **Lopez** database located in the Cases folder on your Data Disk, and then open the Web toolbar.

2. Export the **Car** table to an HTML document in the Cases folder on your Data Disk, using the HTML template named **Lopeztbl**, which is located in the Cases folder on your Data Disk. Use Internet Explorer to open the **Car** HTML document, print the page, and then close Internet Explorer.

Explore

3. Export the **Cars By Model And Year** report to an HTML document in the Cases folder on your Data Disk, using the HTML template named **Lopezrpt**, which is located in the Cases folder on your Data Disk. Use Internet Explorer to open the **Cars By Model And Year** HTML document, print the report, and then close Internet Explorer.

4. Use the AutoPage: Columnar Wizard to create a data access page based on the **Car** table, and then do the following:

   a. Use the data access page to add a new record to the **Car** table with the following values. VehicleID: PAJ9B, Manufacturer: Lexus, Model: SC400, Class: S3, Transmission: A4, Year: 2001, LocationCode: A1, Cost: $37,600, and SellingPrice: $43,000. Save the record.
   b. Sort the data access page in descending order based on the VehicleID field.
   c. Move to the fifth record, and then print this record.
   d. Close the data access page, saving it as **Car Page** in the Cases folder on your Data Disk.

5. Create a custom data access page named **Locations and Cars Page** based on the **Location** and **Car** tables. Use the design in Figure 7-45 as a guide.

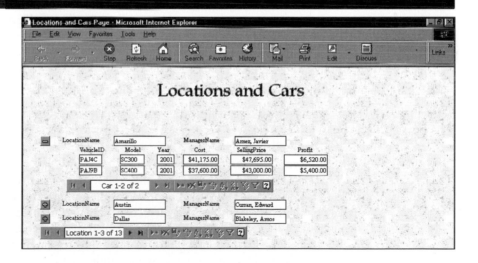

Figure 7-45

   a. Place the LocationName and ManagerName fields from the **Location** table in the Location Header section.

   b. Place the VehicleID, Model, Year, Cost, and SellingPrice fields from the **Car** table (use the first **Car** table in the Related Tables folder) in the Car Header section.

   c. Select the Romanesque theme.

   d. In the Location Header section, move and resize the labels and text boxes, and then reduce the height of the section.

   e. Create a Car Caption section, cut and paste the labels from the Car Header section to the Car Caption section, move and resize the labels and text boxes in the Car Caption and Car Header sections, and then reduce the height of both sections.

Explore   f. Use the Text Box tool on the toolbox to add a calculated control to the Car Header section. Cut the label from the Car Header section and paste it to the Car Caption section, type Profit in the label box, and then move and resize the label. Select the text box in the Car Header section, move and resize it, and then set this control's value to the difference between the SellingPrice and Cost fields. (*Hint*: Set the ControlSource property to-SellingPrice - Cost.)

   g. Use Locations and Cars as the title for the data access page.

Explore   h. Change the default page size to 3 (from 5). (*Hint*: Set the Data Page Size property for the Location group in the Sorting and Grouping dialog box.)

   i. Save the data access page as **Locations and Cars Page** in the Cases folder on your Data Disk.

   j. Close the data access page, use the Web Page Preview command to view the data access page, navigate to the first Location page, expand the first record (Amarillo), print the Web page, and then close Internet Explorer.

Explore   6. The **Mileage** HTML document, which is stored in the Cases folder on your Data Disk, contains fuel mileage data for Lexus models. Import the **Mileage** HTML document into the **Lopez** database as a new table, as follows:

   a. Choose the option for using the column headings as field names in the table.

   b. Let Access assign the primary key.

   c. Name the new table **Mileage**.

   d. Open the **Mileage** table, resize all datasheet columns to fit the data, and then print the table.

   e. Save and close the table.

  7. Maria has created Word documents in the Cases folder on your Data Disk, containing personal reviews about Lexus models. Add a hyperlink field, named Review, to the new **Mileage** table. Add hyperlink field values for each record in the table. The filenames are the names for the models.

  8. Click the hyperlink for the LS400 model. View the personal reviews in the Word document, print the personal reviews, and then close Word.

  9. Print the database relationships in the **Lopez** database.

  10. Close the Web toolbar, close the **Lopez** database, and then exit Access.

Case 5. eACH Internet Auction Site   Chris and Pat Aquino want you to continue your development of their Internet auction site for collectibles. They want you to export some of the **eACH** database data as HTML documents for their registrants to view. They also want you to create two data access pages, and then create a hyperlink field that's linked to Word documents. One of the data access pages will be a custom data access page that buyers can use to view categories with their subcategories when they're searching for items that might be of interest to them. They ask you to make the following changes to the **eACH** database:

  1. Make sure your Data Disk is in the appropriate disk drive, start Access, open the **eACH** database located in the Cases folder on your Data Disk, and then open the Web toolbar.

2. Export the **Item** table to an HTML document in the Cases folder on your Data Disk, using the HTML template named **eACHtbl**, which is located in the Cases folder on your Data Disk. Use Internet Explorer to open the **Item** HTML document, print the page, and then close Internet Explorer.

3. Export the custom report you created in Tutorial 6 to an HTML document in the Cases folder on your Data Disk, using the HTML template named **eACHrpt**, which is located in the Cases folder on your Data Disk. Use Internet Explorer to open the HTML document that you created, print the report, and then close Internet Explorer.

4. Use the AutoPage: Columnar Wizard to create a data access page based on the **Registrant** table, as follows:
    a. Use the data access page to add a new record with your name to the **Registrant** table with additional data that you create.
    b. Sort the data access page in ascending order based on the field that contains the registrant's last name.
    c. Print the first record.
    d. Close the data access page, saving it as **Registrant Page** in the Cases folder on your Data Disk.

5. Design and then create a custom data access page that satisfies the following requirements:
    a. Place all the fields from the **Category** table in the grid.
    b. Place all the fields, except for the common field, from the **Subcategory** table in the grid.
    c. Select the Blueprint theme.
    d. In the Category Header section, move and resize the labels and text boxes, and then reduce the height of the section.
    e. Create a Subcategory Caption section, cut and paste the labels from the Subcategory Header section to the Subcategory Caption section, move and resize the labels and text boxes in the Subcategory Header and Subcategory Caption sections, and then reduce the height of both sections.
    f. Use an appropriate title for the data access page.
    g. Save the data access page as **Categories and Subcategories Page** in the Cases folder on your Data Disk.
    h. Close the data access page, use the Web Page Preview command to view the data access page, expand a record with related records, print the Web page, and then close Internet Explorer.

6. Given the test data you created in Tutorial 5, you should have at least two items you've posted for sale on eACH. To attract bidders to those items, you should include visuals and short descriptions of them by completing the following:
    a. Create at least three Word documents and save them with appropriate filenames in the Cases folder on your Data Disk. In each document, write a short description for one of the items in your database. Also, include an appropriate graphic or picture (that you locate in the Microsoft Clip Gallery or download from the Internet) for the item. Save each document.
    b. Add a hyperlink field named Visual to the **Item** table. Add hyperlink field values for each item that has a corresponding Word document.
    c. Click the hyperlink for one of the items. View the Word document, print it, and then close Word.

7. Print the database relationships in the **eACH** database.

8. Close the Web toolbar, close the **eACH** database, and then exit Access.

INTERNET ASSIGNMENTS

The purpose of the Internet Assignments is to challenge you to find information on the Internet that you can use to create effective documents. The actual assignments are updated and maintained on the Course Technology Web site. Log on to the Internet and use your Web browser to go to the Student Online Companion to accompany this text at **www.course.com/NewPerspectives/office2000**. Click the Access link, and then click the link for Tutorial 7.

QUICK CHECK ANSWERS

Session 7.1

1. The World Wide Web is the collection of HTML documents stored on Web servers linked through the Internet.

2. A Web browser is a program used to view HTML documents.

3. HTML stands for Hypertext Markup Language, the language used to create World Wide Web documents.

4. A hyperlink links one Web document to another.

5. An HTML template is a file that contains HTML instructions for creating a Web page with both text and graphics, together with special instructions that tell Access where to place the Access data on the page.

6. A data access page is a dynamic HTML page that you can open with a Web browser to view or update current data in an Access database.

7. A theme is a predefined style for a data access page.

8. A grouped data access page is a data access page that uses two or more group levels to display information from general categories to specific details. You can view data on grouped data access pages, but you can't add, change, or delete data on them.

Session 7.2

1. Access can import HTML data that is formatted as a table or as a list.

2. AutoNumber

3. a hyperlink to another object

4. a file, a URL, an object in the opened Access database

5. Web browser

6. Click the hyperlink field value to open the hyperlinked document or object.

New Perspectives on

MICROSOFT®
ACCESS 2000

Read This Before You Begin

To the Student

Data Disks

To complete the Level III tutorials, Review Assignments, and Case Problems, you will need access to a folder on your computer's hard drive or a personal network drive. (If you must complete your work using a floppy disk, you will not be able to complete some of the steps due to space limitations. A TROUBLE? paragraph will alert you to these steps.) Your instructor will either provide you with these Data Disk files or ask you to make your own.

You will need to copy a set of folders from a file server or standalone computer or the Web to your folder. Your instructor will tell you which computer, drive letter, and folders contain the files you need. You could also download the files by going to www.course.com, clicking Data Disk Files, and following the instructions on the screen.

The following list shows how to set up your Data Files in the folder that you will use to store them. (If you are storing your Data Files on floppy disks, put each database on a separate disk.)

Contents for the Data Disk folder
Level III (Tutorials 8-10)
Tutorial files
Put this folder in the Data Disk folder:
Tutorial

Level III (Tutorials 8-10)
Review Assignments
Put this folder in the Data Disk folder:
Review

Level III (Tutorials 8-10)
Case Problems 1-5
Cases
Put this folder in the Data Disk folder:
Cases

Additional Cases
Put this folder in the Data Disk folder:
AddCases

When you begin each tutorial, be sure you are using the correct files. Refer to the "File Finder" Chart at the back of this text for more detailed information on which files are used in which tutorials. These Access Level III tutorials use the same files for Tutorials 8-10. See the inside back cover of this book for more information on Data Disk files, or ask your instructor or technical support person for assistance.

Course Labs

The Access Level III tutorials feature an interactive Course Lab to help you understand SQL concepts. There are Lab Assignments at the end of Tutorial 8 that relate to this Lab.

To start a Lab, click the **Start** button on the Windows taskbar, point to **Programs**, point to **Course Labs**, point to **New Perspectives Course Labs**, and click the name of the Lab you want to use.

Using Your Own Computer

If you are going to work through this book using your own computer, you need:

- ■ **Computer System** Microsoft Windows 95, 98, NT, or higher must be installed on your computer. This book assumes a typical installation of Microsoft Access.

- ■ **Data Disks** You will not be able to complete the tutorials or exercises in this book using your own computer until you have your Data Files. It is highly recommended that you work off of your computer's hard drive or your personal network drive.

- ■ **Course Labs** See your instructor or technical support person to obtain the Course Lab software for use on your own computer.

Visit Our World Wide Web Site

Additional materials designed especially for you are available on the World Wide Web. Go to http://www.course.com.

To the Instructor

The Data Files and Course Labs are available on the Instructor's Resource Kit for this title. Follow the instructions in the Help file on the CD-ROM to install the programs to your network or standalone computer. For information on creating Data Disks or the Course Labs, see the "To the Student" section above.

You are granted a license to copy the Data Files and Course Labs to any computer or computer network used by students who have purchased this book.

In this tutorial you will:

- Use Query Wizards to create a crosstab query, a find duplicates query, and a find unmatched query

- Create a top values query

- Create action queries

- Define many-to-many and one-to-one relationships between tables

- View and create indexes for tables

- Join a table using a self-join

- View SQL query statements

- Use replication to create a Design Master and replica of a database

- Synchronize the Design Master and replica databases

LAB

SQL
Queries

USING
QUERY WIZARDS, ACTION QUERIES, AND BRIEFCASE REPLICATION

Enhancing User Interaction with the FineFood Database

CASE

Valle Coffee

Ten years ago Leonard Valle became president of Algoman Imports, a small distributor of inexpensive coffee beans to supermarkets in western Michigan. Since that time, Leonard has transformed the company into a popular distributor of gourmet coffees for restaurants and offices. He took over company ownership, changed the company name to Valle Coffee, and expanded its market area to include Indiana and Ohio.

Leonard has incorporated the use of computers in all aspects of the business, including financial management, inventory, production, and sales. The company has developed the FineFood database of customer information and uses **Microsoft Access 2000** (or simply **Access**) to manage it.

The FineFood database contains tables, queries, forms, and reports. Barbara Hennessey, office manager, uses the FineFood database to keep track of invoices sent to customers. She also periodically publishes tables and reports as HTML files on the company intranet to keep others updated on company activity. Kim Carpenter, director of marketing, uses the FineFood database to keep track of marketing information.

Leonard, Barbara, and Kim have found the FineFood database to be very useful in managing the company's data. They have asked you to continue enhancing the database by creating some advanced queries. Also, Kim is leaving on a business trip to meet with potential customers. During her trip, she wants to have access to the FineFood database so that she can record information about new customers immediately if any potential customers decide to open accounts with Valle Coffee.

<table>
<tr><td>SESSION 8.1</td><td>In this session, you will use Query Wizards to create a crosstab query, a find duplicates query, and a find unmatched query. You'll also create a top values query.</td></tr>
</table>

Creating a Crosstab Query

Leonard is interested in learning how much business Valle Coffee is doing in each state. He also wants to know how the total business in each state varies by month. He asks you to create a crosstab query using the Crosstab Query Wizard to provide the information he needs.

A **crosstab query** performs aggregate function calculations on the values of one database field and displays the results in a spreadsheet format. (**Aggregate functions** perform arithmetic operations on the records in a database.) Figure 8-1 lists the aggregate functions you can use in a crosstab query. A crosstab query can also display one additional aggregate function value that summarizes each row's set of values. The crosstab query uses one or more fields for the row headings on the left and one field for the column headings at the top.

Figure 8-1	AGGREGATE FUNCTIONS USED IN CROSSTAB QUERIES

AGGREGATE FUNCTIONS	DEFINITION
Avg	Average of the field values
Count	Number of the nonnull field values
First	First field value
Last	Last field value
Min	Lowest field value
Max	Highest field value
StDev	Standard deviation of the field values
Sum	Total of the field values
Var	Variance of the field values

Figure 8-2 shows two query results—the first from a select query and the second from a related crosstab query. The title bar indicates the type of query.

| Figure 8-2 | CONTRASTING A SELECT QUERY WITH A CROSSTAB QUERY |

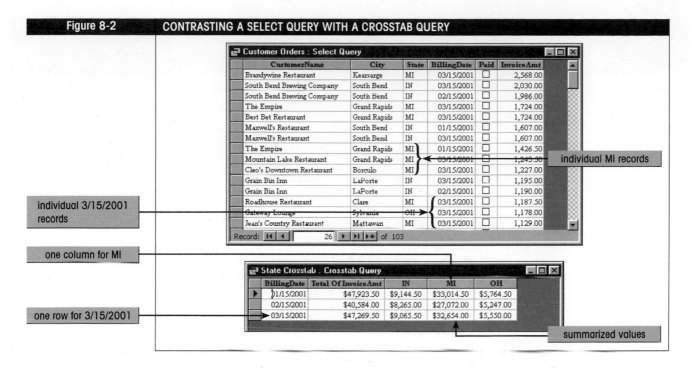

Both queries are based on the Customer Orders query, which joins the Customer and Order tables, but the crosstab query provides more valuable information. For each record in the Customer table, the select query displays the CustomerName, City, and State fields from the Customer table and the BillingDate, Paid, and InvoiceAmt fields from the Order table. Notice that there are many rows for BillingDate 3/15/2001—the select query contains one row for each invoice sent on that date. Some rows with this BillingDate value might not be currently visible on the screen. On the other hand, the crosstab query displays just one row for 3/15/2001. The BillingDate field in the leftmost column identifies each row, and the field values for the State field identify the rightmost columns. The crosstab query uses the Sum aggregate function on the InvoiceAmt field to produce the displayed values in the remainder of the query results. The second column, labeled Total Of InvoiceAmt, represents the total of the InvoiceAmt values for each row. For example, you can use the crosstab query to see that all invoices sent on 3/15/2001 to customers in Michigan totaled $32,654.00. You could extract the same data from a select query, but the crosstab query does it for you automatically. Using the crosstab query results, Leonard can quickly see the amount of business done each month and the amount of business done in each state.

The quickest way to create a crosstab query is to use the **Crosstab Query Wizard**, which guides you through the steps for creating crosstab queries. You could also change a select query to a crosstab query using the Query Type button on the Query Design toolbar. (Refer to the Help system for more information on creating a crosstab query without using a Wizard.)

REFERENCE   WINDOW   **RW**

Using the Crosstab Query Wizard

■ In the Database window, click Queries in the Objects bar to display the Queries list, and then click the New button.

■ Click Crosstab Query Wizard, and then click the OK button.

■ Complete the Wizard dialog boxes to select the table or query on which to base the crosstab query, select the row heading field or fields, select the column heading field or fields, select the calculation field and its aggregate function, and enter a name for the crosstab query.

The crosstab query you create will be like the one shown in Figure 8-2. This crosstab query has the following characteristics:

■ The Customer Orders query in the FineFood database is the basis for the new crosstab query; it includes the CustomerName, City, State, BillingDate, Paid, and InvoiceAmt fields.

■ The BillingDate field from the Order table is the leftmost column and identifies each crosstab query row.

■ The field values that appear in the Customer table for the State field identify the rightmost columns of the crosstab query.

■ The crosstab query applies the Sum aggregate function to the InvoiceAmt field from the Order table and displays the resulting total values in the State columns of the query results. If one state has two or more invoices on the same billing date, then the sum of the invoice amounts appears in the intersecting cell of the query results.

■ The total of the InvoiceAmt values appears for each row in a column with the heading Total Of InvoiceAmt.

You are now ready to create the crosstab query based on the Customer Orders query. The crosstab query will show how much business Valle Coffee is doing in each state and how the total business in each state varies by month.

To start the Crosstab Query Wizard:

1. Make sure you have created your copy of the Access Data Disk, and then place your Data Disk in the appropriate disk drive.

   TROUBLE? If you don't have a Data Disk, you need to get one before you can proceed. Your instructor will either give you one or ask you to make your own. (See your instructor for information.) In either case, be sure you have made a copy of your Data Disk before you begin, so that the original Data Disk files will be available on the copied disk in case you need to start over because of an error or problem.

   TROUBLE? If you are not sure which disk drive to use for your Data Disk, read the "Read This Before You Begin" page on page 8.02 or ask your instructor for help.

2. Start Access and open the **FineFood** database located in the Tutorial folder on your Data Disk. The FineFood database is displayed in the Access window.

3. Click **Queries** in the Objects bar of the Database window, and then click the **New** button. The New Query dialog box opens.

4. Click **Crosstab Query Wizard** and then click the **OK** button. The first Crosstab Query Wizard dialog box opens.

You'll now use the Crosstab Query Wizard to create the crosstab query for Leonard.

To create the crosstab query using the Crosstab Query Wizard:

1. Click the **Queries** option button in the View section to display the list of queries in the FineFood database, and then click **Customer Orders**. See Figure 8-3.

| Figure 8-3 | CHOOSING THE TABLE OR QUERY FOR THE CROSSTAB QUERY |

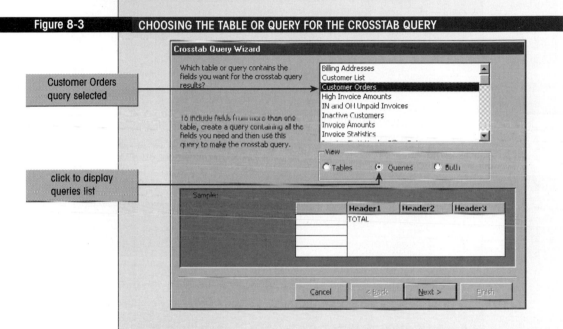

2. Click the **Next** button to open the next Crosstab Query Wizard dialog box, in which you choose the field (or fields) for the row headings. Because Leonard wants the crosstab query to display one row for each BillingDate value, you will select that field for the row headings.

3. In the Available Fields list box, click **BillingDate** and then click the [>] button to move BillingDate to the Selected Fields list box. When you select a field, Access changes the sample crosstab query in the bottom of the dialog box to illustrate your choice.

4. Click the **Next** button to open the next Crosstab Query Wizard dialog box, in which you select the field values that serve as column headings. Leonard wants to see the invoice amounts by state, so you need to select the State field for the column headings.

5. Click **State** in the list box, and then click the **Next** button.

In this Crosstab Query Wizard dialog box, you choose the field that will be calculated for each row and column intersection and the function to use for the calculation. The results of the calculation will appear in the row and column intersections of the query results. Leonard needs to calculate the sum of the InvoiceAmt value for each row and column intersection.

6. Click **InvoiceAmt** in the Fields list box, and then click **Sum** in the Functions list box. Be sure that the **Yes, include row sums** check box is selected. This option creates a column showing the overall totals for the values in each row of the query results. See Figure 8-4.

Figure 8-4	COMPLETED CROSSTAB QUERY DESIGN

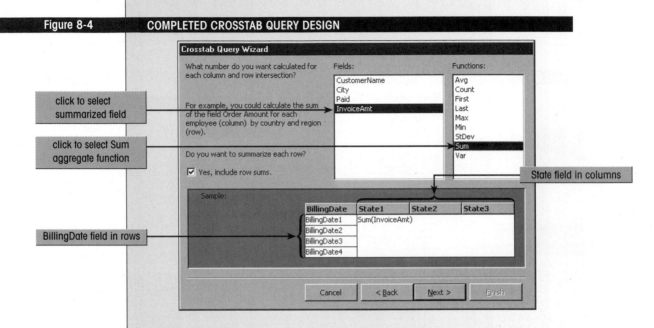

7. Click the **Next** button to open the last Crosstab Query Wizard dialog box, in which you choose the query name.

8. Type **State Crosstab** in the text box, be sure the option button for viewing the query is selected, and then click the **Finish** button. Access saves the crosstab query, and then displays the query results.

9. Resize all the columns in the query results to their best fit, and then click **BillingDate 01/15/2001** to deselect the columns. See Figure 8-5.

Figure 8-5	CROSSTAB QUERY RESULTS

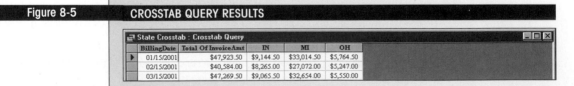

BillingDate	Total Of InvoiceAmt	IN	MI	OH
01/15/2001	$47,923.50	$9,144.50	$33,014.50	$5,764.50
02/15/2001	$40,584.00	$8,265.00	$27,072.00	$5,247.00
03/15/2001	$47,269.50	$9,065.50	$32,654.00	$5,550.00

The query results contain one row for each BillingDate field value. The Total Of InvoiceAmt column shows the total of the invoices for that date. The columns labeled IN, MI, and OH show the total of invoices for each state on that date.

Because this query shows the total of the invoice amounts for each billing date for each state, Leonard can use the information to track the progress of billings in each state. You can now close the completed query results.

To close the query results:

1. Click the **Close** button ☒ on the Query window to close it.

2. Click the **Yes** button to save the changes and return to the Database window.

Access uses unique icons to represent different types of queries. The crosstab query icon appears in the Queries list box to the left of the State Crosstab query. This icon is different in appearance from the icon that appears to the left of the other queries, which are all select queries.

Next, Barbara needs some information from the FineFood database. She is concerned that several customers in Indiana and Ohio have been slow to pay their invoices, and she wants to contact customers who have missed payments. She wants to contact only those customers who consistently don't pay, so she asks you to find out which customers in those states have failed to pay more than one invoice. To find the information Barbara needs, you'll create a find duplicates query.

Creating a Find Duplicates Query

A **find duplicates query** is a select query that locates duplicate records in a table or query. You can create this type of query using the **Find Duplicates Query Wizard**. A find duplicates query searches for duplicates based on the fields you choose as you answer the Wizard's questions. For example, you might want to display all customers who have the same name, all students who have the same phone number, or all products that have the same description. Using this query, you can locate duplicates and avert potential problems (for example, you might have inadvertently assigned two different numbers to the same product), or you can eliminate duplicates that cost money (for example, you could send just one advertising brochure to all the customers having the same address).

You can meet Barbara's request by using the Find Duplicates Query Wizard to display records for customers that appear more than once in the IN and OH Unpaid Invoices query.

REFERENCE WINDOW   RW

Using the Find Duplicates Query Wizard

- In the Database window, click Queries in the Objects bar to display the Queries list, and then click the New button.
- Click Find Duplicates Query Wizard, and then click the OK button.
- Complete the Wizard dialog boxes to select the table or query on which to base the query, select the field or fields to check for duplicate values, select the additional fields to include in the query results, and enter a name for the query.

You can use the Find Duplicates Query Wizard to create and run a new query to display duplicate customer names in the IN and OH Unpaid Invoices query results.

To create the query using the Find Duplicates Query Wizard:

1. Click **Queries** in the Objects bar of the Database window (if necessary), and then click the **New** button to open the New Query dialog box.

2. Click **Find Duplicates Query Wizard**, and then click the **OK** button. The first Find Duplicates Query Wizard dialog box opens. In this dialog box, you select the table or query on which to base the new query. You'll use the IN and OH Unpaid Invoices query.

3. Click the **Queries** option button in the View section to display the list of queries, click **IN and OH Unpaid Invoices**, and then click the **Next** button. Access opens the next Find Duplicates Query Wizard dialog box, in which you choose the fields you want checked for duplicate values.

4. In the Available fields list box, click **CustomerNum** (if necessary), click the ⟩ button to select this field to be checked for duplicate values, and then click the **Next** button to open the next Find Duplicates Query Wizard dialog box, in which you select the additional fields you want displayed in the query results.

   Barbara wants to know the customer's number and name, so you will display the CustomerName field in the query results, as well. Barbara also needs the invoice amount that is outstanding.

5. In the Available Fields list box, click **CustomerName** (if necessary), click the ⟩ button, click **InvoiceAmt**, and then click the ⟩ button. Access moves these fields to the Additional query fields list box.

6. Click the **Next** button to open the final Find Duplicates Query Wizard dialog box, in which you enter a name for the query. You'll use Late IN and OH Payers as the query name.

7. Type **Late IN and OH Payers** in the text box, be sure the option button for viewing the results is selected, and then click the **Finish** button. Access saves the query, and then displays the query results.

8. Resize all the columns in the query results to their best fit, and then click **CustomerNum 624** to deselect the columns. See Figure 8-6. Access displays the records for four customers with more than one unpaid invoice.

Figure 8-6	QUERY RESULTS FOR THE LATE IN AND OH PAYERS QUERY

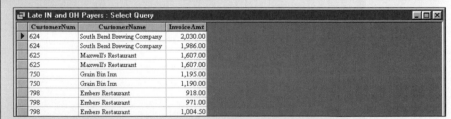

Barbara asks you to print the query before you save and close it.

9. Click the **Print** button 🖨 on the Query Datasheet toolbar to print the query results for Barbara, click the **Save** button 💾 on the Query Datasheet toolbar to save the query, and then click the **Close** button ❌ on the Query window to close it and return to the Database window.

After you give Barbara the list of late payers, she asks you to find the records for any customers who have never been billed. These are customers who have accounts with Valle Coffee, but who have never placed an order. To create this list, you need to create a find unmatched query.

Creating a Find Unmatched Query

A **find unmatched query** is a select query that finds all the records in a table or query that have no related records in a second table or query. For example, you could display all customers who have not placed orders or all nondegree students who are not currently enrolled in classes. Such a query might help you solicit business from the inactive customers or contact the students to find out their future educational plans. You can use the **Find Unmatched Query Wizard** to create this type of query.

REFERENCE WINDOW   **RW**

Using the Find Unmatched Query Wizard

- In the Database window, click Queries in the Objects bar to display the Queries list, and then click the New button.
- Click Find Unmatched Query Wizard, and then click the OK button.
- Complete the Wizard dialog boxes to select the table or query on which to base the query, select the table or query that contains the related records, specify the common field in each table or query, select the additional fields to include in the query results, and enter a name for the query.

Barbara wants to know which customers have never been sent an invoice. These customers are inactive, and she will ask Kim to contact them to determine whether they are still interested in ordering from Valle Coffee. Barbara asks you to create a list of any inactive customers. To create this list, you can use the Find Unmatched Query Wizard to display fields from the Customer table, but only when there are no records in the Order table having a matching CustomerNum field value.

To create the query using the Find Unmatched Query Wizard:

1. Click **Queries** in the Objects bar of the Database window (if necessary), and then click the **New** button to open the New Query dialog box.

2. Click **Find Unmatched Query Wizard**, and then click the **OK** button. The first Find Unmatched Query Wizard dialog box opens. In this dialog box, you select the table or query on which to base the new query. You'll use the Customer table.

3. Click **Customer** (if necessary) in the list box to select this table, and then click the **Next** button to open the next Find Unmatched Query Wizard dialog box, in which you choose the table that contains the related records. You'll select the Order table.

4. Click **Order** in the list box, and then click the **Next** button to open the next dialog box, in which you choose the common field for both tables. Notice that CustomerNum is highlighted in each list box because it is the common field.

5. Click the <=> button to confirm the common field. The Matching fields text box shows CustomerNum <=> CustomerNum to indicate the common field. See Figure 8-7.

Figure 8-7   SELECTING THE COMMON FIELD

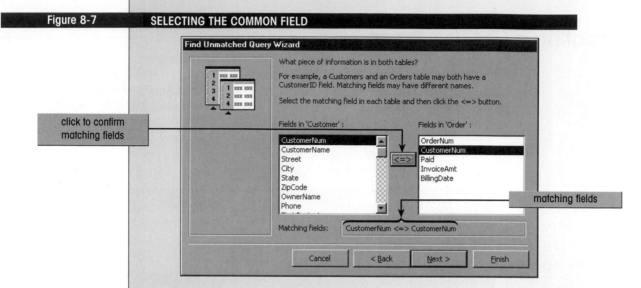

6. Click the **Next** button to open the next Find Unmatched Query Wizard dialog box, in which you choose the fields you want to see in the query results. Barbara wants the query results to display the CustomerName, OwnerName, Phone, and FirstContact fields.

7. Click **CustomerName** in the Available fields list box, and then click the [>] button to select this field. Use the same procedure to select the **OwnerName**, **Phone**, and **FirstContact** fields, and then click the **Next** button to open the final dialog box, in which you enter the query name.

8. Type **Inactive Customers**, make sure the View the results option button is selected, and then click the **Finish** button. Access saves the query, and then displays the query results. Resize all the columns in the query results to their best fit, and then click **CustomerName Pesto Place** to deselect the columns. See Figure 8-8.

Figure 8-8   RESULTS OF THE INACTIVE CUSTOMERS QUERY

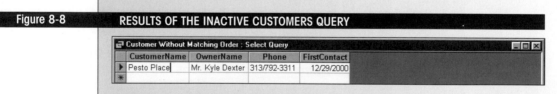

The query results include only the record for Pesto Place, one of the new customers that Kim visited on her recent trip. No other customers are inactive.

9. Click the **Save button** 🖫 on the Query Datasheet toolbar to save the query design, and then click the **Close** button ☒ on the Query window to close it and return to the Database window.

Barbara now knows that Pesto Place did not place any orders, because it was the only record from the Customer table that did not have a matching record in the Order table.

Because Pesto Place is a new customer, Barbara doesn't expect to have an Order record yet, so she does not need to contact Kim about any inactive customers.

Next, Barbara wants to contact those customers who have been placing large orders but who have not paid their invoices. She asks you to create a query to show the largest outstanding invoices. To display the information Barbara wants, you can create a top values query.

Top Values Queries

Whenever you have a query that displays a large group of records, you can limit the number to a more manageable size by displaying just the first 10 records, for example. The **Top Values** property for a query lets you limit the number of records in the query results. For the Top Values property, you enter either an integer (such as 10, to display the first 10 records) or a percent (such as 50%, to display the first half).

Suppose you have a select query that displays 45 records. If you want the query results to show only the first five records, you can change the query by entering a Top Values property of either 5 or 10%. If the query contains a sort, Access displays the records sorted in order by the primary sort key. Whenever the last record that Access can display is one of two or more records with the same value for the primary sort key, Access displays all the records with matching key values.

REFERENCE   WINDOW   **RW**

Creating a Top Values Query
- Create a select query with the necessary fields and selection criteria.
- Enter the number of records (or percentage of records) you want selected in the Top Values text box on the Query Design toolbar.
- Click the Run button on the Query Design toolbar.

Barbara wants to see the CustomerName, OwnerName, Phone, InvoiceAmt, and BillingDate fields for the 10 largest unpaid invoices. You will create a new query and then use the Top Values property to produce this information for her.

To create the query:

1. Click **Queries** in the Objects bar of the Database window (if necessary), and then click the **New** button to open the New Query dialog box.

2. Make sure that Design View is selected, and then click the **OK** button. The Show Table dialog box opens on top of the Query window in Design view.

3. Double-click **Customer** and then double-click **Order** to add both tables to the Query window. Click the **Close** button to close the Show Table dialog box.

   Now you can add the appropriate fields to the design grid.

4. In the Customer field list, double-click **CustomerName**, double-click **OwnerName**, and then double-click **Phone**, scrolling as necessary, to add these three fields to the design grid.

5. In the Order field list, double-click **Paid**, double-click **InvoiceAmt**, and then double-click **BillingDate**, scrolling as necessary, to add these three fields to the design grid.

6. Click the **Paid Criteria** text box, and then type **=No**. The query will select only unpaid invoices.

   Because all the selected Order records are unpaid, you do not need to show the Paid field values in the query results.

7. Click the **Paid Show** check box to remove the check mark.

   Barbara wants to see the 10 largest unpaid invoices, so you need to select a descending sort order for the InvoiceAmt field.

8. Scroll right until the InvoiceAmt field is visible (if necessary), click the right side of the **InvoiceAmt Sort** text box to display the sort order options, and then click **Descending**. The query will display the largest unpaid invoice amounts first.

9. Click the **Run** button [!] on the Query Design toolbar. The query results show the 24 records that represent unpaid invoices. The records appear in descending order sorted by the InvoiceAmt field.

You can now set the Top Values property to limit the query results to the top 10 unpaid invoices, because Barbara wants to focus on the larger outstanding invoices first.

To set the Top Values property of the query:

1. Resize the query results columns to their best fit.

2. Click the **View** button for Design view [⌞] on the Query Datasheet toolbar to switch back to Design view.

3. Click **All** in the Top Values text box on the Query Design toolbar, and then type **10**. See Figure 8-9.

| Figure 8-9 | CREATING THE TOP VALUES QUERY |

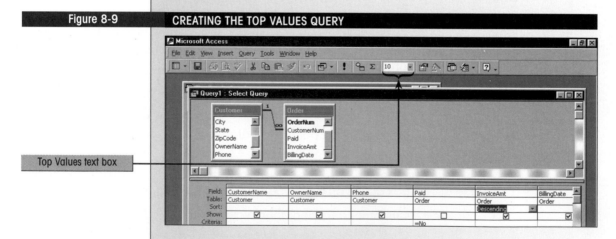

Top Values text box

4. Click the **Run** button [!] on the Query Design toolbar. Access displays the top 10 largest unpaid invoice records in the query results. See Figure 8-10.

Figure 8-10	TOP VALUES QUERY RESULTS

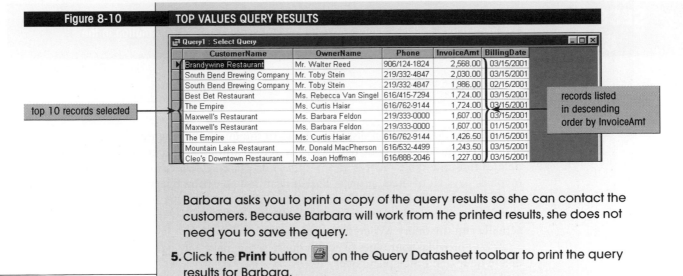

top 10 records selected

records listed in descending order by InvoiceAmt

Barbara asks you to print a copy of the query results so she can contact the customers. Because Barbara will work from the printed results, she does not need you to save the query.

5. Click the **Print** button 🖨 on the Query Datasheet toolbar to print the query results for Barbara.

6. Click the **Close** button ⊠ on the Query window, and then click the **No** button when Access asks if you want to save the query changes. Access closes the Query window and returns to the Database window.

7. Click ⊠ on the Access window title bar to close the FineFood database and to exit Access. You return to the Windows desktop.

Barbara will use the information provided by the queries you created to contact customers, as necessary. In the next session, you'll create queries for Leonard and Kim to meet their needs for information about Valle Coffee's restaurant customers.

Session 8.1 QUICK CHECK

1. What is the purpose of a crosstab query?

2. What aggregate functions can you use in a crosstab query?

3. What are the four Query Wizards you can use to create a new query?

4. What is a find duplicates query?

5. What does a find unmatched query do?

6. What happens if you set the Top Values property of a query to 2 and the first five records have the same value for the primary sort key?

SESSION 8.2

In this session, you will create four different action queries—a make-table query, an append query, a delete query, and an update query—to change information in the FineFood database.

Action Queries

Queries can do more than display answers to the questions you ask; they can also perform actions on the data in your database. An **action query** is a query that adds, changes, or deletes multiple table records at one time. For example, if a customer with several unpaid invoices pays all of them at once, Barbara can use an action query to update all of the customer's Order table records at once to mark them as paid. Because action queries modify many records in a table at a time, Access allows you to preview the query results before you actually run the query. When the query works correctly, you can save it as an action query.

Access provides four types of action queries: the make-table query, the append query, the delete query, and the update query.

A **make-table query** creates a new table from one or more existing tables. The new table can be an exact copy of the records in an existing table, a subset of the fields and records in an existing table, or a combination of the fields and records from two or more tables. Access does not delete the selected fields and records from the existing tables. You can use make-table queries, for example, to create backup copies of tables or to create customized tables for others to use. The new table reflects data at a point in time; future changes made to the underlying tables will not be reflected in the new table. You need to run the make-table query periodically if you want the newly created table to contain current data.

An **append query** adds records from an existing table or query to the end of another table. For an append query, you choose the fields you want to append from one or more tables or queries; the selected data remains in the original tables. Usually you append records to history tables. A **history table** contains data that is no longer needed for current processing but that you might need to reference in the future. Tables containing data about cleared bank checks, former employees, inactive customers, and obsolete products are examples of history tables. Because the records you append to a history table are no longer needed for current processing, you can delete the records from the original table.

A **delete query** deletes a group of records from one or more tables. You choose which records you want to delete by entering selection criteria. Deleting records removes them permanently from the database. Quite often, delete queries are run after append queries have added those same records to history tables, allowing you to verify that you appended the correct records before deleting them.

An **update query** changes selected fields and records in one or more tables. You choose the fields and records you want to change by entering the selection criteria and the update rules. You can use update queries, for example, to increase the salaries of selected employee groups by a specified percent or to change the billing dates of selected customers from one value to another value.

Creating a Make-Table Query

Leonard wants to call the owners of restaurants that are some of Valle Coffee's longstanding customers to thank them for their business. He asks you to create a new table containing the CustomerName, OwnerName, and Phone fields from the Customer table records for all customers whose FirstContact date is before January 1, 1994. He wants a new table so he can modify it for notes that he will take when he calls the restaurant owners.

You can create the new table for Leonard by using a make-table query that modifies the Top Customers query already contained in the FineFood database. (The Top Customers query displays a record if the FirstContact field value is less than 1/1/1994 or if the InvoiceAmt field value is greater than 2000.) When you use a make-table query, you create a new table. The records in the new table are based on the records in the query's underlying tables. The fields in the new table have the data type and field size of the fields in the query's underlying tables. The new table does not preserve the primary key designation or field properties such as format or lookup properties.

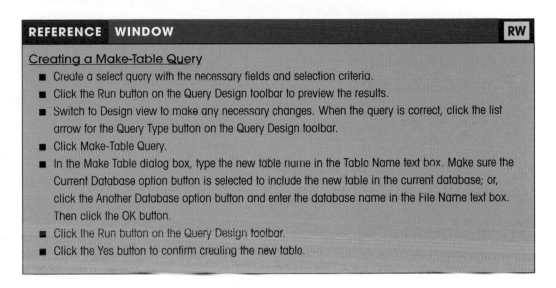

REFERENCE   WINDOW   RW

Creating a Make-Table Query

- Create a select query with the necessary fields and selection criteria.
- Click the Run button on the Query Design toolbar to preview the results.
- Switch to Design view to make any necessary changes. When the query is correct, click the list arrow for the Query Type button on the Query Design toolbar.
- Click Make-Table Query.
- In the Make Table dialog box, type the new table name in the Table Name text box. Make sure the Current Database option button is selected to include the new table in the current database; or, click the Another Database option button and enter the database name in the File Name text box. Then click the OK button.
- Click the Run button on the Query Design toolbar.
- Click the Yes button to confirm creating the new table.

Now you can create the new table using a make-table query. You'll base the make-table query on the Top Customers query to provide the information Leonard wants in the new table.

To open the Top Customers query in Design view:

1. Make sure that Access is running, that the **FineFood** database from the Tutorial folder on your Data Disk is open, and that Queries is selected in the Objects bar of the Database window.

2. Right-click **Top Customers**, and then click **Design View** on the shortcut menu. Access opens the Top Customers query in Design view. See Figure 8-11.

| Figure 8-11 | TOP CUSTOMERS QUERY IN DESIGN VIEW |

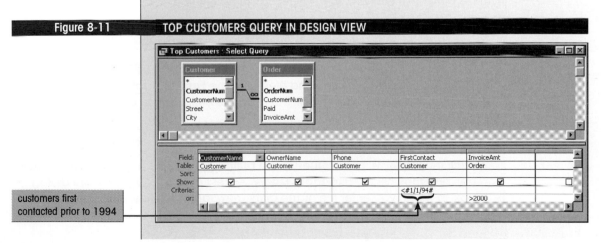

customers first contacted prior to 1994

The Top Customers query contains the fields that Leonard wants from the Customer table. However, he does not need the InvoiceAmt field, which comes from the Order table. You will delete the Order table from the query design so that no fields from that table will appear in the query results.

To remove the Order table from the query design and run the query:

1. Right-click the **Order** table field list, and then click **Remove Table** on the short-cut menu. The Order table field list is removed from the Query window and the InvoiceAmt field is removed from the design grid. See Figure 8-12.

Figure 8-12	MODIFIED QUERY DESIGN

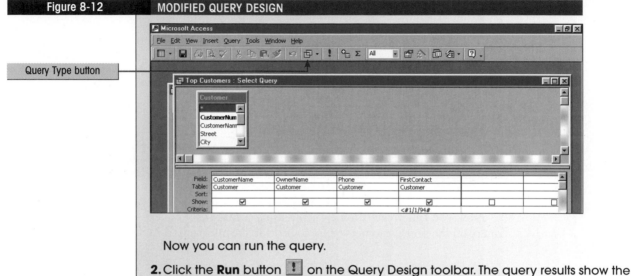

Now you can run the query.

2. Click the **Run** button [!] on the Query Design toolbar. The query results show the CustomerName, OwnerName, Phone, and FirstContact fields for customers whose FirstContact field value is before January 1, 1994.

You can verify that the query is correct because the FirstContact field values are displayed. The FirstContact field is not necessary in the new table, so you will exclude this field from the final query design. Then you can change the query to a make-table query.

To delete the field and change the query type:

1. Click the **View** button for Design view [img] on the Query Datasheet toolbar to switch back to Design view, and then click the **FirstContact Show** check box to remove the check mark from it. The new table will contain only fields with checked Show boxes.

   You are now ready to change the query to a make-table query.

2. Click the list arrow for the **Query Type** button [img] on the Query Datasheet tool-bar, and then click **Make-Table Query**. Access opens the Make Table dialog box, in which you enter the name of the new table. See Figure 8-13.

Figure 8-13	MAKE TABLE DIALOG BOX

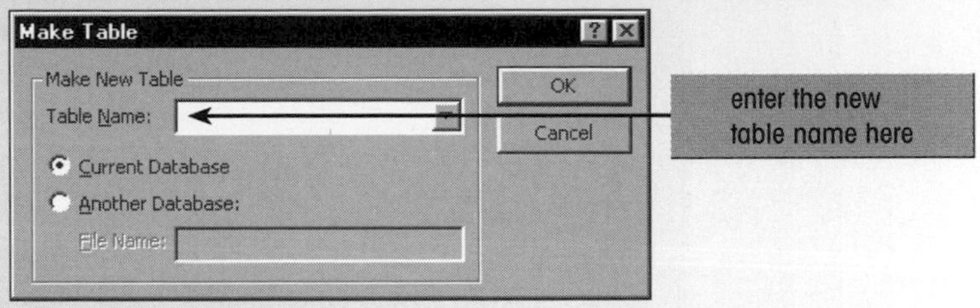

enter the new
table name here

3. In the Table Name text box, type **Special Customers**, make sure the Current Database option button is selected so that the new table will be included in the FineFood database, and then press the **Enter** key.

Now that you have created and tested the query, you can run it to create the Special Customers table. After you run the query, you can save it, and then you can view the new table.

To run and save the make-table query, and then view the Special Customers table:

1. Click the **Run** button [!] on the Query Design toolbar. Access opens a dialog box indicating that you are about to paste 10 new rows into a new table. Because you are running an action query, which alters the contents of the database, Access gives you the opportunity to cancel the operation, if necessary, or to confirm it.

2. Click the **Yes** button. Access closes the dialog box, runs the make-table query to create the Special Customers table, and then displays the Query window in Design view.

3. Click **File** on the menu bar, and then click **Save As**. The Save As dialog box opens.

4. Type **Special Customers Make-Table** in the Save Query To text box, and then press the **Enter** key to name and save the query.

5. Click the **Close** button [X] on the Query window to close it and return to the Database window. Notice that the Special Customers Make-Table query appears in the Queries list with a special icon, indicating that it is a make-table query.

You can now open the Special Customers table to view the results of the make-table query.

6. Click **Tables** in the Objects bar of the Database window, right-click **Special Customers** in the Tables list, and then click **Open** on the shortcut menu.

7. Resize all datasheet columns to their best fit, and then click **CustomerName Meadows Restaurant** to deselect the columns. See Figure 8-14.

Figure 8-14   SPECIAL CUSTOMERS TABLE DATASHEET

The Special Customers table includes the CustomerName, OwnerName, and Phone fields for customers whose FirstContact field value is before January 1, 1994. Notice that the Phone field values do not contain hyphens between the third and fourth digits or between the sixth and seventh digits. The hyphens were part of the Input Mask property for the Phone field in the Customer table; these hyphens were not preserved by the make-table query.

8. Click the **Save** button 🖫 on the Table Datasheet toolbar to save the table design changes, and then click ❌ on the Table window to close it and return to the Database window.

Leonard can now use the Special Customers table records when he contacts the customers. He can make changes to the design of the Special Customers table for his own needs without affecting the Customer table in the FineFood database.

Creating an Append Query

Leonard has decided to expand the list of customers that he will call. He wants to add to the Special Customers table the CustomerName, OwnerName, and Phone fields for all customers who were first contacted in 1994. He asks you to add these new records. You could make this change by modifying the selection criterion in the Special Customers Make-Table query to select customers with FirstContact field values earlier than 1/1/95. If you ran this modified query, however, you would overwrite the existing Special Customers table with a new table. If Leonard had made any changes to the existing Special Customers records, his changes would also be overwritten.

Instead, you will modify the Special Customers Make-Table query to select only those customers with FirstContact dates in 1994, and change the query to an append query. For the selection criterion, you will use the Between comparison operator. The **Between comparison operator** selects records whose field values fit within a range of values. For example, the criterion *Between #1/1/94# And #12/31/94#* selects records with dates between January 1, 1994 and December 31, 1994.

When you run this new query, the selected records will be appended to the records in the existing Special Customers table.

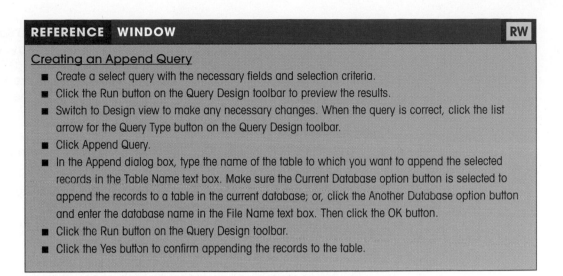

REFERENCE WINDOW   **RW**

Creating an Append Query

- Create a select query with the necessary fields and selection criteria.
- Click the Run button on the Query Design toolbar to preview the results.
- Switch to Design view to make any necessary changes. When the query is correct, click the list arrow for the Query Type button on the Query Design toolbar.
- Click Append Query.
- In the Append dialog box, type the name of the table to which you want to append the selected records in the Table Name text box. Make sure the Current Database option button is selected to append the records to a table in the current database; or, click the Another Database option button and enter the database name in the File Name text box. Then click the OK button.
- Click the Run button on the Query Design toolbar.
- Click the Yes button to confirm appending the records to the table.

You can now modify the Special Customers Make-Table query to create the append query you'll use to include the additional customer data Leonard wants in the Special Customers table.

To create the append query:

1. Click **Queries** in the Objects bar of the Database window, right-click **Special Customers Make-Table**, and then click **Design View** on the shortcut menu to open the query in Design view.

2. Right-click the **FirstContact Criteria** text box, and then click **Cut** on the shortcut menu.

3. In the same Criteria text box, type **Between #1/1/94# And #12/31/94#**. This condition means that the query will select any record with a FirstContact field value between January 1, 1994 and December 31, 1994, inclusive. See Figure 8-15. Notice that only the last part of the criterion is visible.

Figure 8-15	CHANGING THE SELECTION CRITERION

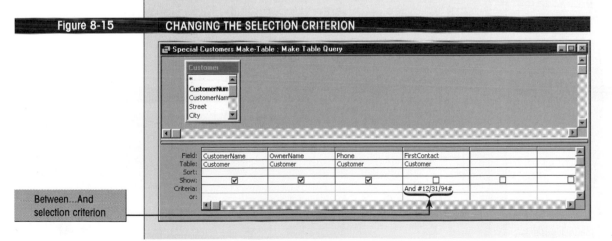

Between...And selection criterion

Before you can run the query to append the records to the Special Customers table, you have to change it to an append query. It is always a good idea to test an action query before you run it, so you will first change the query to a select query and run it to make sure the correct records are selected. Then you will change it to an append query and run it to append the new records to the Special Customers table.

4. Click the **FirstContact Show** check box to select it. You need to include the FirstContact field values in the query results so that you can verify that the correct records are selected.

5. Click the list arrow for the **Query Type** button ⊞! on the Query Design toolbar, and then click **Select Query**.

6. Click the **Run** button ! on the Query Design toolbar. Access runs the query and displays the results. See Figure 8-16.

Figure 8-16	1994 RECORDS SELECTED

Special Customers Make-Table : Select Query

CustomerName	OwnerName	Phone	FirstContact
Bentham's Riverfront Restaurant	Mr. Joe Markovicz	517/792-8040	05/18/1994
Sullivan's Restaurant & Lounge	Ms. Dawn Parker	616/575-6731	05/19/1994
Wagon Train Restaurant	Mr. Carl Seaver	517/111-5545	05/25/1994

The query shows the three records with a FirstContact field value in 1994. These are the additional records you will append to the Special Customers table. Now that the results show that the query is correct, you can remove the FirstContact field from the results, because you don't want to include it in the append query.

7. Click the **View** button for Design view ⊠ on the Query Datasheet toolbar, and then click the **FirstContact Show** check box to remove the check mark from it. You can now change the query to an append query.

8. Click the list arrow for the **Query Type** button ⊞ on the Query Design toolbar, and then click **Append Query**. Access opens the Append dialog box, in which you enter the name of the table to which you want to append the data.

9. Make sure Special Customers appears in the Table Name text box and that the Current Database option button is selected, and then click the **OK** button. Access replaces the Show row with the Append To row between the Sort and Criteria rows in the design grid. See Figure 8-17.

Figure 8-17	QUERY WINDOW FOR THE APPEND QUERY

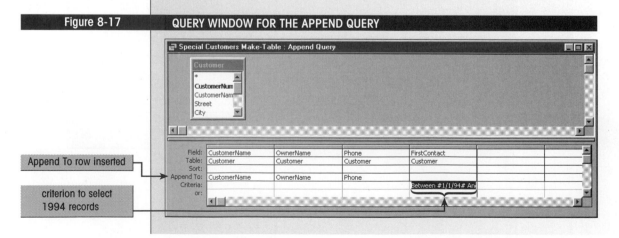

Append To row inserted

criterion to select 1994 records

The Append To row in the design grid identifies the fields that will be appended to the designated table. The CustomerName, OwnerName, and Phone fields are selected to be appended to the Special Customers table, which already contains these three fields for customers with a FirstContact date before January 1, 1994.

You can now run and then save the append query.

To run and save the append query:

1. Click the **Run** button 🔘 on the Query Design toolbar. Access opens a dialog box warning you about the upcoming append operation.

2. Click the **Yes** button to acknowledge the warning. Access closes the dialog box, runs the append query to add the three records to the Special Customers table, and displays the Query window in Design view.

3. Click **File** on the menu bar, and then click **Save As**. The Save As dialog box opens.

4. Type **Special Customers Append** in the Save Query To text box, and then press the **Enter** key. Access saves the query.

5. Click the **Close** button 🅇 on the Query window to close it and return to the Database window. Notice that the Special Customers Append query appears in the Queries list with a special icon indicating that it is an append query.

   Next you'll open the Special Customers table to make sure that the three records were appended to the table.

6. Click **Tables** in the Objects bar of the Database window, right-click **Special Customers** in the Tables list, and then click **Open** on the shortcut menu.

   The new records have been added to the Special Customers table. Because the Special Customers table does not have a primary key, the new records appear at the end of the table. You could arrange the records in a different order by sorting the records using the Sort Ascending or Sort Descending button on the Table Datasheet toolbar.

7. Click 🅇 on the Table window to close it and return to the Database window.

Creating a Delete Query

Leonard has contacted all the customers in the Special Customers table who have phone numbers in the 313 and 517 area codes. He asks you to delete these records from the Special Customers table so that the table contains only records of customers he has not yet contacted. You can either delete the table records individually or create a delete query to remove them.

REFERENCE	WINDOW	RW

Creating a Delete Query
- Create a select query with the necessary fields and selection criteria.
- Click the Run button on the Query Design toolbar to preview the results.
- Switch to Design view to make any necessary changes. When the query is correct, click the list arrow for the Query Type button on the Query Design toolbar.
- Click Delete Query. Access replaces the Show and Sort rows in the design grid with the Delete row.
- Click the Run button on the Query Design toolbar.
- Click the Yes button to confirm deleting the records.

You'll create a delete query to delete the records of all the customers in the Special Customers table who have phone numbers in the 313 and 517 area codes. First, you'll create a select query to choose the correct records based on the area code criteria. Then you'll test the select query and change it to a delete query.

To create the delete query:

1. Click **Queries** in the Objects bar of the Database window, and then click the **New** button to open the New Query dialog box. Make sure that Design View is selected, and then click the **OK** button. The Show Table dialog box opens on top of the Query window in Design view.

2. Double-click **Special Customers** to add the Special Customers field list to the Query window, and then click the **Close** button to close the Show Table dialog box.

3. Double-click the title bar of the Special Customers field list to select all the fields in the table, and then drag the pointer from the highlighted area of the field list to the design grid's first column Field text box. Release the mouse button. Access adds all the fields to the design grid.

4. Click the **Phone Criteria** text box, type **Like "313*"**, press the ↓ key, and then type **Like "517*"**. Access will select a record only if the Phone field value starts with either 313 or 517.

5. Click the **Run** button [!] on the Query Design toolbar. The query results display five records, each one with either a 313 or 517 area code. The select query is correct. See Figure 8-18.

Figure 8-18	FIVE RECORDS TO BE DELETED

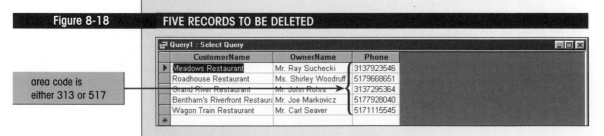

area code is either 313 or 517

TROUBLE? If your query did not select the correct five records, click the View button for Design view [图] on the Query Datasheet toolbar, correct the selection criteria as necessary, and then click the Run button [!] on the Query Design toolbar.

Now that you have verified that the correct records are selected, you can change the query to a delete query.

6. Click the **View** button for Design view [icon] on the Query Datasheet toolbar to switch back to Design view, click the list arrow for the **Query Type** button [icon] on the Query Design toolbar, and then click **Delete Query**. In the design grid, Access replaces the Sort and Show rows with the Delete row. See Figure 8-19.

Figure 8-19	DESIGN VIEW FOR THE DELETE QUERY

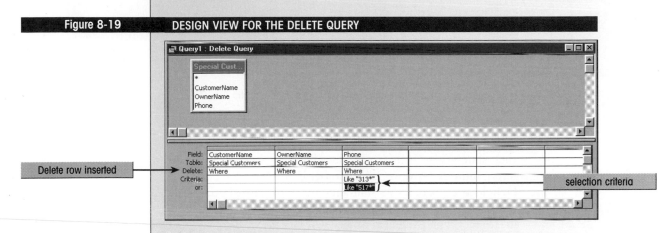

Delete row inserted

selection criteria

Now you can run the query, and then view the results in the Special Customers table.

To run the delete query, and then view the results:

1. Click the **Run** button [icon] on the Query Design toolbar. Access opens a dialog box warning you about the upcoming delete operation.

2. Click the **Yes** button to close the dialog box and run the delete query. Access deletes the five records in the Special Customers table and continues to display the Query window in Design view. Because this query needs to be run only once, you don't have to save it.

3. Click the **Close** button [icon] on the Query window, and then click the **No** button when Access asks if you want to save the query changes.

   You can now open the Special Customers table to verify that the records have been deleted.

4. Click **Tables** in the Objects bar of the Database window, right-click **Special Customers** in the Tables list, and then click **Open**. Access opens the Special Customers table in Datasheet view. Notice that the table now includes only eight records; five records were correctly deleted. See Figure 8-20.

| Figure 8-20 | SPECIAL CUSTOMERS TABLE AFTER DELETING FIVE RECORDS |

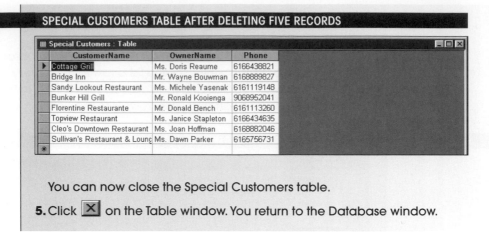

You can now close the Special Customers table.

5. Click 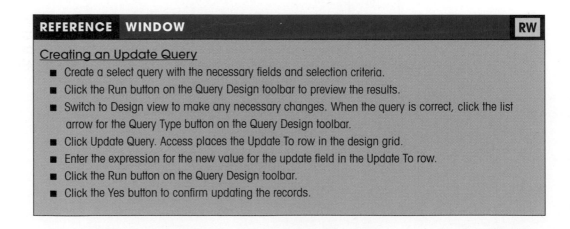 on the Table window. You return to the Database window.

Kim wants to begin holding annual appreciation dinners for Valle Coffee customers in each state where Valle Coffee does business. She has made arrangements to hold three different dinners—one in Ohio, another in Michigan, and the third in Indiana. Each dinner will be held at a customer's restaurant, and all owners of other Valle Coffee customer restaurants in the state will be invited to attend. The Ohio dinner will be held at the Cherry Creek Inn in Toledo. The Michigan dinner will be held at the Sandy Lookout Restaurant in Jenison, and the Indiana dinner will be held at the Embers Restaurant in Goshen. The owners of these restaurants (Mr. Douglas Viereck, Ms. Michele Yasenak, and Mr. Clifford Merritt) will act as contacts between Kim and the other restaurant owners in the state. They will help handle the necessary travel and accommodation arrangements for the out-of-town owners.

Kim asks you to add the new contact information to the FineFood database and then to create a new query that shows which owners will be making arrangements through Mr. Viereck, which through Ms. Yasenak, and which through Mr. Merritt. To produce this information, you'll create an update query.

Creating an Update Query

Recall that an update query changes selected fields and records in one or more tables. In this case, you need to create a new field to contain the contact information for the annual dinners, and then enter the appropriate values in this new field. You could enter the value for every record in the Customer table, but you can accomplish the same thing more quickly and with less chance of error by using an update query to enter the values at one time.

REFERENCE WINDOW | **RW**

Creating an Update Query

- Create a select query with the necessary fields and selection criteria.
- Click the Run button on the Query Design toolbar to preview the results.
- Switch to Design view to make any necessary changes. When the query is correct, click the list arrow for the Query Type button on the Query Design toolbar.
- Click Update Query. Access places the Update To row in the design grid.
- Enter the expression for the new value for the update field in the Update To row.
- Click the Run button on the Query Design toolbar.
- Click the Yes button to confirm updating the records.

First, you will add a field named Contact to the Customer table. This new field will contain either Mr. Viereck's, Ms. Yasenak's, or Mr. Merritt's CustomerNum field value to indicate that this customer is the contact person for the annual dinner being held at their restaurant.

To add the new Contact field to the Customer table:

1. Click **Tables** in the Objects bar of the Database window (if necessary), right-click **Customer**, and then click **Design View** on the shortcut menu. Access opens the Customer table in Design view.

2. If necessary, scroll down the field list until a blank row is visible.

3. Click the **Field Name** text box just below the FirstContact field, type **Contact**, press the **Tab** key twice, and then type **Annual dinner contact for this owner** in the new field's Description text box.

   Because the new field will contain CustomerNum values, which are 3 characters long, you need to change the field size for the new field to 3.

4. Press the **F6** key, and then type **3**. This completes the addition of the Contact field to the Customer table. See Figure 8-21.

Figure 8-21	CONTACT FIELD ADDED TO THE CUSTOMER TABLE

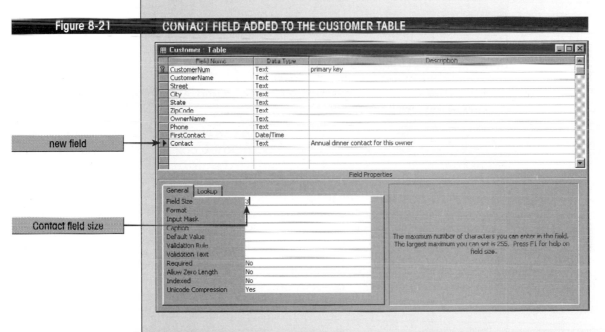

5. Click the **Save** button ▫ on the Table Design toolbar to save the changes to the table design, and then click the **Close** button ☒ on the Table window. Access saves the table structure and returns to the Database window.

Now you can create an update query to update the Contact field for the records in the Customer table. You'll change the Contact field value to 798 (CustomerNum for Embers Restaurant) for each customer in Indiana, to 129 (CustomerNum for Sandy Lookout Restaurant) for each customer in Michigan, and to 742 (CustomerNum for the Cherry Creek Inn) for each customer in Ohio. You will not enter Contact values for Embers Restaurant, Sandy Lookout Restaurant, or Cherry Creek Inn, because the owners of these three restaurants are the three contacts for the dinners.

To create the update query to enter the Contact field values:

1. Click **Queries** in the Objects bar of the Database window, and then click the **New** button to open the New Query dialog box. Make sure that Design View is selected, and then click the **OK** button. The Show Table dialog box opens on top of the Query window in Design view.

2. Double-click **Customer** in the list box to add the Customer field list to the Query window, and then click the **Close** button to close the Show Table dialog box.

   You will select the CustomerNum, State, and Contact fields for the query results. The CustomerNum field allows you to exclude the records for the three contact restaurant owners. The State field allows you to select records for customers in a particular state. The Contact field is the field you want to update.

3. In the Customer field list, double-click the **CustomerNum**, **State**, and **Contact** fields to add these fields to the design grid, scrolling down the field list as necessary.

   You can now select the records for customers in Indiana and update the Contact field value for those records to 798, the CustomerNum for Embers Restaurant.

4. Click the **State Criteria** text box, and then type **"IN"**. Access will select a record only if the State field value is IN.

5. Click the **CustomerNum Criteria** text box, and then type **Not In ("798","129","742")**. Access will not select the records for the host restaurants.

6. Click the list arrow for the **Query Type** button 🗗 on the Query Design toolbar, and then click **Update Query**. In the design grid, Access replaces the Sort and Show rows with the Update To row.

   You tell Access how you want to change a field value for the selected records by entering an expression in the field's Update To text box. An expression is a calculation resulting in a single value. You can type a simple expression directly into the Update To text box. If you need help creating a complicated expression, you can create it using Expression Builder, an Access tool that contains an expression box in which the expression is entered, buttons for common operators, and one or more lists of expression elements, such as table and field names. The expression in this case is simple, so you can type it directly in the Update To text box.

7. Click the **Contact Update To** text box, and then type **798**. This is the CustomerNum field value for Embers Restaurant, which is the host restaurant for the dinner in Indiana. See Figure 8-22.

| Figure 8-22 | UPDATING THE CONTACT FIELD |

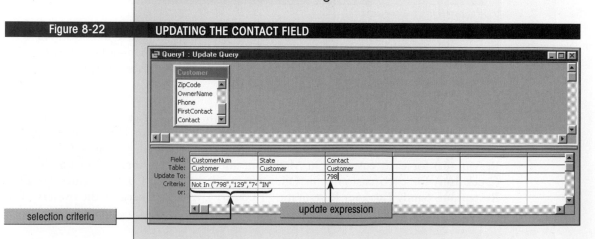

8. Click the **Run** button [!] on the Query Design toolbar. Access opens a dialog box warning you that you are about to update 5 rows.

9. Click the **Yes** button to close the dialog box and run the update query. Access updates the Contact field values for the customers in Indiana and leaves the Query window in Design view open.

Now you need to update the Contact field values for customers located in Michigan and Ohio. To do so, you'll modify the criteria for the existing update query twice.

To update the remaining Contact field values:

1. Double-click **IN** in the State Criteria text box to select it, and then type **MI**. The entry in the State Criteria text box is now "MI", and Access will select a record only if the State field value is MI.

2. Double-click **798** in the Contact Update To text box to select it, and then type **129**. This is the CustomerNum field value for Sandy Lookout Restaurant, the host restaurant for the dinner in Michigan.

3. Click the **Run** button [!] on the Query Design toolbar. Access opens a dialog box warning you that you are about to update 28 rows.

4. Click the **Yes** button to close the dialog box and run the update query. Access updates the Contact field values for the customers in Michigan and leaves the Query window in Design view open.

5. Double-click **MI** in the State Criteria text box to select it, and then type **OH**. Access will select a record only if the State field value is OH.

6. Double-click **129** in the Contact Update To text box to select it, and then type **742**. This is the CustomerNum field value for Cherry Creek Inn, the host restaurant for the dinner in Ohio.

7. Click [!] on the Query Design toolbar, and then click the **Yes** button to confirm the update of the 3 rows.

   You are finished updating the Customer table, so you can close the Query window. Because all the records have been updated, you do not need to save the query.

8. Click the **Close** button [X] on the Query window to close it, and then click the **No** button when Access asks if you want to save the query changes. Access closes the Query window and returns to the Database window.

Now you can view the Customer table to see the results of the update operations.

To view the updated Customer table:

1. Click **Tables** in the Objects bar of the Database window, right-click **Customer** in the Tables list, and then click **Open** on the shortcut menu. Access displays the Customer table in Datasheet view.

2. Scroll the datasheet to the right to see the updated Contact field. See Figure 8-23.

Figure 8-23   CUSTOMER TABLE WITH THE UPDATED CONTACT FIELD VALUES

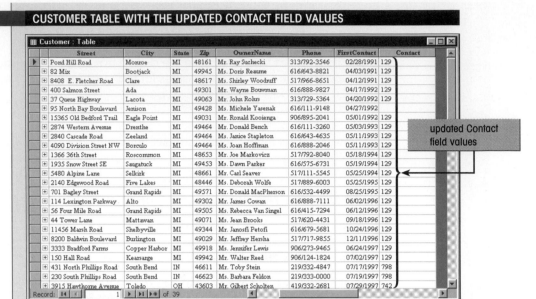

updated Contact field values

3. Scroll through the records to see the new values in the Contact field. Notice that there are no values in the Contact field for records 6, 33, and 38 because the owners of these three restaurants are the three contacts for the dinners.

4. Click the **Close** button ☒ on the Table window to close it and return to the Database window.

5. Click ☒ on the Access window title bar to close the FineFood database and to exit Access. You return to the Windows desktop.

Now that the contact numbers are in place, you can generate the query that shows the information Kim requested: which restaurant owners will contact Mr. Viereck, which will contact Ms. Yasenak, and which will contact Mr. Merritt. You will create this query in the next session.

Session 8.2 QUICK CHECK

1. What is an action query?

2. What precautions should you take before running an action query?

3. What is the difference between a make-table query and an append query?

4. What does a delete query do?

5. What does an update query do?

6. How does the design grid change when you create an update query?

7. What is Expression Builder?

In this session, you will learn about many-to-many and one-to-one relationships between tables. You will then view and create indexes, and learn about the different types of table joins.

Relationships Between Database Tables

As you learned in Tutorial 3, a **one-to-many relationship** (abbreviated as **1:M**) exists between two tables when one record in the primary table matches zero, one, or many records in the related table, and when one record in the related table matches exactly one record in the primary table. For example, Figure 8-24 shows a one-to-many relationship between the Customer and Order tables. Customer 635 has three orders, customer 104 has one order, and customer 741 has zero orders. Every order has a single matching customer.

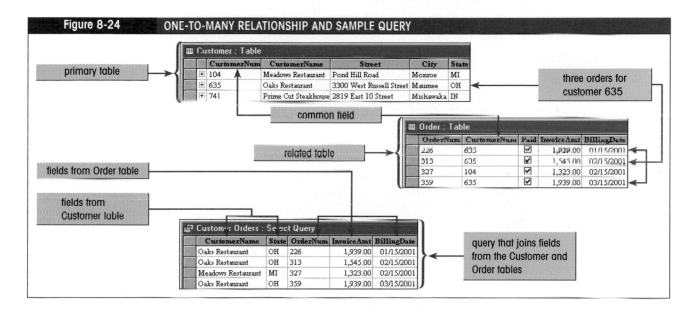

Figure 8-24   ONE-TO-MANY RELATIONSHIP AND SAMPLE QUERY

You use the common field of CustomerNum to form the one-to-many relationship between the Customer and Order tables. When you join the two tables based on CustomerNum field values, you can extract data from them as if they are one larger table. For example, you can join the Customer and Order tables to create the Customer Orders query shown in Figure 8-24. In the Customer Orders query, the CustomerName and State columns are fields from the Customer table, and the OrderNum, InvoiceAmt, and BillingDate columns are fields from the Order table.

In addition to one-to-many relationships between tables, you can also relate tables through many-to-many and one-to-one relationships.

Many-to-Many Relationships

A **many-to-many relationship** (abbreviated as **M:N**) exists between two tables when one record in the first table matches many records in the second table, and one record in the second table matches many records in the first table.

In the FineFood database, the Order table contains one record for each coffee order placed by a customer, and the Product table contains one record for each coffee product sold by Valle Coffee. Because a customer can buy many products with one order, and each product can appear in many orders, the Order and Product tables have a many-to-many relationship, as shown in Figure 8-25.

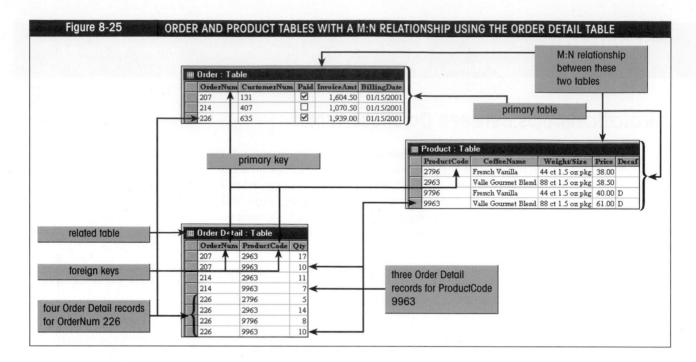

Figure 8-25   ORDER AND PRODUCT TABLES WITH A M:N RELATIONSHIP USING THE ORDER DETAIL TABLE

When you have a many-to-many relationship between two tables, you must create a third table and form one-to-many relationships between the two original tables and the new table. For instance, the Order Detail table exists because the Order and Product tables have a many-to-many relationship. Each record in the Order Detail table contains two foreign keys: the OrderNum field is a foreign key that allows you to join the Order table to the Order Detail table, and the ProductCode field is a foreign key that allows you to join the Product table to the Order Detail table. For example, the last record in the Order Detail table represents Valle Gourmet Blend, a decaffeinated coffee, for OrderNum 226. Decaffeinated Valle Gourmet Blend, which has ProductCode 9963, appears in three records in the Order Detail table. These three Order Detail records appear in three different orders for OrderNum field values of 207, 214, and 226. Also, OrderNum 226 appears in four Order Detail records, each for a different coffee product: French Vanilla, Valle Gourmet Blend, decaffeinated French Vanilla, and decaffeinated Valle Gourmet Blend. The primary key of the Order Detail table is a composite key, consisting of the combination of the OrderNum and ProductCode fields. Each pair of values in this primary key is unique.

When you join tables that have a many-to-many relationship, you can extract data from them as if they were one larger table. For example, you can join the Order, Product, and Order Detail tables to create the Order Detail Data query shown in Figure 8-26.

Figure 8-26   QUERY RESULTS PRODUCED BY JOINING TABLES HAVING A M:N RELATIONSHIP

OrderNum	ProductCode	Qty	Paid	BillingDate	CoffeeName	Price
207	2963	17	☑	01/15/2001	Valle Gourmet Blend	58.50
207	9963	10	☑	01/15/2001	Valle Gourmet Blend	61.00
214	2963	11	☐	01/15/2001	Valle Gourmet Blend	58.50
214	9963	7	☐	01/15/2001	Valle Gourmet Blend	61.00
226	2796	5	☑	01/15/2001	French Vanilla	38.00
226	2963	14	☑	01/15/2001	Valle Gourmet Blend	58.50
226	9796	8	☑	01/15/2001	French Vanilla	40.00
226	9963	10	☑	01/15/2001	Valle Gourmet Blend	61.00

fields from the Order Detail table   fields from the Order table   fields from the Product table

The OrderNum field joins the Order and Order Detail tables, and the ProductCode field joins the Product and Order Detail tables. In the Order Detail Data query, the OrderNum, ProductCode, and Qty fields are from the Order Detail table; the Paid and BillingDate fields are from the Order table; and the CoffeeName and Price fields are from the Product table. The third record in the query results shows data from the third record in the Order Detail table joined with data from the matching second record in the Order table and with data from the matching second record in the Product table.

One-to-One Relationships

A **one-to-one relationship** (abbreviated as **1:1**) exists between two tables when one record in the first table matches at most one record in the second table, and one record in the second table matches at most one record in the first table. Most relationships between tables are either one-to-many or many-to-many; the primary use for one-to-one relationships is as entity subtypes. An **entity subtype** is a table whose primary key is a foreign key to a second table and whose fields are additional fields for the second table. For example, the Customer table and the Billing Address table, which is an entity subtype, have a one-to-one relationship, as shown in Figure 8-27.

Figure 8-27	CUSTOMER AND BILLING ADDRESS TABLES WITH A 1:1 RELATIONSHIP

For most restaurant customers, the Street, City, State, and Zip fields in the Customer table identify both the restaurant's location and billing address, which is where Valle Coffee sends the customer's invoices. In a few cases, however, the billing address is different from the location address; additionally, the customer name used for billing purposes is different from the customer, or restaurant, name. There are two ways to handle these two sets of names and addresses. The first way is to add BillingName, BillingStreet, BillingCity, BillingState, and BillingZip fields to the Customer table, to store values in these fields for those customers who have a different billing name and address, and to leave these fields null for those customers who have identical location and billing names and addresses.

As shown in Figure 8-27, the second way to handle the two sets of addresses is to create the entity subtype named Billing Address. In the Billing Address table, CustomerNum, which is the primary key, is also a foreign key to the Customer table. A record appears in the Billing Address table only for those customers who have a different billing name and address.

When you join tables that have a one-to-one relationship, you can extract data from them as if they were one larger table. For example, you can join the Customer and Billing Address tables to create the Billing Address Data query shown in Figure 8-28.

| Figure 8-28 | QUERY RESULTS PRODUCED BY JOINING TABLES THAT HAVE A 1:1 RELATIONSHIP |

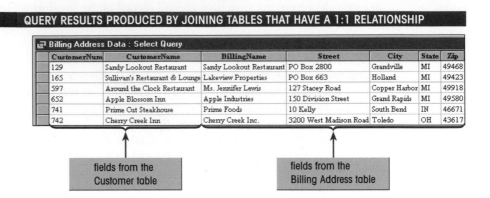

The CustomerNum field joins the Customer and Billing Address tables. In the query, the CustomerNum and CustomerName fields are from the Customer table, and the BillingName, Street, City, State, and Zip fields are from the Billing Address table. Only the six restaurants that have records in the Billing Address table—because they have different billing addresses—appear in the Billing Address Data query results.

Next, you'll define a many-to-many relationship between the Order and Product tables, and a one-to-one relationship between the Customer and Billing Address tables.

Defining M:N and 1:1 Relationships Between Tables

Similarly to how you defined one-to-many relationships in Tutorial 3, you define many-to-many and one-to-one relationships in the Relationships window. First, you'll open the Relationships window and define the many-to-many relationship between the Order and Product tables. You'll define a one-to-many relationship between the Order and Order Detail tables, with Order as the primary table and Order Detail as the related table, and with OrderNum as the common field (the primary key in the Order table and a foreign key in the Order Detail table). Next, you'll define a one-to-many relationship between the Product and Order Detail tables, with Product as the primary table and Order Detail as the related table, and with ProductCode as the common field (the primary key in the Product table and a foreign key in the Order Detail table.)

To define a many-to-many relationship between the Order and Product tables:

1. Make sure that Access is running, that the **FineFood** database from the Tutorial folder on your Data Disk is open, and that Tables is selected in the Objects bar of the Database window.

2. Click the **Relationships** button on the Database toolbar to open the Relationships window.

The Order and Order Detail tables, along with the Customer_1 and Customer tables, already appear in the Relationships window, so you need to add only the Product table to the Relationships window.

3. Click the **Show Table** button ![Show Table icon] on the Relationship toolbar to open the Show Table dialog box, double-click **Product** to add the Product table to the Relationships window, and then click the **Close** button in the Show Table dialog box to close the dialog box and reveal the entire Relationships window.

4. Drag the Product table list title bar to the right until the Product table list is positioned as shown in Figure 8-29.

Figure 8-29	RELATIONSHIPS WINDOW

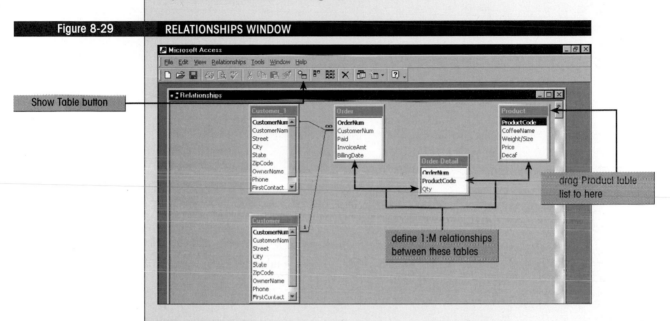

First, you'll define the one-to-many relationship between the Order and Order Detail tables.

5. Click **OrderNum** in the Order table list, and drag it to **OrderNum** in the Order Detail table list. When you release the mouse button, the Edit Relationships dialog box opens.

The primary table, related table, and common field appear at the top of the dialog box. The type of relationship, one-to-many, appears at the bottom of the dialog box. When you click the Enforce Referential Integrity check box, the two cascade options become available. If you select the Cascade Update Related Fields option, Access will change the appropriate foreign key values in the related table when you change a primary key value in the primary table. If you select the Cascade Delete Related Records option, when you delete a record in the primary table, Access will delete all records in the related table that have a matching foreign key value.

6. Click the **Enforce Referential Integrity** check box, click the **Cascade Update Related Fields** check box, and then click the **Cascade Delete Related Records** check box. You have now selected all the necessary relationship options.

7. Click the **Create** button to define the one-to-many relationship between the two tables and close the dialog box. The completed relationship appears in the Relationships window.

8. Repeat Steps 5 through 7 to define the one-to-many relationship between the primary Product table and the related Order Detail table, using ProductCode as the common field. See Figure 8-30.

Figure 8-30   M:N RELATIONSHIP DEFINED BETWEEN THE ORDER AND PRODUCT TABLES

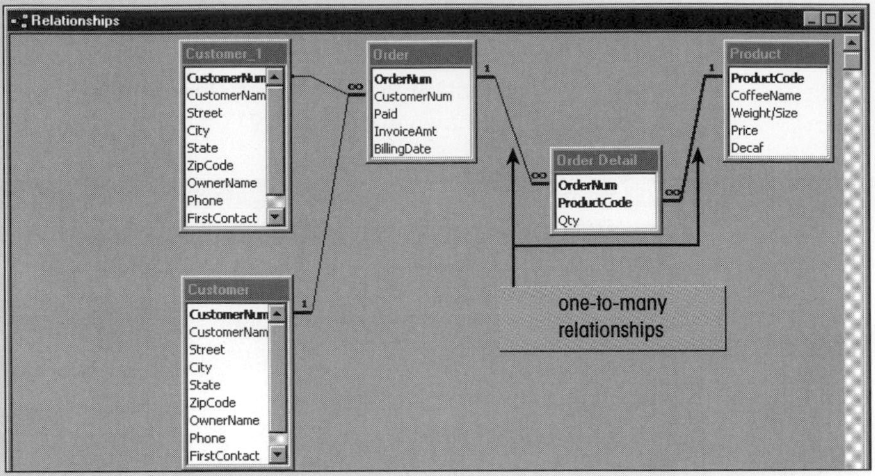

9. Click the **Save** button ⊞ on the Relationship toolbar to save the layout in the Relationships window.

Now you can add the Billing Address table to the Relationships window and then define a one-to-one relationship between the Customer and Billing Address tables.

To define a one-to-one relationship between the Customer and Billing Address tables:

1. Click the **Show Table** button ⊞ on the Relationship toolbar to open the Show Table dialog box, double-click **Billing Address** to add the Billing Address table to the Relationships window, and then click the **Close** button in the Show Table dialog box to close the dialog box and reveal the entire Relationships window.

2. Drag the Billing Address table list title bar down and to the left until the Billing Address table list is positioned to the left of the Customer table list (not the Customer_1 table list) and near the left edge of the Relationships window.

   Now you can define the one-to-one relationship between the primary Customer table and the related Billing Address table.

3. Click **CustomerNum** in the Customer table list, and drag it to **CustomerNum** in the Billing Address table list. When you release the mouse button, the Edit Relationships dialog box opens.

   The primary table, related table, and common field appear at the top of the dialog box. The type of relationship, one-to-one, appears at the bottom of the dialog box.

4. Click the **Enforce Referential Integrity** check box, click the **Cascade Update Related Fields** check box, and then click the **Cascade Delete Related Records** check box. You have now selected all the necessary relationship options.

5. Click the **Create** button to define the one-to-one relationship between the two tables and close the dialog box. The completed relationship appears in the Relationships window. Both sides of the relationship have the digit 1 at their ends to indicate a one-to-one relationship between the two tables. See Figure 8-31.

Figure 8-31	1:1 RELATIONSHIP DEFINED BETWEEN THE CUSTOMER AND BILLING ADDRESS TABLES

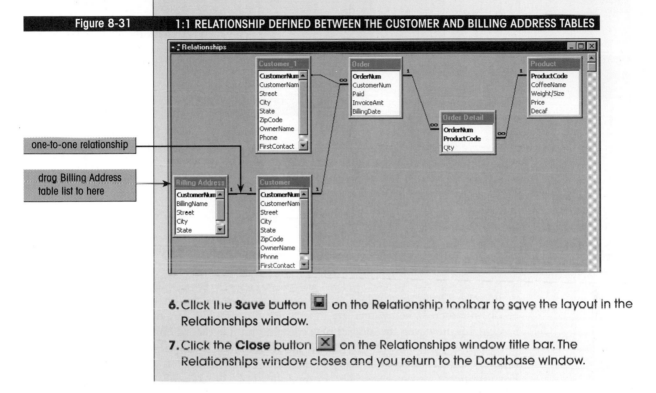

6. Click the **Save** button 🖫 on the Relationship toolbar to save the layout in the Relationships window.

7. Click the **Close** button ⊠ on the Relationships window title bar. The Relationships window closes and you return to the Database window.

Barbara asks you if her staff's work will take longer as the FineFood database grows in size with the addition of more table records. Specifically, she wants to know if queries will take longer to run. You tell her that using indexes will help make her queries run faster.

Using Indexes for Table Fields

Suppose you need to find all the pages in a book that discuss a specific topic. The fastest, most accurate way to perform your search is to look up the topic in the book's index. In a similar fashion, you can create and use indexes to locate all the records in a table that contain specific values for one or more fields. An **index** is a list that relates field values to the records that contain those field values.

Access automatically creates and maintains an index for a table's primary key. (Access also automatically creates and maintains indexes for fields that have been defined explicitly as foreign keys in the Relationships window.) For example, the Order table in the FineFood database includes an index for the OrderNum field, which is the table's primary key. Conceptually, as shown in Figure 8-32, Access identifies each record in the Order table by its record number, and the OrderNum index has two columns. The first column contains an OrderNum value, and the second column contains the number of the record for that OrderNum value. For instance, OrderNum 215 in the index has a record number value of 5, and record number 5 in the Order table contains the data for OrderNum 215.

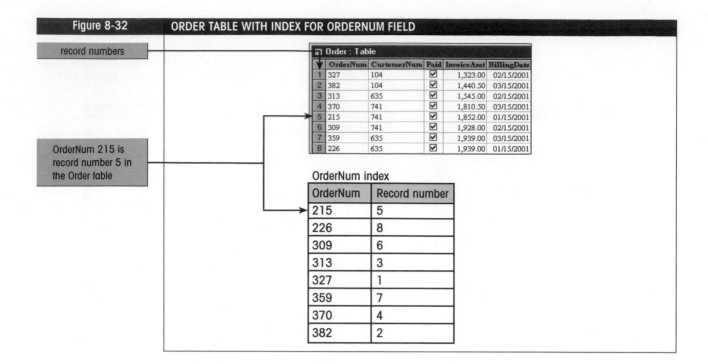

Figure 8-32   ORDER TABLE WITH INDEX FOR ORDERNUM FIELD

Because OrderNum values are unique, each row in the OrderNum index has a single record number. When you create indexes for non-primary-key fields or have an index for a foreign key, however, the indexes may contain multiple record numbers in a row. Figure 8-33 illustrates a CustomerNum index for the Order table. Because a customer can place many orders, each CustomerNum entry in the index can be associated with many record numbers. For instance, CustomerNum 635 in the index has record number values of 3, 7, and 8, and record numbers 3, 7, and 8 in the Order table contain the order data for CustomerNum 635.

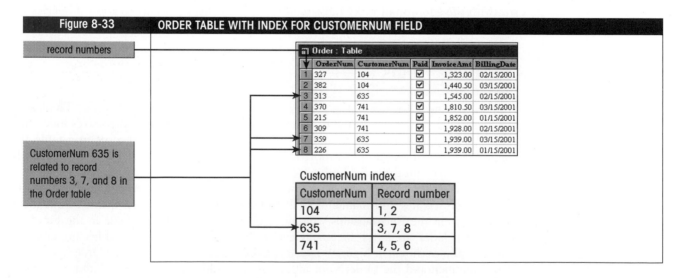

Figure 8-33   ORDER TABLE WITH INDEX FOR CUSTOMERNUM FIELD

If you have an index for the CustomerNum field in the Order table, queries that use CustomerNum as a sort field or as a selection criterion will run faster. This advantage of using an index must be weighed against two disadvantages: the index adds disk storage requirements to the database, and it takes time to update the index as you add and delete records. Except for primary key indexes, you can add and delete indexes at any time. Thus, you can add an index if you believe searching and querying would be faster as the number of records in the database grows. You also can delete an existing index that appears to be unnecessary.

Viewing Existing Indexes

You can view the existing indexes for a table by opening the table in Design view.

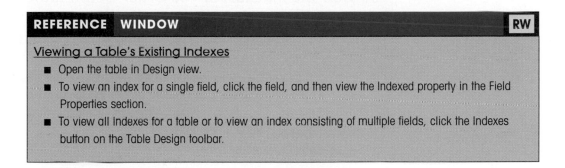

REFERENCE WINDOW   **RW**

Viewing a Table's Existing Indexes
- Open the table in Design view.
- To view an index for a single field, click the field, and then view the Indexed property in the Field Properties section.
- To view all indexes for a table or to view an index consisting of multiple fields, click the Indexes button on the Table Design toolbar.

Barbara wants to view the indexes for the Order table.

To view the indexes for the Order table:

1. If necessary, click the **Tables** object in the Objects bar of the Database window.

2. Right-click **Order** in the Tables list, and then click **Design View** on the shortcut menu. The Order table opens in Design view with the OrderNum field selected.

3. Click the **Indexes** button [icon] on the Table Design toolbar. The Indexes window opens. See Figure 8-34.

Figure 8-34   INDEXES FOR THE ORDER TABLE

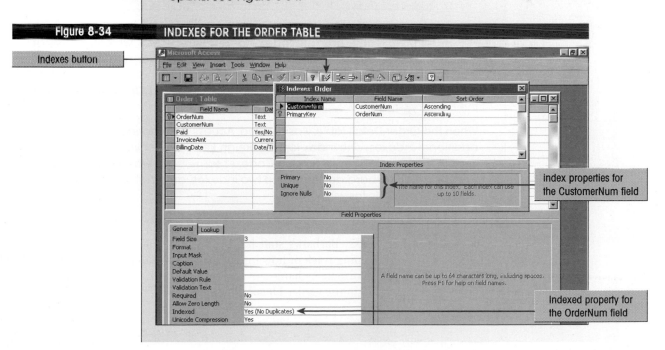

Indexes button

index properties for the CustomerNum field

Indexed property for the OrderNum field

Two indexes appear in the Indexes window: one for the CustomerNum field, which is a foreign key, and one for the OrderNum field, which is the table's primary key. For the CustomerNum index, values in the index do not need to be unique, and all records (even those with null CustomerNum values) are included in the index. For the primary key OrderNum index, values in the index must be unique, and all records are included in the index. Additionally, the Indexed property value of "Yes (No Duplicates)" for the OrderNum field specifies the use of an index with no duplicate values.

Next, Barbara wants to view the indexes for the Order Detail table.

To view the indexes for the Order Detail table:

1. Click the **Close** button ⊠ on the Indexes window title bar, and then click ⊠ on the Table window title bar. Both windows close and you return to the Database window.

2. Right-click **Order Detail** in the Tables list, and then click **Design View** on the shortcut menu. The Order Detail table opens in Design view with the OrderNum field selected.

3. Click the **Indexes** button 📝 on the Table Design toolbar. The Indexes window opens. See Figure 8-35.

| Figure 8-35 | INDEXES WINDOW FOR THE ORDER DETAIL TABLE |

PrimaryKey index consists of these two fields

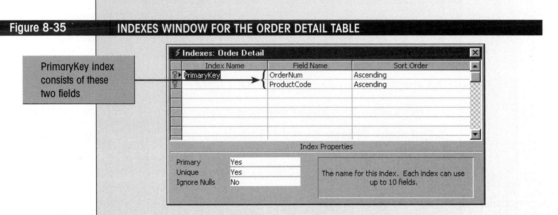

The Order Detail table has one index, named PrimaryKey, which consists of the table's composite key—the combination of the OrderNum and ProductCode fields. Because ProductCode in the second row does not have an Index Name property value, both ProductCode and OrderNum comprise the PrimaryKey index.

When the Order Detail table was created, Access automatically created two additional indexes: one index for the foreign key of OrderNum, and a second index for the foreign key of ProductCode. At some point when the database was still small, Barbara deleted these two indexes, and that's why they no longer appear in the Indexes window.

Over the past few weeks, Barbara's staff has been monitoring the performance of the FineFood database by keeping track of how long it takes to run queries. She wants her staff to let her know if the performance changes over the next few days after an index is created for the ProductCode field in the Order Detail table.

Creating an Index

You can create an index for a single field in the Indexes window or by setting its Indexed property in Design view. For a multiple-field index, however, you must create the index in the Indexes window.

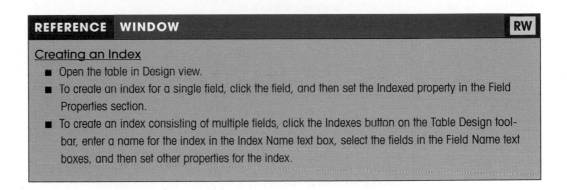

Now, you'll create an index for the ProductCode field in the Order Detail table by setting the field's Indexed property.

To create an index for the ProductCode field:

1. Click the Table window title bar to make it the active window.

2. Click the **ProductCode Field Name** text box to make it the current field.

3. Click the right side of the **Indexed** property, and then click **Yes (Duplicates OK)**. An index for the ProductCode field is created with duplicate values allowed. Setting the Indexed property automatically created the ProductCode index in the Indexes window. See Figure 8-36.

Figure 8-36	AFTER CREATING THE PRODUCTCODE INDEX

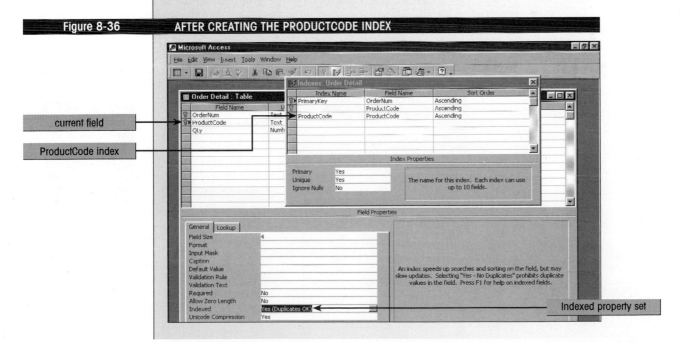

4. Click the **Close** button ☒ on the Indexes window title bar to close the Indexes window.

Now you'll save your changes to the table design and close the Table window.

5. Click the **Save** button 🖫 on the Table Design toolbar, and then click ☒ on the Table window title bar.

Next, you'll generate the query that shows the information Kim requested in the previous session: which restaurant owners will contact Mr. Viereck, which will contact Ms. Yasenak, and which will contact Mr. Merritt about the annual customer appreciation dinners.

Joining Tables

You need to create a query to display the new contact relationships in the Customer table. To do so, you'll create a special join using the Customer table. The design of the FineFood database includes a relationship between the Customer and Order tables using CustomerNum as the common field, which allows you to join the two tables to create a query based on data from both tables. The type of join you have used so far is an inner join. Two other types of joins are the left outer join and the right outer join.

An **inner join** is a join in which Access selects records from two tables only when the records have the same value in the common field that links the tables. For example, in a database containing a table of student information and a table of class information, an inner join would show all students that have a matching class record and all classes that have a matching student record. In the FineFood database, CustomerNum is the common field for the Customer and Order tables. As shown in Figure 8-37, the results of a query based on an inner join of these two tables include only those records that have a matching CustomerNum value. The record in the Customer table with CustomerNum 798 is not included in the query results because it fails to match a record with the same CustomerNum value in the Order table. The inner join is the join you ordinarily use whenever you perform a query from more than one table; it is the default join you have used to this point. (The Order record with OrderNum 382 has been added to illustrate the difference in the various types of joins.)

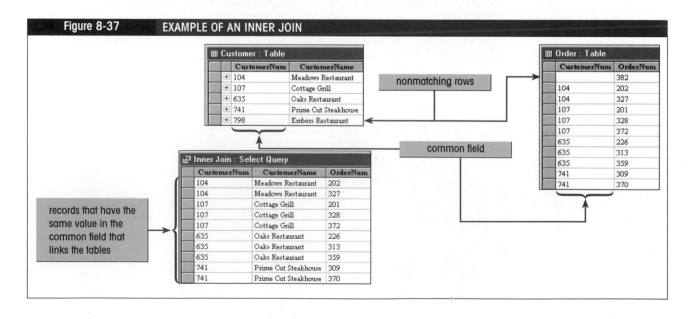

Figure 8-37   EXAMPLE OF AN INNER JOIN

A **left outer join** is a join in which Access selects all records from the first, or left, table and only those records from the second table that have matching common field values. For example, in a database containing a student table and a class table, a left outer join would show all students whether or not the students are enrolled in a class. In the FineFood database, you would use this kind of join if you wanted to see all records from the Customer table and all matching records from the Order table. Figure 8-38 shows a left outer join for the Customer and Order tables. All records from the Customer table, which is the left table, appear in the query results. Notice that the CustomerNum 798 record appears even though it does not match a record in the Order table. The OrderNum 382 record in the Order table does not appear, however, because it does not match a record in the Customer table.

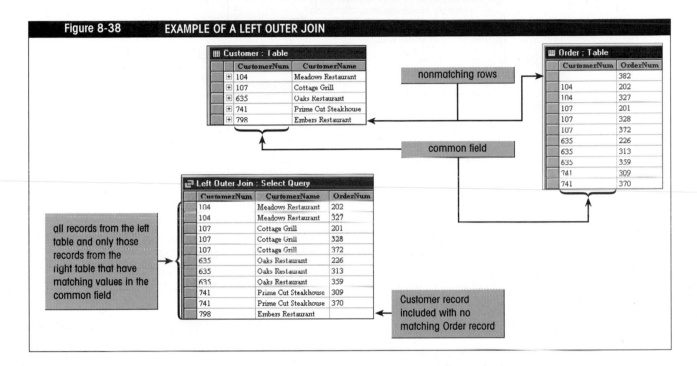

Figure 8-38   EXAMPLE OF A LEFT OUTER JOIN

A **right outer join** is a join in which Access selects all records from the second, or right, table and only those records from the first table that have matching common field values. For example, in a database containing a student table and a class table, a right outer join would show all classes whether or not there are any students enrolled in them. In the FineFood database, you would use this kind of join if you wanted to see all records from the Order table and all matching records from the Customer table. Figure 8-39 shows a right outer join for the Customer and Order tables. All records from the Order table, which is the right table, appear in the query results. The OrderNum 382 record appears even though it does not match a record in the Customer table. The CustomerNum 798 record in the Customer table does not appear, however, because it does not match a record in the Order table.

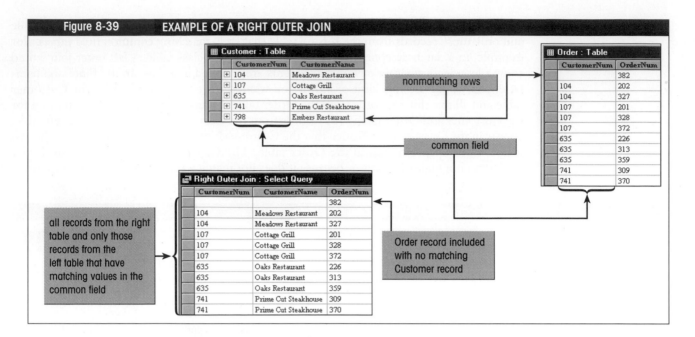

Figure 8-39   EXAMPLE OF A RIGHT OUTER JOIN

A table can also be joined with itself; this join is called a **self-join**. A self-join can be either an inner or outer join. For example, you would use this kind of join if you wanted to see records from the Customer table together with information about the customers' contacts for the annual dinner. Figure 8-40 shows a self-join for the Customer table. In this case, the self-join is an inner join because records appear in the query results only if the Contact field value matches a CustomerNum field value. To create this self-join, you would add two copies of the Customer table to the Query window in Design view, and then link the Contact field of one Customer table to the CustomerNum field of the other Customer table.

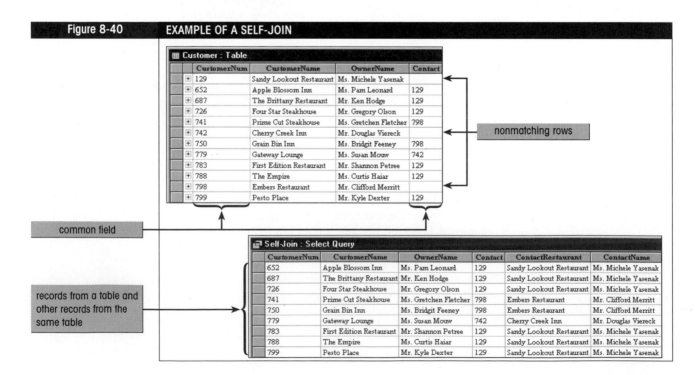

Figure 8-40   EXAMPLE OF A SELF-JOIN

In Figure 8-40, the query results show the record for each customer in the Customer table and the contact information for that customer. The contact information also comes from the Customer table through the Contact field.

To produce the information Kim requested, indicating which restaurant owners will contact which dinner hosts, you need to create a self-join.

Creating a Self-Join

You need to create a query to display the new contact relationships in the Customer table. This query requires a self-join. To create the self-join, you need to add two copies of the Customer field list to the Query window, and then add a join line from the CustomerNum field in one field list to the Contact field in the other. The Contact field is a foreign key that matches the primary key field CustomerNum. You can then create a query that can display Customer information from one table and Contact information from the other table.

REFERENCE WINDOW   **RW**

Creating a Self-Join

- In the Database window, click Queries in the Objects bar to display the Queries list, and then click the New button.
- Click Design View and then click the OK button.
- Click the table for the self-join, and then click the Add button. Click the table for the self-join again, and then click the Add button. Click the Close button.
- Click and drag a field from one field list to the related field in the other field list.
- Right-click the join line between the two tables, and then click Join Properties to open the Join Properties dialog box.
- Click the option button for an inner join, a left outer join, or a right outer join, and then click the OK button.
- Select the fields and define the selection criteria and sort options for the query.

Now you'll create the self-join query to determine which restaurant owners will contact which hosts for the annual dinner.

To create the self-join query:

1. Click **Queries** in the Objects bar of the Database window to display the list of queries, and then click the **New** button to open the New Query dialog box. Make sure that Design View is selected, and then click the **OK** button. The Show Table dialog box opens on top of the Query window in Design view.

2. Click **Customer** and then click the **Add** button.

3. Click the **Add** button again to add a second copy of the Customer field list, and then click the **Close** button. Access identifies the left field list as Customer and the right field list as Customer_1 to distinguish the two copies of the table.

   You will now create a join between the two copies of the Customer table by linking the Contact field in the Customer field list to the CustomerNum field in the Customer_1 field list. The Contact field is a foreign key that matches the primary key field CustomerNum.

4. Scroll the Customer_1 field list until the Contact field is visible. Then click and drag the CustomerNum field from the Customer field list to the Contact field in the Customer_1 field list. Access adds a join line between the two fields. You can verify that this is an inner join query by opening the Join Properties dialog box.

5. Right-click the **join line** between the two tables, and then click **Join Properties** to open the Join Properties dialog box. See Figure 8-41.

Figure 8-41	JOIN PROPERTIES DIALOG BOX

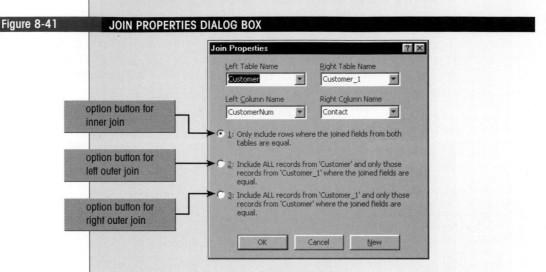

TROUBLE? If right-clicking the join line does not work, click View on the menu bar, and then click Join Properties to open the Join Properties dialog box.

The first option button is selected, indicating that this is an inner join. You would click the second option button for a left outer join or the third option button for a right outer join. Because the inner join is correct, you can cancel the dialog box and then add the necessary fields to the design grid.

6. Click the **Cancel** button and then, scrolling as necessary, double-click the following fields (in order) from the Customer_1 field list: **CustomerNum**, **CustomerName**, **OwnerName**, and **Contact**. Then double-click the following fields (in order) from the Customer field list: **CustomerName** and **OwnerName**.

7. Click the right side of the **CustomerNum Sort** text box, and then click **Ascending** to establish the sort order for the query results.

8. Click the **Run** button ![Run] on the Query Design toolbar. Access displays the query results.

9. Maximize the Query window and then change the font to **Times New Roman 8**. The query results display the records in increasing CustomerNum order and show six fields and 36 records. See Figure 8-42.

Figure 8-42	INITIAL SELF-JOIN ON THE CUSTOMER TABLE

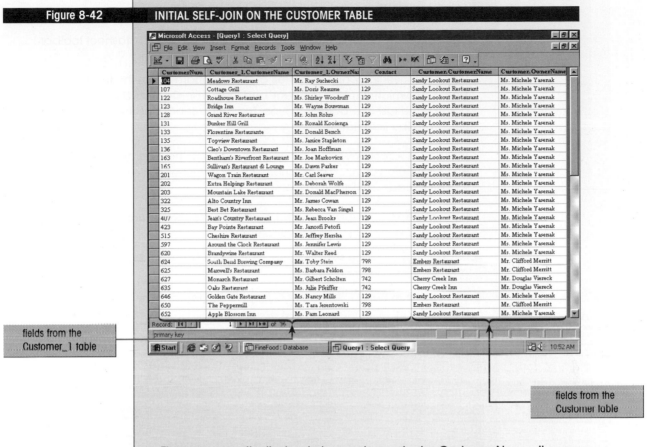

fields from the
Customer_1 table

fields from the
Customer table

The query results display, in increasing order by CustomerNum, all owners
and their contacts, except for the three contact owners who have null Contact
field values.

TROUBLE? If your query results do not match Figure 8-42, click the View button for
Design view to return to Design view. Review the preceding steps and make any
necessary corrections to your query design. Then run the query again.

Access displays 36 of the 39 records from the Customer table. The records for Embers
Restaurant, Sandy Lookout Restaurant, and Cherry Creek Inn have a null Contact field
value and, therefore, are not displayed. Four field names in the query results now have
prefixes indicating either Customer or Customer_1 to distinguish fields in one table from
fields in the other table. For example, the full name of the CustomerName field displayed is
Customer_1.CustomerName, which means the CustomerName field from the Customer_1
(right) table.

Kim asks you to rename some of the fields so that the query results will be easier to read.
After you rename the necessary fields, the field names in the query results, from left to right,
will be CustomerNum, CustomerName, OwnerName, ContactNum, ContactRestaurant,
and ContactName.

To rename the necessary fields:

1. Click the **View** button for Design view 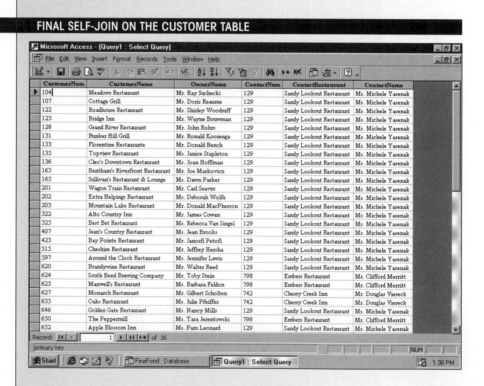 on the Query Datasheet toolbar to switch back to Design view.

2. Place the insertion point to the left of the first character in the fourth column's Field box, which displays Contact, and then type **ContactNum:**. Be sure the colon is the last character you type. The colon separates the caption for this field from the field name.

   TROUBLE? If Access displays the caption Expr1 for the Contact field, you forgot to enter the colon or you made another error in entering the caption. Edit the text so that it reads ContactNum:Contact.

3. Repeat Step 2 for the fifth column, typing **ContactRestaurant:** before the field name (CustomerName) for that column.

4. Repeat Step 2 for the sixth column, typing **ContactName:** before the field name (OwnerName) for that column.

5. Click the **Run** button ! on the Query Design toolbar. The query results display the new names for the renamed columns.

6. Resize all columns to their best fit, and then click **CustomerNum 104** to deselect all columns. See Figure 8-43.

| Figure 8-43 | FINAL SELF-JOIN ON THE CUSTOMER TABLE |

Microsoft Access - [Query1 : Select Query]

File Edit View Insert Format Records Tools Window Help

CustomerNum	CustomerName	OwnerName	ContactNum	ContactRestaurant	ContactName
104	Meadows Restaurant	Mr. Ray Suchecki	129	Sandy Lookout Restaurant	Ms. Michele Yasenak
107	Cottage Grill	Ms. Doris Reaume	129	Sandy Lookout Restaurant	Ms. Michele Yasenak
122	Roadhouse Restaurant	Ms. Shirley Woodruff	129	Sandy Lookout Restaurant	Ms. Michele Yasenak
123	Bridge Inn	Mr. Wayne Bouwman	129	Sandy Lookout Restaurant	Ms. Michele Yasenak
128	Grand River Restaurant	Mr. John Rohrs	129	Sandy Lookout Restaurant	Ms. Michele Yasenak
131	Bunker Hill Grill	Mr. Ronald Kooienga	129	Sandy Lookout Restaurant	Ms. Michele Yasenak
133	Florentine Restaurante	Mr. Donald Bench	129	Sandy Lookout Restaurant	Ms. Michele Yasenak
135	Topview Restaurant	Ms. Janice Stapleton	129	Sandy Lookout Restaurant	Ms. Michele Yasenak
136	Cleo's Downtown Restaurant	Ms. Joan Hoffman	129	Sandy Lookout Restaurant	Ms. Michele Yasenak
163	Bentham's Riverfront Restaurant	Mr. Joe Markovicz	129	Sandy Lookout Restaurant	Ms. Michele Yasenak
165	Sullivan's Restaurant & Lounge	Ms. Dawn Parker	129	Sandy Lookout Restaurant	Ms. Michele Yasenak
201	Wagon Train Restaurant	Mr. Carl Seaver	129	Sandy Lookout Restaurant	Ms. Michele Yasenak
202	Extra Helpings Restaurant	Ms. Deborah Wolfe	129	Sandy Lookout Restaurant	Ms. Michele Yasenak
203	Mountain Lake Restaurant	Mr. Donald MacPherson	129	Sandy Lookout Restaurant	Ms. Michele Yasenak
322	Alto Country Inn	Mr. James Cowan	129	Sandy Lookout Restaurant	Ms. Michele Yasenak
325	Best Bet Restaurant	Ms. Rebecca Van Singel	129	Sandy Lookout Restaurant	Ms. Michele Yasenak
407	Jean's Country Restaurant	Ms. Jean Brooks	129	Sandy Lookout Restaurant	Ms. Michele Yasenak
423	Bay Pointe Restaurant	Mr. Janosfi Petofi	129	Sandy Lookout Restaurant	Ms. Michele Yasenak
515	Cheshire Restaurant	Mr. Jeffrey Hersha	129	Sandy Lookout Restaurant	Ms. Michele Yasenak
597	Around the Clock Restaurant	Ms. Jennifer Lewis	129	Sandy Lookout Restaurant	Ms. Michele Yasenak
620	Brandywine Restaurant	Mr. Walter Reed	129	Sandy Lookout Restaurant	Ms. Michele Yasenak
624	South Bend Brewing Company	Mr. Toby Stein	798	Embers Restaurant	Mr. Clifford Merritt
625	Maxwell's Restaurant	Ms. Barbara Feldon	798	Embers Restaurant	Mr. Clifford Merritt
627	Monarch Restaurant	Mr. Gilbert Scholten	742	Cherry Creek Inn	Mr. Douglas Viereck
635	Oaks Restaurant	Ms. Julie Pfeiffer	742	Cherry Creek Inn	Mr. Douglas Viereck
646	Golden Gate Restaurant	Ms. Nancy Mills	129	Sandy Lookout Restaurant	Ms. Michele Yasenak
650	The Peppermill	Ms. Tara Jerentowski	798	Embers Restaurant	Mr. Clifford Merritt
652	Apple Blossom Inn	Ms. Pam Leonard	129	Sandy Lookout Restaurant	Ms. Michele Yasenak

Record: 1 of 36

primary key   NUM

Start   FineFood : Database   Query1 : Select Query   1:38 PM

Kim asks you to print a copy of the query results in landscape orientation.

7. Click **File** on the menu bar, click **Page Setup**, click the **Page** tab, click the **Landscape** option button in the Orientation section, and then click the **OK** button.

8. Click the **Print** button 🖨 on the Query Datasheet toolbar to print the query results for Kim.

You can now give Kim a list of customers and their contacts for the appreciation dinner. Kim can give this list to the restaurant owners so that they can contact Mr. Viereck, Ms. Yasenak, and Mr. Merritt. You are finished with the query, so you can save it as Annual Dinner Contact and then return to the Database window.

To save and close the query:

1. Click the **Save** button 🖫 on the Query Datasheet toolbar. The Save As dialog box opens.

2. In the Query Name text box, type **Annual Dinner Contact**, and then press the **Enter** key. Access saves the new self-join query.

3. Click the **Close** button ☒ on the Query window to close it and return to the Database window.

4. Click ☒ on the Access window title bar to close the FineFood database and to exit Access. You return to the Windows desktop.

You have created and saved many queries that Leonard, Barbara, Kim, and others can use to help them manage Valle Coffee's customer and order records. In the next session, you will learn about the SQL language that Access uses behind the scenes when performing many of its operations, and how to replicate a database.

Session 8.3 QUICK CHECK

1. What are the three types of relationships you can define between tables?

2. What is an entity subtype?

3. What is an index?

4. What is the difference between an inner join and an outer join?

5. What is a self-join?

Figure 8-44	

TELEPHONE	PHONE CALL
TelephoneNumber	CallingTelephoneNumber
BillingName	CalledTelephoneNumber
BillingAddress	CallDate
	CallStartTime
	CallEndTime
	BilledTelephoneNumber

6. Figure 8-44 lists the field names from two tables: Telephone and Phone Call.

   a. What is the primary key for each table?

   b. What type of relationship exists between the two tables?

   c. Is an inner join possible between the two tables? If so, give one example of an inner join.

   d. Is either type of outer join possible between the two tables? If so, give one example of an outer join.

   e. Is a self-join possible for one of the tables? If so, give one example of a self-join.

SESSION 8.4

In this session, you will view the SQL statements Access creates when you design a query. You will use replication to convert the FineFood database to a Design Master and to create a replica of the database. Then you will make changes to the data in the replica and update the Design Master.

Introduction to SQL

SQL
Queries

SQL (Structured Query Language) is a standard language used in querying, updating, and managing relational databases. Every full-featured relational DBMS has its own version of the current standard SQL, which is called SQL-92. If you learn SQL for one relational DBMS, it's a relatively easy task to begin using SQL for other relational DBMSs. This is particularly important when you work with two or more relational DBMSs, which is the case in most companies.

Much of what Access accomplishes behind the scenes is done with SQL. Whenever you create a query in Design view, for example, Access automatically constructs an equivalent SQL statement. When you save a query, Access saves the SQL statement version of the query.

When you are working in Design view or viewing the results of a query, you can see the SQL statement that is equivalent to your query by clicking the SQL View button or by selecting SQL View from the View menu. In response, Access displays the SQL statement in the SQL window.

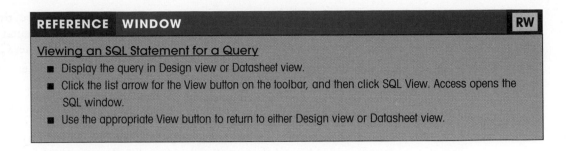

REFERENCE   WINDOW   RW

Viewing an SQL Statement for a Query
- Display the query in Design view or Datasheet view.
- Click the list arrow for the View button on the toolbar, and then click SQL View. Access opens the SQL window.
- Use the appropriate View button to return to either Design view or Datasheet view.

Next you'll examine the SQL statements that are equivalent to two existing queries: Customer List and Customer Orders.

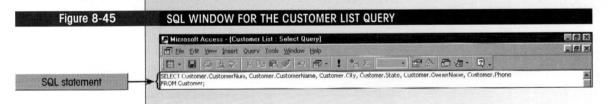

To view the SQL statements for the Customer List query:

1. Make sure that Access is running, that the **FineFood** database from the Tutorial folder on your Data Disk is open, and that Queries is selected in the Objects bar of the Database window.

2. Right-click **Customer List** in the Queries list, and then click **Open** on the short-cut menu. Access opens the query results in Datasheet view and displays the 39 records from the Customer table. The fields displayed are CustomerNum, CustomerName, City, State, OwnerName, and Phone.

3. Click the list arrow for the **View** button 📖 on the Query Datasheet toolbar, and then click **SQL View** to open the SQL window.

4. Maximize the SQL window, and then click the line below the SQL statement to deselect the statement. See Figure 8-45.

Figure 8-45	SQL WINDOW FOR THE CUSTOMER LIST QUERY

Microsoft Access - [Customer List : Select Query]

File Edit View Insert Query Tools Window Help

SQL statement → SELECT Customer.CustomerNum, Customer.CustomerName, Customer.City, Customer.State, Customer.OwnerName, Customer.Phone
FROM Customer;

SQL uses the **SELECT statement** to define what data it retrieves from a database and how it presents the data. For the work you've done so far, the Access menu commands and dialog box options have sufficed. If you learn SQL to the point where you can use it efficiently, you will be able to enter your own SELECT and other SQL statements in the SQL window. If you work with more complicated databases, you might find that you need the extra power of the SQL language to implement your database strategies fully.

The rules that SQL uses to construct a statement similar to the SELECT statement shown in Figure 8-45, are summarized as follows:

- The basic form of a SQL statement is: SELECT-FROM-WHERE-ORDER BY. After SELECT, list the fields you want to display. After FROM, list the tables used in the query. After WHERE, list the selection criteria. After ORDER BY, list the sort keys.
- If a field name includes a space, enclose the field name in brackets.

■ Precede a field name with the name of its table. Connect the table name to the field name with a period. For example, you would enter the CustomerNum field in the Customer table as "Customer.CustomerNum."

■ Separate field names and table names by commas, and end a statement with a semicolon.

The SQL statement shown in Figure 8-45 selects the CustomerNum, CustomerName, City, State, OwnerName, and Phone fields from the Customer table. The SQL statement does not contain a WHERE clause or an ORDER BY clause, so all records are included in the query results and they are listed in the default order, which is in ascending order by primary key.

You can enter or change SQL statements directly in the SQL window. If you enter a SQL statement and then switch to the Query window in Design view, you will see its equivalent in the design grid.

Next, you'll examine the SQL statement for the Customer Orders query.

To view the SQL statements for the Customer Orders query:

1. Click the **Close** button ☒ on the menu bar to close the SQL window and return to the Database window.

2. Right-click **Customer Orders** in the Queries list, and then click **Design View** on the shortcut menu. Access opens the query in Design view. The query selects records from the joined Customer and Order tables in descending order by the Paid field as the primary sort key and in descending order by the InvoiceAmt field as the secondary sort key. The fields displayed are CustomerName, City, and State from the Customer table, and BillingDate, Paid, and InvoiceAmt from the Order table.

3. Click the list arrow for the **View** button ☒ on the Query Design toolbar, and then click **SQL View** to open the SQL window.

4. Click the line below the SQL statement to deselect the statement. See Figure 8-46.

Figure 8-46   SQL WINDOW FOR THE CUSTOMER ORDERS QUERY

The SELECT statement for this query is similar to the one shown in Figure 8-45, except for the following added features:

■ The ORDER BY clause specifies the sort order for the records.

■ The notation DESC indicates a descending sort order. If DESC does not follow a sort key field, then SQL uses an ascending sort order.

■ The clause INNER JOIN links the two tables with an inner join. The syntax for this clause is INNER JOIN between the two table names, followed by ON, and then followed by the names of the fields serving as the common field, connected by an equals sign. (Access is using the ON clause here instead of the standard SQL WHERE clause.)

The SQL SELECT statements mirror the query options you select in Design view. In effect, every choice you make in Design view is reflected as part of the SQL SELECT statement. Viewing the SQL statements generated from queries that you design is an effective way to begin learning SQL.

To close the SQL window:

1. Click the **Close** button ☒ on the menu bar to close the SQL window and return to the Database window.

2. Click the **Restore** button ⊡ on the menu bar to restore the Database window.

You are ready to present your information to Kim so that she can finalize the plans for the appreciation dinners. If you want to pursue SQL further, you can also use the Access Help system to find additional information on SQL.

Creating a Replica of a Database

Kim wants to take a copy of the FineFood database with her on her business trip. She wants to be sure that while she is away, any changes that she or anyone else makes to the database will be updated, keeping the database accurate and current.

If you simply created a copy of the FineFood database file and gave it to Kim, her copy would not include any changes made by other Valle Coffee employees while she is away, nor would the changes she makes to her copy of the database be included in the original database. Instead, you'll create a special copy of the FineFood database called a **replica**. When you create a replica of a database, the original copy of the database becomes the **Design Master**. The Design Master and all of its replicas are called the **replica set**. Access adds special tables and fields to the Design Master database to keep track of changes made to data and to the design of the database. Anyone using the Design Master can make changes to the design of database tables, queries, and other objects. Any changes in the data or design of database objects in the Design Master can then be automatically updated in a replica. Anyone using a replica of the database can make changes to the data in any of the database tables. A replica prevents the user from changing the structure or the design of an existing table, query, or other database object. Any changes in the data in any replicas can be updated automatically in the Design Master. The process of updating the Design Master and the replicas is called **synchronization**.

REFERENCE WINDOW   **RW**

Creating a Replica of a Database

- Open the database you want to replicate.
- Click Tools on the menu bar, point to Replication, and then click Create Replica.
- Click the Yes button to close the database.
- Click the Yes button to make a backup copy of the database.
- Select the location where you want to store the new replica.
- Click the OK button.

You need to convert the FineFood database to a Design Master and create a replica of the database to give to Kim.

To convert the FineFood database to a Design Master and create a replica of it:

1. Click **Tools** on the menu bar, point to **Replication**, and then click **Create Replica**. Access opens a dialog box asking if you want to close the database, convert it to a Design Master, and create a replica of the database.

2. Click the **Yes** button. Access closes the database and, after a few moments, opens a dialog box asking if you want to make a backup copy of the FineFood database. See Figure 8-47.

Figure 8-47	CREATING A BACKUP COPY OF THE FINEFOOD DATABASE

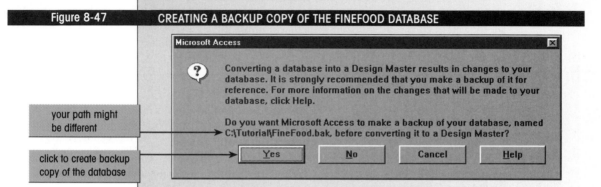

your path might be different

click to create backup copy of the database

Access can make a backup copy of your database on your Data Disk. This backup can serve as an extra copy of the FineFood database in case anything goes wrong when Access creates the replica. You'll make a backup copy and, at the end of this tutorial, you'll change the extension of the backup copy from bak to mdb, so you can use it instead of the Design Master for later tutorials.

TROUBLE? If you're using drive A for your Data Disk, you won't have enough space for a backup copy of the FineFood database. Click the Cancel button, close the FineFood database, and then copy the FineFood database from the Tutorial folder on drive A to a folder on your hard drive. If you don't have access to a hard drive, then you won't be able to complete the remaining steps in this tutorial. You should read through the steps, however, to learn how to create and work with a Design Master and a replica.

TROUBLE? If Access opens a dialog box indicating that it cannot start SQL dialogs and that this feature is not currently installed, insert your Microsoft Office 2000 CD into the appropriate disk drive, and then click the Yes button. If you do not have this CD, ask your instructor or technical support person for help.

3. Click the **Yes** button. The Location of New Replica dialog box opens. See Figure 8-48.

Figure 8-48	LOCATION OF NEW REPLICA DIALOG BOX

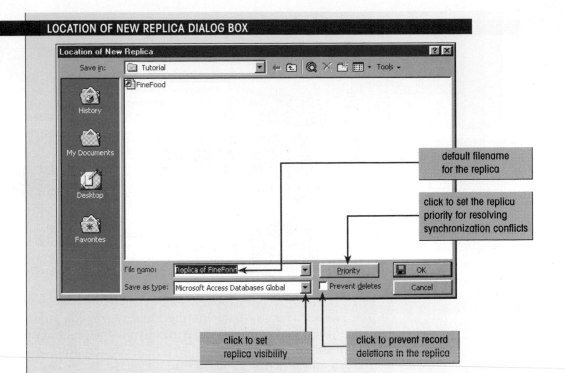

In the Location of New Replica dialog box, you choose the location and name for the replica. You also can set options for the **replica priority** (when multiple replicas update the same record, only the change for the replica with the highest priority is made), the **replica visibility** (choices are global, local, and anonymous), and **replica record deletion** (a check mark in the Prevent deletes check box prevents a user from deleting a record in the replica). The default settings are sufficient, so you can continue creating the replica.

4. Click the **OK** button. Access creates the replica, naming it Replica of FineFood, converts the FineFood database to the Design Master, and opens a dialog box informing you of these actions. See Figure 8-49.

Figure 8-49	AFTER CREATING THE FINEFOOD DESIGN MASTER AND REPLICA

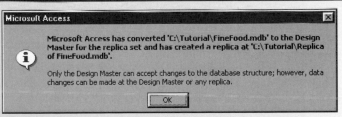

5. Click the **OK** button. The dialog box closes, and the Design Master version of the FineFood database opens. See Figure 8-50.

Figure 8-50   DATABASE WINDOW FOR THE FINEFOOD DATABASE DESIGN MASTER

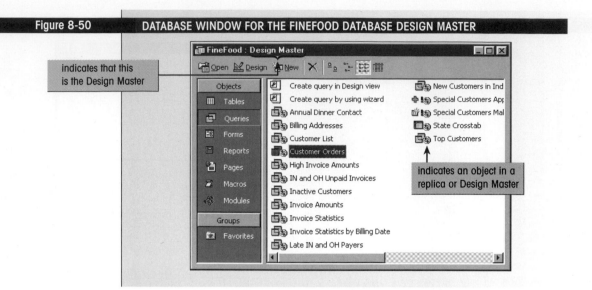

The phrase "Design Master" in the Database window title bar indicates that this is a replica of the FineFood database. A new symbol appears next to the query icons in the Queries list to indicate that these objects have been replicated.

You can now give Kim a copy of the FineFood database replica on a disk to take with her on her trip.

Synchronizing the Replica and the Design Master

While she is on her trip, Kim visits several restaurants that are potential Valle Coffee customers. Her visit to Steamer's is successful, and the owner decides to open an account with Valle Coffee. Kim adds a new record for Steamer's in the Customer table of the FineFood database replica.

To add the new record to the replica of the FineFood database:

1. Click the **Close** button ☒ on the Database window title bar to close the Design Master of the FineFood database.

2. Open the **Replica of FineFood** database from the Tutorial folder on your Data Disk, and then click **Forms** in the Objects bar of the Database window.

   The word "Replica" in the Database window title bar indicates that this is a replica of the FineFood database.

   You can now enter Kim's new record using the Customer Data form.

3. Right-click **Customer Data**, and then click **Open** on the shortcut menu to display the first Customer record in the form.

4. Click the **New Record** button ▶* on the Form View toolbar to display a blank form.

5. Enter the data for the new record, as shown in Figure 8-51.

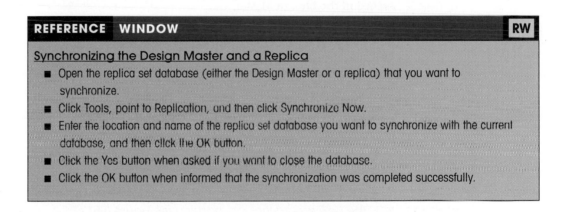

Figure 8-51   NEW CUSTOMER RECORD FOR STEAMER'S

6. Click ☒ on the Form window title bar to close the form.

The replica of the FineFood database now contains a new record that is not recorded in the Design Master. When Kim returns from her trip, you can update the Design Master by synchronizing the Design Master and the replica. The synchronizing process compares the Design Master to the replica and checks for any differences. Access updates the Design Master with any changes that have been made to the data in the replica, and updates the replica with any changes that have been made to the data or to the design of any database objects in the Design Master. This process ensures that the Design Master and the replica are consistent.

REFERENCE WINDOW   **RW**

Synchronizing the Design Master and a Replica

- Open the replica set database (either the Design Master or a replica) that you want to synchronize.
- Click Tools, point to Replication, and then click Synchronize Now.
- Enter the location and name of the replica set database you want to synchronize with the current database, and then click the OK button.
- Click the Yes button when asked if you want to close the database.
- Click the OK button when informed that the synchronization was completed successfully.

Kim has returned from her trip, so now you must synchronize the open replica of the FineFood database with the Design Master to enter the new Customer record.

To synchronize the replica and the Design Master:

1. Click **Tools** on the menu bar, point to **Replication**, and then click **Synchronize Now**. The Synchronize Database dialog box opens.

2. Make sure the **Directly with Replica** check box is selected. If the Directly with Replica list box does not display the name of the Design Master of the FineFood database, use the Browse button to select it. See Figure 8-52.

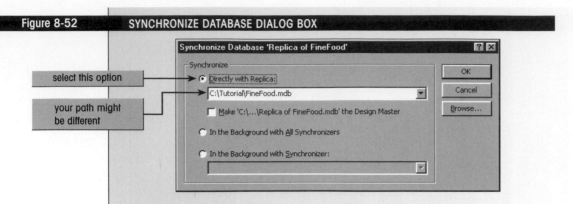

Figure 8-52   SYNCHRONIZE DATABASE DIALOG BOX

TROUBLE? The path statement in the Directly with Replica list box on your screen might not match the one in the figure. Be sure that it is accurate for your system and the location of your Data Files.

3. Click the **OK** button, and then click the **Yes** button when asked if you want to close the replica. After a few seconds Access opens a dialog box indicating that the synchronization is complete.

4. Click the **OK** button to close the dialog box and reopen the replica.

The Design Master and the replica are now synchronized. The new record that Kim added to the replica copy of the FineFood database has been added to the Design Master. You can now open the Customer table using the Customer Data form and display the new record in the Design Master.

To find and display the new record in the Customer table:

1. Click the **Close** button ☒ on the Database window title bar to close the replica of the FineFood database.

2. Open the **FineFood** database from the Tutorial folder on your Data Disk, and then click **Forms** in the Objects bar of the Database window.

3. Right-click **Customer Data**, and then click **Open** on the shortcut menu to display the first Customer record in the form.

4. Click the **Last Record** navigation button ▶❙ to display the last record. This is the new record that Kim added (see Figure 8-51).

5. Click ☒ on the Form window to close it and return to the Database window.

Now that you have synchronized the databases, you can delete the replica of the FineFood database. You can easily create another replica whenever Kim needs to take the database with her on future business trips. Even though you delete the replica of the FineFood database, the original Design Master of the database remains a Design Master. Because there can be many replicas of a database in a replica set, the Design Master keeps track of any changes you make to the database, so that other replicas can be synchronized at any time.

In future tutorials you won't use the Design Master of the FineFood database; you'll use the original version of the FineFood database (before you converted it to a Design Master and created the replica). Therefore, you'll also rename both versions of the FineFood database.

To delete the replica of the FineFood database and rename databases:

1. Click the **Close** button ☒ on the Access window title bar to close the Design Master and to exit Access. You return to the Windows desktop.

2. Use Windows Explorer or My Computer to open the Tutorial folder on your Data Disk.

3. Right-click the **Replica of FineFood** database, click **Delete**, and then click the **Yes** button to delete the replica of the FineFood database.

4. Right-click the **FineFood** database, click **Rename**, type **FineFood Design Master**, and then press the **Enter** key.

   TROUBLE? If a dialog box opens and tells you that changing the filename extension might make the file unusable, click the No button, and then repeat Step 4 and type FineFood Design Master.mdb, with the filename extension, before pressing the Enter key.

5. Right-click the **FineFood.bak** database, click **Rename**, type **FineFood.mdb**, and then press the **Enter** key.

6. Close the Windows Explorer or My Computer windows to return to the Windows desktop.

The new queries that you created and the other work you completed will make it much easier for Leonard, Barbara, and Kim to enter, retrieve, and view information in the FineFood database.

Session 8.4 QUICK CHECK

1. _____ is a standard language used in querying, updating, and managing relational databases.

2. What is the basic format of an SQL statement?

3. What is the purpose of the ORDER BY clause in an SQL SELECT statement?

4. What is a replica set?

5. How does a Design Master differ from a replica?

6. What does Access do when you synchronize a Design Master and a replica?

REVIEW ASSIGNMENTS

The **Coffees** database in the Review folder on your Data Disk contains information about Valle Coffee products. The **Coffee** table in the database contains records of the various types of coffee that Valle Coffee sells. The **Product** table contains pricing information, and the **Weight** table contains packaging information. Finally, the **Supplier** table contains records of the companies that supply coffee to Valle Coffee, and the **Coffee Supplier** table contains records indicating which suppliers provide which coffees to Valle Coffee.

The database contains several other objects, including queries, forms, and reports. Barbara wants you to define a many-to-many relationship between the **Supplier** and **Coffee** tables, to create some new queries for her, and to make a replica of the database. Complete the following:

1. Make sure your Data Disk is in the appropriate disk drive, start Access, and then open the **Coffees** database located in the Review folder on your Data Disk.

2. Define a many-to-many relationship between the **Supplier** and **Coffee** tables, using the **Coffee Supplier** table as the related table. Select the referential integrity option and both cascade options for the relationships.

Explore ▶ 3. Open the **Supplier** table in Design view, delete the ContactName index, save the table, and then close the table.

4. Create a query based on the **Coffee**, **Product**, and **Weight** tables. Display the CoffeeType, Decaf (from the **Product** table), and Weight/Size fields in the query results. Save the query as **Coffee Types and Weights**, run the query, print the first page of the query results, and then close the query.

5. Create a crosstab query based on the **Coffee Types and Weights** query. Use the CoffeeType field values for the row headings, the Decaf field values for the column headings, and the count of the Weight/Size field as the summarized value. Save the query as **Summary of CoffeeType by Decaf Crosstab**, view the query, resize the columns in the query results to their best fit, print the query results, and then save and close the query. (*Note*: The <> symbol is used for the column heading for a null value; in this case, where the Decaf field value is No. The column heading "D" represents a Yes value in the Decaf field.)

6. Barbara informs you that coffee prices have increased, and Valle Coffee will have to raise the price of its least expensive products. Create an update query that increases the price of all records in the **Product** table where the Price field value is 7.99; the new price is 8.59. After you run the update query, close it and save it as **Price Update**.

7. Create a make-table query based on the **Coffee** table, saving the results as **Decaf Coffee** in the current database. Select all fields for Decaf coffees. (*Hint*: Decaf coffees have a Decaf value of Yes.) Run the query, close the query, and then save the make-table query as **Decaf Coffee Make-Table**. Open the **Decaf Coffee** table, change the font to Times New Roman 8, resize the columns to their best fit, print the table records, and then save and close the table.

8. Create a delete query that deletes all records from the **Decaf Coffee** table where the CoffeeType field value is not Flavored. Run the query, close the query, and then save the delete query as **Delete Non-Flavored**. Rename the **Decaf Coffee** table as **Flavored Decaf Coffee**. Open the table, resize the columns in the query results to their best fit, print the datasheet, and then save and close the table.

9. Create a find unmatched query that finds all records in the **Product** table for which there is no matching record in the **Flavored Decaf Coffee** table. Select all fields from the **Product** table in the query results. Save the query as **Product Without Matching Flavored Decaf Coffee**, print the first page of the query results, and then close the query.

Explore ▶ 10. Create an outer join query between the **Flavored Decaf Coffee** and **Product** tables, selecting all records from the **Product** table and any matching records from the **Flavored Decaf Coffee** table. Display the CoffeeCode, CoffeeName, and the CoffeeType fields from the **Flavored Decaf Coffee** table, and the ProductCode field from the **Product** table in the query results. Save the query as **Product and Flavored Decaf Coffee Outer Join**, run the query, resize all columns to their best fit, print the first page of the query results, and then save and close the query.

Explore

11. Open the **Special Imports** query and view the SQL statement in the SQL window. Answer the following questions:

    a. Which tables are used in the query?
    b. Which fields are displayed in the query results?
    c. What type of join is used between the tables?
    d. What selection criteria are used?
    e. How are the query results sorted?

    Close the SQL window.

12. Create a replica of the **Coffees** database in the Review folder on your Data Disk, making a backup of the database in the same folder. Accept the default settings in the Location of New Replica dialog box.

13. Close the Design Master, and then open the replica. Add the record shown in Figure 8-53 to the **Coffee** table.

Figure 8-53

COFFEECODE	COFFEENAME	COFFEETYPE	DECAF
VALS	Valle Special Blend	Blended	No

14. Close the **Coffee** table, and then synchronize the replica with the Design Master. Close the replica, open the Design Master, verify that the new record was added to the **Coffee** table, close the Design Master, and then exit Access.

15. Use Windows Explorer or My Computer to open the Review folder on your Data Disk. Rename the **Coffees** database as **Coffees Design Master**, rename the **Coffees.bak** database as **Coffees.mdb**, and then close Windows Explorer or My Computer.

CASE PROBLEMS

Case 1. Ashbrook Mall Information Desk   The Mall Operations Office is responsible for everything that happens in the Ashbrook Mall in Phoenix, Arizona. To maintain a catalog of job openings at the mall stores and to track maintenance work done at the mall, Sam Bullard, director of the Mall Operations Office, has created the **Mall** database. The **Job** table contains records of the various jobs available at the mall, the **Store** table contains information about the mall stores, and the **Location** table identifies the location of all stores and other areas in the mall. The **Repairer** table contains maintenance worker information, the **Maintenance Job** table contains maintenance request information, and the **Maintenance Job Repairer** table contains records indicating which maintenance workers are assigned to which maintenance jobs. The database contains several other objects, including queries, forms, and reports. Sam asks you to define a many-to-many relationship between the **Maintenance Job** and **Repairer** tables, to create some new queries for him, and to make a replica of the database. To help Sam with his requests, you'll complete the following:

1. Make sure your Data Disk is in the appropriate disk drive, start Access, and then open the **Mall** database located in the Cases folder on your Data Disk.

2. Define a many-to-many relationship between the **Maintenance Job** and **Repairer** tables, using the **Maintenance Job Repairer** table as the related table. Select the referential integrity option and both cascade options for the relationships.

3. Open the **Maintenance Job Repairer** table in Design view, create an index for the Repairer field with duplicates allowed, save the table, and then close the table.

4. Create a make-table query based on the **Job** table, saving the table as **Salesclerk Job** in the current database. Select all fields for the Salesclerk position. Run the query, close the query, and then save the make-table query as **Salesclerk Job Make-Table**. Open the **Salesclerk Job** table, resize the columns to their best fit, print the datasheet, and then save and close the table.

5. Create a crosstab query based on the **Store Jobs** query. Use the Location field values for the row headings, the Position field values for the column headings, and the count of the StoreName field as the summarized value. Save the query as **Location by Position Crosstab**, view the query, resize the columns in the query results to their best fit, print the query results in landscape orientation, and then save and close the query.

6. Create a find unmatched query that finds all records in the **Store** table for which there is no matching record in the **Job** table. Select all fields from the **Store** table in the query results. Save the query as **Store Without Matching Job**, run the query, resize the columns in the query results to their best fit, print the query results, and then save and close the query.

Explore ▶ 7. Open the **Clerk Jobs** query and view the SQL statement in the SQL window. Answer the following questions:

   a. Which tables are used in the query?
   b. Which fields are displayed in the query results?
   c. What type of join is used between the tables?
   d. What selection criteria are used?
   e. How are the query results sorted?

   Close the SQL window.

Explore ▶ 8. Create a replica of the **Mall** database in the Cases folder on your Data Disk, making a backup of the database in the same folder and accepting the defaults in the Location of New Replica dialog box. Then complete the following:

   a. Close the Design Master, and then open the replica.
   b. Create a delete query that deletes all records from the **Job** table where the Position field value is Salesclerk. Run the query, save the delete query as **Delete Salesclerks**, and then close the query.
   c. Synchronize the replica with the Design Master, close the replica, and then open the Design Master.
   d. Open the **Job** table, verify that the records for the Salesclerk position have been deleted, print the table records, close the table, close the Design Master, and then exit Access.
   e. Use Windows Explorer or My Computer to open the Cases folder on your Data Disk. Rename the **Mall** database as **Mall Design Master**, rename the **Mall.bak** database as **Mall.mdb**, and then close Windows Explorer or My Computer.

Case 2. Professional Litigation User Services Professional Litigation User Services (PLUS) creates all types of visual aids for judicial proceedings. To track daily payments received from the firm's clients, Raj Jawahir has created the **Plus** database. The **Firm** table contains client information, and the **Payment** table contains records of the payments made by clients. The **Project** table contains information about the projects for each client, the **Employee** table contains PLUS employee information, and the **Time Billed** table contains records of the time spent by employees on various projects. The database contains several other objects, including queries, forms, and reports. Raj wants you to define a many-to-many relationship between the **Project** and **Employee** tables, and to create several new queries. To help Raj with his requests, you'll complete the following:

1. Make sure your Data Disk is in the appropriate disk drive, start Access, and then open the **Plus** database located in the Cases folder on your Data Disk.

2. Define a many-to-many relationship between the **Project** and **Employee** tables, using the **Time Billed** table as the related table. Select the referential integrity option and both cascade options for the relationships.

3. Raj has assigned a new PLUS account representative to Sunil Jain's accounts. The new representative is Cathy Cunningham. Create an update query to update the PLUSAcctRep field in the **Firm** table, updating the PLUSAcctRep field value to Cunningham, Cathy where the current field value is Jain, Sunil. Run the query, save the query as **Rep Name Update**, and then close the query. Open the **Firm** table, resize the columns to their best fit, print the table, and then save and close the table.

4. Create a crosstab query based on the **Account Representatives** query. Use the PLUSAcctRep field values for the row headings, the FirmName field values for the column headings, and the sum of the AmtPaid field as the summarized value. Save the query as **AcctReps by Firm Crosstab**, view the query, resize the columns in the query results to their best fit, print the first page of the query results in landscape orientation, and then save and close the query.

5. Create a make-table query based on the **Payment** table, saving the table as **Early June Payment** in the current database. Select all fields for payments made before June 8, 2001. Run the query, save the make-table query as **Early June Payment Make-Table**, and then close the query. Open the **Early June Payment** table, print the first page of the datasheet, and then close the table.

6. Create an append query to select all records from the **Payment** table where the DatePaid field value is between June 8, 2001 and June 10, 2001 and append them to the **Early June Payment** table. After you run the query, close the query, and then save the append query as **June Payment Append**. Open the **Early June Payment** table, print the table records, and then close the table.

7. Create a delete query to delete all records from the **Early June Payment** table where the AmtPaid is less than $1500.00. Run the query, close the query, and then save the delete query as **Delete Small Payments**. Rename the **Early June Payment** table as **Large Early June Payment**, open the table, print the table records, and then close the table.

8. Create a query based on the **Payment** table. Display the Payment#, Firm#, and AmtPaid fields in the query results. Sort the query results in descending order by the AmtPaid field. Use the Top Values property to select the top 5% of records based on the AmtPaid field. Save the query as **Top Values Payments**, run the query, print the query results, and then close the query.

Explore   9. Create an outer join query between the **Firm** and **Large Early June Payment** tables, selecting all records from the **Firm** table and any matching records from the **Large Early June Payment** table. Display the Firm#, FirmName, and PLUSAcctRep fields from the **Firm** table and the AmtPaid field from the **Large Early June Payment** table in the query results. Save the query as **Firm and Large Early June Payment Outer Join**, run the query, print the query results, and then close the query.

10. Close the **Plus** database, and then exit Access.

Case 3. Best Friends   Best Friends is a not-for-profit organization that trains hearing and service dogs for people with disabilities. To raise funds, Best Friends periodically sponsors walk-a-thons. These fundraisers have been so popular that Noah and Sheila Warnick, the founders of Best Friends, have created the **Friends** database to keep track of walkers and their pledges. The **Friends** database has been a useful tool for Noah and Sheila.

The **Walker** table contains information about people who participate in the walk-a-thons, the **Pledge** table contains pledge information for each walker, and the **Walker Biography** table contains background information on some of the walkers. The database contains several other objects, including queries, forms, and reports. Now, Noah and Sheila want you to define a one-to-one relationship between the **Walker** and **Walker Biography** tables, to create several new queries, and to create a replica of the database. To help them with their requests, you'll complete the following:

1. Make sure your Data Disk is in the appropriate disk drive, start Access, and then open the **Friends** database located in the Cases folder on your Data Disk.

2. Define a one-to-one relationship between the **Walker** and **Walker Biography** tables. Select the referential integrity option and both cascade options for the relationship.

3. Create an update query to select all records in the **Walker** table where the Distance field value is greater than 2.6. Update the Distance field value to 3.0. Run the query, save the query as **Distance Update**, and then close the query. Open the **Walker** table, print the table, and then close the table.

4. Create a find unmatched query to select all records in the **Walker** table for which there are no matching records in the **Pledge** table. Select the WalkerID, LastName, and FirstName fields for display in the query results and save the query as **Walker Without Matching Pledge**. Run the query, print the query results, and then close the query.

5. Open the **Walker Distance** query in Design view and sort the query results in ascending order by Distance. Use the Top Values property to select the top 5 records. Save the query as **Short Walks**, run the query, and print the query results. Why does the query select records with the smallest Distance values? Why does the query select more than 5 records?

6. Switch to SQL view to view the SQL statement that creates the **Short Walks** query. What SQL phrase is used to select the top 5 records? Close the **Short Walks** query.

> **Explore**

7. Create a make-table query based on the **Difference** query, saving the table as **Per Mile Pledge**. Select all fields and select those records where the PerMile field value is greater than 0. Run the query, save the make-table query as **Per Mile Pledge Make-Table**, and then close the query. Open the **PerMile Pledge** table, resize the columns in the query results to their best fit, print the records, and then save and close the table.

> **Explore**

8. Create a replica of the **Friends** database in the Cases folder on your Data Disk, making a backup of the database in the same folder and accepting the default settings in the Location of New Replica dialog box. Then complete the following:

   a. Close the Design Master, and then open the replica.
   b. Open the **Walker** table, change the phone number for Kim Shah to 723-5778, and then close the table.
   c. Synchronize the replica with the Design Master, close the replica, and then open the Design Master.
   d. Open the **Walker** table, verify that the phone number for Kim Shah was changed, print the table records, close the table, close the Design Master, and then exit Access.
   e. Use Windows Explorer or My Computer to open the Cases folder on your Data Disk. Rename the **Friends** database as **Friends Design Master**, rename the **Friends.bak** database as **Friends.mdb**, and then close Windows Explorer or My Computer.

Case 4. Lopez Lexus Dealerships Maria and Hector Lopez own a chain of Lexus dealerships throughout Texas. They have used a computer in their business for several years to handle their payroll and normal accounting functions. To keep track of their car inventory, they have developed the **Vehicles** database. The database has four tables: **Car**, **Customer**, **Location**, and **Purchase**. The **Car** table contains information about each car in the inventory, and the **Customer** table contains information about purchasers of cars. The **Location** table contains information about each of the Lopez dealership lots, and the **Purchase** table contains information about each car purchased by a customer. The database contains several other objects, including queries, forms, and reports. Maria and Hector ask you to define a many-to-many relationship between the **Car** and **Customer** tables, to create several new queries, and to create a replica of the database. To help them with their requests, you'll complete the following:

1. Make sure your Data Disk is in the appropriate disk drive, start Access, and then open the **Vehicles** database located in the Cases folder on your Data Disk.

2. Define a many-to-many relationship between the **Car** and **Customer** tables, using the **Purchase** table as the related table. Select the referential integrity option and both cascade options for the relationships.

Explore   3. Open the **Customer** table in Design view, delete the LastName index, save the table, and then close the table.

4. Create a query using the **Car** and **Location** tables. Display the Model and Cost fields from the **Car** table, and display the LocationName field from the **Location** table. Save the query as **Models by Location**, run the query, print the query results, and then close the query.

5. Create a crosstab query based on the **Models by Location** query. Use the LocationName field values for the row headings, the Model field values for the column headings, and the sum of the Cost field values as the summarized value. Save the query as **Models by Location Crosstab**, view the query, resize the columns in the query results to their best fit, print the query results, and then save and close the query.

6. Create a top values query based on the **Car** table. Display all fields from the table in the query results, sort the records in descending order by the SellingPrice field, and select the 10 most expensive cars. Save the query as **Most Expensive Cars**, run the query, print the query results in landscape orientation, and then close the query.

Explore   7. Lopez Lexus Dealerships is having a sale on GS300 model cars. The selling price is reduced by $1,000. Create an update query to reduce the SellingPrice for all GS300 model cars. Use the Expression Builder to create the expression [SellingPrice]-1000 as the update value. (*Hint*: Read the Help topic Expression Builder to learn more about the Expression Builder.) Save the query as **GS300 Model Update**, run the query, and then close the query. Open the **Car** table, print the table records in landscape orientation, and then close the table.

8. Create a find duplicates query based on the **Car** table. Select LocationCode as the field that might contain duplicates, and select all other fields as additional fields in the query results. Save the query as **Find Duplicate Locations**, view the query, print the query results, and then close the query.

Explore   9. Create a replica of the **Vehicles** database in the Cases folder on your Data Disk, making a backup of the database in the same folder and accepting the default settings in the Location of New Replica dialog box. Then complete the following:

   a. Close the Design Master, and then open the replica.
   b. Open the **Location** table, change the name of the manager at the San Antonio location to Hunsley, Betsey, and then close the table.

c. Open the **Car** table, delete the record for the car with VehicleID 888TL, and then close the table.

d. Synchronize the replica with the Design Master, close the replica, and then open the Design Master.

e. Open the **Location** table, verify that the name of the manager at the San Antonio location was changed, print the table records, and then close the table. Open the **Car** table, verify that the record for VehicleID 888TL was deleted, close the table, close the Design Master, and then exit Access.

f. Use Windows Explorer or My Computer to open the Cases folder on your Data Disk. Rename the **Vehicles** database as **Vehicles Design Master**, rename the **Vehicles.bak** database as **Vehicles.mdb**, and then close Windows Explorer or My Computer.

Case 5. eACH Internet Auction Site Chris and Pat Aquino own a successful Internet service provider and want to expand their business to host an Internet auction site named eACH. Before people can sell items and bid on items, they must register with eACH. After a seller posts an item for sale, it is sold at the auction site by accepting bids from buyers. Each item is listed by subcategory within category—for example, the general category of collectibles consists of several subcategories, including advertising, animation characters, comic books, and bears.

To keep track of these auctions, Chris and Pat have developed the **BuySell** database. The database has four tables: **Category**, **Subcategory**, **Registrant**, and **Item**. The **Category** table contains information about categories, and the **Subcategory** table contains information about subcategories. The **Registrant** table has one record for each person who sells and/or bids on items, and the **Item** table has one record for each item that is posted for sale. The database contains several other objects, including queries, forms, and reports.

Chris and Pat want you to add a new table, named **Bid**, to the database to keep track of the bids placed by people on the items for sale. Also, they want you to define a many-to-many relationship between the **Item** and **Registrant** tables and to create several new queries. To help them with their requests, you'll complete the following:

1. Make sure your Data Disk containing the **BuySell** database is in the appropriate drive, start Access, and then open the **BuySell** database located in the Cases folder on your Data Disk.

2. Create the new **Bid** table by defining the following fields:

   ■ Bid#, an AutoNumber field, is the primary key field.

   ■ Item#, a Number (Long Integer field size) field, is a foreign key to the **Item** table. This field stores the item on which the bidder is placing a bid.

   ■ Bidder, a Number (Long Integer field size) field, is a foreign key to the **Registrant** table. This field stores the registrant who's making the bid.

   ■ BidTime, a Date/Time (General Date format) field, stores the exact date and time the bid is made.

   ■ Bid, a Currency (Currency format with 2 decimal places), stores the amount of the bid.

3. Define a many-to-many relationship between the **Item** and **Registrant** tables, using the **Bid** table as the related table. Select the referential integrity option and both cascade options for the relationships.

Explore   4. If the Bid# field was deleted from the **Bid** table, what would be the primary key of the **Bid** table? (*Hint*: A registrant can bid on many items, and an item can have many registrants as bidders. However, it's possible for a registrant to place two or more bids on a single item.)

5. Open the **Bid** table in Design view, create an index for the Bidder field with duplicates allowed, save the table, and then close the table.

Explore

6. Design test data for the **Bid** table, and then add the test data to the table. (*Hint*: Be sure you have at least one item without any bids, at least one item with a single bid, and at least three items with two or more bids. Also, be sure you have at least one registrant who's not placed a bid and not posted an item for sale, at least one registrant who's only a seller, at least one registrant who's only a bidder, at least one registrant who's placed bids on two or more items, and at least one registrant who's placed multiple bids on a single item.)

7. Create a crosstab query based on the **Bid** table. Use the Item# field values for the row headings, the Bidder field values for the column headings, and the maximum of the Bid field as the summarized value. Save the query as **Bid Crosstab**, resize the columns in the query results to their best fit, print the query results in landscape orientation, and then save and close the query.

8. Create a find duplicates query based on the **Bid** table. Select the Item# and Bidder fields as the fields that might contain duplicates, and select all other fields as additional fields in the query results. Save the query as **Find Duplicate Bids**, print the query results, and then close the query.

9. Create a find unmatched query that finds all records in the **Item** table for which there is no matching record in the **Bid** table. Select the Item#, Seller, Subcategory#, Title, MinimumBid, and Opened fields in the query results. Save the query as **Item Without Matching Bid**, print the query results, and then close the query.

10. Create a make-table query based on the **Subcategory** table, saving the table as **Special Subcategory** in the current database. Select all fields in the **Subcategory** table, and select those records with a Category# field value of 2. Run the query, close the query, and then save the make-table query as **Category 2 Make-Table**. Open the **Special Subcategory** table, resize the columns to their best fit, print the table records, and then save and close the table.

11. Create an append query to select all records from the **Subcategory** table where the Category# field value is either 4 or 6 and append them to the **Special Subcategory** table. After you run the query, close the query, and then save the append query as **Category 4 or 6 Append**. Open the **Special Subcategory** table, print the table records, and then close the table.

12. Close the **BuySell** database, and then exit Access.

INTERNET ASSIGNMENTS

The purpose of the Internet Assignments is to challenge you to find information on the Internet that you can use to create effective documents. The actual assignments are updated and maintained on the Course Technology Web site. Log on to the Internet and use your Web browser to go to the Student Online Companion to accompany this text at **www.course.com/NewPerspectives/office2000**. Click the Access link, and then click the link for Tutorial 8.

LAB ASSIGNMENTS

These Lab Assignments are designed to accompany the interactive Course Lab for SQL. To start the SQL Lab, click the Start button on the Windows taskbar, point to Programs, point to Course Labs, point to New Perspectives Applications, and then click SQL. If you do not see Course Labs on your Programs menu, see your instructor or technical support person.

SQL Queries To query many relational databases, you use SQL (usually pronounced by saying the letters of the acronym, "S Q L"). IBM developed SQL in the mid 1970s for use in mainframe relational database products such as DB2. In 1986 the American National Standards Institute (ANSI) adopted SQL as the standard relational database language, and it is now used extensively on microcomputer databases as well. Understanding how to use SQL is an important skill for many data management jobs. In this Lab, you will get a taste of this powerful and flexible database language. To gain further expertise, you should refer to the course offerings at your school.

1. Click the Steps button to learn how to formulate SQL queries. As you proceed through the steps, answer the Quick Check questions. After you complete the Steps, you will see a Quick Check Summary Report. Follow the instructions on the screen to print this report.

2. In Explore, use the scroll bar to browse through the database to find the answers to the following questions:

   a. What are the names of the staff physicians? (*Hint*: The JobCode for staff physicians is SMD.)
   b. How many LPNs are in the database?
   c. Who makes more than $20 an hour?
   d. What is Ralph Smith's job?
   e. When was Tony Jackson hired?

3. In Explore, try the following queries and indicate if each accomplishes the result listed:

   a. **QUERY:** SELECT * FROM Employee order by Hourlywage
      RESULT: Displays employees beginning with the person who is the lowest paid
   b. **QUERY:** SELECT * FROM Employee where Gender = 'F' AND Jobcode = 'SMD'
      RESULT: Displays all the female staff physicians
   c. **QUERY:** SELECT * FROM Employee where LastName between 'C' and 'M'
      RESULT: Displays all the employees with last names that begin with a C, D, E, F, G, or H
   d. **QUERY:** SELECT * FROM Employee where Gender = 'M' or Hourlywage > 20.00
      RESULT: Displays only the men who make more than $20 an hour
   e. **QUERY:** SELECT * FROM Employee where DeptCode <> 'OB' order by BirthDate
      RESULT: Displays all the obstetricians' birthdays

4. In Explore, suppose that the database contains thousands of records and it is not practical to browse through all of the records using the scroll bar. Write down the queries you use to do the following:

   a. Find the record for Angela Peterson.
   b. Find the records for all the RNs.
   c. Find all the employees who work in Intensive Care (IC).
   d. Find all the employees who make less than $15 an hour.
   e. Find all the employees who do not work in obstetrics (OB).

5. In Explore, suppose that the database contains thousands of records and it is not practical to browse through all of the records using the scroll bar. Write down the queries you use to do the following:

   a. Find the name of the oldest employee.
   b. Find the departments that have female employees.

    c. Find out how many employees work in Intensive Care.

    d. Find the last names of the female employees who make between $10 and $15 per hour.

    e. Get an alphabetized list of male employees who work as RNs or LPNs.

6. Circle the errors in the following SQL queries:

    a. SELECT * FROM Employee where DeptCode <> OB order by BirthDate

    b. SELECT * FROM Employee where Wages between 10 and 50

    c. SELECT * FROM Employee where order = LastName

    d. SELECT * FROM Employee where DeptCode <> 'OB' and Hourly Wage > '$10.00' order by LastName

    e. SELECT * FROM Employee where FirstName like T*

QUICK | CHECK ANSWERS

Session 8.1

1. A crosstab query performs aggregate function calculations on the values of one database field and displays the results in a spreadsheet format.

2. Avg, Count, First, Last, Min, Max, StDev, Sum, Var

3. Simple Query Wizard, Crosstab Query Wizard, Find Duplicates Query Wizard, Find Unmatched Query Wizard

4. A select query that locates duplicate records in a table or query

5. A find unmatched query is a select query that finds all the records in a table or query that have no related records in a second table or query.

6. Access displays the first five records.

Session 8.2

1. A query that adds, changes, or deletes multiple table records at one time

2. You should preview the query results before running the action query.

3. A make-table query creates a new table from one or more existing tables. An append query adds records from an existing table or query to the end of another table.

4. deletes groups of records from one or more tables

5. changes selected field values in one or more tables

6. Access places the Update To row in the design grid.

7. Expression Builder is an Access tool that contains an expression box in which the expression is entered, buttons for common operators, and one or more lists of expression elements, such as table and field names.

Session 8.3

1. one-to-many (1:M), many-to-many (M:N), one-to-one (1:1)

2. a table whose primary key is a foreign key to a second table and whose fields are additional fields for the second table

3. a list that relates field values to the records that contain those field values

4. An inner join selects records from two tables when they have matching values in the common field(s). An outer join selects all records from one table and records from a second table whose common field value(s) match records in the first table.

5. a join between a table and itself

6. a. The primary key for the Telephone table is TelephoneNumber. There is no single field that serves as the primary key for the Phone Call table. A primary key can be constructed using a combination of the CallingTelephoneNumber, CallDate, and CallStartTime fields.

   b. There is a one-to-many relationship between the primary Telephone table and the related Phone Call table.

   c. Yes, an inner join is possible. Examples use these common fields: TelephoneNumber and CallingTelephoneNumber, TelephoneNumber and CalledTelephoneNumber, TelephoneNumber and BilledTelephoneNumber.

   d. Yes, an outer join is possible. Assume that the primary keys are defined as in Quick Check 6-a and that Telephone is the left table. Examples of a left outer join use these common fields: TelephoneNumber and CallingTelephoneNumber, TelephoneNumber and CalledTelephoneNumber, TelephoneNumber and BilledTelephoneNumber.

   e. No, a self-join is not possible for either of these tables.

Session 8.4

1. SQL (Structured Query Language)

2. The basic format of an SQL statement is SELECT-FROM-WHERE-ORDER BY. The SELECT clause identifies the fields selected; the FROM clause specifies the table(s) from which the fields are selected; the WHERE clause specifies the selection criteria; the ORDER BY clause specifies the sort sequence.

3. specifies the sort order for the records

4. When you create a replica of a database, the Design Master and all of its replicas are called the replica set.

5. Anyone using the Design Master can make changes to the design of the database tables, queries, and other objects. A replica prevents the user from changing the structure or design of an existing table, query, or other database object.

6. The synchronizing process compares the Design Master to the replica and checks for any differences. Access updates the Design Master with any changes that have been made to the data in the replica, and updates the replica with any changes that have been made to the data or to the design of any database objects in the Design Master.

AUTOMATING TASKS WITH MACROS

Creating a User Interface for the FineFood Database

CASE

Valle Coffee

At a recent office automation conference, Leonard saw several database applications developed by database designers. The designers' applications used several advanced Access features to automate and control how a user interacts with Access. These features allowed the designers to create a custom user interface for a database. This Interface made it much easier for inexperienced users to access the database, and it minimized the chance that an unauthorized user could change the design of any database objects.

Leonard would like to implement a similar user interface for the FineFood database. He would like the interface to display a list of available forms, reports, and queries in the database that the user can select by clicking a command button. This Interface will make it much easier for Valle Coffee employees to use the FineFood database, and It will reduce the chance that database users will make undesirable changes to the design of the database objects.

SESSION 9.1

In this session, you will review the design of a graphical user interface for the FineFood database. You also will run, modify, test, create, and save macros.

Implementing a Graphical User Interface

A **user interface** is what you see and how you communicate with a computer program. Not too long ago, most users communicated with a program by typing words that represented commands. You had to remember these commands, which were part of a command language. Most of the programs developed for today's popular operating environments, such as Microsoft Windows, provide graphical user interfaces. A **graphical user interface** (**GUI**; pronounced "gooey") displays windows, menu bars, pull-down menus, dialog boxes, and graphical pictures, called **icons**, which you use to communicate with the program. All Microsoft Windows programs use a similar visual interface, so once you learn one program, you can easily learn another. Overall, a GUI benefits a user by simplifying work, improving productivity, and decreasing errors.

Leonard wants to provide an easier way to work with the FineFood database. The type of user interface you need for working with a database is called a switchboard.

Switchboards

A **switchboard** is a form that appears when you open a database. It provides controlled access to the database's tables, forms, queries, and reports. When a user opens the database, Access opens a switchboard from which the user can choose an option. When you create a switchboard, you are essentially creating a new interface, and it's up to you to decide what options you want to give the user. Figure 9-1 shows the finished FineFood Database switchboard, which you will begin in this tutorial and finish in Tutorial 10.

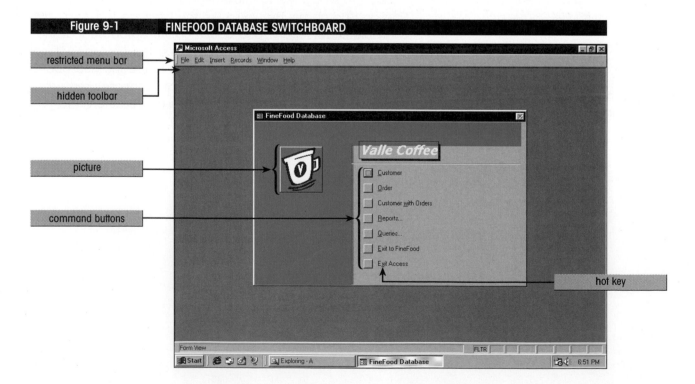

Figure 9-1   FINEFOOD DATABASE SWITCHBOARD

A typical switchboard provides the following items:

- Command buttons for all the options available to the user. In the switchboard shown in Figure 9-1, for example, you can click command buttons to open one of three forms (Customer, Order, or Customers with Orders), to open another switchboard with report options, to open a list of available queries, to close the switchboard and return to the Database window for the FineFood database, or to exit Access. When a selected form, query list, or report switchboard is closed, Access redisplays the FineFood Database switchboard, so you can choose the next option. In other words, you start and end with the switchboard and navigate between options from the switchboard.

- A restricted menu bar. Only the options that a user needs for manipulating data appear on these menus; there are no menu options for changing the database design.

- A hidden toolbar. Because many toolbar buttons alter the database design, the toolbar is hidden from the user.

- **Shortcut keys** (or **hot keys**), which are the underlined letters in the words next to each command button option. You can use shortcut keys to make a selection by holding down the Alt key while typing the underlined letter, instead of clicking a command button. You also can provide shortcut keys for menu names, menu options, and toolbar buttons.

- Text boxes and pictures that provide identification and visual appeal. The display of a small number of attractively designed pictures and text boxes can help users understand the switchboard's functions, but keep in mind that too many can be confusing or distracting.

A switchboard provides an attractive appearance to a user interface, but there are two more important reasons to use a switchboard instead of the Database window to work with a database. First, a switchboard lets you customize the organization of the user interface. Second, a switchboard prevents users from changing the design of tables, forms, queries, reports, and other objects. By hiding the Database window and toolbar and using a restricted menu bar, you limit users to just those database features that you want them to use. If you do not include any menu, toolbar, or command button options that let users open database objects in Design view, users cannot inadvertently or purposely change the design of the database.

The Reports and Queries command buttons on the FineFood Database switchboard include ellipses after the button names. As you know from your work in Windows, these ellipses signify that a dialog box containing additional options opens when you click that command button. To display the list of available reports, you will create another switchboard, as shown in Figure 9-2, which is similar in appearance to the FineFood Database switchboard.

Figure 9-2   REPORTS SWITCHBOARD

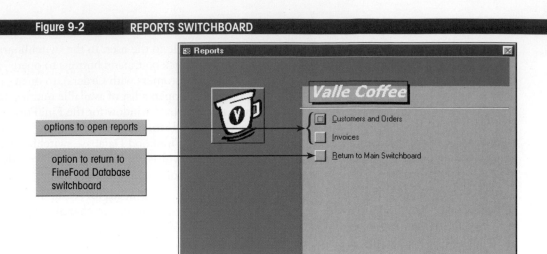

options to open reports

option to return to
FineFood Database
switchboard

The Reports switchboard contains command buttons to open the Customers and Orders report and the Invoices report. It also has a command button to return to the FineFood Database switchboard, which is the main switchboard.

To display the list of available queries and their options, you will create a custom dialog box.

Dialog Boxes

A **custom dialog box** is a form that resembles a dialog box, both in appearance and function. You use a custom dialog box to ask for user input, selection, or confirmation before performing an action, such as opening the results of a query or printing a query. Figure 9-3 shows the finished Queries dialog box that you will create later in this tutorial for the FineFood database user interface.

Figure 9-3   QUERIES DIALOG BOX

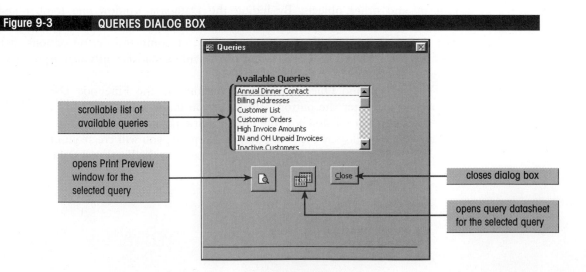

scrollable list of
available queries

opens Print Preview
window for the
selected query

closes dialog box

opens query datasheet
for the selected query

You will add a list box, which displays the queries available for selection, to the dialog box. You also will add three command buttons. A **command button** is a control on a form that starts an action (or set of actions) when you click it. Command buttons can contain text, standard pictures available from Access, or pictures you supply, to indicate their functions. Clicking the Close command button in the Queries dialog box returns you to the FineFood

Database switchboard. The other command buttons contain pictures to identify their functions. The command button on the left has an icon of a magnifying glass over a piece of paper. This is the same icon shown on the Print Preview button on the Standard toolbar in Access. Just as the Print Preview button opens the Print Preview window, this command button opens the Print Preview window for the selected query. When you click the middle command button, the selected query opens in Datasheet view.

Introduction to Macros

The command buttons and custom dialog boxes on the FineFood Database switchboard gain their power from macros—and from Visual Basic for Applications code. A **macro** is a command or a series of commands that you want Access to perform automatically for you. Macros automate repetitive tasks, such as opening forms, printing selected form records, and running queries. Each command in a macro is called an action. An **action** is an instruction to Access to perform an operation, such as opening a form or displaying a query in the Print Preview window. For example, clicking the Order command button on the FineFood Database switchboard causes Access to run a macro containing the action that opens the Order form.

Access lets you automate most tasks using either macros or **Visual Basic for Applications (VBA)**, the programming language for Microsoft applications. As a beginner, you will find it easier to write macros than to create programs using VBA. With macros, you simply select a series of actions from a list so that the macro does what you want it to do. To use VBA, you need to understand the VBA command language well enough to be able to write your own code. VBA does provide advantages over using macros, such as better error-handling capabilities and making your application easier to change. Macros, however, are useful for small applications and for simple tasks, such as opening and closing objects. Additionally, you cannot use VBA to assign actions to a specific key or key combination or to open an application in a special way, such as displaying a switchboard. For these types of actions, you must use macros.

Before you begin creating the FineFood Database switchboard and its supporting macros, you'll run an existing macro, named Customer, that Leonard created after he returned from the conference.

Running a Macro

You can run an existing macro in three different ways:

- In the Macro window, click the Run button on the Macro Design toolbar.
- Click Tools on the menu bar, point to Macro, click Run Macro, scroll through the Macro Name list box, click the desired macro name, and then click the OK button.
- In the Database window, click Macros in the Objects bar, right-click the macro name, and then click Run.

You'll use the last method to run the Customer macro.

To run the Customer macro:

1. Place your Data Disk in the appropriate disk drive, start Access, and then open the **FineFood** database located in the Tutorial folder on your Data Disk.

2. Click **Macros** in the Objects bar of the Database window, right-click **Customer**, and then click **Run**. A message box opens. See Figure 9-4.

Figure 9-4

| Figure 9-4 | USING A MACRO ACTION TO OPEN A MESSAGE BOX |

Opening the message box is the first action in the Customer macro. The message box specifies that the next macro action will open the Customer form. When you click the OK button, the message box closes, and the macro resumes with the next action.

3. Click the **OK** button. The next two actions in the Customer macro are performed: the Customer form opens, and the second message box opens. See Figure 9-5.

| Figure 9-5 | SECOND AND THIRD ACTIONS IN THE CUSTOMER MACRO |

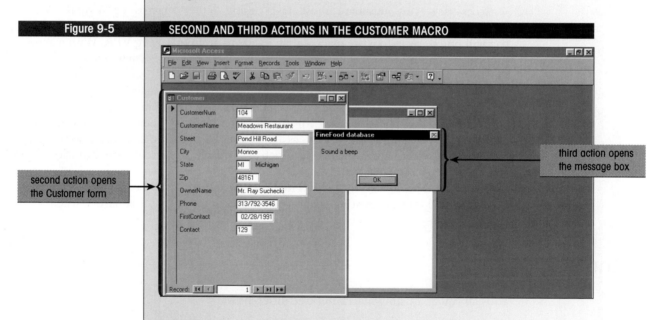

4. Click the **OK** button. A beep sounds, and the third message box opens. These are the fourth and fifth actions in the Customer macro.

5. Click the **OK** button. The Customer form is maximized, and the fourth message box opens. These are the sixth and seventh actions in the Customer macro.

6. Click the **OK** button. The Customer form is restored, and the fifth message box opens. These are the eighth and ninth actions in the Customer macro.

7. Click the **OK** button. The Customer form now displays record 21 for Around the Clock Restaurant, and the sixth message box opens. These are actions 10 and 11 in the Customer macro.

8. Click the **OK** button. The Customer form closes (action 12—the last action in the Customer macro), the Customer macro ends, and the Database window becomes the active window.

Leonard suggests that you add some actions to the Customer macro to learn about the Macro window and the way to modify an existing macro.

Adding Actions to a Macro

To modify the Customer macro, you need to open it in the Macro window.

To open the Macro window:

1. Right-click **Customer** in the Macros list, and then click **Design View** on the shortcut menu. The Customer macro opens in the Macro window. See Figure 9-6.

| Figure 9-6 | MACRO WINDOW |

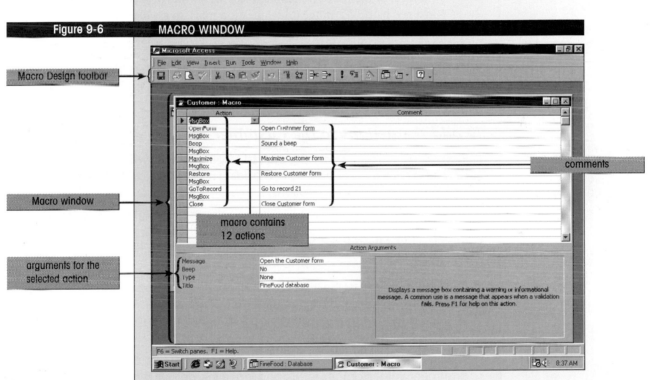

In the **Macro window**, you create and modify macros. Both the menu bar and toolbar for the Macro window have options that are specifically related to macros. The Macro window also includes an **Action column**, in which you enter the action you want Access to perform, and a **Comment column**, in which you enter optional comments to document the specific action. You usually don't enter comments for actions that are self descriptive.

The first MsgBox action is the current action. Access displays a hint for the current action in the bottom pane (Action Arguments) of the Macro window on the right. On the left, Access lists the arguments associated with the current action. **Arguments** are additional facts Access needs to execute an action. The action for opening a message box, for example, needs the wording of the message to be displayed and the title bar name as arguments.

You'll add two actions, the MsgBox and FindRecord actions, to the Customer macro between the GoToRecord and the last MsgBox actions. For the FindRecord action, you'll find the record for CustomerNum 798. You use the **FindRecord action** to find the first record that meets the criteria specified by the FindRecord arguments.

The **MsgBox action** causes Access to open a message box—a special type of dialog box with a message and command button but no options. The message box remains on the screen until you click the OK button. The macro containing a MsgBox action does not proceed to the next action until you click the OK button, so when you add this action to the Customer macro, you'll have as much time as you need to read and react to the message box.

The MsgBox action requires four arguments: Message, Beep, Type, and Title, described as follows:

- Message contains the text that will appear in the message box when it is displayed.

- Beep is a Yes/No argument that specifies whether a beep will sound when the message box is opened.

- Type determines which icon appears in the message box, signifying the critical level of the message. Icon choices are: None (no icon), Critical (white X in a red ball), Warning? (blue question mark in a white balloon), Warning! (black exclamation point in a yellow triangle), and Information (blue letter I in a white balloon).

- Title contains the title that appears in the message box title bar.

You'll now add the MsgBox and FindRecord actions to the Customer macro.

To add the actions to the Customer macro:

1. Right-click the **row selector** for the last MsgBox action, which is the 11th action, and then click **Insert Rows**. Access adds a new, blank row between the GoToRecord and MsgBox actions.

   Because you'll be adding two actions, you need to insert a second blank row.

2. Repeat Step 1 to add a second blank row.

   You'll add the MsgBox action to the first blank row.

3. Click the right side of the first blank row's **Action** text box to display the list of actions, scroll down the list, and then click **MsgBox**. The list box closes as MsgBox becomes the new action, and four arguments for this action appear in the Action Arguments pane.

   You'll enter values for the Message and Title arguments, change the Beep argument value from Yes to No, and leave the default Type argument value of None unchanged. The description to the right of the argument text boxes changes as you move from one action argument to the next. The description is a brief explanation of the current macro argument. If you need a more detailed explanation, press the F1 key. You can also use Help to learn about specific actions and their arguments, and about macros in general.

4. Press the **F6** key, type **Find CustomerNum 798** in the Message text box, press the **Tab** key, click the **Beep** list arrow, click **No**, press the **Tab** key twice, and then type **FineFood database** in the Title text box. See Figure 9-7.

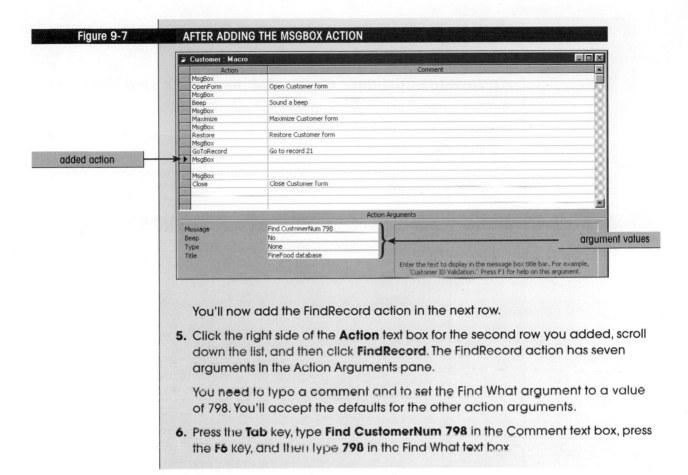

Figure 9-7 — AFTER ADDING THE MSGBOX ACTION

added action

argument values

You'll now add the FindRecord action in the next row.

5. Click the right side of the **Action** text box for the second row you added, scroll down the list, and then click **FindRecord**. The FindRecord action has seven arguments in the Action Arguments pane.

You need to type a comment and to set the Find What argument to a value of 798. You'll accept the defaults for the other action arguments.

6. Press the **Tab** key, type **Find CustomerNum 798** in the Comment text box, press the **F6** key, and then type **798** in the Find What text box.

When you create complicated macros with many actions, you'll find it useful to be able to run through a macro one step at a time.

Single Stepping a Macro

Single stepping executes a macro one action at a time, pausing between actions. You use single stepping to make sure you have placed actions in the right order and with the correct arguments. If you have problems with a macro, you can use single stepping to find the cause of the problems and to determine their proper corrections. The Single Step button on the Macro Design toolbar is a toggle you use to turn single stepping on and off. Once you turn on single stepping, it stays on for all macros until you turn it off.

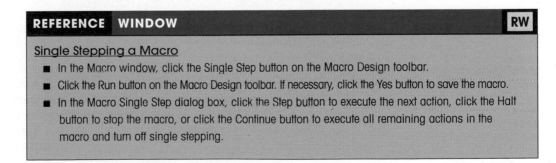

REFERENCE WINDOW **RW**

Single Stepping a Macro
- In the Macro window, click the Single Step button on the Macro Design toolbar.
- Click the Run button on the Macro Design toolbar. If necessary, click the Yes button to save the macro.
- In the Macro Single Step dialog box, click the Step button to execute the next action, click the Halt button to stop the macro, or click the Continue button to execute all remaining actions in the macro and turn off single stepping.

To get a clearer view of the effects of the actions in the Customer macro, you can single step through it. First you need to save your macro changes.

To save the Customer macro and then single step through it:

1. Click the **Save** button on the Macro Design toolbar.

2. Click the **Single Step** button on the Macro Design toolbar to turn on single stepping.

3. Click the **Run** button on the Macro Design toolbar. The Macro Single Step dialog box opens. See Figure 9-8.

Figure 9-8	MACRO SINGLE STEP DIALOG BOX

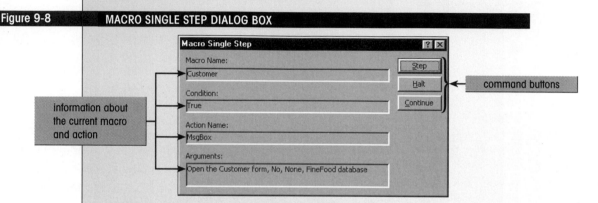

TROUBLE? If the first message box opens instead of the Macro Single Step dialog box, then you turned off single stepping in Step 2 when you clicked the button. Click the OK button as needed to run the macro, and then repeat Steps 2 and 3.

When you single step through a macro, Access opens the Macro Single Step dialog box before performing each action. This dialog box shows the macro's name and the action's condition, name, and arguments. The action will be executed or not executed, depending on whether the condition is true or false. The three command buttons let you step through the macro one action at a time, halt the macro and return to the Macro window, or continue by executing all remaining actions without pausing. Note that single stepping is turned off if you click the Continue button.

4. Click the **Step** button. Access runs the first action (MsgBox). Because the MsgBox action pauses the macro, the Macro Single Step dialog box remains hidden until you click the OK button in the message box.

5. Click the **OK** button to close the message box. The Macro Single Step dialog box shows the macro's second action (OpenForm).

6. Click the **Step** button. Access runs the second action by opening the Customer form and shows the macro's third action (MsgBox) in the Macro Single Step dialog box.

7. Click the **Step** button nine more times, and click the **OK** button four more times. Make sure you read the Macro Single Step dialog box carefully and observe the actions that occur. At this point, the message box you added (Find CustomerNum 798) is open, and record 21 is the current record in the Customer form.

8. Click the **OK** button, and then click the **Step** button. The FindRecord action runs, record 38 for CustomerNum 798 is now the current record in the Customer form, and the Macro Single Step dialog box shows the macro's last action (MsgBox).

9. Click the **Step** button two more times, and the **OK** button once. The Macro Single Step dialog box closes automatically after completing the last macro action.

Leonard suggests that you complete your practice with macros by creating a new macro and adding an action to it by dragging an object from the Database window.

Creating a Macro

You use the Macro window to create and modify macros. To create the new macro, you'll create a blank macro and then add the actions to it.

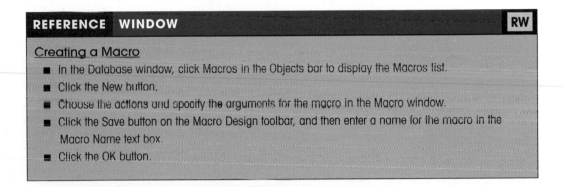

REFERENCE WINDOW   **RW**

Creating a Macro
- In the Database window, click Macros in the Objects bar to display the Macros list.
- Click the New button.
- Choose the actions and specify the arguments for the macro in the Macro window.
- Click the Save button on the Macro Design toolbar, and then enter a name for the macro in the Macro Name text box.
- Click the OK button.

Before you create the new macro, you need to turn off single stepping and close the Customer macro.

To turn off single stepping and close the Customer macro:

1. Click the **Single Step** button 📇 on the Macro Design toolbar to turn off single stepping.

2. Click the **Close** button ☒ on the Macro window to close it and return to the Database window.

You'll create a macro named Order; this macro will contain actions to open and close the Order form.

To create the Order macro:

1. Click the **New** button in the Database window. The Macro window opens.

   Because you can save a macro at any time, you'll save the blank macro immediately and name it Order.

2. Click the **Save** button 💾 on the Macro Design toolbar. The Save As dialog box opens.

3. Type **Order** in the Macro Name text box, and then press the **Enter** key.

Adding Actions by Dragging

Another way to add an action to a macro is by dragging an object from the Database window to a new row in the Macro window. When you do this, Access adds the appropriate action and specifies its default argument values. Figure 9-9 describes the effect of dragging each of the six Access objects to a new row in the Macro window. For example, dragging a table creates an OpenTable action that opens the table in Datasheet view and permits editing or updating. To use this dragging technique, be sure that the Macro and Database windows are both visible. You can move the two windows until you see all the critical components of each window, or use the Tile Horizontally or Tile Vertically command on the Window menu.

Figure 9-9	ACTIONS CREATED BY DRAGGING OBJECTS FROM THE DATABASE WINDOW	
OBJECT DRAGGED	**ACTION CREATED**	**ARGUMENTS AND THEIR DEFAULT VALUES**
Table	OpenTable	View: Datasheet Data Mode: Edit
Query	OpenQuery	View: Datasheet Data Mode: Edit
Form	OpenForm	View: Form Filter Name: none Where Condition: none Data Mode: none Window Mode: Normal
Report	OpenReport	View: Print Filter Name: none Where Condition: none
Data Access Page	OpenDataAccessPage	View: Browse
Macro	RunMacro	Repeat Count: none Repeat Expression: none
Module	OpenModule	Procedure Name: none

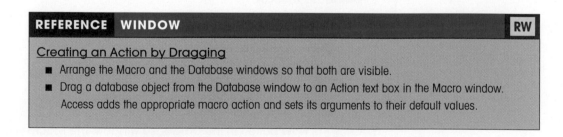

REFERENCE WINDOW   **RW**

<u>Creating an Action by Dragging</u>
- Arrange the Macro and the Database windows so that both are visible.
- Drag a database object from the Database window to an Action text box in the Macro window. Access adds the appropriate macro action and sets its arguments to their default values.

Next, you'll use the dragging technique to add actions that open and close the Order form.

To add actions using the dragging method:

1. Click **Window** on the menu bar, and then click **Tile Vertically** to tile the Macro window and the Database window. See Figure 9-10.

| Figure 9-10 | MACRO AND DATABASE WINDOWS TILED VERTICALLY |

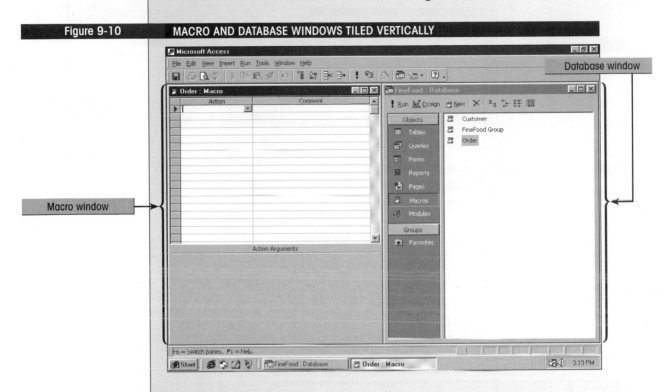

2. Click **Forms** in the Objects bar of the Database window to display the Forms list.

3. Drag **Order** from the Forms list box to the first row's Action text box in the Macro window. Access adds the OpenForm action for the Order form and sets the arguments to their default values.

4. Press the **Tab** key, and then type **Open Order form** in the Comment text box.

   Next, you'll add the MsgBox action so that you'll be able to see the opened Order form before you close it. You use the default values for the Beep and Type arguments.

5. Press the **Tab** key, click the **Action** list arrow, scroll down the list, and then click **MsgBox**.

6. Press the **F6** key, type **Close Order form** in the Message text box, press the **Tab** key three times, and then type **FineFood database** in the Title text box.

   You'll select Close as the final action in the Order macro, and set its arguments by dragging the Order form from the Database window to the Object Name text box in the Action Arguments pane of the Macro window.

7. Click the right side of the third row's **Action** text box, click **Close**, press the **Tab** key, and then type **Close Order form** in the Comment text box.

8. Drag **Order** from the Forms list in the Database window to the Object Name text box in the Macro window. When you release the mouse button in the Object Name text box, Access automatically sets the Object Type argument to Form and the Object Name argument to Order. See Figure 9-11.

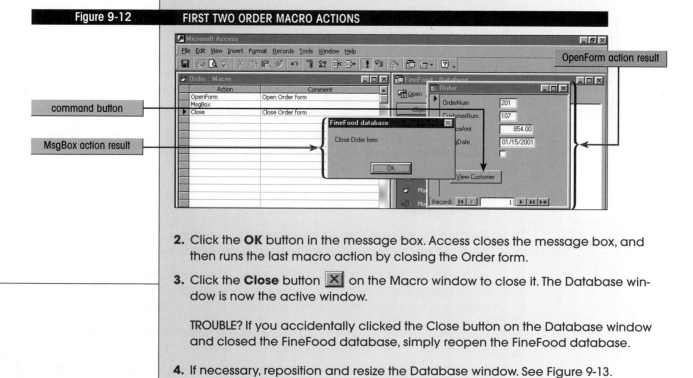

| Figure 9-11 | MACRO WINDOW WITH ACTION ARGUMENTS SET BY DRAGGING |

Close action selected

Object Name text box

form selected for dragging

The macro is now complete, so you'll run it to be sure it is correct.

To run the Order macro:

1. Click the **Run** button ! on the Macro Design toolbar, and then click the **Yes** button to save the modified macro. Access runs the first two macro actions by opening the message box after opening the Order form. See Figure 9-12.

| Figure 9-12 | FIRST TWO ORDER MACRO ACTIONS |

command button

MsgBox action result

OpenForm action result

2. Click the **OK** button in the message box. Access closes the message box, and then runs the last macro action by closing the Order form.

3. Click the **Close** button ✕ on the Macro window to close it. The Database window is now the active window.

   TROUBLE? If you accidentally clicked the Close button on the Database window and closed the FineFood database, simply reopen the FineFood database.

4. If necessary, reposition and resize the Database window. See Figure 9-13.

Figure 9-13	DATABASE WINDOW REPOSITIONED AND RESIZED

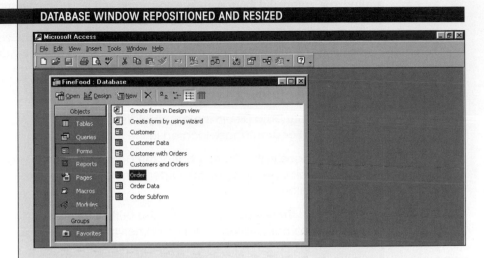

5. Click the **Close** button ⊠ on the Access window title bar to close the FineFood database and exit Access. You return to the Windows desktop.

The Order form (see Figure 9-12) that Leonard created contains a command button that uses a macro. In the next session, you'll use this macro and the command button, and then you'll add a command button with an attached macro to the Customer form. You'll also define data validation criteria for the State field in the Customer table.

Session 9.1 QUICK CHECK

1. Define a switchboard and provide two reasons for using one.

2. What is a hot key and how do you use it?

3. What is a macro, and what is the relationship between a macro and an action?

4. What is an action argument? Give an example of an action argument.

5. What does the MsgBox action do?

6. What are you trying to accomplish when you single step through a macro?

SESSION 9.2

In this session, you'll review a macro that's attached to a command button and learn about events and macro groups. You'll also add a macro to a macro group, add a command button with an attached macro to a form, and set validation properties for a table field.

Using a Command Button with an Attached Macro

Leonard created a macro that he associated, or attached, to a command button on the Order form that you opened in Session 9.1. In Session 9.1, you learned how to create a macro with actions that open and close forms, find records, and open message boxes. You can also add a command button to a form to execute a set of actions. To add a command button to a form, you open the form in Design view and use the Command Button tool on the toolbox. After adding the command button to the form and while still in Design view, you attach the macro with the desired actions to the button. Then, when a user clicks the command button, the macro's actions are executed. Leonard asks you to use the command button to view how the macro attaches to the command button, and then to view the macro.

To use the View Customer command button:

1. Place your Data Disk in the appropriate disk drive, start Access, and then open the **FineFood** database located in the Tutorial folder on your Data Disk.

2. Click **Forms** in the Objects bar of the Database window, right-click **Order**, and then click **Open** to open the Order form for the first order with OrderNum 201 and CustomerNum 107.

3. Click the **View Customer** command button. The Order form remains open, and the Customer form opens for CustomerNum 107. See Figure 9-14.

Figure 9-14   AFTER OPENING THE CUSTOMER FORM WITH THE VIEW CUSTOMER COMMAND BUTTON

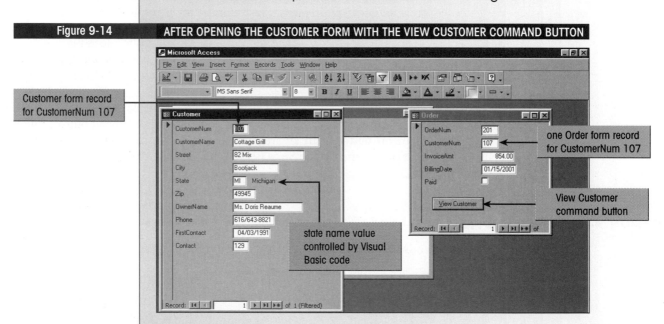

Customer form record for CustomerNum 107

state name value controlled by Visual Basic code

one Order form record for CustomerNum 107

View Customer command button

Clicking the View Customer command button triggered an attached macro that opened the Customer form. The record displayed in the Customer form is for the customer (CustomerNum 107) who placed the order displayed in the Order form. The text "Record 1 of 1 (Filtered)" that appears around the navigation buttons in the Customer form indicates that you can view only the record for CustomerNum 107 in the Customer form at this point. Notice that the full state name of Michigan appears in red letters to the right of the state abbreviation in the Customer form. VBA code controls the state name's value and color. You'll learn more about this specific code and VBA in Tutorial 10.

As you navigate through the Order form, the contents of the Customer form do not change unless you click the View Customer command button.

4. Click the **Last Record** navigation button ▶❙ in the Order form. The last record, record 103 for CustomerNum 202, is now the current record, but the Customer form is unchanged—it still shows the record for CustomerNum 107.

5. Click the **View Customer** command button. The record for CustomerNum 202 is now the current record in the Customer form, and the Order record still displays record 103.

6. Click the **Close** button ☒ on the Customer form to close it. The Order form is now the active window.

Clicking the View Customer command button is an event, and the opening of the Customer form is controlled by setting an event property.

Events

An **event** occurs when you take an action, such as clicking a button, using the mouse, or pressing a key to choose an option. In your work with Access, you've initiated hundreds of events on forms, controls, records, and reports. For example, three form events are: Open, which occurs when you open a form; Activate, which occurs when the form becomes the active window; and Close, which occurs when you close a form and it is removed from the screen. Each event has an associated event property. An **event property** specifies how an object responds when an event occurs. For example, each form has OnOpen, OnActivate, and OnClose event properties associated with the Open, Activate, and Close events, respectively.

Event properties appear in the property sheet when you create forms and reports. Unlike most properties you've used previously in property sheets, event properties do not have an initial value. If an event property contains no value, it means that the event property has not been set. In this case Access takes no *special action* when the associated event occurs. For example, if a form's OnOpen event property is not set and you open the form, then the Open event occurs (the form opens), but no *special action* occurs beyond the opening of the form. You can set an event property value to a macro name, and Access will execute the macro when the event occurs. For example, you could write a macro that automatically selects a particular field in a form when you open it. You also can create a group of statements using VBA code and set the event property value to the name of that group of statements. Access will then execute the group of statements, or **procedure**, when the event occurs. Such a procedure is called an **event procedure**.

When you clicked the View Customer command button on the Order form, the Click event occurred and triggered the attached macro. The View Customer command button contains an OnClick event property, which you will examine next.

To view the OnClick event property for the View Customer command button:

1. Click the **View** button for Design view 🖳 on the Form View toolbar to display the Order form in Design view.

2. Scroll down the form, right-click the **View Customer** command button, and then click **Properties** to open the property sheet.

You might notice that event properties, such as OnEnter and OnClick, do not contain a space, but the property sheet shows them as On Enter and On Click, with the spaces. In this case, OnClick and the On Click property in the property sheet are the same.

3. Click the **Event** tab (if necessary), right-click the **On Click** text box, click **Zoom** to open the Zoom dialog box, and then click to the right of the selected text to deselect it. See Figure 9-15.

Figure 9-15   **MACRO ATTACHED TO THE ONCLICK EVENT PROPERTY**

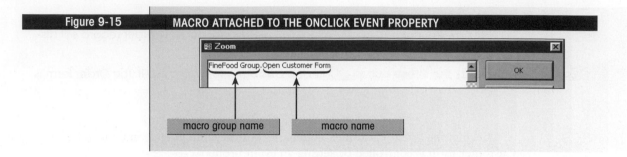

The OnClick event property value shown in the Zoom dialog box is *FineFood Group.Open Customer Form*. This is an example of a reference to a macro in a macro group.

Macro Groups

Instead of creating several separate macros, you can combine them in a macro group. A **macro group** is a macro that contains other macros. Macro groups allow you to consolidate related macros and to manage large numbers of macros. For the OnClick event property value shown in Figure 9-15, FineFood Group is the macro group name, and Open Customer Form is the macro name. A period separates the two names. When you click the View Customer command button on the Order form, Access processes the actions contained in the Open Customer Form macro, which is located in the FineFood Group macro group.

You'll now close the Zoom dialog box, and then open the Macro window from the property sheet.

To open the FineFood Group macro in the Macro window:

1. Click the **Close** button ⊠ on the Zoom dialog box to close it. The OnClick event property value is selected in the property sheet, and the On Click text box contains a list arrow and Build button on its right edge. See Figure 9-16.

Figure 9-16   **ONCLICK EVENT PROPERTY VALUE FOR THE VIEW CUSTOMER COMMAND BUTTON**

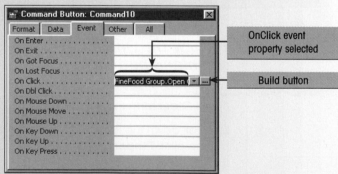

You click the list arrow if you want to change the current macro to a different macro, and you click the Build button if you want to view or change the existing macro in the Macro window. The Build button is also called the **Macro Builder** when you use it to work with macros.

2. Click the **Build** button ▦ on the right edge of the On Click text box. The Macro window opens and displays the FineFood Group macro. See Figure 9-17.

Figure 9-17	MACRO WINDOW FOR THE FINEFOOD GROUP MACRO

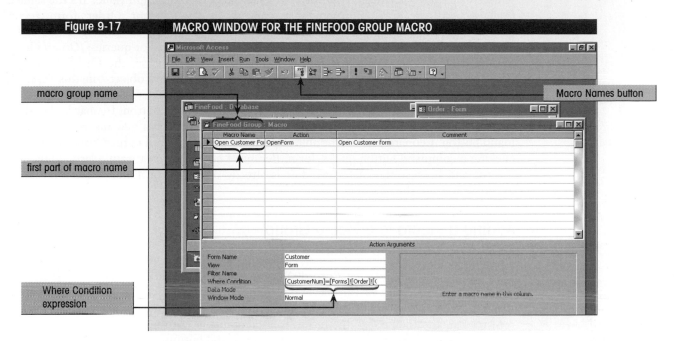

The Macro window has an additional column, the **Macro Name column**, which lets you distinguish macros in a macro group. Each separate macro is identified with a name in the Macro Name column. If a macro contains several actions, you leave the Macro Name column blank for actions added after the first one.

The Open Customer Form macro consists of a single action, OpenForm, which opens the Customer form (the Form Name argument value is Customer). The **Where Condition argument** value specifies the record to display in the form. You'll use the Zoom dialog box to view the entire Where Condition argument value.

To view the Where Condition argument value in the Zoom dialog box:

1. Right-click the **Where Condition** text box, click **Zoom** to open the Zoom dialog box, and then click to the right of the selected text to deselect it. See Figure 9-18.

Figure 9-18	WHERE CONDITION EXPRESSION FOR OPEN CUSTOMER FORM MACRO

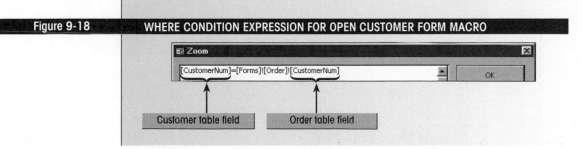

The Where Condition argument value contains the expression *[CustomerNum]=[Forms]! [Order]![CustomerNum]*. In simple terms, the expression asks Access to find the record in the Customer form with the same CustomerNum as the current record in the Order form. The expression, however, is complex. The OpenForm action in the macro opens the Customer form, so the value of *[CustomerNum])* to the left of the equals sign determines which record will be displayed in the Customer form. What is this CustomerNum value? It's the same as (equals sign) the CustomerNum that appears in the current Order form record (*[Forms]![Order]![CustomerNum]*) to the right of the equals sign. On the right side of the equals sign, *[Forms]* identifies the object collection, such as forms or queries; *[Order]* identifies the specific object within the object collection—in this case, the Order form; and *[CustomerNum]* identifies the specific field within the specified object—in this case, the Order form.

Now that you've seen a macro that's attached to a command button, Leonard asks you to add a command button to the Customer form, and then attach a new macro to the command button. Leonard wants to be able to print the current record in the Customer form by clicking a command button on the form. Because Leonard doesn't want a large number of macros and because the Macro window is already open for the FineFood Group macro group, you'll add the new macro to it.

Adding a Macro to a Macro Group

To print the contents of a form's current record, you have to click File on the menu bar, click Print, click the Selected Record(s) option button, and then click the OK button—a process that takes four steps and several seconds. Instead of following this process, you can create a command button on the form and a macro that prints the contents of a form's current record, and then attach the macro to the command button on the form. To print the form's current record, you'd simply click the command button.

First, you'll add a macro to the FineFood Group macro group. You'll use the PrintOut action for the new macro. The **PrintOut action** lets you print the contents of an object; you can choose to print the selected record, a page range, or the entire contents of the object. You'll use a macro name of Print Current Record when you add it to the FineFood Group macro group, so that the macro's function is obvious.

REFERENCE WINDOW   **RW**

Adding a Macro to a Macro Group
- Open the macro group in the Macro window. (For a macro group, the Macro Names button is already selected.)
- Type the macro name in the Macro Name column, select the action in the Action column, type an optional comment in the Comment column, and then set the arguments for the action.
- If the macro consists of more than one action, enter the remaining actions in the rows immediately following the first macro action. Leave the Macro Name column blank for each additional action.
- Click the Save button on the Macro Design toolbar.

You'll now add the Print Current Record macro to the FineFood Group macro group.

To add the Print Current Record macro to the FineFood Group macro group:

1. Click the **Close** button ☒ on the Zoom dialog box to close it.

2. Click the second row's **Macro Name** text box, type **Print Current Record**, press the **Tab** key, click the **Action** list arrow, scroll down the list, click **PrintOut**, press the **Tab** key, and then type **Print current record** in the Comment column.

You need to set only the Print Range argument; you'll set its value to Selection.

3. Press the **F6** key, click the **Print Range** list arrow, and then click **Selection**. You've completed the action, which is the only action in the Print Current Record macro. The macro group now contains two macros. See Figure 9-19.

Figure 9-19	MACRO GROUP CONTAINING TWO MACROS

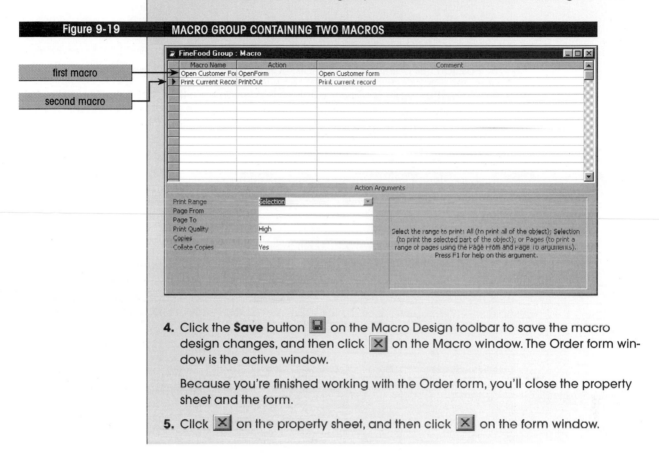

4. Click the **Save** button 🖫 on the Macro Design toolbar to save the macro design changes, and then click ✖ on the Macro window. The Order form window is the active window.

Because you're finished working with the Order form, you'll close the property sheet and the form.

5. Click ✖ on the property sheet, and then click ✖ on the form window.

Next, you'll add a command button to the Customer form. After you attach the Print Current Record macro to the command button, you'll be able to click the command button to print the current Customer form record.

Adding a Command Button to a Form

You use the Command Button tool on the toolbox to add a command button to a form. If the Control Wizards tool is selected when you click the Command Button tool, the Command Button Wizard guides you through the process of adding the command button. Instead, you'll add the command button directly to the Customer form without using the Wizard. Then you'll set the command button's properties in the property sheet.

To add a command button to the Customer form:

1. Right-click **Customer** in the Forms list box, and then click **Design View** to open the Customer form in Design view.

2. Click ▼ on the form's vertical scroll bar so that you can see the bottom of the Detail section.

3. If necessary, click the **Toolbox** button ✶ on the Form Design toolbar to open the toolbox.

4. Make sure the **Control Wizards** tool 🔨 on the toolbox is not selected, and then click the **Command Button** tool ▭ on the toolbox.

5. Position the pointer in the Detail section. The pointer changes to a ⁺▭ shape.

6. When the pointer's plus symbol (+) is positioned in the Page Header section at the 1-inch mark on the horizontal ruler and at the 2.75-inch mark on the vertical ruler, click the mouse button. Access adds a command button to the form. See Figure 9-20.

| Figure 9-20 | AFTER ADDING A COMMAND BUTTON TO THE CUSTOMER FORM |

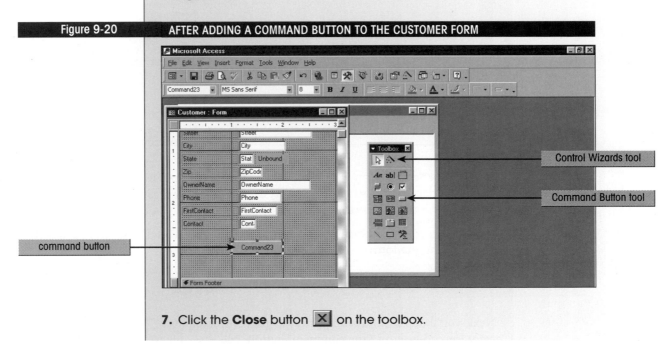

7. Click the **Close** button ✕ on the toolbox.

You can now attach the Print Current Record macro to the command button.

Attaching a Macro to a Command Button

You created the Print Current Record macro and added the command button to the Customer form. You'll attach the macro to the command button's On Click property, so that the macro is executed when the command button is clicked.

To attach the Print Current Record macro to the command button:

1. Right-click the command button, click **Properties** on the shortcut menu, and then click the **Event** tab (if necessary).

2. Click the right edge of the **On Click** text box, and then click **FineFood Group.Print Current Record**.

   TROUBLE? If the On Click list box is too narrow to see which macro is the correct one, drag the right or left property sheet border to make the box wider, and then repeat Step 2.

   You can change the text that appears on the command button by changing its Caption property, or you can replace the text with a picture by setting its Picture property. Leonard wants you to place a picture of a printer on the command button.

3. Click the **Format** tab, click the **Picture** text box, and then click the **Build** button ![...] that appears next to the text box. The Picture Builder dialog box opens. See Figure 9-21.

Figure 9-21   PICTURE BUILDER DIALOG BOX

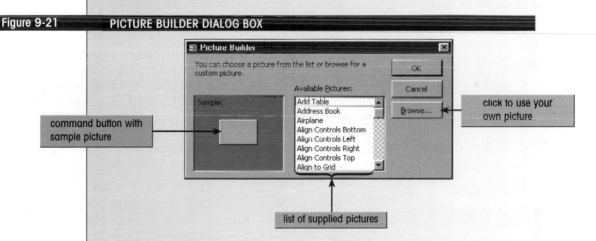

command button with sample picture

click to use your own picture

list of supplied pictures

The Picture Builder dialog box contains an alphabetical list of pictures supplied with Access. You can scroll the list and select one of the pictures, or you can click the Browse button to select your own picture. When you select a picture, a sample of the picture on the command button appears in the Sample box on the left.

4. Scroll down the Available Pictures list box, and then click **Printer**. A printer picture appears on the command button in the Sample box.

5. Click the **OK** button. The Picture Builder dialog box closes, and the picture of a printer appears on a resized command button.

6. Click the **Close** button ![X] on the property sheet.

Next, you'll save the Customer form and test the command button.

> *To save the form and test the command button:*
>
> **1.** Click the **Save** button 🔲 on the Form Design toolbar.
>
> **2.** Click the **View** button for Form view 🔳 on the Form View toolbar.
>
> **3.** Click the **Last Record** navigation button ▶❙ in the Customer form, and then click the **Print** command button on the form. The last record for Pesto Place prints.
>
> **4.** Click the **Close** button ☒ on the Customer form.

As he viewed the Customer form, Leonard remembered that his staff wanted to know if it is possible to limit the entries in the State field to values of IN, MI, and OH so that the database will reject any other value. To provide this capability, you'll set the validation properties for the State field.

Defining Data Validation Criteria

You've now used macros to make it easier for employees to use the FineFood database. You could create a macro to limit the entries in the State field in the Customer form to values of IN, MI, and OH. However, you would have to attach the macro to every form and query that allowed updates to the State field, and you would have to remember to attach the macro to all such forms and queries that you create in the future. To prevent a user from entering a value other than IN, MI, or OH, a better solution is to set the Validation Rule and the Validation Text properties for the State field in the Customer table. The **Validation Rule** property value specifies the valid values that users can enter in a field. The **Validation Text** property value will be displayed in a dialog box if a user enters an invalid value (in this case, a value other than IN, MI, or OH). After setting these two State field properties in the Customer table, users will be prevented from entering an invalid State field value in all current and future forms and queries. So even though macros are powerful tools, when field properties exist to handle a specific task, directly setting them is always the preferred solution.

You'll now set the Validation Rule and Validation Text properties for the State field in the Customer table.

> *To set the Validation Rule and Validation Text properties for the State field:*
>
> **1.** Click **Tables** in the Objects bar of the Database window, right-click **Customer**, click **Design View**, and then click the **State Field Name** text box. The Customer table opens in Design view and the State field is the current row.
>
> To make sure that the only values entered in the State field are IN, MI, or OH, you'll specify a list of valid values in the Validation Rule text box.
>
> **2.** Click the **Validation Rule** text box, and then type **"IN" Or "MI" Or "OH"**.
>
> The Validation Text text box allows you to enter a message box that will open if the user enters a value not listed in the Validation Rule text box.
>
> **3.** Press the **Tab** key, and then type **Must be IN, MI, or OH** in the Validation Text text box. See Figure 9-22.

Figure 9-22	VALIDATION PROPERTIES FOR THE STATE FIELD

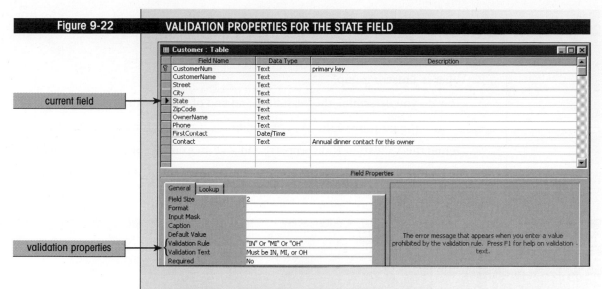

current field

validation properties

You can now save the table design changes, and then test the validation properties.

4. Click the **Save** button 🖫 on the Table Design toolbar, and then click the **Yes** button when asked if you want Access to test the existing State field values against the new validation rule.

Next, you'll test the new validation rule.

5. Click the **View** button for Datasheet view 🖩 on the Table Design toolbar.

6. Double-click **MI** in the first row's State field text box, type **TX**, and then press the **Tab** key. A dialog box opens containing the message "Must be IN, MI, or OH," which is the Validation Text property setting you just entered.

7. Click the **OK** button, and then click the **Undo Typing** button ↶ on the Table Datasheet toolbar. The first row's State field value reverts back to its original value of MI.

8. Click the **Close** button ✕ on the Table window title bar.

9. Click ✕ on the Access window title bar to close the FineFood database and exit Access. You return to the Windows desktop.

You've now completed your initial work with macros and defined the validation criteria for the State field. In the next session, you'll start to develop the user interface for the FineFood database. You'll create the dialog box to display the queries in the FineFood database, and then add command buttons and a list box to it. Finally, you'll use an SQL statement to select the values for the list box.

Session 9.2 QUICK CHECK

1. What is an event property?

2. What is a macro group?

3. How do you determine the beginning and end of a macro in a macro group?

4. What is the purpose of the Where Condition argument for the OpenForm action?

5. Define the Validation Rule property and give an example of when you would use it.

6. Define the Validation Text property and give an example of when you would use it.

SESSION 9.3

In this session, you will create the Queries dialog box, which will contain command buttons and a list box. You also will use an SQL statement to retrieve the query names for the list box.

Creating the Queries Dialog Box Form

To create the user interface for the FineFood database, you need to create the FineFood Database and Reports switchboards and the Queries dialog box. First, you'll create the dialog box shown in Figure 9-23.

Figure 9-23   QUERIES DIALOG BOX

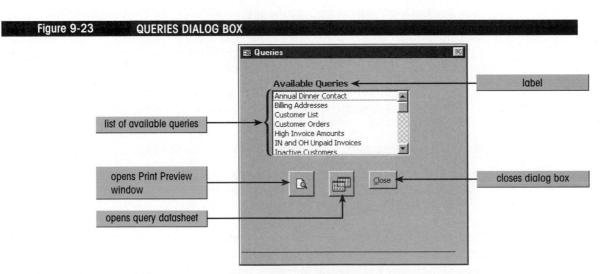

The Queries dialog box is actually a form that you will create. You'll add a label, a list box, and three command buttons to the form, and enter an SQL statement that will determine the contents of the list box. The Valle Coffee staff will use the dialog box as follows:

- Scroll the list box until the desired query name is visible.
- Click the query name, and then click the command button with the Print Preview icon to open the query in Print Preview. Alternatively, double-click the query name to open the query in Print Preview.
- Click the query name, and then click the command button with the Datasheet icon to display the query results.

■ Click the Close button to close the dialog box and activate the FineFood Database switchboard. The underlined letter "C" in the Close command button identifies the button's hot key. Pressing Alt + C will close the dialog box, just as clicking the Close command button will.

To create the Queries dialog box, you'll begin by creating a blank form. Because none of the form controls need data from a table or query (an SQL statement will supply the list box with its values), you will not select a table or query as the basis for the blank form.

To create the Queries Dialog Box form:

1. Place your Data Disk in the appropriate disk drive, start Access, and then open the **FineFood** database located in the Tutorial folder on your Data Disk.

2. Click **Forms** in the Objects bar of the Database window, and then click the **New** button. The New Form dialog box opens.

3. Make sure that Design View is selected, and then click the **OK** button. Access opens the Form window in Design view.

4. Click the **Save** button 🖫 on the Form Design toolbar, type **Queries Dialog Box** in the Form Name text box, and then press the **Enter** key. The title bar displays the saved form's name.

Before adding any controls to the form, you need to set the overall form properties so that the form matches Leonard's design. You will set the Caption property to Queries, which will appear in the title bar for the form. You will also set the Shortcut Menu, Record Selectors, Navigation Buttons, and Close Button properties to No, because Leonard doesn't want the form to include these elements. You will set the Auto Resize property to No so that Access will not resize the form when it is opened, which maintains a consistent form size for all users. Also, Leonard does not want users to be able to open the form in Design view, so you will set the Modal property to Yes. Finally, after you have completed the form's design, you will set the Border Style property to Dialog so that the form will look like a dialog box that users cannot resize using the pointer. Figure 9-24 shows the form property settings you will use to create the Queries Dialog Box form for Leonard.

Figure 9-24	QUERIES DIALOG BOX FORM PROPERTIES	
PROPERTY	**SETTING**	**FUNCTION**
Auto Resize	No	Opens a form using the last saved size
Border Style	Dialog	Prevents users from resizing the form
Caption	Queries	Value that appears in the form's title bar
Close Button	No	Disables display of the Close button
Modal	Yes	Prevents users from opening the form in Design view
Navigation Buttons	No	Disables display of navigation buttons
Record Selectors	No	Disables display of record selectors
Shortcut Menu	No	Disables display of shortcut menu if the user right-clicks the form

Working from this list, you can use the property sheet to set the form properties.

To set the properties for the form:

1. Right-click the form selector, which is the gray box immediately to the left of the horizontal ruler in the Form window, and then click **Properties** to open the property sheet for the form (as indicated by the word "Form" in the title bar).

2. If necessary, click the **All** tab to display the All page of the property sheet.

   You can now set the Caption property for the form. The Caption property value will appear in the title bar when the form is displayed.

3. Scroll to the top of the property sheet (if necessary), click the **Caption** text box, and then type **Queries**.

   Next, you'll set the Record Selectors property so that record selectors will not be displayed on the form. Because the form does not display any records, there's no need to include selectors.

4. Scroll down until the Record Selectors property is visible, click the right side of the **Record Selectors** text box, and then click **No**.

   You'll now set the remaining form properties.

5. Continue scrolling as necessary, and set the **Navigation Buttons** property to **No**, set the **Auto Resize** property to **No**, set the **Modal** property to **Yes**, set the **Close Button** property to **No**, and then set the **Shortcut Menu** property to **No**.

6. Click the **Close** button [X] on the property sheet to close it.

7. Click the **Save** button [🖫] on the Form Design toolbar.

Now that you have set the form's properties, you can add a label and a list box to it. The label will identify the list box for the user, and the list box will display the list of queries from which to choose. You will not use the Control Wizards tool for the list box because you'll be using an SQL statement to provide the query names for the list box.

Adding a List Box to a Form

A **list box** is a control that displays a list of values. The list box in the Queries Dialog Box will display the list of queries that the user can print preview or view. Clicking the name of a query selects it, and then the user can click one of the command buttons to print preview or view the query. Double-clicking a query name in the list box will open the query in the Print Preview window.

REFERENCE WINDOW   RW

Adding a List Box to a Form

- If necessary, click the Control Wizards tool on the toolbox so that it is appropriately selected or deselected.
- Click the List Box tool on the toolbox.
- Position the pointer where you want the list box to appear in the form, and then click the left mouse button.
- If you used the List Box Wizard, complete the dialog boxes to choose the source of the list, select the fields to appear in the list box, size the columns, select the field that will provide the data for the field in the main form, choose to remember the value for later use or store it in a field, and then enter the value to appear in the list box label.

First you'll add the label "Available Queries" to the form. Then you'll add the list box to display the list of queries from which to choose.

To add the label to the form:

1. If the toolbox is not displayed, click the **Toolbox** button 🛠 on the Form Design toolbar.

2. If necessary, drag the toolbox to the right side of the Form window.

3. Click the **Label** tool *Aa* on the toolbox.

4. Position the pointer in the Detail section and, when the center of the pointer's plus symbol (+) is positioned at the .5-inch mark on the horizontal ruler and the .25-inch mark on the vertical ruler, click the mouse button. A small label box opens on the form with the insertion point positioned inside it.

5. Type **Available Queries** and then press the **Enter** key.

   Leonard wants the label to stand out more, so you'll change the label's font size from the default of 8 to 10, make the label boldface, and then resize the label box.

6. Click the **Font Size** list arrow on the Formatting toolbar, click **10**, and then click the **Bold** button **B** on the Formatting toolbar.

7. Click **Format** on the menu bar, point to **Size**, and then click **To Fit**.

Now you can add the list box to the form.

To add the list box to the form:

1. If the Control Wizards tool is selected, click the **Control Wizards** tool ⟍ on the toolbox to deselect it.

2. Click the **List Box** tool 📇 on the toolbox, position the center of the pointer's plus symbol (+) in the row of grid dots below the left edge of the Available Queries label box, and then click the mouse button. Access adds a list box and attached label box to the form. See Figure 9-25.

Figure 9-25	FORM DESIGN AFTER ADDING THE LABEL AND THE LIST BOX

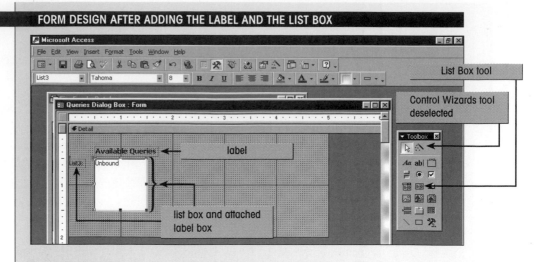

TROUBLE? If your list box is sized or positioned differently, resize it or move it until it matches the list box shown in Figure 9-25.

You can now save the form and then check your progress by switching to Form view.

3. Click the **Save** button 🔲 on the Form Design toolbar.

4. Click the **View** button for Form view 🔲 on the Form Design toolbar to display the form in Form view. See Figure 9-26.

Figure 9-26	QUERIES DIALOG BOX DISPLAYED IN FORM VIEW

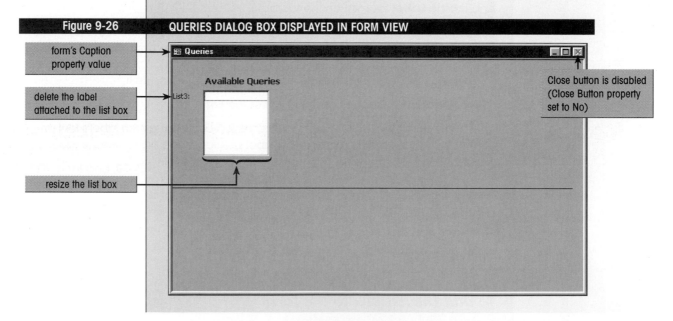

After viewing the form, Leonard asks you to make two changes to it. Because the form already includes the label "Available Queries," the label attached to the list box is unnecessary. Leonard asks you to delete this label. He'd also like you to resize the list box by making it wider, so that it will accommodate the list of queries better.

> *To delete the label attached to the list box and resize the*
> *list box:*
>
> 1. Click the **View** button for Design view ▨ on the Form Design toolbar to switch to Design view.
>
> 2. Right-click the label box for the attached label to open the shortcut menu, and then click **Cut** to delete it.
>
> 3. Click the list box to select it.
>
> 4. Use the middle-right sizing handle to drag the right border to the 2.5-inch mark on the horizontal ruler.
>
> 5. Click the **Save** button 🖫 on the Form Design toolbar.

You now can enter the SQL statement that will provide the query names for the list box.

Using an SQL Statement for a List Box

Recall from your work in Tutorial 8 that SQL uses the SELECT statement to define what data it retrieves from a database and how it presents the data. You'll use a SELECT statement to retrieve the list of query names from one of the Access system tables. **System tables** are special tables maintained by Access that store information about the characteristics of a database and about the structure of the objects in a database. Although system tables do not appear in the Database window's Tables list box, you can retrieve information from system tables by using SELECT statements. One of the system tables, the **MSysObjects table**, keeps track of the names, types, and other characteristics of every object in your database. The Name and Type fields are the two MSysObjects table fields you'll use in the SELECT statement. The Name field contains a query name when the Type field value is 5, as shown in Figure 9-27.

Figure 9-27	MSYSOBJECTS TABLE TYPE FIELD VALUES

OBJECT TYPE	TYPE FIELD VALUE IN MSYSOBJECTS TABLE
Table	1
Query	5
Form	-32768
Report	-32764
Page	-32756
Macro	-32766
Module	-32761

Access creates its own queries to handle a number of tasks for you; each of these queries has a name that begins with the "~" character. Because you want to exclude these special system queries from the list box, you'll also need to use the Left function in your SELECT statement. The **Left function** provides the first character(s) in a text string. The format of the Left function is *Left(text string, number of characters)*. You'll use *Left([Name],1)* to retrieve the first character of the Name field. To include only those queries whose names do not begin with the "~" character, you'll use the expression *Left([Name],1)<>"~"*. In this expression, the <> operator is the not equal operator. Access interprets the expression as "the first character of the Name field does not equal the ~ character." Figure 9-28 shows the Zoom dialog box, which contains the complete SELECT statement that you will use to select the list of query names.

Figure 9-28	SELECT STATEMENT FOR THE LIST BOX

The **Row Source property** specifies how to provide data to a list box, so you'll enter the SELECT statement as the value for the list box's Row Source property.

To set the Row Source property for the list box:

1. Right-click the list box to open the shortcut menu, click **Properties** to open the property sheet, and then click the **All** tab (if necessary).

2. Right-click the **Row Source** text box, and then click **Zoom**. The Zoom dialog box opens.

3. Type **SELECT [Name] FROM MSysObjects WHERE [Type]=5 And Left([Name],1)<>"~" ORDER BY [Name];** in the Zoom dialog box, and then click the **OK** button.

4. Click the **Close** button ☒ on the property sheet to close it.

5. Click the **Save** button 🖫 on the Form Design toolbar.

   You can now view the scrollable list box in Form view.

6. Click the **View** button for Form view ▦ on the Form Design toolbar to display the form in Form view. See Figure 9-29.

Figure 9-29	COMPLETED LIST BOX

query names retrieved from an SQL statement and the MSysObject table →

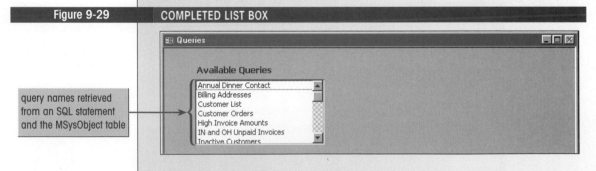

TROUBLE? If a syntax-error message appears, switch to Design view, click the OK button, right-click the list box, click Properties, right-click the Row Source text box, and then click Zoom. Correct the SELECT statement until it's the same as the statement shown in Figure 9-28, click the OK button, and then repeat Steps 4 through 6.

You now can add the command buttons to the form.

Adding Command Buttons to a Form

First, you'll add the Print Preview command button to the form. A macro cannot handle the complex interaction that is involved in the actions of selecting a report or query in a list box and clicking a command button. This task requires VBA code. So, the Print Preview and Datasheet command buttons for the list box will be attached using VBA code instead of macros.

In the next steps, you will add the Print Preview command button to the form. You can add a command button to a form by placing the button directly on the form or by using the Control Wizards tool. If you use the Control Wizards tool, you can attach a standard Access action (such as opening a specific query or closing a window) or a macro to the button. You cannot use a standard Access action for this command button, because the query to be opened will depend on the query the user has selected in the list box. Instead, you will add the command button directly to the form now and attach VBA code to it in the next tutorial.

To add the Print Preview command button to the form:

1. Click the **View** button for Design view on the Form Design toolbar to switch to Design view.

2. Make sure the **Control Wizards** tool on the toolbox is not selected, and then click the **Command Button** tool on the toolbox.

3. Position the pointer in the Detail section and, when the pointer's plus symbol is positioned at the .75-inch mark on the horizontal ruler and the 1.75-inch mark on the vertical ruler, click the mouse button. Access adds a command button to the form.

4. Right-click the command button, and then click **Properties** on the shortcut menu to open the property sheet.

   TROUBLE? If the property sheet is covering the form, drag it out of the way.

   You can now change the picture that appears on the command button to the Print Preview picture, which is the same picture that appears on the Print Preview button on the Form Design toolbar.

5. Click the **Format** tab, click the **Picture** text box, and then click the **Build** button that appears next to the Picture text box. The Picture Builder dialog box opens.

6. Scroll down the Available Pictures list box, and then click **Preview Document**. Access shows the picture on the command button in the Sample box.

7. Click the **OK** button. Access closes the Picture Builder dialog box, resizes the command button, places the picture on the command button, and increases the height of the form's Detail section.

Instead of repeating the steps to add the command button for viewing a query, you can copy the first command button and paste it in the Detail section. After moving the copied button into position, you can change the picture on it to show the query datasheet icon.

To place the query datasheet command button on the form:

1. Right-click the command button, and then click **Copy** on the shortcut menu.

2. Click the **Paste** button 🖺 on the Form Design toolbar. Access adds a copy of the command button below the original command button in the Detail section.

3. Move the new command button into position to the right of the original command button. See Figure 9-30.

Figure 9-30	AFTER ADDING A COPY OF THE COMMAND BUTTON

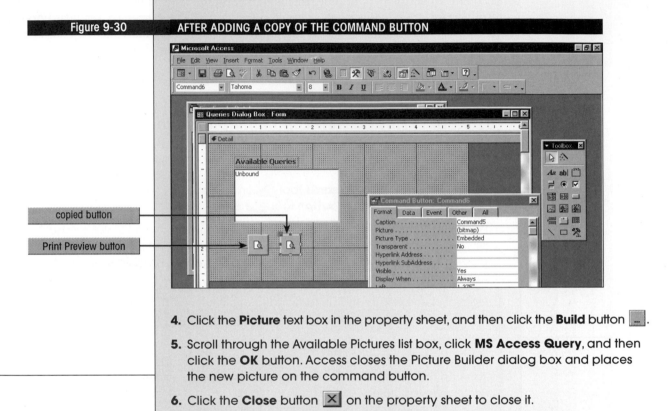

copied button

Print Preview button

4. Click the **Picture** text box in the property sheet, and then click the **Build** button 📄.

5. Scroll through the Available Pictures list box, click **MS Access Query**, and then click the **OK** button. Access closes the Picture Builder dialog box and places the new picture on the command button.

6. Click the **Close** button ❎ on the property sheet to close it.

7. Click the **Save** button 🖫 on the Form Design toolbar to save the form changes.

You can now add the final command button using Control Wizards. This button will close the dialog box when the user clicks it.

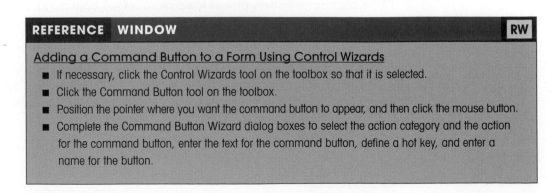

REFERENCE WINDOW RW

<u>Adding a Command Button to a Form Using Control Wizards</u>

- If necessary, click the Control Wizards tool on the toolbox so that it is selected.
- Click the Command Button tool on the toolbox.
- Position the pointer where you want the command button to appear, and then click the mouse button.
- Complete the Command Button Wizard dialog boxes to select the action category and the action for the command button, enter the text for the command button, define a hot key, and enter a name for the button.

To define the Close button, you'll use the Control Wizards tool, because the tool automatically attaches the correct VBA code (for closing the dialog box) to the command button. Standard operations, such as opening and closing forms, are good candidates for using the Control Wizards tool. Leonard also wants a user to be able to close the dialog box using a keyboard combination, so you will specify the letter "C" as the hot key for the Close button. To underline the letter C and make it the hot key, you need to enter &Close as the Caption property value for the command button control on the form. Placing an ampersand (&) to the left of a character in a caption underlines the character on the open form and makes it that control's hot key. Note that you can specify any character in a button's name, not just the first, as the hot key, and each command button on a specific form needs a unique hot key.

To add the Close command button using the Control Wizards tool:

1. Click the **Control Wizards** tool ⬚ on the toolbox to select it.

2. Click the **Command Button** tool ▢ on the toolbox, position the pointer's plus symbol at the 2-inch mark on the horizontal ruler and the 1.75-inch mark on the vertical ruler, and then click the mouse button. Access adds a command button to the form and, after a few seconds, opens the first Command Button Wizard dialog box. The Sample box shows how the command button will appear. See Figure 9-31.

| Figure 9-31 | FIRST COMMAND BUTTON WIZARD DIALOG BOX |

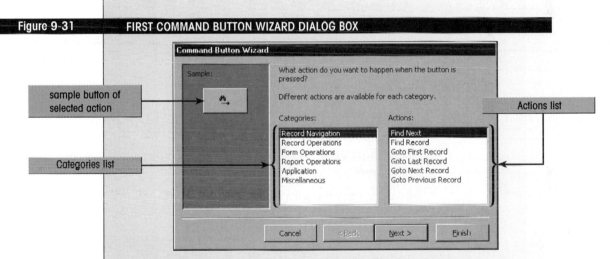

You'll now select the command that will be attached to the command button. The dialog box form must close when the user clicks the Close button, so you'll select the Close Form action in the Form Operations category for this button.

3. Click **Form Operations** in the Categories list box, click **Close Form** in the Actions list box, and then click the **Next** button. Access opens the next Command Button Wizard dialog box, in which you specify the text or picture you want to appear on the button. In this case, Leonard wants the button to display the word "Close," with the letter "C" identified as the hot key.

4. Click the **Text** option button, select **Close Form** in the text box, and then type **&Close**. Notice that the sample button changes to show the word "Close" with an underlined "C." See Figure 9-32.

Figure 9-32   SPECIFYING THE TEXT ON THE COMMAND BUTTON

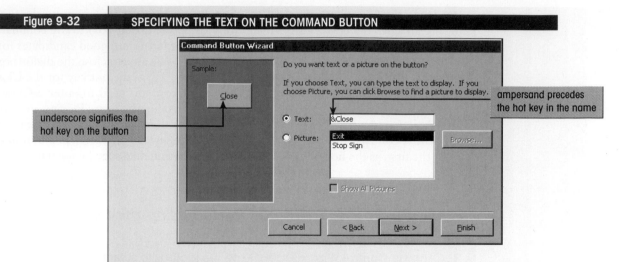

underscore signifies the hot key on the button

ampersand precedes the hot key in the name

5. Click the **Next** button to open the next Command Button Wizard dialog box, in which you enter a name for the button.

6. Type **Close** in the text box, and then click the **Finish** button. Access closes the final Command Button Wizard dialog box and shows the new command button on the form.

In the next tutorial, you will create the VBA code for the Print Preview and Datasheet command buttons. This code will define what Access should do when a user clicks each button. The VBA code you will create later will need to refer to the list box control. It is a good idea to give meaningful names to controls on your forms, so now you will enter the name QueryList Control for the list box control.

To set the Name property for the list box:

1. Right-click the list box control, and then click **Properties** to open the property sheet.

2. If necessary, click the **All** tab.

3. If necessary, scroll to the top of the property sheet, and then double-click the **Name** text box to select the current value for this property.

4. Type **QueryList Control** in the Name text box, and then click the **Close** button ☒ on the property sheet to close it.

You've completed your work with the list box and command buttons for now, so you'll finish your initial work with the Queries Dialog Box form by modifying some its form properties.

Modifying Form Properties

Next, you'll resize and position the form and set the form's Border Style property to Dialog, according to Leonard's design.

To set the form properties, and then resize and position the form:

1. Drag the right edge of the form's Detail section to the 3.25-inch mark on the horizontal ruler, and then drag the bottom edge of the form's Detail section to the 3-inch mark on the vertical ruler.

2. Click the **View** button for Form view on the Form Design toolbar.

3. Position and resize the form until it is approximately in the same position and is approximately the same size as the form in Figure 9-33.

Figure 9-33	RESIZED AND REPOSITIONED FORM

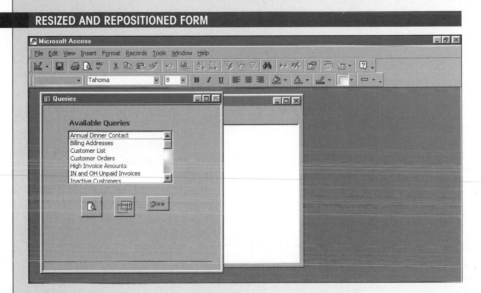

TROUBLE? If scroll bars appear on the form, enlarge the form until the scroll bars disappear.

4. Click the **Save** button 🖫 on the Form View toolbar, and then click the **View** button for Design view 🔳 on the Form View toolbar to switch back to Design view.

You'll now set the form's Border Style property to Dialog, which will prevent a user from resizing the form.

5. In the Form window, right-click the form selector, click **Properties** to display the property sheet, and then click the **All** tab (if necessary).

6. Scroll down the property sheet, click the right side of the **Border Style** text box, and then click **Dialog**.

7. Click the **Close** button ☒ on the property sheet to close it, click ☒ on the tool-box to close it, and then click 🖫 on the Form Design toolbar.

8. Click ☒ on the Form window to close it and return to the Database window.

You'll now test the work you've completed for the Queries Dialog Box form.

Testing the Queries Dialog Box Form

You can now test the form by opening it in Form view. Clicking the Print Preview command button, clicking the Datasheet command button, or double-clicking a query name in the list box should have no effect, because you have not yet added the VBA code for these actions. However, you can click the Close button or press Alt + C to close the form.

To test the form's design:

1. Right-click **Queries Dialog Box** in the Forms list, and then click **Open**. The form opens in Form view.

   TROUBLE? If the form is not the correct size or if scroll bars appear on the form, switch to Design view and set the form's Border Style property to Sizable. Switch back to Form view and resize the form. Save the form changes, switch to Design view, set the form's Border Style property to Dialog, and then save the form again. Close the Form window, and then repeat Step 1.

2. Double-click any report name in the list, click the **Print Preview** command button, and then click the **Datasheet** command button. Each double-click or click makes that control the currently active control but does not execute any other action.

3. Either click the **Close** command button or press **Alt + C**. The form closes, and you return to the Database window.

4. Click the **Close** button ☒ on the Access window title bar to close the FineFood database and exit Access. You return to the Windows desktop.

You've completed the initial work with the Queries Dialog Box form. In the next session, you'll create the two switchboards and the macros for the switchboards.

Session 9.3 QUICK CHECK

1. What is the purpose of setting a form's Border Style property value to Dialog?

2. What is the purpose of setting a form's Modal property value to Yes?

3. What is a list box control?

4. What are system tables?

5. How do you change the picture on a command button?

6. How do you make a duplicate copy of a form control in Design view?

SESSION 9.4

In this session, you will create a macro group that will be associated with command buttons on the switchboard. You also will use the Switchboard Manager to create switchboard forms for the FineFood Database switchboard and the Reports switchboard.

Reviewing the Requirements for the FineFood Database Switchboard

Recall that a switchboard is a form that provides controlled access to a database's tables, forms, queries, reports, and other objects. You need to create the switchboard form that will serve as the primary user interface for the FineFood database. Figure 9-34 shows the finished FineFood Database switchboard form.

Figure 9-34   FINEFOOD DATABASE SWITCHBOARD FORM

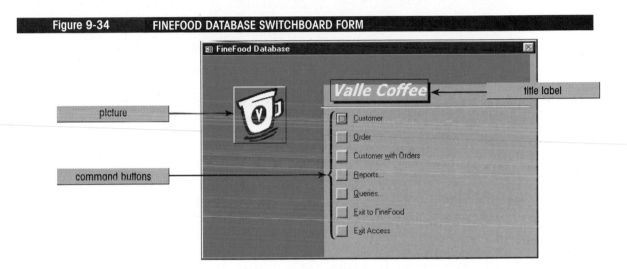

Leonard has the following design specifications for the FineFood Database switchboard:

- The form will not include Minimize, Restore, or Close buttons, scroll bars, navigation buttons, record selectors, or sizing buttons.
- The form cannot be resized.
- A picture of the Valle Coffee cup will appear in the left section of the form.
- The picture of the Valle Coffee cup will have the raised special effect applied to it.
- "FineFood Database" will appear in the form's title bar, and "Valle Coffee" with a shadowed special effect applied to it will be the form's title.
- The command buttons will all be the same size.
- Macros will be attached to each command button to specify the actions that Access should take when the command button is clicked.

You'll also create the Reports switchboard, which will look similar to the FineFood Database switchboard. The Reports switchboard will have three command buttons: one to open the Customers and Orders report, a second to open the Invoices reports, and a third to return to the FineFood Database switchboard.

Your first step in creating the switchboards is to create the macros you need to attach to the command buttons in the switchboard forms.

Creating the Macro Group for the Switchboard

You'll place the macros for the switchboards in a macro group. The Macro Name column in the Macro window lets you distinguish macros in a macro group. Because a macro can contain many actions, the macro name tells Access where the macro begins. First you'll name one macro and list the actions for that macro. Then you'll name the second macro, list the actions for the second macro, and so on. You can define the macros in any order, and you can group as many macros as you want in the Macro window.

You will use the name Switchboard Macros for the macro group. Figure 9-35 shows the names and actions for the six macros in the macro group. For example, the Customer macro will execute the OpenForm action to open the Customer form when a user clicks the Customer button on the switchboard. Notice that both the ExitToFineFood and ExitAccess macros each contain two actions.

| Figure 9-35 | MACROS AND ACTIONS IN THE SWITCHBOARD MACROS MACRO GROUP |

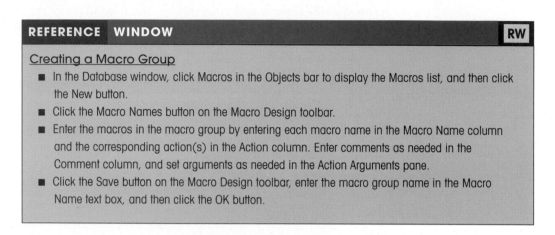

MACRO NAME	ACTIONS	FORM NAME
Customer	OpenForm	Customer
Order	OpenForm	Order
CustomerWithOrders	OpenForm	Customer with Orders
Queries	OpenForm	Queries Dialog Box
ExitToFineFood	Close SendKeys	Switchboard
ExitAccess	Close Quit	Switchboard

You will not use macros for the Reports command button on the FineFood Database switchboard or for any of the three buttons on the Reports switchboard. After you create the six macros, you'll use the Switchboard Manager to create the two switchboard forms and to handle the four buttons without macros.

You'll now create the Switchboard Macros macro group for the six command buttons on the switchboard form that use macros. First, you'll start a new macro, enter two of the macros (ExitAccess and Customer), and then save the macro group.

To create the macro group:

1. Make sure that Access is running, that the **FineFood** database from the Tutorial folder on your Data Disk is open, and that Macros is selected in the Objects bar of the Database window.

2. Click the **New** button to open the Macro window, and then click the **Macro Names** button on the Macro Design toolbar. Access adds the Macro Name column to the left of the Action column.

   Next, you'll enter the ExitAccess macro and its two actions: the Close action to close the switchboard form and the Quit action to exit Access.

3. Type **ExitAccess**, press the **Tab** key, click the **Action** list arrow, click **Close**, press the **Tab** key, and then type **Close Switchboard**.

   You need to specify the arguments for the Close action. In the Object Type text box, you specify the type of object to close, in this case, a form. In the Object Name text box, you specify which object to close. Even though you haven't created the Switchboard form yet, you can specify it as the object to close.

4. In the Action Arguments pane, click the right side of the **Object Type** text box, and then click **Form**. Click the **Object Name** text box, and then type **Switchboard**. This completes the first action for the first macro. Next, you'll define the second action for this macro, which will exit the Access program.

5. Click the right side of the second row's **Action** text box, scroll through the list, and then click **Quit**. This completes the first macro, which contains two actions: the first to close the Switchboard form and the second to exit Access. These two actions will occur in sequence when a user clicks the Exit Access command button on the switchboard.

   Next, you'll define the second macro, Customer, which will open the Customer form.

6. Click the third row's **Macro Name** text box, type **Customer**, press the **Tab** key, click the list arrow, scroll through the list, click **OpenForm**, press the **Tab** key, and then type **Open Customer form**.

   Next, you'll specify the name of the form to open.

7. In the Action Arguments pane, click the right side of the **Form Name** text box, and then click **Customer**. This completes the second macro, which contains one action.

8. Click the **Save** button on the Macro Design toolbar, type **Switchboard Macros** in the Macro Name text box, and then press the **Enter** key. See Figure 9-36.

Figure 9-36	TWO MACROS IN THE MACRO GROUP

macro with two actions

macro with one action

macro group name

The macro name, which appears in the Macro window title bar, is Switchboard Macros. This also is the name of the macro group, because the Switchboard Macros macro contains more than one macro. The first macro in the macro group is ExitAccess, and the second macro in the macro group is Customer. A macro in a macro group starts in the row containing the macro name and continues until the next macro name or a blank row.

When Access executes the ExitAccess macro, it runs the Close action, it runs the Quit action, and then the macro ends. The Customer macro begins with the OpenForm action and then ends when it reaches the end of the macro group.

Next, you'll enter three more macros—the first to open the Order form, the second to open the Customer with Orders form, and the third to open the Queries Dialog Box form.

To add three macros to the macro group:

1. Click the next row's **Macro Name** text box, type **Order**, press the **Tab** key, click the **Action** list arrow, scroll through the list, click **OpenForm**, press the **Tab** key, and then type **Open Order form**.

2. In the Action Arguments pane, click the **Form Name** text box, click the list arrow, and then click **Order**. This completes the third macro, which contains one action to open the Order form.

3. Click the next row's **Macro Name** text box, type **CustomerWithOrders**, press the **Tab** key, click the **Action** list arrow, click **OpenForm**, press the **Tab** key, and then type **Open Customer with Orders form**.

4. In the Action Arguments pane, click the **Form Name** text box, click the list arrow, and then click **Customer with Orders**. This completes the fourth macro, which contains one action to open the Customer with Orders form.

5. Click the next row's **Macro Name** text box, type **Queries**, press the **Tab** key, click the **Action** list arrow, click **OpenForm**, press the **Tab** key, and then type **Open Queries Dialog Box**.

6. In the Action Arguments pane, click the **Form Name** text box, click the list arrow, and then click **Queries Dialog Box**. This completes the fifth macro, which contains one action to open the Queries Dialog Box form.

The final macro you need to define is the ExitToFineFood macro, which will execute two actions: the Close action to close the switchboard and the **SendKeys action**, which simulates keystrokes. In this macro, you will use the SendKeys action to simulate pressing the F11 key, which activates the Database window, because Leonard wants users to return to the Database window after closing the switchboard.

To finish creating the macro group:

1. Click the next row's **Macro Name** text box, type **ExitToFineFood**, press the **Tab** key, click the **Action** list arrow, click **Close**, press the **Tab** key, and then type **Close Switchboard**.

2. In the Action Arguments pane, click the **Object Type** text box, click the list arrow, click **Form**, click the **Object Name** text box, and then type **Switchboard**.

3. Click the right side of the next row's **Action** text box, scroll the list, click **SendKeys**, press the **Tab** key, and then type **Activate Database window**.

   For the SendKeys action, you need to specify the Keystrokes argument value {F11}, which is the same as pressing the F11 key, so that the action will return to the Database window after closing the Switchboard form.

4. In the Action Arguments pane, click the **Keystrokes** text box, and then type **{F11}**. Be sure to type the braces, but not the period. This completes the second of the two actions for the final macro. See Figure 9-37.

Figure 9-37   COMPLETED MACRO GROUP CONTAINING SIX MACROS

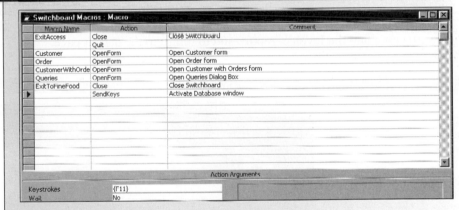

TROUBLE? Check your macros carefully against those in the figure. If any of your macros are not correct, click the appropriate text box and use the list arrow to select the correct option, or edit the text to correct it.

5. Click the **Save** button on the Macro Design toolbar, and then click the **Close** button on the Macro window to close it and return to the Database window.

Now that you've defined all the macros that will execute the necessary actions for the command buttons on the switchboard, you can create the form for the switchboard.

Creating a Switchboard

To create the switchboard, you'll use the Access Switchboard Manager. The **Switchboard Manager** is a Microsoft Access add-in tool that helps you create and customize a switchboard. When you use the Switchboard Manager, you specify the command buttons that will appear on the switchboard. For each button, you identify the command to execute when the button is clicked. The Switchboard Manager automatically attaches the command to the OnClick property for that command button; this property specifies the action to take when the command button is clicked. Some commands require one or more arguments, which you can specify as well. When you complete the switchboard design, the Switchboard Manager creates a form for your switchboard with the default name Switchboard. The Switchboard Manager also creates a table, named **Switchboard Items**, which contains records describing the command buttons on the switchboard.

The Switchboard Manager allows you to create only one switchboard form for a database, but the switchboard can contain many pages. You can designate only one of the switchboard pages as the default page. The **default page**, or **main page**, is the switchboard page that will appear when you open the switchboard form. You can place command buttons on the default page to open other switchboard pages.

You will use the Switchboard Manager to create the switchboard form for the FineFood database. Review the design of the form shown in Figure 9-34. Notice that each command button has an associated hot key, which is indicated by the underlined letter in the button's label. As you use the Switchboard Manager to create the form, you'll place the appropriate command buttons on the switchboard, define the hot keys, and associate the corresponding macros from the Switchboard Macros macro group with the buttons.

The FineFood Database switchboard shown in Figure 9-34 will be the default page. You'll create a second switchboard page for the Reports switchboard. As shown in Figure 9-38, this switchboard page will contain command buttons to print the Customers and Orders report and the Invoices report, and to return to the default page.

| Figure 9-38 | REPORTS SWITCHBOARD AS A SECOND SWITCHBOARD PAGE |

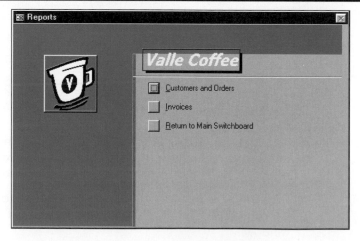

First, you'll create the switchboard form and two switchboard pages.

To create the switchboard form with two pages:

1. Click **Tools** on the menu bar, point to **Database Utilities**, and then click **Switchboard Manager**. Access opens a dialog box asking if you want to create a switchboard.

   TROUBLE? If you do not see the Switchboard Manager in the Database Utilities menu list, it might not be installed on your computer. See your instructor or technical support person for assistance.

2. Click the **Yes** button. The Switchboard Manager dialog box opens. See Figure 9-39.

Figure 9-39   **SWITCHBOARD MANAGER DIALOG BOX**

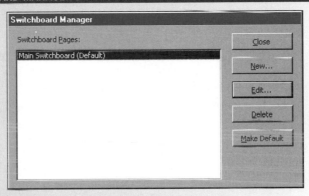

The Main Switchboard page, which is the default page, is created with the switchboard. You use the Switchboard Manager dialog box to add new pages, edit or delete existing pages, or to change the default page. You will add a new page next.

3. Click the **New** button. The Create New dialog box opens.

4. Type **Reports** in the Switchboard Page Name text box, and then click the **OK** button. The Create New dialog box closes, and the Switchboard Pages list box now shows the original default page and the new Reports page.

   Next, you'll edit the default page to change its name to FineFood Database.

5. Make sure the Main Switchboard (Default) page is selected, and then click the **Edit** button. The Edit Switchboard Page dialog box opens on top of the Switchboard Manager dialog box. This dialog box lets you edit the name for the switchboard page and add command buttons to the page.

6. Select the current entry in the Switchboard Name text box, and then type **FineFood Database**. See Figure 9-40.

Figure 9-40   EDIT SWITCHBOARD PAGE DIALOG BOX

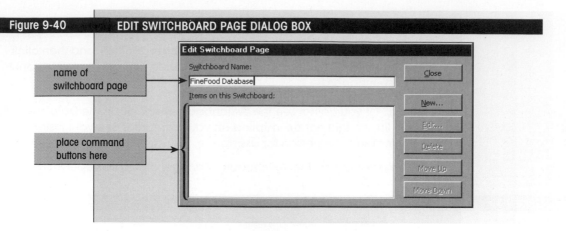

Adding Command Buttons to a Switchboard Page

You can now add the command buttons for each of the macros in the Switchboard Macros macro group. Each command button will carry out the actions in its associated macro when the command button is clicked.

To add the first command button to the switchboard page:

1. Click the **New** button. The Edit Switchboard Item dialog box opens.

   The first button you will add is the Customer button, which will open the Customer form. According to Leonard's design, the hot key for this button is C.

2. Type **&Customer** in the Text box. This text will appear to the right of the command button. Recall that the ampersand (&) creates the hot key.

   Next, you need to specify the command that will be executed when the user clicks the button. In this case, you want Access to run the Customer macro, which opens the Customer form. This macro is part of the Switchboard Macros group.

3. Click the **Command** list arrow, and then click **Run Macro**. The third text box in the Edit Switchboard Item dialog box now displays the label "Macro." In this text box you need to specify the macro to run when the button is clicked. When you click the Macro list arrow, you will see a list of all the macros defined for the database. The names of all the macros that are part of the macro group you created are preceded with the text "Switchboard Macros" to identify them as belonging to the group.

4. Click the **Macro** list arrow, and then click **Switchboard Macros.Customer**. The first command button definition is now complete. See Figure 9-41.

Figure 9-41   EDIT SWITCHBOARD ITEM DIALOG BOX

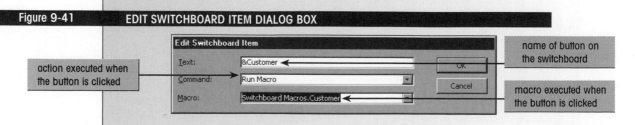

5. Click the **OK** button. The Switchboard Manager returns to the Edit Switchboard Page dialog box. Notice that the Items on this Switchboard list now shows the Customer command button.

Five of the remaining six command buttons in the FineFood Database switchboard page have associated macros in the Switchboard Macros group; the Reports button does not. Next, you'll add these five command buttons to the switchboard.

To add five additional buttons to the switchboard page:

1. Click the **New** button. The Edit Switchboard Item dialog box opens.

2. Type **&Order** in the Text box.

3. Click the **Command** list arrow, and then click **Run Macro**.

4. Click the **Macro** list arrow, scroll down the list, and then click **Switchboard Macros.Order**.

5. Click the **OK** button. The definition of the second command button, Order, is now complete. When clicked, the button will run the Order macro in the Switchboard Macros macro group, which opens the Order form in Form view.

6. Repeat Steps 1 through 5 to define the **Customer &with Orders** command button to run the macro named **Switchboard Macros.CustomerWithOrders**.

The next command button you need to define is the button for opening the Queries Dialog Box form. According to Leonard's design, the name of this button includes the ellipsis after the word "Queries" to indicate that a dialog box will open when the button is clicked.

7. Repeat Steps 1 through 5 to define the **&Queries...** command button (be sure to include the ellipsis in the button name) to run the macro named **Switchboard Macros.Queries**.

8. Repeat Steps 1 through 5 to define the **&Exit to FineFood** command button to run the macro named **Switchboard Macros.ExitToFineFood**.

9. Repeat Steps 1 through 5 to define the **E&xit Access** command button to run the macro named **Switchboard Macros.ExitAccess**. The switchboard design now contains six command buttons. See Figure 9-42.

Figure 9-42	EDIT SWITCHBOARD PAGE DIALOG BOX

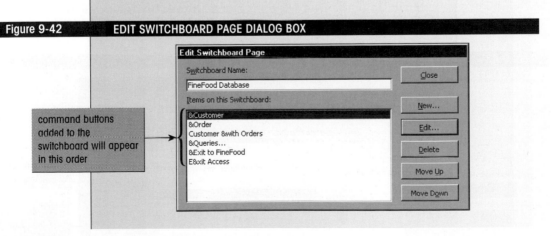

command buttons added to the switchboard will appear in this order

TROUBLE? Compare your Edit Switchboard Page dialog box with Figure 9-42. If any of your command buttons are incorrect, click the button name and then click the Edit button. Make the necessary changes, and then click the OK button to return to the dialog box.

The FineFood Database switchboard page is complete, except for the Reports command button. You'll add this command button next.

To add the last button to the switchboard page:

1. Click the **New** button. The Edit Switchboard Item dialog box opens.

2. Type **&Reports...** in the Text box. Be sure to include the ellipsis in the button name.

   Because you do not have a macro in the Switchboard Macros macro group for this command button, you will not select Run Macro in the Command text box. Instead, you'll accept the default command, Go to Switchboard, which allows you to change from one switchboard page to another.

3. Click the **Switchboard** list arrow, and then click **Reports**.

4. Click the **OK** button. The switchboard design for the FineFood Database switchboard page now contains all the necessary command buttons.

In Leonard's design for the FineFood Database switchboard page, the Reports command button precedes the Queries command button. You'll need to move the Reports command button to its correct position in the switchboard page.

Moving Command Buttons in a Switchboard Page

You can delete and move command buttons in a switchboard page by selecting an entry in the Items on this Switchboard list box and then clicking the Delete, Move Up, or Move Down buttons. You'll use the Move Up button to reposition the Reports command button.

To reposition the Reports command button:

1. Click **&Reports...** in the Items on this Switchboard list box, and then click the **Move Up** button. The &Reports... entry moves up one position in the list box and remains selected. See Figure 9-43.

Figure 9-43	MOVING A COMMAND BUTTON

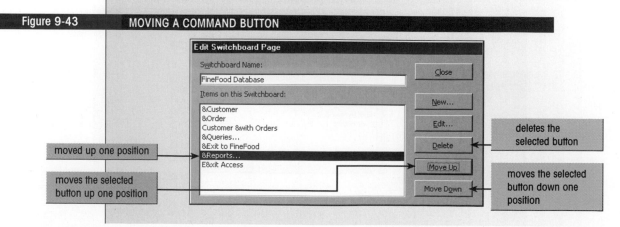

2. Click the **Move Up** button two more times to correctly position the &Reports... entry above the &Queries... entry.

You've finished the FineFood Database switchboard page, so you can close the Edit Switchboard Page dialog box.

3. Click the **Close** button to close the Edit Switchboard Page dialog box. The Switchboard Manager dialog box is now active.

Next, you'll add the command buttons to the Reports switchboard page.

Adding Command Buttons in a Second Switchboard Page

You've already used the Run Macro and Go to Switchboard options in the Edit Switchboard Item dialog box. Six other Command text box options in this dialog box that you can use are: Open Form in Add Mode, Open Form in Edit Mode, Open Report, Design Application, Exit Application, and Run Code. For the Reports switchboard page, you'll use the Open Report option for the first two command buttons (Customers and Orders, Invoices) and the Go to Switchboard option for the Return to Main Switchboard command button.

To add command buttons to the Reports switchboard page:

1. Click **Reports** in the Switchboard Pages list box, and then click the **Edit** button. The Edit Switchboard Page dialog box opens on top of the Switchboard Manager dialog box.

2. Click the **New** button. The Edit Switchboard Item dialog box opens.

3. Type **&Customers and Orders** in the Text box.

4. Click the **Command** list arrow, and then click **Open Report**. The third text box in the Edit Switchboard Item dialog box now displays the label "Report." In this text box, you specify the report to open when the button is clicked. When you click the Report list arrow, you see a list of all the reports defined for the database.

5. Click the **Report** list arrow, click **Customers and Orders**, and then click the **OK** button.

6. Repeat Steps 2 through 5 to define the **&Invoices** command button to open the report named **Invoices**.

7. Click the **New** button, type **&Return to Main Switchboard**, click the **Switchboard** list arrow, click **FineFood Database**, and then click the **OK** button. The Reports switchboard page now contains all the necessary command buttons. See Figure 9-44.

Figure 9-44   COMPLETED REPORTS SWITCHBOARD PAGE

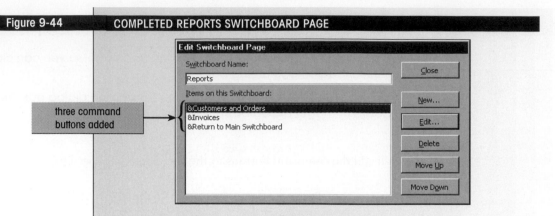

three command
buttons added

TROUBLE? Compare your Edit Switchboard Page dialog box with Figure 9-44. If any of your command buttons are incorrect, click the button name and then click the Edit button. Make the necessary changes, and then click the OK button to return to the dialog box.

Viewing and Testing a Switchboard

You are finished using the Switchboard Manager, so you can now exit the Switchboard Manager and view the new switchboard.

To exit the Switchboard Manager and view the Switchboard form:

1. Click the **Close** button to close the Edit Switchboard Page dialog box.

2. Click the **Close** button to close the Switchboard Manager dialog box and return to the Database window.

3. If necessary, click **Forms** in the Objects bar of the Database window to display the Forms list.

4. Right-click **Switchboard**, and then click **Open**. Access opens the Switchboard form. See Figure 9-45.

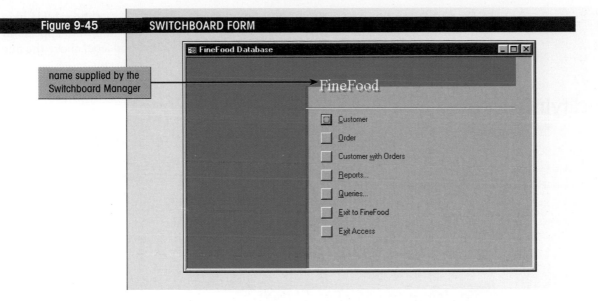

Figure 9-45   **SWITCHBOARD FORM**

The Switchboard form contains the seven command buttons you defined for the FineFood Database switchboard page, using the Switchboard Manager. Each command button has an attached label displaying the button name. The underscore in the button name indicates the hot key for that button. The name "FineFood" appears in white text in a label above the buttons; the Switchboard Manager automatically supplied this label for the form. Behind the FineFood label is another copy of the FineFood label displaying the text in gray letters, creating a shadowed effect. The Switchboard Manager also added the large green areas on the switchboard, which are green rectangle objects.

Overall, Leonard is pleased with the appearance of the Switchboard form, but there are some changes he would like you to make. Before you make these changes, you will test some of the command buttons to make sure that they work properly.

To test the command buttons:

1. Click the **Customer** command button. Access displays the record for the Meadows Restaurant in the Customer form in Form view.

2. Click the **Close** button ☒ on the Customer window title bar to close it and return to the switchboard.

3. Press and hold down the **Alt** key, and then press the letter **O**. Access opens the Order form and displays the first Order record.

4. Click ☒ on the Order window title bar to close it and return to the switchboard.

5. Click the **Reports** command button. Access replaces the FineFood Database switchboard page with the Reports switchboard page.

6. Click the **Invoices** command button. Access opens the Invoices report in Print Preview.

7. Click ☒ on the Report window title bar to close it and return to the Reports switchboard page.

8. Click the **Return to Main Switchboard** command button to replace the Reports switchboard page with the FineFood Database switchboard page.

Leonard wants you to make some changes to the design of the switchboard. He likes the layout of the buttons, but he wants you to make sure that the form always appears in the same size on the screen. He also wants you to remove the FineFood label above the buttons and add a new label, Valle Coffee, and a picture of the Valle Coffee cup.

Modifying a Switchboard

Because the switchboard is a form, you can make Leonard's changes in Design view. However, you need to be careful not to make any changes to the command buttons that would affect the actions and macros associated with them. You should only make these types of changes using the Switchboard Manager. If you were to change the definitions of any of the command buttons in Design view, the Switchboard Manager would not be able to make the necessary updates, and the switchboard would not function correctly.

Next, you'll delete the FineFood label, place the new "Valle Coffee" label on the form, and add the Valle Coffee cup picture.

To delete the FineFood label:

1. Click the **View** button for Design view 🖎 on the Form View toolbar. Access displays the Switchboard form in Design view.

2. Right-click the **FineFood** label above the command buttons to open the shortcut menu, and then click **Cut**. The label is deleted. Notice that there is a second FineFood label now visible. This label appeared as the shadow of the first label in the switchboard.

3. Right-click the **FineFood** label above the command buttons to open the shortcut menu, and then click **Cut**. The second label is deleted.

You can now add the Valle Coffee label in the green area above the command buttons.

To add the Valle Coffee label to the switchboard:

1. If the toolbox is not displayed, click the **Toolbox** button 🛠 on the Form Design toolbar. Move the toolbox if it covers any part of the Form window.

2. Click the **Label** tool 𝐴𝑎 on the toolbox. Position the pointer in the Detail section and, when the center of the pointer's plus symbol (+) is positioned at the 2-inch mark on the horizontal ruler and the ⅜-inch mark on the vertical ruler, click the mouse button.

3. Type **Valle Coffee** and then press the **Enter** key.

   Leonard wants the title to stand out, so he asks you to format it in bold and italics, increase its font size, change its font color to yellow, and apply the shadowed special effect.

4. Click the **Bold** button 𝐁 on the Form Design toolbar, click the **Italic** button 𝐼 on the Form Design toolbar, click the **Font Size** list arrow on the Formatting toolbar, and then click **18**.

5. Click the list arrow for the **Font/Fore Color** button 🅰 on the Formatting toolbar to display the palette of available colors.

6. Click the bright yellow color box (the third button in the fourth row). The Valle Coffee label now appears bright yellow.

7. Click the list arrow for the **Special Effect** button on the Formatting toolbar, and then click the **Shadowed** button.

8. Click **Format** on the menu bar, point to **Size**, and then click **To Fit**. Access resizes the label box to display the entire label.

Next, you'll add the picture of the Valle Coffee cup to the form, and then you'll apply the raised special effect to the picture to enhance it.

To add the Valle Coffee cup picture to the switchboard:

1. Click the **Image** button on the toolbox, position the pointer's plus symbol (+) at the ½-inch mark on the horizontal ruler and the ½-inch mark on the vertical ruler, and then click the mouse button to place the picture. The Insert Picture dialog box opens.

2. In the Look in list box, click the **Tutorial** folder on your Data Disk (if necessary), click **ValleCup** in the file list, and then click the **OK** button. Access inserts the ValleCup picture on the form.

3. Click the list arrow for the **Special Effect** button on the Formatting toolbar, and then click the **Raised** button. The raised effect is applied to the button. You've finished making the necessary changes to the layout of the Switchboard form. See Figure 9-46.

Figure 9-46	MODIFIED SWITCHBOARD FORM LAYOUT

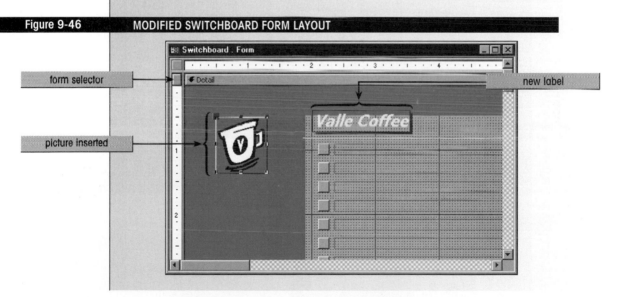

Now you can change the form properties so that the form will be correctly sized and positioned on the screen.

To change the Switchboard form properties:

1. Click the **Close** button ☒ on the toolbox to close it.

2. Right-click the form selector, and then click **Properties** to display the property sheet for the form.

   First you'll set the Auto Resize property to No so that Access will not resize the form when it is opened.

3. Click the **Format** tab, click the right side of the **Auto Resize** text box, and then click **No**.

   Now you'll set the Border Style property to Dialog to prevent users from resizing the form.

4. Click the right side of the **Border Style** text box, and then click **Dialog**.

   Setting the Close Button property to No disables the Close button in the title bar of the form. You'll disable this button because Leonard wants users to close the form by clicking the Exit to FineFood or Exit Access command buttons.

5. Click the right side of the **Close Button** text box, and then click **No**.

6. Click ☒ on the property sheet.

7. Click the **Save** button 🖫 on the Form Design toolbar.

8. Click ☒ on the Form window to close it and return to the Database window.

Leonard wants to view the modified switchboard, so you'll open the switchboard in Form view to see its appearance.

To view the switchboard:

1. In the Forms list of the Database window, right-click **Switchboard**, and then click **Open**. The switchboard opens in Form view. See Figure 9-47.

| Figure 9-47 | MODIFIED SWITCHBOARD IN FORM VIEW |

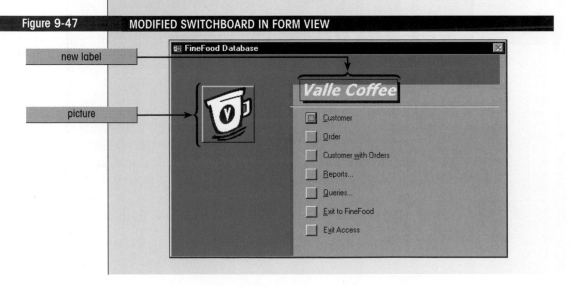

new label

picture

> **2.** Click the **Exit to FineFood** command button. Access closes the switchboard and returns to the Database window.
>
> **3.** Click the **Close** button ☒ on the Access window title bar to close the FineFood database and to exit Access. You return to the Windows desktop.

Leonard's design for the FineFood database user interface also includes a restricted menu bar and hides the toolbar. In the next tutorial, you'll add these features to the switchboard and create the necessary VBA code for the Queries Dialog Box form command buttons.

Session 9.4 QUICK | CHECK

1. What does the SendKeys action do?

2. What is the Switchboard Manager?

3. To which property does the Switchboard Manager automatically assign commands for each command button?

4. When using the Command Button Wizard, how do you define a hot key for a command button?

5. How do you specify that a form is a dialog box?

6. What are two special effects you can use for a control?

REVIEW ASSIGNMENTS

Barbara wants you to create a switchboard interface for the **Coffees** database. You can create the interface by completing the following steps:

1. Make sure your Data Disk is in the appropriate disk drive, start Access, and then open the **Coffees** database located in the Review folder on your Data Disk.

2. Design and create a dialog box form named **Reports Dialog Box** that has the following components and characteristics:

   a. The text "Print Reports" appears in the title bar.

   Explore

   b. A list box (with a Name property value of ReportList Control) displays all the report names contained in the **Coffees** database. To place the report names in the list box, use an SQL SELECT statement to retrieve the report names from the MSysObjects table.

   c. The text "Reports Available" appears as a heading above the list box.

   d. Two command buttons appear below the list box. The left command button displays the Preview Document icon, and the right command button displays the word "Close" with the letter "C" underlined.

   e. Double-clicking a report name has the same effect as selecting a report name in the list box and clicking the left command button. Both events cause Access to display the Print Preview window for the selected report. (You will add the VBA code for these events in the next tutorial. For now, double-clicking or clicking should cause no action to occur.)

   f. Clicking the Close command button causes Access to close the dialog box. The letter "C" is the hot key.

   g. Set form properties that are appropriate for a dialog box.

3. Design and create a switchboard form named **Switchboard**. Use Figure 9-48 and the following descriptions as a guide in designing the switchboard.

Figure 9-48

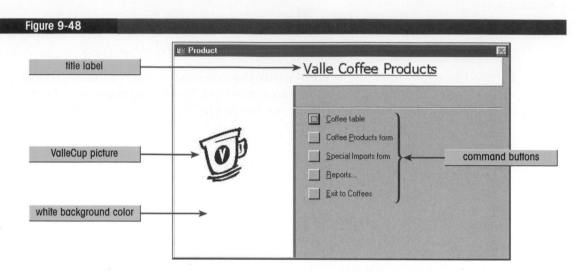

a. Create a macro group named **Switchboard Macros** for the command buttons. The command buttons perform these actions: open the **Coffee** table, open the **Coffee Products** form, open the **Special Imports** form, open the **Reports Dialog Box** form, and close the switchboard and activate the Database window. Define hot keys for each command button.
b. Create the switchboard and place the command buttons on the form.
c. Specify "Product" as the name to appear in the title bar. Delete the default label in the form and place a label at the top of the switchboard. The label should read "Valle Coffee Products" and should be underlined with a 16-point font size in a font color of your choice.
d. Add the **ValleCup** picture from the Review folder on your Data Disk to the appropriate position in the switchboard.

Explore

e. Set the background color and visual effects for the switchboard and its components, as shown in Figure 9-48, and then set form properties that are appropriate for a switchboard.

4. Save the **Switchboard** form, and then test the command buttons and the Reports Dialog Box form to make sure that your switchboard items work correctly. If necessary, return to the Switchboard Manager and make any corrections.

5. Click the Exit to Coffees command button to close the **Switchboard** form, and then exit Access.

CASE PROBLEMS

Case 1. Ashbrook Mall Information Desk Sam Bullard wants the **Mall** database to include an easy-to-use interface. He asks you to create a switchboard interface for the **Mall** database by completing the following:

1. Make sure your Data Disk is in the appropriate disk drive, start Access, and then open the **Mall** database located in the Cases folder on your Data Disk.

2. Define data validation criteria for the Status field in the **Maintenance Job** table. Acceptable field values for the Status field are A, C, and O. Use a message of "Status values must be A, C, or O" that appears if a user enters an invalid Status field value.

3. Design and create a switchboard form named **Switchboard**. Use Figure 9-49 and the following descriptions as a guide in designing the switchboard.

Figure 9-49

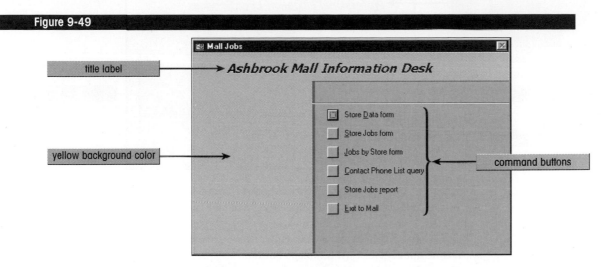

Explore

a. Create a macro group named **Switchboard Macros** for the command buttons. The command buttons perform these actions: open the **Store Data** form, open the **Store Jobs** form, open the **Jobs by Store** form, open the **Contact Phone List** query, open the **Store Jobs** report in the Print Preview window, and close the switchboard and activate the Database window. Define hot keys for each command button.

b. Create the switchboard and place the command buttons on the form.

c. Specify "Mall Jobs" as the name to appear in the title bar. Delete the default label in the form and place a label at the top of the switchboard. The label should read "Ashbrook Mall Information Desk" and should be in italics and boldface with a 14-point font size.

Explore

d. Set the background color for the switchboard, as shown in Figure 9-49, and then set form properties that are appropriate for a switchboard.

4. Save the **Switchboard** form, and then test the command buttons to make sure that your switchboard items work correctly. If necessary, return to the Switchboard Manager and make any corrections.

5. Click the Exit to Mall command button to close the **Switchboard** form, and then exit Access.

Case 2. Professional Litigation User Services To make the **Plus** database easier to use, Raj Jawahir wants you to create a switchboard interface for it. To create the interface, you will complete the following:

1. Make sure your Data Disk is in the appropriate disk drive, start Access, and then open the **Plus** database located in the Cases folder on your Data Disk.

2. Design and create a switchboard form named **Switchboard**. Use Figure 9-50 and the following descriptions as a guide in designing the switchboard.

Figure 9-50

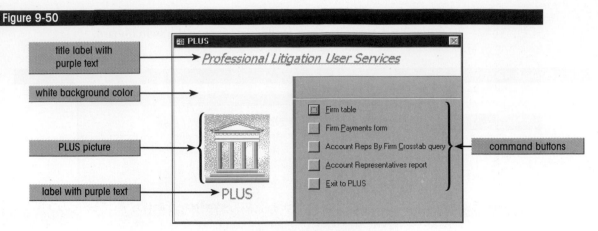

Explore

a. Create a macro group named **Switchboard Macros** for the command buttons. The command buttons perform these actions: open the **Firm** table, open the **Firm Payments** form, open the **AcctReps by Firm Crosstab** query, open the **Payments By Account Representative** report in the Print Preview window, and close the switchboard and activate the Database window. Define hot keys for each command button.

b. Create the switchboard and place the command buttons on the form.

c. Specify "PLUS" as the name to appear in the title bar. Delete the default label in the form and place a label at the top of the switchboard. The label should read "Professional Litigation User Services" and should be underlined and in italics with a 14-point font size. Set the label's font color to purple.

d. Add the **PLUS** picture from the Cases folder on your Data Disk to the appropriate position in the switchboard.

e. Add the label PLUS below the picture. Set the label's font color to purple with a 16-point font size.

Explore

f. Set the background color for the switchboard, as shown in Figure 9-50, and then set form properties that are appropriate for a switchboard.

3. Save the **Switchboard** form, and then test the command buttons to make sure that your switchboard items work correctly. If necessary, return to the Switchboard Manager and make any corrections.

4. Click the Exit to PLUS command button to close the **Switchboard** form, and then exit Access.

Case 3. Best Friends Noah and Sheila Warnick, the founders of Best Friends, want the **Friends** database to have an interface that is easier to use. They ask you to create a switchboard interface for the database by completing the following:

1. Make sure your Data Disk is in the appropriate disk drive, start Access, and then open the **Friends** database located in the Cases folder on your Data Disk.

2. Design and create a switchboard form named **Switchboard**. Use Figure 9-51 and the following descriptions as a guide in designing the switchboard.

Figure 9-51

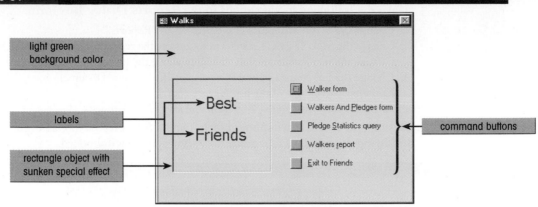

Explore

a. Create a macro group named **Switchboard Macros** for the command buttons. The command buttons perform these actions: open the **Walker** form, open the **Walkers And Pledges** form, open the **Pledge Statistics** query, open the **Walkers** report in the Print Preview window, and close the switchboard and activate the Database window. Define hot keys for each command button.

b. Create the switchboard and place the command buttons on the form.

c. Specify "Walks" as the name to appear in the title bar. Delete the default label in the form and place two labels at the left of the switchboard. The first label is "Best" and the second label is "Friends." Set the labels' font color to red with an 18-point font size.

Explore

d. Set the background color and visual effects for the switchboard and its components, as shown in Figure 9-51, resize the form, and then set form properties that are appropriate for a switchboard. (*Hint*: Delete the rectangle objects created by the Switchboard Manager on the **Switchboard** form before setting the Detail section Back Color property.)

3. Save the **Switchboard** form, and then test the command buttons to make sure that your switchboard items work correctly. If necessary, return to the Switchboard Manager and make any corrections.

4. Click the Exit to Friends command button to close the **Switchboard** form, and then exit Access.

Case 4. Lopez Lexus Dealerships Marie and Hector Lopez want you to create a user-friendly interface for the **Vehicles** database. They ask you to create a switchboard for the **Vehicles** database by completing the following:

1. Make sure your Data Disk is in the appropriate disk drive, start Access, and then open the **Vehicles** database located in the Cases folder on your Data Disk.

2. Design and create a dialog box form named **Queries Dialog Box** that has the following components and characteristics:

a. The text "Queries" appears in the title bar.

Explore

b. A list box (with a Name property value of QueryList Control) displays all the query names contained in the **Vehicles** database. To place the query names in the list box, use an SQL SELECT statement to retrieve the query names from the MSysObjects table.

c. The text "Queries Available" appears as a heading above the list box.

d. Two command buttons appear below the list box. The left command button displays the MS Access Query icon, and the right command button displays the word "Close" with the letter "C" underlined.

e. Double-clicking a query name has the same effect as selecting a query name in the list box and clicking the left command button. Both events cause Access to display the query datasheet for the selected query. (You will add the VBA code for these events in the next tutorial. For now, double-clicking or clicking should cause no action to occur.)

f. Clicking the Close command button causes Access to close the dialog box. The letter "C" is the hot key.

g. Set form properties that are appropriate for a dialog box.

Explore ▸ 3. Create a copy of the **Queries Dialog Box** form and name it **Reports Dialog Box**. Make the following modifications to the **Reports Dialog Box** form:

  a. Change the text that appears in the title bar to "Reports."
  b. Change the SQL SELECT statement to retrieve the report names from the MSysObjects table.
  c. Change the text that appears as a heading above the list box to "Reports Available."
  d. Change the left command button to display the Preview Document icon, and change the Name property value of the list box to ReportList Control.
  e. Close the **Reports Dialog Box** form and save your changes.

4. Design and create a switchboard form named **Switchboard**. Use Figure 9-52 and the following descriptions as a guide in designing the switchboard.

Figure 9-52

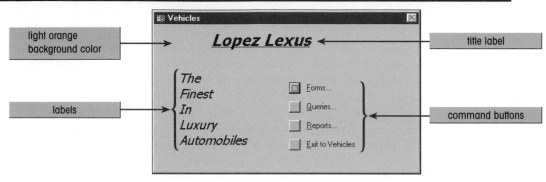

  a. Create one macro named Exit Switchboard for the fourth command button, but do not create macros for the other command buttons. The macro should close the switchboard and activate the Database window.
  b. The switchboard should have two pages. Specify "Vehicles" as the name to appear in the title bar for the first, default page. Delete the default label in the form and place a label at the top of the switchboard. The label should read "Lopez Lexus" and should be underlined, in boldface, and italics with an 18-point font size.
  c. On the left side of the form, enter the labels shown in Figure 9-52. Set the labels' font size to 14-point and italics. (*Hint*: You can enter the labels as one label by pressing Shift + Enter after each word and then resizing the label box after you're done.)
  d. Specify "Forms" as the name to appear in the title bar for the second switchboard page. Place three command buttons on the second page. The command buttons perform these actions: open the **Car Data** form, open the **Locations And Cars** form, and return to the main switchboard. Define hot keys for each command button. Do not use macros for this second switchboard page.

Explore ▸ e. Place four command buttons on the first switchboard page. The command buttons perform these actions: switch to the second switchboard page, open the **Queries Dialog Box** form, open the **Reports Dialog Box** form, and close the switchboard and activate the Database window. Define hot keys for each command button.

Explore ▸ f. Set the background color and visual effects for the switchboard and its components, as shown in Figure 9-52, and then set form properties that are appropriate for a switchboard. (*Hint*: Delete the rectangle objects created by the Switchboard Manager on the **Switchboard** form before setting the Detail section Back Color property.)

5. Save the **Switchboard** form, and then test the command buttons to make sure that your switchboard items and dialog boxes work correctly. If necessary, return to the Switchboard Manager and make any corrections.

6. Click the Exit to Vehicles command button to close the **Switchboard** form, and then exit Access.

Case 5. eACH Internet Auction Site Chris and Pat Aquino want you to create a friendly user interface for the **BuySell** database. They ask you to create a switchboard for the **BuySell** database by completing the following:

1. Make sure your Data Disk that contains the **BuySell** database is in the appropriate drive, start Access, and then open the **BuySell** database located in the Cases folder on your Data Disk.

2. Design and create a switchboard form named **Switchboard**. Use Figure 9-53 and the following descriptions as a guide in designing the switchboard.

Figure 9-53

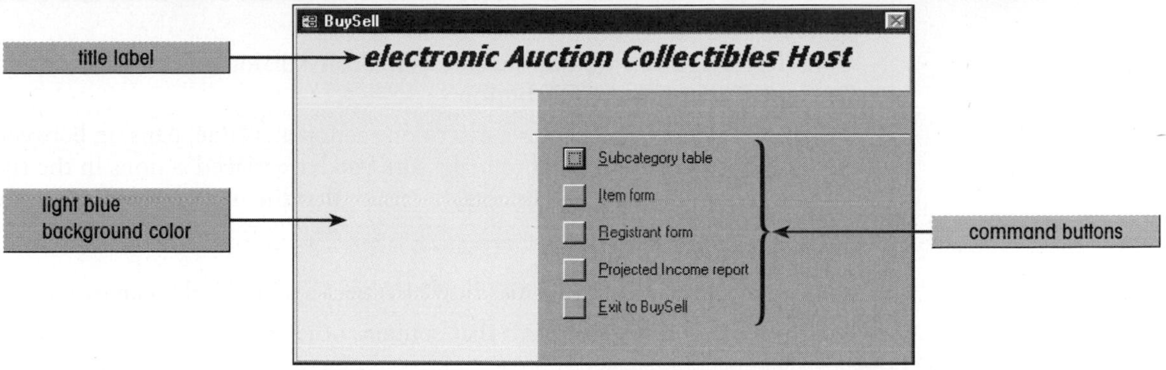

Explore

a. Create a macro group named **Switchboard Macros** for the command buttons. The command buttons perform these actions: open the **Subcategory** table, open the **Item** form, open the **Registrant** form, open the **Projected Income Based on Minimum Bid** report in the Print Preview window, and close the switchboard and activate the Database window. Define hot keys for each command button.

b. Create the switchboard and place the command buttons on the form.

c. Specify "BuySell" as the name to appear in the title bar. Delete the default label in the form and place a label at the top of the switchboard. The label should read "electronic Auction Collectibles Host" and should be in italics and boldface with a 16-point font size.

Explore

d. Set the background color for the switchboard, as shown in Figure 9-53, and then set form properties that are appropriate for a switchboard.

3. Save the **Switchboard** form, and then test the command buttons to make sure that your switchboard items work correctly. If necessary, return to the Switchboard Manager and make any corrections.

4. Click the Exit to BuySell command button to close the **Switchboard** form, and then exit Access.

INTERNET ASSIGNMENTS

The purpose of the Internet Assignments is to challenge you to find information on the Internet that you can use to create effective documents. The actual assignments are updated and maintained on the Course Technology Web site. Log on to the Internet and use your Web browser to go to the Student Online Companion to accompany this text at **www.course.com/NewPerspectives/office2000**. Click the Access link, and then click the link for Tutorial 9.

QUICK | CHECK ANSWERS

Session 9.1

1. A switchboard is a form that appears when you open a database and that provides controlled access to the database's tables, forms, queries, and reports. It lets you customize the organization of the user interface, and prevents users from changing the design of tables, forms, queries, reports, and other objects.

2. A hot key is an underlined letter in a command button, menu name, menu option, or toolbar button that provides a keyboard shortcut to a common operation. You can use shortcut keys by holding down the Alt key while typing the underlined letter to make a selection.

3. A macro is a command or a series of commands that you want Access to perform automatically for you. Each command in a macro is called an action.

4. Action arguments are additional facts Access needs to execute an action. The action for opening a form, for example, needs the form name and the appropriate view as arguments.

5. The MsgBox action causes Access to open a dialog box that remains on the screen until you click the OK button.

6. Single stepping executes a macro one action at a time, pausing between actions. You use single stepping to make sure you have placed actions in the right order and with the right arguments, to ensure that the macro works correctly.

Session 9.2

1. An event property specifies how an object responds when an event occurs.

2. A macro group is a macro that contains other macros.

3. The beginning of each macro in a macro group has an entry in the Macro Name column; subsequent actions in the macro do not have entries in the Macro Name column. The macro ends with the start of a new macro or at the end of the macro group, whichever comes first.

4. The Where Condition specifies which record to display in the form.

5. The Validation Rule property specifies the valid values that can be entered in a field. For example, you could use this property to specify that only positive numeric values can be entered in a numeric field.

6. The Validation Text property value will be displayed in a message box if the user enters an invalid value. For example, you could display the message "Must be a positive integer" if the user enters a value less than or equal to zero.

Session 9.3

1. Users will not be able to resize the form using the pointer.

2. to prevent users from opening the form in Design view

3. a control that displays a list of values

4. special tables maintained by Access that store information about the characteristics of a database and about the structure of its objects

5. In Design view, open the property sheet for the command button. Click the All tab in the property sheet, click the Picture text box, and then click the Build button. Select the picture from the Picture Builder dialog box, and then click the OK button.

6. Right-click the object, click Copy on the shortcut menu, and then click the Paste button on the toolbar.

Session 9.4

1. The SendKeys action simulates keystrokes in a macro.

2. The Switchboard Manager is a Microsoft add-in tool that helps you create and customize a switchboard.

3. OnClick

4. Type an ampersand (&) to the left of the hot key character to create the hot key.

5. Open the form in Design view, open the form's property sheet, and then set the Border Style property to Dialog.

6. shadowed and raised

OBJECTIVES

In this tutorial you will:

- Learn about Function procedures, Sub procedures, and modules

- Review and modify an existing Sub procedure in an event procedure

- Create Function procedures in a standard module

- Create event procedures

- Compile and test Function procedures, Sub procedures, and event procedures

- Hide text and change display colors

- Encrypt and decrypt a database

- Set and unset a database password

- Analyze a database

- Split a database

- Set database startup options

USING
AND WRITING VISUAL
BASIC FOR
APPLICATIONS CODE

Completing the FineFood Database User Interface

CASE

Valle Coffee

Leonard reviews your progress in developing the graphical user interface for the FineFood database. So far, you have created the switchboard that contains command buttons for opening forms, displaying dialog boxes, and exiting the switchboard. You have created a macro group that contains the macros attached to the command buttons on the switchboard. You have also created a dialog box for displaying the list of available queries.

You'll complete the user interface by modifying the Queries Dialog Box form so that its command buttons carry out the appropriate operations, and by modifying the Customer and Order forms to make data entry easier and to highlight important information on the forms. To make these modifications, you will write Visual Basic for Applications code to perform the necessary operations, and then attach the code to the appropriate event properties for the buttons and forms.

Leonard has some concerns about database security, encryption, and the database's overall performance. To address his concerns, you will implement Access security features, such as passwords and encryption, and use Access analysis features, such as the Performance Analyzer. Finally, you'll use the Database Splitter Wizard and set the startup options for the Switchboard form so that it opens automatically when a user opens the FineFood database.

Introduction to Visual Basic for Applications

You are ready to finish the graphical user interface for the FineFood database. Your next task is to refine the user interface further by adding a procedure to ensure proper capitalization of data entered using the Customer form. Leonard wants to make sure that all values entered in the State field using this form will be stored in the Customer table using uppercase letters. He asks you to modify the form so that it will automatically convert any lowercase letters entered in the State field to uppercase. To accomplish this, you will use Visual Basic.

Visual Basic for Applications (VBA) is the programming language provided with Access and the other Office 2000 programs. The process of writing VBA instructions is called **coding**. You write VBA instructions, called **statements**, to respond to events that occur with the objects in a database. A language such as VBA is, therefore, called both an **event-driven language** and an **object-oriented language**. Your experience with macros, which are also event-driven and object-oriented, should facilitate your learning of VBA. You can do almost anything with Visual Basic that you can do with macros, but Visual Basic gives you more control over commands and objects than you have with macros. For example, with Visual Basic you can create your own procedures to perform special calculations. You can also change an object's properties dynamically; for example, VBA code can change the color on a form when the user enters a specific field value.

Events

Recall from Tutorial 9 that an **event** occurs when you take some action, such as clicking a button using the mouse or pressing a key to choose an option. An **event property** specifies how an object responds when an event occurs. In Tutorial 9, you set event property values to macro names, and Access executed the macros when those events occurred. You can also create a group of statements using VBA code and set an event property value to the name of that group of statements. Access will then execute the group of statements, or **procedure**, when the event occurs. Such a procedure is called an **event procedure**.

Access has 44 events and associated event properties. As with actions, you do not need to learn all 44 events. You will gain experience with several event properties in this text, and if you need information on other event properties, you can use the Help system as a reference tool.

Next, you'll use Help to review two particularly useful topics about events.

To review two Help topics for events:

1. Place your Data Disk in the appropriate disk drive, start Access, and then open the **FineFood** database located in the Tutorial folder on your Data Disk.

2. Click the **Microsoft Access Help** button [?] on the Database toolbar to open the Office Assistant.

3. Type **What are events?** in the text box, and then click the **Search** button. The Office Assistant displays a list of relevant topics.

4. Click **Events and Event Properties Reference** in the list of topics. The Office Assistant opens the topic in the Microsoft Access Help window. This topic displays events grouped by task and listed alphabetically. You can use this topic whenever you need more information about a specific event and its associated event property.

5. After reviewing the topic, click the **See Also** link at the top of the page. The Topics Found dialog box opens.

6. Click **Find out when events occur** and then click the **Display** button. The selected topic opens in the Microsoft Access Help window. This topic describes the order in which events occur. Review the contents of this window and any of the links that interest you.

7. Click the **Close** button ⊠ on the Microsoft Access Help window to close it and return to the Database window.

8. Right-click the **Office Assistant**, and then click **Hide** on the shortcut menu. The Office Assistant closes.

Procedures

When you work with VBA, you code a group of statements that performs an operation or calculates a value, and then you attach the group to the event property of an object. Access then executes, or **calls**, these statements every time the event occurs for that object. Each group of statements is called a **procedure**. The two types of procedures are Function procedures and Sub procedures.

A **Function procedure**, or **function**, performs operations, returns a value, can accept input values, and can be used in expressions (recall that an expression is a calculation resulting in a single value). For example, some of the FineFood database queries use built-in Access functions, such as Sum, Count, and Avg, to calculate a sum, a record count, or an average. To meet Leonard's request, you will create a function named CapAll by entering the appropriate VBA statements. The CapAll function will accept the value entered in a field—in this case, the State field—as an input value, capitalize all characters of the field value, and then return the changed field value to be stored in the database.

A **Sub procedure**, or **subroutine**, performs operations and can accept input values, but does not return a value and cannot be used in expressions. In the next session, you will create a Sub procedure that displays a message on the Order form only when the data for an unpaid invoice is displayed in the form.

Modules

You store a group of related procedures together in a **module**. Figure 10-1 shows the structure of a typical module.

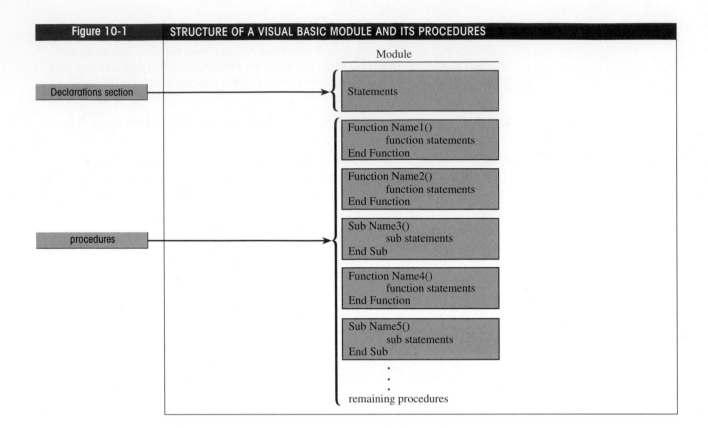

Figure 10-1   STRUCTURE OF A VISUAL BASIC MODULE AND ITS PROCEDURES

Each module starts with a **Declarations section**, which contains statements that apply to all procedures in the module. One or more procedures, which follow the Declarations section, constitute the rest of the module. The two basic types of modules are standard modules and class modules.

A **standard module** is a database object that is stored in memory with other database objects when you open the database. You can use the procedures in standard modules from anywhere in a database—even from procedures in other modules. A procedure that more than one object can use is called a **public** procedure. For example, the CapAll procedure that you will create capitalizes all letters in the value passed to it. Although you are creating this procedure specifically to work with the State field value, you will place it in a standard module and make it public. You could then use the CapAll procedure for any object in the database. All standard modules are listed on the Modules tab of the Database window.

A **class module** is usually associated with a particular form or report. When you create the first event procedure for a form or report, Access automatically creates an associated form or report class module. When you add additional event procedures to the form or report, Access adds them to the class module for that form or report. The event procedures in a class module are **local**, or **private**, which means that only the form or report for which the class module was created can use the event procedures.

Using Help and Sample Databases

The most difficult part of becoming proficient with Access is learning how to code effective VBA procedures. VBA is a powerful programming language containing hundreds of statements and built-in functions, along with hundreds of event properties, object properties, and built-in procedures. Deciding when and how to use each VBA feature can be intimidating to programming novices and even to experts. Fortunately, you can perform many fundamental operations without using VBA, by setting control properties and by using macros, as you have done in previous tutorials.

When you use VBA to create new procedures, you can take advantage of the excellent Access Help system as a reference tool. Three particularly useful Help topics are "Programming Information," "Visual Basic Conceptual Topics," and "Visual Basic Language Reference." You can also find Help for every VBA statement, function, and property—most of these topics even have a corresponding example that displays sample VBA code. If you find sample code similar to what you need, you can simply copy the statements to the Office Clipboard, paste them into a procedure in your own database, and modify the statements to work for your special case.

Another source for sample VBA code is the set of sample databases that you can install with Access. When installed, the following four sample databases appear in the Program Files\Microsoft Office\Office\Samples folder: Northwind, Contact, Addrbook, and Inventry. Each database has a variety of simple and complex VBA procedures. You can view the effects of these procedures by using them in the sample databases. Microsoft encourages you to copy and use the proven procedures in the sample databases as a way to learn and use VBA more quickly.

Using an Existing Procedure

Before creating the CapAll procedure for Leonard, you'll use an existing procedure that Leonard created in the class module for the Customer form. This procedure displays the full state name in a label box to the right of the State field value—Michigan appears in red, Indiana in blue, and Ohio in magenta.

You'll navigate the Customer form to observe the effects of the procedure.

To navigate a form that uses a VBA procedure:

1. Click **Forms** in the Objects bar of the Database window, right-click **Customer**, and then click **Open**. The Customer form opens and displays the first record for Meadows Restaurant. The state name of Michigan displays in red to the right of the State field value of MI.

2. Select the record number of **1** between the navigation buttons, type **32**, and then press the **Enter** key. The Customer form displays record 32 for Prime Cut Steakhouse. The state name of Indiana displays in blue to the right of the State field value of IN.

3. Click the **Next Record** navigation button ▶ to display record 33 for Cherry Creek Inn. The state name of Ohio displays in magenta to the right of the State field value of OH.

Leonard asks you to change the magenta color for Ohio to black to make it more readable.

Displaying an Event Procedure

The VBA procedure that controls the display of the state name and its color for each record is in the class module for the Customer form. Access processes the statements in the procedure when you open the Customer form and also when the focus leaves one record and moves to another. **Focus** refers to the record and control that is currently active and awaiting user action. Because the **Current event** occurs when a form opens and when the focus moves to another record, the VBA procedure is associated as an event procedure with the form's **OnCurrent property**.

To change the color of Ohio from magenta to black, you'll modify the event procedure for the form's OnCurrent property. First, you'll switch to Design view, and then you'll display the event procedure.

To display the event procedure for the form's OnCurrent property:

1. Click the **View** button for Design view 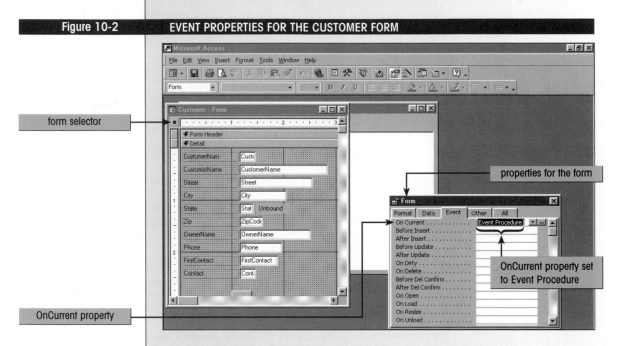 on the Form View toolbar to display the Customer form in Design view.

2. Right-click the form selector, and then click **Properties** to open the property sheet for the form.

3. If necessary, click the **Event** tab to display the Event page of the property sheet. See Figure 10-2.

| Figure 10-2 | EVENT PROPERTIES FOR THE CUSTOMER FORM |

form selector

properties for the form

OnCurrent property set to Event Procedure

OnCurrent property

The OnCurrent property is set to (Event Procedure), indicating that a VBA procedure is processed when the Current event occurs. You'll click the Build button to display the procedure.

4. Click the **Build** button to the right of the On Current text box. The Code window opens in the Visual Basic window. See Figure 10-3.

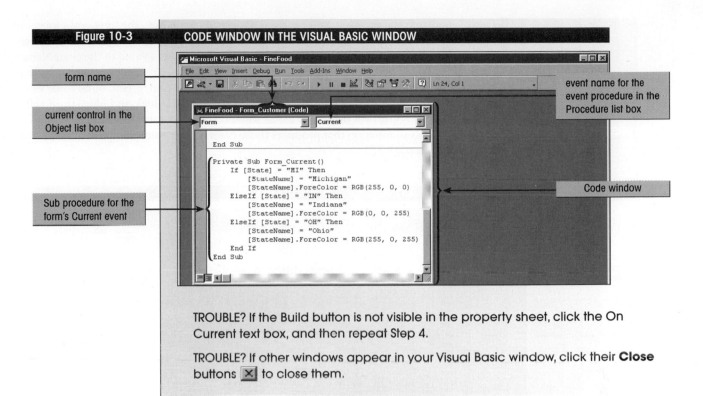

| Figure 10-3 | CODE WINDOW IN THE VISUAL BASIC WINDOW |

form name

current control in the
Object list box

Sub procedure for the
form's Current event

event name for the
event procedure in the
Procedure list box

Code window

```
Private Sub Form_Current()
    If [State] = "MI" Then
        [StateName] = "Michigan"
        [StateName].ForeColor = RGB(255, 0, 0)
    ElseIf [State] = "IN" Then
        [StateName] = "Indiana"
        [StateName].ForeColor = RGB(0, 0, 255)
    ElseIf [State] = "OH" Then
        [StateName] = "Ohio"
        [StateName].ForeColor = RGB(255, 0, 255)
    End If
End Sub
```

TROUBLE? If the Build button is not visible in the property sheet, click the On
Current text box, and then repeat Step 4.

TROUBLE? If other windows appear in your Visual Basic window, click their **Close**
buttons ☒ to close them.

The program you use to create and modify VBA code is called **Visual Basic Editor**
(**VBE**, or **editor** for short), and the **Visual Basic window** is the program window that
opens when you use VBE. The **Code window** is the window in which you create, modify,
and display VBA code. You can have as many Code windows open as you have modules in
the database. In the Code window, the Object list box (the upper-left list box) indicates the
current control, and the Procedure list box (the upper-right list box) indicates the event
name for the event procedure you are viewing.

All event procedures are Sub procedures. A horizontal line visually separates each procedure in the Code window. Each Sub procedure begins with a **Sub statement** and ends with
an **End Sub statement**. The Sub statement includes the **scope** of the procedure (private or
public), the name of the procedure (Form_Current, which means the Current event for the
form control), and an opening and closing parenthesis.

The remaining statements in the procedure shown in Figure 10-3 use only two controls
in the form: the State field from the Customer table; and StateName, which is the text-box
control that displays the full state name. Depending on the State field value, the statements
in the procedure do the following:

- If the State field value is MI, then set StateName to Michigan and set its
  font color to red.

- If the State field value is not MI but is IN, then set StateName to Indiana
  and set its font color to blue.

- If the State field value is neither MI nor IN but is OH, then set StateName
  to Ohio and set its font color to magenta.

Statements such as *[StateName]* = *"Michigan"* are assignment statements. An **assignment
statement** assigns the value of an expression—Michigan, in this case—to a field or property—
the StateName field, in this case.

Because a property is associated with a control, you use the general form of ControlName.PropertyName to specify a property for a control. An assignment statement such as *[StateName].ForeColor = RGB(255, 0, 0)*, for example, assigns a value to the StateName's ForeColor (font color) property. The expression in this assignment statement uses a built-in VBA function named RGB. The **RGB function** returns an RGB (red, green, blue) color value, indicating the relative intensity of red (first value), green (second value), and blue (third value) in a control's color. Figure 10-4 displays a list of some common colors and the red, green, and blue values for the RGB function that produces those colors. Each color component value must be in the range 0 through 255.

Figure 10-4	RGB FUNCTION VALUES FOR SOME COMMON COLORS		
COLOR	**RED VALUE**	**GREEN VALUE**	**BLUE VALUE**
Black	0	0	0
Blue	0	0	255
Cyan	0	255	255
Green	0	255	0
Magenta	255	0	255
Red	255	0	0
White	255	255	255
Yellow	255	255	0

Modifying an Event Procedure

Because Leonard wants you to change the magenta color for Ohio to black, you'll modify the last set of RGB function values in the event procedure. Then you'll close the Visual Basic window, and save and test your modification.

To modify, save, and test the event procedure:

1. Select **255, 0, 255** in the last RGB function, and then type **0,** (be sure you type the comma after the zero). A banner opens below the function and displays syntax information for the RGB function. See Figure 10-5.

Figure 10-5	MODIFYING A BUILT-IN VBA FUNCTION

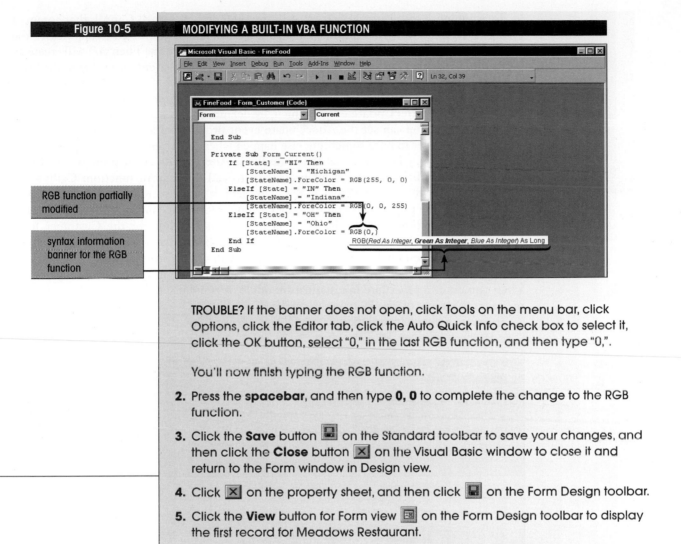

RGB function partially modified

syntax information banner for the RGB function

TROUBLE? If the banner does not open, click Tools on the menu bar, click Options, click the Editor tab, click the Auto Quick Info check box to select it, click the OK button, select "0," in the last RGB function, and then type "0,".

You'll now finish typing the RGB function.

2. Press the **spacebar**, and then type **0, 0** to complete the change to the RGB function.

3. Click the **Save** button 🔲 on the Standard toolbar to save your changes, and then click the **Close** button ✖ on the Visual Basic window to close it and return to the Form window in Design view.

4. Click ✖ on the property sheet, and then click 🔲 on the Form Design toolbar.

5. Click the **View** button for Form view 🔳 on the Form Design toolbar to display the first record for Meadows Restaurant.

6. Select the record number of **1** between the navigation buttons, type **33**, and then press the **Enter** key. The Customer form displays record 33 for Cherry Creek Inn. The state name of Ohio displays in black to the right of the State field value of OH. Your modification to the event procedure was completed successfully.

7. Click ✖ on the Form window to close the Customer form and return to the Database window.

You've completed your modification to the event procedure. Next, you'll create the CapAll function.

Creating Functions in a Standard Module

Leonard wants you to create a VBA procedure for the Customer form that will automatically convert the values entered in the State field to uppercase. That is, if a user enters "mi" for the state, the procedure should automatically convert it to "MI." Leonard feels that this will make data entry easier and reduce the number of data-entry errors. Users might not always be consistent about capitalizing entries in the State field, and using this procedure to capitalize entries will ensure consistency.

To accomplish this, you will first create a simple function, named CapAll, that accepts a **string** (text) input value and returns that string with all letters converted to uppercase. You create the function by typing the statements in the Module window. Then you will create an event procedure that calls the CapAll function whenever the user enters a value in the State field using the Customer form.

Whenever a user enters or changes a field value in a control on a form, Access automatically triggers the **AfterUpdate event**, which, by default, simply accepts the new or changed entry. However, you can set the AfterUpdate event property of a field to a specific event procedure, in order to have something else happen when a user enters or changes the field value. In this case, you need to set the State field's AfterUpdate event property to [Event Procedure], and then code an event procedure to call the CapAll function. Calling the CapAll function will cause the entry in the State field to be converted to uppercase letters.

You will use the CapAll function with the Customer form, so you could add it to the class module for that form. Adding the function to the class module for the Customer form would make it a private function; that is, it could not be used in other forms or database objects. Because you might use the CapAll function in other forms in the FineFood database, you'll place it in a new standard module named FineFood Procedures. Generally, when you enter a procedure in a standard module, it is public, and you can use it in event procedures for any other object in the database.

To create a new standard module, you'll begin by opening the Module window.

REFERENCE WINDOW	RW

Creating a New Standard Module
- In the Database window, click Modules in the Objects bar to display the Modules list.
- Click the New button. A new Code window, in which you create a new module, opens in the Visual Basic window.

To create a new standard module:

1. Click **Modules** in the Objects bar, and then click the **New** button. A new Code window opens in the Visual Basic window on top of the Code window for the Customer form's class module. See Figure 10-6.

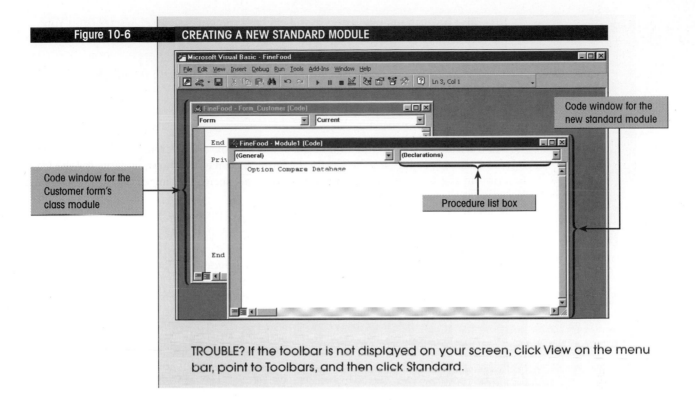

Figure 10-6   **CREATING A NEW STANDARD MODULE**

Labels in figure:

Code window for the new standard module

Code window for the Customer form's class module

Procedure list box

TROUBLE? If the toolbar is not displayed on your screen, click View on the menu bar, point to Toolbars, and then click Standard.

In the Code window for the new standard module, the Procedure list box displays the Declarations section as the current procedure in the module. Access automatically includes the Option Compare statement in the Declarations section of a new module. The **Option Compare statement** designates the technique Access uses to compare and sort text data. The default method, Database, as shown in Figure 10-6, means that Access compares and sorts letters in normal alphabetical order, using the language settings specified for Access running on your computer.

The CapAll function is a simple function that does not require additional statements in the Declarations section.

Creating a Function

Each function begins with a **Function statement** and ends with an **End Function statement**. Access visually separates each procedure in the Code window with a horizontal line. You can view a procedure's statements by selecting the procedure name from the Procedure list box.

The CapAll function begins with the statement "Function CapAll (FValue)." CapAll is the function name, and FValue is used as a placeholder for the input value in the function definition. When the user enters a value for the State field in the Customer form, that value will be passed to the CapAll function and substituted for FValue in the function definition. A placeholder like FValue is called a **parameter**. The value passed to the function and used in place of the parameter when the function is executed is called an **argument** (similar to an action in a macro). In other words, the value passed to the function is the argument, which is assigned to the parameter named FValue.

All VBA function names, Sub procedure names, argument names, and other names you create must conform to the following rules:

- They must begin with a letter.
- They cannot exceed 255 characters.

- They can include letters, numbers, and the underscore character (_). You cannot use a space, period (.), exclamation mark (!), or the characters @, &, $, or #.

- They cannot contain keywords, such as Function, Sub, If, and Option, that VBA uses as part of its language.

- They must be unique; that is, you can't declare the same name twice within the same procedure.

You'll enter the CapAll function in the Code window and then test it. Then you'll attach it to an event procedure for the Customer form. As you enter the statements for the CapAll function in the Code window, remember that capitalization is important in all statements. You now can start entering the CapAll function.

To start a new function:

1. With the insertion point two lines below the Option Compare statement, type **Function CapAll (FValue)** and then press the **Enter** key. The editor displays a dividing line that visually separates the new function from the Declarations section. See Figure 10-7.

Figure 10-7	STARTING A NEW FUNCTION

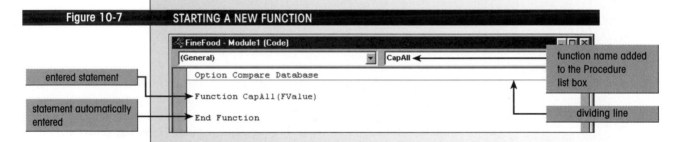

The function name CapAll now appears in the Procedure list box. The editor automatically added the End Function statement and moved the insertion point to the beginning of a blank line between the two statements. This is where you will enter the procedure statements. The editor displays the reserved words Function and End Function in blue. The function name and the parameter name appear in black.

The CapAll function will consist of a single executable assignment statement that you will place between the Function and End Function statements. You'll enter the following assignment statement: CapAll = UCase(FValue). The value of the expression, which is UCase(FValue), will be assigned to the function, which is CapAll.

The expression in the assignment statement uses a built-in Access function named UCase. The **UCase function** accepts a single string argument as input, converts the value of the argument to uppercase, and then returns the converted value. The assignment statement assigns the converted value to the CapAll function. Figure 10-8 illustrates this process.

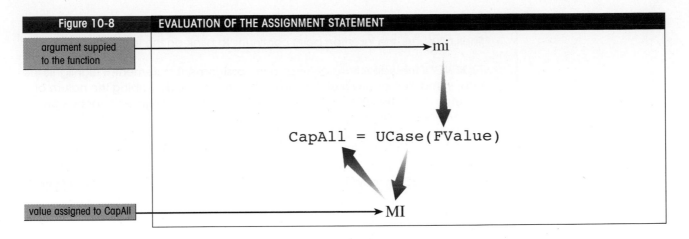

Figure 10-8   **EVALUATION OF THE ASSIGNMENT STATEMENT**

argument supplied to the function

value assigned to CapAll

Before entering the assignment statement, you will add a comment line to explain the procedure's purpose. You can include comments anywhere in a VBA procedure to describe what the procedure or a statement does, to make it easier for you and other programmers to identify the purpose of statements in your code. You begin a comment with the word Rem (for "Remark") or with a single quotation mark ('). VBA ignores anything following the word Rem or the single quotation mark on a single line. Because VBA ignores comments, you can include spaces, special characters, and mixed-case letters in your comments. Also, you will indent these lines; indenting statements is a common practice that makes code easier to read.

To add comments and statements to the function:

1. Press the **Tab** key to indent the line.

2. Type **'Capitalize all letters of a field value** and then press the **Enter** key. Notice that the editor displays the comment in green and indents the new line. After entering the comment line, you can enter the assignment statement, which is the executable statement in the function that performs the actual conversion of the argument to uppercase.

3. Type **CapAll = UCase(FValue)**. See Figure 10-9. The editor provides assistance as you enter the statement. After you type UCase and the opening parenthesis, the editor displays a banner with a reminder that UCase accepts a single string argument.

Figure 10-9   **CAPALL FUNCTION IN THE CODE WINDOW**

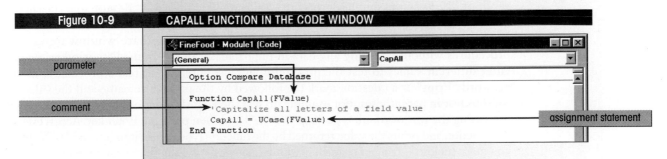

parameter

comment

assignment statement

The editor scans each statement for errors when you press the Enter key or change the focus to another statement. Because the function is complete and you want the editor to scan for errors, you can move the insertion point to another line.

4. Press the ↓ key to move the insertion point to the next line. Because Access finds no errors, the insertion point continues to blink on the last line.

TROUBLE? If the editor finds an error in the assignment statement, it highlights the error in red and opens a dialog box with a message describing the nature of the error. Click the OK button and then change the highlighted error by comparing your entries with those shown in Steps 2 and 3. Then repeat Step 4 to scan the statement for errors again.

You have finished entering the function, so you'll save it before continuing with your work.

Saving a Module

When you click the Save button in the Visual Basic window, the editor saves the module and its procedures. If you are entering a long procedure, it's a good idea to save your work periodically.

To save the module:

1. Click the **Save** button 🖫 on the Standard toolbar, type **FineFood Procedures** in the Module Name text box, and then press the **Enter** key. The editor saves the module and places the new module name in the title bar.

Before making the changes to the Customer form so that the CapAll function automatically acts on every entry in the State field, you can test the function using the Immediate window.

Testing a Procedure in the Immediate Window

When you finish entering a VBA statement, the editor checks the statement to make sure its syntax is correct. Although you may have entered all procedure statements with the correct syntax, the procedure may still contain logic errors. A **logic error** occurs when the procedure produces incorrect results. For example, the CapAll function would have a logic error if you typed mi and the function changed it to mI, Mi, or anything other than the correct result of MI. Even the simplest procedure can contain logic errors. Be sure to test each procedure thoroughly to ensure that it does exactly what you expect it to do in all situations.

When working in the Code window, you can use the **Immediate window** to test VBA procedures without changing any data in the database. In the Immediate window, you can enter different values to test the procedure you just entered. To test a procedure, use the keyword "Print" or a question mark (?), followed by the procedure name and the value you want to test in parentheses. For example, to test the CapAll function in the Immediate window using the test word mi, type *?CapAll ("mi")* and then press the Enter key. Access executes the function and prints the value returned by the function (you expect it to return MI). Note that you must enclose a string of characters within quotation marks in the test statement.

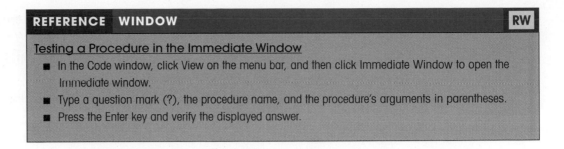

REFERENCE WINDOW   RW

Testing a Procedure in the Immediate Window

- In the Code window, click View on the menu bar, and then click Immediate Window to open the Immediate window.
- Type a question mark (?), the procedure name, and the procedure's arguments in parentheses.
- Press the Enter key and verify the displayed answer.

Now you can use the Immediate window to test the CapAll function.

To test the function in the Debug window:

1. Click **View** on the menu bar, and then click **Immediate Window**. The editor opens the Immediate window across the bottom of the screen and places the insertion point inside the window.

   The Immediate window allows you to run individual lines of VBA code for **debugging** (testing). You will use the Immediate window to test the CapAll function.

2. Type **?CapAll("mi")** and then press the **Enter** key. The editor executes the function and prints the function result, MI, on the next line. See Figure 10-10.

Figure 10-10   **CAPALL FUNCTION EXECUTED IN THE IMMEDIATE WINDOW**

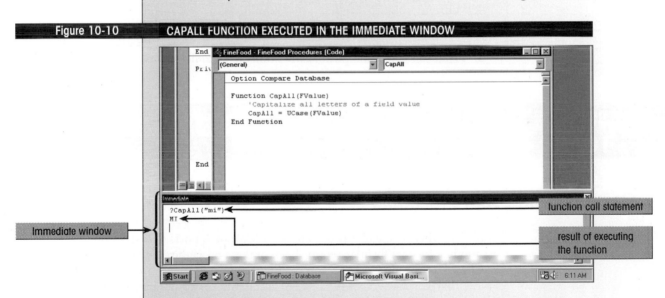

TROUBLE? If Access displays a dialog box with an error message, click the OK button in the dialog box and correct the error in the Immediate window. If the function does not produce the correct output (MI), correct the CapAll function statements in the Code window, and then repeat Steps 1 and 2.

To test the CapAll function further, you can enter several other test values, retyping the entire statement each time. Instead, you'll select the current test value, type another value, and then press the Enter key.

3. Select the characters **mi** in the first line of the Immediate window.

4. Type **oH** and then press the **Enter** key. The editor executes the function and prints the function result, OH, on the next line.

5. Repeat Steps 1 and 2 two more times, using **In** and then **MI** as the test values. The editor prints the correct values, IN and MI.

6. Click the **Close** button ☒ on the Immediate window to close it, and then click ☒ on the Visual Basic window to return to the Database window.

7. Click ☒ on the Access window to close the FineFood database and exit Access. You return to the Windows desktop.

Your initial test of the CapAll function is successful. In the next session, you'll modify the Customer form to call the CapAll function for the State field.

Session 10.1 QUICK CHECK

1. Why is Visual Basic for Applications called an event-driven, object-oriented language?

2. What is an event procedure?

3. What are the differences between a Function procedure and a Sub procedure?

4. What are the two different types of modules?

5. The _____ of a procedure is either private or public.

6. What can you accomplish in the Immediate window?

SESSION 10.2

In this session, you'll create, compile, and test an event procedure. You'll also add a second function to a standard module. You will write the function in VBA, compile it, and then call the function from an event procedure.

Creating an Event Procedure

Recall that when you add a procedure to a form or report, Access automatically creates a class module for that form or report. Each of these procedures is called an event procedure; Access runs a procedure when a specific event occurs.

Now that you have created the CapAll function as a public procedure in the standard module named FineFood Procedures, you can create an event procedure for the Customer form to call the CapAll function for the State field's AfterUpdate event. Whenever a user enters or changes a State field value, the **AfterUpdate event** occurs and Access runs your event procedure.

What exactly happens when Access calls a procedure? There is an interaction between the calling statement and the function statements, as represented by a series of steps. Figure 10-11 shows the process for the CapAll procedure.

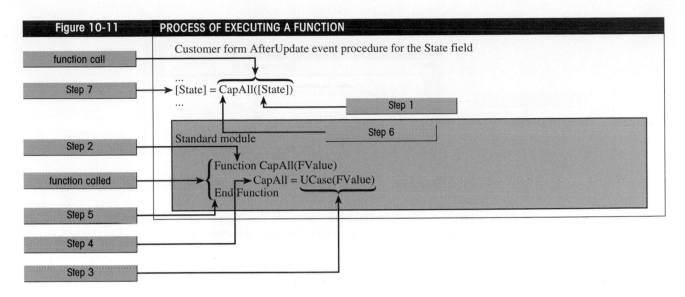

Figure 10-11 PROCESS OF EXECUTING A FUNCTION

The steps in Figure 10-11 are numbered in the order in which they occur as Access processes the statement and the function. Access goes through the following steps:

- Step 1. The call to the function CapAll passes the value of the argument [State]. This is the value of the State field that is entered by the user.
- Step 2. The function CapAll begins, and the parameter FValue receives the value of [State].
- Step 3. FValue is changed to uppercase.
- Step 4. The value of CapAll is set equal to the result of Step 3.
- Step 5. The function CapAll ends.
- Step 6. The value of CapAll is returned to the point of the call to the function.
- Step 7. The value of [State] is set equal to the returned value of CapAll.

Although it looks complicated, the general function process is simple—the statement contains a function call. When the statement is executed, Access performs the function call, executes the function, returns a single value back to the original statement, and completes that statement's execution. Study the steps in Figure 10-11 and trace their execution until you understand the complete process.

Designing an Event Procedure

Whenever a user enters a new value or modifies an existing value in the State field using the Customer form, Leonard wants Access to execute the CapAll function to ensure that all State field values appear in uppercase. After a user changes a State field value, the AfterUpdate event automatically occurs. You can set the AfterUpdate event property to run a macro, call a built-in Access function, or execute an event procedure. Because you want to call your user-defined function from within the event procedure, instead of calling the default AfterUpdate event, you will set the AfterUpdate event property to [Event Procedure].

All event procedures are Sub procedures. Access automatically adds the Sub and End Sub statements to an event procedure. All you need to do is place the statements between the Sub and End Sub statements. Figure 10-12 shows the completed event procedure. The following text describes the parts of the procedure.

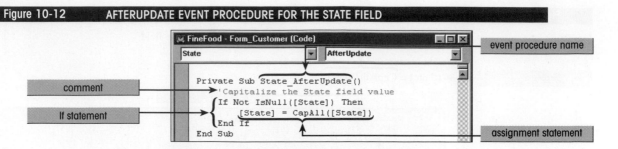

Figure 10-12   AFTERUPDATE EVENT PROCEDURE FOR THE STATE FIELD

Access names each event procedure in a standard way: the name of the control, an underscore (_), and the event name. No parameters are passed to an event procedure, so Access places nothing in the parentheses following the name of the Sub procedure. If the name of the control contains spaces, Access substitutes underscores for the spaces in the event procedure name.

A user might delete an existing State field value so that it contains no value, or becomes **null**. In this case, calling the function accomplishes nothing. The procedure is designed to call the CapAll function only when a user changes the State field to a value that is not null. The If statement screens out the null values. In its simplest form, an **If statement** executes one of two groups of statements according to a condition, as in common English usage. For example, consider the English statements, "If I work the night shift, then I'll earn extra spending money. Otherwise, I'll go to the movies, and I'll dip into my savings." In these sentences, the two groups of statements come before and after the "otherwise,"depending on the condition, "if I work the night shift." The first group of statements consists of the clause "I'll earn extra spending money." This is called the **true-statement group** because it's what happens if the condition ("I work the night shift") is true. The second group of statements contains "I'll go to the movies, and I'll dip into my savings." This is called the **false-statement group** because it is what happens if the condition is false. VBA uses the keyword If to precede the condition. The keyword Then precedes the true-statement group, and the keyword Else precedes the false-statement group. The general syntax, or valid form, of a VBA If statement is:

> If condition Then
>   true-statement group
> [Else
>   false-statement group]
> End If

Access executes the true-statement group when the condition is true and the false-statement group when the condition is false. Bracketed portions of a statement's syntax are optional parts of the statement. Therefore, you must omit the Else and its related false-statement group when you want Access to execute a group of statements only when the condition is true.

In Figure 10-12, the If statement uses the VBA **IsNull function**, which returns True when the State field value is null, and False when it is not null. The Not is the same logical operator you've used before to negate an expression. So, Access executes the statement [State] = CapAll([State]) only when the State field value is not null.

You are ready to make your changes to the Customer form.

Adding an Event Procedure

To add an event procedure to the State field's AfterUpdate event property, you need to open the Customer form in Design view.

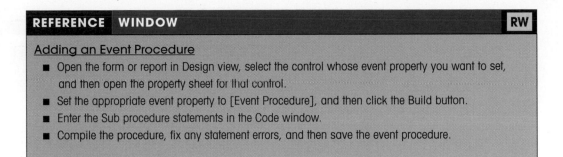

REFERENCE WINDOW   RW

Adding an Event Procedure

- Open the form or report in Design view, select the control whose event property you want to set, and then open the property sheet for that control.
- Set the appropriate event property to [Event Procedure], and then click the Build button.
- Enter the Sub procedure statements in the Code window.
- Compile the procedure, fix any statement errors, and then save the event procedure.

You can now add the event procedure to the Customer form.

To add the event procedure:

1. Place your Data Disk in the appropriate disk drive, start Access, and then open the **FineFood** database located in the Tutorial folder on your Data Disk.

2. Click **Forms** in the Objects bar of the Database window, right-click **Customer**, and then click **Design View** to open the Customer form in Design view.

3. Right-click the field-value text box for the **State** field to display the shortcut menu, and then click **Properties** to open the property sheet.

4. If necessary, click the **Event** tab. Access shows only the event properties in the property sheet. You need to set the AfterUpdate property.

5. Click the right side of the **After Update** text box, click **(Event Procedure)**, and then click the **Build** button ![...] to the right of the After Update text box. The Code window opens in the Visual Basic window. See Figure 10-13.

Figure 10-13	INITIAL EVENT PROCEDURE IN THE CODE WINDOW

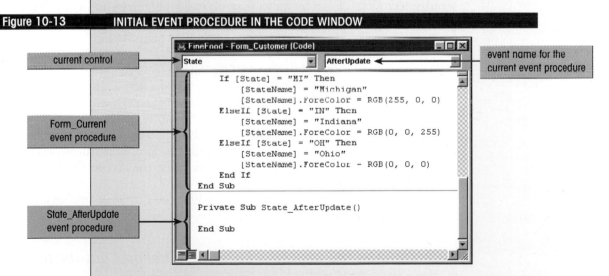

The new event procedure for the State field's AfterUpdate event property contains the Private Sub and End Sub statements, and it follows the form's Current event procedure. You can now enter the statements to call the CapAll function.

6. Enter the statements shown in Figure 10-14. Press the **Enter** key at the end of each line and use the Tab key to indent the lines, as shown in the figure, and the Backspace key to move one tab stop to the left. Compare your screen with Figure 10-14, and make any necessary corrections.

Figure 10-14   COMPLETED EVENT PROCEDURE

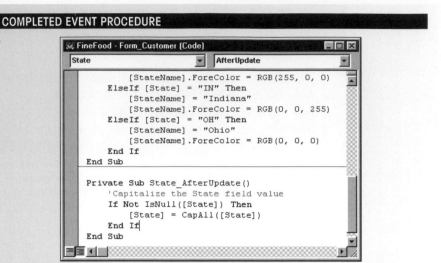

TROUBLE? If your event procedure contains errors, correct them by highlighting the error and typing the correction. Use the Backspace or Delete keys to delete characters.

Before saving the event procedure, you'll compile it.

Compiling Modules

The VBA programming language is not your native language, nor is it the computer's native language. Although you can learn VBA and become fluent in it, computers cannot understand or learn VBA. For a computer to understand the statements in your VBA modules, the statements must be translated to a form that the computer can run. The process of translating modules from VBA to a translated form is called **compilation**; you say that you **compile** the module when you translate it.

When you run a procedure for the first time, Access compiles it for you automatically and opens a dialog box only when it finds syntax errors in the procedure. If it finds an error, Access does not translate the procedure statements. If no errors are detected, Access translates the procedure and does not display a confirmation. You also can compile a procedure at any point, as you enter it, by clicking the Compile command on the Debug menu. In response, Access compiles the procedure and all other procedures in all modules in the database. It's best to compile modules after you've made changes to them, to make sure they don't contain syntax errors.

You'll now compile the procedures in the FineFood database and save the class module for the Customer form.

To compile the procedures in the FineFood database and save the class module:

1. Click **Debug** on the menu bar, and then click **Compile FineFood**. Access compiles all the modules in the FineFood database. Because you have no syntax errors, Access translates the VBA statements and returns control to the Visual Basic window.

> **TROUBLE?** If Access identifies any errors in your code, correct the errors and repeat Step 1.
>
> **2.** Click the **Save** button 🔲 on the Standard toolbar.
>
> **3.** Click the **Close** button ✖ on the Visual Basic window to close it, and then click ✖ on the property sheet to close it.
>
> **4.** Click ✖ on the Form window to return to the Database window.

You have created the function and the event procedure and have set the event property. Next, you'll test the event procedure to make sure it works correctly.

Testing an Event Procedure

You need to display the Customer form in Form view and test the State field's event procedure by entering a few different test State field values in the first record of the form. Moving the focus to another control on the form or to another record triggers the AfterUpdate event for the State field and executes your attached event procedure. Because the CapAll function is attached only to the Customer form, the automatic capitalization of State field values is not in effect when you enter them in the Customer table or any other object in the FineFood database.

> ### To test the event procedure:
>
> **1.** Make sure Customer is selected in the Forms list in the Database window, and then click the **Open** button.
>
> **2.** Select the **State** field value (MI), type **mi** in the State text box, and then press the **Enter** key. Access executes the AfterUpdate event procedure for the State field and changes the State field value to "MI." See Figure 10-15.

| Figure 10-15 | CUSTOMER FORM AFTER EXECUTING THE EVENT PROCEDURE |

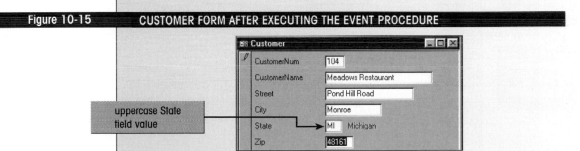

uppercase State field value

> **3.** Repeat Step 2 three more times, entering **Mi**, then **ml**, and finally **MI** in the State field box. Access displays the correct value "MI" each time.
>
> **4.** Click the **Close** button ✖ on the Form window to return to the Database window.

Leonard wants you to create a more complicated function for the CustomerName field in the Customer form.

Adding a Second Function to a Standard Module

Leonard wants to make it easier for users to enter a customer's name when using the Customer form, so he asks you to create a second function that will automatically correct the case of letters entered in the CustomerName field. This function, named CapAllFirst, will capitalize the first letter of each word in the field and change all other letters to lowercase. An event procedure attached to the AfterUpdate event for the CustomerName field will use this function. When a user enters or edits a customer name in the Customer form, the event procedure will use the CapAllFirst function to correct any capitalization errors in the CustomerName field value. For example, if the user enters "meadOWs reStaurant" as the CustomerName field value, the event procedure will use the CapAllFirst function to correct the field value to "Meadows Restaurant."

The Design of the CapAllFirst Function

Figure 10-16 shows the CapAllFirst function that you will create. You've already seen several of the statements in this function in your work with the CapAll function. Except for the function name, the Function and End Function statements are the same. The next two lines of the function are comments; these comments are specific to the CapAllFirst function. You'll learn about each new statement as you enter it to code this procedure.

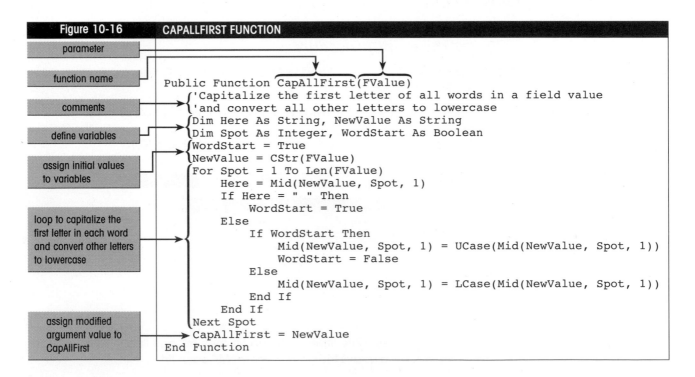

Figure 10-16 — CAPALLFIRST FUNCTION

- parameter
- function name
- comments
- define variables
- assign initial values to variables
- loop to capitalize the first letter in each word and convert other letters to lowercase
- assign modified argument value to CapAllFirst

```
Public Function CapAllFirst(FValue)
    'Capitalize the first letter of all words in a field value
    'and convert all other letters to lowercase
    Dim Here As String, NewValue As String
    Dim Spot As Integer, WordStart As Boolean
    WordStart = True
    NewValue = CStr(FValue)
    For Spot = 1 To Len(FValue)
        Here = Mid(NewValue, Spot, 1)
        If Here = " " Then
            WordStart = True
        Else
            If WordStart Then
                Mid(NewValue, Spot, 1) = UCase(Mid(NewValue, Spot, 1))
                WordStart = False
            Else
                Mid(NewValue, Spot, 1) = LCase(Mid(NewValue, Spot, 1))
            End If
        End If
    Next Spot
    CapAllFirst = NewValue
End Function
```

The CapAllFirst function has a single parameter, named FValue. When the AfterUpdate event procedure for the CustomerName field calls the CapAllFirst function, the CustomerName field value entered by the user is passed to the function, and this value is used in place of FValue when CapAllFirst is executed. So, the CustomerName field value is the argument passed to the function.

The CapAllFirst function capitalizes the first letter in each word of the parameter and converts all other letters to lowercase. You will learn about the function in detail as you enter the function statements in the following steps. Basically, the function works by examining the parameter, character by character. Whenever a space is encountered, the function "knows" that the next letter encountered should be capitalized, because a space immediately precedes the first letter of a word. When the next letter is found, it is capitalized. After the entire parameter has been examined, the modified parameter is returned to the event procedure that called the function.

Creating a Second Function

You'll add the CapAllFirst function to the FineFood Procedures module, which is a standard module, so that the CapAllFirst function will be available for use with any object in the FineFood database. Once you have added the function to the FineFood Procedures module, you will be able to attach it to an event procedure for the AfterUpdate event of the CustomerName field in the Customer form.

REFERENCE WINDOW   `RW`

Adding a New Procedure to a Standard Module
- In the Database window, click Modules in the Objects bar, right-click the module name, and then click Design View.
- In the Code window, click the list arrow for the Insert Module button on the Standard toolbar, and then click Procedure.
- Type the new procedure name, click the Sub or Function option button, and then click the OK button.
- Enter the new procedure, click Debug on the menu bar, and then click Compile <database name>.
- Click the Save button on the Standard toolbar.

As you enter the statements in the following steps, refer to Figure 10-16 to verify that you are entering the statements correctly. You'll begin by adding the descriptive comments to the function.

To begin creating the CapAllFirst function and add the comments:

1. Click **Modules** in the Objects bar, right-click **FineFood Procedures**, click **Design View**, and then click the **Maximize** button ▣ on the Code window for the FineFood Procedures module.

2. Click the list arrow for the **Insert Module** button ▨ on the Standard toolbar, and then click **Procedure** to open the Add Procedure dialog box.

   This dialog box allows you to name the new procedure and define its type and scope. The new procedure can be a Sub procedure, a function, or a new property definition for an existing object. The scope of the new procedure can be either public or private. The new procedure you will create is a function, and you want it to be public so that you can use it in an event procedure for the Customer form.

3. Type **CapAllFirst** in the Name text box, make sure the Function and Public option buttons are selected, and then click the **OK** button. The editor starts a new procedure named CapAllFirst and displays the Function and End Function statements in the Code window. See Figure 10-17.

Figure 10-17   CAPALLFIRST FUNCTION STARTED IN THE CODE WINDOW

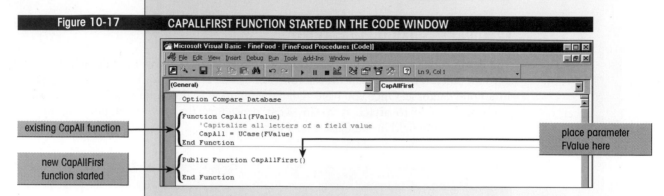

existing CapAll function

new CapAllFirst function started

place parameter FValue here

The CapAllFirst function will accept one argument passed to the parameter FValue. When the function is called by an event procedure, FValue will hold the string value that CapAllFirst will process. You must place the parameter inside the parentheses after the function name.

4. Click between the parentheses in the function statement, type **FValue**, press the ↓ key, and then press the **Tab** key.

5. Type **'Capitalize the first letter of all words in a field value** and then press the **Enter** key to enter the first comment.

6. Type **'and convert all other letters to lowercase** and then press the **Enter** key to enter the second comment.

The next two lines of the CapAllFirst function declare the variables that the function uses. A **variable** is a named location in computer memory that can contain a value. If you use a variable in a module, you must explicitly declare it in the Declarations section or in the function definition where the variable is used. The **Dim statement** is used to declare variables in a procedure. The variables in the CapAllFirst function are Here, NewValue, Spot, and WordStart. (You'll see what these variables do in a moment.) Each variable is assigned an associated data type. Figure 10-18 shows the primary data types for Visual Basic variables.

FIGURE 10-18 | **STANDARD VBA DATA TYPES**

DATA TYPE	STORES
Boolean	True/False values
Byte	Integer values from 0 to 255
Currency	Currency values from -922,337,203,685,477.5808 to 922,337,203,685,477.5807
Date	Date and time values from 1 January 100 to 31 December 9999
Decimal	Noninteger values with 0 to 28 decimal places
Double	Noninteger values from $-1.79769313486231*10^{308}$ to $-4.94065645841247*10^{-324}$ for negative values, from $4.94065645841247*10^{-324}$ to $1.79769313486232*10^{308}$ for positive values, and 0
Integer	Integer values from -32,768 to 32,767
Long	Integer values from -2,147,483,648 to 2,147,483,647
Object	Any object reference
Single	Noninteger values from $-3.402823*10^{38}$ to $-1.401298*10^{-45}$ for negative values, from $1.401298*10^{-45}$ to $3.402823*10^{38}$ for positive values, and 0
String	Text values up to 2 billion characters in length
Variant	Any numeric or string data type

You specify the data type for a variable by following the variable name with the word "As" and the data type. In the CapAllFirst function, for example, the two variables Here and NewValue are string variables. The **string type** is the equivalent of the Access text data type. Spot is an integer variable, and WordStart is a Boolean variable. The **Boolean type** is the equivalent of the yes/no type used to define the data type of a table record field. The Boolean type can take one of two values: True or False. If a module does not include an Option Explicit statement in the Declarations section and you create a variable without specifying a data type, VBA assigns the variant data type to the variable. The variant data type is the default data type; a variant variable can store any value.

The variable Here is a string variable that will temporarily hold a copy of the character that is being examined. The variable NewValue is a string that holds a copy of the argument. The first character in each word of NewValue is converted to uppercase as the function executes. Spot is an integer that is used as a counter to keep track of which character is being examined. Spot counts from 1 to the number of characters in the argument. Finally, WordStart is a Boolean variable that records whether to capitalize the next letter. When WordStart is True, the next letter encountered in the argument should be capitalized. When WordStart is False, the next letter is not capitalized.

You'll now enter the Dim statements to declare the variables.

To enter the Dim statements:

1. With the insertion point positioned on the line below the second comment line and indented one tab stop, type **Dim Here As Str**. When you press the space-bar after typing the word "As," a list of available data types opens. As you type each letter in the data type, the entries in the list change to those entries whose starting letters match those you've typed. See Figure 10-19.

Figure 10-19	ENTERING THE FIRST DIM STATEMENT

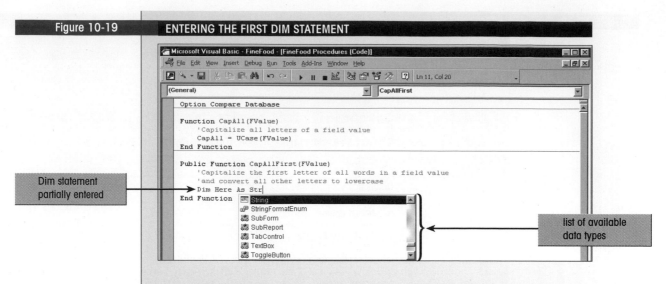

TROUBLE? If the list box does not open, click Tools on the menu bar, click Options, click the Editor tab, click the Auto List Members check box to select it, and then click the OK button.

The **Complete Word IntelliSense feature** helps you enter or complete a VBA keyword. When a keyword list opens, you can type the complete entry, or you can scroll the list and select an entry. You also can type the first one or more letters of the keyword and, when the desired entry is highlighted in the list, press the Tab key to select it as your entry.

You'll now finish typing the first Dim statement.

2. Press the **Tab** key, type **, NewValue As Str** and then press the **Tab** key.

3. Press the **Enter** key to start a new indented line, type **Dim Spot As Integer, WordStart As Boolean** and then press the **Enter** key.

The next two lines of the CapAllFirst function assign WordStart and NewValue their initial values. WordStart is initialized to True because the next letter encountered (the first letter in the parameter) should be capitalized. The next line uses the **CStr function** to convert the value of the parameter FValue, which has the variant data type, to a string and assigns this converted value to the variable NewValue. Because CapAllFirst is a public function, a value of any type could be passed to FValue when the function is called. The CStr function ensures that the value in FValue is converted to a string. This must happen because the value in FValue is assigned to NewValue, which must contain a string.

You'll now enter the initial assignment statements.

To enter the initial assignment statements:

1. Type **WordStart = True** and then press the **Enter** key.

2. Type **NewValue = CStr(FValue)** and then press the **Enter** key.

The main body of the CapAllFirst function consists of a group of statements that are executed repeatedly to examine and process each character in NewValue (the CustomerName value entered by the user). A group of statements executed repeatedly is called a **loop**. The statement For Spot = 1 To Len(FValue) marks the beginning of the loop, and the statement Next Spot marks the end of the loop. The group of statements between the For and Next statements is called the **loop body**.

The For statement establishes how many times to repeat the loop body. In this case, the For statement uses the variable Spot as a counter to keep track of how many times to repeat the loop body. The For Spot = 1 To Len(FValue) statement sets the starting value of Spot, which is an integer variable, to 1 and the ending value of Spot to Len(FValue). The **Len function** returns the number of characters in a string. For example, if FValue is the string "Restaurant Name," Len(FValue) returns 15 as the number of characters, including spaces. In this case, Access executes the statements in the loop 15 times.

Then Access executes the loop body, ending with the statement before the Next Spot statement. After reaching the Next Spot statement, Access adds 1 to Spot, goes back to the For statement, and compares the value of Spot to Len(FValue). If Spot is less than or equal to Len(FValue), then there are still more characters to check to determine if any should be capitalized, so Access executes the loop statements again, reaches the Next Spot statement, and repeats the cycle. When Spot becomes greater than Len(FValue), then there are no more characters to check in the field entry, so Access terminates the loop and executes the statement following the Next Spot statement.

The loop body is executed once for each value of Spot, that is, once for each character in NewValue. The statement Here = Mid(NewValue, Spot, 1) uses the built-in **Mid function** to copy a single character, as specified by the argument "1" in the statement, from NewValue and store it in Here. The character selected is indicated by the value of Spot. So, if the current value of Spot is 3, then the third character in NewValue is copied into Here. For example, if the user enters Pesto Place in the CustomerName field of the Customer form, and Spot equals 3, the value of "s" is assigned to the variable Here so that the function can determine if "s" needs to be capitalized.

The next statement is an If statement that decides which operations to perform, depending on the value of Here. If Here is a space, then the value of WordStart is set to True (indicating that the next letter encountered should be capitalized), and the Else part of the If statement is skipped. If Here is not a space, then the current character is a letter that might need to be capitalized. A second If statement checks to see if WordStart is True. If WordStart is True, then the next statement uses the UCase function to convert Here to uppercase and assigns it to the appropriate position in NewValue. If WordStart is not True, then the next statement uses the LCase function to convert Here to lowercase and assigns it to the appropriate position in NewValue. The UCase and LCase functions have no effect on characters that are not letters.

When the loop body has finished processing the current character, the Next Spot statement increments Spot and returns control to the For Spot = 1 to Len(NewValue) statement. If Spot is less than or equal to the length of NewValue, the loop body is executed again, processing the next character in NewValue.

When the loop has processed the last character in NewValue, the loop ends and control is passed to the statement following the Next Spot statement. NewValue now has the first letter of each word capitalized and all other letters converted to lowercase.

Next, you'll enter the statements for the loop in the Module window.

To enter the loop statements in the CapAllFirst function:

1. Type **For Spot = 1 To Len(FValue)** and then press the **Enter** key.

2. Enter the remaining loop statements, ending with the statement Next Spot, as shown in Figure 10-20. Be sure to use the Tab key to indent lines as necessary. Recall that pressing the Backspace key moves the insertion point one tab stop to the left. When you are finished, your screen should look like Figure 10-20.

Figure 10-20   AFTER ENTERING THE LOOP STATEMENTS IN THE CAPALLFIRST FUNCTION

loop statements →

```
Function CapAll(FValue)
    'Capitalize all letters of a field value
    CapAll = UCase(FValue)
End Function

Public Function CapAllFirst(FValue)
    'Capitalize the first letter of all words in a field value
    'and convert all other letters to lowercase
    Dim Here As String, NewValue As String
    Dim Spot As Integer, WordStart As Boolean
    WordStart = True
    NewValue = CStr(FValue)
    For Spot = 1 To Len(FValue)
        Here = Mid(NewValue, Spot, 1)
        If Here = " " Then
            WordStart = True
        Else
            If WordStart Then
                Mid(NewValue, Spot, 1) = UCase(Mid(NewValue, Spot, 1))
                WordStart = False
            Else
                Mid(NewValue, Spot, 1) = LCase(Mid(NewValue, Spot, 1))
            End If
        End If
    Next Spot

End Function
```

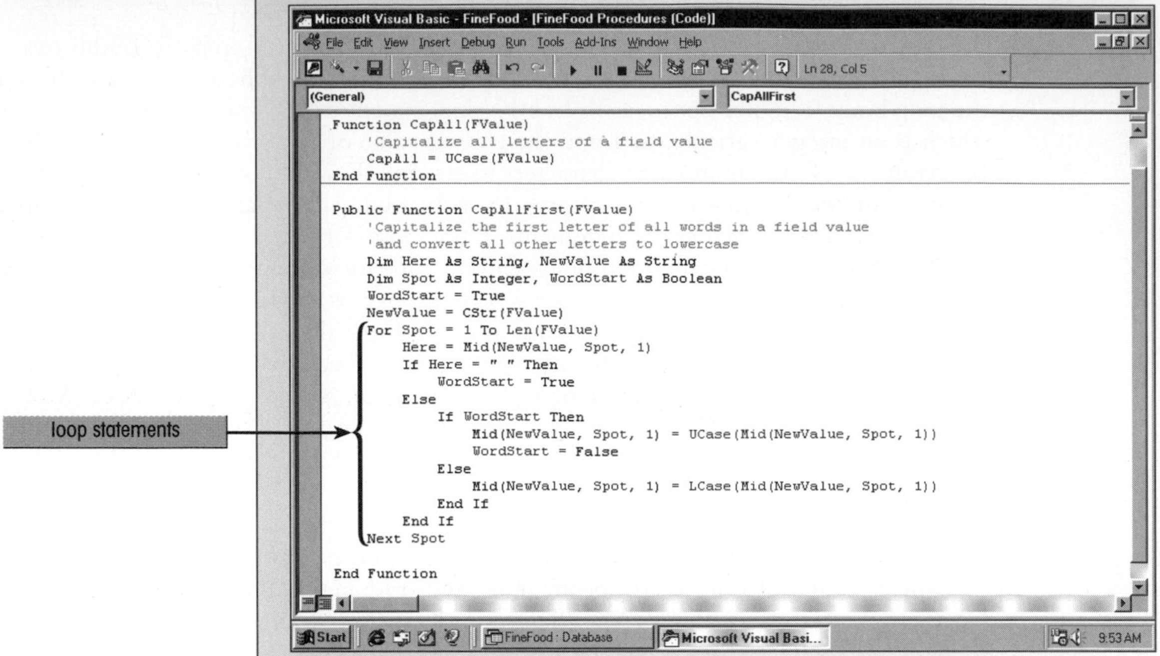

TROUBLE? If your statements contain errors, position the insertion point in the Code window to the right of the error. Use the Backspace key to delete characters. Reenter any incorrect statements until your screen looks like Figure 10-20.

When the loop ends, NewValue contains words with capitalized first letters and lowercase for the remaining letters. The final step in the CapAllFirst function assigns the NewValue to CapAllFirst, to be returned to the event procedure that called the CapAllFirst function. In the case of the Customer form, the CustomerName field's event procedure will call the CapAllFirst function, which will return the customer name with the correct capitalization. You'll now enter this final statement.

To enter the final function statement:

1. Type **CapAllFirst = NewValue** and then press the ↓ key. See Figure 10-21.

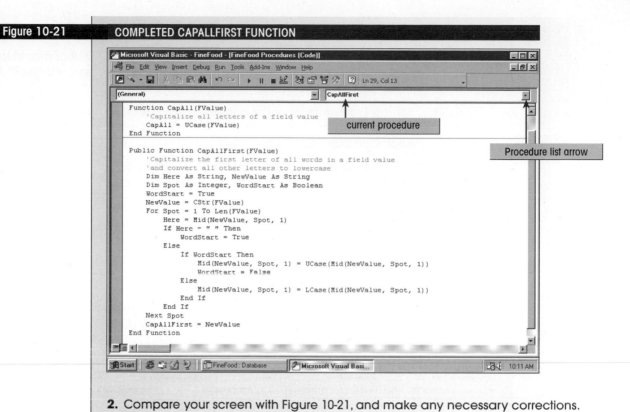

Figure 10-21   COMPLETED CAPALLFIRST FUNCTION

2. Compare your screen with Figure 10-21, and make any necessary corrections.

You'll now compile the modules in the FineFood database and save the FineFood Procedures module.

To compile the procedures in the FineFood database and save the FineFood Procedures module:

1. Click **Debug** on the menu bar, and then click **Compile FineFood**. Access compiles all the modules in the FineFood database.

TROUBLE? If Access finds an error, it highlights the error and opens a dialog box with a message describing the nature of the error. Click the OK button and change the statement contained in the highlighted area by comparing each character you entered to what should be entered. Then repeat Step 1.

2. Click the **Save** button 🖫 on the Standard toolbar to save the FineFood Procedures module.

The FineFood Procedures module now contains the Declarations, the CapAll function, and the CapAllFirst function. You can view each procedure in a module by clicking the Procedure list arrow and selecting a procedure.

To view the procedures in the FineFood Procedures module:

1. Click the **Procedure** list arrow, and then click **CapAll**. The editor moves the insertion point to the first statement after the Function statement in the CapAll function and displays CapAll in the Procedure text box.

2. Click the **Procedure** list arrow, and then click **(Declarations)**. The editor displays the module's Declarations section and moves the insertion point to the Option Compare statement.

3. Click the **Procedure** list arrow, and then click **CapAllFirst** to display the CapAllFirst function and move the insertion point to its first statement.

4. Click the **Close** button ☒ on the Visual Basic window to return to the restored Database window.

Adding a Second Event Procedure

The function that you just created ensures that each word in the customer name begins with a capital letter and that all other letters are lowercase. Next, you'll open the Customer form in Design view and add an event procedure for the CustomerName field's AfterUpdate event property. Recall that the AfterUpdate property determines the actions Access will take after the user has entered or edited the specified field value. Access will execute the event procedure whenever a value in the CustomerName field is entered or updated.

To add the event procedure for the CustomerName field in the Customer form:

1. Click **Forms** in the Objects bar of the Database window, right-click **Customer**, and then click **Design View** to open the form in Design view.

2. Right-click the **CustomerName** field-value text box to display the shortcut menu, and then click **Properties** to open the property sheet.

3. If necessary, click the **Event** tab in the property sheet.

4. Click the right side of the **After Update** text box, click **[Event Procedure]**, and then click the **Build** button ⌐ to the right of the After Update text box. The Code window, which is maximized and contains new Private Sub and End Sub statements, opens in the Visual Basic window. Notice that the Code window also contains the event procedure for the form's Current property, which you modified earlier. The Code window also displays the procedures for other events for the Customer form. These event procedures were automatically created by Access when you created the form.

5. Press the **Tab** key, and then type the Sub procedure statements exactly as shown in Figure 10-22.

Figure 10-22	EVENT PROCEDURE FOR THE CUSTOMERNAME FIELD

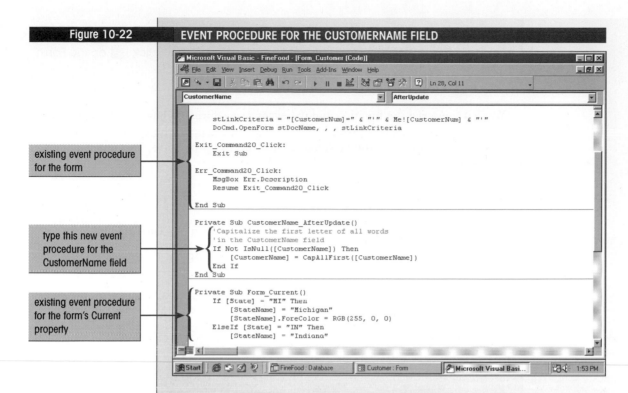

existing event procedure for the form

type this new event procedure for the CustomerName field

existing event procedure for the form's Current property

The CustomerName field AfterUpdate event procedure works the same as the State field AfterUpdate event procedure. If the CustomerName field is not null (empty), then the CustomerName field value is passed to the CapAllFirst function. The CapAllFirst function capitalizes the first letter of each word in the CustomerName field value, converts all other letters to lowercase, and then returns the value to the event procedure. The event procedure assignment statement then assigns the converted value to the CustomerName field.

6. Click the **Save** button 🖫 on the Standard toolbar. The Save dialog box opens. See Figure 10-23.

Figure 10-23	SAVE DIALOG BOX WITH THE LIST OF MODULES

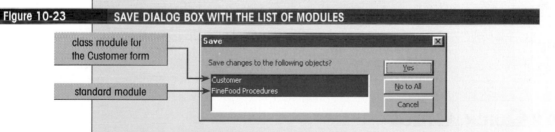

class module for the Customer form

standard module

TROUBLE? If the Save dialog box doesn't open, skip to Step 8.

The Save dialog box displays a list of all the modules in the FineFood database. You can save as many of the listed modules as you want. Because you changed only the Customer class module, you save only that module.

7. Click **FineFood Procedures** to deselect it, and then click the **Yes** button to save your changes to the Customer class module and close the dialog box.

8. Click **Debug** on the menu bar, and then click **Compile FineFood**. Access compiles all the modules in the FineFood database.

9. Click the **Close** button ⊠ on the Visual Basic window to return to the Form window, click ⊠ on the property sheet to close it, and then click ⊠ on the Form window to return to the Database window.

You have entered the function and the event procedure and have set the event property. You can now test the event procedure. To do so, you'll open the Customer form in Form view and test the CustomerName field's event procedure by entering different CustomerName field values.

To test the new event procedure:

1. Right-click **Customer**, and then click **Open** to open the form in Form view.

2. Click the **Last Record** navigation button ▶I to display the record for the Pesto Place restaurant.

3. Select the value in the CustomerName text box, type **test restaurant name**, and then press the **Enter** key. Access executes the AfterUpdate event procedure for the CustomerName field and correctly changes the CustomerName field value to "Test Restaurant Name."

4. Press the ↑ key to highlight the CustomerName field value.

5. Repeat Steps 3 and 4 two more times, entering **sECond test namE** (correctly changed to "Second Test Name"), and then entering **pesto place** (correctly changed to "Pesto Place").

6. Click the **Close** button ⊠ on the Form window to return to the Database window.

7. Click ⊠ on the Access window title bar to close the FineFood database and exit Access. You return to the Windows desktop.

   TROUBLE? If a dialog box opens, asking if you want to save changes to the design of the FineFood Procedures module, click the Yes button to save your changes and exit Access.

Now that you've finished coding the functions to facilitate the use of the Customer form, you're ready to put the finishing touches on the FineFood database user interface, which you'll do starting in the next session.

Session 10.2 QUICK CHECK

1. What happens when you compile a module?

2. What does the UCase function do?

3. What is the purpose of a Dim statement?

4. How many times would the following loop be executed?

   For MyCounter = 2 to 11

5. What is the Boolean data type?

6. What is the string data type?

7. What does the CStr function do?

In this session, you will learn how to hide text and change the color of a form during the execution of a procedure. You also will create an event procedure for the **Queries Dialog Box** form.

Hiding **Text and Changing Display Color**

Barbara wants you to add a message to the Order form that will remind users when an invoice is unpaid. Access will display the message, in red, only when the invoice is unpaid. Also, she wants you to display the value in the InvoiceAmt text box in red for unpaid invoices and in black for paid invoices. The red display will help to draw attention to those invoices that have not yet been paid. See Figure 10-24.

Figure 10-24	ORDER FORM WITH THE UNPAID MESSAGE AND AMOUNT IN RED

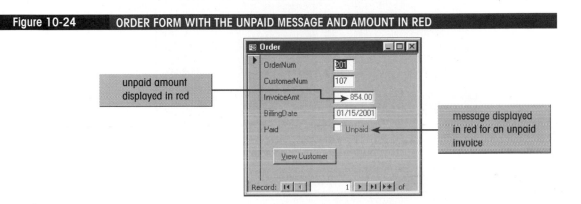

The **Visible property** determines when Access displays a control. Access displays a control when its Visible property is True, which is the default, and hides a control when its Visible property is False. A field's **ForeColor property** determines the field's foreground, or text, color. In the Order form, you will add a label to the right of the Paid check box. The text "Unpaid" will appear in red letters. Because Barbara wants the text to appear only when the Paid column has the value No, you will change the label's Visible property during execution. You will also change the foreground color of the InvoiceAmt field to red for unpaid invoices and to black for paid invoices.

Because the change to the Visible property takes place during execution, you will add code to the Current event procedure in the Order form. To set a property in a Visual Basic statement, you enter the object name followed by the property name, separating the two with a period. For example, if the label name for the message is UnpaidMsg, then [UnpaidMsg].Visible = False hides the label on the form.

First, you'll add a label to the Order form that will display a message in red for unpaid invoices and will be hidden for paid invoices.

To add the message to the Order form:

1. Place your Data Disk in the appropriate disk drive, start Access, and then open the **FineFood** database located in the Tutorial folder on your Data Disk.

2. Click **Forms** in the Objects bar of the Database window (if necessary), right-click **Order**, and then click **Design View** to open the Order form in Design view.

3. If necessary, click the **Toolbox** button on the Form Design toolbar to open the toolbox, and then click the **Label** tool on the toolbox.

4. Position the pointer in the Detail section and, when the center of the pointer's plus symbol (+) is positioned in the grid dots to the right of the Paid field-value text box and aligned with its top edge, click the mouse button.

5. Click the **Close** button ☒ on the toolbox to close it.

6. Type **Unpaid** and then press the **Enter** key. See Figure 10-25.

Figure 10-25	POSITION OF THE LABEL BOX

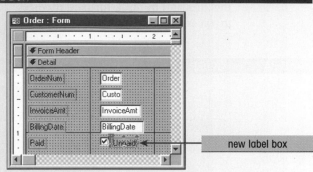

new label box

You'll now add the Current event procedure to the Order form.

To add the Current event procedure to the Order form:

1. Right-click the **Unpaid** label to display the shortcut menu, and then click **Properties** to open the property sheet.

2. Click the **All** tab (if necessary), select the value in the **Name** text box (if necessary), and then type **UnpaidMsg**.

   You can now set the ForeColor property for the label so that the message is displayed in red.

3. Scroll the property sheet, click the **Fore Color** text box, and then click the **Build** button ... Access opens the Color dialog box.

4. Click the **red** color box (the first color box in the second row of Basic Colors), click the **OK** button, and then press the **Enter** key. Access sets the ForeColor property value to the code for red (255). Notice that Access changes the foreground (text) color of the Unpaid label to red.

   TROUBLE? If the property sheet blocks your view of the form, drag it to an open area of the screen.

   You'll now enter the event procedure for the form's OnCurrent event. This event procedure will be executed whenever the Order form is opened or the focus moves from one record to another record.

5. Click the form selector, scroll down the property sheet to the OnCurrent property, click the right side of the **On Current** text box, click [**Event Procedure**], and then click the **Build** button ▭. Access opens the Code window in the Visual Basic window, displaying the Sub and End Sub statements.

6. Press the **Tab** key, and then type the Sub procedure statements exactly as shown in Figure 10-26.

<table>
<tr><td>Figure 10-26</td><td>CURRENT EVENT PROCEDURE FOR THE ORDER FORM</td></tr>
</table>

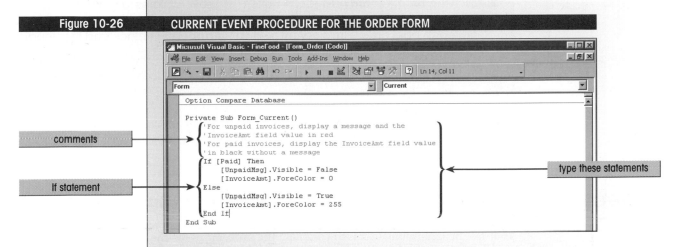

The Sub Form_Current procedure uses an If statement to decide whether the current value of the Paid field is True or False. If the current value of the Paid field is True, the procedure sets the UnpaidMsg Visible property to False (which means the Unpaid message will not appear on the Order Data form), and it sets the InvoiceAmt ForeColor property to 0 (black). If the current value of the Paid field is False, the procedure sets the UnpaidMsg Visible property to True, making the Unpaid message visible on the form, and sets the InvoiceAmt ForeColor property to 255 (red).

7. Click **Debug** on the menu bar, and then click **Compile FineFood**. Access compiles all the modules in the FineFood database.

8. Click the **Save** button 🖫 on the Standard toolbar.

9. Click the **Close** button ☒ on the Visual Basic window, click ☒ on the property sheet, and then click ☒ on the Form window to return to the Database window.

You'll now test the Current event procedure for the Order form.

To test the Current event procedure for the Order form:

1. Right-click **Order** in the Forms list, and then click the **Open** button to display the Order form in Form view. Access displays the first record for OrderNum 201, which is unpaid. The message "Unpaid" appears in red, as does the InvoiceAmt field value of 854.00.

TROUBLE? If Access opens a dialog box indicating a run-time error, Access could not execute the event procedure. Click the Debug button in the dialog box. Access displays the event procedure in the Code window and highlights the line containing the error. Check the statements carefully and make sure that they are exactly like those in Figure 10-26. Make the necessary changes, compile the module, save the module, and then close the Code window. Then repeat Step 1.

2. Click the **Next Record** navigation button ▶ several times to make sure that each unpaid order's message and InvoiceAmt field value appear in red, and that each paid order's InvoiceAmt field value appears in black and the Unpaid message does not appear.

3. Click the **Close** button ✕ on the Form window to return to the Database window.

You have finished all your work on the Current event procedure for the Order form. Next, you'll create the necessary procedures for the command buttons in the Queries Dialog Box form.

Creating the Procedures for the Queries Dialog Box Form

Your last programming task is to complete the procedures for the Queries Dialog Box form. Leonard wants Access to highlight the first item in the list box, when the Queries Dialog Box form first opens, by placing the focus on it. Next, when a user double-clicks a query name in the list box or highlights a query name and then clicks the Print Preview command button, that query should be displayed in the Print Preview window. Finally, when a user selects a query name in the list box and then clicks the Datasheet command button, the selected query should open in Datasheet view. You'll create the three procedures for the Queries Dialog Box form to perform these processes. Figure 10-27 shows the names for the three procedures.

Figure 10-27   QUERIES DIALOG BOX FORM'S PROCEDURES

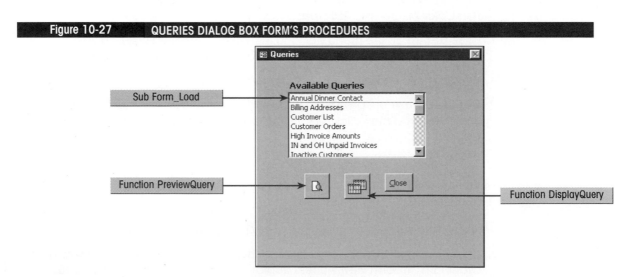

Coding the Load Event Procedure for the Queries Dialog Box

When a user opens the Queries Dialog Box form, Leonard wants Access to place the focus on the top query in the list box automatically. To accomplish this, you need to specify the form's Load event. Figure 10-28 shows the code for the form's Load event.

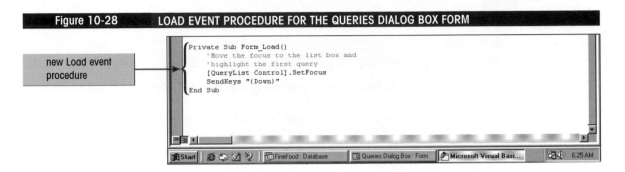

| Figure 10-28 | LOAD EVENT PROCEDURE FOR THE QUERIES DIALOG BOX FORM |

new Load event procedure

```
Private Sub Form_Load()
    'Move the focus to the list box and
    'highlight the first query
    [QueryList Control].SetFocus
    SendKeys "{Down}"
End Sub
```

The **Load event** occurs when Access opens a form. Anything you specify for this event will happen whenever the form is opened. **SetFocus** is a method that moves the focus to the specified object or control. A **method** is an action that operates on specific objects or controls. The statement [QueryList Control].SetFocus moves the focus to QueryList Control—which is the name for the form's list box—but does not set the focus to any specific query name. The SendKeys "{Down}" statement sends the down arrow keystroke to the list box; Access highlights the top query in the list box in response to this statement. The end result of these statements is that when the user opens the dialog box, the top query is highlighted and has the focus.

You'll open the Queries Dialog Box form in Design view and create the Load event procedure.

To add the Load event procedure for the Queries Dialog Box form:

1. Click **Forms** in the Objects bar of the Database window (if necessary), right-click **Queries Dialog Box**, and then click **Design View** to open the Queries Dialog Box form in Design view.

2. Right-click the form selector, and then click **Properties** to open the property sheet.

3. Click the **Event** tab (if necessary), scroll the property sheet (if necessary), click the right side of the **On Load** text box, click **[Event Procedure]**, and then click the **Build** button ... . Access opens the Code window in the Visual Basic window, displaying the Sub and End Sub statements.

4. Press the **Tab** key, and then type the Sub procedure statements as shown in Figure 10-29.

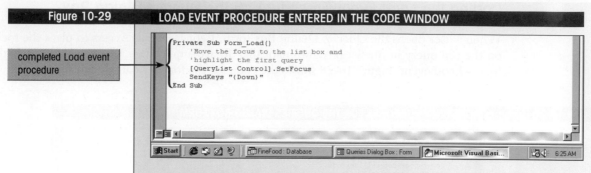

Figure 10-29   LOAD EVENT PROCEDURE ENTERED IN THE CODE WINDOW

completed Load event procedure

```
Private Sub Form_Load()
    'Move the focus to the list box and
    'highlight the first query
    [QueryList Control].SetFocus
    SendKeys "{Down}"
End Sub
```

Start | FineFood : Database | Queries Dialog Box : Form | Microsoft Visual Basi... | 6:25 AM

The word "Private" in the first line of the Sub procedure definition indicates that it can be used only in the class module for this form. Form_Load indicates that this Sub procedure is the event procedure for the Load event. Make sure you type curly braces in the SendKeys statement.

5. Click **Debug** on the menu bar, click **Compile FineFood**, and then click the **Save** button 🖫 on the Standard toolbar.

6. Close the Visual Basic window, close the property sheet, and then close the Form window to return to the Database window.

   Next you'll test the procedure by opening the Queries Dialog Box form in Form view and verifying that the first query in the list box is selected.

7. Right-click **Queries Dialog Box**, and then click **Open** to open the Queries Dialog Box form in Form view. Notice that the top query in the list box is selected.

   TROUBLE? If the top query in the list box is not highlighted, you probably did not use the curly braces { } in the SendKeys statement. Click the View button for Design view 🖾, and then open the properties list for the form. Click the On Load event text box, click the Build button ⋯, and then correct the event procedure. Then repeat Steps 5 through 7.

8. Click the **Close** command button in the dialog box to close it and return to the Database window.

You have finished your work with the Load event procedure for the Queries Dialog Box form. Next, you need to create the form's PreviewQuery and DisplayQuery procedures.

Coding the PreviewQuery and DisplayQuery Procedures for the Queries Dialog Box

Double-clicking a query name in the list box or selecting a query name and then clicking the Print Preview command button must open that query in the Print Preview window. Selecting a query name in the list box and then clicking the Datasheet command button must open that query in Datasheet view. Figure 10-30 shows the code to handle these procedures.

Figure 10-30   PREVIEWQUERY AND DISPLAYQUERY FUNCTIONS FOR THE FORM

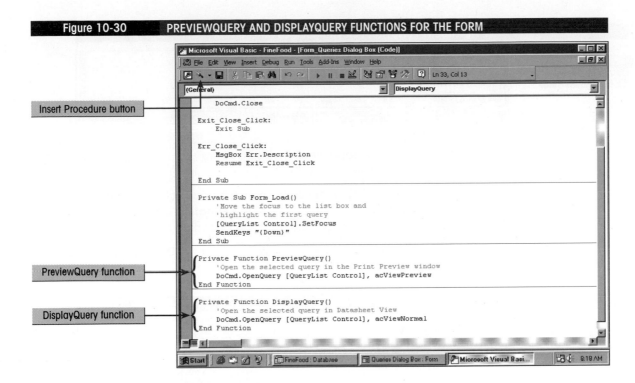

The **DoCmd statement** executes an action in a function. You use the DoCmd statements in these functions to run the OpenQuery action. The parameter choices for the selected query of [QueryList Control] in the OpenQuery action are: acViewPreview to open the Print Preview window, acViewDesign to open the query in Design view, and acViewNormal to open the query in Datasheet view. Because the OpenQuery action and its parameter values acViewPreview, acViewDesign, and acViewNormal are standard features of Access, you do not have to define them in a Dim statement as you do for variables you create.

Next you'll open the Queries Dialog Box form in Design view, create the two functions, and attach the functions to the appropriate control properties.

To add the two functions to the Queries Dialog Box form:

1. Click the **Design** button to display the Queries Dialog Box form in Design view, and then click the **Code** button 📖 on the Form Design toolbar to open the Code window for the form's class module in the Visual Basic window.

2. Click the list arrow for the **Insert Module** button 📖 on the Standard toolbar, and then click **Procedure**. The Add Procedure dialog box opens.

3. Type **PreviewQuery** in the Name text box, click the **Function** option button, click the **Private** option button, and then click the **OK** button. Access displays the Function and End Function statements for a new procedure.

4. Press the **Tab** key, and then type the statements for the PreviewQuery function exactly as shown in Figure 10-31.

Figure 10-31 — PREVIEWQUERY FUNCTION FOR THE QUERIES DIALOG BOX FORM

completed PreviewQuery function

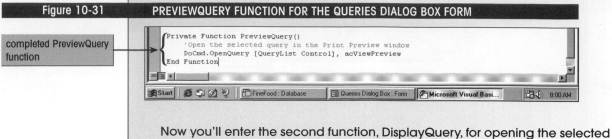

```
Private Function PreviewQuery()
    'Open the selected query in the Print Preview window
    DoCmd.OpenQuery [QueryList Control], acViewPreview
End Function
```

Now you'll enter the second function, DisplayQuery, for opening the selected query in Datasheet view.

5. Click the list arrow for ⚙ on the Standard toolbar, click **Procedure**, type **DisplayQuery** in the Name text box, click the **Function** option button, click the **Private** option button, and then click the **OK** button.

6. Press the **Tab** key, and then type the statements for the DisplayQuery function exactly as shown in Figure 10-32.

Figure 10-32 — DISPLAYQUERY FUNCTION FOR THE QUERIES DIALOG BOX FORM

completed DisplayQuery function

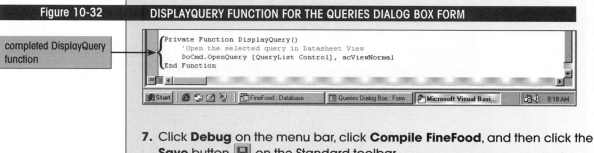

```
Private Function DisplayQuery()
    'Open the selected query in Datasheet View
    DoCmd.OpenQuery [QueryList Control], acViewNormal
End Function
```

7. Click **Debug** on the menu bar, click **Compile FineFood**, and then click the **Save** button 🖫 on the Standard toolbar.

8. Close the Visual Basic window.

Next you'll attach the appropriate procedure to the correct properties for the form objects.

To specify the functions for the event properties:

1. Right-click the form's list box (the box containing the word "Unbound") to display the shortcut menu, and then click **Properties** to open the property sheet.

2. Make sure the Event tab is selected, scroll the property sheet as necessary, click the **On Dbl Click** text box, and then type **=PreviewQuery()**. This specifies that Access will execute the procedure for previewing a query whenever a user double-clicks a query name in the list box. See Figure 10-33.

Figure 10-33 — SETTING THE LIST BOX'S ONDBLCLICK PROPERTY

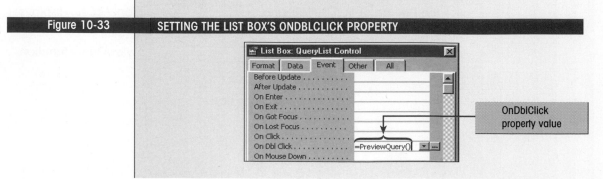

OnDblClick property value

3. Click the form's **Print Preview** command button, click the property sheet's **On Click** text box, and then type **=PreviewQuery()**. This specifies that Access will execute the procedure for previewing a query whenever a user selects a query name and then clicks the Print Preview command button.

4. Click the form's **Datasheet** command button, click the property sheet's **On Click** text box, and then type **=DisplayQuery()**. This specifies that Access will execute the procedure for opening the query datasheet whenever a user selects a query name and then clicks the Datasheet command button.

5. Click the **Save** button 🖫 on the Standard toolbar to save the form changes, close the property sheet, and then close the form to return to the Database window.

You'll now test the changes you made to the Queries Dialog Box form.

To test the changes to the Queries Dialog Box form:

1. Right-click **Queries Dialog Box** in the Forms list, and then click **Open** on the shortcut menu to open the form in Form view.

2. Double-click a few of the query names in the list box, in turn, to verify that the correct query opens in Print Preview. From the Print Preview window, click the **Close** button ☒ on the Print Preview window to return to the dialog box in Form view.

3. Click a query name in the list box, and then click the **Print Preview** command button to verify that the correct query opens in the Print Preview window. From the Print Preview window, click ☒ on the Print Preview window to return to the dialog box in Form view.

4. Repeat Step 3 for several more query names in the form's list box.

5. Click a query name in the list box, and then click the **Datasheet** command button to verify that the correct query datasheet opens. From the Query Datasheet window, click ☒ on the Query window to return to the dialog box in Form view.

6. Repeat Step 5 for several more query names in the form's list box.

7. Click the **Close** command button in the dialog box to close it and return to the Database window.

Leonard stops by and views your results. He is very pleased with the modifications to the Customer form and the Order form and to the Queries Dialog Box form. Next, he wants you to make access to the FineFood database more secure, and he wants you to make the final enhancements to the database and the user interface. In the next session, you'll complete your work with the FineFood database.

Session 10.3 QUICK CHECK

1. What does the Visible property determine?

2. What does the ForeColor property determine?

3. When does the Current event occur?

4. When does the Load event occur for an object?

5. What is a method?

6. What is the purpose of the DoCmd statement?

SESSION 10.4

In this session, you will use the password and encryption security features for Access databases. You also will use the Performance Analyzer and the Database Splitter tools, and then you will set the FineFood database startup options.

Securing an Access Database

Security refers to the protection of a database against unauthorized access, either intentional or accidental. Access provides several security features, including encryption and passwords.

Encryption converts the data in a database to a format that's indecipherable to a word processor or other program and stores it in that format. If unauthorized users attempt to bypass Access and get to the data directly, they will be able to see only the encrypted version of the data. However, users accessing the data using Access will have no problem working with the data. Any time a user stores or modifies data in a database, Access will encrypt the data before updating the database. Before a user retrieves data using Access, the data will be decrypted and presented to the user in the normal format. Once you've encrypted a database, you can use Access to decrypt it. **Decrypting** a database reverses the encryption. If your encrypted database takes longer to respond to your requests as it gets larger, you might consider decrypting it to improve its responsiveness.

To prevent access to a database using Access by an unauthorized user, you can assign a password to the database. A **password** is a word assigned to a database that users must enter before they can open the database. As long as the password is known only to authorized users of the database, unauthorized access to the database is prevented. It's best if you use a password that's easily remembered by authorized users but not obvious and easily guessed by others.

Leonard wants to restrict access to the FineFood database to authorized employees at Valle Coffee and also wants to prevent people from using other programs to access the data in the FineFood database.

Encrypting a Database

First, you'll encrypt the FineFood database for Leonard.

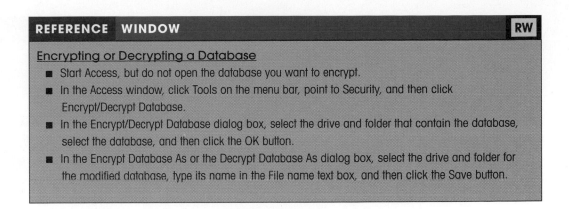

You'll encrypt the FineFood database, so you need to start Access without opening the FineFood database.

To encrypt the FineFood database:

1. Make sure that Access is running. If a database is open, close it by clicking the **Close** button ☒ on the Database window.

2. Click **Tools** on the menu bar, point to **Security**, and then click **Encrypt/Decrypt Database**. The Encrypt/Decrypt Database dialog box opens.

3. If necessary, use the Look in list arrow to select the Tutorial folder on your Data Disk.

4. Click **FineFood** in the list box, and then click the **OK** button. The Encrypt Database As dialog box opens.

   You can use the same name, drive, and folder for the original and encrypted versions of the database. If an error occurs during the encryption operation, Access doesn't delete the original file. If the operation is successful, Access replaces the original database with the encrypted version. If you use a different name, drive, or folder for the encrypted database, both the original and encrypted databases are retained.

   You'll replace the original database by using the same name, drive, and folder for the encrypted database.

5. Click **FineFood** in the list box, click the **Save** button, and then click the **Yes** button when asked if you want to replace the existing file. The dialog box closes, Access encrypts the FineFood database, and you return to the Access window.

Even though the FineFood database is encrypted, it won't look any different when you use Access to open it. However, if you attempt to open the FineFood database with another program, the data in the FineFood database will be indecipherable.

Next, you'll set a password for the FineFood database.

Setting a Database Password

Encrypting a database does not prevent unauthorized users from using Access to open the FineFood database and viewing or changing its data. Leonard asks you to set a password for the FineFood database to prevent such unauthorized access.

REFERENCE   WINDOW   RW

Setting a Database Password

- Start Access, click the Open button on the Database toolbar, select the drive and folder that contain the database, and then click the database.
- Click the Open list arrow, and then click Open Exclusive.
- Click Tools on the menu bar, point to Security, and then click Set Database Password.
- Type the password in the Password text box, type the same password in the Verify text box, and then press the Enter key.

The way you usually open an Access database allows **shared** access of the database with others; that is, two or more users can open and use the same database at the same time. When you set a password for the FineFood database, you need to open the database with exclusive access. When you open an Access database with **exclusive access**, you prevent other users from opening and using the database at the same time. You must open the database with exclusive access in order to set a password, so that you can guarantee that only one copy of the database is open when you set the password.

You'll now set the password for the FineFood database to Mocha.

To set the password for the FineFood database:

1. Click the **Open** button 📂 on the Database toolbar. The Open dialog box opens.

2. Make sure that **FineFood** is selected in the list box, and then click the **Open** list arrow. See Figure 10-34.

Figure 10-34	OPENING A DATABASE WITH EXCLUSIVE ACCESS

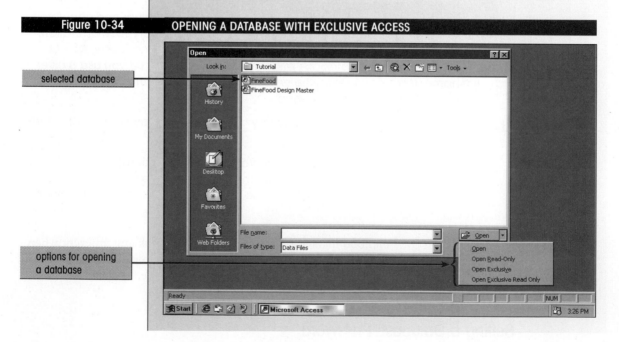

selected database

options for opening a database

Clicking the Open option opens the selected database with shared access for both reading and updating, whereas clicking the Open Read-Only option opens the selected database with shared access for reading only. **Reading** includes any action that does not involve updating the database, such as running queries and viewing table records. Actions that are prohibited when you open a database as Read-Only (because they involve updating the database) include changing the database design and updating table records. The other two options in the Open list open the selected database with exclusive access for reading and updating (Open Exclusive) or for reading only (Open Exclusive Read Only).

3. Click **Open Exclusive**. The FineFood database opens in the Access window.

4. Click **Tools** on the menu bar, point to **Security**, and then click **Set Database Password**. The Set Database Password dialog box opens. See Figure 10-35.

| Figure 10-35 | SET DATABASE PASSWORD DIALOG BOX |

type password here

type same
password here

You must type the password twice: once in the Password text box, and once in the Verify text box. Passwords are case-sensitive, so you must type the password in exactly the same way in both text boxes.

5. Type **Mocha** in the Password text box, press the **Tab** key, type **Mocha** in the Verify text box, and then press the **Enter** key. The dialog box closes, and Access sets the FineFood database password to Mocha.

TROUBLE? If a dialog box opens, asking you to verify the new password by retyping it in the Verify text box, click the OK button, type Mocha in the Verify text box, and then press the Enter key.

Next, you'll close and open the FineFood database to verify that the password has been set. Then you'll unset, or remove, the password. Unsetting a password eliminates the password protection from the database. It also permits you to modify the password; after unsetting the password, you can set a new password.

To test and unset the password for the FineFood database:

1. Click the **Close** button ☒ on the Database window.

Because you'll be unsetting the password, you need to open the FineFood database with exclusive access.

2. Open the FineFood database with exclusive access. The Password Required dialog box opens. See Figure 10-36.

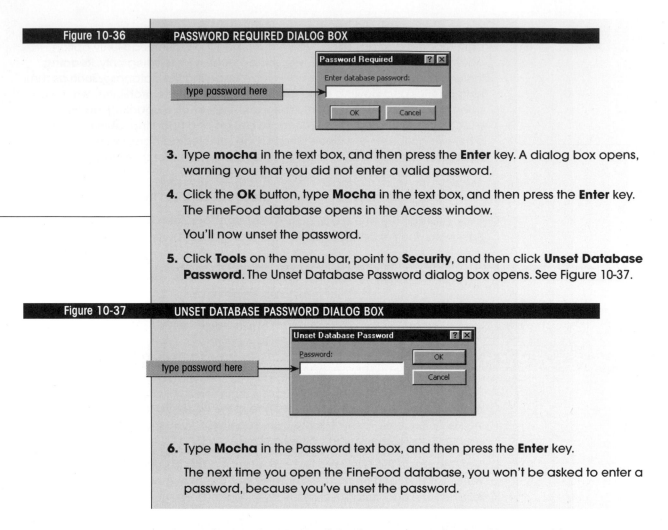

Figure 10-36   PASSWORD REQUIRED DIALOG BOX

type password here

3. Type **mocha** in the text box, and then press the **Enter** key. A dialog box opens, warning you that you did not enter a valid password.

4. Click the **OK** button, type **Mocha** in the text box, and then press the **Enter** key. The FineFood database opens in the Access window.

You'll now unset the password.

5. Click **Tools** on the menu bar, point to **Security**, and then click **Unset Database Password**. The Unset Database Password dialog box opens. See Figure 10-37.

Figure 10-37   UNSET DATABASE PASSWORD DIALOG BOX

type password here

6. Type **Mocha** in the Password text box, and then press the **Enter** key.

The next time you open the FineFood database, you won't be asked to enter a password, because you've unset the password.

Leonard wants the FineFood database to respond as quickly as possible to user requests, such as running queries and opening reports. You'll use the Performance Analyzer to check the performance of the FineFood database.

Analyzing **Database Performance with the Performance Analyzer**

To analyze the performance of the FineFood database, you'll use the Performance Analyzer. The **Performance Analyzer** is an Access add-in tool that you can use to optimize the performance of an Access database. You select the database objects you want to analyze for performance, you run the Performance Analyzer, and then the Performance Analyzer lists three types of analysis results: recommendation, suggestion, and idea. Access can complete the recommendation and suggestion optimizations for you, but you must do the idea optimizations.

Using the Performance Analyzer
- Start Access and open the database you want to analyze.
- Click Tools on the menu bar, point to Analyze, and then click Performance.
- Select the objects you want to analyze, and then click the OK button.
- Select the analysis results you want the Performance Analyzer to complete for you, and then click the Optimize button.
- Click the Close button.

You'll use the Performance Analyzer to optimize the performance of the FineFood database.

To use the Performance Analyzer to optimize the performance of the FineFood database:

1. Click **Tools** on the menu bar, point to **Analyze**, and then click **Performance**. The Performance Analyzer dialog box opens. See Figure 10-38.

Figure 10-38   PERFORMANCE ANALYZER DIALOG BOX

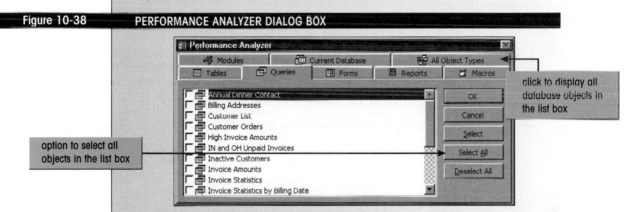

click to display all database objects in the list box

option to select all objects in the list box

TROUBLE? If a dialog box opens and asks if you would like to install this feature, insert your Microsoft Office 2000 CD in the correct drive, and then click the Yes button. If you do not have the Office 2000 CD, see your instructor or technical support person for assistance.

You want to analyze all the objects in the FineFood database.

2. Click the **All Object Types** tab, and then click the **Select All** button. All objects in the FineFood database appear in the list box, and all of them are now selected.

3. Click the **OK** button. The Performance Analyzer analyzes all the objects in the FineFood database and, after finishing, displays its analysis results. See Figure 10-39.

Figure 10-39   PERFORMANCE ANALYZER ANALYSIS RESULTS

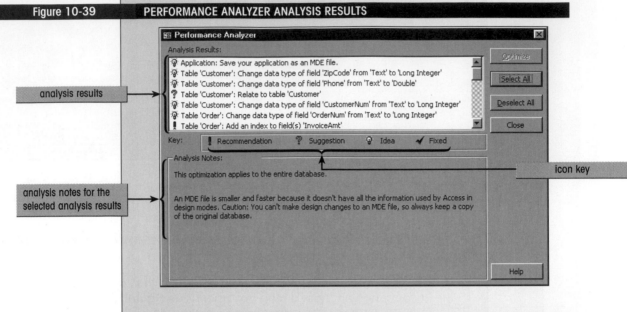

analysis results

analysis notes for the
selected analysis results

icon key

Most of the analysis results are ideas that you'd have to do yourself. The Performance Analyzer can perform the one suggestion (relate the two copies of the Customer table) and the two recommendations (add an index to the InvoiceAmt and Paid fields in the Order table) for you automatically. You don't want to form a relationship between the two copies of the Customer table in the Relationships window, because it's the same table, but you'll let the Performance Analyzer create the two indexes in the Order table.

4. Click several of the entries in the Analysis Results list box, and read the entries and change their analysis notes.

5. Click the first recommendation (its icon is a red exclamation point) to select it, press and hold down the **Ctrl** key and click the second recommendation to select both recommendations, release the **Ctrl** key, and then click the **Optimize** button. Access adds indexes for the InvoiceAmt and Paid fields in the Order table, and the icons for the two selected items change to blue check marks.

6. Click the **Close** button to close the dialog box and return to the Database window.

Leonard wants to create several queries for the FineFood database, but he doesn't want the user interface for other users to be cluttered with queries they won't need to use. He asks if there's a way for him to have a special user interface to access the data in the FineFood database.

Using the Database Splitter Wizard

Users might want to customize their own versions of the user interface, while accessing the same central table data. The **Database Splitter Wizard** splits an Access database into two files: one file contains the tables, and the other contains the queries, forms, and other database objects. Although a single master copy of the file containing the tables is stored and accessed, users can have their own copies of the other file and add their own queries, reports, and other objects to handle their processing needs.

People who develop databases to sell to multiple companies have a more important reason to split a database. When a developer delivers a split database, the initial file that contains the tables does not include the company's data, and the initial file that contains all the other database objects, including the user interface, is complete as created by the developer. Companies use the user interface to update the data in the database, but they do not modify the user interface in any way. Periodically, the database developer improves the user interface by modifying and adding queries, reports, and other objects without changing the structure of the tables. In other words, the user interface file changes, but the file that contains the tables does not change. The developer gives its client companies replacement user interface files, which continue to work with the split file that contains the company's data.

REFERENCE WINDOW	RW

<u>Using the Database Splitter Wizard</u>
- Make a backup copy of the database that you want to split.
- Start Access and open the database you want to split.
- Click Tools on the menu bar, point to Database Utilities, and then click Database Splitter.
- Click the Split Database button, select the drive and folder for the back-end database, type a name for the database in the File name text box, and then click the Split button.
- Click the OK button.

You'll use the Database Splitter Wizard to split the FineFood database into two files. Even though you should usually make a backup copy of a database before you split it, you will not make a backup copy of the FineFood database before you use the Database Splitter Wizard.

To use the Database Splitter Wizard:

1. Click **Tools** on the menu bar, point to **Database Utilities**, and then click **Database Splitter**. The Database Splitter dialog box opens. See Figure 10-40.

Figure 10-40   **DATABASE SPLITTER DIALOG BOX**

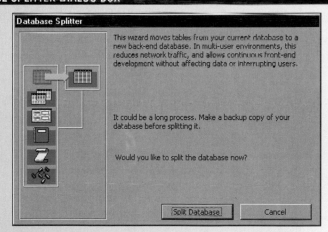

TROUBLE? If a dialog box opens and asks if you would like to install this feature, insert your Office 2000 CD in the correct drive, and then click the Yes button. If you do not have the Office 2000 CD, see your instructor or technical support person for assistance.

2. Click the **Split Database** button. The Create Back-end Database dialog box opens. The back-end database will contain the tables from the FineFood database. You'll use the default filename for the back-end database.

3. Click the **Split** button. After several seconds, a dialog box informs you that the database was successfully split.

4. Click the **OK** button to close the dialog box and return to the Database window. See Figure 10-41.

Figure 10-41	LINKED TABLES IN THE FINEFOOD DATABASE

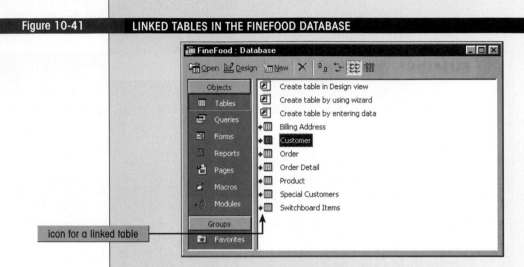

icon for a linked table

Each table in the FineFood database has an icon next to its name that signifies that there's a link to that table in another database file. The tables are no longer stored in the FineFood database; they are stored in the FineFood_be database file you just created with the Database Splitter Wizard. You can use the tables as if they were stored in the FineFood database, except that you cannot change a table's design from the FineFood database. You have to close the FineFood database and open the FineFood_be database to change a table's design.

5. Right-click **Customer** in the Tables list, and then click **Design View**. A dialog box informs you that the Customer table is a linked table and has some properties that you cannot modify.

6. Click the **No** button to close the dialog box and return to the Database window.

7. Click **Queries** in the Objects bar of the Database window. The queries you've created appear in the Queries list box. The queries and objects other than tables are still stored in the FineFood database.

You'll close the FineFood database and then open the FineFood_be database to verify which objects are stored in the new split database.

To verify the contents of the back-end database:

1. Click the **Close** button ☒ on the Database window to close the FineFood database, and then open the **FineFood_be** database located in the Tutorial folder on your Data Disk. The tables from the FineFood database appear with their usual icons in the Tables list box. The tables are now stored in the FineFood_be database.

2. Right-click **Customer** in the Tables list, and then click **Design View** to open the Customer table in Design view. You can modify the design of the tables in the FineFood_be database because they are stored in that database; they are not linked, as they are in the FineFood database.

3. Click ☒ on the Table window to close the Customer table.

4. Click **Queries** in the Objects bar of the Database window. No queries are listed because they are stored in the FineFood database.

5. Click ☒ on the Database window to close the FineFood_be database, and then open the **FineFood** database located in the Tutorial folder on your Data Disk.

Leonard stops by and views your results. He is very pleased with the work you've completed. As a final enhancement to the user interface, he asks whether you can have Access open the Switchboard form automatically when a user opens the FineFood database.

Setting the Database Startup Options

Access allows you to specify certain actions, called **startup options**, that take place when a database opens. For example, you can specify the name that appears in the Access window title bar, prevent users from using the Database window, or specify a form that is automatically displayed. If you want to bypass the startup options, you can press and hold down the Shift key when you open the database.

Leonard wants users to be able to open the FineFood database and have the switchboard appear automatically. This way, users won't need to use the Forms list to access the Switchboard form.

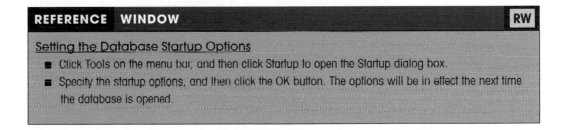

REFERENCE WINDOW   **RW**

Setting the Database Startup Options
- Click Tools on the menu bar, and then click Startup to open the Startup dialog box.
- Specify the startup options, and then click the OK button. The options will be in effect the next time the database is opened.

You need to set the FineFood database startup options so that the switchboard appears automatically when the database is opened, and so that the Database window is hidden from view. You'll also set startup options to provide users with restricted menus, to eliminate the toolbars, and to prevent users from making changes to toolbar and menu options.

To change the FineFood database startup options:

1. Click **Tools** on the menu bar, and then click **Startup**. The Startup dialog box opens. See Figure 10-42.

Figure 10-42	STARTUP DIALOG BOX

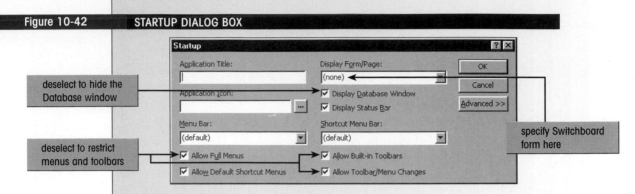

2. Click the **Display Form/Page** list arrow, scroll down the list, and then click **Switchboard**. This setting specifies that the Switchboard form will be displayed upon startup.

3. Click the **Display Database Window** check box to remove the check mark. This setting specifies that the Database window will not be displayed upon startup.

4. Click the **Allow Full Menus** check box to remove the check mark. This setting eliminates menus and commands that enable users to change the design of the objects in the FineFood database. Only a subset of the built-in menus will be available.

5. Click the **Allow Built-in Toolbars** check box to remove the check mark. This setting eliminates the toolbars from all windows in the FineFood database.

6. Click the **Allow Toolbar/Menu Changes** check box to remove the check mark. This setting prevents users from customizing toolbars, menu bars, and shortcut menus.

7. Click the **OK** button to close the Startup dialog box.

To test the startup options, you need to close and then open the FineFood database.

To test the startup options:

1. Click the **Close** button ☒ on the Database window to close the FineFood database.

2. Click **File** on the menu bar, and then click **1 FineFood** to open the FineFood database. See Figure 10-43.

   TROUBLE? The path might be different in your menu option, depending on the location of your Data Disk.

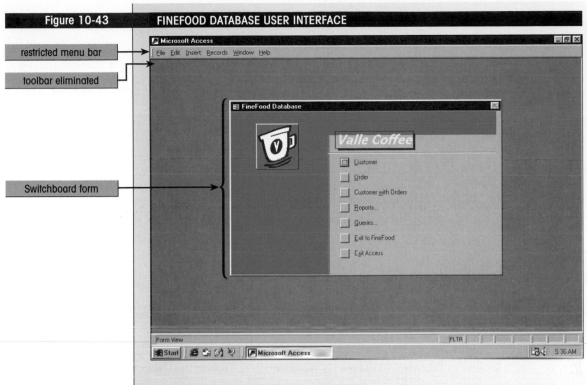

| Figure 10-43 | FINEFOOD DATABASE USER INTERFACE |

restricted menu bar

toolbar eliminated

Switchboard form

Access opens the FineFood database, displays the Switchboard form, hides the
Database window, displays a restricted menu bar, and eliminates the built-in
Form View toolbar. Your test shows that the startup options are correctly set.

Now you can make one final test of the FineFood database user interface. When you finish your final testing, you can exit Access.

To test the features of the FineFood database user interface:

1. Make one final pass through all the command button options to verify that all
features work properly on the FineFood database user interface.

2. Click the **Exit Access** command button on the FineFood Database switchboard as your last test to close the form, close the FineFood database, and
then exit Access.

The FineFood database user interface is complete. Leonard reviews the final interface
with Barbara and Kim, and they all agree that the interface will give them controlled, easy
access to the database's forms, queries, and reports. After working with the interface and
making any final adjustments, they can use the Switchboard Manager to remove the Exit to
FineFood command button from the Switchboard form. In this way, the FineFood
Database switchboard will be the only interface that users will see when they work with the
FineFood database. (Recall that you can press and hold down the Shift key when you open
a database if you need to bypass the startup options.)

Session 10.4 QUICK CHECK

1. _____ refers to the protection of a database against unauthorized access, either intentional or accidental.

2. Name two ways of providing security for an Access database.

3. What is the Performance Analyzer?

4. What does the Database Splitter Wizard accomplish?

5. What is a startup option?

6. How do you display a form automatically when a database opens?

REVIEW ASSIGNMENTS

Barbara asks you to complete the switchboard interface for the **Coffees** database. You can complete it by doing the following:

1. Make sure your Data Disk is in the appropriate disk drive, start Access, and then open the **Coffees** database located in the Review folder on your Data Disk.

2. Complete the **Reports Dialog Box** form design by doing the following:
   a. Create a Load event procedure that moves the focus to the first report name in the list box when the **Reports Dialog Box** form opens.

   Explore
   b. Create a PreviewReport function to open a report in the Print Preview window.
   c. Attach the PreviewReport function to the OnDblClick property for the **Reports Dialog Box** form list box.
   d. Attach the PreviewReport function to the OnClick property for the Print Preview command button on the **Reports Dialog Box** form.
   e. Open the **Reports Dialog Box** form in Form view, and then test all the form options. Save and close the form.

   Explore
3. Modify the **Enhanced Coffee Multi-page** form to display the Coffee Type field value in red when the value is "Flavored," and in black otherwise. Test the modified form, and then save and close it.

4. Set the database password to Amaretto.

5. Set the startup options to hide the Database window and open the **Switchboard** form whenever you open the **Coffees** database.

6. Test the database password and startup options, and then make one more pass through all the command button options on the **Switchboard** form.

7. Exit Access.

CASE PROBLEMS

Case 1. Ashbrook Mall Information Desk Sam Bullard asks you to complete the switchboard interface for the **Mall** database. You can complete it by doing the following:

1. Make sure your Data Disk is in the appropriate disk drive, start Access, and then open the **Mall** database located in the Cases folder on your Data Disk.

Explore   2. Modify the **Store Jobs** form to display a label to the right of the Position field-value text box. The label should be visible when the Position field value is "Assistant Manager," and hidden otherwise. The label should display the message "Management Position!" in red when it is visible. Test the modified form, and then save and close it.

Explore   3. Use the Office Assistant to ask the following question: "What is Name AutoCorrect?" Choose the topic "Automatically repair errors caused by renaming." Read the information, and then read the information in the link at the bottom of the topic. Close the Help window and hide the Office Assistant. Open the **Job** table in Design view, change the field name of Hours/Week to HoursPerWeek, and then save and close the table. Open the **Store Jobs** query, review the query results, close the query, and then do the same for the **Store Jobs** form. Describe your findings in terms of the effects of using the Name AutoCorrect feature.

4. Encrypt the Mall database by overwriting the existing **Mall** database in the Cases folder on your Data Disk, and then set the database password to Ashbrook.

5. Use the Performance Analyzer to analyze the entire **Mall** database, but do not implement any of the analysis results. How many analysis results of the recommendation type did the Performance Analyzer find? Of the suggestion type? Of the idea type?

6. Use the Database Splitter Wizard to split the **Mall** database. Use the default name for the back-end database and store it in the Cases folder on your Data Disk.

7. Set the startup options to hide the Database window and open the **Switchboard** form whenever you open the **Mall** database.

8. Test the database password and startup options, and then make one more pass through all the command button options on the **Switchboard** form.

9. Close the database, and then reopen the database while bypassing the startup options.

10. Exit Access.

Case 2. Professional Litigation User Services Raj Jawahir asks you to complete the switchboard interface for the Plus database. You can complete it by doing the following:

1. Make sure your Data Disk is in the appropriate disk drive, start Access, and then open the **Plus** database located in the Cases folder on your Data Disk.

Explore   2. Cathy Cunningham and David Abelson are partners at Professional Litigation User Services. Add the message "Partner's Account" to the **Enhanced Firm Multi-page** form so that the message appears to the right of the PLUSAcctRep field-value text box. Use the ForeColor value of blue, and make the font bold. Display the message only when the PLUSAcctRep field value is "Cunningham, Cathy" or "Abelson, David." Test the modified form, and then save and close it.

3. Encrypt the **Plus** database by overwriting the existing **Plus** database in the Cases folder on your Data Disk, and then set the database password to pLuS.

4. Use the Performance Analyzer to analyze the entire **Plus** database, but do not implement any of the analysis results. How many analysis results of the recommendation type did the Performance Analyzer find? Of the suggestion type? Of the idea type?

Explore ▶

5. Use the Office Assistant to ask the following question: "What is the Documenter?" Choose the topic "View, print, output, or save the design characteristics of database objects." Read the information, and then close the Help window and hide the Office Assistant. Use the Documenter to document the **Firm** table, print the report produced by the Documenter, and then close the Object Definition window.

6. Set the startup options to hide the Database window and open the **Switchboard** form whenever you open the **Plus** database.

7. Test the database password and startup options, and then make one more pass through all the command button options on the **Switchboard** form.

8. Exit Access.

Case 3. Best Friends Noah and Sheila Warnick ask you to complete the switchboard interface for the **Friends** database. You can complete it by doing the following:

1. Make sure your Data Disk is in the appropriate disk drive, start Access, and then open the **Friends** database located in the Cases folder on your Data Disk.

Explore ▶

2. Modify the **Enhanced Walker Information Multi-page** form to display the message "Long Distance" to the right of the Distance field-value text box. Use the ForeColor value of yellow, and make the font bold. Display the message only when the Distance field value is greater than 2.5. Test the modified form, and then save and close it.

3. Set the database password to BestFriends.

4. Use the Database Splitter Wizard to split the **Friends** database. Use the default name for the back-end database and store it in the Cases folder on your Data Disk.

5. Set the startup options to hide the Database window, restrict menus, eliminate the built-in toolbars, and open the **Switchboard** form whenever you open the **Friends** database.

6. Test the database password and startup options, and then make one more pass through all the command button options on the **Switchboard** form.

7. Exit Access.

Case 4. Lopez Lexus Dealerships Hector and Maria Lopez ask you to complete the switchboard interface for the **Vehicles** database. You can complete it by doing the following:

1. Make sure your Data Disk is in the appropriate disk drive, start Access, and then open the **Vehicles** database located in the Cases folder on your Data Disk.

2. Complete the **Reports Dialog Box** form design by doing the following:

   a. Create a Load event procedure that moves the focus to the first report name in the list box when the **Reports Dialog Box** form opens.

Explore ▶

   b. Create a PreviewReport function to open a report in the Print Preview window.

   c. Attach the PreviewReport function to the OnDblClick property for the **Reports Dialog Box** form list box.

   d. Attach the PreviewReport function to the OnClick property for the Print Preview command button on the **Reports Dialog Box** form.

   e. Open the **Reports Dialog Box** form in Form view, and then test all the form options. Save and close the form.

3. Complete the **Queries Dialog Box** form design by doing the following:

   a. Create a Load event procedure that moves the focus to the first query name in the list box when the **Queries Dialog Box** form opens.

   b. Create a DisplayQuery function to open a query in Datasheet view.

   c. Attach the DisplayQuery function to the OnDblClick property for the **Queries Dialog Box** form list box.

   d. Attach the DisplayQuery function to the OnClick property for the Datasheet command button on the **Queries Dialog Box** form.

   e. Open the **Queries Dialog Box** form in Form view, and then test all the form options. Save and close the form.

4. Lopez Lexus Dealerships has honored Soon Hong as manager of the year. Add the message "Manager of the Year!" to the **Enhanced Location Information Multi-page** form. Use the ForeColor value of orange, make the font 14-point bold, and position the message to the right of the ManagerName field-value text box. Display the message only when the ManagerName field value is "Hong, Soon." Save and close the form.

5. Set the startup options to hide the Database window and open the **Switchboard** form whenever you open the **Vehicles** database.

6. Test the database startup options, and then make one more pass through all the command button options on the **Switchboard** form.

7. Exit Access.

Case 5. eACH Internet Auction Site   Chris and Pat Aquino ask you to complete the switchboard interface for the **BuySell** database. You can complete it by doing the following:

1. Make sure your Data Disk is in the appropriate disk drive, start Access, and then open the **BuySell** database located in the Cases folder on your Data Disk.

Explore   2. Modify the **Item** form to display the message "Very High Reserve" to the right of the ReservePrice field-value text box. Use the ForeColor value of blue, and make the font bold. Display the message only when the ReservePrice field value is greater than 1000. Test the modified form, and then save and close it.

3. Set the database password to eACH.

4. Use the Database Splitter Wizard to split the **BuySell** database. Use the default name for the back-end database and store it in the Cases folder on your Data Disk.

5. Set the startup options to hide the Database window, restrict menus, eliminate the built-in toolbars, and open the **Switchboard** form whenever you open the **BuySell** database.

6. Test the database password and startup options, and then make one more pass through all the command button options on the **Switchboard** form.

7. Exit Access.

INTERNET ASSIGNMENTS

The purpose of the Internet Assignments is to challenge you to find information on the Internet that you can use to create effective documents. The actual assignments are updated and maintained on the Course Technology Web site. Log on to the Internet and use your Web browser to go to the Student Online Companion to accompany this text at **www.course.com/NewPerspectives/office2000**. Click the Access link, and then click the link for Tutorial 10.

QUICK CHECK ANSWERS

Session 10.1

1. Visual Basic for Applications statements respond to events that occur with the objects in a database.
2. a procedure that runs when a specific event occurs
3. A Function procedure performs operations, returns a value, can accept input values, and can be used in expressions. A Sub procedure performs operations and can accept input values, but does not return a value and cannot be used in expressions.
4. A standard module is a database object that is stored in memory with other database objects when you open the database. A class module is associated with a specific database object, such as a form or report.
5. scope
6. You use the Immediate window to test VBA procedures when you are coding them.

Session 10.2

1. Access checks the modules in your database for syntax errors. If no syntax errors are found, Access translates the VBA code into machine language.
2. The UCase function converts its argument to uppercase letters. It has no effect on characters that are not letters.
3. A Dim statement is used to declare variables and their types.
4. 10 times
5. VBA equivalent of the yes/no data type
6. VBA equivalent of the text data type
7. converts its argument to a String data type

Session 10.3

1. when Access displays a control
2. a control's foreground, or text, color
3. when the object opens and every time you move to another record
4. when the object opens
5. an action that operates on specific objects or controls
6. executes an action in a function

Session 10.4

1. security
2. encryption and passwords
3. The Performance Analyzer is an Access add-in tool that you can use to optimize the performance of an Access database.
4. The Database Splitter Wizard splits an Access database into two files: one file contains the tables, and the other contains the other database objects.
5. an action that takes place when a database opens
6. In the Startup dialog box, click the Display Form/Page list arrow, and then select the form.

OBJECTIVES

In this case you will:

- Change field properties

- Add a table to a database and define relationships between tables

- Create select, parameter, and crosstab queries

- Create a form using the Form Wizard

- Create custom forms

- Create custom reports

- Prepare a chart

- Design and create a switchboard

- Add macros and event procedures

COMPANY FINANCIAL INFORMATION BY FINSTAT INC.

CASE

FINSTAT Inc.

When Pat Mitchell graduated from a prestigious business college, she had her pick of job offers. Employers could see from her internship record and her grades that she was a bright, ambitious worker who would be an asset to their company. Pat had always dreamed of being her own boss, however, so after careful market analysis and planning she founded FINSTAT Inc., an electronic information service that markets financial information to its clients. Since the time Pat started her company, competing vendors have appeared on the market offering similar databases of financial information.

Pat and her team of financial analysts are now realizing that to remain competitive, their products must supply current and complete data. Also their clients must be able to access the data effortlessly and with as many options as possible. Pat decides to take the current databases she has and upgrade them with ease of use in mind. Her most successful database contains recent financial statement data on several of the leading U.S. corporations. She starts her new campaign by reorganizing the financial statement information to make it more accessible, and then designing an interface that is easier for clients to use.

Pat's corporation database currently consists of two tables, Company and Finance. Figure 1 shows the structure of the Company table, which stores general data about each company. The Company table contains an ID number and name for each company, a code classifying the company's industry, and a symbol that uniquely identifies the company on the stock exchange and in financial publications.

Figure 1	STRUCTURE OF THE COMPANY TABLE

Field Name	Data Type	Properties
CompanyID	Text	Field Size—3
		Caption—Company ID
CompanyName	Text	Field Size—30
		Caption—Company Name
Industry	Text	Field Size—2
Symbol	Text	Field Size—6

Figure 2 shows the structure of the Finance table, which tracks the yearly financial data for each company. The Finance table contains the same ID numbers used in the Company table and contains additional data on the sales, assets, and profits for each company for a given year, 1999 or later.

Figure 2	STRUCTURE OF THE FINANCE TABLE

Field Name	Data Type	Properties
CompanyID	Text	Field Size—3
		Caption—Company ID
Year	Number	Field Size—Integer
		Decimal Places–Auto
Sales	Currency	Description—Rounded to the nearest million
		Decimal Places—0
Assets	Currency	Description—Rounded to the nearest million
		Decimal Places—0
Profits	Currency	Description—Rounded to the nearest million
		Decimal Places—0

Pat wants to create a new customized version of the database so that clients can choose information more easily. She formulates the following plan: she will modify the field properties in the Company and Finance tables, add a table for industry codes and descriptions, define relationships for the three tables, and create and save four queries. She will then create the form shown in Figure 3, using the Form Wizard. This new form will make it easier for both her own staff and her clients to add current financial data to the database.

Figure 3	COMPANY FINANCES FORM CREATED BY THE FORM WIZARD

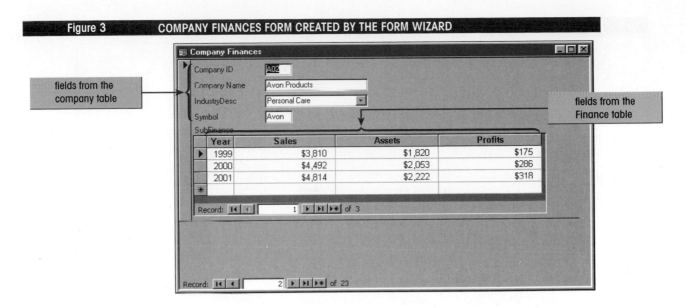

fields from the company table

fields from the Finance table

Pat plans to create a custom form, shown in Figure 4, that uses all three tables to display a company's financial information, a year at a time. Calculations are included on this form for the company's rate of return and profit margin.

Figure 4	ANNUAL FINANCIALS FORM

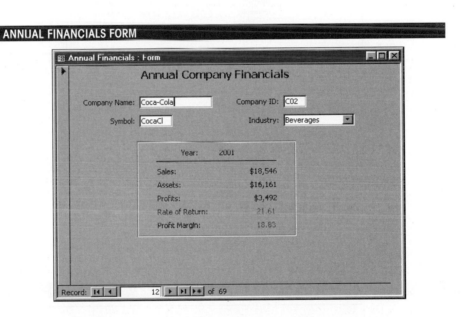

Next, Pat plans to create two reports that are easy to generate and are of presentation quality. The first report, shown in Figure 5, groups companies by industry and provides industry and overall totals.

Figure 5   CUSTOM INDUSTRY 2001 REPORT

FINSTAT

Financial Analysis for 2001
Figures rounded to the nearest million

Industry: Apparel

Company Name	Sales	Assets	Profits
Reebok International	$3,483	$1,786	$139
Nike	$6,471	$3,952	$553
Liz Claiborne	$2,217	$1,382	$155
Fruit of the Loom	$2,447	$2,547	$151
Industry Total:	$14,618	$9,667	$998

Industry: Beverages

Company Name	Sales	Assets	Profits
Coca-Cola	$18,546	$16,161	$3,492
PepsiCo	$31,645	$24,512	$1,149
Anheuser-Busch	$10,884	$10,464	$1,190
Industry Total:	$61,075	$51,137	$5,831

Industry: Cars & Trucks

Company Name	Sales	Assets	Profits
Chrysler	$61,397	$56,184	$3,529
Ford Motor	$146,991	$262,867	$4,446
General Motors	$168,369	$222,142	$4,963
Industry Total:	$376,757	$541,193	$12,938

Industry: Chemicals

Company Name	Sales	Assets	Profits
Du Pont	$39,689	$37,987	$3,636
Monsanto	$9,262	$11,191	$385
Dow Chemical	$20,053	$24,673	$1,907
Industry Total:	$69,004	$73,851	$5,928

Industry: Discount Retailing

Company Name	Sales	Assets	Profits
J.C. Penney	$23,649	$22,088	$565
Home Depot	$19,535	$9,342	$938
Wal-Mart Stores	$106,147	$39,501	$3,056
Kmart	$31,437	$14,286	($220)
Sears, Roebuck	$38,236	$36,167	$1,271
Toys "R" US	$9,932	$8,023	$427
Industry Total:	$228,936	$129,407	$6,037

Industry: Personal Care

Company Name	Sales	Assets	Profits
Procter & Gamble	$35,284	$27,730	$3,046
Colgate-Palmolive	$8,749	$7,902	$635
Avon Products	$4,814	$2,222	$318
Gillette	$9,698	$10,435	$949
Industry Total:	$58,545	$48,289	$4,948
Grand Total:	$808,935	$853,544	$36,680

The second report, shown in Figure 6, summarizes sales, assets, and profits by industry.

Figure 6   CUSTOM INDUSTRY 2001 SUMMARY REPORT

FINSTAT

Industry Summary for 2001
Figures rounded to the nearest million

Industry	Sales	Assets	Profits
Apparel	$14,618	$9,667	$998
Beverages	$61,075	$51,137	$5,831
Cars & Trucks	$376,757	$541,193	$12,938
Chemicals	$69,004	$73,851	$5,928
Discount Retailing	$228,936	$129,407	$6,037
Personal Care	$58,545	$48,289	$4,948
Grand Total:	$808,935	$853,544	$36,680

Pat also plans to create a chart showing profits by industry by year, for all industries. This chart is shown in Figure 7.

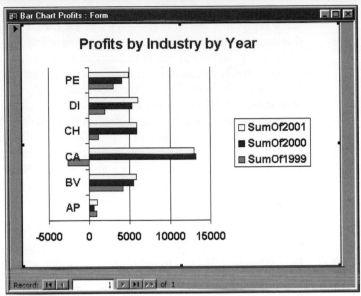

After creating a crosstab query showing the profits by company name and by year, and a bar chart showing average sales and average profits by year, Pat plans to design and create a switchboard, set the startup options, and create an event procedure for one of the new forms. Figure 8 shows the finished switchboard.

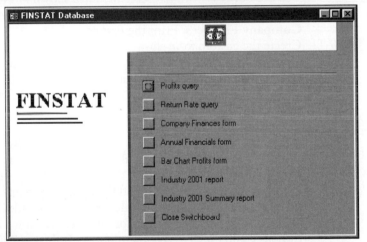

Complete the following to create the customized database:
1. Make sure you have created your copy of the Access Data Disk, place your Data Disk in the appropriate drive, start Access, and then open the **Finstat** database in the AddCases folder on your Data Disk.
2. Review the **Company** and **Finance** tables to become familiar with their structures and datasheet contents. If you are unfamiliar with any property setting, use the Access Help system for an explanation of that property.
3. For the **Company** table, make CompanyName a required field and make CompanyID the primary key. For the **Finance** table, add a validation rule for the Year field to allow values greater than or equal to 1999, add an appropriate validation text message, and make the combination of CompanyID and Year the primary key. Finally, define a one-to-many relationship between the primary **Company** table and the related **Finance** table, using CompanyID as the common field and enforcing referential integrity and both cascade options.

4. The **Company** table contains the Industry field, which stores a two-character industry code. The acceptable industry codes and associated industry descriptions are: AP (Apparel), BV (Beverages), CA (Cars & Trucks), CH (Chemicals), DI (Discount Retailing), and PE (Personal Care). Design and create a new table to store the industry codes and industry descriptions, using the field names Industry and IndustryDesc and making Industry the primary key. Name this table **Industry** and add the six industry records to the table. Define a one-to-many relationship between the primary **Industry** table and the related **Company** table, using the two-character industry code as the common field and enforcing referential integrity and both cascade options. Print the six records from the **Industry** table.

5. Change the Industry field in the **Company** table to a Lookup Wizard field. Display the IndustryDesc field from the **Industry** table.

6. Create and save a query named **Profits** that displays the CompanyID, CompanyName, Year, IndustryDesc, Sales, and Profits fields for all companies with sales above 4000 and profits above 300. Print the query results in ascending order by Profits.

7. For all companies, create a query named **Return Rate** to display the CompanyName, Sales, Assets, Profits, and RateOfReturn for the year 2001. Calculate RateOfReturn by dividing Profits by Assets. Format RateOfReturn as a percent. Print the query results in descending order by RateOfReturn.

8. For all companies, create a query named **Company Data** to display the CompanyID, CompanyName, Industry, Symbol, Year, Sales, Assets, Profits, RateOfReturn, and ProfitMargin. Calculate RateOfReturn by dividing Profits by Assets and then multiplying by 100. Calculate ProfitMargin by dividing Profits by Sales and then multiplying by 100. For both RateOfReturn and ProfitMargin, use a fixed format. Print the query results in ascending order by CompanyName as the primary sort key, and Year as the secondary sort key.

9. Create and save a parameter query named **Profits Parameter** that displays the CompanyName, Symbol, Sales, Assets, Profits, and Industry fields for companies during 2001 in a selected industry (use Industry as the parameter). Print the query results in ascending order by Profits, using the parameter value PE.

10. Use the Form Wizard to create the form shown in Figure 3. Use the **Company** and **Finance** tables. Save the subform as **SubFinance**, and save the main/subform form as **Company Finances**. Print the first record.

Explore ▶ 11. Create the custom form shown in Figure 4 and save it as **Annual Financials**. Use the **Company Data** query as the basis for the form. Position the label boxes and text boxes as shown in Figure 4, and draw a rectangle around the financial information. Set the Back Style property to Transparent and the Special Effect property to Flat to remove the boxes from the financial text boxes. Print the first and last records of the custom form.

Explore ▶ 12. Create a query named **Industry 2001** using the **Company**, **Finance**, and **Industry** tables to select all the financial records for the year 2001. Refer to Figure 5 to determine which fields to include in the query and which fields to use as sort keys. Then create the custom report shown in Figure 5, using the **Industry 2001** query as the basis for the report. Save the report as **Industry 2001**, and then print the report. (*Note:* The FINSTAT logo at the top of the report is stored as **Finlogo.bmp** in the AddCases folder on your Data Disk.)

13. Create the Industry Summary for 2001 report shown in Figure 6. Base the report on the **Industry 2001** query. Save the report as **Industry 2001 Summary**. Print the report. (*Hint:* Use the report from Step 12 as a guide, but include only summary information for this report.)

14. Create a crosstab query showing the profits by industry by year. Include a Total of Profits column. Base the query on the **Company Data** query. Save the query as **Profit Crosstab**, and then print the query results.

Explore ▶ 15. Create the form with a bar chart showing profits by industry by year for all industries, as shown in Figure 7. Base the chart form on the **Profit Crosstab** query. Add appropriate titles and a legend. Save the form as **Bar Chart Profits**, and then print the form.

Explore

16. Design and create a switchboard, using Figure 8 as a model. Provide the wording for the title bar. Add the **Finmoney.bmp** and **Finlogo.bmp** pictures from your Data Disk to the locations shown on the switchboard in the figure. On the switchboard, place eight command buttons to perform the following actions:
    - Open the **Profits** query
    - Open the **Return Rate** query
    - Open the **Company Finances** form
    - Open the **Annual Financials** form
    - Open the **Bar Chart Profits** form
    - Open the **Industry 2001** report in the Print Preview window
    - Open the **Industry 2001 Summary** report in the Print Preview window
    - Close the switchboard and activate the Database window

    Create a macro group named **Switchboard Macros** for these command buttons. Use appropriate background and foreground colors and visual effects for the switchboard and its components, and size and position the switchboard in Form view. Test the switchboard.

17. Set the startup options to hide the Database window and open the **Switchboard** form whenever the **Finstat** database is opened.

18. For the **Annual Financials** form, display the RateOfReturn field value with a Fore Color value of red when the field value is over 10, and with the default black color otherwise. Similarly, display the ProfitMargin field value with a Fore Color value of red when the field value is over 10, and with the default black color otherwise. Test the form.

OBJECTIVES

In this case you will:

- Create select queries

- Create a form using the Form Wizard

- Create custom forms

- Create custom reports

- Design and create a switchboard

CUSTOMER ORDERS FOR PET PROVISIONS

CASE

Pet Provisions

Pet Provisions, started by Manny Cordova in 1993, sells pet food and pet supplies to pet shops around the world. His company has enjoyed steady annual increases in sales, but profits have lagged behind. Manny asks his office manager, Kerri Jackson, to tighten the company's collection methods as a first step in improving profits.

Currently the office maintains an Access database named Pet that contains information on its customers. After looking over the database, Kerri realizes that there is no easy way to tell which client accounts are paid in full and which have outstanding balances. She decides to create the necessary forms, queries, and reports to automate the collection process. Her work will include creating an invoice report that she can automatically generate to send to any client with an outstanding balance.

Kerri uses the Pet database as the starting point for her work. Among the tables in the Pet database are the Customer and Order tables. Figure 9 shows the structure for the Customer table, which contains one record for each customer. CustomerNum is the primary key for the table, which has 26 customer records. The other fields in the table are CustomerName, Street, City, State/Prov, Zip/PostalCode, Country, Phone, and FirstContact.

Figure 9	STRUCTURE OF THE CUSTOMER TABLE

Field Name	Data Type	Properties
CustomerNum	Number	Primary Key Field Size—Integer Format—Fixed Decimal Places—0 Caption—Customer Num Required—Yes
CustomerName	Text	Field Size—35 Caption—Customer Name
Street	Text	Field Size—30
City	Text	Field Size—20
State/Prov	Text	Field Size—20
Zip/PostalCode	Text	Field Size—10 Caption—Zip/Postal Code
Country	Text	Field Size—20
Phone	Text	Field Size—15
FirstContact	Date/Time	Format—mm/dd/yyyy Caption—First Contact

Figure 10 shows the structure for the Order table, which contains one record for each customer order. OrderNum is the table's primary key. CustomerNum is a foreign key in the Order table, and the Customer table will have a one-to-many relationship with the Order table.

Figure 10   STRUCTURE OF THE ORDER TABLE

Field Name	Data Type	Properties
OrderNum	Number	Primary Key Field Size—Integer Format—Fixed Decimal Places—0 Caption—Order Num Required—Yes
CustomerNum	Number	Field Size—Integer Format—Fixed Decimal Places—0 Caption—Customer Num Required—Yes Foreign Key
SaleDate	Date/Time	Format—mm/dd/yyyy Caption—Sale Date
ShipVia	Text	Field Size—7 Caption—Ship Via
TotalInvoice	Number	Field Size—Double Format—Standard Decimal Places—2 Caption—Total Invoice
AmountPaid	Number	Field Size—Double Format—Standard Decimal Places—2 Caption—Amount Paid
PayMethod	Text	Field Size—5 Caption—Pay Method

Kerri plans to create special queries, forms, and reports to help her analyze the 144 orders in the Order table. One of the special forms, shown in Figure 11, displays all orders for a customer along with totals for the customer's invoices, amount paid, and amount owed.

Figure 11   CUSTOMER WITH ORDERS FORM

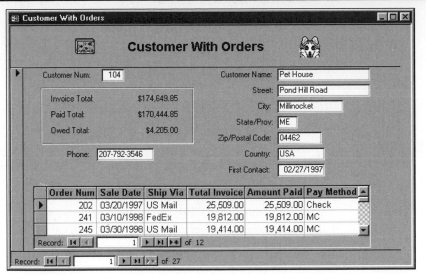

Kerri also wants to create a special report, shown in Figure 12, that she can send to customers owing money to Pet Provisions.

Figure 12   CUSTOM CUSTOMER STATEMENT REPORT

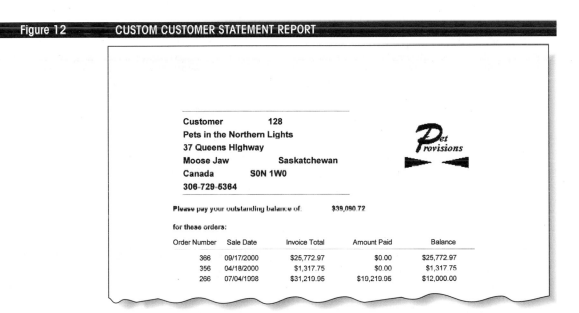

Complete the following to analyze profits at Pet Provisions:

1. Make sure you have created your copy of the Access Data Disk, place your Data Disk in the appropriate drive, start Access, and then open the **Pet** database in the AddCases folder on your Data Disk.
2. Review the **Customer** and **Order** tables to become familiar with their structures and datasheet contents. If you are unfamiliar with any property settings, use the Access Help system for an explanation of that property.
3. Define a one-to-many relationship between the primary **Customer** table and the related **Order** table.

4. Create and save a query named **Order Totals** that displays the grand total number of orders and grand totals for the TotalInvoice, AmountPaid, and AmountOwed fields. AmountOwed, a calculated field, is the difference between the TotalInvoice and AmountPaid fields. Format the grand total fields as currency. Use column names of Number of Orders, Sum of TotalInvoice, Sum of AmountPaid, and Sum of AmountOwed. Print the query results.

5. For all orders that have not been paid in full, create a query named **Open Orders** to display the CustomerName, Phone, SaleDate, TotalInvoice, AmountPaid, and AmountOwed fields. Print the query results in descending order by AmountOwed.

Explore ▶ 6. For all orders that have not been paid in full, create and save a query named **Owed By Customer** that displays the total number of orders and totals for the TotalInvoice, AmountPaid, and AmountOwed fields, grouped by CustomerName. Format the three sum columns as currency. Print the query results. *(Hint:* Use the **Open Orders** query as the basis for this query.) The query contains five columns to be displayed: CustomerName, Number of Orders, Sum of Total Invoice, Sum of AmountPaid, and Sum of Amount Owed.

Explore ▶ 7. Use the Form Wizard to create linked forms to maintain all fields in the **Customer** table and all fields in the **Order** table. Select all fields from the **Customer** table and all fields from the **Order** table. When the Form Wizard asks you how to display the forms, choose the Linked forms option. Save the forms as **Customer Data** and **Linked Orders**, respectively. Use the forms to add the records shown in Figure 13 to the tables, and then print the new records from each table.

Figure 13	NEW CUSTOMER AND ORDER RECORDS

Customer record:

CustomerNum	CustomerName	Street	City	State/Prov
790	Fuzzy Friends	3333 Binford	Corvallis	OR

Zip/PostalCode	Country	Phone	FirstContact
97332	USA	503-273-8998	6/23/2001

Order record:

OrderNum	CustomerNum	SaleDate	ShipVia	TotalInvoice	AmountPaid	PayMethod
375	790	7/24/2001	UPS	12,437.44	4000.00	Check

8. Create and save two queries that will be used with the form shown in Figure 11. For the first query, use the **Order** table to display totals for the TotalInvoice, AmountPaid, and AmountOwed fields, grouping by CustomerNum and using the column names Invoice Total, Paid Total, and Owed Total, respectively. Save the query as **Customer Order Totals**, and then print the query results. For the second query, use the **Customer Order Totals** query and the **Customer** table; display the CustomerNum, InvoiceTotal, PaidTotal, OwedTotal, CustomerName, Street, City, State/Prov, Zip/PostalCode, Country, Phone, and FirstContact fields; sort in ascending order by CustomerNum. Save the query as **Customer With Totals**, and then print the query results.

Explore

9. Create the custom form shown in Figure 11 and save it as **Customer With Orders**. Create an initial approximation of the form using the **Customer With Totals** query for the main form. Using the Subform/Subreport tool on the toolbox, create a subform based on the **Order** table, and place it on the form as shown in the figure. Select all the fields from the **Customer** table for the main form and all the fields from the **Order** table except CustomerNum for the subform. Save the subform as **SubOrder**. Then change the form so that it looks similar to the form shown in Figure 11. Use the Flat Special Effect property value, the Transparent Border Style property value, and the Transparent Back Style property value to remove the boxes from the three text boxes between the Customer Num and Phone boxes. Print the first record of the custom form. (*Note*: The pictures that appear on the top of the form are stored as **Petfish.bmp** and **Petdog.bmp** on your Data Disk.)

Explore

10. Create and save a query named **For Special Report** that selects customers who owe money to Pet Provisions and the unpaid orders for these customers. Refer to Figure 12 to determine which fields to include in the query. (*Hint*: Use the **Customer With Totals** query and the **Order** table to create this query; create a join line between the CustomerNum fields; and sort in ascending order by CustomerNum as the primary sort key and OrderNum as the secondary sort key.) Then create the custom report shown in Figure 12, using the **For Special Report** query as the basis for the report. Include a Group Header section based on CustomerNum, and place orders in the Detail section. Set the Force New Page property in the Group Header section to the value "Before Section" so that one customer statement is printed per page. Save the report as **Customer Statement**, and then print pages 5 through 7 of the report. (*Note*: The logo in the upper-right corner of the report is stored as **Petlogo.bmp** on your Data Disk.)

Explore

11. Design and create a switchboard, using Figure 14 as a model. Place command buttons on the switchboard to coordinate the running of two forms (**Customer Data** and **Customer With Orders**), three queries (**Open Orders, Order Totals,** and **Owed By Customer**), and one report (**Customer Statement**). Also provide a command button to close the switchboard and return to the Database window. Test the switchboard.

Figure 14   PET PROVISIONS SWITCHBOARD

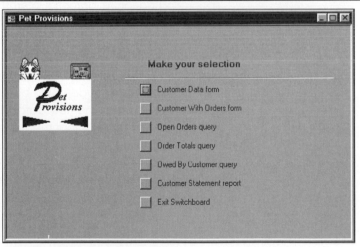

OBJECTIVES

OBJECTIVES

In this case you will:

- Design a database and draw its entity-relationship diagram

- Create the tables and relationships for the database

- Create forms to maintain the database

- Design and enter test data for the database

- Create queries and reports from the database

- Design and create a switchboard

INTERNSHIP PROGRAM FOR PONTIAC COLLEGE

CASE

Pontiac College

Pontiac College provides students with opportunities for professional development and field study through its internship program, which is administered by the Office of Internships and Field Experience. Students complement their courses with a structured training experience provided by qualified professionals in selected fields. Internships are offered in many different areas, including law, counseling, government, administration, public relations, communications, health care, computer programming, and marketing.

Anjali Bhavnani has just been hired as Pontiac College's new Internship Coordinator. She is eager to make information about the sponsoring agencies, potential internships, and current student interns more readily available to her office and to the students who qualify for the program. Anjali's most ambitious project is to develop a computerized database for the internship program to help meet these goals.

Instead of visually scanning all internship possibilities, Anjali, her staff, and interested students will be able to select internships of specific interest to them. The new database will allow potential interns to view only the internships that meet the criteria they specify. Anjali asks Roula Mendes, an information systems major working in the Office of Internships and Field Experience, to help the office develop a computerized database system for the internship program.

Anjali first outlines the steps in the internship program process for Roula:

- Identify and document the available internships
- Arrange for student intern placements
- Assign and track student interns

As the first step in the internship program process, Anjali receives a letter or phone call from a potential sponsoring agency. After some discussions, a sponsoring agency proposes an internship possibility and fills out the Agency/Internship Information form, shown in Figure 15. (Anjali's office currently maintains this form on a word processor.)

Figure 15　**AGENCY/INTERNSHIP INFORMATION FORM**

AGENCY/INTERNSHIP INFORMATION

AGENCY INFORMATION

NAME OF AGENCY _____

DEPARTMENT _____

ADDRESS _____
　　　　　Street

　　　　　City　　　　　　　　　　　State　　　Zip

CONTACT _____ PHONE _____

INTERNSHIP INFORMATION

TITLE _____

DESCRIPTION OF _____
DUTIES _____
_____

ORIENTATION & _____
TRAINING _____
_____

ACADEMIC _____
BACKGROUND _____
REQUIRED _____

SUPERVISOR _____ PHONE _____

Office Use
Agency ID　　_____
Internship ID　_____
Category　　_____

Many agencies offer more than one type of internship possibility. For each possible internship, the agency fills out a separate form and assigns one person as the contact for all internship questions and problems. In addition, each internship lists a supervisor who will work with the student intern. The internship remains active until the agency notifies the Office of Internships and Field Experience that the internship is filled or no longer available.

Anjali assigns a three-digit Agency ID to each new agency and a four-digit Internship ID to each new internship. These are sequential numbers. She also classifies each internship into a category that helps students identify internships that are related to their major or interests. For example, a student might be interested in health care, accounting, social service, or advertising.

A copy of each Agency/Internship Information form is placed in reference books in the Office of Internships and Field Experience. Students browse through these books to find internships that are of interest to them. If an internship interests a student, the student copies the information about the internship and contacts the sponsoring agency directly to request an interview.

When a student gets an internship, the student and agency establish a Learning Contract, outlining the goals to be accomplished during the internship. The student then fills out the Student Internship form, shown in Figure 16, to provide basic information on the student for the office files.

Figure 16   STUDENT INTERNSHIP FORM

STUDENT INTERNSHIP

NAME _____ SS# _____

ADDRESS _____
         Street

         _____
         City   State   ZIP

PHONE _____

MAJOR _____GPA _____ CLASS ____ Junior _____ Senior

Office Use

Internship ID   _____
Internship Term   ____ Fall ____ Spring ____ Summer
Internship Year   _____

Anjali enters the Internship ID and year on the Student Internship form and checks the term for the internship. Next, a clerk enters information from the form into a word processor to prepare lists of current interns and internships, and then places the form in a binder.

Anjali and Roula determine that getting these two forms into an Access database is their first priority, and then they will work on creating several new reports. The first report, the design of which is shown in Figure 17, lists all student interns alphabetically by last name for a selected term. In order to identify the student interns who should be included in the report, the system prompts the user for the term and year.

Figure 17   STUDENT INTERNS REPORT DESIGN

<today's date>	**Student Interns**		Page x
	As of <term><year>		

Last Name	First Name	Agency Name	Internship Title
X_____X	X_____X	X_____X	X_____X
X_____X	X_____X	X_____X	X_____X
X_____X	X_____X	X_____X	X_____X
X_____X	X_____X	X_____X	X_____X

End of Report

A second new report lists all agencies in the database alphabetically by agency name. Figure 18 shows the design of this report.

Figure 18	INTERNSHIP AGENCIES REPORT DESIGN

<today's date>   **Internship Agencies**   Page x

Agency Name	Department	Contact	Phone
X_____X	X_____X	X_____X	X_____X
X_____X	X_____X	X_____X	X_____X
X_____X	X_____X	X_____X	X_____X
X_____X	X_____X	X_____X	X_____X

End of Report

The Internship by Category report, the design of which is shown in Figure 19, lists internships grouped by category. The staff will use this report when talking with students about the internship program.

Figure 19	INTERNSHIP BY CATEGORY REPORT DESIGN

<today's date>   **Internship by Category**   Page x

Category x_____ x

Internship ID	Internship Title	Internship Description
XXXX	X_____X	X_____X
		X_____X
		X_____X
XXXX	X_____X	X_____X
XXXX	X_____X	X_____X
		X_____X

Category x_____ x

Internship ID	Internship Title	Internship Description
XXXX	X_____X	X_____X
XXXX	X_____X	X_____X
		X_____X
		X_____X

End of Report

At the end of an internship, the intern's supervisor evaluates the intern's work experience, using an evaluation form mailed from the Office of Internships and Field Experience. Anjali needs mailing labels addressed to the supervisor of each intern for the current term and year. The mailing labels should contain the supervisor's name on the first line; the agency name on the second line; the agency's street on the third line; and the agency's city, state, and zip code on the fourth line.

Complete the following to create the complete database system:

Explore 1. Read the appendix titled "Relational Databases and Database Design."

Explore 2. Identify each entity (relation) in the database for the internship system.

Explore 3. Draw an entity-relationship diagram showing the entities and the relationships between the entities.

Explore 4. Design the database for the internship system. For each relation, list the fields and their attributes, such as data types, field sizes, and validation rules. Place the set of relations in third normal form and identify all primary, alternate, and foreign keys.

5. Create the database structure using Access and the database name **Intern**. Be sure to define relationships between appropriate tables.

6. Create and save forms to maintain data on agencies, internships, student interns, and any other entity in your database structure. The forms should be used to view, add, edit, and delete records in the database.

7. Create test data for each table in the database and add the test data, using the forms you created in Step 6.

8. Create and save the **Student Interns** report, **Internship Agencies** report, **Internship by Category** report, and mailing labels report. The layouts shown in Figures 17 through 19 are guides—improve them as you see fit.

9. Design, create, and save a form that a student can use to view internships for a selected category. Display one internship at a time on the screen. For each internship, display the category, internship ID, title, description of duties, orientation and training, academic background, agency name, department, agency address, contact name, and contact phone. Provide an option to print the internship displayed on the screen. (*Note*: The AddCases folder on your Data Disk contains two picture files, **Intmatch.bmp** and **Inttrack.bmp**, which you can include on this form.)

10. Design, create, and save a switchboard to coordinate the running of the internship system. (*Note*: The AddCases folder on your Data Disk contains two picture files, named **Intmatch.bmp** and **Inttrack.bmp**, which you can include on the switchboard if you want.)

11. Test all the features of the internship system.

OBJECTIVES

In this appendix you will:

- Learn the characteristics of a relation

- Learn about primary, candidate, alternate, foreign, and composite keys

- Study one-to-one, one-to-many, and many-to-many relationships

- Learn to describe relations and relationships with entity-relationship diagrams and with a shorthand method

- Study database integrity constraints for primary keys, referential integrity, and domains

- Learn about determinants, functional dependencies, anomalies, and normalization

RELATIONAL DATABASES AND DATABASE DESIGN

This appendix introduces you to the basics of database design. Before trying to master this material, be sure you have an understanding of the following concepts: data, information, field, field value, record, table, relational database, common field, database management system (DBMS), and relational database management system.

Relations

A relational database stores its data in tables. A **table** is a two-dimensional structure made up of rows and columns. The terms table, row, and column are the popular names for the more formal terms **relation** (table), **tuple** (row), and **attribute** (column), as shown in Figure 1.

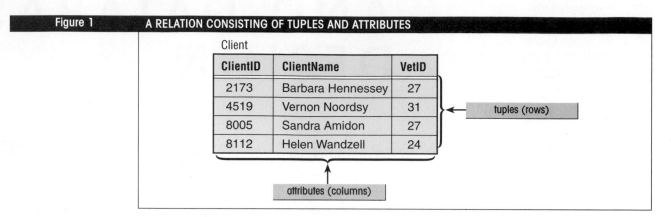

Figure 1 — A RELATION CONSISTING OF TUPLES AND ATTRIBUTES

Client

ClientID	ClientName	VetID
2173	Barbara Hennessey	27
4519	Vernon Noordsy	31
8005	Sandra Amidon	27
8112	Helen Wandzell	24

tuples (rows)

attributes (columns)

The Client table shown in Figure 1 is an example of a relation, a two-dimensional structure with the following characteristics:

- Each row is unique. Because no two rows are the same, you can easily locate and update specific data. For example, you can locate the row for ClientID 8005 and change the ClientName value, Sandra Amidon, or the VetID value, 27.

- The order of the rows is unimportant. You can add or view rows in any order. For example, you can view the rows in ClientName order instead of ClientID order.

- Each table entry contains a single value. At the intersection of each row and column, you cannot have more than one value. For example, each row in Figure 1 contains one ClientID, one ClientName, and one VetID.

- The order of the columns is unimportant. You can add or view columns in any order.

- Each column has a unique name called the **attribute name**. The attribute name allows you to access a specific column without needing to know its position within the relation.

- The entries in a column are from the same domain. A **domain** is a set of values from which one or more columns draw their actual values. A domain can be broad, such as "all legitimate names of people" for the ClientName column, or narrow, such as "24, 27, or 31" for the VetID column. The domain of "all legitimate dates" could be shared by the BirthDate, StartDate, and LastPayDate columns in a company's employee relation.

- Each row in a relation describes, or shows the characteristics of, an entity. An **entity** is a person, place, object, event, or idea for which you want to store and process data. For example, ClientID, ClientName, and VetID are characteristics of the clients of a pet-sitting company. The Client relation represents all the client entities and their characteristics. That is, the sets of values in the rows of the tblClient relation describe the different clients of the company. The Client relation includes only characteristics of a client. Other relations would exist for the company's other entities. For example, a Pet relation might describe the clients' pets and an Employee relation might describe the company's employees.

Knowing the characteristics of a relation leads directly to a definition of a relational database. A **relational database** is a collection of relations.

Keys

Primary keys ensure that each row in a relation is unique. A **primary key** is an attribute, or a collection of attributes, whose values uniquely identify each row in a relation. In addition to being *unique*, a primary key must be *minimal* (that is, contain no unnecessary extra attributes) and must not change in value. For example, in Figure 2 the State relation contains one record per state and uses StateAbbrev as its primary key.

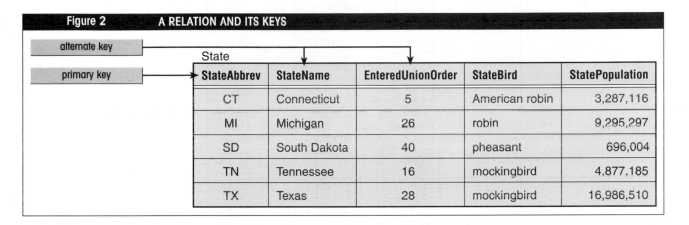

| Figure 2 | A RELATION AND ITS KEYS |

State

StateAbbrev	StateName	EnteredUnionOrder	StateBird	StatePopulation
CT	Connecticut	5	American robin	3,287,116
MI	Michigan	26	robin	9,295,297
SD	South Dakota	40	pheasant	696,004
TN	Tennessee	16	mockingbird	4,877,185
TX	Texas	28	mockingbird	16,986,510

Could any other attribute, or collection of attributes, be the primary key of the State relation?

- Could StateBird serve as the primary key? No, because the column does not have unique values (for example, the mockingbird is the state bird of more than one state).
- Could StatePopulation serve as the primary key? No, because the column values change periodically and are not guaranteed to be unique.
- Could StateAbbrev and StateName together serve as the primary key? No, because the combination is not minimal. Something less, StateAbbrev by itself, can serve as the primary key.

■ Could StateName serve as the primary key? Yes, because the column has unique values. In a similar way, you could select EnteredUnionOrder as the primary key for the State relation. One attribute, or collection of attributes, that can serve as a primary key is called a **candidate key**. The candidate keys for the State relation are StateAbbrev, StateName, and EnteredUnionOrder. You choose one of the candidate keys to be the primary key, and the remaining candidate keys are called **alternate keys**.

Figure 3 shows a City relation containing the attributes StateAbbrev, CityName, and CityPopulation.

Figure 3	A RELATION WITH A COMPOSITE KEY

City   primary key

StateAbbrev	CityName	CityPopulation
CT	Hartford	139,739
CT	Madison	14,031
CT	Portland	8,418
MI	Lansing	127,321
SD	Madison	6,257
SD	Pierre	12,906
TN	Nashville	488,374
TX	Austin	465,622
TX	Portland	12,224

What is the primary key for the City relation? The values for CityPopulation periodically change and are not guaranteed to be unique, so CityPopulation cannot be the primary key. Because the values for each of the other two columns are not unique, StateAbbrev alone cannot be the primary key and neither can CityName (for example, there are two Madisons and two Portlands). The primary key is the combination of StateAbbrev and CityName. Both attributes together are needed to identify, uniquely and minimally, each row in the City relation. A multiple-attribute primary key is called a **composite key** or a **concatenated key**.

The StateAbbrev attribute in the City relation is also a **foreign key**. A **foreign key** is an attribute, or a collection of attributes, in one relation whose values must match the values of the primary key of some relation. As shown in Figure 4, the values in the City relation's StateAbbrev column match the values in the State relation's StateAbbrev column. Thus, StateAbbrev, the primary key of the State relation, is a foreign key in the City relation. Although the attribute name StateAbbrev is the same in both relations, the names could be different. Most people give the same name to an attribute stored in two or more tables to broadcast clearly they are really the same attribute.

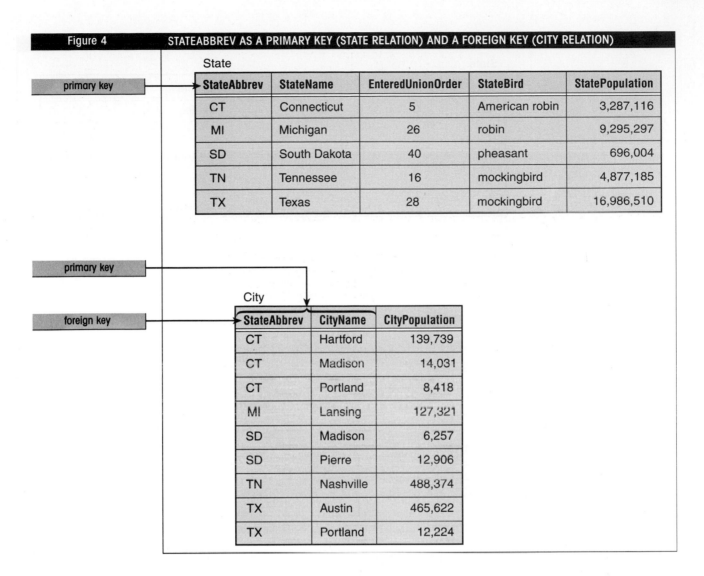

Figure 4	STATEABBREV AS A PRIMARY KEY (STATE RELATION) AND A FOREIGN KEY (CITY RELATION)

State

StateAbbrev	StateName	EnteredUnionOrder	StateBird	StatePopulation
CT	Connecticut	5	American robin	3,287,116
MI	Michigan	26	robin	9,295,297
SD	South Dakota	40	pheasant	696,004
TN	Tennessee	16	mockingbird	4,877,185
TX	Texas	28	mockingbird	16,986,510

primary key

primary key

foreign key

City

StateAbbrev	CityName	CityPopulation
CT	Hartford	139,739
CT	Madison	14,031
CT	Portland	8,418
MI	Lansing	127,321
SD	Madison	6,257
SD	Pierre	12,906
TN	Nashville	488,374
TX	Austin	465,622
TX	Portland	12,224

A **nonkey attribute** is an attribute that is not part of the primary key. In the two relations shown in Figure 4, all attributes are nonkey attributes except StateAbbrev in the State and City relations and CityName in the City relation. *Key* is an ambiguous word because it can refer to a primary, candidate, alternate, or foreign key. When the word key appears alone, however, it means primary key and the definition for a nonkey attribute consequently makes sense.

Relationships

The Capital relation, shown in Figure 5, has one row for each state capital. The CapitalName and StateAbbrev attributes are candidate keys; selecting CapitalName as the primary key makes StateAbbrev an alternate key. The StateAbbrev attribute in the Capital relation is also a foreign key, because its values match the values in the State relation's StateAbbrev column.

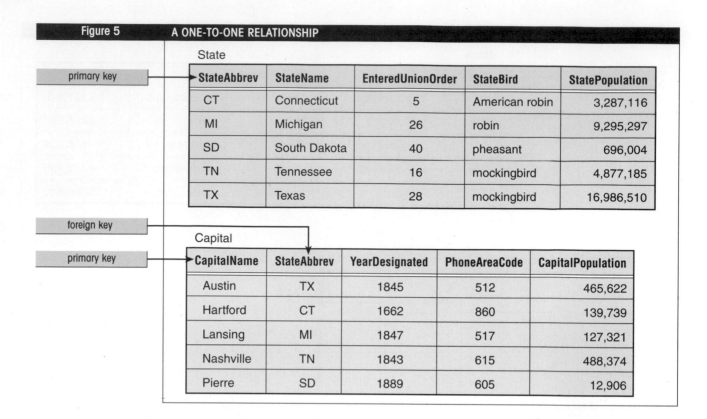

Figure 5   **A ONE-TO-ONE RELATIONSHIP**

State

StateAbbrev	StateName	EnteredUnionOrder	StateBird	StatePopulation
CT	Connecticut	5	American robin	3,287,116
MI	Michigan	26	robin	9,295,297
SD	South Dakota	40	pheasant	696,004
TN	Tennessee	16	mockingbird	4,877,185
TX	Texas	28	mockingbird	16,986,510

Capital

CapitalName	StateAbbrev	YearDesignated	PhoneAreaCode	CapitalPopulation
Austin	TX	1845	512	465,622
Hartford	CT	1662	860	139,739
Lansing	MI	1847	517	127,321
Nashville	TN	1843	615	488,374
Pierre	SD	1889	605	12,906

One-to-One

The State and Capital relations, shown in Figure 5, have a one-to-one relationship. A **one-to-one relationship** (abbreviated 1:1) exists between two relations when each row in one relation has at most one matching row in the other relation. StateAbbrev, which is a foreign key in the Capital relation and the primary key in the State relation, is the common field that ties together the rows of each relation.

Should the State and Capital relations be combined into one relation? Although the two relations in any 1:1 relationship can be combined into one relation, each relation describes different entities and should usually be kept separate.

One-to-Many

The State and City relations, shown once again in Figure 6, have a one-to-many relationship. A **one-to-many relationship** (abbreviated 1:M) exists between two relations when one row in the first relation matches many rows in the second relation and one row in the second relation matches only one row in the first relation. Many can mean zero rows, one row, or two or more rows. StateAbbrev, which is a foreign key in the City relation and the primary key in the State relation, is the common field that ties together the rows of each relation.

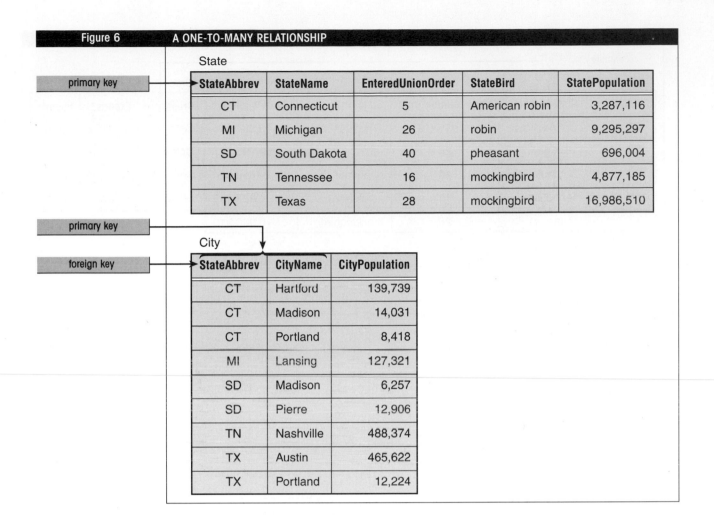

Figure 6   **A ONE-TO-MANY RELATIONSHIP**

State

StateAbbrev	StateName	EnteredUnionOrder	StateBird	StatePopulation
CT	Connecticut	5	American robin	3,287,116
MI	Michigan	26	robin	9,295,297
SD	South Dakota	40	pheasant	696,004
TN	Tennessee	16	mockingbird	4,877,185
TX	Texas	28	mockingbird	16,986,510

City

StateAbbrev	CityName	CityPopulation
CT	Hartford	139,739
CT	Madison	14,031
CT	Portland	8,418
MI	Lansing	127,321
SD	Madison	6,257
SD	Pierre	12,906
TN	Nashville	488,374
TX	Austin	465,622
TX	Portland	12,224

primary key

primary key

foreign key

Many-to-Many

In Figure 7, the State relation with a primary key of StateAbbrev and the Crop relation with a primary key of CropName have a many-to-many relationship. A **many-to-many relationship** (abbreviated as M:N) exists between two relations when one row in the first relation matches many rows in the second relation and one row in the second relation matches many rows in the first relation. In a relational database, you must use a third relation to serve as a bridge between the two M:N relations; the third relation has the primary keys of the M:N relations as its primary key. The original relations now each have a 1:M relationship with the new relation. The StateAbbrev and CropName attributes represent the primary key of the Production relation that is shown in Figure 7. StateAbbrev, which is a foreign key in the Production relation and the primary key in the State relation, is the common field that ties together the rows of the State and Production relations. Likewise, CropName is the common field for the Crop and Production relations.

Figure 7   A MANY-TO-MANY RELATIONSHIP

primary key

State

StateAbbrev	StateName	EnteredUnionOrder	StateBird	StatePopulation
CT	Connecticut	5	American robin	3,287,116
MI	Michigan	26	robin	9,295,297
SD	South Dakota	40	pheasant	696,004
TN	Tennessee	16	mockingbird	4,877,185
TX	Texas	28	mockingbird	16,986,510

Crop

CropName	Exports	Imports
Corn	$4,965.8	$68.5
Cotton	$2,014.6	$11.4
Soybeans	$4,462.8	$15.8
Wheat	$4,503.2	$191.1

primary key

foreign key

Production

StateAbbrev	CropName	Quantity
MI	Corn	241,500
MI	Soybeans	47,520
MI	Wheat	35,280
SD	Corn	377,200
SD	Soybeans	63,000
SD	Wheat	119,590
TN	Corn	79,360
TN	Soybeans	33,250
TN	Wheat	13,440
TX	Corn	202,500
TX	Cotton	3,322
TX	Soybeans	12,870
TX	Wheat	129,200

Entity Subtype

Figure 8 shows a special type of one-to-one relationship. The Shipping relation's primary key is StateAbbrev and contains one row for each state having an ocean shoreline. Because not all states have an ocean shoreline, the Shipping relation has fewer rows than the State relation. However, each row in the Shipping relation has a matching row in the State relation with StateAbbrev serving as the common field; StateAbbrev is the primary key in the State relation and is a foreign key in the Shipping relation.

| Figure 8 | AN ENTITY SUBTYPE |

State

StateAbbrev	State Name	EnteredUnionOrder	StateBird	StatePopulation
CT	Connecticut	5	American robin	3,287,116
MI	Michigan	26	robin	9,295,297
SD	South Dakota	40	pheasant	696,004
TN	Tennessee	16	mockingbird	4,877,185
TX	Texas	28	mockingbird	16,986,510

primary key →

Shipping

StateAbbrev	OceanShoreline	ExportTonnage	ImportTonnage
CT	618	3,377,466	2,118,494
TX	3,359	45,980,912	109,400,314

primary key →
foreign key →

The Shipping relation, in this situation, is called an **entity subtype**, a relation whose primary key is a foreign key to a second relation and whose attributes are additional attributes for the second relation. You can create an entity subtype when a relation has attributes that could have null values. A **null value** is the absence of a value. A null value is not blank, nor zero, nor any other value. You give a null value to an attribute when you do not know its value or when a value does not apply. For example, instead of using the Shipping relation, you could store the OceanShoreline, ExportTonnage, and ImportTonnage attributes in the State relation and allow them to be null for states not having an ocean shoreline. You should be aware that database experts are currently debating the validity of the use of nulls in relational databases and many experts insist that you should never use nulls. Part of this warning against nulls is based on the inconsistent way different relational DBMSs treat nulls and part is due to the lack of a firm theoretical foundation for how to use nulls. In any case, entity subtypes are an alternative to the use of nulls.

Entity-Relationship Diagrams

A common shorthand method for describing relations is to write the relation name followed by its attributes in parentheses, underlining the attributes that represent the primary key and identifying the foreign keys for a relation immediately after the relation. Using this method, the relations that appear in Figures 5 through 8 are described in the following way:

State (StateAbbrev, StateName, EnteredUnionOrder, StateBird, StatePopulation)
Capital (CapitalName, StateAbbrev, YearDesignated, PhoneAreaCode,
    CapitalPopulation)
    Foreign key: StateAbbrev to State relation
City (StateAbbrev, CityName, CityPopulation)
    Foreign key: StateAbbrev to State relation
Crop (CropName, Exports, Imports)

Production (<u>StateAbbrev</u>, <u>CropName</u>, Quantity)
    Foreign key: StateAbbrev to State relation
    Foreign key: CropName to Crop relation
Shipping (<u>StateAbbrev</u>, OceanShoreline, ExportTonnage, ImportTonnage)
    Foreign key: StateAbbrev to State relation

Another popular way to describe relations *and their relationships* is with entity-relationship diagrams. An **entity-relationship diagram (ERD)** shows a database's entities and the relationships among the entities in a symbolic, visual way. In an entity-relationship diagram, an entity and a relation are equivalent. Figure 9 shows an entity-relationship diagram for the relations that appear in Figures 5 through 8.

Figure 9	AN ENTITY-RELATIONSHIP DIAGRAM

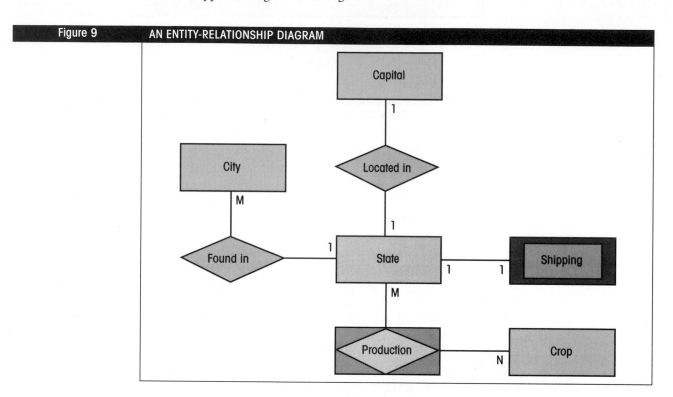

Entity-relationship diagrams have the following characteristics:

- Entities, or relations, appear in rectangles and relationships appear in diamonds. The entity name appears inside the rectangle and a verb describing the relationship appears inside the diamond. For example, the City rectangle is connected to the State rectangle by the Found in diamond and is read: "a city is found in a state."

- The 1 by the State entity and the M by the City entity identify a 1:M relationship between these two entities. In a similar manner, an M:N relationship exists between the State and Crop entities and 1:1 relationships exist between the State and Capital entities and between the State and Shipping entities.

- A diamond inside a rectangle defines a composite entity. A **composite entity** is a relationship that has the characteristics of an entity. For example, Production connects the State and Crop entities in an M:N relationship and acts as an entity by containing the Quantity attribute, along with the composite key of the StateAbbrev and CropName attributes.

■ An entity subtype, for example, Shipping, appears in a double rectangle and is connected without an intervening diamond directly to its related entity, for example, State.

You can also show attributes in an ERD by placing each individual attribute in a bubble connected to its entity or relationship. However, typical ERDs have large numbers of entities and relationships, so including the attributes might confuse rather than clarify the ERD.

Integrity Constraints

A database has **integrity** if its data follows certain rules, known as **integrity constraints**. The ideal is to have the DBMS enforce all integrity constraints. If a DBMS can enforce some integrity constraints but not others, the other integrity constraints must be enforced by other programs or by the people who use the DBMS. Integrity constraints can be divided into three groups: primary key constraints, referential integrity, and domain integrity constraints.

■ One primary key constraint is inherent in the definition of a primary key, which says that the primary key must be unique. The **entity integrity constraint** says that the primary key cannot be null. For a composite key, none of the individual attributes can be null. The uniqueness and nonnull properties of a primary key ensure that you can reference any data value in a database by supplying its table name, attribute name, and primary key value.

■ Foreign keys provide the mechanism for forming a relationship between two tables, and referential integrity ensures that only valid relationships exist. **Referential integrity** is the constraint specifying that each nonnull foreign key must match a primary key value in the related relation. Specifically, referential integrity means that you cannot add a row with an unmatched foreign key value. Referential integrity also means that you cannot change or delete the related primary key value and leave the foreign key orphaned. In some relational DBMSs, if you try to change or delete a primary key value, you can specify one of these options: restricted, cascades, or nullifies. If you specify **restricted**, the DBMS updates or deletes the value only if there are no matching foreign key values. If you choose **cascades** and then change a primary key value, the DBMS changes the matching foreign keys to the new primary key value, or, if you delete a primary key value, the DBMS also deletes the matching foreign-key rows. If you choose **nullifies** and then change or delete a primary key value, the DBMS sets all matching foreign keys to null.

■ A domain is a set of values from which one or more columns draw their actual values. **Domain integrity constraints** are the rules you specify for an attribute. By choosing a data type for an attribute, you impose a constraint on the set of values allowed for the attribute. You can create specific validation rules for an attribute to limit its domain further. As you make an attribute's domain definition more precise, you exclude more and more unacceptable values for an attribute. For example, in the State relation you could define the domain for the EnteredUnionOrder attribute to be a unique integer between 1 and 50 and the domain for the StateBird attribute to be any name containing 25 or fewer characters.

Dependencies and Determinants

Relations are related to other relations. Attributes are also related to other attributes. Consider the StateCrop relation shown in Figure 10. Its description is:

StateCrop (StateAbbrev, CropName, StateBird, BirdScientificName, StatePopulation, Exports, Quantity)

| Figure 10 | A RELATION COMBINING SEVERAL ATTRIBUTES FROM OTHER RELATIONS |

null value

primary key

StateCrop

StateAbbrev	CropName	StateBird	BirdScientificName	StatePopulation	Export	Quantity
CT	Corn	American robin	Planesticus migratorius	3,287,116	$4,965.8	
MI	Corn	robin	Planesticus migratorius	9,295,297	$4,965.8	241,500
MI	Soybeans	robin	Planesticus migratorius	9,295,297	$4,462.8	47,520
MI	Wheat	robin	Planesticus migratorius	9,295,297	$4,503.2	35,280
SD	Corn	pheasant	Phasianus colchicus	696,004	$4,965.8	277,200
SD	Soybeans	pheasant	Phasianus colchicus	696,004	$4,462.8	63,000
SD	Wheat	pheasant	Phasianus colchicus	696,004	$4,503.2	119,590
TN	Corn	mockingbird	Mimus polyglottos	4,977,185	$4,965.8	79,360
TN	Soybeans	mockingbird	Mimus polyglottos	4,977,185	$4,462.8	33,250
TN	Wheat	mockingbird	Mimus polyglottos	4,977,185	$4,503.2	13,440
TX	Corn	mockingbird	Mimus polyglottos	16,986,510	$4,965.8	202,500
TX	Cotton	mockingbird	Mimus polyglottos	16,986,510	$2,014.6	3,322
TX	Soybeans	mockingbird	Mimus polyglottos	16,986,510	$4,462.8	12,870
TX	Wheat	mockingbird	Mimus polyglottos	16,986,510	$4,503.2	129,200

The StateCrop relation combines several attributes from the State, Crop, and Production relations that appeared in Figure 7. The StateAbbrev, StateBird, and StatePopulation attributes are from the State relation. The CropName and Exports attributes are from the Crop relation. The StateAbbrev, CropName, and Quantity attributes are from the Production relation. The BirdScientificName attribute is a new attribute for the StateCrop relation, whose primary key is the combination of the StateAbbrev and CropName attributes.

Notice the null value in the Quantity attribute for the state of Connecticut (StateAbbrev CT). If you look back to Figure 7, you can see that there were no entries for Quantity for the state of Connecticut, which is why Quantity is null in the StateCrop table. However, note that CropName requires an entry because it is part of the composite key for the relation. If you want the state of CT to be in the relation, you need to assign a dummy CropName for the CT entry, in this case, Corn.

In the StateCrop relation, each attribute is related to other attributes. For example, a value for StateAbbrev determines the value of StatePopulation, and a value for StatePopulation depends on the value of StateAbbrev. In database discussions, the word functionally is used, as in: "StateAbbrev functionally determines StatePopulation" and

"StatePopulation is functionally dependent on StateAbbrev." In this case, StateAbbrev is called a determinant. A **determinant** is an attribute, or a collection of attributes, whose values determine the values of another attribute. We also state that an attribute is functionally dependent on another attribute (or collection of attributes) if that other attribute is a determinant for it.

You can graphically show a relation's functional dependencies and determinants in a bubble diagram. Bubble diagrams are also called data model diagrams and functional dependency diagrams. Figure 11 shows the bubble diagram for the StateCrop relation.

Figure 11	A BUBBLE DIAGRAM FOR THE STATECROP RELATION

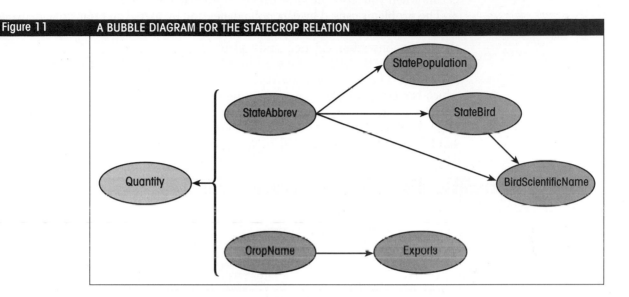

- StateAbbrev is a determinant for StatePopulation, StateBird, and BirdScientificName.
- CropName is a determinant for Exports.
- Quantity is functionally dependent on StateAbbrev and CropName together.
- StateBird is a determinant for BirdScientificName.

Only Quantity is functionally dependent on the relation's full primary key, StateAbbrev and CropName. StatePopulation, StateBird, and BirdScientificName have partial dependencies, because they are functionally dependent on StateAbbrev, which is part of the primary key. A **partial dependency** is a functional dependency on part of the primary key, instead of the entire primary key. Does another partial dependency exist in the StateCrop relation? Yes, Exports has a partial dependency on CropName.

Because StateAbbrev is a determinant of both StateBird and BirdScientificName, and StateBird is a determinant of BirdScientificName, StateBird and BirdScientificName have a transitive dependency. A **transitive dependency** is a functional dependency between two nonkey attributes, which are both dependent on a third attribute.

How do you know which functional dependencies exist among a collection of attributes, and how do you recognize partial and transitive dependencies? The answers lie with the questions you ask as you gather the requirements for a database application. For each attribute and entity, you must gain an accurate understanding of its meaning and relationships in the context of the application. **Semantic object modeling** is an entire area of study within the database field devoted to the meanings and relationships of data.

Anomalies

When you use a DBMS, you are more likely to get results you can trust if you create your relations carefully. For example, problems might occur with relations that have partial and transitive dependencies, whereas you won't have as much trouble if you ensure that your relations include only attributes that are directly related to each other. Also, when you remove data redundancy from a relation, you improve that relation. **Data redundancy** occurs when you store the same data in more than one place.

The problems caused by data redundancy and by partial and transitive dependencies are called **anomalies**, because they are undesirable irregularities of relations. Anomalies are of three types: insertion, deletion, and update.

To examine the effects of these anomalies, consider the Client relation that is shown in Figure 12. The Client relation represents part of the database for Pet Sitters Unlimited, which is a company providing pet-sitting services for homeowners while they are on vacation. Pet Sitters Unlimited keeps track of the data about its clients and the clients' children, pets, and vets. The attributes for the Client relation include the composite key ClientID and ChildName, along with ClientName, VetID, and VetName.

Figure 12	THE CLIENT RELATION WITH INSERTION, DELETION, AND UPDATE ANOMALIES

primary key

Client

ClientID	ChildName	ClientName	VetID	VetName
2173	Ryan	Barbara Hennessey	27	Pet Vet
4519	Pat	Vernon Noordsy	31	Pet Care
4519	Dana	Vernon Noordsy	31	Pet Care
8005	Dana	Sandra Amidon	27	Pet Vet
8005	Dani	Sandra Amidon	27	Pet Vet
8112	Pat	Helen Wandzell	24	Pets R Us

- An **insertion anomaly** occurs when you cannot add a row to a relation because you do not know the entire primary key value. For example, you cannot add the new client Cathy Corbett with a ClientID of 3322 to the Client relation when you do not know her children's names. Entity integrity prevents you from leaving any part of a primary key null. Because ChildName is part of the primary key, you cannot leave it null. To add the new client, your only option is to make up a ChildName, even if the client does not have children. This solution misrepresents the facts and is unacceptable, if a better approach is available.

- A **deletion anomaly** occurs when you delete data from a relation and unintentionally lose other critical data. For example, if you delete ClientID 8112 because Helen Wandzell is no longer a client, you also lose the only instance of VetID 24 in the database. Thus, you no longer know that VetID 24 is Pets R Us.

- An **update anomaly** occurs when you change one attribute value and either the DBMS must make more than one change to the database or else the database ends up containing inconsistent data. For example, if you change the ClientName, VetID, or VetName for ClientID 4519, the DBMS must change multiple rows of the Client relation. If the DBMS fails to change all the rows, the ClientName, VetID, or VetName now has two different values in the database and is inconsistent.

Normalization

Database design is the process of determining the precise relations needed for a given collection of attributes and placing those attributes into the correct relations. Crucial to good database design is understanding the functional dependencies of all attributes; recognizing the anomalies caused by data redundancy, partial dependencies, and transitive dependencies when they exist; and knowing how to eliminate the anomalies.

The process of identifying and eliminating anomalies is called **normalization**. Using normalization, you start with a collection of relations, apply sets of rules to eliminate anomalies, and produce a new collection of problem-free relations. The sets of rules are called **normal forms**. Of special interest for our purposes are the first three normal forms: first normal form, second normal form, and third normal form. First normal form improves the design of your relations, second normal form improves the first normal form design, and third normal form applies even more stringent rules to produce an even better design.

First Normal Form

Consider the Client relation shown in Figure 13. For each client, the relation contains ClientID, which is the primary key; the client's name and children's names; the ID and name of the client's vet; and the ID, name, and type of each client's pets. For example, Barbara Hennessey has no children and three pets, Vernon Noordsy has two children and one pet, Sandra Amidon has two children and two pets, and Helen Wandzell has one child and one pet. Because each entry in a relation must contain a single value, the structure shown in Figure 13 does not meet the requirements for a relation, therefore it is called an **unnormalized relation**. ChildName, which can have more than one value, is called a **repeating group**. The set of attributes that includes PetID, PetName, and PetType is a second repeating group in the structure.

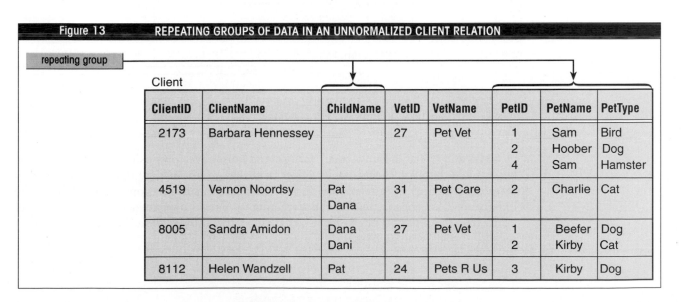

Figure 13   REPEATING GROUPS OF DATA IN AN UNNORMALIZED CLIENT RELATION

repeating group

Client

ClientID	ClientName	ChildName	VetID	VetName	PetID	PetName	PetType
2173	Barbara Hennessey		27	Pet Vet	1 2 4	Sam Hoober Sam	Bird Dog Hamster
4519	Vernon Noordsy	Pat Dana	31	Pet Care	2	Charlie	Cat
8005	Sandra Amidon	Dana Dani	27	Pet Vet	1 2	Beefer Kirby	Dog Cat
8112	Helen Wandzell	Pat	24	Pets R Us	3	Kirby	Dog

First normal form addresses this repeating-group situation. A relation is in **first normal form (1NF)** if it does not contain repeating groups. To remove a repeating group and convert to first normal form, you expand the primary key to include the primary key of the repeating group. You must perform this step carefully, however. If the unnormalized relation has independent repeating groups, you must perform the conversion step separately for each.

The repeating group of ChildName is independent from the repeating group of PetID, PetName, and PetType. That is, the number and names of a client's children are independent of the number, names, and types of a client's pets. Performing the conversion step to each independent repeating group produces the two 1NF relations shown in Figure 14.

Figure 14   AFTER CONVERSION TO 1NF

primary key

Child

ClientID	ChildName	ClientName	VetID	VetName
4519	Pat	Vernon Noordsy	31	Pet Care
4519	Dana	Vernon Noordsy	31	Pet Care
8005	Dana	Sandra Amidon	27	Pet Vet
8005	Dani	Sandra Amidon	27	Pet Vet
8112	Pat	Helen Wandzell	24	Pets R Us

primary key

Client

ClientID	PetID	ClientName	VetID	VetName	PetName	PetType
2173	1	Barbara Hennessey	27	Pet Vet	Sam	Bird
2173	2	Barbara Hennessey	27	Pet Vet	Hoober	Dog
2173	4	Barbara Hennessey	27	Pet Vet	Sam	Hamster
4519	2	Vernon Noordsy	31	Pet Care	Charlie	Cat
8005	1	Sandra Amidon	27	Pet Vet	Beefer	Dog
8005	2	Sandra Amidon	27	Pet Vet	Kirby	Cat
8112	3	Helen Wandzell	24	Pets R Us	Kirby	Dog

The alternative way to describe the 1NF relations is:

Child (<u>ClientID</u>, <u>ChildName</u>, ClientName, VetID, VetName)
Client (<u>ClientID</u>, <u>PetID</u>, ClientName, VetID, VetName, PetName, PetType)

Child and Client are now true relations and both have composite keys. Both relations, however, suffer from insertion, deletion, and update anomalies. (Find examples of the three anomalies in both relations.) In the Child and Client relations, ClientID is a determinant for ClientName, VetID, and VetName, so partial dependencies exist in both relations. It is these partial dependencies that cause the anomalies in the two relations, and second normal form addresses the partial-dependency problem.

Second Normal Form

A relation in 1NF is in **second normal form (2NF)** if it does not contain any partial dependencies. To remove partial dependencies from a relation and convert it to second normal form, you perform two steps. First, identify the functional dependencies for every attribute in the relation. Second, if necessary, create new relations and place each attribute in a relation, so that the attribute is functionally dependent on the entire primary key. If you need to create new relations, restrict them to ones with a primary key that is a subset of the original composite key. Note that partial dependencies occur only when you have a composite key; a relation in first normal form with a single-attribute primary key is automatically in second normal form.

Figure 15 shows the functional dependencies for the 1NF Child and Client relations.

Figure 15	A BUBBLE DIAGRAM FOR THE 1NF CHILD AND THE CLIENT RELATIONS

ClientID is a determinant for ClientName, VetID, and VetName in both relations. The composite key ClientID and PetID is a determinant for PetName and PetType. ChildName is not a determinant, nor is PetID. Is the composite key of ClientID and ChildName a determinant? No, it is not a determinant. What happens, however, if you do not have a relation with this composite key? You lose the names of the children of each client. You need to retain this composite key in a relation to preserve the important 1:M attribute relationship between ClientID and ChildName. Performing the second conversion step produces the three 2NF relations shown in Figure 16.

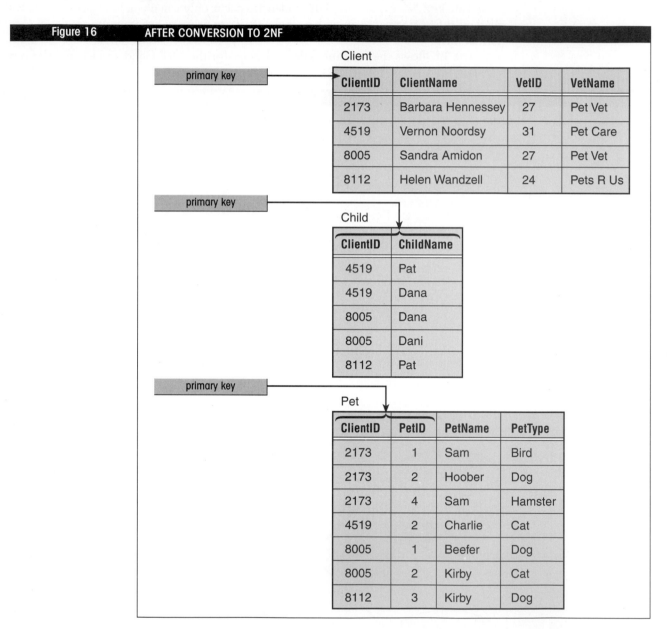

Figure 16   AFTER CONVERSION TO 2NF

Client

primary key

ClientID	ClientName	VetID	VetName
2173	Barbara Hennessey	27	Pet Vet
4519	Vernon Noordsy	31	Pet Care
8005	Sandra Amidon	27	Pet Vet
8112	Helen Wandzell	24	Pets R Us

primary key

Child

ClientID	ChildName
4519	Pat
4519	Dana
8005	Dana
8005	Dani
8112	Pat

primary key

Pet

ClientID	PetID	PetName	PetType
2173	1	Sam	Bird
2173	2	Hoober	Dog
2173	4	Sam	Hamster
4519	2	Charlie	Cat
8005	1	Beefer	Dog
8005	2	Kirby	Cat
8112	3	Kirby	Dog

The alternative way to describe the 2NF relations is:

Client (<u>ClientID</u>, ClientName, VetID, VetName)
Child (<u>ClientID</u>, <u>ChildName</u>)
    Foreign key: ClientID to Client relation
Pet (<u>ClientID</u>, <u>PetID</u>, PetName, PetType)
    Foreign key: ClientID to Client relation

All three relations are in second normal form. Do anomalies still exist? The Child and Pet relations show no anomalies, but Client suffers from anomalies caused by the transitive dependency between VetID and VetName. (Find examples of the three anomalies caused by the transitive dependency.) You can see the transitive dependency in the bubble diagram shown in Figure 15; VetID is a determinant for VetName and ClientID is a determinant for VetID and VetName. Third normal form addresses the transitive-dependency problem.

Third Normal Form

A relation in 2NF is in **third normal form (3NF)** if every determinant is a candidate key. This definition for 3NF is referred to as **Boyce-Codd normal form (BCNF)** and is an improvement over the original version of 3NF.

To convert a relation to third normal form, remove the attributes that depend on the non-candidate-key determinant and place them into a new relation with the determinant as the primary key. For the Client relation, you remove VetName from the relation, create a new Vet relation, place VetName in the Vet relation, and then make VetID the primary key of the Vet relation. Note that only VetName is removed from the Client relation; VetID remains as a foreign key in the Client relation. Figure 17 shows the database design for the four 3NF relations.

Figure 17	AFTER CONVERSION TO 3NF

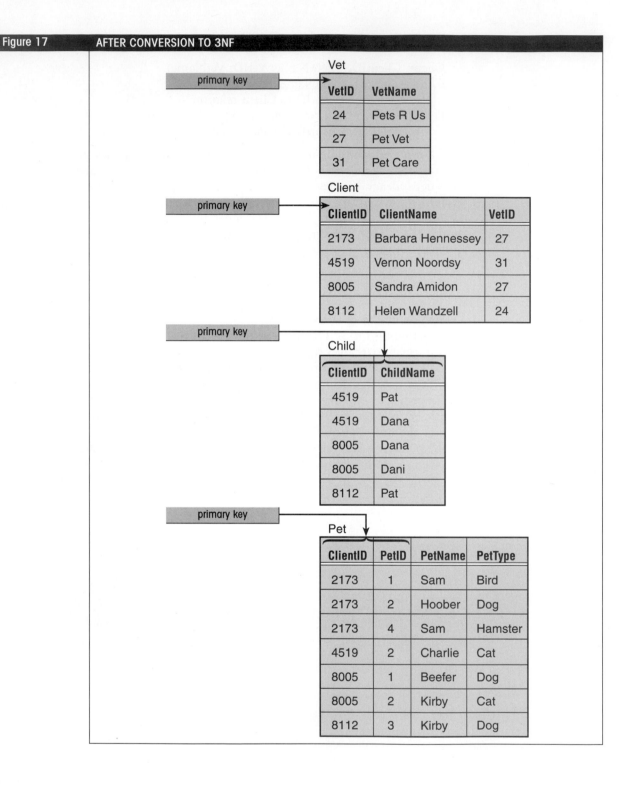

Vet

primary key →

VetID	VetName
24	Pets R Us
27	Pet Vet
31	Pet Care

Client

primary key →

ClientID	ClientName	VetID
2173	Barbara Hennessey	27
4519	Vernon Noordsy	31
8005	Sandra Amidon	27
8112	Helen Wandzell	24

primary key →

Child

ClientID	ChildName
4519	Pat
4519	Dana
8005	Dana
8005	Dani
8112	Pat

primary key →

Pet

ClientID	PetID	PetName	PetType
2173	1	Sam	Bird
2173	2	Hoober	Dog
2173	4	Sam	Hamster
4519	2	Charlie	Cat
8005	1	Beefer	Dog
8005	2	Kirby	Cat
8112	3	Kirby	Dog

The alternative way to describe the 3NF relations is:

Vet (<u>VetID</u>, VetName)
Client (<u>ClientID</u>, ClientName, VetID)
    Foreign key: VetID to Vet relation
Child (<u>ClientID</u>, <u>ChildName</u>)
    Foreign key: ClientID to Client relation
Pet (<u>ClientID</u>, <u>PetID</u>, PetName, PetType)
    Foreign key: ClientID to Client relation

The four relations have no anomalies, because you have eliminated all the data redundancy, partial dependencies, and transitive dependencies. Normalization provides the framework for eliminating anomalies and delivering an optimal database design, which you should always strive to achieve. You should be aware, however, that experts often denormalize relations to improve database performance—specifically, to decrease the time it takes the database to respond to a user's commands and requests. When you denormalize a relation, you reintroduce redundancy to the relation. At the same time, you reintroduce anomalies. Thus, improving performance exposes a database to potential integrity problems. Only database experts should denormalize relations, but even experts first complete the normalization of their relations.

REVIEW QUESTIONS

1. What are the formal names for a table, for a row, and for a column?

2. What is a domain?

3. What is an entity?

4. What is the relationship between a primary key and a candidate key?

5. What is a composite key?

6. What is a foreign key?

Explore

7. Look for an example of a one-to-one relationship, an example of a one-to-many relationship, and an example of a many-to-many relationship in a newspaper, magazine, book, or everyday situation you encounter. For each one, name the entities and select the primary and foreign keys.

8. When do you use an entity subtype?

9. What is a composite entity in an entity-relationship diagram?

10. What is the entity integrity constraint?

11. What is referential integrity?

12. What does the cascades option, which is used with referential integrity, accomplish?

13. What are partial and transitive dependencies?

14. What three types of anomalies can be exhibited by a relation, and what problems do they cause?

15. Figure 18 shows the Vet, Client, and Child relations with primary keys VetID, ClientID, and both ClientID and ChildName, respectively. Which two integrity constraints do these relations violate and why?

Figure 18

Vet

VetID	VetName
24	Pets R Us
27	Pet Vet
31	Pet Care

Client

ClientID	ClientName	VetID
2173	Barbara Hennessey	27
4519	Vernon Noordsy	31
8005	Sandra Amidon	37
8112	Helen Wandzell	24

Child

ClientID	ChildName
4519	Pat
4519	Dana
8005	
8005	Dani
8112	Pat

16. The State and Capital relations, shown in Figure 5, are described as follows:

    State (StateAbbrev, StateName, EnteredUnionOrder, StateBird,
        StatePopulation)
    Capital (CapitalName, StateAbbrev, YearDesignated, PhoneAreaCode,
        CapitalPopulation)
        Foreign key: StateAbbrev to State relation

    Add the attribute CountyName for the county or counties containing the state capital
    to this database, justify where you placed it (that is, in an existing relation or in a new
    one), and draw the entity–relationship diagram for all the entities. The counties for the
    state capitals shown in Figure 5 are Travis and Williamson counties for Austin TX;
    Hartford county for Hartford CT; Clinton, Eaton, and Ingham counties for Lansing
    MI; Davidson county for Nashville TN; Hughes county for Pierre SD.

17. Suppose you have a relation for a dance studio. The attributes are dancer's identification
    number, dancer's name, dancer's address, dancer's telephone number, class identification
    number, day that the class meets, time that the class meets, instructor name, and
    instructor identification number. Assume that each dancer takes one class, each class
    meets only once a week and has one instructor, and each instructor can teach more than
    one class. In what normal form is the relation currently, given the following shorthand
    description?

    Dancer (DancerID, DancerName, DancerAddr, DancerPhone, ClassID, ClassDay,
    ClassTime, InstrName, InstrID)
    Convert this relation to 3NF and then draw an entity–relationship diagram for this
    database.

18. Store the following attributes for a library database: AuthorCode, AuthorName,
    BookTitle, BorrowerAddress, BorrowerName, BorrowerCard Number,
    CopiesOfBook, ISBN (International Standard Book Number), LoanDate,
    PublisherCode, PublisherName, and PublisherAddress. A one-to-many relationship
    exists between publishers and books. Many-to-many relationships exist between
    authors and books and between borrowers and books.

    a. Name the entities for the library database.
    b. Create the relations for the library database and describe them using the shorthand method.
       Be sure the relations are in third normal form.
    c. Draw an entity–relationship diagram for the library database.

ADDITIONAL ACCESS PROJECTS

Inventory for Global Crafts

Global Crafts is a non-profit organization based in Montreal that sells crafts made by artisans all over the world. The profits from the sales are invested back into the artisans' communities to be used to build schools and hospitals, finance agricultural projects, and operate social programs. You are in charge of monitoring the inventory levels and placing orders with the suppliers who work directly with the artisans to distribute their products. For this project, you will create a small database consisting of a Products table that contains 15 records and a Suppliers table that contains four records. Your principal goal in this project is to find out which products you need to order and the supplier you need to contact to place the order. Four activities are required to build an inventory database for Global Crafts and then produce a list of the products to order.

Project Activities

Set Up Products Table

The Products table shown in Figure P1-1 lists 15 of the products sold by Global Crafts. This table consists of seven fields, including a field for Units in Stock. You will use the Table Wizard to create the Products table.

Set Up Suppliers Table

The Suppliers table lists the four suppliers who obtain the products from the artisans and then ship them to Global Crafts. You will use the Form Wizard to enter the data required for the Suppliers table. Figure P1-2 shows a form created to enter the data for one of the suppliers.

Create Queries

You will create queries to find information listed in the Products table and Suppliers table of the Global Crafts database. You will be most concerned with the data entered in the Units in Stock field.

Format and Print an Order Report

You will create a query that lists all the products that you need to order, along with the distributors you need to contact. You will then create and format a report that presents this information in an easy-to-read and attractive format. Figure P1-3 shows the Order report you will create.

Clues to Use

Database Design

A "real" database for a viable company such as Global Crafts would, of course, contain considerably more records because the company would need to sell more than 15 products to stay in business. However, the number of products has been reduced to minimize the amount of time you need to spend entering data.

FIGURE P1-1: Datasheet View of Products table for Global Crafts Database

Field names

Records

FIGURE P1-2: Form for Supplier 1

FIGURE P1-3: Completed Order report

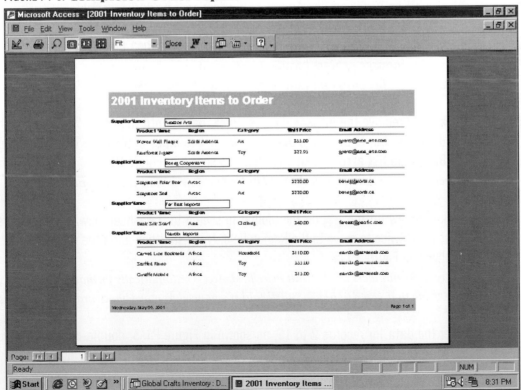

activity:

Set Up Products Table

You first need to enter the data required for the Products table.

steps:

1. Start Access, click the **Blank Access database option button** in the Microsoft Access dialog box, click **OK**, find the directory containing your disk (if necessary), type **Global Crafts Inventory** in the File name box, then click **Create**

2. Double-click **Create table by using wizard**

   You could go directly to a blank datasheet; however, the Table Wizard automatically enters selected fields into your table, thereby saving you time.

3. Click **Products** in the Sample Tables list box, make sure **ProductID** is selected in the **Sample Fields** list box, then click the **Select Single Field button** [>]

   The ProductID field appears in the "Fields in my new table" list box.

4. Click [>] to select **ProductName**, click **CategoryID**, click [>], click **Rename Field** under the Fields in my new table list box, type **Region**, click **OK**, then select the following fields: **SupplierID**, **UnitsInStock**, and **UnitPrice**

   If you select the wrong field, click the Remove Single Field button [<] to return the field to the Sample Fields list.

5. Click **Next**, type **Global Crafts Products** for the table name, accept the default to let the Wizard set a primary key, click **Next**, accept the default to enter data directly into the table, then click **Finish**

   The Datasheet View appears. At present, no data appears in the six fields.

6. Press [Tab], type **Jade Earrings**, press [Tab], type **Asia**, then press [Tab]

   A warning message appears because you have entered the wrong kind of data into the Region field. Originally this field was called CategoryID, which Access formats as a field that contains only numbers.

7. Click **OK** to remove the message, press [**Backspace**] until you erase "Asia," click the **View button** [ ] on the toolbar to switch to Design View, click **Number** in the Data Type column for Region, click the **Data Type list arrow**, then click **Text**, as shown in Figure P1-4

   You changed the data type of the field in Design view so that you can enter text data.

8. Click the **View button** [ ] on the toolbar to switch to Datasheet View, click **Yes** to save the table, press [**Tab**] twice to move to the Region field, type **Asia**, then enter the remaining data for Record 1, as shown in Figure P1-5

   Just type the numbers for the Unit Price field. Access automatically formats the number in the Currency style. Note that you can press [Shift][Tab] if you need to move backwards to a previous cell.

9. Enter the data for records 2 to 15, as shown in Figure P1-5, double-click on each column divider to resize the columns, click **File** on the menu bar, click **Close**, then click **Yes** if a Save message appears

   You can also click the Close button that appears at the top right corner of the Datasheet window.

FIGURE P1-4: Design View of the Products table

View button

Primary Key field

Region field

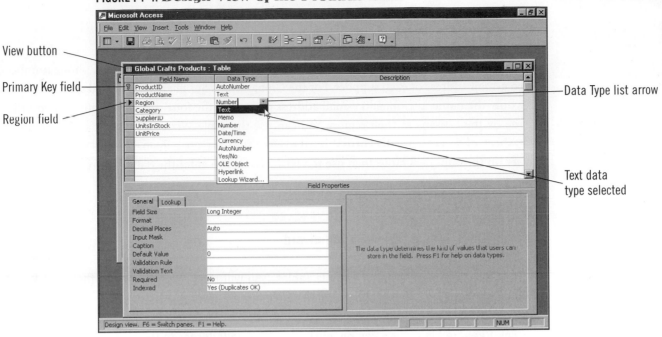

Data Type list arrow

Text data type selected

FIGURE P1-5: Data for records 1 to 15

Data for record 1

Unit price field formatted automatically as Currency

To adjust column width, position ←||→ between the field names, then double-click

activity:

Set Up Suppliers Table

The Suppliers table you created for a "real" business would include the address, phone numbers, and even e-mail address of each supplier. For the Global Crafts Suppliers table, you'll save time by including only the name, region, and e-mail address of each of the four suppliers who send you the crafts made by the artisans in their region. You can use the Table Wizard to enter data for a table into a datasheet, or you can use the Form Wizard to enter the data into a form. You will use the Table Wizard to set up the Suppliers table, then use the Form Wizard to enter the data required.

steps:

1. Double-click **Create table by using wizard**

2. Click **Suppliers** in the list of Sample Tables (you will need to scroll down), then add **SupplierID**, **SupplierName**, and **ContactName** to the Fields in my new table list box

3. Click **Rename Field**, type **Region**, click **OK**, add **EmailAddress** to the table, click **Next**, type **Global Crafts Suppliers**, then click **Next**

Access asks you if your new table is related to any other tables in your current database. Tables that contain at least one common field can be related. Both the Products table and the Suppliers table contain two common fields: Region and SupplierID.

4. Click **Relationships**, click **One record in the 'Global Crafts Suppliers' table**, as shown in Figure P1-6, click **OK**, click **Next**, check that the **Enter data directly into the table option button** is selected, then click **Finish**

In a few moments the Datasheet view of the Suppliers table appears.

5. Click **File** on the menu bar, click **Close**, click **Forms** in the Database window, then double-click **Create form by using wizard**

6. Click the **Tables/Queries list arrow**, click **Table: Global Crafts Suppliers**, click the **Select All Fields button** >> , click **Next**, click **Next** to accept the **Columnar** layout, click **Ricepaper**, click **Next**, make sure the **Open the form to view or enter information option button** is selected, then click **Finish**

In a few seconds a blank form appears.

7. Press [**Tab**], type **Far East Imports** for the Supplier Name, press [**Tab**], type **Asia**, press [**Tab**], type **fareast@pacific.com**, then press [**Tab**] twice to move to the Supplier Name field in form 2

8. Enter the data for the next three forms, as shown in Figures P1-7, P1-8, and P1-9

9. Close the last form

You can now view the data for the Global Crafts Suppliers in both individual forms and in a datasheet.

FIGURE P1-6: **Relationships dialog box**

Click here ———

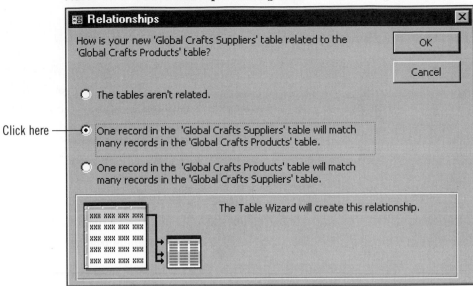

FIGURE P1-7: **Data for Supplier 2**

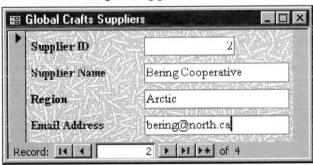

FIGURE P1-8: **Data for Supplier 3**

FIGURE P1-9: **Data for Supplier 4**

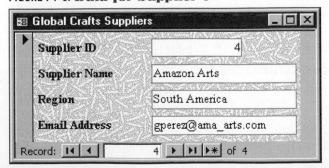

activity:

Create Queries

Now that you've set up the two tables for the Global Crafts database, you will ask three questions, called **queries** in database language. These queries relate to specific actions you wish to perform using the data stored in the two tables. First you want to make a quick count of the products made in Asia. The fastest method of obtaining this information is to use the Filter tool in the Datasheet view of the Global Crafts Products table.

steps:

1. Click **Tables** in the Database window, double-click **Global Crafts Products** to open it, click the first **Asia** entry in the Region field, then click the **Filter By Selection button** ▧ on the Standard toolbar
   As you can see, four of the products are made in Asia.

2. Click the **Remove Filter button** ▽

3. Click the **View button** ▨ on the toolbar to switch to Design View, click the row selector to the left of SupplierID, **right-click** the mouse, click **Insert Rows**, click the blank **Field Name cell**, type **Category**, then press **[Tab]**
   The default data type is Text, which is fine in this case. You can always add new fields to a table just by working in Design View.

4. Click the **View button** ▦ on the toolbar to switch to Datasheet View, click **Yes** to save the table, enter the category for each product, as shown in Figure P1-10, click **File** on the menu bar, then click **Close**

5. Click **Queries** in the Database window, double-click **Create query by using wizard**, click the **Table/Queries list arrow**, click **Table: Global Crafts Products**, click the **Select All Fields button** ⟩⟩ to select all the fields in the Global Crafts Products table, click **Next**, click **Next** to accept a Detail query, click the **Modify the query design option button**, then click **Finish**
   The design grid appears.

6. As shown in Figure P1-11, click the **Region Criteria cell**, type **Africa**, click the **Category Criteria cell**, type **Toy**, then click the **Run button** ▯
   Two of the products from Africa are toys — the Stuffed Rhino and the Giraffe Mobile.

7. Click **File** on the menu bar, click **Close**, then click **No**
   You don't save the constraints for this query because you will not use it again. Often you create queries to find a specific piece of information that you read off the screen before closing the query. If you need to view the information again, you can easily modify the query.

8. Double-click **Global Craft Products Query**, switch to Design View, scroll to and click the **UnitsInStock Criteria cell**, type **<10**, then click ▯
   A datasheet listing all the products with fewer than 10 units in stock appears, as shown in Figure P1-12. These are the items that you need to order.

9. Click **File** on the menu bar, click **Close**, then click **No**

FIGURE P1-10: Category records for the Global Crafts Products table

Plus signs indicate that the table is related to the suppliers table

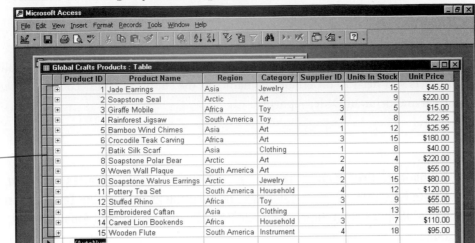

FIGURE P1-11: Design grid for Query 2

Run button

"Africa" entered in the Region Criteria cell

"Toy" entered in the Category Criteria cell

Quotes are automatically inserted when you exit the cell

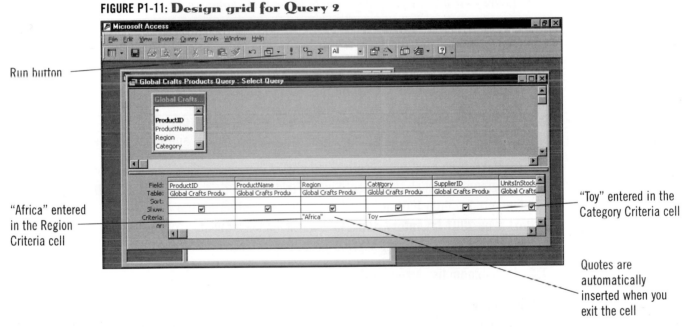

FIGURE P1-12: Datasheet view of Query 3 results

Product ID	Product Name	Region	Expr1	Supplier ID	Units In Stock	Unit Price
2	Soapstone Seal	Arctic		2	9	$220.00
3	Giraffe Mobile	Africa		3	5	$15.00
4	Rainforest Jigsaw	South America		4	8	$22.95
7	Batik Silk Scarf	Asia		1	8	$40.00
8	Soapstone Polar Bear	Arctic		2	4	$220.00
9	Woven Wall Plaque	South America		4	8	$55.00
12	Stuffed Rhino	Africa		3	9	$55.00
14	Carved Lion Bookends	Africa		3	7	$110.00

Record: 1 of 8

activity:

Format and Print an Order Report

You will create a query from both the Global Crafts Products table and the Suppliers table to list the products you need to order and the names of the suppliers you need to contact, and then you will format and print an Order report.

steps:

1. Double-click **Create query by using wizard**, click the **Tables/Queries list arrow**, click **Table: Global Crafts Products**, click the **Select All Fields button** >> , click the **Tables/Queries list arrow**, click **Table: Global Crafts Suppliers**, then select **SupplierName** and **EmailAddress** for inclusion in the table

2. Click **Next**, click **Next** again, type **Items to Order** as the Query table name, then click **Finish**

3. Switch to **Design View**, click the **UnitsInStock Criteria cell**, type **<10**, click the **SupplierName Sort cell**, click the **Sort Cell list arrow**, click **Ascending**, then click the **Run button** !

   You have your list of eight products to order and the names and e-mail addresses of the suppliers to contact sorted by supplier name. Note that you may need to scroll right to view all the fields in the query table.

4. Click **File** on the menu bar, click **Close**, click **Yes**, click **Reports**, then double-click **Create report by using wizard**

5. Click the **Tables/Queries list arrow**, click **Query: Items to Order**, then select the following fields: **ProductName**, **Region**, **Category**, **UnitPrice**, **SupplierName**, and **EmailAddress**

6. Click **Next**, click **by Global Crafts Products**, if necessary, click **Next**, click **Supplier Name** in the list of groupings, click the **Select Single Field button** > , click **Next**, click **Next** again, click the **Align Left 1 option button**, click the **Landscape option button**, click **Next**, click **Soft Gray**, click **Next**, type **2001 Inventory Items to Order**, then click **Finish**

   The Unit Price field heading appears too far to the right.

7. Click the **Zoom list arrow** on the Print Preview toolbar, then click **Fit**

8. Click the **View button** 🔍 to switch to Design View, click the **Unit Price** label, press and hold **[Shift]**, click the **Unit Price** field, move the mouse over a selected label until the ✋ appears, then drag the ✋ to move the two selected labels to the left, as shown in Figure P1-13

9. Click the **Print Preview button** 🔍 on the Standard toolbar, maximize the report window, check the positioning of the Unit Price labels, as shown in Figure P1-14, click the **Print button** 🖨 on the Standard toolbar, close the report, click **Yes**, then close the database

Clues to Use

Formatting Reports

If you want to modify the positioning of the Unit Price labels or any other labels, switch back to Design View, make the adjustments required, then view the results in the Print Preview screen. To format a report in Access, you need to switch frequently between Design View and the Print Preview screen.

FIGURE P1-13: **Position of the Unit Price labels in Design View**

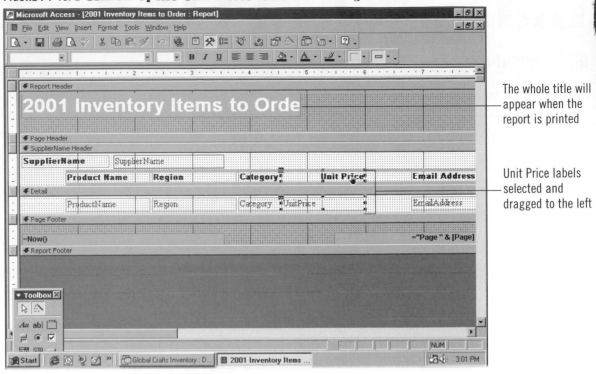

The whole title will appear when the report is printed

Unit Price labels selected and dragged to the left

FIGURE P1-14: **Completed report in the Print Preview screen**

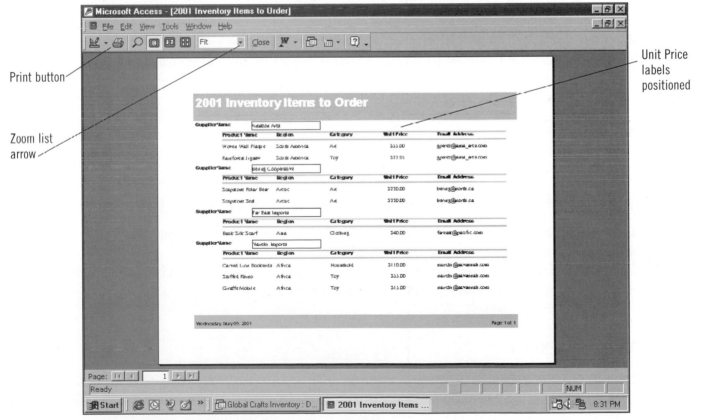

Print button

Zoom list arrow

Unit Price labels positioned

Independent Challenges

INDEPENDENT CHALLENGE 1

Create a report based on tables that contain information about 20 to 30 products stocked by a company of your choice. For example, you could create a report for a small company that sells classic videos or gourmet coffee. Follow the steps provided to create the database, create a Products table and a Suppliers table, make two or three queries, then create a report.

1. You need to know the name of your company and the type of products it sells. For example, you could call your company Waves and describe it as a retail operation that sells water sports equipment, such as surfboards, bathing suits, and inflatable water toys. Write the name of your company and a brief description of it in the box below:

Company name:_____

Description:_____

2. Create a database called [Company name] Inventory.
3. Create a Products table. Use the Table Wizard to create a Products table similar to the table you created for Project 1. Include at least six fields, including the UnitsInStock field. If necessary, rename some of the fields to match the type of data you plan to enter.
4. Create a Suppliers table. Use the Form Wizard to enter the data for a Suppliers table. Include at least four or five fields. Make sure that at least one of the fields in the Suppliers table is the same as a field in the Products table. Use the Copy and Paste commands to minimize typing time.
5. Create relationships between the two tables.
6. In the box below, write four queries you plan to make based on the Products and Suppliers tables. For example, you could ask which products are handled by a certain supplier, which products conform to a specific category, and which suppliers are located in a specific area. The queries you make will depend upon the type of data you included in your Products and Suppliers tables and the relationships you have created between the two tables.

Query 1:_____

Query 2:_____

Query 3:_____

Query 4:_____

7. Use the Query Wizard to create the queries. Make sure you specify the criteria for each query in Design View.
8. Select the query table that you will use to create your Inventory Report.
9. Use the Report Wizard to create your report. Experiment with the many features available in Report Design view. Remember that you will need to switch frequently between Report Design view and the Print Preview screen to check your progress.
10. Print the report then close the database.

INDEPENDENT CHALLENGE 2

Create an Event database that contains information about an event of your choice. For example, you could create tables that contain information about a concert or a conference that you are helping to organize. Plan and then create the database as follows:

1. Create a database called [Event Name]. For example, a database for a local computer users conference could be called "Seattle Computer Users Conference."

2. Open the Table Wizard and select the Events sample table.

3. Plan your database on paper:

   a. Write down the fields from the Events sample table that you plan to include in a table.

   b. Determine additional fields for a second table.

   c. List a few of the records you plan to include in the two tables.

   d. Determine two or three queries that you could make based on the data in the two tables.

   e. Identify the information that you would like to show in a report. For example, you could create a report that lists the total amount of money made at the event from three categories of people who attended (e.g., adults, seniors, and students). Spend a fair bit of time planning your Events database so that when you begin working in Access, you will know exactly what kinds of fields and records you need to enter in order to create the type of report you require.

4. Create the tables required for your database.

5. Establish relationships between the tables.

6. Make two or three queries based on the data in the two tables.

7. Create and print an attractively formatted report based on one of the query tables you created.

INDEPENDENT CHALLENGE 3

Create a database that contains information about all the sales made in the past month by a company of your choice. Suppose, for example, that you owned a pet store. You could create three tables related to sales: Pet Sales, Buyers, and Accessories. The Pet Sales table, for example, could look similar to the table shown in Figure IC-1.

Spend some time designing your Sales Information database, then create three tables, make two or three queries, and create a report based on one of the queries. Use your imagination and Access skills to create a database that you can use to produce an informative and useful report regarding some aspect of your product sales. Refer to the database you created for Castaway Cruises in Project 3 for ideas.

FIGURE IC-1: Pet Sales table

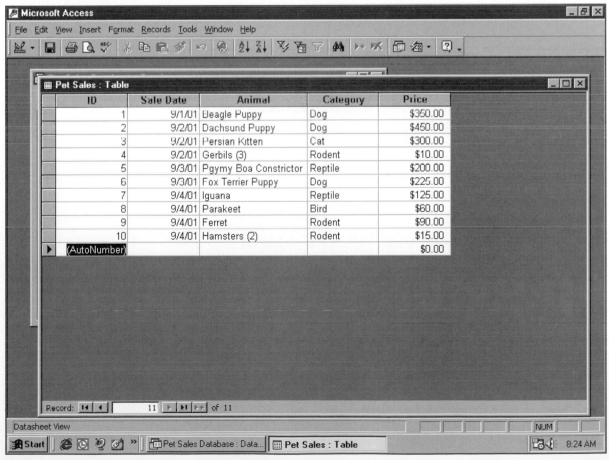

APPENDIX: TECHNOLOGY TOOLS

Enhance your learning experience with technology tools

The New Perspectives team and Course Technology pride themselves on developing quality learning tools—not just textbooks. There's a lot more to the textbook you're holding than these pages. Here are just a few of the highlights.

CBT (Computer-Based Training)/WBT (Web-Based Training)

Explore!

In the back of this textbook you will find a FREE sample of Explore!, an exciting new learning product. Explore! places you, the student, as an intern in a working company, AdZ, Incorporated. You will gain computer skills through helping the other AdZ employees solve their business problems. The CD contained in your textbook contains a CBT that teaches you the basic operating system and file management skills of Microsoft Windows 2000 Professional. (You do not need Microsoft Windows 2000 Professional to run Explore!, but the content may not match what you see on your computer if it is running Windows 95, 98, or NT.)

Explore! is also available for Word, Access, Excel, PowerPoint, and Office 2000. Each Explore! CBT is organized to match your New Perspectives textbook, so it makes an excellent companion study tool or independent learning system.

For more information, or to use the WBT version of Explore!, go to *www.npexplore.com*. (Instructors: Go to www.npexplore.com for all support materials.) Or, continue with this appendix for step-by-step instructions on how to use Explore!

MyCourse.com

www.mycourse.com

MyCourse.com allows you to enhance and supplement your classroom learning through additional course content made available online. You can use MyCourse.com to go beyond traditional learning by accessing and completing online readings, tests, and other assignments. A complete description of MyCourse.com and step-by-step instructions on how to us it are provided later in this appendix.

On the Web

The Office 2000 Student Online Companion
http://www.course.com/NewPerspectives/office2000/

The Internet Assignments at the end of each tutorial point you to the Student Online Companion for your textbook. These assignments give you an opportunity to combine the skills gained in the tutorial with Web research. But the Student Online Companion provides more than just additional case projects. You also can obtain your data files and updates to the text. And the Additional Resources section is constantly updated to bring you the latest news and tips on using Office 2000. A helpful and comprehensive Computer Buyer's Guide is also available on the Student Online Companion; just click the link for the guide.

Welcome to Explore!

Explore! is a system of discovery learning.

Explore! challenges you to take control of your own learning. You'll participate in solving realistic business problems and discover skills along the way. Through videos, animations, interactive graphics, guided work in the live application, and a wealth of resources online, Explore! puts the fun back in learning.

Launching the CD and Logging into the Web

You can use Explore! either via the Web or through this CD. You can even switch between the two versions at any time! All your information will be saved on your tracking disk (explained on pages 2 and 3).

To take the course over the Web

- You will need the keycode at the back of this folder and an active e-mail account.
- Get connected to the Internet through your ISP, and go to www.npexplore.com.
- Click **Take a Course** and follow the onscreen instructions.

To take the course from the CD

- Put your CD into the CD-ROM drive, label side up.
- If your machine supports AutoPlay, insert this CD into the CD-ROM drive. The course will start automatically. Follow the onscreen instructions.
- If your machine does not support AutoPlay:
  1. Click **Start**.
  2. Click **Run**.
  3. Type **d:\IST_Player.exe** (where "d" is your CD-ROM drive).
  4. Click **OK**.

Logging In and Setting Up Your Tracking Disk

- Once you enter the course (either via the Web or CD), you will need to log in if you want your progress tracked.

  As a new user, you will be required to set up your profile. You'll do this by entering your First Name, Last Name, Student ID number, and Class section number in the appropriate fields. Your Student ID must be unique to you.
- Then you will be asked to choose and confirm a password.

■ Once you've set up your profile, you only need to put your tracking disk in your floppy drive to access your profile every time you start the course. This disk will bookmark where you are in the course and save your quiz results.

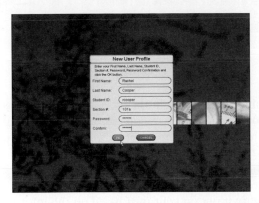

Much of the work you do will be recorded on your tracking disk and your instructor will be checking it from time to time. This disk will be proof of the work you do. So please be sure to save your disk and keep any other files (such as Portfolio Project files, explained on pages 4 and 5) on a separate disk.

Navigating Explore! Getting Started

Explore! will take you inside a working company—AdZ, Inc. As an intern at this fictional Seattle-based advertising agency, you will participate in training, listen to voicemails, and create project files for clients live in the application. If you are using Explore! in a public setting (such as a computer lab), we recommend you use headphones.

Explore! is divided into Tutorials, each of which is designed to be completed in about 90 minutes. Each Tutorial consists of several learning objectives or lessons.

■ To launch a Tutorial, click the name of that tutorial in the menu screen.

Navigating Explore! Courses, Tutorials, Lessons, and Sections

Once inside the Tutorial, you can navigate your way through the course using the navigation box at the lower-right corner of your screen.

Menu   Pause   Previous Page

Exit   Next Page

Help

Show/Hide
Display Window   Options   Replay   Play

Each Lesson (learning objective) is further divided into Sections. You can move through the Sections of a Lesson by clicking the menu tab, and then clicking the link. We highly recommend you follow the Tutorial in the order in which topics are presented, at least for the first time through.

When navigation buttons are gray, they are inactive. This typically means you need to complete a task on screen before the course will proceed. Often this task is not stated outright—you need to figure it out on your own based on the information provided. But don't worry if you aren't 100% sure—just try something! Explore! will often supply hints and help if you get it wrong. And if you ever need it, help is accessible just by clicking the Help button.

Self-evaluation and Quick Checks

At the end of every Tutorial, you will be prompted to do a self-evaluation that checks whether you are confident enough to take the quiz on this Tutorial.

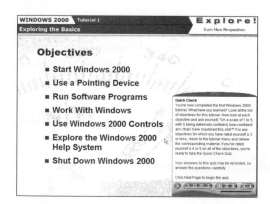

Each quiz consists of 20 questions, designed to test your understanding of the concepts and mastery of the skills included in the lessons. Before you start the quiz, be sure your tracking disk is in the floppy drive. Quizzes are scored upon completion, and encoded on your tracking disk. You can review a quiz as many times as you like, until you feel confident of your skills.

Portfolio Projects and Turning in Files

Most Tutorials include work in the live application throughout the instruction, but all include a live application Portfolio Project at the very end of the Tutorial.

This Portfolio Project allows you to apply what you've learned in the Tutorial to another situation at AdZ, Inc. Unlike total simulation products, the Portfolio Project gives you and your instructor tangible proof of your progress.

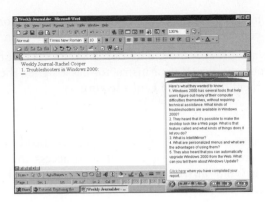

You can hand in tutorial data files, portfolio project files, and tracking disk files on a floppy disk or send them via e-mail to your instructor.

- To e mail any data or project files, simply attach the *student ID*.txt file from your project disk to the e-mail message, where *student ID* is the same student ID number you used to set up your profile (see pages 2 and 3).

Explore! on the Web

Our community of users is always accessible on the Web at www.npexplore.com. Here you'll find FAQs for any technical support questions, information about Discovery Learning, an online demo, and much more!

AdZ, Inc. also has a Web site for you to explore. Go to the intern's corner for additional resources and data to work on your project and to interact with other users of Explore!. Or just browse the company background, client list, description of services, and more.

We're excited about Explore! and we think that after you work with it, you will be too.

It's time to Explore!

MyCourse.com

MyCourse.com offers instructors and students an opportunity to supplement classroom learning through additional course content online. As a student, you can use MyCourse.com to expand your traditional learning by accessing and completing short readings, Practice tests, and other assignments through this customized, comprehensive Web site.

MyCourse.com provides five types of course content: Objectives, Case Projects, Assignments, Practice Tests, and Links. Your instructor may choose to assign any combination of these activities.

- **Objectives** outline the material to be covered within the tutorial. Topic Reviews, which are listed below each Objective, guide you to the area of the tutorial you need to focus on in order to achieve the given objective.

- **Case Projects** are detailed assignments that let you apply the knowledge gained in the tutorial. There are typically two case projects per tutorial. The first case project provides hands-on practice and application of the concepts, whereas the second case project is more research-based.

- Your instructor may choose to create **Assignments** specifically for your course that build upon previous exercises or assignments, or that investigate completely new areas of the subject matter. Your instructor will direct you to turn in the completed Assignments either in class or by e-mail.

- The **Practice Tests** allow you to test your knowledge with brief quizzes that directly correspond to the Objectives. Practice Tests are graded as soon as you complete them, so you know instantly how well you're doing. Practice

Tests are for self-testing only—results are not tracked or consolidated, although you can e-mail your results to your instructor.

■ Your instructor may want you to look at Web sites that have content relevant to your course topics. If your instructor has assigned these sites, you can easily access them through the **Links** feature.

Getting Started

If you are using MyCourse.com for the first time, you will need to create an individualized MyCourse.com user profile. You use this profile to access the course information and assignments created by your instructor. In order to reach the User Profile page, go to http://www.mycourse.com and click the New User link.

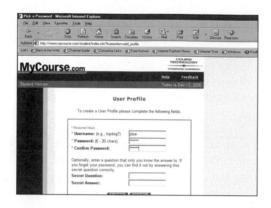

The User Profile page summarizes specific information about you and creates your username and password, which you will need in order to access your MyCourse.com account. There are five fields on this page:

Username (required)	Create a username that consists of at least six characters. It is recommended to use a combination of your first and last names. For example, if your name is Sally Student, you would enter Sstudent. You will use this username to log in to MyCourse.com on subsequent visits.
Password (required)	Enter a password that contains at least six characters. You will use this password to log in to MyCourse.com on subsequent visits.
Confirm Password (required)	Re-enter the password for confirmation.
Secret Question (optional)	Enter a question that has an answer only you would know.
Secret Answer (optional)	Type the answer to the secret question.

You must complete the first three fields. Completing the optional fields for the Secret Question and Secret Answer will provide MyCourse.com with an easy way to help you if you forget your username and password. Once you have completed the User Profile fields, click Submit. The next screen, the Student Information page, prompts you to provide your contact information. After completing the required fields on this page, click Submit.

You will now need to enroll in your MyCourse.com course. Each course has its own Access Key, which is a coded password. Your instructor will provide you with the appropriate Access Key for your course. To enroll in your course, type the appropriate Access Key in the Access Key field, and click Submit.

Another way to enroll in a MyCourse.com course is to enter your textbook's ISBN in the Access Key field. This option is available for students who want to access the extra course content available in MyCourse.com, even if their instructor is not using MyCourse.com to supplement the course.

Once you enroll in your MyCourse.com course, you are launched into your MyCourses home page, which is your customized starting point for all of the MyCourse.com features.

Once you have registered for at least one course, MyCourse.com creates an individual-ized MyCourse.com home page for you, called MyCourses. From this page, you can use the buttons at the bottom of the screen to enter a course, add or enroll in a new MyCourse.com course, or delete an existing course. Any time you log on to MyCourse.com as a returning user to view your assignments, update your student information, or revise your registration information, you will be launched into your MyCourses home page. Once you have entered your course, you have the option to return to your MyCourses home page at any time by clicking the MyCourses link in the left-hand navigation bar.

Navigating Around MyCourse.com

The left-hand navigation bar in any MyCourse.com screen provides navigation options based on your current location. For example, when you are in the Day at a Glance page of a Calendar-Organized course, the left-hand navigation bar shows eight options:

- Zoom Calendar – When you are working in a Calendar-Organized course, you can click Zoom Calendar to enlarge the Day at a Glance calendar for easier readability.

- Announcements – Your instructor may broadcast information such as class-room changes or assignment reminders using the Announcement feature. Any time you enter a course, you will see announcements for that course displayed on the course's opening screen. You can click the Announcement link in the left-hand navigation bar to display the announcement dates.

- Course Syllabus – The Course Syllabus page lists details about the course for which you are registered, including the course name, instructor, Access Key, course number, semester, start and finish dates, office hours, class times, course description, texts, grading policies, and any other policies spec-ified by the instructor.

- Instructor Information – The Instructor Information page shows you all of the information the instructor included in his or her user profile. The page includes his or her name and school, and might also include phone numbers, e-mail address, office location, and other information.

- Student Information – You can use the Student Information link to update your user profile name and contact information.

- Publisher Resources – Clicking Publisher Resources loads the Course Technology Web page that provides an overview of the textbook you are using in your MyCourse.com online course, as well as access to any addi-tional materials you may need such as data files.

- MyCourses – This link returns you to your MyCourses home page, your starting point for entering, adding, or deleting online courses.
- Log Out – This link exits you from the MyCourse.com Web site.

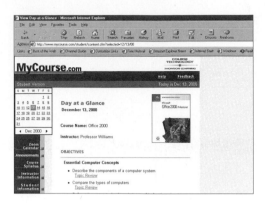

Course Organization Methods

Each course is organized either by Textbook Chapter, Calendar, or Session. Your instructor selects the method of organization. The way you enter a course varies with the way your course is organized, although the course content and the way you add and delete courses are the same, regardless of how the course is organized. The icon in the Org column to the right of each course's period indicates the course organization method.

A **Textbook Chapter-Organized course** is typically used for courses using only one textbook. You can view the content of each chapter that is assigned to the course. Assignments are not tied to a date or any other information. To enter a Textbook Chapter-Organized course, select the option button to the left of the appropriate course. Click the Enter a Course button at the bottom of the page. You are now launched into the Chapter at a Glance page for your selected course. The course name and instructor are shown in addition to the list of assigned content for the first chapter of the textbook. To access the Chapter at a Glance page for another chapter, click the Table of Contents link on the left-hand navigation menu, and then select the chapter whose content you want to see.

The **Calendar-Organized course** option is the default organizational method for MyCourse.com online courses. It allows your instructor to assign readings, projects, or other work based on your class calendar. The MyCourse.com Day at a Glance calendar is the primary tool you use to manage your Calendar-Organized courses. You can click a date to see that day's assignments. Days that have work assigned to them appear on the Day at a Glance calendar with a gray background. To enter a Calendar-Organized course, select the option button to the left of the appropriate course. Click the Enter a Course button at the bottom of the page, which launches you into the Day at a Glance page for your selected course. The course name, instructor name, and a graphic of the textbook are shown in addition to the Day at a Glance calendar. Click a date to see the content assigned for that day.

If your instructor is simultaneously teaching more than one session of your course, he or she may choose to designate different content for each session using the **Session-Organized course** option. To enter a Session-Organized course, select the option button to the left of the appropriate course and click the Enter a Course button at the bottom of the page. You are then launched into the Session at a Glance page for the selected course. This page automatically defaults to Session 1, which is indicated by the red 1 in the Sessions box in the upper-left corner of the page. If you are not enrolled in Session 1, click the appropriate session number in the Sessions box. The currently selected session number appears in red with a box around it. The Session at a Glance page shows information about your course, including course name and instructor name, and also lists the content assigned for each session.

TASK REFERENCE

TASK	PAGE #	RECOMMENDED METHOD
Access, exit	AC 1.13	Click ☒ on the program window
Access, start	AC 1.07	Click Start, point to Programs, click Microsoft Access
Action, add by dragging	AC 9.12	See Reference Window: Creating an Action by Dragging
Action, add to macro	AC 9.07	In the Macro window, click the Action list arrow, click the action
Aggregate functions, use	AC 3.34	Display the query in Design view, click Σ
And operator, enter in selection criteria	AC 3.27	Enter selection criteria in the same Criteria row in the design grid
Append query, create	AC 8.21	See Reference Window: Creating an Append Query
AutoForm, create	AC 4.02	Click Forms in the Objects bar, click New, click an AutoForm Wizard, choose the table or query for the form, click OK
AutoFormat, change	AC 4.05	See Reference Window: Changing a Form's AutoFormat
AutoReport, create	AC 4.19	Click Reports in the Objects bar, click New, click an AutoReport Wizard, choose the table or query for the form, click OK
Calculated field, add to a query	AC 3.31	See Reference Window: Using Expression Builder
Caption, change for a label	AC 5.30	See Reference Window: Changing a Label's Caption
Character, insert	WIN 98 2.6	Click where you want to insert the text, type the text
Chart, edit	AC 6.42	Right-click the chart object, point to Chart Object, click Edit
Chart, embed in a report	AC 6.40	See Reference Window: Embedding a Chart in a Report
Chart Wizard, activate	AC 6.41	Click Reports in the Objects bar, click New, click Chart Wizard, choose the table or query for the form, click OK
Color, change an object's background	AC 5.38	See Reference Window: Changing the Background Color of an Object
Column, adjust width of	AC 3.23	Double-click the right border of the column heading
Command button, add to a form	AC 9.21	Click ▭ on the toolbox, position the pointer in the form, click the left mouse button
Command button, add to a form using Control Wizards	AC 9.34	See Reference Window: Adding a Command Button to a Form Using Control Wizards
Conditional formatting rules, define	AC 6.26	See Reference Window: Defining Conditional Formatting for a Control
Control, resize	AC 5.32	Select the control, click and drag a sizing handle, release the mouse button
Controls, align	AC 5.43	See Reference Window: Aligning Controls on a Form
Controls, move	AC 5.28	See Reference Window: Selecting and Moving Controls
Controls, select	AC 5.28	See Reference Window: Selecting and Moving Controls
Crosstab query, create	AC 8.06	See Reference Window: Using the Crosstab Query Wizard
Data Access Page Wizard, activate	AC 7.08	Click Pages in the Objects bar, click New, click AutoPage: Columnar or Page Wizard, choose the table or query to use, click OK
Data access page, custom, create	AC 7.13	See Reference Window: Creating a Data Access Page in Design View

TASK	PAGE #	RECOMMENDED METHOD
Data access page, update with a browser	AC 7.10	See Reference Window: Viewing and Updating a Data Access Page Using Internet Explorer
Data access page, view with a browser	AC 7.10	See Reference Window: Viewing and Updating a Data Access Page Using Internet Explorer
Data, find	AC 4.08	See Reference Window: Finding Data
Data, group in a report	AC 6.29	See Reference Window: Sorting and Grouping Data in a Report
Data, sort in a report	AC 6.29	See Reference Window: Sorting and Grouping Data in a Report
Database, compact on close	AC 1.26	Click Tools on the menu bar, click Options, click the General tab, click Compact on Close, click OK
Database, compact and repair	AC 1.25	Click Tools on the menu bar, point to Database Utilities, click Compact and Repair
Database, compile	AC 10.20	Click Debug, click Compile database name
Database, decrypt	AC 10.43	See Reference Window: Encrypting or Decrypting a Database
Database, encrypt	AC 10.43	See Reference Window: Encrypting or Decrypting a Database
Database relationships, print	AC 7.15	In the Relationships window, click File, click Print Relationships, click 🖨, click Close
Database, split	AC 10.49	See Reference Window: Using the Database Splitter Wizard
Database startup options, set	AC 10.51	See Reference Window: Setting the Database Startup Options
Datasheet view, switch to	AC 2.17	Click 🖩
Date, add to a report	AC 6.19	See Reference Window: Adding the Date to a Report
Delete query, create	AC 8.24	See Reference Window: Creating a Delete Query
Design Master and replica, synchronize	AC 8.57	See Reference Window: Synchronizing the Design Master and a Replica
Design view, switch to	AC 2.22	Click 📐
Desktop, access	WIN 98 1.14	Click 🗔 on the Quick Launch toolbar
Dialog box form, create	AC 9.27	Display the form in Design view, open the form's property sheet, set the Border Style property to Dialog
Disk, copy	WIN 98 2.25	See Reference Window: Copying a Disk
Disk, format	WIN 98 2.2	Open My Computer, right-click 3 ½ Floppy (A:), click Format, click Start
Duplicate values, hide	AC 6.37	See Reference Window: Hiding Duplicate Values in a Report
Event procedure, add	AC 10.19	See Reference Window: Adding an Event Procedure
Explorer windows, navigate	WIN 98 2.23	Click ⇐, ⇒, or ⬆
Field, add to a form or report	AC 5.27	Drag the field from the field list to the form or report in Design view
Field, add to a table	AC 2.23	See Reference Window: Adding a Field Between Two Existing Fields
Field, define	AC 2.08	See Reference Window: Defining a Field in a Table

TASK	PAGE #	RECOMMENDED METHOD
Field, delete	AC 2.21	Display the table in Design view, right-click the field's row selector, click Delete Rows, click Yes
Field, move	AC 2.22	Display the table in Design view, click the field's row selector, drag the field with the pointer
File, copy	WIN 98 2.22	See Reference Window: Copying a File
File, delete	WIN 98 2.24	Right-click the file, click Delete
File extensions, hide	WIN 98 2.20	Open My Computer click View, click Folder Options, click View tab, make sure the Hide file extensions for known file types check box is checked, click OK
File, move	WIN 98 2.21	See Reference Window: Moving a File
File, open from My Computer	WIN 98 2.9	Open My Computer, open the window containing the file; in Web style, click the file; in Classic style, click the file then press Enter
File, print	WIN 98 2.10	Click 🖨
File, rename	WIN 98 2.24	See Reference Window: Renaming a File
File, save	WIN 98 2.7	Click 💾
Filter, save as a query	AC 5.52	See Reference Window: Saving a Filter as a Query
Filter, saved as a query, apply	AC 5.53	See Reference Window: Applying a Filter that Was Saved as a Query
Filter By Form, activate	AC 5.49	Click 🔃
Filter By Form, create	AC 5.50	See Reference Window: Selecting Records Using Filter By Form
Filter By Selection, activate	AC 3.18	See Reference Window: Using Filter By Selection
Find duplicates query, create	AC 8.09	See Reference Window: Using the Find Duplicates Query Wizard
Find unmatched query, create	AC 8.11	See Reference Window: Using the Find Unmatched Query Wizard
Folder, create	WIN 98 2.21	See Reference Window: Creating a New Folder
Form, custom, create	AC 5.23	See Reference Window: Creating a Form in Design View
Form Footer, add	AC 5.34	Click View, click Form Header/Footer
Form Footer, remove	AC 5.34	Click and drag the bottom edge of the footer up until the section area disappears
Form Header, add	AC 5.34	Click View, click Form Header/Footer
Form Header, remove	AC 5.34	Click and drag the bottom edge of the header up until the section area disappears
Form Wizard, activate	AC 4.02	Click Forms in the Objects bar, click New, click Form Wizard, choose the table or query for the form, click OK
Function, create	AC 10.11	Enter function statements in the Code window
Group totals, calculate in a report	AC 6.31	See Reference Window: Calculating Totals in a Report
Help, display topic from Contents tab	WIN 98 1.28	From Help, click the Contents tab, click 📖 until you see the topic you want, click ❓ to display topic
Help, display topic from Index tab	WIN 98 1.28	From Help, click the Index tab, scroll to locate topic, click topic, click Display

TASK	PAGE #	RECOMMENDED METHOD
Help, return to previous Help topic	WIN 98 1.30	Click ⬅
Help, start	WIN 98 1.27	Click 🔲 Start , click Help
Hot key, create	AC 9.35	Type an ampersand (&) to the left of the hot key letter in the object's name
HTML document, export an Access object as	AC 7.04	See Reference Window: Exporting an Access Object to an HTML Document
HTML document, import as a table	AC 7.26	See Reference Window: Importing an HTML Document as an Access Table
HTML document, view	AC 7.05	See Reference Window: Viewing an HTML Document in a Web Browser
Hyperlink, use	AC 7.35	Click the hyperlink field value
Hyperlink field, create	AC 7.32	See Reference Window: Creating a Hyperlink Field in a Table
Hyperlink field value, enter	AC 7.33	See Reference Window: Entering a Hyperlink Field Value in a Table
Index, create	AC 8.41	See Reference Window: Creating an Index
Indexes, view a table's existing	AC 8.39	See Reference Window: Viewing a Table's Existing Indexes
Input Mask Wizard, activate	AC 5.11	Click the field's Input Mask text box, click ... , specify your choices in the Input Mask Wizard dialog boxes
Insertion point, move	WIN 98 2.5	Click the location in the document to which you want to move
Label, add to a form or report	AC 5.35	See Reference Window: Adding a Label to a Form
Line, add to a form or report	AC 6.25	See Reference Window: Adding a Line to a Report
List box, add to a form	AC 9.29	See Reference Window: Adding a List Box to a Form
List box, change option	WIN 98 1.24	Click ▼ , then click option you want in list that appears
Lookup Wizard field, create	AC 5.04	Click the Data Type list arrow, click Lookup Wizard, specify your choices in the Lookup Wizard dialog boxes
Macro, add to a macro group	AC 9.20	See Reference Window: Adding a Macro to a Macro Group
Macro, attach to a command button	AC 9.22	Open the property sheet for the command button, click the right edge of the event property text box, click the macro name
Macro, create	AC 9.11	See Reference Window: Creating a Macro
Macro, run from the Database window	AC 9.05	Click Macros in the Objects bar, right-click the macro, click Run; or click Tools, point to Run Macro, select the macro from the list, click OK
Macro, run from the Macro window	AC 9.10	Click ❗ on the Macro Design toolbar
Macro, single step	AC 9.09	See Reference Window: Single Stepping a Macro
Macro group, create	AC 9.40	See Reference Window: Creating a Macro Group
Make-table query, create	AC 8.17	See Reference Window: Creating a Make-Table Query
Menu option, select	WIN 98 1.8	Click the menu option, or, if it is a submenu, point to it

TASK	PAGE #	RECOMMENDED METHOD
Module, create	AC 10.10	See Reference Window: Creating a New Standard Module
Module, save	AC 10.14	Click 💾 on the VBA Standard toolbar, enter the module name, press Enter
My Computer, open	WIN 98 2.14	In Web style, click My Computer on the desktop; in Classic style, click My Computer on the desktop then press Enter
Object, embedded or linked, insert in a form or report	AC 6.47	See Reference Window: Inserting a Linked Object in a Report
Object, embedded or linked, update manually	AC 6.50	Click Edit, click OLE/DDE Links, select the object, click Update Now, click Close
Object, export to an HTML document	AC 7.04	See Reference Window: Exporting an Access Object to an HTML Document
Office Assistant, use to get Help	AC 1.20	See Reference Window: Using the Office Assistant
Or operator, enter in selection criteria	AC 3.28	Enter selection criteria in the Criteria and "or" rows in the design grid
Overall totals, calculate in a report	AC 6.31	See Reference Window: Calculating Totals in a Report
Page numbers, add to a report	AC 6.21	See Reference Window: Adding Page Numbers to a Report
Parameter query, create	AC 5.21	See Reference Window: Creating a Parameter Query
Password, set a database	AC 10.44	See Reference Window: Setting a Database Password
Performance Analyzer, use	AC 10.47	See Reference Window: Using the Performance Analyzer
Picture, add to a form or report	AC 5.37	See Reference Window: Adding a Picture to a Form
Picture, change on a command button	AC 9.23	Open the property sheet for the command button, click the Picture text box, click ⋯, select the picture, click OK
Picture, insert on a report	AC 4.27	Click Insert on the menu bar, click Picture, select the picture file, click OK
Primary key, specify	AC 2.15	See Reference Window: Specifying a Primary Key for a Table
Procedure, create	AC 10.23	See Reference Window: Adding a New Procedure to a Standard Module
Procedure, test in the Immediate window	AC 10.15	See Reference Window: Testing a Procedure in the Immediate Window
Program, close	WIN 98 1.12	Click ✖
Program, close inactive	WIN 98 1.15	Right-click program button then click Close
Program, start	WIN 98 1.11	See Reference Window: Starting a Program
Program, switch to another	WIN 98 1.14	Click the program button on the taskbar that contains the name of the program to which you want to switch
Query, define	AC 3.03	Click Queries in the Objects bar, click New, click Design View, click OK
Query, export as an Excel worksheet	AC 6.52	See Reference Window: Exporting an Access Table or Query to Excel
Query, run	AC 3.05	Click ❗

TASK	PAGE #	RECOMMENDED METHOD
Query results, sort	AC 3.15	See Reference Window: Sorting a Query Datasheet
Record, add a new one	AC 2.17	Click ▶∗
Record, delete	AC 2.30	Right-click the record's row selector, click Delete Record, click Yes
Record, move to first	AC 1.12	Click ◀◀
Record, move to last	AC 1.12	Click ▶▶
Record, move to next	AC 1.12	Click ▶
Record, move to previous	AC 1.12	Click ◀
Record, move to a specific one	AC 1.12	Type the record number in the Specific Record box, press Enter
Records, redisplay all after filter	AC 3.19	Click ▽
Relationship, define between tables	AC 3.08	Click 🖧
Replica, create	AC 8.53	See Reference Window: Creating a Replica of a Database
Report, custom, create	AC 6.07	See Reference Window: Creating a Report in Design View
Report, preview	AC 6.16	Click 🔍
Report Footer, add	AC 6.31	Click View, click Report Header/Footer
Report Footer, remove	AC 6.31	Click and drag the bottom edge of the footer up until the section area disappears
Report Header, add	AC 6.31	Click View, click Report Header/Footer
Report Header, remove	AC 6.31	Click and drag the bottom edge of the header up until the section area disappears
Report Wizard, activate	AC 4.19	Click Reports in the Objects bar, click New, click Report Wizard, choose the table or query for the report, click OK
Self-join, create	AC 8.45	See Reference Window: Creating a Self-Join
Sort, specify ascending	AC 3.13	Click ⬇
Sort, specify descending	AC 3.13	Click ⬇
Special effect, create	AC 9.53	Select the object, click the list arrow for ▭ , click the special effect
SQL statement, use for a list box	AC 9.31	Open the property sheet for the list box, right-click the Row Source text box, click Zoom, enter the SQL statement, click OK
SQL statement, view	AC 8.51	See Reference Window: Viewing an SQL Statement for a Query
Subdatasheet, display related records	AC 5.09	Click ➕
Subdatasheet, hide related records	AC 5.11	Click ➖
Subform/Subreport Wizard, activate	AC 5.44	Make sure ⟋ is selected, click 🔲 , click at the upper-left corner for the subform/subreport
Switchboard Manager, activate	AC 9.44	Click Tools, point to Database Utilities, click Switchboard Manager

TASK	PAGE #	RECOMMENDED METHOD
Start menu, open	WIN 98 1.7	Click **Start** *or* press Ctrl-Esc
Student Disk, create	WIN 98 2.15	Click **Start**, point to Programs, point to NP on Microsoft Windows 98 – Level I, click Disk 1, click OK
Tab control, add to a form	AC 5.41	Click 🗔, click at the upper-left corner for the tab control
Table, create	AC 2.07	Click Tables in the Objects bar, click New, click Design View, click OK
Table, export as an Excel worksheet	AC 6.52	See Reference Window: Exporting an Access Table or Query to Excel
Table, open	AC 1.11	Click Tables in the Objects bar, click the table name, click Open
Table, print	AC 1.13	Click 🖨
Table structure, save	AC 2.16	See Reference Window: Saving a Table Structure
Template, use	AC 7.04	Click the Save formatted check box in the Export dialog box
Text, select	WIN 98 2.6	Drag the pointer over the text
Theme, select data access page	AC 7.22	Click Format, click Theme, select desired theme, click OK
Title, add to a form or report	AC 5.36	Click Aa, click at the upper-left corner for the title, type the title, press Enter
Top values query, create	AC 8.13	See Reference Window: Creating a Top Values Query
Toolbar button, select	WIN 98 1.24	Click the toolbar button
Toolbars, control display	WIN 98 2.17	Click View, point to Toolbars, then select the toolbar options you want
ToolTip, view	WIN 98 1.7	Position the pointer over the tool
Update query, create	AC 8.26	See Reference Window: Creating an Update Query
Validation rule, create	AC 9.24	Display the table in Design view, select the field, enter the rule in the Validation Rule text box
Validation text, create	AC 9.24	Display the table in Design view, select the field, enter the text in the Validation Text text box
View, change	WIN 98 2.18	Click View then click the view option you want
Web style, switch to	WIN 98 2.12	Click **Start**, point to Settings, click Folder Options, click Web style, click OK
Web view, switch to	WIN 98 2.18	Open My Computer, click View then click as Web Page
Window, maximize	WIN 98 1.20	Click ☐
Window, minimize	WIN 98 1.18	Click ▬
Window, move	WIN 98 1.21	Drag the title bar
Window, redisplay	WIN 98 1.20	Click the program button on the taskbar
Window, resize	WIN 98 1.21	Drag ◿
Window, restore	WIN 98 1.20	Click 🗗
Windows 98, shut down	WIN 98 1.15	Click **Start**, click Shut Down, click the Shut Down option button, click OK
Windows 98, start	WIN 98 1.4	Turn on the computer

Standardized Coding Number	Certification Skill Activity Activity	Tutorial Number (page numbers)	End-of-Tutorial Practice	
			Exercise	Step Number
AC2000.1	**Planning and designing databases**			
AC2000.1.1	Determine appropriate data inputs for your database	2 (2.02-2.06) 5	5: Case Problem 5	2, 3
AC2000.1.2	Determine appropriate data outputs for your database	2 (2.02-2.06) 5	5: Case Problem 5	2, 3
AC2000.1.3	Create table structure	2 (2.04-2.17) 5	2: Review Assignment Case Problem 1 Case Problem 2 Case Problem 3 Case Problem 4 5: Case Problem 5	3, 15, 16 3 3 3 3 6
AC2000.1.4	Establish table relationships	3 (3.06-3.12) 5	3: Review Assignment Case Problem 1 Case Problem 2 Case Problem 3 Case Problem 4 5: Case Problem 5	3 2 2 2 2 6
AC2000.2	**Working with Access**			
AC2000.2.1	Use the Office Assistant	1 (1.19-1.22)	Review Assignment Case Problem 2	3, 4, 6 6
AC2000.2.2	Select an object using the Objects Bar	1 (1.11, 1.14, 1.18, 1.24)	Review Assignment Case Problem 1 Case Problem 2 Case Problem 3 Case Problem 4	5, 7, 8, 11 3, 4, 5, 6 3, 4, 7, 8 3, 4, 6, 7 3, 5, 8, 9
AC2000.2.3	Print database objects (tables, forms, reports, queries)	1 (1.13, 1.14, 1.17,1.19, 1.25)	Review Assignment Case Problem 1 Case Problem 2 Case Problem 3 Case Problem 4	6, 7, 10, 11 3, 4, 5, 6 3, 6, 7, 10 3, 5, 6, 9 4, 7, 8, 9
AC2000.2.4	Navigate through records in a table, query, or form	1 (1.12, 1.19) 4 (4.07-4.08)	Review Assignment Case Problem 2 Case Problem 3 Case Problem 4	9 7 6 8
AC2000.2.5	Create a database (using a Wizard or in Design View)	2 (2.02-2.04) 5	2: Review Assignment 5: Case Problem 5	2 6
AC2000.3	**Building and modifying tables**			
AC2000.3.1	Create tables by using the Table Wizard	2 (2.07)	Case Problem 4	8
AC2000.3.2	Set primary keys	2 (2.02-2.03, 2.09-2.10, 2.14-2.16) 5	2: Review Assignment Case Problem 1 Case Problem 3 Case Problem 4 5: Case Problem 5	4, 15e, 16c 4 3b 3d, 8c 6
AC2000.3.3	Modify field properties	2 (2.04-2.06, 2.08-2.14, 2.24-2.26)	Review Assignment Case Problem 3 Case Problem 4	16 3a, 3b, 4b 5a, 5b, 5c

Standardized Coding Number	**Certification Skill Activity** Activity	Tutorial Number (page numbers)	**End-of-Tutorial Practice** Exercise	Step Number
AC2000.3.4	Use multiple data types	2 (2.04-2.05) 5	2: Review Assignment Case Problem 1 Case Problem 2 Case Problem 3 5: Case Problem 5	3 3 3 4a, 4b 6
AC2000.3.5	Modify tables using Design View	2 (2.21-2.27)	Review Assignment Case Problem 1 Case Problem 2 Case Problem 3 Case Problem 4	6, 12, 16 7 5 3, 4 5
AC2000.3.6	Use the Lookup Wizard	5 (5.04-5.09)	Review Assignment Case Problem 1 Case Problem 2 Case Problem 3 Case Problem 4	2 2 2 2 2
AC2000.3.7	Use the input mask wizard	5 (5.11-5.14)	Case Problem 2 Case Problem 3 Case Problem 5	3 3 13
AC2000.4	**Building and modifying forms**			
AC2000.4.1	Create a form with the Form Wizard	4 (4.02-4.05) 5	4: Review Assignment Case Problem 1 Case Problem 2 Case Problem 3 Case Problem 4 5: Case Problem 5	2, 6 2, 6 2 2, 5 2 8
AC2000.4.2	Use the Control Toolbox to add controls	5 (5.26-5.28)	Review Assignment Case Problem 1 Case Problem 2 Case Problem 3 Case Problem 4	8, 10 8, 10 9, 10, 12, 13, 14 8, 9, 10, 12, 13 7, 8, 10, 11
AC2000.4.3	Modify Format Properties (font, style, font size, color, caption, etc.) of controls	5 (5.30-5.31, 5.36, 5.43-5.44)	Review Assignment Case Problem 1 Case Problem 2 Case Problem 3 Case Problem 4	8, 11a, 11b 10b, 10d 10, 13a, 13c, 14a, 14b, 14c 9, 13a, 13b, 13c, 13d 8, 11a, 11b, 11c, 11d
AC2000.4.4	Use form sections (headers, footers, detail)	5 (5.33-5.35)	Review Assignment Case Problem 1 Case Problem 2 Case Problem 3 Case Problem 4	10, 11b 10 12, 13 12 10
AC2000.4.5	Use a Calculated Control on a form	3 (3.30-3.37) 5	5: Case Problem 2 Case Problem 3	12 10

Standardized Coding Number	Certification Skill Activity — Activity	Tutorial Number (page numbers)	End-of-Tutorial Practice — Exercise	Step Number
AC2000.5	**Viewing and organizing information**			
AC2000.5.1	Use the Office Clipboard	2 (2.29-2.30)	Review Assignment	9
			Case Problem 1	6
			Case Problem 2	7
AC2000.5.2	Switch between object Views	2 (2.17)	Review Assignment	15c, 15e, 16d
			Case Problem 1	8, 10
			Case Problem 3	3c
AC2000.5.3	Enter records using a datasheet	2 (2.17-2.19)	Review Assignment	5, 7, 15b
			Case Problem 1	5, 9a, 9b
			Case Problem 2	4, 6b
			Case Problem 3	5
			Case Problem 4	6
AC2000.5.4	Enter records using a form	4 (4.13-4.14)	Review Assignment	4c
			Case Problem 1	5
			Case Problem 3	3
AC2000.5.5	Delete records from a table	2 (2.30-2.31)	Review Assignment	11
			Case Problem 1	9c
			Case Problem 2	10
			Case Problem 4	6c
AC2000.5.6	Find a record	4 (4.08-4.11)	Review Assignment	4b
			Case Problem 1	4
			Case Problem 2	5, 6
			Case Problem 3	3a, 3d
			Case Problem 4	5, 6
AC2000.5.7	Sort records	3 (3.12-3.17)	Review Assignment	2, 4
			Case Problem 1	3
			Case Problem 2	3, 6
			Case Problem 3	3, 5
			Case Problem 4	3, 4, 6
AC2000.5.8	Apply and remove filters (filter by form and filter by selection)	3 (3.17-3.19) 5 (5.49-5.52)	3: Review Assignment	6, 7
			Case Problem 1	4
			5: Review Assignment	9
			Case Problem 1	9
			Case Problem 2	11
			Case Problem 3	11
			Case Problem 4	9
AC2000.5.9	Specify criteria in a query	3 (3.20-3.23, 3.26-3.30) 6	3: Review Assignment	4, 8, 10, 11
			Case Problem 1	5, 6
			Case Problem 2	3, 4, 5
			Case Problem 3	3, 4, 5, 6
			Case Problem 4	3, 4, 5, 6, 7, 8
			6: Case Problem 5	2
AC2000.5.10	Display related records in a subdatasheet	5 (5.09-5.11)	Case Problem 1	2
			Case Problem 2	2
			Case Problem 3	2
			Case Problem 4	2

MOUS CERTIFICATION GRID

Standardized Coding Number	Certification Skill Activity Activity	Tutorial Number (page numbers)	End-of-Tutorial Practice	
			Exercise	Step Number
AC2000.5.11	Create a calculated field	3 (3.30-3.37) 6	3: Review Assignment Case Problem 3 Case Problem 4 6: Case Problem 5	9 5 6 2
AC2000.5.12	Create and modify a multi-table select query	3 (3.06-3.12) 6	3: Review Assignment Case Problem 1 Case Problem 2 Case Problem 3 Case Problem 4 6: Case Problem 5	4 3 3, 5, 6 3, 4, 5, 6 3, 4, 5, 6 2
AC2000.6	**Defining relationships**			
AC2000.6.1	Establish relationships	3 (3.06-3.11) 5	3: Review Assignment Case Problem 1 Case Problem 2 Case Problem 3 Case Problem 4 5: Case Problem 5	3 2 2 2 2 4, 6
AC2000.6.2	Enforce referential integrity	3 (3.06-3.11) 5	3: Review Assignment Case Problem 1 Case Problem 2 Case Problem 3 Case Problem 4 5: Case Problem 5	3 2 2 2 2 6
AC2000.7	**Producing reports**			
AC2000.7.1	Create a report with the Report Wizard	4 (4.18-4.27)	Review Assignment Case Problem 1 Case Problem 2 Case Problem 3 Case Problem 4	7 8 7 8 7
AC2000.7.2	Preview and print a report	4 (4.29-4.32)	Review Assignment Case Problem 1 Case Problem 2 Case Problem 3 Case Problem 4	9 8 11 9 8
AC2000.7.3	Move and resize a control	6 (6.11-6.13)	Review Assignment Case Problem 1 Case Problem 2 Case Problem 3 Case Problem 4	2 2 3 2, 8 9, 10
AC2000.7.4	Modify format properties (font, style, font size, color, caption, etc.)	6 (6.13-6.16, 6.32-6.33, 6.34-6.36)	Review Assignment Case Problem 1 Case Problem 2 Case Problem 3 Case Problem 4	2, 4 2, 9 3, 5 4, 5, 6, 7 2

Standardized Coding Number	Certification Skill Activity — Activity	Tutorial Number (page numbers)	End-of-Tutorial Practice — Exercise	Step Number
AC2000.7.5	Use the Control Toolbox to add controls	6 (6.19-6.26)	Review Assignment	2, 4
			Case Problem 1	2
			Case Problem 2	3, 4, 17
			Case Problem 3	2
AC2000.7.6	Use report sections (headers, footers, detail)	6 (6.02-6.04)	Review Assignment	3, 4, 6
			Case Problem 1	2, 4
			Case Problem 2	3
			Case Problem 3	3
			Case Problem 4	8
			Case Problem 5	3
AC2000.7.7	Use a Calculated Control in a report	6 (6.05-6.07, 6.30-6.35)	Review Assignment	8
			Case Problem 2	12
			Case Problem 4	13
AC2000.8	**Integrating with other applications**			
AC2000.8.1	Import data to a new table	2 (2.07) 7 (7.26-7.30)	2: Review Assignment	16
			Case Problem 3	3
			Case Problem 4	3
			7: Review Assignment	6
			Case Problem 1	6
			Case Problem 2	5
			Case Problem 3	5
			Case Problem 4	6
AC2000.8.2	Save a table, query, form as a Web page	7 (3-7, 9-28)	Review Assignment	2, 3
			Case Problem 1	2, 3
			Case Problem 2	2, 3
			Case Problem 3	2, 3
			Case Problem 4	2, 3
			Case Problem 5	2,3
AC2000.8.3	Add Hyperlinks	7 (7.31-7.38)	Review Assignment	7, 8
			Case Problem 1	7, 8
			Case Problem 2	6, 7, 8
			Case Problem 3	6, 7
			Case Problem 4	7, 8
			Case Problem 5	6
AC2000.9	**Using Access Tools**			
AC2000.9.1	Print Database Relationships	7 (7.15-7.16)	Case Problem 2	9
			Case Problem 4	9
			Case Problem 5	7
AC2000.9.2	Backup and Restore a database	1 (1.27)	<none>	
AC2000.9.3	Compact and Repair a database	1 (1.25-1.26)	Review Assignment	12
			Case Problem 1	7
			Case Problem 2	11
			Case Problem 3	10
			Case Problem 4	10

Expert Standardized Coding Number	Certification Skill Activity Activity	Tutorial Number (page numbers)	End-of-Tutorial Practice	
			Exercise	Step Number
AC2000E.1.	**Building and modifying tables**			
AC2000E.1.1	Set validation text	9 (9.24–9.25)	Case Problem 1	2
AC2000E.1.2	Define data validation criteria	9 (9.24–9.25)	Case Problem 1	2
AC2000E.1.3	Modify an input mask	5 (5.11–5.14)	Case Problem 2 Case Problem 3 Case Problem 5	3 3 13
AC2000E.1.4	Create and modify Lookup Fields	5 (5.04–5.09)	Review Assignment Case Problem 1 Case Problem 2 Case Problem 3 Case Problem 4 Case Problem 5	2 3 2 2 2 2
AC2000E.1.5	Optimize data type usage (double, long, int, byte, etc.)	2 (2.04–2.06) 5 8	2: Review Assignment Case Problem 1 Case Problem 2 Case Problem 3 Case Problem 4 5: Case Problem 5 8: Case Problem 5	3 3 3 3–4 5 3–6 2
AC2000E.2	**Building and modifying forms**			
AC2000E.2.1	Create a form in Design View	5 (5.23–5.30)	Review Assignment Case Problem 1 Case Problem 2 Case Problem 3 Case Problem 4	8, 10 8, 10 9, 10, 13 8, 9, 12 7, 8, 10, 11
AC2000E.2.2	Insert a graphic on a form	5 (5.36–5.38)	Review Assignment	11c
AC2000E.2.3	Modify control properties	5 (5.32–5.33, 5.35–5.36, 5.43)	Review Assignment Case Problem 1 Case Problem 2 Case Problem 3 Case Problem 4	8, 10, 11 8, 10 9, 10, 13, 14 8, 9, 12, 13 7, 8, 10, 11
AC2000E.2.4	Customize form sections (headers, footers, detail)	5 (5.33–5.35)	Review Assignment Case Problem 1 Case Problem 4	10, 11 10 8
AC2000E.2.5	Modify form properties	5 (5.30–5.31, 5.38–5.39)	Review Assignment Case Problem 1 Case Problem 2 Case Problem 3 Case Problem 4	8 8, 10 9, 10, 13, 14 8, 9, 12, 13 7, 8, 10, 11

Standardized Coding Number	Certification Skill Activity — Activity	Tutorial Number (page numbers)	End-of-Tutorial Practice — Exercise	Step Number
AC2000E.2.6	Use the Subform Control and synchronize forms	5 (5.44–5.49)	Review Assignment	10
			Case Problem 1	10
			Case Problem 2	13
			Case Problem 3	12
			Case Problem 4	10
AC2000E.2.7	Create a Switchboard	9 (9.02–9.04, 9.39–9.55)	Review Assignment	3
			Case Problem 1	3
			Case Problem 2	2
			Case Problem 3	2
			Case Problem 4	4
			Case Problem 5	2
AC2000E.3	**Refining queries**			
AC2000E.3.1	Apply filters (filter by form and filter by selection) in a query's recordset	3 (3.17–3.19)	Review Assignment	6
			Case Problem 1	4
AC2000E.3.2	Create a totals query	3 (3.34–3.36)	Case Problem 2	7
			Case Problem 3	6
AC2000E.3.3	Create a parameter query	5 (5.21–5.22)	Review Assignment	7
			Case Problem 1	7
			Case Problem 2	8
			Case Problem 3	7
			Case Problem 4	6
			Case Problem 5	14
AC2000E.3.4	Specify criteria in multiple fields (AND vs. OR)	3 (3.27–3.30) 5 (5.19–5.20)	3: Review Assignment	8, 10
			Case Problem 1	6
			Case Problem 3	4
			Case Problem 4	5
AC2000E.3.5	Modify query properties (field formats, caption, input masks, etc.)	3 (3.23–3.24)	Case Problem 3	5, 6
			Case Problem 4	7
AC2000E.3.6	Create an action query (update, delete, append)	8 (8.16–8.30)	Review Assignment	6, 8
			Case Problem 1	8b
			Case Problem 2	3, 6, 7
			Case Problem 3	3
			Case Problem 4	7
			Case Problem 5	11
AC2000E.3.7	Optimize queries using indexes	8 (8.37–8.42)	Case Problem 1	3
			Case Problem 5	5

Standardized Coding Number	Certification Skill Activity Activity	Tutorial Number (page numbers)	End-of-Tutorial Practice Exercise	Step Number
AC2000E.3.8	Specify join properties for relationships	3 (3.06–3.11) 5 8 (8.42–8.47)	3: Review Assignment	3
			Case Problem 1	2
			Case Problem 2	2
			Case Problem 3	2
			Case Problem 4	2
			5: Case Problem 5	6
			8: Review Assignment	2
			Case Problem 1	2
			Case Problem 2	2
			Case Problem 3	2
			Case Problem 4	2
			Case Problem 5	3
AC2000E.4	**Producing reports**			
AC2000E.4.1	Insert a graphic on a report	4 (4.27–4.30)	Review Assignment	8
			Case Problem 2	8, 9
AC2000E.4.2	Modify report properties	6 (6.29–6.30)	Review Assignment	5, 6
			Case Problem 1	5, 9
			Case Problem 2	7
			Case Problem 3	5, 7
AC2000E.4.3	Create and modify a report in Design View	6 (6.02–6.16)	Review Assignment	2–11
			Case Problem 1	2–10
			Case Problem 2	3–14
			Case Problem 3	2–11
			Case Problem 4	6–14
			Case Problem 5	3
AC2000E.4.4	Modify control properties	6 (6.10–6.16, 6.21–6.25)	Review Assignment	4, 6, 8, 9
			Case Problem 1	4, 5, 7, 9
			Case Problem 2	5–9, 11
			Case Problem 3	4–7, 9
			Case Problem 4	9–11, 13
			Case Problem 5	3
AC2000E.4.5	Set section properties	6 (6.02–6.04)	Review Assignment	3–9
			Case Problem 1	3–7
			Case Problem 2	4–11
			Case Problem 3	3–9
			Case Problem 4	3, 8–13
			Case Problem 5	3
AC2000E.4.6	Use the Subreport Control and synchronize reports	5 (5.44–5.49) 6	6: Case Problem 2	17
AC2000E.5	**Defining relationships**			
AC2000E.5.1	Establish one-to-one relationships	8 (8.33–8.37)	Case Problem 3	2

Standardized Coding Number	Certification Skill Activity		Tutorial Number (page numbers)	End-of-Tutorial Practice	
	Activity			**Exercise**	**Step Number**
AC2000E.5.2	Establish many-to-many relationships		8 (8.31–8.33, 8.34–8.36)	Review Assignment Case Problem 1 Case Problem 2 Case Problem 4 Case Problem 5	2 2 2 2 3
AC2000E.5.3	Set Cascade Update and Cascade Delete options		3 (3.08–3.10) 5	3: Review Assignment Case Problem 1 Case Problem 2 Case Problem 3 Case Problem 4 5: Case Problem 5	3 2 2 2 2 6
AC2000E.6	**Utilizing web capabilities**				
AC2000E.6.1	Create hyperlinks		7 (7.31–7.38)	Review Assignment Case Problem 1 Case Problem 2 Case Problem 3 Case Problem 4 Case Problem 5	7 7, 8 6–8 6, 7 7, 8 6
AC2000E.6.2	Use the group and sort features of data access pages		7 (7.11–7.12, 7.20–7.22)	Review Assignment Case Problem 1 Case Problem 2 Case Problem 3 Case Problem 4 Case Problem 5	5 4, 5 4c 4, 5 4, 5 4, 5
AC2000E.6.3	Create a data access page		7 (7.08–7.15, 7.16–7.25)	Review Assignment Case Problem 1 Case Problem 2 Case Problem 3 Case Problem 4 Case Problem 5	4, 5 4, 5 4 4 4, 5 4, 5
AC2000E.7	**Using Access tools**				
AC2000E.7.1	Set and modify a database password		10 (10.43–10.46)	Review Assignment Case Problem 1 Case Problem 2 Case Problem 3 Case Problem 5	4, 6 4, 8 3, 7 3, 6 2, 6
AC2000E.7.2	Set startup options		10 (10.51–10.53)	Review Assignment Case Problem 1 Case Problem 2 Case Problem 3 Case Problem 4 Case Problem 5	5, 6 7, 8 6, 7 5, 6 5, 6 5, 6

Standardized Coding Number	Certification Skill Activity Activity	Tutorial Number (page numbers)	End-of-Tutorial Practice Exercise	Step Number
AC2000E.7.3	Use Add-ins (Database Splitter, Analyzer, Link Table Manager)	10 (10.46–10.51)	Case Problem 1 Case Problem 2 Case Problem 3 Case Problem 5	5, 6 4 4 4
AC2000E.7.4	Encrypt and Decrypt a database	10 (10.42–10.43)	Case Problem 1 Case Problem 2	4 3, 7
AC2000E.7.5	Use simple replication (copy for a mobile user)	8 (8.53–8.58)	Review Assignment Case Problem 1 Case Problem 3 Case Problem 4	12–15 8 8 9
AC2000E.7.6	Run macros using controls	9 (9.05–9.07, 9.15–9.17, 9.21–9.24, 9.34–9.36, 9.46–9.48, 9.49–9.52)	Review Assignment 2d, 2f Case Problem 1 Case Problem 2 Case Problem 3 Case Problem 4 Case Problem 5	 3b, 3c 2d, 2e 2c, 2d 2d, 2f, 4d 2c
AC2000E.7.7	Create a macro using the Macro Builder	9 (9.11–9.14, 9.18–9.21, 9.40–9.43)	Review Assignment Case Problem 1 Case Problem 2 Case Problem 3 Case Problem 4 Case Problem 5	2, 3c, 3d 3a 2e 2d 2d, 2f, 4d 2b, 2c
AC2000E.7.8	Convert database to a previous version	4 (4.32)	<none>	
AC2000E.8	**Data Integration**			
AC2000E.8.1	Export database records to Excel	6 (6.52–6.54)	Review Assignment Case Problem 1 Case Problem 2 Case Problem 3 Case Problem 4 Case Problem 5	13 11 15 12 16 5
AC2000E.8.2	Drag and drop tables and queries to Excel	6	Case Problem 1 Case Problem 2	11 15
AC2000E.8.3	Present information as a chart (MS Graph)	6 (6.40–6.46)	Review Assignment Case Problem 4	12 15
AC2000E.8.4	Link to existing data	6 (6.39–6.40, 6.46–6.51) 7	6: Review Assignment Case Problem 1 Case Problem 2 Case Problem 3 Case Problem 4 7: Case Problem 2	10 10 13 10 12, 17 8

File Finder

Location in Tutorial	Name and Location of Data File	Student Creates New File
ACCESS LEVEL 1		
Tutorial 1		
Session 1.1	Disk1\Tutorial\Restaurant.mdb	
Session 1.2	Disk1\Tutorial\Restaurant.mdb *(Continued from Session 1.1)*	
Review Assignments	Disk2\Review\Customer.mdb	
Case Problem 1	Disk3\Cases\MallJobs.mdb	
Case Problem 2	Disk4\Cases\Payments.mdb	
Case Problem 3	Disk5\Cases\Walks.mdb	
Case Problem 4	Disk6\Cases\Lexus.mdb	
Tutorial 2		
Session 2.1	Disk1\Tutorial\Restaurant.mdb *(Continued from Session 1.2)*	
Session 2.2	Disk1\Tutorial\Restaurant.mdb *(Continued from Session 2.1)* Disk1\Tutorial\Valle.mdb	
Review Assignments	Disk2\Review\Barbara.mdb Disk2\Review\Coffee.dbf	Disk2\Review\Valle Products.mdb
Case Problem 1	Disk3\Cases\MallJobs.mdb *(Continued from Tutorial 1)* Disk3\Cases\Openings.mdb	
Case Problem 2	Disk4\Cases\Payments.mdb *(Continued from Tutorial 1)* Disk4\Cases\PlusPays.mdb	
Case Problem 3	Disk5\Cases\Walks.mdb *(Continued from Tutorial 1)* Disk5\Cases\Pledge.db	
Case Problem 4	Disk6\Cases\Lexus.mdb *(Continued from Tutorial 1)* Disk6\Cases\Lopez.xls	
Tutorial 3		
Session 3.1	Disk1\Tutorial\Restaurant.mdb *(Continued from Session 2.2)*	
Session 3.2	Disk1\Tutorial\Restaurant.mdb *(Continued from Session 3.1)*	
Review Assignments	Disk2\Review\Valle Products.mdb *(Continued from Tutorial 2)*	
Case Problem 1	Disk3\Cases\MallJobs.mdb *(Continued from Tutorial 2)*	
Case Problem 2	Disk4\Cases\Payments.mdb *(Continued from Tutorial 2)*	
Case Problem 3	Disk5\Cases\Walks.mdb *(Continued from Tutorial 2)*	
Case Problem 4	Disk6\Cases\Lexus.mdb *(Continued from Tutorial 2)*	
Tutorial 4		
Session 4.1	Disk1\Tutorial\Restaurant.mdb *(Continued from Session 3.2)*	
Session 4.2	Disk1\Tutorial\Restaurant.mdb *(Continued from Session 4.1)* Disk1\Tutorial\ValleCup.bmp	
Review Assignments	Disk2\Review\Valle Products.mdb *(Continued from Tutorial 3)* Disk2\Review\ValleCup.bmp	
Case Problem 1	Disk3\Cases\MallJobs.mdb *(Continued from Tutorial 3)*	
Case Problem 2	Disk4\Cases\Payments.mdb *(Continued from Tutorial 3)* Disk4\Cases\PLUS.bmp	
Case Problem 3	Disk5\Cases\Walks.mdb *(Continued from Tutorial 3)*	
Case Problem 4	Disk6\Cases\Lexus.mdb *(Continued from Tutorial 3)*	
ACCESS LEVEL II		
NOTE: New Data Disks required for Tutorials 5-7; numbering starts over.	It is highly recommended that students work off of their hard drive or personal network drive for the Level II tutorials.	
Tutorial 5		
Session 5.1	Disk1\Tutorial\Dining.mdb	
Session 5.2	Disk1\Tutorial\Dining.mdb *(Continued from Session 5.1)* Disk1\Tutorial\ValleCup.bmp	
Session 5.3	Disk1\Tutorial\Dining.mdb *(Continued from Session 5.2)*	
Review Assignments	Disk2\Review\Products.mdb Disk2\Review\ValleCup.bmp	
Case Problem 1	Disk3\Cases\Ashbrook.mdb	
Case Problem 2	Disk4\Cases\FirmPays.mdb	

File Finder

Location in Tutorial	Name and Location of Data File	Student Creates New File
ACCESS LEVEL II		
Tutorial 5		
Case Problem 3	Disk5\Cases\Pledges.mdb	
Case Problem 4	Disk6\Cases\Lopez.mdb	
Case Problem 5		Disk7\Cases\eACH.mdb
Tutorial 6		
Session 6.1	Disk1\Tutorial\Dining.mdb *(Continued from Session 5.3)*	
Session 6.2	Disk1\Tutorial\Dining.mdb *(Continued from Session 6.1)*	
Session 6.3	Disk1\Tutorial\Dining.mdb *(Continued from Session 6.2)* Disk1\Tutorial\ChartTxt.doc	Disk1\Tutorial\Invoice Statistics by Billing Date.xls
Review Assignments	Disk2\Review\Products.mdb *(Continued from Tutorial 5)*	Disk2\Review\Coffee Report Description.doc
Case Problem 1	Disk3\Cases\Ashbrook.mdb *(Continued from Tutorial 5)*	Disk4\Cases\Store Jobs Report Description.doc Disk4\Cases\Ashbrook Stores.xls
Case Problem 2	Disk4\Cases\FirmPays.mdb *(Continued from Tutorial 5)*	Disk4\Cases\Account Representatives Report Description.doc Disk4\Cases\PLUS Account Representatives.xls
Case Problem 3	Disk5\Cases\Pledges.mdb *(Continued from Tutorial 5)*	Disk5\Cases\Walkers Report Description.doc Disk5\Cases\Pledge Statistics by Walker.xls
Case Problem 4	Disk6\Cases\Lopez.mdb *(Continued from Tutorial 5)* Disk6\Cases\3N4TA.bmp Disk6\Cases\79XBF.bmp Disk6\Cases\AAEAF.bmp	Disk6\Cases\Cars Report Description.doc Disk6\Cases\Cost vs Selling.xls
Case Problem 5	Disk7\Cases\eACH.mdb *(Continued from Tutorial 5)*	Disk7\Cases\Projected Income.xls
Tutorial 7		
Session 7.1	Disk1\Tutorial\Dining.mdb *(Continued from Session 6.3)* Disk1\Tutorial\Valletbl.htm Disk1\Tutorial\ValleCup.bmp	Disk1\Tutorial\Customer Page.htm* Disk1\Tutorial\Customer.htm Disk1\Cases\Customers and Orders Page.htm
Session 7.2	Disk1\Tutorial\Dining.mdb *(Continued from Session 7.1)* Disk1\Tutorial\NewRest.htm Disk1\Tutorial\Java.doc Disk1\Tutorial\Taza.doc Disk1\Tutorial\Peterson.doc Disk1\Tutorial\Dinner.gif Disk1\Tutorial\Cup.gif Disk1\Tutorial\CoffCup.jpg Disk1\Tutorial\TazaLink.htm Disk1\Tutorial\Pesto.htm	
Review Assignments	Disk2\Review\Products.mdb *(Continued from Tutorial 6)* Disk2\Review\Valletbl.htm Disk2\Review\Vallerpt.htm Disk2\Review\Wwfoods.gif Disk2\Review\ValleCup.bmp	Disk2\Review\Product.htm Disk2\Review\Coffee Types.htm Disk2\Review\Pricing Query.htm* Disk2\Review\Coffee Products.htm*
	Disk2\Review\Importer.htm Disk2\Review\CoffCup.jpg Disk2\Review\Johnson.gif Disk2\Review\Wwfoods.htm Disk2\Review\Johnson.htm	Disk2\Review\Pricing.xls

File Finder

Location in Tutorial	Name and Location of Data File	Student Creates New File
ACCESS LEVEL II		
Tutorial 7		
Case Problem 1	Disk3\Cases\Ashbrook.mdb *(Continued from Tutorial 6)* Disk3\Cases\Jobtbl.htm Disk3\Cases\Jobrpt.htm Disk3\Cases\Wages.htm Disk3\Cases\Baker.doc Disk3\Cases\Cashier.doc Disk3\Cases\Clerk.doc Disk3\Cases\FryCook.doc	Disk3\Cases\Job.htm Disk3\Cases\Store Jobs.htm Disk3\Cases\Job Page.htm Disk3\Cases\Available Jobs.htm*
Case Problem 2	Disk4\Cases\FirmPays.mdb *(Continued from Tutorial 6)* Disk4\Cases\PLUStbl.htm Disk4\Cases\PLUCrpt.htm Disk4\Cases\NewFirms.htm Disk4\Cases\Dupont.htm Disk4\Cases\Dupont.gif Disk4\Cases\Services.mdb	Disk4\Cases\Firm.htm Disk4\Cases\Payments By Account Representative.htm Disk4\Cases\Payment.htm*
Case Problem 3	Disk5\Cases\Pledges.mdb *(Continued from Tutorial 6)* Disk5\Cases\Walktbl.htm Disk5\Cases\Walkrpt.htm Disk5\Cases\Malls.htm Disk5\Cases\Southgat.htm Disk5\Cases\PLUS.bmp Disk5\Cases\PLUS.jpg Disk5\Cases\Southgat.gif	Disk5\Cases\Walker.htm Disk5\Cases\Walkers.htm Disk5\Cases\Walker Page.htm*
Case Problem 4	Disk6\Cases\Lopez.mdb *(Continued from Tutorial 6)* Disk6\Cases\Lopeztbl.htm Disk6\Cases\Lopezrpt.htm Disk6\Cases\Mileage.htm Disk6\Cases\ES300.doc Disk6\Cases\GS300.doc Disk6\Cases\LS400.doc Disk6\Cases\SC300.doc Disk6\Cases\SC400.doc	Disk6\Cases\Car.htm Disk6\Cases\Cars By Model And Year.htm Disk6\Cases\Car Page.htm* Disk6\Cases\Locations and Cars Page.htm*
Case Problem 5	Disk7\Cases\eACH.mdb (Continued from Tutorial 6) Disk7\Cases\eACHtbl.htm Disk7\Cases\eACHrpt.htm	Disk7\Cases\Item.htm Disk7\Cases\Custom Report filename Disk7\Cases\Registrant Page.htm Disk7\Cases\Categories and Subcategories Page.htm Students will create and save three Word documents in the folder Disk7\Cases.
ACCESS LEVEL III NOTE: Students will not be able to complete all steps working off of a floppy disk.	They should copy the files to their hard drive or personal network drive to complete the steps.	
Tutorial 8		
Session 8.1	Tutorial\FineFood.mdb	
Session 8.2	Tutorial\FineFood.mdb *(Continued from Session 8.1)*	
Session 8.3	Tutorial\FineFood.mdb *(Continued from Session 8.2)*	
Session 8.4	Tutorial\FineFood.mdb *(Continued from Session 8.3)*	Tutorial\Replica of FineFood.mdb (deleted in a later step) Tutorial\FineFood Design Master.mdb Tutorial\FineFood.bak (renamed to FineFood.mdb in a later step)

Note: When students create this data access page, a folder with the same name is created and contains the files needed to create the Web page.

File Finder

ACCESS LEVEL III

Tutorial 8

Review Assignments	Review\Coffees.mdb	Review\Replica of Coffees.mdb
		Review\Coffees Design
Master.mdb		
		Review\Coffees.bak (renamed to Coffees.mdb in a later step)
Case Problem 1	Cases\Mall.mdb	Cases\Replica of Mall.mdb
		Cases\Mall Design Master.mdb
		Cases\Mall.bak (renamed to Mall.mdb in a later step)
Case Problem 2	Cases\Plus.mdb	
Case Problem 3	Cases\Friends.mdb	Cases\Friends Design Master.mdb
		Cases\Replica of Friends.mdb
		Cases\Friends.bak (renamed to Friends.mdb in a later step)
Case Problem 4	Cases\Vehicles.mdb	Cases\Replica of Vehicles.mdb
	Cases\3N4TA.bmp	Cases\Vehicles Design Master.mdb
	Cases\79XBF.bmp	Cases\Vehicles.bak (renamed to
	Cases\AAEAF.bmp	Vehicles.mdb in a later step)
Case Problem 5	Cases\BuySell.mdb	

Tutorial 9

Session 9.1	Tutorial\FineFood.mdb *(Continued from Session 8.4)*	
Session 9.2	Tutorial\FineFood.mdb *(Continued from Session 9.1)*	
Session 9.3	Tutorial\FineFood.mdb *(Continued from Session 9.2)*	
Session 9.4	Tutorial\FineFood.mdb *(Continued from Session 9.3)*	
	Tutorial\ValleCup.bmp	
Review Assignments	Review\Coffees.mdb *(Continued from Tutorial 8)*	
	Review\ValleCup.bmp	
Case Problem 1	Cases\Mall.mdb *(Continued from Tutorial 8)*	
Case Problem 2	Cases\Plus.mdb *(Continued from Tutorial 8)*	
	Cases\PLUS.jpg	
Case Problem 3	Cases\Friends.mdb *(Continued from Tutorial 8)*	
Case Problem 4	Cases\Vehicles.mdb *(Continued from Tutorial 8)*	
Case Problem 5	Cases\BuySell.mdb *(Continued from Tutorial 8)*	

Tutorial 10

Session 10.1	Tutorial\FineFood.mdb *(Continued from Session 9.4)*	
Session 10.2	Tutorial\FineFood.mdb *(Continued from Session 10.1)*	
Session 10.3	Tutorial\FineFood.mdb *(Continued from Session 10.2)*	
Session 10.4	Tutorial\FineFood.mdb *(Continued from Session 10.3)*	Tutorial\FineFood_be.mdb
Review Assignments	Review\Coffees.mdb *(Continued from Session 9.4)*	
Case Problem 1	Cases\Mall.mdb *(Continued from Tutorial 9)*	Cases\Mall_be.mdb
Case Problem 2	Cases\Plus.mdb *(Continued from Tutorial 9)*	
Case Problem 3	Cases\Friends.mdb *(Continued from Tutorial 9)*	Cases\Friends_be.mdb
Case Problem 4	Cases\Vehicles.mdb *(Continued from Tutorial 9)*	
Case Problem 5	Cases\BuySell.mdb *(Continued from Tutorial 9)*	Cases\BuySell_be.mdb
Additional Case 1	AddCases\Finstat.mdb	
	AddCases\Finlogo.bmp	
	AddCases\Finmoney.bmp	
Additional Case 2	AddCases\Pet.mdb	
	AddCases\Petfish.bmp	
	AddCases\Petdog.bmp	
	AddCases\Petlogo.bmp	
Additional Case 3		AddCases\Intern.mdb
		AddCases\Intmatch.bmp
		AddCases\Inttrack.bmp